Multitool Linux

Multitool Linux

Practical Uses for Open Source Software

Michael Schwarz
Jeremy Anderson
Peter Curtis
Steven Murphy
with Jose Nazario

Addison-Wesley

Boston • San Francisco • New York • Toronto • Montreal
London • Munich • Paris • Madrid
Capetown • Sydney • Tokyo • Singapore • Mexico City

The publisher offers discounts on this book when ordered in quantity for special sales. For more information, please contact:

Pearson Education Corporate Sales Division
201 W. 103rd Street
Indianapolis, IN 46290
(800) 428-5331
corpsales@pearsoned.com

Visit AW on the Web: www.aw.com/cseng/

Library of Congress Cataloging-in-Publication Data

Multitool Linux : practical uses for open source software /Michael Schwarz . . . [et al].

ISBN 0-201-73420-6 (alk. paper)
1. Linux. 2. Operating systems (Computers). I. Schwarz, Michael.
QA76.76.O63 M84553 2002
005.4'32—dc21 2002001318

ISBN 0-201-73420-6
Text printed on recycled paper
1 2 3 4 5 6 7 8 9 10—CRS—0605040302
First printing, April 2002

To the memory of my father, Gene Schwarz.

—Michael Schwarz

To my lovely bride, Angela,
who put up with seeing far less of me than normal
while I wrote this book and who encouraged me to keep going
every time I was ready to pooh-pooh the whole project.
To my dad, who taught me how to program
in BASIC at age 7 on a Bally BASIC
(and who actually made me use good programming style).
And to my mom, who taught me that no task is insurmountable:
It's just a matter of digging in and doing it.

—Jeremy Anderson

To Tom, Amy, Jane, and Annie
for supporting me, encouraging me, and teaching me that
knowledge is the best thing one can attain in life.

—Peter Curtis

To my wife, Ramona,
for her infinite patience while I was writing this book.

—Steven Murphy

Contents

Preface

You've Been Hoodwinked!

You picked this book up thinking it was about Linux. Hah! We fooled you completely! This book is only tangentially about Linux. It is really about a number of pieces of Free Software (note the capitals—there's more about this in Chapter 1) that are frequently packaged with Linux in common distributions.

There are quite a few books out there on how to install Linux, how to administer Linux, how to program for Linux, and how to secure Linux. What we believed was lacking, however, was some guide for those who are new to Free Software and Open Source software as to just what you can *do* with a Linux system once you have one.

This book is all about things you can do either with a base Linux distribution or with software that is readily available on the Web for the Linux platform. Every single piece of software we cover in this book is available under one or another "open source" license, meaning that you can get the software for free and redistribute it freely. In all cases the source code is available for you to see and modify for your own use. The differences in the licenses tend to govern what you are allowed to do with the modified source code.

The authors have a definite bias (which you should know about up front) in favor of the GNU Public License (the GPL), which allows you to do anything with the source code except refuse to give away any work derived from it. We cover some of the reasoning behind various source code licenses in Chapter 1.

Now, how, exactly, did we fool you? Well, although all of the software we cover here runs on Linux on Intel-based PCs, most of it will run on any flavor of Unix, from the BSD-derived systems of FreeBSD, NetBSD, and OpenBSD (all of which are freely available and open source and run on Intel PCs), on up to the most closed and expensive commercial proprietary versions of Unix running on the most expensive high-speed massively parallel hardware.

Why You Want This Book

Let's face it: It's a Windows world. If you have an Intel-based PC, the odds are you own a copy of one or another of the dozens of versions of Microsoft Windows. The odds are, also, that you didn't have any choice in the matter. The hardware comes with Windows preinstalled. There are tons of software packages available for from $20 to $20,000 for PCs running that operating system, and they are right there in your local SuperCompuMegaHut. What more could you want?

In the most selfish sense, you might want all of that software for from $0 to $0. You can do that with the commercial software. This is called "piracy," and it is, quite rightly, against the law. It turns out, however, that those of us who write software also would like to get software for free. So some of us started writing code and giving it away. We get paid back in the form of the other free software written by other programmers.

At this point, thanks to people like Richard Stallman of the Free Software Foundation and Linus Torvalds (author of the Linux kernel), you can now have a complete multiuser network server operating system and a whole slew of applications for free. You can also, if you are a programmer, get all the source code for all of it and add features or fix bugs yourself, if you are so inclined.

Even if you are not a programmer, you benefit from this openness because bugs get found and fixed much more rapidly in this model than in the closed, commercial, distributed media model. And you don't have to pay an upgrade price every few months.

Still, as we said, it is a Windows world. People who are not computer scientists know Windows. They know Microsoft Office. They know only this way of doing things. And Linux is different. So how do I do useful things like I do with my Windows PC? And what can I do with a Linux PC that I never even imagined doing with my Windows PC?

That's what the rest of this book is about. At one of our darkest hours, we thought of calling this book *Hooray! I've installed Linux . . . Now What?* Fortunately, our editors stared at us dumbfounded until we came to our senses. But that is still what the book is about. It is about some of the practical things you can do with Free Software.

How This Book Is Organized

This book is organized as follows:

- An introductory section (which consists of this Preface and Chapter 1).
- The "toolbox," in which each chapter covers a single application or piece of software at some length. This toolbox is further divided into sections covering:
  - Networking and Communications (Chapters 2–9)
  - Privacy and Security (Chapters 10–14)
  - Miscellaneous Applications (Chapters 15–17)
  - Music and Audio (Chapters 18–21)
  - Graphics and Photography (Chapters 22–23)
  - Video (Chapter 24)
- Afterword (Chapter 25 and About the Authors)

The bulk of the book is the toolbox section. Each chapter begins with a resource box, which includes our "patented" *Difficult-o-Meter*, a list of the programs being presented, their versions, and URLs where the software may be obtained. Every effort has been made to provide accurate and timely information. But because this book was over a year in the making, there will be newer versions of most of these packages by the time you read this.

Why You Might Not Want This Book

If you are looking for a book to help you install or administer Linux, this is not the one for you. There are many such books on the market, frequently on the same shelf where you found this one. This book is meant to show you some interesting things you can *do* with a Linux box.

Naturally, we think this is a great book to acquire while you're getting that book on installing and administering Linux.

Acknowledgments

We want to thank our editors and reviewers for their invaluable help in improving this book. A special thanks to Jose Nazario for contributing Chapter 8.

Chapter 1
INTRODUCTION

Linux as a Tool

Linux isn't really an operating system. Let me put that another way: Linux is more than an operating system—or less—or not.

You may think I'm confused, but I'm not. You see, pundits throughout the computer industry have been predicting the death of Unix since it was created. Bill Gates and company of Microsoft are merely the latest in a series of computer industry powers who wanted the future to come to their platform and, in an effort to do so, have either dismissed Unix or claimed that their product is better than Unix or done both at once. The claim that Windows NT "will be a better Unix than Unix" serves more to indicate the durability of Unix than the benefits of a new version of Windows.

So why does Unix not die? With a series of industry powerhouses gunning for it and a number of legitimate criticisms out there, one would think predicting the end would be a safe thing, with only the dying day uncertain. But it isn't so.

Unix (and, by extension, Linux) is not the best at anything. It isn't the easiest to understand. It isn't the fastest. It isn't the richest in features for business, science, or mathematics. So, for the final rhetorical time, why does it live on? Because, in spite of centuries of progress, of science and engineering, of decades of electronics and miniaturization, if you have a board and a nail you still want a hammer to make them work together. I haven't seen a digital hammer worth the price.

Linux is a tool. In fact, the metaphor we have chosen is, I think, a very apt one. Linux is the *multitool* of computing. We certainly cannot take credit for inventing this metaphor (I've been hearing it for years now), but we do intend to prove the truth of it.

Unix, and the "Unix way" of doing things, has produced tools that allow you to do things that are quite simply impossible on other platforms. For example, can your operating system do this?

```
$ perl -e 's/http:\/\/www.reknown.org\/playbyplay\//http:\/\
    /www.play.org\//gi' -p -i.bak *.html
```

Now, I will be the first to admit that this is an intimidating-looking command line. What does it do? Suppose you have a large and complex Web site and you have many links to another Web site, whose current URL begins:

```
http://www.reknown.org/playbyplay
```

You have just learned that everything at "playbyplay" and below is moving to its own server at:

```
http://www.play.org/
```

You've got over 100 links to the old address scattered over 30 html files! What do you do? Well, you type in that first command, which will find and replace every occurrence of the old base URL with the new base URL in all the html files in the current directory all at once. It will leave behind unchanged files with the same name but with a new ".bak" extension. Try that with Notepad or MS Office!

But wait, there's more. Put that command line in a shell script named *movelink* that looks like this:

```
#!/bin/bash

cd $1
perl -e 's/http:\/\/www.reknown.org\/playbyplay\//http:\/\/www.play.org\
    //gi' -p -i.bak *.html
```

Now you can make that change to any directory on your system by typing the directory name as the first command line argument:

```
$ movelink /var/www
```

Now how much would you pay? But wait, there's more! Suppose you wanted to do that for your whole Web site at once. Supposing that Web site begins at /var/www, you could now do that with this command line:

```
$ find /var/www -type d -exec movelink {} \;
```

Now, granted, Perl is not Linux, or even Unix, but Perl is very, well, Unix-y. You see, the Linux kernel and all the GNU (and other) tools that run with it are based on decades of experience in doing the real-world things that programmers and IT professionals have found themselves doing repetitively. At this point, whenever I hear someone over a cubicle wall typing the same keystrokes over and over again (Up-arrow, del, del, Up-arrow, del, del, etc.), I take the opportunity to offer to help. With vi, or sed, or awk, or Perl, I am usually able to do in one command line what this person was doing with mind-numbing repetition. You are sitting at a computer, for goodness sake! It should do the repetitive work for you.

Unix does not die, because it provides a rich set of tools and a way to combine those tools rapidly to make new and more powerful tools.

To some, Linux is just a kernel that provides a base set of services and APIs. To us, Linux (and Unix) are a philosophy of computer operation and programming. Installing Linux is the computer equivalent of getting a complete wood, metals, and automotive shop, absolutely jammed full of the finest, shiniest, best tools you can buy. And the best part is you didn't have to buy it.

Defining *Free*

Difficult-o-Meter: 1 (monkeys can do it)

Covers:

Free software	*http://www.gnu.org/philosophy/free-sw.html*
GPL	*http://www.gnu.org/copyleft/gpl.html*
LGPL	*http://www.gnu.org/copyleft/lesser.html*

Free Means Different Things to Different People

The most immediately noticable thing about "Free Software" is that it is "free" in the cost sense. You don't have to pay anything to anybody to get Linux and/or any of the software mentioned in this book. *Free* can certainly mean "gratis."

The more subtle and easy-to-overlook thing about "Free Software" is that it is "free" in the liberated sense. You can use the code from one program in a program of your own devising. *Free* can certainly mean "liberated."

Free Means Different Things in Different Licenses

These different meanings of *free* are given form in the licenses under which Free Software is distributed. Only software declared to be in the public domain is "up for grabs." All other software is distributed under one or another of the "free" licenses out there.

So why license free software? Just because you don't care if you get paid for the use of software you write doesn't mean that you don't care about how it may ultimately be used. For this reason, you use the ownership rights given you implicitly by law by the act of authorship to specify limits (or specify the lack of limits) on what a user of your work may do with the work.

The IANAL Declaration

IANAL means "I am not a lawyer." None of the authors of this book are lawyers. Some of us watch *Law & Order* on TV, but that's about as close as we get. Do not take the following capsule summaries of various licenses as legal advice. Don't even take them as accurate representations of the intent of the licenses. Read each license yourself. If you want to use the code and you are not sure what a license means, I suggest you seek legal advice.

All of that said, don't be too paranoid if all you want to do is use the program yourself or give away copies. All of the licenses we cover here give you at least those rights. If you plan to use the source code in a program of your own, be more alert. This is where these licenses differ wildly.

The GPL

GPL stands for GNU Public License. GNU stands for "GNU's not Unix." GNU is a project launched by the founder of the Free Software Foundation (FSF), one Richard M. Stallman, or RMS, as he is often called. He believes that all software should be free. He does not mean that all software should be gratis, but rather that all software should be "liberated." The phrase Stallman uses is "Think free speech, not free beer."

Stallman is often denounced as at best naive, at worst communist. This arises from a misunderstanding of Stallman's philosophy. To Stallman, the notion of "owning" an algorithm is as bizzare as the notion of "owning" the Pythagorean theorem. To Stallman, you have bought the software. You should have the "parts."

Furthermore, you should have the full ability to build on the work of others. You should be able to take that code and improve and extend it. This is not, in Stallman's philosophy, stealing. The only way you could steal from the author is if you took his open work, added it to your project, and then distributed the result *without* the original author's source or your extensions. That would be stealing.

The GPL reflects this philosophy. It grants the recipient all rights to use the source code in any way *except*:

- You may not refuse to pass the same rights to the source code on to any third party.
- If you compile or link any GPL'ed code to your code, you must also provide your code under the same terms as the GPL.

It is this latter point that leads some people to condemn the GPL as a "viral" license. Some critics of the GPL are bothered by the fact that using GPL'ed code requires you to release your code under the GPL.

There is a very simple remedy to this, however: Don't use GPL'ed code. The GPL is very hostile to closed or proprietary software. If you believe that you will develop a new piece of software and it will be so special that no one else will be able to reproduce it, and that keeping it secret is the best way to make you as rich as, well, Bill Gates or Larry Ellison, then get on with it and good luck! It is certainly within Stallman's rights (or those of anyone else who chooses to use the GPL) to refuse you the right to use any of his code on your path to proprietary riches.

The GPL protects not just the author's immediate interest of keeping her code open, it also protects her broader interest, in that there is an ever-growing body of free software out there to learn from and build from.

Now, this may not be your philosophy. That's fine. You don't have to use the GPL. But people who have elected to use the GPL have decided not to allow you to exploit their generosity by using their work to make you rich. In this sense, the GPL is as conservative a license as you are ever likely to find.*

The LGPL

Of course, this idealism is all well and good. But in a world where you want people to use your software, including people who may wish to write closed and proprietary software, you may find that your philosophy *prevents* this from happening. The GNU

*Note that these terms of the GPL come into play only when you want to distribute software. If you are developing code for yourself or for a client to use privately, it is not an issue. There is nothing wrong with refusing to share the source code if you also refuse to share the binary code!

C compiler (gcc) faced this very barrier. In many cases, gcc offered a better compiler than any offered by the actual vendor of a *nix-type operating system. Many people didn't want to use it, however, because they didn't want to have to open their applications just because they linked with the gcc C library.

Stallman and the FSF caved in to some of this pressure and created the LGPL (variously called the Lesser GPL or Library GPL). This license permitted you to link with an LGPL'ed library without its forcing you to release your own source code. The logic was that a library is a complete thing in itself. The mere act of linking an application to use the library was not really extending the library code.

Stallman has since come out publicly against using the LGPL. Still, many products are released under the LGPL.

The BSD Licenses

The Berkeley Software Distribution (BSD) licenses are the other major class of "open source" license. Although I'm making the following number up, I would say roughly 80% of all "open source" code is released under either the GPL or the BSD license.

The BSD license differs from the GPL primarily in that it does allow you to modify the code and then keep the modifications closed. In other words, you cannot take away the rights to the original code, but you can modify that code and then not share the results. For critics of the GPL, this is the perfect solution.

For fans of the GPL (and by now it should be clear I am such a fan—objectivity is a myth), this denies the original author a fundamental right—namely, the right to control how the code is used. Nonetheless, many major free software products have been released under the BSD license. And while this has led to closed commercial variants of some products, it certainly hasn't been a death knell to free software. Both licenses give you full-use rights to the released version.

The Artistic License

The major package released under the Artistic License is Perl. This license is practically a public domain license, except it does try to prevent you from calling your derived closed version the same thing as the original open version.

Public Domain

This allows anyone to do anything he or she wishes with the code.

Other Licenses

There are a host of licenses out there. For a lengthy list and critique (from the possibly biased creators of the GPL), visit *http://www.gnu.org/philosophy/license-list.html.*

The Great Schism

As with any field, leaders tend to become iconoclasts. Some are born iconoclasts. Some have iconoclasism thrust upon 'em. There is a single major split in the philosophies of free software. (Note the lowercase letters: When we use lowercase, we mean software that is free and for which you get the source code.) The split is between Richard Stallman and his "Free Software" philosophy and Eric Raymond and Bruce Perens with their "Open Source" philosophy.

Richard Stallman

We have already talked about RMS, the father of the GPL and the first to codify a philosophy of "liberated" software. People had shared source code in the past; he certainly did not invent that. What he did was to articulate what it means for software to be "Free." It boils down to the two main thrusts of the GPL. First, you have the right to get all the source code with any software, whether it is "gratis" or not. Giving someone binary code only is like giving them an encrypted book or a car with a hood that is welded shut. The other thrust is that if you use code shared in this way, you do not have the right to hide your source code additions. Part of the price you pay for the labor of the original programmer is that everyone else shall benefit from your code. If you don't want to pay that price, fine. But then you don't get to use the original author's code.

Eric Raymond and Bruce Perens

Bruce Perens created the original Open Source Definition (OSD) as the Debian Free Software Guidelines (DFSG). Debian is a Linux distribution that consists entirely of software that meets these guidelines. Some Linux distributions include closed, commerical, or marginally open software. Debian never has and never will.

Eric S. Raymond wrote a number of seminal papers on the phenomenon of what he and Bruce call *open source development* but what I think may be more generally called *Internet-distributed software development*. Eric tends to come to fairly far-reaching conclusions from a limited number of data points, but it doesn't change the fact that *The Cathedral and the Bazaar* has become what may be the single most influential essay on the whole phenomenon of free software.

Bruce and Eric maintain a Web site, *opensource.org*, where they push the notion of *Open Source* and downplay the term *Free Software*.

They also created an "Open Source Certification and Mark" program that would assure a consumer that a product's license met their Open Source Definition.

They argue that the term *Free Software* is scary to business and hard to sell.

What's a Pagan Boy to Do?

The truth is that this is largely a tempest in a teapot. The DFSG is used to decide what software may be included in Debian, and it remains one of the most robust Linux distributions around. Stallman continues to call it "Free Software," and ESR (as Eric Raymond is often called) continues to call it "Open Source."

The GPL meets the DFSG and the OSD. The reverse would not necessarily be true. Eric's and Bruce's points about the marketing of the ideas are well taken, and there is no doubt that Eric and Bruce have been instrumental in pushing many of these ideas into the corporate arena at a much faster pace than they would have been taken up on their own.

In this book we will call the products "free software," and we will capitalize it when we talk about GPL'ed software. This is not to join the ranks of iconoclasts, but rather to honor RMS, who really made all of this happen. ESR and Bruce Perens have been staunch and successful advocates, but there would have been nothing for them to advocate without Stallman and the FSF.

Get Comfortable with Source Code

Difficult-o-Meter: 3 (moderate Linux skill required)

"Just compile it!" is probably a slogan we'll never see from an overpriced-sneaker company—particularly not now that tech stocks are in the toilet and most dot-commers can't even afford Ramen noodles, much less $90 sneakers. But there's another reason we'll never see it as a shoe slogan:

Shoe company slogans are always exhorting us to go do difficult things. They want us to run to strange, isolated places and stop and do sit-ups, or to race traffic lights while on foot. I'm afraid I'm not that type of person. When I want to race traffic lights, I play some variant of "Need for Speed." When I get to strange, isolated places, I tend to spend my time enjoying the view by rubbernecking. I guess I don't like all the hard work associated with "TV Commercial" exercise.

This is why I often exhort people to "Just compile it!" It's easier than figuring out the switches to something like RPM (RedHat package manager, a utility that is *supposed* to work quite well, but with which I'm always having some type of argument). Almost every GPL'ed project I've downloaded has configured and compiled easily, with nary a wasted neuronal discharge on my part (a neuronal discharge is a thought, for those of you not up on your medical terminology). A casual perusing of the README file has traditionally told me which packages were prerequisites, generally where said prerequisites can be found, and then what commands should be used to configure, compile, and install the package.

I could devote a whole chapter to why I don't like RPM, but I can sum it up in one sentence: Most people who make RPMs are exceedingly careless. They require all sorts of other packages—most of which aren't required at all. RedHat, Mandrake, and TurboLinux should be ashamed for this. Installing one of their .rpm files will undoubtedly drive you to the brink of insanity, because it requires their version of every package in the world. SuSE is smarter. They put only the real requirements in the requirement list. As a result, I find myself using some .rpm files from SuSE. Too bad SuSE has stopped distributing free iso's* of their distribution. But I digress.

Being comfortable with compiling and installing source code is rather equivalent to being able to put oil and coolant in your own car—it's a skill that isn't absolutely required but that will certainly make your life simpler—and it will certainly give you a better understanding of how your computer works.

Compiling your kernel from scratch is one of my big bugaboos. I've put a bit of a write-up online at

```
http://www.jurai.net/~patowic/computer/pre-kernel.html
```

explaining why I don't think you should use a precompiled kernel. I'll save you the effort of heading off to that URL by reproducing the text here.

> At least once a week, I answer the question "Why shouldn't I use a precompiled kernel?" It's a simple question, with a fairly simple answer.

---

*ISO stands for International Standards Organization. In this case, it is common shorthand for ISO-9660, the CD-ROM file system standard, so "an iso" is an image of a CD-ROM that may be downloaded and burned to a CD-R or CD-RW. See Chapter 18.

> The short answer is this: Don't trust your vendor.
>
> The long answer goes something like this: All Linux distributors have to make certain decisions when making their distribution. They have to decide what software to include and what kernel options to enable. They don't know anything about your hardware. They don't have much idea what you intend to do with your Linux box. They do have to worry about supporting the widest range of hardware possible.
>
> Out of this need grew kernel modules—which give you the ability to insert code into the kernel on the fly. This is really great for assembling a generic system. This has less utility for Joe Average. Joe Average, you see, does not change his PC hardware that often. He builds a system and installs an operating system (OS). Ideally, he should have some idea of what is in his system.
>
> A kernel based on modules is kind of like a generic engine that can be placed in any car. A custom-built kernel would (for the purposes of this analogy) be a tuned engine that only fits in your car. Which do you think will be faster and work better?
>
> After speed, security is a concern. RedHat is infamous for leaving nice fat security holes all over their distribution. Their kernel is no different. A while back, they left a debugging feature enabled in all kernels. This was a feature that would be used by far less than 1% of Linux users, but it *did* open up a hole to the outside. This is what most people would call "bad."
>
> Upgrading one's kernel should also be done fairly regularly. When new kernels come out, look at the features and fixes they offer. Try to decide if you should have them. When kernel 2.2.16 came out, fixing a nice big security hole that had existed in all previous versions, it was a week before the major vendors had new kernels available for upgrade. I had all my machines upgraded within a matter of hours after hearing the announcement—because I build my own kernels.
>
> Building your own kernel is like having a tailor-made suit for the same price as a regular one. Who would pick off-the-rack over tailor-made?

Do you see why I don't like precompiled kernels? I feel this way about most precompiled software. I'd rather download the source, compile it myself, and run from there.

Compiling Software

Compiling software under Linux generally follows one of three patterns: autoconf, makefiles, and imakefiles. Before I cover each one, I want to point out a few commonalities. In every case, the INSTALL and README files should be carefully read. The answers to any questions you may have are undoubtedly in them. The configure and compile should be done using a normal user account, and *only the install should be done as root.*

Avoid using the root account whenever possible. The root account is basically the .44 magnum of your Linux box. Screwing up with a normal account can be painful. Screwing up with the root account can cost you a limb.

I keep all my source code under `/usr/src`. It's a logical place, and it helps keep my home directory slightly less cluttered. Files that end in *.tar.gz* or *.tgz* or *.tar.bz2* are generally called *tarballs*. Yep—that's a real word (at least in the Unix world). *Tar* is a Tape ARchival program that's been around since the beginning of time, and it's the de facto standard for distributing non-RPM'd files. Note that RPM files are generally only available for RedHat or its derivatives—so you'd never find an RPM file for slackware or OpenBSD or FreeBSD. Oops, we're talking about Linux, aren't we? Just strike those last two names from your mind for a while.

Imakefiles

Developed for X Windows, the only package I've run into that uses Imake is XFree86. This was intended to be a platform-independent version of make, but it never really took off. Imake has a neat O'Reilly book on it that I've never read, and (I suspect) I'm not alone in this. It's complex, it's different from what's out there, and Gnu Autoconf pretty much does away with the need for it. Even XFree86 can now be built without fiddling with Imake at all—download the source code and run "make World" from the top directory. Things seem to go just fine from there.

Basic Makefiles

Plain-Jane make files may require modification to compile on your system. Try them first to see if they work:

```
tar zxvf mypackage.tar.gz
cd mypackage
more README
more INSTALL
[make config]
make
su -c "make install"
make clean
```

As always, we read the instructions first, and remember that `/usr/src` is a good place to put all that source code. The next step, `make config`, is optional. Many packages don't use it. Some do. Some have other options as well—it'll say in the README or INSTALL files. The `make config` step will generally mean you'll have a variety of questions asked of you. You'll have to figure out the correct answers (for example, it may ask "What is the path to md5sum?"), or the compile will fail.

For packages that do not have a config option and that don't compile the first time, you'll have to open up the Makefile with an editor and look for variables that can be changed. Generally it'll be something minor, like adjusting the path to a binary. It's also worth looking at the makefile to see just *where* it intends to put the compiled binaries. Big problems with the Makefile will require either in-depth knowledge of Makefiles (which few people seem to have) or e-mail to the package maintainer. The latter is generally the better course of action, since if there is a genuine problem, the main developer needs to know. Don't go crying wolf, though, and be polite about e-mailing the guy or gal.

Autoconf

Gnu autoconf is one of the more clever pieces of software out there. Basically, it's a way for the software package to ask a couple of hundred questions about your system—and to ask the system directly. The configure program (which is what autoconf uses) checks the location of binaries, checks compiler behavior, and does everything short of washing the windows. Autoconf'd packages are really, really nice to compile, particularly in comparison to the manual editing of Makefiles.

The pattern for autoconf'd packages looks like this:

```
tar zxvf myswfr2.tar.gz
cd mysfwr-2
more README
more INSTALL
./configure --help
./configure [options]
make
su -c "make install"
make clean
```

Note the [options]—many autoconf'd packages have a gaggle of extra information you can manually pass to the configure script. You can generally ignore this, but there are times it's a distinct advantage. In the XMMS (Cross-platform Multi-Media System) package, for example, there is a switch to enable 3DNOW! Optimizations—which is great if you have an Athlon, Duron, K6, K6/2, or K6-III microprocessor, but useless if you have an Intel or Cyrix chip. Here's an example of using some command line flags to the configure script:

```
tar zxvf xmms-1.2.4.tar.gz
cd xmms-1.2.4
./configure --with-x --enable-3dnow
make
su -c "make install"
make clean
```

Simple, eh? Astute readers will also note that I included X-windows support, too. These flags are all different from package to package, so doing a "configure--help" is really the only way (besides reading documentation) to figure them out.

If something gets fouled up in your compile and you need to rerun configure, be sure to erase the old results! These are stored in the files `config.cache` or `.config.cache` and the files will need to be removed before you run configure again.

How to Roll Your Own Kernel

Many new to Linux are seriously intimidated by the prospect of compiling their own operating system kernel. There is no doubt that if you are not a programmer, this is a more complex undertaking than you probably have ever attempted with a computer.

Even though it may seem an awesome prospect, this doesn't have to be as nerve-wracking as it sounds. Before we actually get into kernel compilation, we are going to show you around a few directories and files so you know something about how Linux sets itself up on your hard drive and how it starts itself up. We'll then show you how a little preparation can allow you to safely get back where you started, even if you totally mess up the configuration and compilation of your new kernel. Once you have this safe recovery point, you need never worry again. You can compile the kernel again and again, certain that even if you screw up, you can always boot from your working original kernel. Let's start that tour.

The /etc/lilo.conf *File*

The following discussion pertains, alas, only to Linux on Intel processors. I would love to be equally knowledgeable about other platforms, but Intel machines are all I work with when it comes to Linux. Also, Intel machines will be what the vast majority of our readers are using. For these reasons, we have followed the herd and written about "Lintel" platforms. Be aware as you read the following that Linux on Alpha, PowerPC, Sparc, or any other processor platform will have similar structures and capabilities, but they will *not* be the same.

Every Linux distribution with which I am familiar uses the LILO boot loader by default. What is a boot loader? You may not know it, but your PC has two invisible programs in it. They show up in no directory and have no file name. One of them is probably familiar to you. It is called the BIOS, which stands for *basic input/output system*. It resides in read-only memory (ROM), which is a "burned-in" (or, in newer machines, "flashed") separate memory chip on your motherboard. The second is the boot loader.

When the BIOS starts up, it knows how to find a special little bit of disk called the *superblock*. The superblock contains two important things. One is the *partition table*. The other is a little data area called the *master boot record*, or MBR.

The BIOS reads the data from the MBR into a particular place in random-access memory (RAM) and then executes the instructions stored there. You could write your own little assembly language program and put it in the MBR of your hard drive, and then your computer would be able to execute only your little program. Nasty little creatures called *boot sector viruses* do precisely this.

Since most machines ship with some variety of Windows preinstalled, the default MBR program consists of enough code to determine which partition is marked as "bootable" and then to boot the operating system stored there.

When Linux is installed on a machine, it generally replaces this silent and invisible boot loader program with a verbose and configurable boot loader called LILO.

What LILO does is determined by a configuration file called */etc/lilo.conf*. Here is a sample file:

```
boot     = /dev/hda
vga = normal
read-only
linear
prompt
timeout  = 30

  image  = /boot/vmlinuz
  label  = linux
  root   = /dev/hda3

  image  = /boot/vmlinuz.suse
  label  = suse
  root   = /dev/hda3

  other  = /dev/hda1
  label  = win
```

I separate the global options from the bootable regions by indenting the bootable specifications. This isn't a requirement for LILO; I just do it to keep them clear. The vertical whitespace I use is also optional.

Here's the meaning of some of the global options you might use.

Option	Description
boot	This option specifies which device is the boot device. In this case, it is the first IDE hard drive (/dev/hda).
default	This option names the image that will be booted by default. If omitted, the first image specified is booted.
delay	Specifies the number of tenths of seconds to wait before booting the default image.
read-only	The read-only option is actually a Linux kernel parameter, not a LILO option. It specifies that the root partition is initially to be mounted as read only. This allows for file system checking and cleaning.
linear	The linear option tells LILO to use logical sector addresses instead of so-called cylinder/head/sector (CHS) addressing. This is a rather esoteric point. You should never have to add or remove this option if your lilo.conf is working.
lock	This option causes LILO to "remember" any kernel options you apply manually at boot and to use them the next time that image is booted. In other words, it makes the Linux kernel options you type at the boot prompt "sticky."
prompt	Normally LILO boots directly into the default image, unless a Shift key is pressed. When a Shift key is pressed during boot, the "boot:" prompt is given. If this option is specified, the "boot:" prompt always appears. Note that you cannot have an unattended reboot if this option is specified and the "timeout" option is not specified.

Running LILO

To install LILO, you will have to be root, and then, assuming the *lilo.conf* file you wish to use is in */etc/lilo.conf*, simply type:

```
# lilo
Added linux *
Added suse
Added win
#
```

The output you see here are the names of the images defined in the *lilo.conf* file. The asterisk denotes the default image.

The /boot *Directory (Maybe)*

Most distributions place a number of files of relevance to the kernel and to LILO in the */boot* directory. This is often where default kernels (precompiled kernels) for your distribution are installed. Also to be found here are kernel maps, boot sector images, backups of old boot sector contents, and so forth.

Welcome to /usr/src/linux

Now we take the plunge! Let's visit */usr/src/linux*. Take a look at Figure 1-1. This is the base directory of the 2.2.x Linux kernel source. This is an actual look at the 2.2.16 kernel on my Linux-based laptop. You don't need to know all that much about the kernel to compile it as you need. Even so, let me introduce you to this base directory so that you can use it as a launching point should you ever want to dig into the depths.

The README file gives a very brief introduction to the kernel and how to compile it. The Makefile file is the "formula" for building the kernel (similar to those cases described earlier in this chapter, although the Linux kernel make process does not exactly match any of the "standard" make styles we talked about earlier).

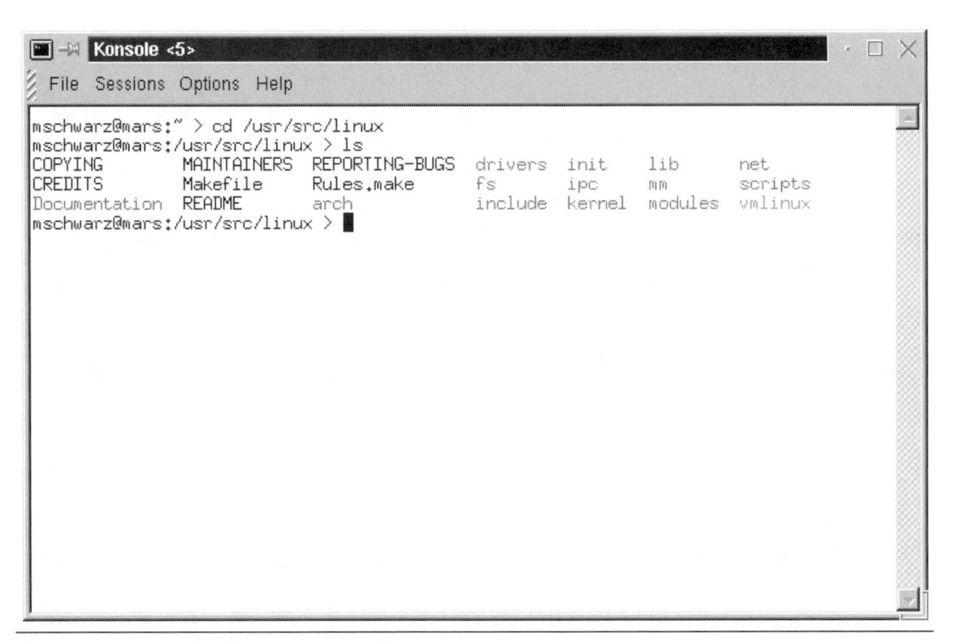

Figure 1-1 Our first look at */usr/src/linux.*

Directory	Description
Documentation	This is, as you may have guessed, a collection of documentation on the Linux kernel and its subsystems. This documentation varies quite a bit. Some of it is written to be understood by end users; some of it is written to be understood only by other kernel developers. Some of it is a bit out of date. As is often the case with programs everywhere, documentation tends to lag behind coding. Still, this is a rich mine of information, and often the best place to turn when you are having problems using some kernel feature for the first time.
arch	This is where architecture-specified code (read: processor-specific code) is kept. Subdirectories of this directory include: ■ *i386* ■ *alpha* ■ *arm* ■ *m68k* ■ *mips* ■ *ppc* ■ *s390* ■ *sparc* ■ *sparc64* So, as you can see, Linux runs on quite a range of hardware. Soon you will see something like "ia64," which will be support for the next generation of Intel processors (the "Itanium"). That "s390" is none other than the IBM mainframe S/390. So Linux runs on everything from the smallest 386's right on through IBM mainframes.
drivers	The *drivers* directory contains code for driving various devices, from serial ports to network cards, from floppy drives to RAID arrays, and everything in between.
fs	The *fs* directory contains the code to implement the various file systems Linux supports. Linux supports many file systems. Its preferred native file system, *ext2*, is here, along with several others, including FAT, NTFS, and HPFS and such network file systems as *smbfs*, *nfs*, and *coda*.
include	This has the header files (*.h* files, or "include files") that are used throughout the kernel source. This can be interesting to poke around in, since data structures are generally defined in such files.
init	Duh, gee, Tennessee . . . this is the kernel initialization code.
ipc	The code that implements the System V InterProcess Communication APIs is in here (semaphores, message queues, and shared memory).
kernel	This is where the "core" kernel code lives. Here is where you will find the code that does process scheduling, resource allocation, signals, kernel modules, etc.

(continued)

Directory	Description
lib	Here you will find code for kernel versions of some familiar standard C library function calls, including ctype, sprintf, and so forth. The kernel cannot call user-space versions of these functions for thread-safety reasons (among others), so it must have its own implementations of them.
mm	This directory contains the memory management system of Linux. You might well think that memory management was about as "core" a kernel feature as you can get, so why isn't it in "kernel"? The simple answer is that the memory management system contains as much code by itself as the rest of the "core" kernel. Keeping it apart makes it easier to figure out which source files are involved in this critical function. The more complex answer has to do with the fact that this is both a complex system and one where bugs will have disastrous consequences. It is always easier to maintain and debug code "off by itself."
net	As you may have guessed, the implementation of the various network protocols supported by the Linux kernel are to be found here. Note that this is code for the protocols, not for the network devices themselves (ethernet cards, etc.). Code for these is to be found in the *drivers* directory.
scripts	Various "support" scripts for the configuration and make process are kept here. For example, Perl/Tk scripts that implement the xconfig configuration tool are to be found here.

Friendly Kernel Configuration (menuconfig, xconfig)

The Linux kernel is configurable in thousands of ways. The complexity is such that an interactive configuration system is built into the kernel's make file. Making the Linux kernel is quite dissimilar to any other build I have seen (although Perl's make process comes close).

There are three ways to run the interactive configuration. The most basic is to type *make config*, which will ask a question about every single possible configuration option. I don't recommend this. You'll start going completely nuts long before you get to the options you want to change. The other two options are *make menuconfig*, which is a text-based "point-and-shoot" interface, and *make xconfig*, which is an X-windows–based GUI point-and-click configuration interface.

The *make menuconfig* interface looks like Figure 1-2. The *make xconfig* interface looks like Figure 1-3.

Generally, you will need to be root to configure, build, and install a new kernel.

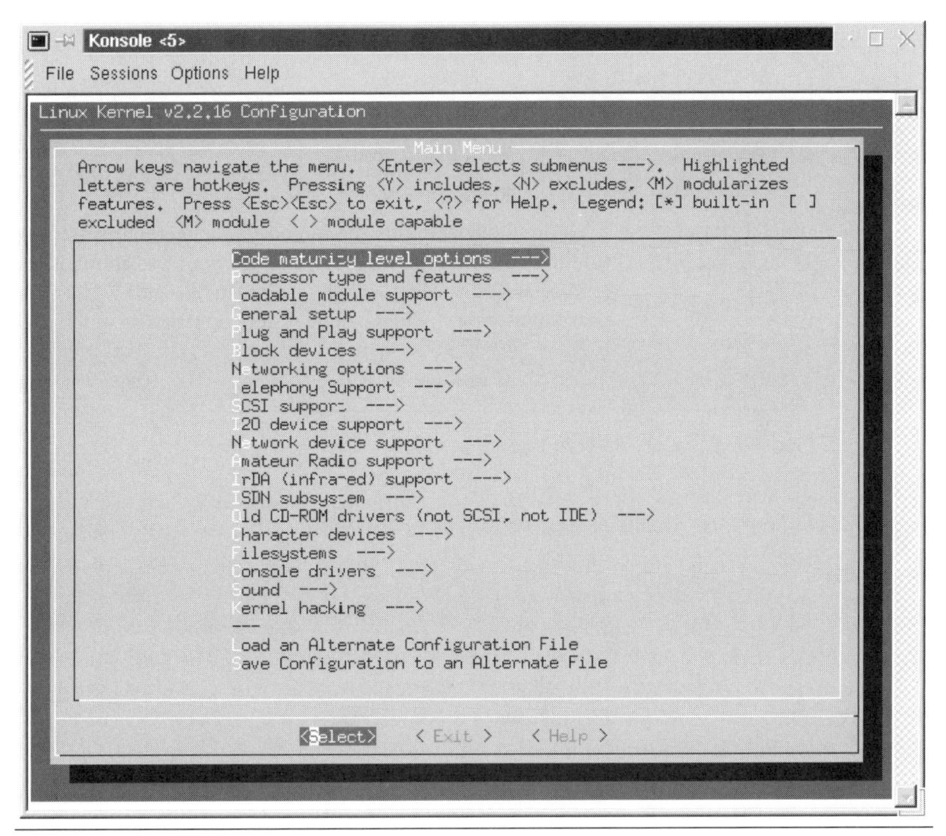

Figure 1-2 Sample menuconfig.

Most optional code in the Linux kernel can be disabled, compiled in to the kernel, or built as modules. Modules offer greater flexibility, but they do involve a small performance cost to get loaded; and if you wish to load and unload them, you must use a set of commands (*insmod*, *rmmod*, etc.) to manipulate them. I find it much simpler to actually directly compile in everything I need, and then, if I need different things, to boot between two or three different kernels. One of the great things about Linux is you can do it your own way. You can go either route.

Several chapters in this book will take you through configuring the kernel to enable such features as IP Masquerading and Parallel Line Internet Protocol (PLIP). Those chapters will just tell you what settings to change. This chapter is the only one in the book that will actually walk you through compiling and deploying a new kernel. Refer back to this chapter when you read later chapters that tell you to reconfigure your kernel if you are not comfortable with the process. We will try to make this as painless as possible.

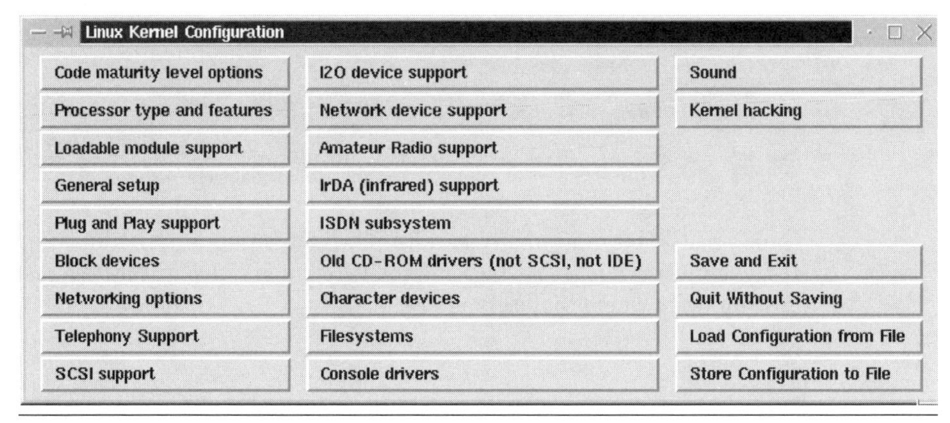

Figure 1-3 Sample xconfig.

Using *make menuconfig* or *make xconfig* you will be able to reconfigure your Linux kernel in a great many ways.

As a general principle, be sure to write down exactly which configuration parameters you change, what they used to be set to, and what you changed them to. This allows you to confidently "undo" your changes (assuming you can boot the system to change them back! More about how to be sure that you can, even if you screw up the new kernel, will appear later).

Also, as another general rule, change as few things at a time as possible. If you wish, for example, to install your Intel EtherExpress Pro *and* set up PLIP networking, do one first, compile and deploy the kernel, and then do the other. If one doesn't work, you then know which one.

Building the New Kernel

Now that you have set your configuration, you must run *make dep* to rebuild the dependencies. What does this mean? Well, some code requires that other code be built and linked to the kernel. If that code was not included for any other reason, then the compilation would fail. Running *make dep* causes such prerequisite code to be compiled for any of your configuration changes.

Now you can make your kernel. There are a number of build targets (the arguments to *make* that build a kernel). Some of them build and install the kernel for you. We won't use those options here. We will do this all "manually" because I don't know which distribution you have and I don't know if some of the installs will work correctly with what you have. So we will do it by the numbers, by the book. Most kernels have enough code in them that compressed images are required. These targets are *zImage* or *bzImage*. The *bzImage* kernel will use *bzip* to compress the kernel. It gets them smaller, and almost all distributions support it. That's the one I'll use. Note that while running, *make bzImage* should be all that is necessary; some people, out of paranoia, want to have every single bit of code rebuilt. They like to run a *make clean* before they run their *make bzImage*. This should not be necessary, but it will do no harm (other than to make the compile take quite a long time).

There's a little bit more that you must do. If any options are set to compile as modules, you must run *make modules* and then you must run *make modules_install* to install those modules where they belong.

You can string all of these commands together on one command line and do it in such a way that subsequent commands will not run if an earlier one fails for some reason. Here's how you could do this:

```
# make dep && make clean && make bzImage && make modules && make
    modules_install
```

When this finishes (and it will take several minutes even on the fastest machines), you have a compressed compiled kernel and you have the modules installed where they belong. You will now need to install the kernel.

Installing the New Kernel

To install the new kernel, you must set up an entry in */etc/lilo.conf* that points at the new kernel.

In most distributions I have seen, kernels reside either in the root directory or in */boot*. Since this is a new kernel (and perhaps your first kernel), we should not replace any existing kernel, especially not your current default, so that your system will properly boot into one of your old kernels if something is wrong.

Let's assume you are working with the machine from which came the sample lilo.conf earlier in this chapter.

Your new compiled kernel will be found in */usr/src/linux/arch/i386/boot* (remember, we are assuming an Intel-compatible PC here) and will be named *bzImage*. Let's copy it into the boot directory and call it *vmlinuz.new*:

```
# cp arch/i386/boot/bzImage /boot/vmlinuz.new
```

You might also want to copy down the kernel memory map, System.map, (which is used to resolve addresses to kernel function names in the event of a kernel panic). We won't bother with that here.

Now add the new kernel to your */etc/lilo.conf* file. (The new lines are in bold type):

```
boot     = /dev/hda
vga = normal
read-only
linear
prompt
timeout  = 30

  image  = /boot/vmlinuz
  label  = linux
  root   = /dev/hda3

  image  = /boot/vmlinuz.suse
  label  = suse
  root   = /dev/hda3

  image  = /boot/vmlinuz.new
  label  = new
  root   = /dev/hda3

  other  = /dev/hda1
  label  = win
```

Next, be sure to run lilo, or your new kernel won't be accessible on boot:

```
# lilo
Added linux *
Added suse
Added new
Added win
#
```

Next comes the moment of truth.

Booting the New Kernel

Okay, are you ready? Then gird your loins, or whatever it is you do, and type the fateful:

```
# init 6
```

Or, if you have actual users on your system:

```
# shutdown -r 5
```

This latter will give users five minutes to get off the system before it reboots. When it reboots, you should see the LILO prompt:

```
LILO:
```

Type:

```
LILO: new
```

Typing "new" and pressing Enter will cause LILO to boot your newly built and installed kernel instead of the default (which is still the kernel named "linux"). If all goes well, your system should boot normally.

Yikes! Or Booting the Old Kernel

But what if it doesn't? Becuase of the way we set up */etc/lilo.conf*, all you should have to do in the event of a crash is cold-boot the machine. Your old (and known to be working) Linux kernel will boot instead of the new one and the system should recover.

So, what went wrong? Because of the wide variety of PC configurations and Linux kernels I really cannot hazard a guess.

None of the changes this book tells you to make should prevent your kernel from working. If you changed other kernel configuration parameters, you may have dropped some driver needed by your hardware. Before you reboot into the old kernel, take a look at the kernel messages output just before the crash (if they are still visible). Which subsystem was starting may provide a clue about what you are missing or have misconfigured.

Another possible cause of difficulty is if the default kernel setup in */usr/src/linux* does not, in fact, match the configuration of your boot kernel.

This isn't a book on the Linux kernel. If you can't boot your modified kernel and you can't figure out why, your best bets are to try any of the following:

1. A friend who is into Linux. This is often the best possible resource. Most Linux people are thrilled to help people have good experiences with Linux and will take any opportunity to help out.
2. A local Linux user's group.
3. A Web site like LinuxCare or the Web site for your Linux distribution.
4. The linux newsgroups.
5. A Web search engine, like google.com.

One nice thing is that almost every possible problem has been encountered and solved by at least one person before you. Help can be found.

Finding Source

The Freshmeat Web site, at *http://www.freshmeat.net/* is a major repository and announcement site for open source projects. Sourceforge, at *http://www.sourceforge.net/*, is another repository, and it too has an announcement section. Yet another way to find open source projects is by searching on my favorite search engine, google, at *http://www.google.com/*.

Source Is Good!

Downloading the source can lead to other good habits—like looking through the source code when you find a problem. I've seen almost no Linux/open source projects that aren't currently under development. Usually, at least one person is actively looking into improving a given project. Source code isn't that hard to learn. It's basically another language, remember—but one tailored to solving problems. Learning source code is much like learning a limited subset of a foreign language—for example, learning only enough Turkish to be able to read a Turkish recipe.

There are a lot of really good books on various programming languages. I tend to get O'Reilly books when I need some programming reference books. Note that I said *reference* books. For actually learning a language, there are generally hundreds, if not thousands, of free lesson sets and tutorials available on the Web. The primary languages used for Linux and open source projects are C, C++, Perl, and Python.

What this means is that I can dig through small programs and find the answers to certain compilation problems. While working on the chapter about Wine (Chapter 17), I found myself unable to compile the Wine debugger. It kept erroring out, saying that a shared library (.so files under Linux) did not contain needed functions. "That's odd," I thought, and I did a quick find to see if that was a library compiled by Wine. Sure enough, it was. My compile was failing because the compilation process was using an old version of the library. Once I copied the new library into place, the compile hummed along happily.

Someday, "when I have more time" (which generally translates to never), I hope to start digging through C++ code for things like Wine and for fixing small bugs. Most open source projects have 'FIXME!' notes tagged in their source code. These notes mark code that needs to be fixed but that wasn't a high enough priority for someone to get to it yet. If you want to learn to program, these things are often a great place to start.

How does one get comfortable with source code? By downloading and installing things from source. You've read my rant, and hopefully you understand some of the rationale behind it.

Eschew RPM, I say! Use the Source, Luke!

Requirements

Difficult-o-Meter: 2 (light Linux skill required)

So, you ask, what do you actually *need* to make sense of this book? The answer comes in three parts: the knowledge you're required to possess, the hardware you're required to obtain, and the software to which we'll refer.

Knowledge

Not much preexisting knowledge is required. Some experience with Linux is handy, but it isn't absolutely required. We do not cover installing Linux on your PC, so it'd be best if you had the ability to install Linux and get it running on your own machine before you begin delving into the chapters. In fact, that's really a prerequisite for the entire book. You wouldn't be expected to learn advanced driving techniques if you couldn't drive in the first place. While I'd love to offer to help each and every one of you install Linux on your machine, it simply isn't possible. If you can't get Linux installed and running on your machine, check one of the other help sources: Read the documentation, talk to your local Linux user's group, call up your friends who run Linux, or access any of the thousands of pieces of online documentation. You could even go to one of the interactive help sites to ask an expert for help.

The primary knowledge required is this:

- A general idea of the hardware in your PC
- Enough know-how to get a working installation of Linux going
- Ability to follow directions

That's about it, really. Bear in mind that the second item has no time limits associated with it—if it took you a week to get XFree86 configured, don't worry about it—you got it working, and that's all that counts.

Hardware

As for hardware, this entire book assumes that you're working with x86-compatible hardware: Intel Pentiums, Pentium II/IIIs, AMD K5/K6/K6-2/K6-3/Athlon/Duron, any of the Cyrix chips, even 486s (however, a 486 will be a bit short on power for Chapter 24, Video Production). You must have some free disk space. A couple of hundred megs would be nice, but you can probably get by with less if you're careful.

Chapter 20 (Music Production), for instance, is predicated a bit on the assumption that you've got a lot of spare space—it'll still work without it, but your MP3 Jukebox won't be nearly as cool.

You must have a video card capable of running Xfree86 (don't worry, I've yet to run into one that won't drive *any* Xserver).

Since this book assumes that you've got enough smarts to get Linux up and running in the first place, you can probably figure out ways around the lack of disk space or the lack of a video card. It can be done. The only real hardware requirement is this: *a Linux box on which you can freely play, test, and make mistakes*. If you've got that, you're golden. An Internet connection, for downloading new software and updates, would be nice too—as always, the faster the better.

Software

At the beginning of each chapter, we'll do our best to mention the software you'll need to build what we built. You'll need a relatively recent Linux distribution. I recommend SuSE, because I really like their installer and runtime setup. One author prefers Debian—the most GNU-ish of the distributions. None of us particularly care for RedHat or Mandrake—both are unstable and needlessly different from the others. Something based on at least kernel 2.2 would sure be nice, because 2.2 has been the standard for a couple of years now. Kernel 2.4 is all good, too. And if you really like RedHat, or it's the only distribution you have, that's okay. It's still very usable. Everything in this book was tested on either SuSE, TurboLinux, or Debian—and most everything was tested on Debian. Three of the four authors of this book prefer Debian, and the remaining author is simply difficult to get along with.

Web Sites

The three big Web sites to get familiar with are:

> *http://www.freshmeat.net/*—an announcement site for GPL'ed and non-GPL'ed software projects
>
> *http://www.sourceforge.net/* (another open-source repository)
>
> *http://www.linuxdoc.org/*—the core Linux documentation repository

These are three fabulous places to go when you're either looking for software or trying to figure out how to use it. Also, there is a web site for this book: *http://www.multitool.net/mtl*.

Chapter 2

Remote-Control Your Computer from Anywhere, Anytime, and Any Operating System, Even OS/2!

Difficult-o-Meter: 2 (light Linux skill required)

Covers:

vncserver 3.3.3	*http://www.uk.research.att.com/vnc/*
vncclient	*http://www.uk.research.att.com/vnc/*
Java client, Web VNC	*http://www.uk.research.att.com/vnc/*

Question: I have Linux and I know that with X-windows I can run applications from anywhere on the Internet. My problem is that I'm usually working on systems that do not have an X-server, so I can't use the network capabilities of X to do my work remotely. Are there any solutions?

Answer: There must be, or this chapter wouldn't be here! Read on, MacDuff . . .

When X Doesn't Cut It

I'm a consultant. Please don't hold that against me. This simple fact means that I move around a lot. I move from place to place many times each year. In each place, I am forced to use different hardware, software, networks, and so forth.

You already know, because you are reading this book, that I use Linux. I use Linux a lot. I tend to use Linux to develop software for every environment, including Windows, because I like the tools Linux gives me.

I recently had occasion to work in an environment that I would consider quite atypical. A client was using OS/2 to build and deploy a 16-bit Powerbuilder application that connected over a token-ring network to a middle tier implemented using CICS on AIX! Over time, I managed to get a PC reassigned to running RedHat for a variety of internal documentation (another adventure, recounted in Chapter 9). Now I had continuous access to my favorite tools. OS/2 even has an X-server, called PMX, so I could run applications on the Linux box and display them on my desktop—almost.

What Is a Window Manager?

X-windows is a system that divides the labor up quite a bit. An X-windows application draws and controls only the area "inside" the window, the so-called client area. A totally separate program, called a "window manager" paints the borders and controls (such as resizing edges, maximize, minimize, and close buttons). You can have only one window manager program per X server, and that window manager provides these window "decorations" on behalf of all windows.

The window manager and the X-application communicate in standard ways. For example, when you resize a window by dragging an edge, all the work is done by the window manager program until you release the edge; then the window manager tells the X application about it by sending it a resize message. The application then must repaint itself in the new client area. (This is a bit theoretical: Some window managers send repaint messages while you drag the edge, so the application repaints several times, but you get the idea.) The application is also able to tell the window manager certain things, such as whether or not the window may be resized.

The division of labor has some distinct advantages, especially when you consider X's network capabilities. If the window manager is local, then when, for example, resizing the window of a remote application, only the final "window resize" and screen repaint need go over the network. None of the mouse events or border animation need to generate network traffic. (Again, if your window manager sends repaint messages as it goes, this benefit is lost.)

The other advantage is that you can change window managers. You might have an industrial application that is always maximized and should not be closed. You could write a window manager that doesn't have a close button or resizing decorations and that always sets the client area size to the full screen. Heck, some existing window managers can be configured to do this without any programming.

The details of window managers and their interaction with applications can get quite complex. There is a sort of "minimum standard" set of features a window manager must provide, and there is a "minimum standard" set of window manager messages an X-application must support, but many applications go well beyond this. The increasingly common "desktop" systems for X (KDE and GNOME, for example) extend this set quite, er, extensively. This means that applications that use these features either will run only with that one window manager or will have some functionality unavailable when running under other window managers.

If you want to know more, it is time for you to delve into X-windows programming.

VNC is available from the URLs noted at the beginning of the chapter. As for X-servers for Windows, a number of commercial ones are available. Since this book is about Free Software, however, we will not lead you to those.

A free X-server for Windows is available as part of a product called Cygwin, which is a complete POSIX-compliant programming environment for Windows. Cygwin actually makes Windows itself into a decent Unix-like environment. The X-server for Cygwin is the same X-server shipped with most Linux distributions: Xfree86.

Cygwin is available from Cygnus Software, which was purchased by RedHat last year. The URL is *http://sources.redhat.com/cygwin*.

I found that a great many "normal" applications, such as Wine (see Chapter 17) and the GIMP (see Chapter 22) would crash the OS/2 PMX server. Not only that, but the OS/2 PMX server insists on using OS/2 Presentation Manager as the window manager. (If you do not know what this means, see the "Window Manager" sidebar.) I found myself with a classic problem: How, if Linux is not my primary system, do I get a decent X-server?

This problem exists for Windows users as well. There are a couple of free X-servers out there for Windows, but they are quite limited in capability. There are some excellent commercial X-servers for Windows, but if you are like me, your software budget is limited (nonetheless, we will list URLs for a few of the commercial ones as well).

I began looking for alternatives. I was already familiar with something called *VNC*, which stands for "virtual network console" and is similar to PC-Anywhere. It basically allows you to access another machine's console as if you were sitting at that machine. To understand the differences, we will have to review the design of X and of VNC (Figure 2-1).

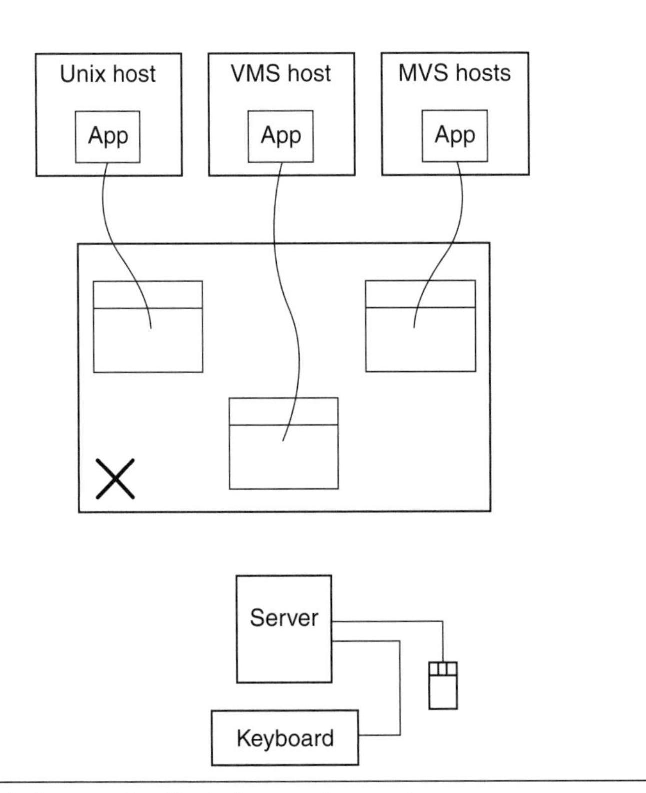

Figure 2-1 Block diagram of an X-windows environment.

X Basics

As you can see, the X-model revolves around the familiar client–server arrangement. The X-application is the client and generally runs on a box considered a "server" for all other purposes. The X-application controls only the "client area" of the window. The window frame, controls, resize handles, and so forth are all actually drawn and maintained by the window manager program. Thus, three applications—the X-server, the X-application (or client), and the window manager—are involved in presenting an application. The X-server resides on the box the user is sitting at. Beyond that, all bets are off. The window manager may be running on the same box as the X-server, on the same box as the application, or on a totally different box. The application may be running on the same box as the X-server, on the same machine as window manager, or on a totally different box. That's the beauty of X: It literally doesn't matter where you are in relation to the running program. You get what you want where you want it.

X-programs use a "display" specification (which may be set by the DISPLAY environment variable or may be specified as a command line argument using the -display switch) to determine where the X-server is. The format of a display specification is:

```
address:device number.display number
```

The address is the host address of the box on which the desired X-server is running. The device number refers to which display controller on that host is to be used (X supports multiple display cards). The display number refers to which monitor (sometimes called a *head*) attached to that display device is to be used (X supports multihead displays, which are cards that can drive multiple monitors). X-servers start sockets listening on port 6000 + device. In other words, if you have an X-server handling display device 1, it is listening on tcp port 6001.

On most PC hardware, there is only one display device, and that device has only one monitor, so the numeric portion of most display specifications is ":0.0". When the X-server is on the same host as the application, you may leave the address portion empty, thus ":0.0" would be the entire display specifcation.

If we consider the case in Figure 2-1, the display specification for the window manager is ":0.0" because it is on the same box as the X-server. The "xcpuinfo" program, however, has "flour.kitchen.org:0.0" as its display specification because it is being displayed on the host "flour," but it is being run on the host "soda."

The flexibility X-windows offers by assuming that the elements of the user interface are distributable over a network makes X-windows running on Unix platforms (and, thus, a Unix-like platform such as Linux) one of the most powerful and flexible environments in all of computing. Why? Because by virtue of this design element of X, combined with the full integration of TCP/IP networking into the operating system, we have a software environment where your geographical location has *absolutely nothing* to do with your ability to use a given computing resource.

In other words, if you are traveling in Hong Kong and get a call saying "We can't figure out why the check printing system is cutting hundreds of ten-thousand-dollar checks, all made out to you! Can you take a look at the production box?" all you need is a computer with an X-server and an Internet connection and you are as able to work with the "production box" as if you were right there. That's X, and it is a wonderful thing.

But what if you don't have an X-windows server available to you? Or what if the X-server you have access to is a few versions behind and you just can't run the applications you need—like maybe being stuck on OS/2? Trying to run the GIMP? Watching your desktop crash?

Enter VNC

The other major graphical platform on the market, Microsoft Windows, had a very different evolution. It grew out of an environment that was almost totally ignorant of networking in general and of TCP/IP internetworking in particular. It grew up in an environment that assumed one user and only one user would be making full use of the computer resources and that that user would be sitting next to the box.

In a Windows-based PC, applications must run on the same box as they are being displayed. There is no distinction between the program's "server" (the operating system) and the user interface's server (the display API). In X, the display API is a set of services offered by a server that is actually network available. The program API is provided by the OS of the host on which the program runs. On a Windows PC, both sets of services are assumed to be local.

An entire class of applications arose to work around this deficiency in Windows. From Close-up to PC Anywhere, these programs essentially "poll" the display of a host PC and, using an entirely proprietary protocol, send the changes over a link (originally a modem, later an IP network). On the client side, they capture keystrokes and mouse movements and send them back over the link and then "regenerate" them as if they were performed on the host PC.

Such programs were used (and often still are used) to remote-control Windows-based PCs. This is nothing like X. It replicates an entire desktop. You cannot have windows open showing applications running on multiple hosts at the same time on the same desktop. Still, it gave Windows users something approaching the capabilities of X for remote computing.

AT&T developed an open standard for such transfer of a graphical desktop and user input. They called this *VNC*, or virtual network console. They developed servers and clients for a number of platforms and, luckily for the world of Linux, they put the code out under the GNU Public License.

Before we go into the details of the Linux implementation, let's examine the generic model of a VNC session (Figure 2-2). In our diagram of a simple VNC session, we have a box running a VNC client (host *salt.kitchen.org*) and a box running a VNC server (*pepper.kitchen.org*). Both of these boxes are Windows 98 machines. Pepper has a VNC server running. VNC servers have "names," similar to (but not identical to) X-windows server names.

A VNC server name is of the form:

```
address:desktop
```

where "address" is the name of the server host, and "desktop" is a number specifying which VNC server session on that box to talk to. VNC servers start listening sockets

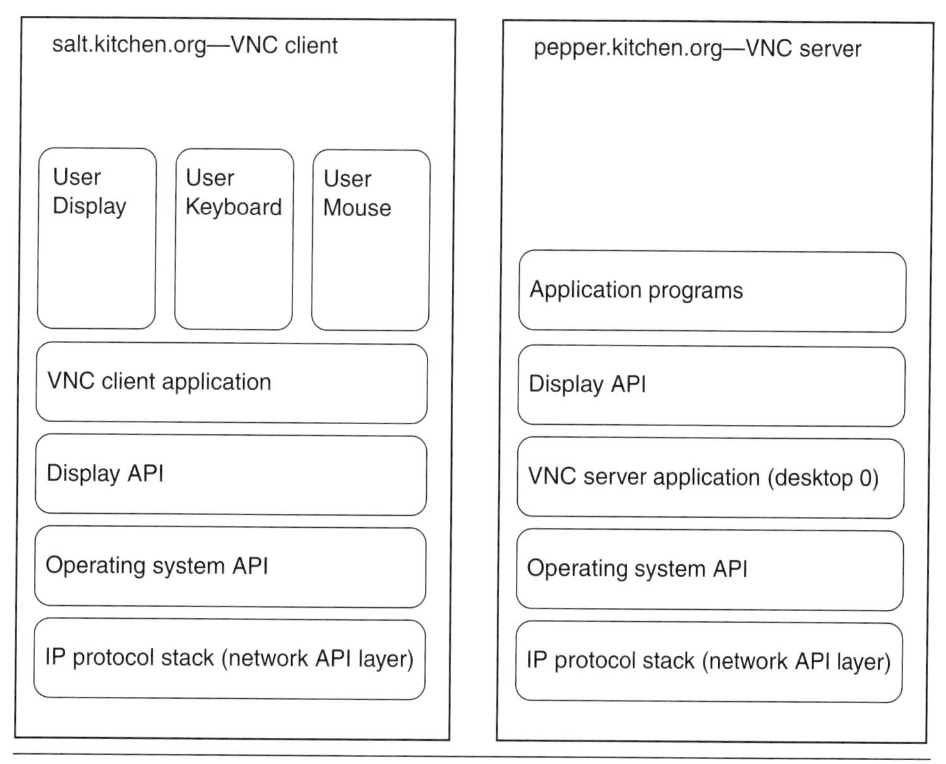

Figure 2-2 Block diagram of a VNC environment.

on port 5900 plus desktop number. In other words, to contact desktop 2, a VNC client must connect to tcp port 5902.

Data bound for the server flows down the left-side layers, is sent over the Internet to the right side, where it moves up the layers. Data bound for the client moves down the right side, over the net, then up the left. All of this is invisible to the user. The user on the client just sees a window on "salt" that appears to have "pepper"'s desktop displayed in it.

So, as we can see, VNC is quite different from X. But that's okay. It serves a different need. When you have a good X-server and X-applications, X is all that you need. Remember, though, if you use Windows 98 and aren't made out of money, you probably do not have a decent X-server. And what about that poor schlep stuck on OS/2? What is he going to do? Don't worry—we'll get there. Have patience.

VNC is, of course, available for all versions of Microsoft Windows. It is, happily for this book, also available for Linux. The generic model of a VNC session covers most of what's going on when you use VNC on Windows platforms. On Linux platforms, it is a little bit more interesting.

XVNC—The Best of Both Worlds

The program that implements a VNC server for Linux is actually called Xvnc. It is a complicated little beastie with literally hundreds of possible configurations. More often than not, it is started with a shell script called "vncserver" that reads a configuration file and sets up an Xvnc instance with settings most users will want (Figure 2-3).

VNC on Linux has a bit of a twist: Xvnc is not only a VNC server; it is also an X-server. That's right. When you run a VNC server on Linux you are actually running a full-blown X-server. This X-server provides a complete, self-contained X-desktop. It has a unique X-display specification.

How is this done? Most Linux boxes already have a running X-server, the default graphical console. It does this by setting up each VNC server as a separate display number. Remember, your standard console X-server is probably:

```
flour.kitchen.org:0.0
```

Your first VNC server instance will set up its "X self" as:

```
flour.kitchen.org:1.0
```

If you point an application at the former, it will display on the console. If you point it at the latter, it will display on the VNC console. Neat, eh?

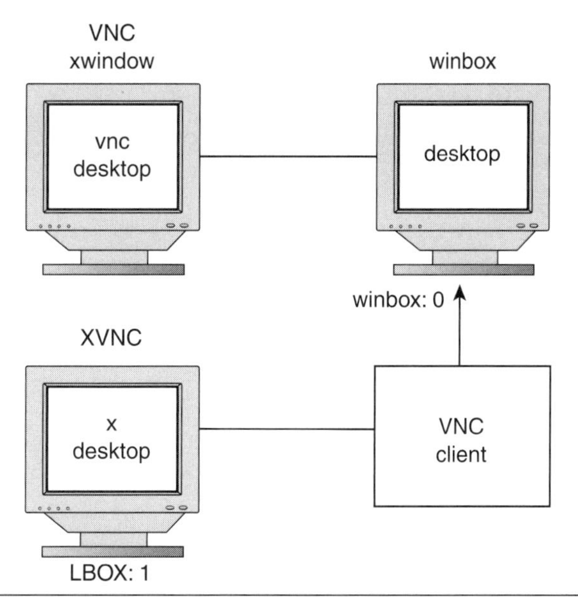

Figure 2-3 Block diagram of an Xvnc environment.

Wait! It gets better. Your standard X-desktop looks like Figure 2-4. That same X-desktop with a VNC client running looks like Figure 2-5. That client shows the VNC desktop, running a totally different desktop environment.

It gets better yet! You can connect to a VNC server from a totally different OS (Figure 2-6). Figure 2-7 shows a Windows 98 desktop running a Windows VNC client, with that client connected to a Linux box. So even if you don't have a decent X-server for Windows, you're able, as you can see, to make full use of X within the VNC client.

So what about OS/2 or even some other orphaned platform? What about that? Well, it so happens that there is an experimental OS/2 VNC client for Presentation Manager, but there is an even better solution. Not only does Xvnc provide an X-server listening on X port 1 (which, just for those who are dying to know, is actually TCP port 6001) and a VNC port listening on port 5901, it also opens an HTTP server listening on TCP port 5801. An HTTP server? A *Web* server? Yup. A Web server. It doesn't serve up much in the way of HTML, however. What it serves up is a Web page containing a Java applet. That Java applet is a full-blown VNC client!

That's right. If the platform you are on has a Java-enabled Web browser, then you can connect to a Linux VNC server. It is just that easy. Take a look at Figure 2-8. I'm still an X bigot, but I must admit that VNC provides a certain level of cross-platform, not just cross-continent, functionality that I am already unable to live without.

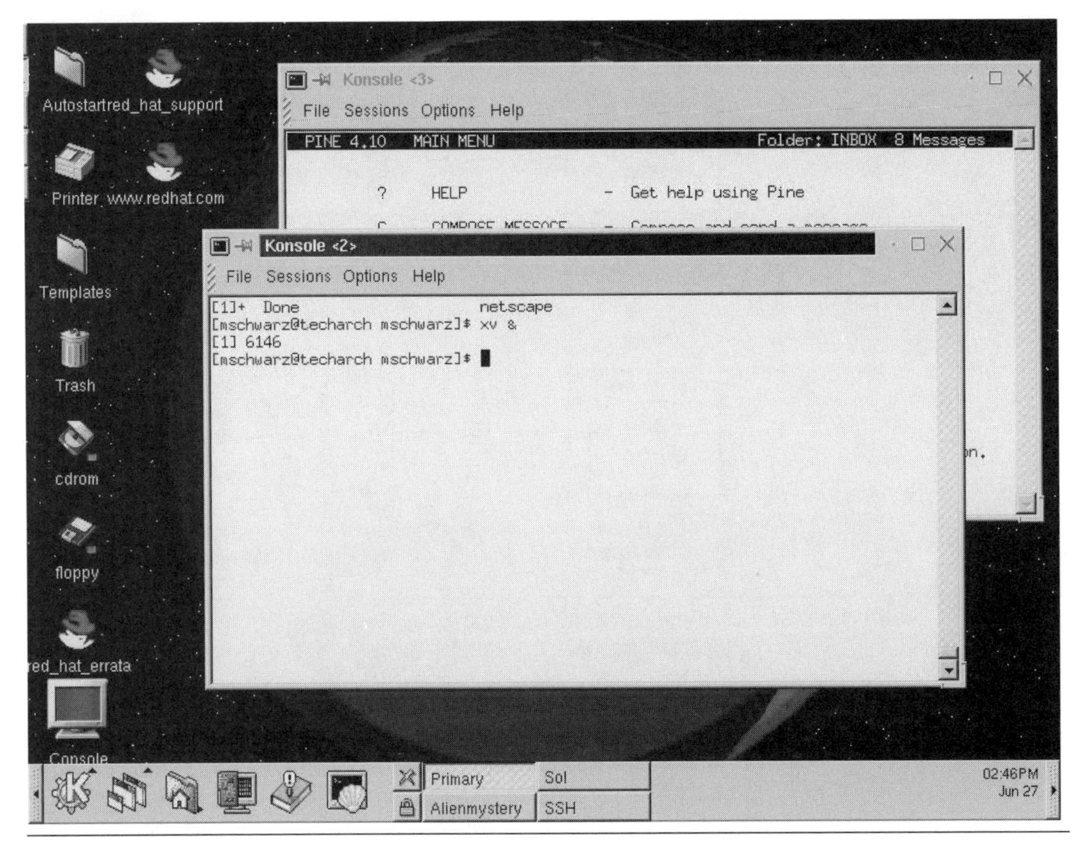

Figure 2-4 Image of an X-desktop, probably a KDE desktop, but I'm not picky.

VNC is not without limitations. It can't forward sounds (but then, X can't forward digital sound either). It is not terribly secure (but we'll cover using SSH to lock down this and many other protocols later in the book), being protected by a simple password and having no encryption. It is often set to lower color depth to make the protocol faster, limiting the usefulness of the protocol for remote multimedia work. The screen "paints" top to bottom and left to right as fast as the communications medium allows. This painting effect makes VNC rather useless for full-motion-animation applications. Still, it allowed me to make full use of a Linux platform, even through my severely limited desktop environment.

One exciting thread: Apparently, there is a VNC client for the Palm organizer! That's right: Use Windows, X, anything, right from your Palm-connected organizer. Maybe in the next book.

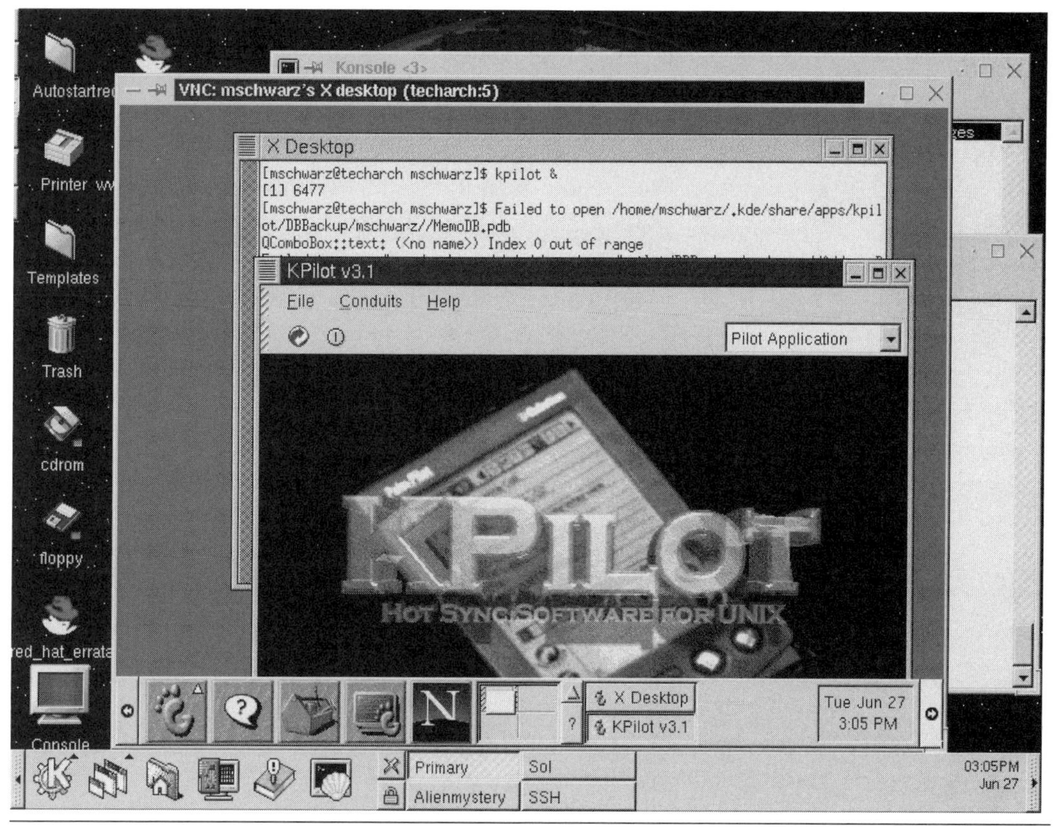

Figure 2-5 Image of the same X-desktop as in Figure 2-4, but this time with a VNC client showing a GNOME desktop.

Using VNC with Linux

Meanwhile, let's walk you through using *vncserver*, the two Linux vnc clients, and finally through using your browser to connect to a VNC server.

To run an X VNC server, you would generally just type:

```
$ vncserver
```

If you have never run a vncserver session before, the response should look like this:

```
$ vncserver

You will require a password to access your desktops.
```

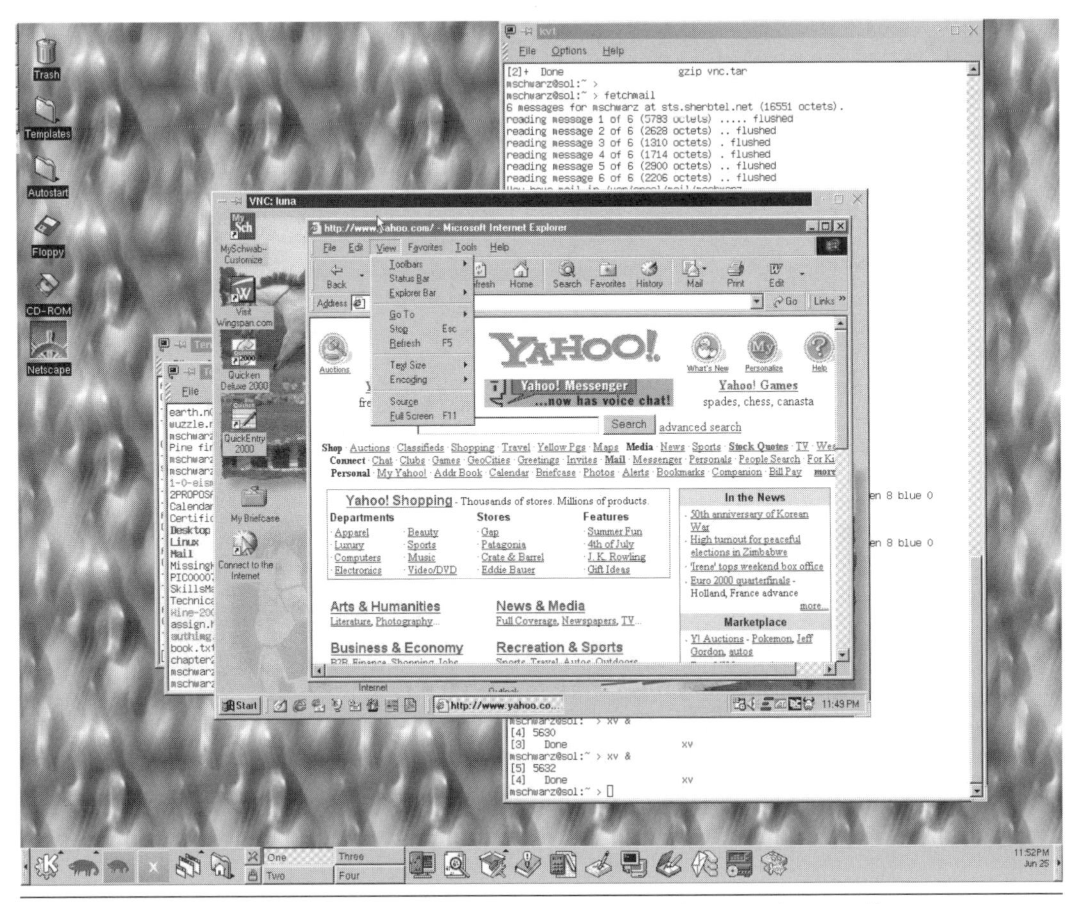

Figure 2-6 Same desktop again as in Figure 2-4, except this time the VNC client is talking to a Windows box.

```
Password:
Verify:

New 'X' desktop is roux.kitchen.org:1

Starting applications specified in /etc/X11/Xsession
Log file is /home/mschwarz/.vnc/roux.kitchen.org:1.log

$
```

You must type and then retype a password. If they don't match, you will have to rerun vncserver. This password is then permanently set for this user. The home directory of

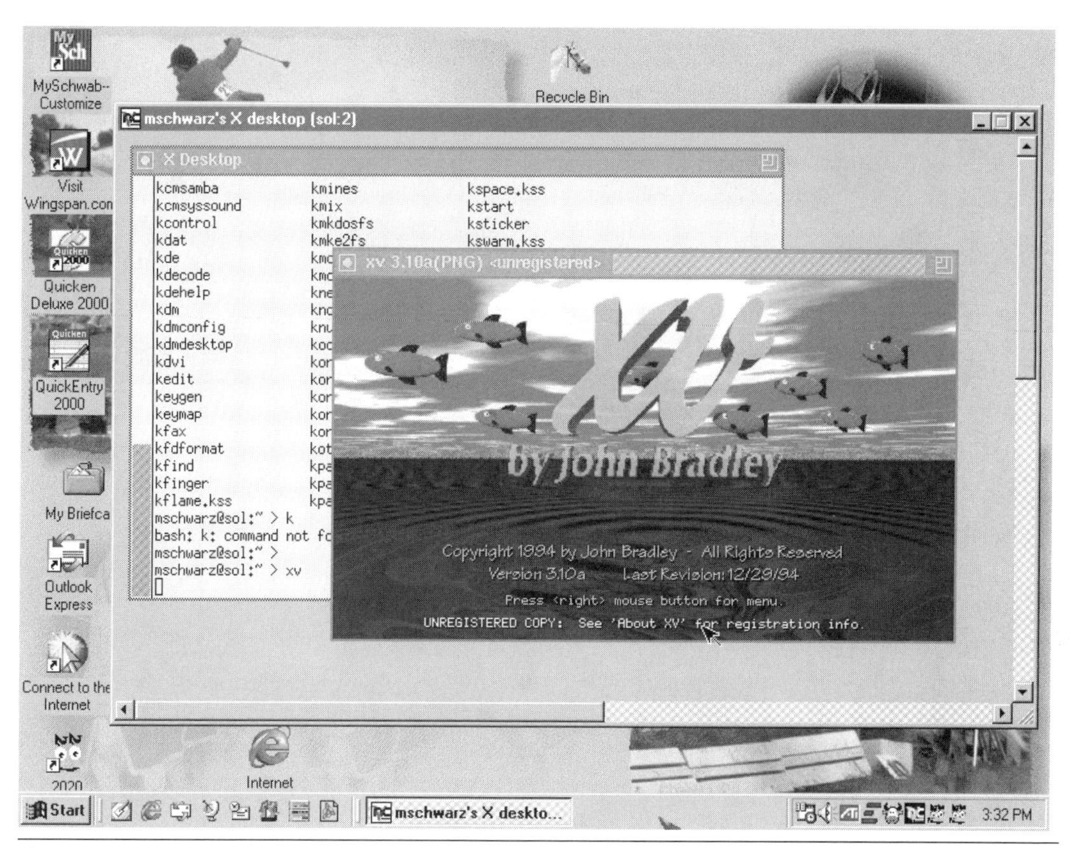

Figure 2-7 Windows 98 desktop running VNC to a Linux box.

your user account will now contain a *.vnc* directory. That directory contains control files and logs for VNC. Feel free to explore these files at your leisure.

If you want to change your VNC password, use the *vncpasswd* command.

The vncserver session keeps running until the machine is rebooted or until you kill it. Here's how you kill a VNC session on Linux:

```
$ vncserver -kill :1
Killing Xvnc process ID 13824
$
```

When you run vncserver you will get the first available desktop number. This is generally :1 (since :0 is probably taken by the system's "real" X-server console). If you wish to run one on a specific desktop number, try:

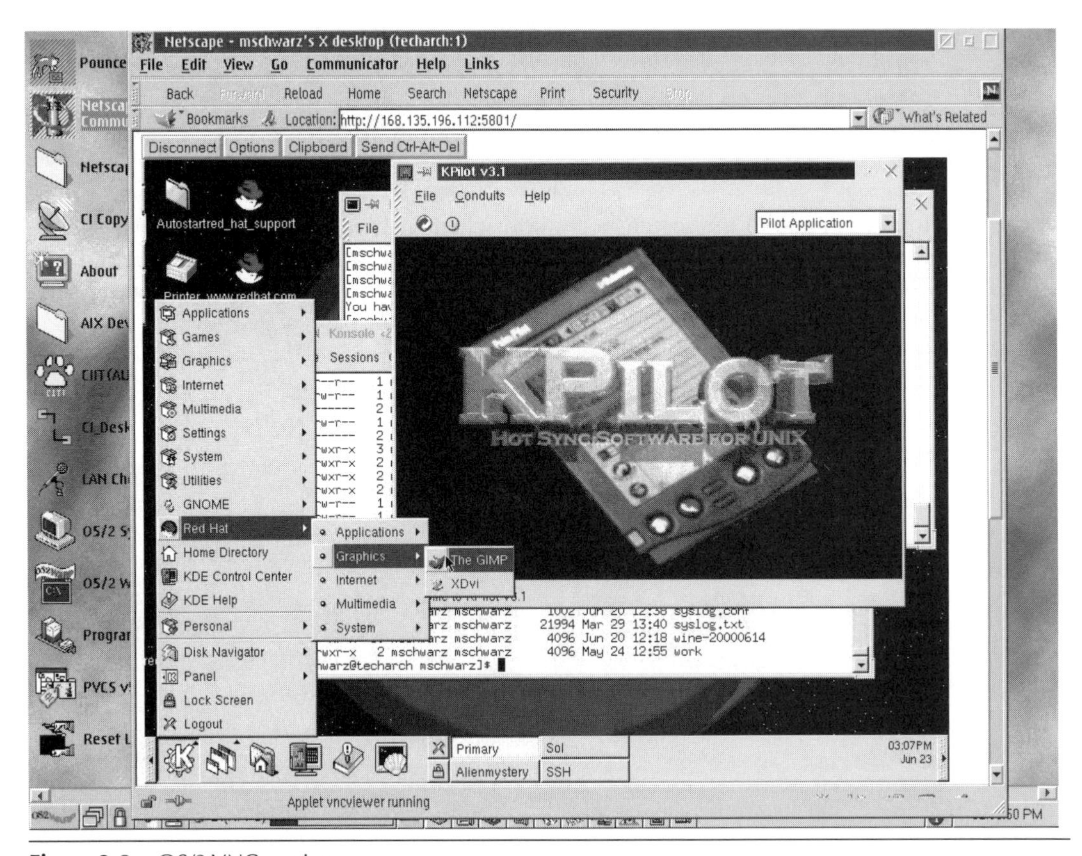

Figure 2-8 OS/2 VNC session.

```
$ vncserver :8

New 'X' desktop is roux.kitchen.org:8

Starting applications specified in /etc/X11/Xsession
Log file is /home/mschwarz/.vnc/roux.kitchen.org:8.log

$
```

There are quite a few options and choices to set on VNC. Where these are set depends on how you install VNC. Debian sets you up with an entry in /etc for VNC server configuration. This is very nice, because it gives you one place to set defaults for the entire system.

On RedHat (and other RPM-based distributions), the defaults are all set in */usr/bin/vncserver*, which is a Perl script that runs the real VNC X-server (which is called *Xvnc*). Here you must edit the actual script.

One convention that is often used but that is by no means required is to set the VNC X-server display size to be "one smaller" than the client display. That convention is followed in all of the screenshots in this chapter. If you have an 800 × 600-pixel display, set your VNC server to 640 × 480. If you have a 1024 × 768-pixel client display, set your VNC server to 800 × 600, and so on. This ensures that the entire server desktop will fit on your client screen with room to spare, and you won't have to use scroll bars to move around the server desktop. That works, but it does get both distracting and annoying.

While only Mandrake and Debian ship with VNC on their installation media, the source code is available, and RPM packages are available from the usual suspects.

To make use of a VNC server, you must run a VNC client.

There are actually three clients for Linux VNC. Some packages include only two of these three. The three clients are:

- *vncviewer/xvncviewer:* This is an X-windows client for VNC. This one is included in every VNC package I have seen.
- *svncviewer:* This is an SVGA (or console) version of the VNC client. This can be run from a text-mode console on your Linux box. Debian optionally includes this one. Otherwise, compile it from the source.
- *The Java client:* The Xvnc server can offer an HTTP server that pushes a Java VNC client to a browser. Thus, any Java-enabled browser can be used to access the VNC server! We discuss this in depth later.

When you use the X vncviewer, you may launch it as in Figure 2-9. Once vncviewer (or xvncviewer) is running, your desktop might look as it does in Figure 2-5.

The svncviewer works much the same, except it will run only on the text-mode console of a Linux box. It uses the SVGA library support (which is shipped with every Linux distribution I know of, including very old ones) to present a VNC graphical desktop on the console. The only reason to obtain or compile the SVGA client is if you need a VNC client on a Linux box that doesn't have an X-server.

You run svncviewer in exactly the same way as vncviewer/xvncviewer, but when it runs it will not open a window with a desktop in it; it will instead take over the entire screen with the VNC desktop. You may find this useful on older machines

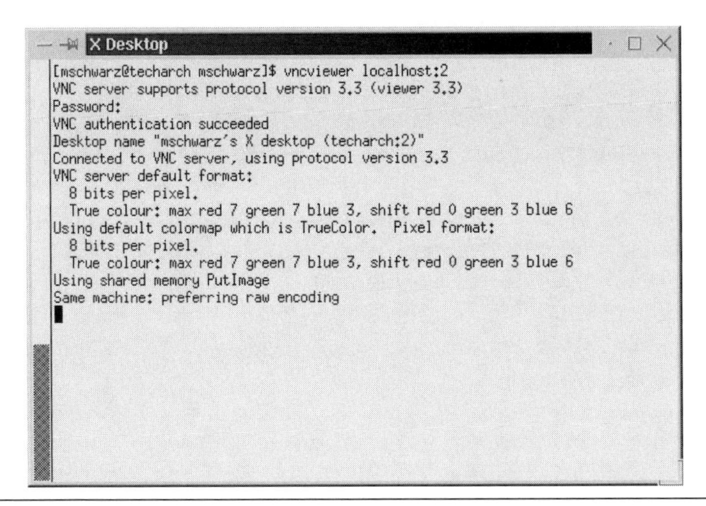

Figure 2-9 xviewer xterm.

(386/486-class machines) with limited memory (16M or less), where running an X-server would be a major burden.

Finally, let's cover the Java client. Let's assume you've started an Xvnc server on your Linux box at *soda.kitchen.org*. Let's assume it is desktop :2. To use the Java client, just point your browser at:

```
http://soda.kitchen.org:5802/
```

and you will get the login screen of Figure 2-10.

Once logged in, you will get a browser window with a VNC client inside that looks just like Figure 2-7. That's how I used Linux with a fully functional X-desktop from my OS/2 box!

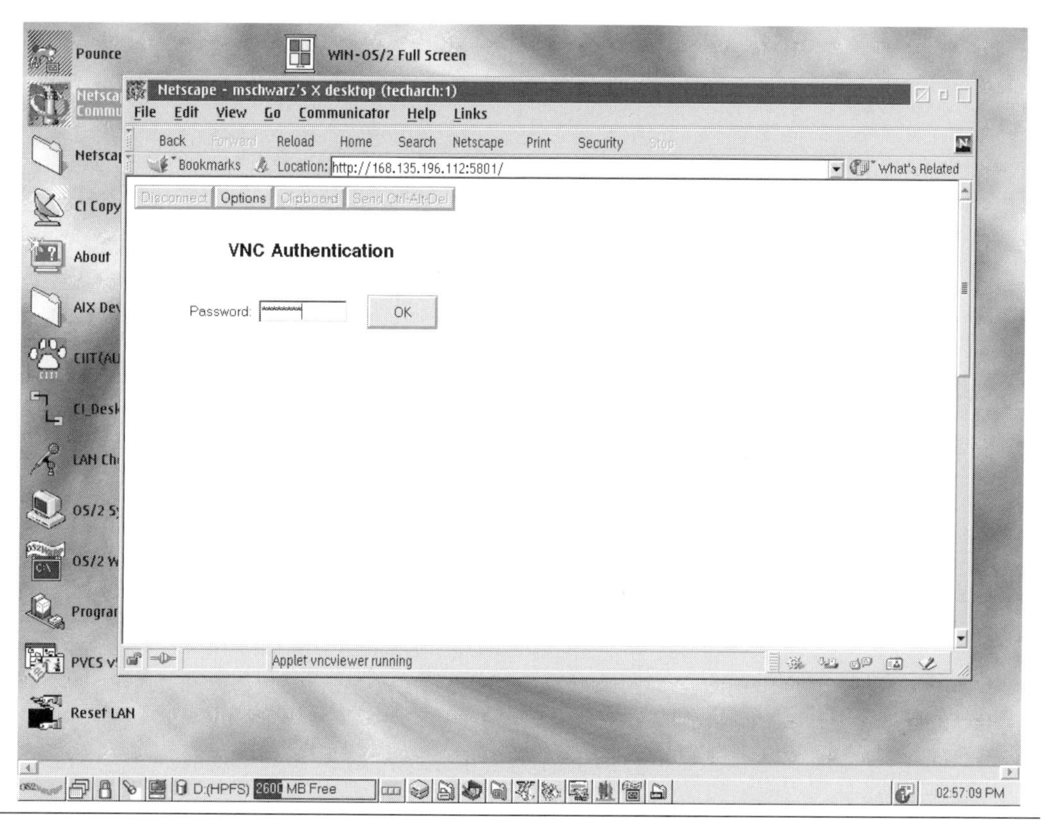

Figure 2-10 Browser with VNC login screen.

Chapter 3

Run a Whole Network with One IP Address

Difficult-o-Meter: 5 (this is a tad bit of work)

Covers:

ipchains	*http://netfilter.filewatcher.org/ipchains/*
ipmasqadm	*http://juanjox.kernelnotes.org/*
diald	*http://netfilter.filewatcher.org/ipchains/*
Prerequisites	A working TCP/IP network and a working connection to your ISP. A rough understanding of the differences between static and dynamic IP addresses.

Problem: I've got a whole herd of machines, but only one externally addressable IP address. What do I do?

Solution: Well, you could shell out a lot of money, buy a T-1 connection, and then get yourself a Class C address from an ISP. Or you could enable something called IP Masquerading (see the next section, What the Heck Is IPMasquerading) and go to town with what you've already got.

Preamble

Cable providers and many Internet service providers (ISPs) don't like to give out multiple IP addresses to customers for free. Most of them don't like to give out static IP addresses at all. They do this for several reasons:

1. It's easier to configure.
2. It helps prevent customers from running servers on their home systems and soaking up ISP resources without paying for the extra bandwidth.
3. It allows them to oversell. With 254 static IP addresses, they could have only 254 customers; with 254 dynamic IP addresses, they can have a lot more, since not all 254 people will be logged in at once.
4. It allows them to reconfigure their networks on the fly, without affecting end users.

Bear in mind that cable companies do it primarily for reason 2. They want their money, and I guess I can't blame them. Some cable companies will also tell you that running any sort of network address translation (NAT) is strictly against their terms of service and will even claim that they can detect it. As of this writing, I have seen no way in which they would be able to reliably detect a NAT'ed network. The cable companies in question want you to buy one IP per machine, you see—generally at $30–$50 a pop. Seeing as they're willing to let you hook up an infinite number of TVs these days, this pay-per-PC thing seems a bit . . . greedy, doesn't it?

This chapter covers two different but somewhat similar setups: The network that is connected via a Linux box and a modem, and the network that is permanently connected. I'll cover both static and dynamic IP addresses for the router's connection, but I'm going to assume that your own network is running with static IP addresses. It's simpler that way, you see. If you really want to run DHCP, head over to the DHCP HOWTO at *http://www.ibiblio.org/pub/Linux/docs/HOWTO/mini/DHCP* and go to town.)

What the Heck Is IP Masquerading?

IP Masquerading is the act of hiding an entire network behind a single machine. Basically, the IP Masquerading host takes all the packets from one side of the network and passes them on to the other side—like any router. Unlike routers, however, the IPMasq host rewrites each packet so that it appears as if the IPMasq host itself sent it. When it receives a reply to one of these rewritten packets, it rewrites it once again, passing it back to the correct host on the hidden network. This means that for a single valid IP address, you can have dozens, hundreds, or even thousands of machines with full access to the other side—all while remaining completely hidden.

NAT vs. IP Masquerade

Some sources will tell you that NAT is different from IPMasquerading—including the IP Masquerade-HOWTO at *http://www.linuxdoc.org/*! They are, however, incorrect. As of RFC 2663, NAT and IP Masquerading are the same thing. Once upon a time, NAT required your own externally addressable subnet (you'd have had to pay for your own class A, B, or C address block). This is, however, no longer true. Official NAT is now more than happy to work with the nonrouted subnets of 192.168.x.x, 172.16.x.x, and 10.x.x.x . While I used to say that for all intents and purposes, NAT is IP Masquerading is NAT, I can now correctly say that they are indeed the same thing. Linux just insists on calling NAT by the name of IP Masquerading. What did old Will Shakespeare say? A rose by any other name . . . ?

Stand-Alone Masqing Boxes

Since we've acknowledged that you have more than one machine in your house, I have to recommend setting up a dedicated IP Masquerading box. You don't need anything big. A discarded P75 with a few hundred megabites of disk space is plenty. My Masqing host is a Pentium 75 with 16MB of RAM and 350MB of disk space. It's always been much more than I really need (though I will say that when compiling a new kernel on the firewall, I can detect a slowdown in the network). One could use a minimal Linux distribution like Trinux, and do away with the hard drive entirely. But Trinux (*http://www.trinux.org/*) and the Linux router project (*http://www.linuxrouter.org/*) are both beyond the scope of this chapter.

I recommend that your stand-alone router have one Network Information Card (NIC) for your internal network and one NIC for your external network (if you're doing this over a modem, skip ahead and look at the next section). There are a variety of very usable $10 1/100 PCI Ethernet NICs available. Head over to your local SuperMegaMicroComputerMaxHutDepot, and pick up as many as you need.

The Modem-Connect IPMasq'd Network

The first thing you'll need to do is get Point-to-Point Protocol (PPP) up and running. You'll also want to configure diald so that your Linux router will dial up your ISP whenever a connected machine needs to get out. Configuring diald and the modem are really beyond the scope of this chapter, I'm afraid. Instead, you'll have to head over to the Diald HOWTO, available at *http://www.ibiblio.org/pub/Linux/docs/HOWTO/Diald-HOWTO*.

The Router-Connect IPMasq'd Network

The first thing to bear in mind is that no matter how many times you hear people (including myself) refer to cable modems and DSL modems, *there is no such thing* as a cable modem or a DSL modem. Modems are pretty much used only on phone lines (*modem* is short for modulator/demodulator, and this modulation is required to convert digital data to analog data—since normal phone lines can only handle analog data). So-called cable modems and DSL modems are actually routers—they merely route packets from your internal network (or PC) to the external world. Now, that said, for pretty much all intents and purposes, you can get away with calling a cable router a cable modem. This is rather similar to the definition of *pistol*. Technically, a revolver is *not* a pistol. A *pistol* is a handgun whose chamber is integral with the barrel (check it out at *http://www.m-w.com/*), while a *revolver* has multiple chambers (usually six). For all intents and purposes, a revolver is a pistol—it's a handgun (and that's usually what people think of when they say *pistol*). For virtually everyone, a modem is a gadget that gets plugged into your home somewhere that lets you access the Internet or another computer. I think that's enough hair-splitting, don't you?

For consistency and simplicity, I will not cover IP Masquerading under kernel 2.0.x—it's time to upgrade to a newer version of the kernel, my friend. Kernel 2.0.x is quite old now. Since (as of this writing) no updates have been done to it since January 9, 2001, it seems safe to say that not much more development work is going into it. If it helps convince you at all, I noticed small speed increases when I upgraded from kernel 2.0.36 to kernel 2.2.x. That explains why I'm not using the old 2.0 series of kernel. But why wouldn't I use the new 2.4 kernel? I've always followed a rather simple saying: The early bird may get the worm, but the second mouse gets the cheese. For this reason, I tend to stay one kernel revision behind on my servers. The only time I violate that rule is when the new kernel has some feature that I desperately need.

If that line of argument hasn't convinced you to go with kernel 2.2, then that's okay. Kernel 2.2's ipchain rules can be read natively by kernel 2.4's netfilter tool. Doing so is beyond the scope of this chapter, however.

Okay, so you've got yourself a machine with a kernel 2.2 distribution (or, conceivably, a 2.4 distribution). You've got yourself a working DSL or cable connection. Now you need to get ipchains up and running.

Kernel Configuration

Yep, you'll once again be compiling your kernel. We need to add some specific configuration items. We need:

- Network firewalls
- IP Firewalling
- IP transparent proxy support
- IP Masquerading
- ICMP Masquerading (so ping will work)
- Optimization as a router
- TCP Syncookie support
- procfs
- sysctl support

Thankfully, we can almost complete this little shopping list in the "Networking Options" of our kernel configuration. As you can see in Figure 3-1, just about everything we need (and more—see the upcoming section, Port Forwarding) can be enabled from one screen. You'll find procfs under "proc filesystem support" in the filesystems section of the kernel config. Sysctl support is found under "general setup." What do these things do?

Network firewalls and IP Firewalling allow us to use ipchains to block certain packets. They're a required piece of foundation for all the rest. If IP: firewalling is not selected, you aren't allowed to compile masquerading in either. It is, at least as far as I can ascertain, the kernel code that allows you to take a really close look at network packets and to reject or accept them.

IP transparent proxy support is also used in masquerading, and it is what allows the kernel to modify packets as they go through. This is required for IP Masquerading.

IP Masquerading is . . . well, isn't it obvious that we'd have to enable this in order to do IP Masquerading? This code actually allows the kernel to do packet rewriting, using the rules defined by ipchains. This will also compile the standard ipmasq modules, for such things as vdolive, irc, ftp, and quake—which do not work under normal ipchains rules.

ICMP Masquerading lets you use ping and traceroute from masq'd machines—very handy when checking out networking problems. You want this.

Optimization as a router is definitely a good thing to enable—it'll result in a good throughput, provided you're using a dedicated IPMasqing box (which I already highly recommended). Speed is a good thing, right?

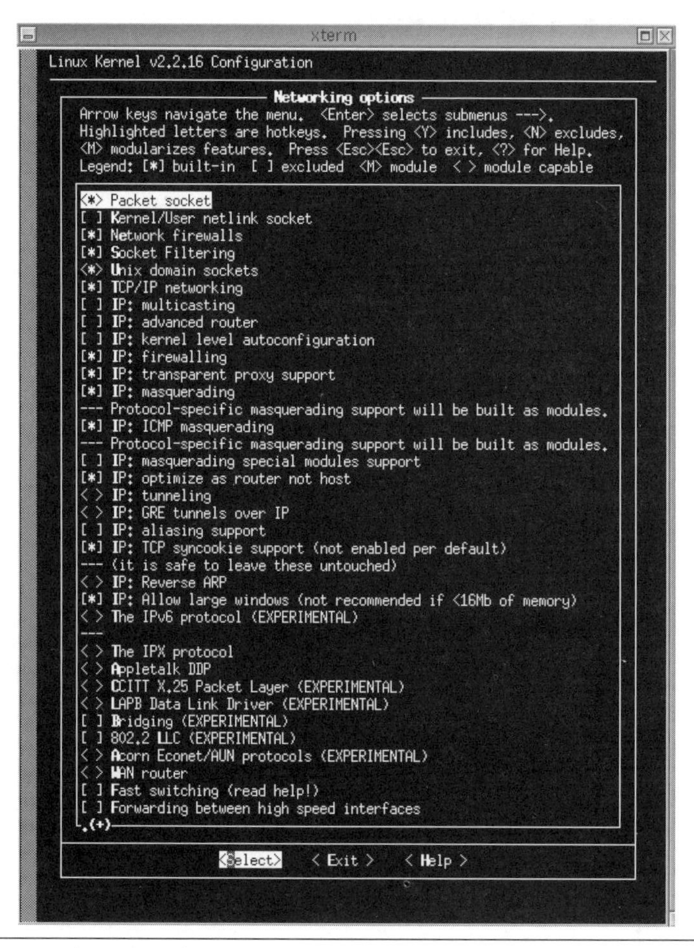

Figure 3-1 Linux kernel configuration.

TCP Syncookie support is a basic survival strategy. We enable this in the kernel so that when the inevitable denial-of-service attack comes, we'll be prepared. What's a denial-of-service attack? Picture this nightmarish situation: a parent cursed to answer every question, and put in charge of 35 3-year-olds. Flooded with thousands upon thousands of "why?" questions, the parent is incapable of doing anything but responding. That's a denial-of-service attack in a nutshell. It's easy to do, it's usually fairly pointless, and it's quite annoying. TCP Syncookie support will let your internal users continue using the Internet even while you're under attack. Cool, eh?

Procfs is the Proc filesystem. It's required for enabling IP Forwarding and for that syncookie support we just talked about.

Sysctl support allows you to change some kernel parameters on the fly, which is what we'll need to do to . . . you guessed it . . . enable IP Forwarding and syncookie support.

Now that you've got these things enabled, go ahead and recompile your kernel and install it. Go ahead and reboot, and when the system comes back up, issue these two commands as root:

```
echo 1>/proc/sys/net/ipv4/ip_forward
echo 1>/proc/sys/net/ipv4/tcp_syncookies
```

Test those two commands, and once you've verified that they work, pick a configuration file (I like /etc/rc.d/rc.inet myself) and add those two lines into it somewhere near the beginning. Syncookie and IP_Forwarding support will now be enabled on the next boot as well. Congratulations! Your system now has the basic kernel configuration required for IP Masquerading.

IPChains

Well, now that we've got a working kernel, we've got two things left to do: install IPChains, and put some rules together. First, installing IPChains.

Head off to *http://netfilter.filewatcher.org/ipchains/* and download and install the latest version. When I grabbed 1.3.10, I noticed there was already a version of ipchains compiled in the directory. Being the paranoid sod that I am, I deleted that binary, and recompiled from source with a simple "make." Even on my P75, compilation took less than a minute. Then a "make install" as root, and you'll be ready to install some ipchains rulesets.

IPChains Rulesets

Well, the simplest possible set of rules would look like this:

```
/sbin/ipchains -F forward
/sbin/ipchains -P forward DENY
/sbin/ipchains -A forward -j MASQ -s 192.168.2.0/24 -d 0.0.0.0/0
```

Basically, the first line flushes all forwarding rules. The second line says, "Our standard reaction to forwarding requests is to deny them." The third line says, "Anyone coming from 192.168.2.0 is AOK by me. They can send packets anywhere and get responses." Obviously, you'd want to substitute your own internal IP address space for 192.168.2.0. If you use the 192.168.0.x space, simply replace 192.168.2.0 with 192.168.0.0. The terminating 0 means "anyone whose IP address starts with the preceding three numbers." (Actually, the combination of the subnet mask (24) and the IP subnet (192.168.2.0) are what determine that, but if you don't understand subnet masks and subnets, that's okay.)

Throw those rules up on your firewall and go to town. You should now be able to connect from any internal machine to any external *provided* you have set the firewall's IP address as that machine's default gateway. To set your default gateway on Linux, type

```
route add default gw xxx.yyy.www.zzz
```

where xxx.yyy.www.zzz is the internal IP address of your firewall. The internal IP address is the IP address assigned to the NIC that is attached to your internal network. The other NIC will have some ISP-assigned IP address, about which we don't care. For MS Windows, you can set the default gateway in the TCP/IP properties section of the network control panel.

If your internal machines can't connect, there are several things to check:

1. Does the internal machine have the correct default route set?
2. Are you *sure* you typed the ipchains commands properly on the firewall? Use ipchains -L to verify the currently running rules.
3. Are you running the right kernel on the firewall machine (you remember, the one you compiled with IP Masquerading support)?
4. Did you remember to turn on IP Forwarding, as mentioned earlier?
5. Can the firewall itself reach the site you're using to test?
6. Can your firewall ping the default route on its external NIC?
7. Do you have network connectivity between the firewall and internal machines?

If all those things are true, and you *still* can't reach the outside world from the internal network, then . . . well, it's time to hit the documents. Take a look at the IPChains-HOWTO and the IP-Masquerading-HOWTO, available from *http://www.linuxdoc.org/*, or from the homepage listed at the beginning of the chapter.

If, however, everything is working fine at this point, go ahead and put the three earlier commands into something /etc/rc.d/rc.ipchains or /etc/rc.d/rc.firewall, make sure the file is executable, and call it from your rc.local file (on RedHat, Mandrake, and Turbolinux, at least; on SuSE, you'll need to create a start-up and shutdown script—just copy one of the existing ones, and change the relevant bits).

Secure IPChains Rules

The next set of rules I'll give you will help secure your system a bit better, but it's no catch-all. The first thing you have to do is go through your firewall box and deactivate *all* unnecessary services. */etc/inetd.conf* has lots of things listed, and go ahead and deactivate pretty much all of them. For connecting to your firewall, you should install openssh (see Chapter 14 on SSH). *Never* use Telnet or File Transfer Protocol (FTP) to connect to your firewall, and certainly not from the outside. Go into your */etc/rc.d* directory and make a new directory called *unused*. At the very least move the nfs and smb and nfsserver scripts into the *unused* directory. Delete the symbolic links from */etc/rc.d/rcX.d*. You can even get away with deactivating inetd entirely. This will help avoid inetd-based DoS attacks, since inetd can't swamp the system if it's not even running (sshd isn't usually started from inetd, so sshd can still be running without needing inetd). Basically, don't run *anything* unnecessary on your firewall. I run openssh and the distributed.net client. Why do I consider the distributed.net client? Because I have a chance of winning $1000 by running it. Anyway, those two applications are it—I don't run anything else. Anything else is a security hole.

On to the secure rules:

```
/sbin/ipchains -F input

#stuffed masquerading?  no thanks
/sbin/ipchains -A input -i eth1 -s 192.168.2.0/24 -d 0.0.0.0/0 -l -j
    REJECT
#inbound stuffed routing?  no way
/sbin/ipchains -F output
/sbin/ipchains -A output -i eth1 -s 0.0.0.0/0 -d 192.168.2.0/24 -l -j
    REJECT

/sbin/ipchains -F forward
/sbin/ipchains -P forward DENY
/sbin/ipchains -A forward -j MASQ -s 192.168.2.0/24 -d 0.0.0.0/0
```

The first thing this does is to flush all input rules, then it sets up a rule that rejects IP packets that come from the outside but have internal IP addresses. Since it's impossible for one of your internal machines to be on the outside, someone is doing something nasty. It also logs any such request into /var/log/messages.

Next, all output rules are flushed, and then a rule that forbids stuffed routing—packets that have been specially constructed to breach your network. Obviously, it's not hard to see why we're rejecting those. No upstanding netizen has any use for those sorts of packets.

The last three rules should look familiar to you—they're the rules that are already running on your firewall. They still do the same thing.

Blocking Specific Ports

You can add additional rules to kill specific services on your firewall. A rule like

```
ipchains -A input -p tcp -i eth1 -s 0.0.0.0/0 21 -l -j REJECT
```

will deny any port 21 (FTP) packets that try to come in via eth1. This will also kill your outgoing FTP connections, since it's going to terminate any incoming FTP data. Basically, you'll make an FTP connection out, but all replies from the remote server will be rejected (and logged) by the firewall.

"Gee Whiz, Wally, I can't block only incoming FTP packets?" Nope, Beav, you can't. But that's not such a big deal, unless you insist on running an FTP server on your firewall—which you should *not* be doing. The preceding rule isn't necessary in 99.9% of network setups. If you don't have it, and the firewall isn't running ftpd, those FTP request packets won't do anything. Why? Basically, the FTP request will come into your firewall, but since there are no forwarding rules set up for FTP (see the next section, Port Forwarding) and your firewall doesn't have any software running on port 21, the packet is denied. A really clever attacker might try stuffed routing to get past this, but . . . well, we already blocked stuffed routing.)

Where the per-port rules come in handy is in blocking your internal users from doing specific things. You may not want them to be able to use Gopher (port 70) or Usenet News (port 119). You may want to block AIM (AOL Instant Messenger), but it really can't be done. The programmers at AOL thought of you already, and they've built in the ability to use all the common ports that people don't dare block (like port 80 for www and port 25 for smtp). Simply set your user's PC speakers on maximum, and run around pummeling anyone whose machine generates the AIM login sound.

You can also block the ports that backdoor software might use, like the cDc's Back-Orifice program. Of course, since BO2K doesn't have a default port (the old version uses 31337 as the default port), you're going to end up blocking a lot of ports. It'd probably be easier just to alter your first three rules so that you're allowing only a few services and blocking all others. Remember to leave icmp and the Domain Naming System (DNS) open! Without DNS, your machines won't be able to figure out the IP address to which they should send requests.

Port Forwarding

Since we aren't running any services on the firewall, we can't run our own FTP or Hypertext Transfer Protocol (HTTP) server. At least, we can't unless we tell the firewall where it should send those inbound requests for HTTP traffic. Basically, we're going to do port forwarding, which is to say that the firewall will take all requests on a certain port and forward them to a machine hidden on the internal network. Once again, your network will appear as if it is only one machine.

This can lead to confusing responses for crackers. They'll do a scan on your firewall and determine that it is running Linux, but the WWW server on it seems to be Microsoft Internet Information Server. That isn't possible! Your Linux box is simply forwarding traffic from port 80 to some NT server on your network. Granted, any cracker worth his weight in lint will quickly figure out what's going on.

Actually Getting PORTFW Installed in the Kernel

Well, this is easier said than done! First, make sure you have "experimental drivers" enabled, as seen in Figure 3-2. Then go down to network and enable "Masquerading special modules support (NEW)." *Then* go down and enable "IP: ipportfw masq support (EXPERIMENTAL) (NEW)" (Figure 3-3).

Recompile. Install. Reboot.

For what it's worth, I tried to enable ipportfw *without* enabling experimental/incomplete drivers. All it did was waste two hours. But it did show me how fast my P75 router can reboot: 60 seconds. That's not too shabby.

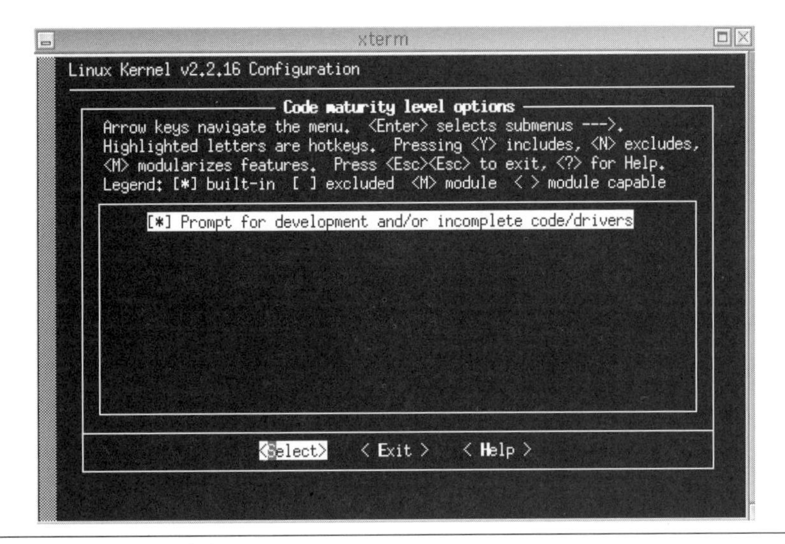

Figure 3-2 Experimental drivers.

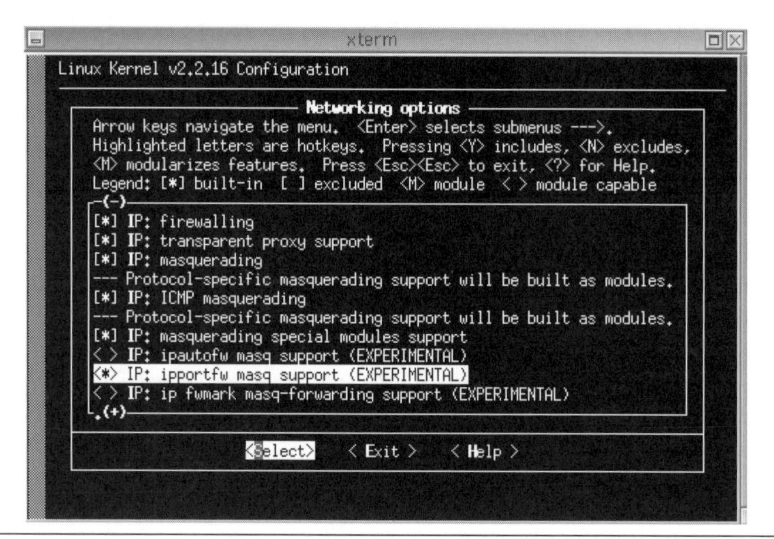

Figure 3-3 Port forward support.

Compiling ipmasqadm

I downloaded ipmasqadm from *http://freshmeat.net/projects/ipmasqadm/altdownload/ipmasqadm-0.4.2.tar.gz*, and the only change I had to make was to edit the *Common.mk* file and change KSRC so that it pointed at my Linux kernel source—*/usr/src/linux*. After that, it compiled okay.

Forwarding HTTP Traffic

Once the kernel and ipmasqadm were properly configured, all I did to forward the ports to my Web server was thus:

```
ipmasqadm portfw -a -P tcp -L 24.26.178.68 80 -R 192.168.2.102 80
```

As you'll note, my externally addressable IP was 24.26.178.68, and the internal Web server is at 192.168.2.102. Simple, eh?

Rogue Spear Games

Rogue Spear is one of my great weaknesses. But one of the things that really irked me was that I could not *host* a game. I'm not that strong a player—any sort of lag really, really trips me up. And since the only way to avoid lag in Rogue Spear is to host a game, I had to do some thinking. After poking through the game settings, I found that it used three ports: 2346, 2347, and 2348. After that, it was just a matter of slapping together these rules:

```
ipmasqadm portfw -a -P tcp -L 24.26.178.68 2346 -R 192.168.2.101 2346
ipmasqadm portfw -a -P tcp -L 24.26.178.68 2347 -R 192.168.2.101 2347
ipmasqadm portfw -a -P tcp -L 24.26.178.68 2348 -R 192.168.2.101 2348
```

Simple, eh?

Kernel 2.4 and IPMASQ

Remember when I mentioned kernel 2.4? I had hoped we'd get this book wrapped up and in your hands before 2.4 hit the streets. Alas, it was not meant to be. The good news is that kernel 2.4 will be happy with your old ipchains rules!

Netfilter is the name of the kernel 2.4 ipchains-equivalent, and it's a complete rewrite of the old stuff. It's generally just cooler. Here's what I've learned from various documentation. The pros are huge (and I stole this list from the IP-Masquerade-HOWTO):

- Offers TRUE 1:1 NAT functionality for those who have TCP/IP subnets to play with.
- Built-in PORT Forwarding, which makes IPMASQADM no longer required.
- The new built-in PORTFWing ability works for both external and internal traffic. This means that users using PORTFW for external traffic and REDIR for internal redirection don't have to use two tools any more!
- Full policy-based routing features (source-based TCP/IP address routing).
- Compatible with the Linux FastRoute feature for significantly faster packet forwarding (aka Linux network switching).
- Fully supports TCP/IP v4, v6, and even DECnet (ack!).
- Supports wildcard interface names like ppp* for PPP0, PPP1, etc.
- Supports filtering on both input and output INTERFACES.
- Ethernet MAC filtering.
- Denial-of-Service (DoS) packet rate limiting.
- Very simple and generic Stateful-like inspection functionality.
- Packet REJECTs now have user-selectable return ICMP messages.
- Variable levels of logging (different packets can go to different SYSLOG levels.

The only real con is that it is so new that most of the ip_masq modules haven't yet been ported—so cuseeme, icq, irc, realaudio, quake, and vdolive won't work yet. This isn't really the end of the world, however. Documentation is hard to come by, and even though kernel 2.4 is fully accepted, I have this to say: Run kernel 2.2.19 or later on your firewall. Don't upgrade to the kernel 2.4 series until all the little modules you need to use have been ported. If you just *must* run it, however, then you can get information from *http://netfilter.filewatcher.org/unreliable-guides/NAT-HOWTO.html.*

Hardware Firewall/NAT Boxes

Now that you've read this far, I have a suggestion: Consider purchasing a hardware firewall/router/NAT box (as produced by Linksys, Dlink, and Netgear, among others). In the past year they've become quite inexpensive, and they're very easy to set up. They are not, however, as flexible as a software router such as can be built with ipchains. For the average small local area network (LAN) and home user, however, they are more than sufficient. Three of the four authors use such devices, for yet another reason: Because hardware firewalls have no moving parts, their power consumption is quite low. I figure that my hardware router will pay for itself in about six months, in lower electric bills. A disadvantage of these hardware devices is that they may have security holes in them, and one may find oneself suddenly vulnerable. Depending on how long it takes the vendor to come up with a patch that solves the problem, one's exposure may be longer than one would like.

Summary

There! You've got all the information you need to get all your machines up and onto the Internet in a relatively secure fashion. Don't forget to turn off every service you can live without on that firewall, and don't allow Telnet into it. Use SSH instead, as detailed in Chapter 14. Happy surfing!

Chapter 4

Soup Cans and String: Last-Ditch Communications Methods

Difficult-o-Meter: 5 (as difficult as this book gets!)

Covers:

Parallel-Line IP

Advanced network configuration

Kernel compiling

agetty and mgetty

We've got two problems in this chapter. The first is what can you do when you find yourself confronted with a stubbornly incompatible network, as I did when I had to integrate my laptop with a token-ring network. The second is how to keep control of your home network without access to an IP network, either because none is available or because your own network is under attack by bored teenagers.

The two techniques we cover in this chapter are quite different, but they are alike in that they are both rather primitive but nonetheless effective means of communication and control.

Did you ever as a kid take two soup cans and a length of string and make a telephone? We're going to show how to do that as an adult. But this time, it's digital!

I recently bought myself a preloaded Linux laptop. I hadn't owned a laptop before, I had never had need of one. Because I was getting back into consulting following a stint as an employee on the Web applications design team that still employs two of my co-authors, I knew I would often be unable to control my desktop. Given this, I wanted the laptop so I could have Linux with me, whatever level of control was maintained over the client-provided computers.

It has served me well. With a 10/100 ethernet card and a basic Linux laptop, I was always able to have my Linux, even when I was not allowed to install it on my desktop.

Then I came to my first pure "Big Blue" shop in some time. They used OS/2 on their desktops, AIX on their mid-tier, OS/390 on their mainframes, and, of course, token-ring to link it all together. I don't know if you've ever priced token-ring cards and multistation access units (MAUs), but they are quite expensive, especially PCMCIA and Cardbus ones. There was no way I was going to pay almost as much as I paid for the laptop just to hook up to a token-ring network, even though Linux will do token-ring just fine. Time for the soup cans and string.

Problem 1: Parallel Line Internet Protocol (PLIP) Networking

Linux supports something called *PLIP*, which stands for Parallel Line Internet Protocol. Most modern parallel ports are capable of two-way communication. PLIP takes advantage of this fact by using this two-way capability to pass IP network packets.

In order to get PLIP going, we need to cover the following:

- Parallel port basics
- BIOS printer port setup
- Two-way printer port cables
- Compiling the Linux kernel (don't be scared!)
- Setting up the PLIP tunnel
- (Optional) Setting up masquerading

Don't be intimidated by the kernel compilation. We will hold your hand through the process, outlining how to make the selections, how to deploy the new kernel, and how to keep your old kernel around to boot from in case you make a mistake.

Before we leap into the fray, let's cover some basics of parallel ports so you are up on the terminology.

Parallel Port Basics

Most communications devices that do not plug into a bus (ISA, VLB, PCI, USB, etc.) are "serial" devices. More specifically, they are RS-232 serial devices. Without getting overly detailed, a serial device is a device where the bits of a byte are sent as separate pulses, one after another, down a single wire. A parallel device, on the other hand, is one with eight wires, one for each bit of a byte, on which all the bits of a byte are sent in a single pulse, all at the same time.

Of course, serial ports have more than one wire, and parallel ports have more than eight. There are lines in both for control signals and grounds, and serial ports have two data wires, one for input and another for output. The point is, the names *serial* and *parallel* come from the idea that a byte is presented as as series of pulses (hence *serial*), or in parallel, as a group of bit pulses all sent at once.

You may have noticed that while serial devices have a line for input and a line for output, I mentioned only one set of eight lines for parallel port data. That's because the specification of the parallel interface was set almost 30 years ago by a company called Centronics for use as a printer interface only. At that time, printers were fairly dumb devices that just received and printed data. They had nothing to say back to the computer (except on those control lines I mentioned—lines like "Out Of Paper"). The parallel port was never intended for two-way communication. Since when has that stopped anyone?

The Four Kinds of Parallel Ports

Since PLIP is a nitty-gritty, "close to the metal" little hack to network machines that could not otherwise communicate, you are, I'm afraid, about to be confronted with a little bit of hard technical reality.

It turns out there is more than one kind of parallel port on PCs. In fact, there are four of them:

- SPP (standard)
- PS/2
- EPP
- ECP

I'll tell you a little bit about each one.

SPP: Standard Parallel Port

The SPP is a purely unidirectional interface—or so it was intended. Remember how I said a standard parallel cable has eight bits of data and some control lines? The control lines set values in the status register of the parallel port controller. What a parallel port link cable does is to link five outbound data lines from one side of the interface to the five status lines on the other. The reverse is done in the other direction. Data is sent four bits at a time. (The fifth bit is used for *handshaking*—a term that means "control signaling." The two sides must be told when a character is ready to be read and when that character has been read; otherwise, characters could be lost or duplicated.) This is the type of interface that PLIP is written to work with, for it is the lowest common denominator of parallel interfaces.

PS/2: IBM's Beloved Mutants

IBM attempted to rectify many of the design flaws in the original PC creating an entirely new set of design flaws. The result was the PS/2 family of PCs. PS/2's running IBM's powerhouse OS/2 were going to reassert IBM's dominance over the SOHO (small office/home office) PC market. Since the odds are you have neither a PS/2 nor OS/2, I think you can deduce what happened to that.

The success or failure of IBM's ambitious plans for world reconquest do not concern us here. What does concern us, however, is the PS/2 parallel port and its differences from the SPP. IBM decided that a bidirectional parallel port would be a good idea, so they added the ability to "tri-state" the drivers that put signals on the parallel data lines, allowing the computer port not only to send zeroes and ones, but also to listen.

Both the SPP and PS/2 modes transfer only unstructured byte data directly between a computer and a peripheral.

EPP: Enhanced Parallel Port

The EPP interface adds some protocol to the two-way communications channels. Four kinds of transfers are possible with EPP-capable parallel interfaces:

- Data read cycles
- Data write cycles
- Address read cycles
- Address write cycles

This ability to read and write data and to send "addresses" allows the parallel port to be used essentially like a bus, connecting multiple peripherals or complex devices with more than one "port" on them. So, in addition to being bidirectional, this specification allows you to attach devices where you can pass data and/or command and control information. This lets you control more complex devices, like disk drives and network interfaces, through your parallel port.

The EPP specification was developed by an ad hoc group of industry members, including Xircom and Zenith Data Systems. One of its important features is that each cycle can be completed in one ISA bus cycle. This allows devices connected on the EPP port to be treated in certain ways as if they were Industry Standard Architecture devices. This makes it easier both for driver programmers and for device manufacturers, who can now port ISA bus devices to EPP devices with minimal additional hardware.

ECP: Enhanced Capability Port

The ECP standard was developed jointly by Hewlett-Packard and Microsoft Corporation. It may come as a surprise to some of us more hardcore Linux folks (who tend to dislike and mistrust Microsoft), but despite Microsoft's participation, ECP is the first parallel port specification since the original SPP to go through an open standards process. Now known as the IEEE 1284 Extended Capabilities Port Protocol and ISA Interface Standard, this standard defines a fully ISA-compatible bus protocol for parallel ports. It also defines a number of performance-enhancing protocol and design improvements, including RLE compression, FIFOs for inbound and outbound channels, DMA and programmed I/O. This standard offers considerable performance improvements over the earlier standards.

So what does all of this mean? Alas, not all that much. The Linux PLIP code is written to work with all of these modes of parallel operation. It does not take advantage of the greater capabilities of the PS/2, EPP, and ECP modes. It is still valuable to know about them, however. While PLIP doesn't use them, the Parallel Port IDE driver in Linux, which allows you to connect parallel Zip drives, CD-ROM drives, external hard drives, and scanners, does use these capabilities.

Also, some ECP-capable parallel port controllers will use the FIFO buffers even in SPP mode, thus improving throughput, so it may still be an advantage to use the more advanced modes.

Two-Way Printer Port Cables

Since PLIP is written to be the lowest common denominator of SPP, to do two-way PLIP requires a custom cable. The simplest way to get going is to go to your local Super Mongo Mega Electrode Hut and buy a *Laplink cable*. This is a common name for these cables, since an old MS-DOS program called Laplink was the first to take advantage of this tricky way to link computers using a special parallel cable and special software.

If you are a radical do-it-yourselfer, you can make your own. You will need:

- 2 DB-25 male connectors and hoods
- 12-conductor cable (see the nearby table)
- Crimping and/or soldering tools appropriate to the DB-25 connector type you have selected

I recommend, first, that you not make your own cable and just buy the Laplink cable. It will not cost that much more. If, however, you enjoy inhaling lead from solder, then buy shielded 12-conductor cable. Use the shortest length of cable you possibly can. Longer cables are more susceptible to radio-frequency interference. After that, connect the cables as follows:

Connector 1 pin	Connects to connector 2 pin
2	15
3	13
4	12
5	10
6	11
10	5
11	6
12	4
13	3
15	2
17	17
25	25

Compiling the Linux Kernel to Support PLIP

Changes Needed for PLIP

Most optional code in the Linux kernel can be disabled, compiled into the kernel, or built as modules. Modules offer greater flexibility, but they do involve a small performance cost to get loaded. And if you wish to load and unload them, you must use a set of commands (*insmod*, *rmmod*, etc.) to manipulate them. Personally, I find it much simpler to compile directly in everything I need and then, if I need different things, to boot between two or three different kernels. One of the great things about Linux is you can do it your own way. You can go either route.

In this case, the real problem with the PLIP driver is that it will *not* coexist with the parallel port printer driver. If you will often be switching between PLIP and a parallel printer, then you will probably want to use modules. This was not the case for me, so I am going to show you how to explicitly disable the parallel port and enable PLIP.

I'll show you some of the changes made with the *make menuconfig* interface and some with the *make xconfig* interface so you can get a flavor of each. No matter which tool you see used in the examples here, *all* of these changes must be made.

Settings I do not specifically mention should be left as they are in your present kernel. Do not change them to match the figures here. The settings you see here are from a specific installation and may not match your needs at all. If you don't know what changing an option will do, do not change it! You'd think I wouldn't need to say this, but not every reader is as bright as you.

Let's go over the changes in the order they appear. First, go to General Settings (Figure 4-1). When you enter this section (by pressing Return in *menuconfig* or by clicking on it with your mouse in *xconfig*), you will see the options shown in Figure 4-2. The ones that concern us are "Parallel port support" and "PC-style hardware." Both of these should be compiled in.

The next section to go to is Network Options, as shown in Figure 4-3 (this time, in *xconfig*, just for variety).

This is a pretty large subsection, so we will look at more than one screenshot. Figure 4-4 is the first. The item that concerns us here is "Network firewalls." This item must be compiled in.

Figure 4-5 shows the next part, which is just a scroll down from the screenshot of Figure 4-4. The items that concern us here are "IP: firewalling," "IP: masquerading," and "IP: ICMP masquerading." The first two must be compiled in. The last one is optional, but if you want your PLIP client box to be able to ping hosts out on the rest of the network, you will want this compiled in.

You can now build and install the new kernel as described in Chapter 1 in the section Get Comfortable with Source Code.

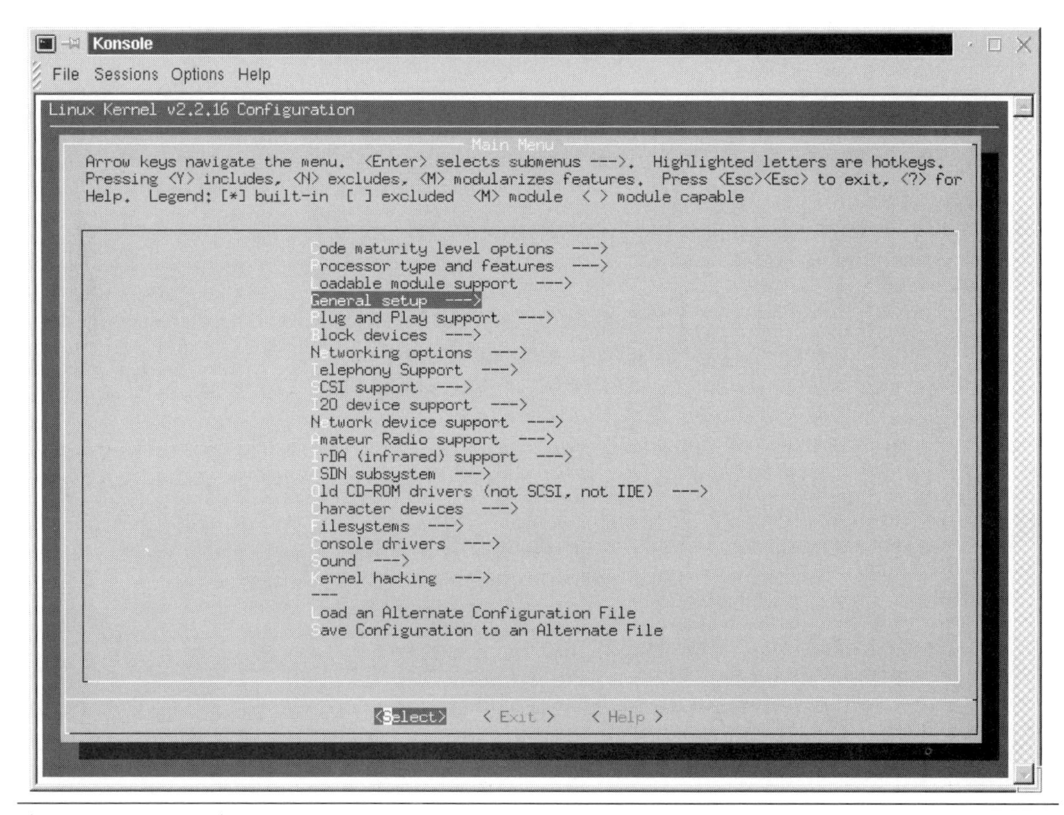

Figure 4-1 General options.

Installing the New Kernel

Or can you? There is a wrinkle in setting up a PLIP kernel. That wrinkle is in adding an entry for the new kernel to */etc/lilo.conf*. The new lines are in bold type:

```
boot     = /dev/hda
vga      = normal
read-only
linear
prompt
timeout  = 30

  image  = /boot/vmlinuz
  label  = linux
  root   = /dev/hda3
```

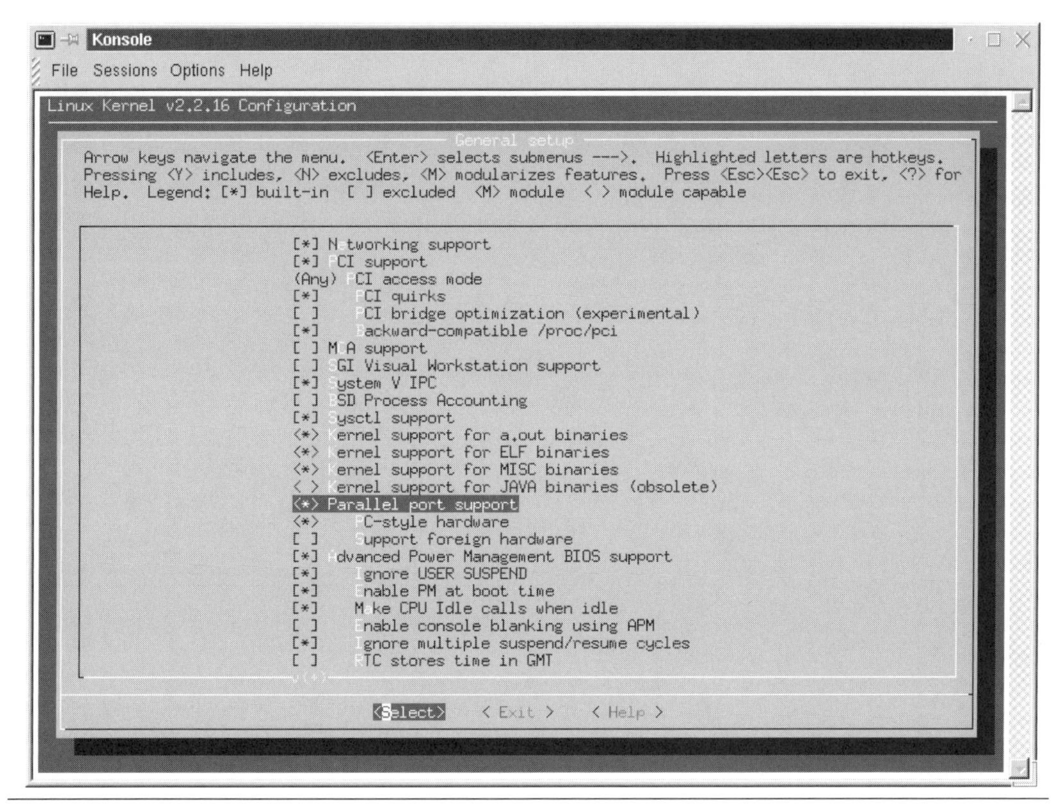

Figure 4-2 General details.

Linux Kernel Configuration

Code maturity level options	I2O device support	Sound
Processor type and features	Network device support	Kernel hacking
Loadable module support	Amateur Radio support	
General setup	IrDA (infrared) support	
Plug and Play support	ISDN subsystem	
Block devices	Old CD-ROM drivers (not SCSI, not IDE)	Save and Exit
Networking options	Character devices	Quit Without Saving
Telephony Support	Filesystems	Load Configuration from File
SCSI support	Console drivers	Store Configuration to File

Figure 4-3 Network options.

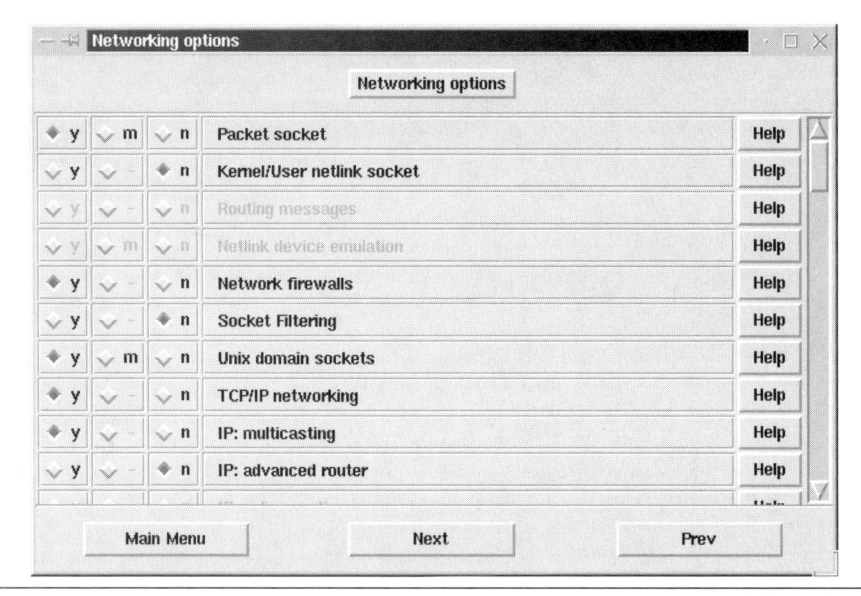

Figure 4-4 Network options, detail 1.

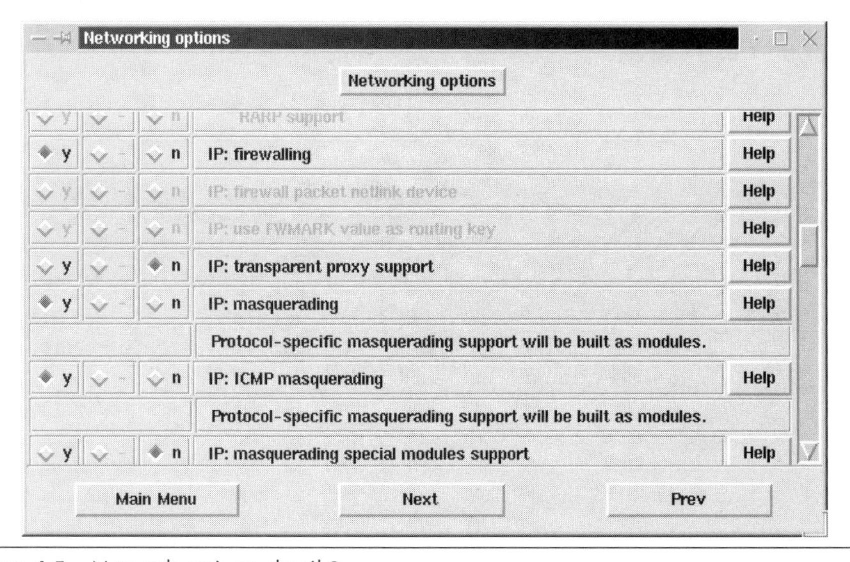

Figure 4-5 Network options, detail 2.

```
image  = /boot/vmlinuz.suse
label  = suse
root   = /dev/hda3

image  = /boot/vmlinuz.new
label  = new
root   = /dev/hda3
append = "parport=0x378,7"

other  = /dev/hda1
label  = win
```

That last new line needs some explaining. The "append=" option of lilo allows you to specify "kernel parameters." Think of the text that follows as the kernel's "command line arguments." The Linux kernel by default uses a polling driver for the parallel ports. *Polling* is where the system "looks" at the port every time it gets a chance to see if it can send or receive a character. This is as opposed to *interrupts*, where the system ignores the port completely until the port sends an "interrupt," indicating that the status of the device has changed. The computer then drops everything to handle the event at the port.

Linux uses the polling driver by default because on many (especially older) machines it is not possible to discover what "IRQ" (or interrupt number) the parallel port uses. The polling driver works just fine for plain old printing. (The worst thing that will ever happen is the printer will have to wait for the computer to send some data.) When doing two-way data traffic, however, the worst thing that will happen is that some data will be lost because the computer doesn't get to the port before the data is overwritten by more data. This is deadly for networking.

If you want PLIP to work at all, you need to activate the interrupt driver. You do this by telling the driver (called *parport*) what the port address and IRQ number of your parallel ports are. In this case, we have one lp port and it is at the PC standard of address 0x0378, and it is on the standard IRQ of 7. Be sure to check if this is correct for your hardware. If you have more than one parallel port, you can specify them here.

Be sure to do this! If you set everything else up and nothing seems to work, check the port and IRQ settings first. PLIP simply won't work right with the polling driver.

Setting Up the PLIP Tunnel

To use PLIP, you must make those enabling modifications on two boxes. For the rest of this discussion we will refer to these two boxes as *plipserver* and *plipclient*.

First, in the */etc/hosts* file of both machines, create an entry for both hosts:

```
10.0.0.1        plipserver
10.0.0.2        plipclient
```

I like to use the nonrouting IP subnet of 10.x.x.x. No machines on the Internet have any addresses in this range. There are other nonrouting ranges, but this one is quite easily remembered.

In this part of the discussion, we will be setting up only the connection from the client to the server. The client will not be able to reach any host other than the server. The next section will detail how to let the client through to the rest of the Internet.

Server-Side Setup

First, you must set up the interface. That is done with the *ifconfig* command. Here's the command to use (issue this command on plipserver):

```
# ifconfig plip0 plipserver pointopoint plipclient netmask 255.255.255.0
    up
```

Here's what ifconfig might show after issuing this command:

```
eth0      Link encap:Ethernet  HWaddr 00:04:AC:D9:05:7F
          inet addr:168.135.196.112  Bcast:168.135.199.255
            Mask:255.255.252.0
          UP BROADCAST RUNNING MULTICAST  MTU:1500  Metric:1
          RX packets:15357136 errors:0 dropped:0 overruns:0 frame:2
          TX packets:5981809 errors:0 dropped:0 overruns:0 carrier:17241
          collisions:2629247 txqueuelen:100
          Interrupt:10

lo        Link encap:Local Loopback
          inet addr:127.0.0.1  Mask:255.0.0.0
          UP LOOPBACK RUNNING  MTU:3924  Metric:1
          RX packets:2736675 errors:0 dropped:0 overruns:0 frame:0
          TX packets:2736675 errors:0 dropped:0 overruns:0 carrier:0
          collisions:0 txqueuelen:0

plip0     Link encap:Ethernet  HWaddr FC:FC:0A:00:00:FE
          inet addr:10.0.0.1  P-t-P:10.0.0.2  Mask:255.255.255.0
          UP POINTOPOINT RUNNING NOARP  MTU:1500  Metric:1
          RX packets:985771 errors:0 dropped:308 overruns:0 frame:0
          TX packets:942471 errors:350 dropped:0 overruns:0 carrier:350
          collisions:253 txqueuelen:10
          Interrupt:7 Base address:0x378
```

(Those packet counts are a bit high—I ran this on a box that had been up for a few days!) Note that I used a class C netmask (255.255.255.0). You can use any netmask value valid for the 10.x.x.x network, such as 255.0.0.0; just be sure to use the same netmask on both sides of the interface.

Client-Side Interface

We are assuming the client side has only the loopback interface set up, so there are no entries in plipclient's routing table. To enable the plip interface and to route all network packets over the plip interface, we execute the following two commands:

```
# ifconfig plip0 plipclient pointopoint plipserver netmask 255.255.255.0
    up
# route add default gw plipserver
```

Next, we attempt to ping the server from the client:

```
# ping plipserver
PING plipserver (10.0.0.1): 56 data bytes
64 bytes from plipserver: icmp_seq=0 ttl=255 time=13.301 ms
64 bytes from plipserver: icmp_seq=1 ttl=255 time=13.734 ms
64 bytes from plipserver: icmp_seq=2 ttl=255 time=13.709 ms
--- plipserver ping statistics ---
3 packets transmitted, 3 packets received, 0% packet loss
round-trip min/avg/max = 13.301/13.581/13.734 ms
#
```

You should also now be able to ping the client from the server.

Setting Up NAT (aka IP Masquerade)

If all you want is to reach the server from the client, you are done. If, however, you wish to access any and all other machines the server can reach, you need to do a little bit more on both sides.

The setup outlined here is *extremely* basic. We are going to show you just enough to enable your PLIP "client" machine to use the "host" machine's connection to the rest of your network and/or the Internet. We will be setting up transparent network address translation, aka IP Masquerading. We will not be setting up a true configurable firewall.

Server-Side Setup

Let's do this backwards. I'll show you all the commands you need to execute up front, then I will explain what each of them means and does. If you've been reading this book in order from cover to cover, (a) I'm impressed, and (b) this is a mere refresher on topics covered in much greater depth in Chapter 3. If you would like, you can treat all of these commands as a magic incantation and skip the rest of this section. I recommend you read this section, but don't worry too much if you don't understand it.

These commands should be run as root on the server side:

```
# modprobe ip_masq_ftp
# echo "1" > /proc/sys/net/ipv4/ip_forward
# echo "1" > /proc/sys/net/ipv4/ip_always_defrag
# /sbin/ipchains -M -S 7200 10 160
# /sbin/ipchains -P forward DENY
# /sbin/ipchains -A forward -s 10.0.0.0/24 -j MASQ
```

The first command installs a module that supports masquerading of the FTP protocol. Since FTP requires that the remote end be able to open connections *back* to the client, this protocol requires special support to enable the return path. There are other such protocols, including cuseeme and, of course, Quake. FTP is the only one I chose to enable. I left these as modules. That's why modprobe is used to enable it.

The second command enables IP forwarding.

The third command tells the server side always to defragment fragmented IP datagrams. If you don't know what this means, don't worry—you don't have to know. The 10-second version is that the actual low-level protocol of the Internet is called IP. IP packets are called *datagrams*. In theory, an IP datagram may be up to 64 kilobytes in length. Every network interface (Ethernet, token-ring, AX.25, etc.) has an *MTU*, or *maximum transmission unit*, which is the largest packet size the physical network can carry. In the case of Ethernet, this is generally set at 1500 bytes. When an IP datagram is routed over an interface, if the datagram is larger than the interface's MTU, the datagram is broken into "fragments" that are small enough to go over the interface. Generally, once fragmented, a datagram stays fragmented, since it would take more time and resources to reassemble them, only possibly to have to fragment them again at a later point in their journey. Thus, they may be made smaller and smaller on their journey, but they are never made larger again. They are only reassembled to full size at their final destination.

This is a problem, however, when the IP datagram carries TCP stream or UDP datagram data. Only the first such fragment has the information about which port is to receive the data. Subsequent fragments do not have this information. Suppose you have two FTP sessions being masqueraded and the two different clients are talking to the same server. Fragment 1 of session 1 comes in; it is sent to the correct client. Fragment 1 of session 2 comes in; it is sent to the correct client. Now fragment 2 of session 2 comes in. There is no way to tell if this fragment belongs to session 1 or session 2.

For this reason, the box that is doing the masquerading must "break with tradition" and must reassemble (defragment) all IP datagrams so that they can be routed as a unit. If you want to know more about this, read the excellent book *Internetworking with TCP/IP* by Douglas E. Comer.

The third command is the first of three "ipchains" commands. The ipchains command sets up "firewall rules." The first is:

```
ipchains -M -S 7200 10 160
```

Here's what this does: The -M argument tells ipchains this is a masquerade request. The -S argument tells ipchains that we are setting masquerade parameters. Remember that in order to do masquerading, the "server" box must "remember" the host and port that actually originated a request and the port number on the server box that it used to "resend" the request from the server box (remember that masquerading hides an entire network behind the server box). The three numbers that follow the "-S" are:

- The number of seconds to "remember" a TCP connection.
- The number of seconds to "remember" a TCP connection for which an FIN has been received (see the previously cited book by Comer).
- The number of seconds to "remember" a UDP session. UDP is technically sessionless, but some request/reply protocols (like DNS) do exist.

The values shown here seem to work well. You must remember that masquerading is a "trick." It will mess you up sometimes. If you, for example, Telnet to another host while masqueraded and then you leave that socket idle for longer than the TCP timeout, you will find the connection up but frozen when you come back to it. This isn't a network failure! Your computer thinks the connection is still there. The far end thinks the connection is still there, but the proxy machine in the middle has forgotten that far end should be connected to your computer!

The next ipchains command is:

```
ipchains -P forward DENY
```

The "-P" option specifies a policy. We are setting a policy on the "forward" chain. (This chain is "active" when we have a packet that has been accepted for input on one network interface that must be forwarded to another interface in order to reach its destination. We are here setting a policy that all such packets be silently dropped [that's what DENY means]. We could have said REJECT, which would have sent an ICMP-host or network-unreachable message back to the sender. We don't want such traffic.)

This sounds like we are disabling all routing from PLIP to eth0 and back! Well, we are. But this is just a default policy. We are about to add a specific rule to open the one and only path we want. That's the final ipchains command. Here it is:

```
/sbin/ipchains -A forward -s 10.0.0.0/24 -j MASQ
```

So what's all this, then? The "-A" says we are going to append a rule to a chain. The "forward" argument is the chain we are appending a rule to. The "-s" specifies a source to which this rule shall be applied. In this case, it is the 10.x.x.x network with a 24-bit netmask (this is an alternate way to say a netmask of 255.255.255.0). The "-j" specifies a "jump." Any packet that matches the rule up to this point will be sent to the chain named after the "-j" parameter. The "MASQ" chain is a special "pre-existing" chain that masquerades the packet (just as DENY is a special chain that drops packets and REJECT is a special chain that drops packets with an ICMP report, and so on).

Notice we didn't really attempt to teach you the intricacies of firewalls here. You should have read all about this in Chapter 3.

Client-Side Setup

Actually, no further configuration is required on the client side. You now have full connectivity from the client through the server to the rest of the world the server can reach.

In fact, the kernel configuration need not have been the same on both sides. The client side did not need firewalling and masquerading enabled. However, by configuring these capabilities on the client box, you can now configure the client to be a server if ever you need to do so.

Problem 2: Non-IP Dialup (getty)

So you've got your Linux box up and running. Maybe you're on a 24–7 connection like DSL or a cable modem. You've got your firewall configured and a whole network behind it, with a happy spouse and maybe happy children. Every inch the bucolic postmillennial family. Nice, isn't?

You are away at a sales convention (you're in sales—don't take it personally, this is an imaginary scenario) and you're secure-shelled into your home network, in a talk session with your spouse when suddenly everything starts moving in slow motion. It's like you're typing through molasses.

X is so sluggish that it takes several minutes to open an X-term. Your spouse has stopped responding. You manage to launch a primitive sniffer, perhaps tcpdump, and you see that your whole network is pumping out traffic to some IP address. You do a whois and find that your network is spewing traffic at *www.irs.ustreas.gov*.

The IRS? You had better get off your dead backside before the men in dark suits, sunglasses, and little earpieces show up to tell you how much more fun they can have in your home than you can! Trouble is, at this point, your network is so congested that you can't type anything. You are dead in the water. Or are you?

I'm going to show you how you can maintain another communications channel of last resort. You can actually connect to your Linux box like an old-style BBS system. If you were into computers in the 1970s and 1980s, you remember a time before the Internet came to such lows as SLIP, CSLIP, and PPP. You remember using terminal programs (perhaps PROCOMM, perhaps Smarterm, perhaps something you wrote yourself {ahem!}) to issue ATDT commands to your Hayes-compatible modem and connecting to modems on other computers directly, one to one.

In our scenario, you pop your PCMCIA Ethernet card out of your laptop and slam in your PCMCIA modem. You fire up a terminal program (such as Minicom), dial your home analog modem number, and are greeted with:

```
sol login:
```

You log in, become root, disable the network, and start looking for what went wrong. You are saved!

Well, maybe. Your system is probably hopelessly compromised. Once someone has gotten in and done something naughty with your system, it is almost certainly impossible to secure it again, simply because there is an almost infinite number of holes and back doors that may now be open. It's easy to open additional locked doors once you get through the first one. You'll have to leave the network down until you can get home and reinstall from scratch. (And don't bother restoring from backups. You have no way of knowing how long ago your system was compromised. You can restore, but you might be restoring their access as well.) This isn't a book about computer incident response, so I won't spend much more time on this. I will say, however, that you should make every effort to apply all security patches that have come out since you last built your system from scratch. You should also report the incident to your ISP. Finally, you should try to find how the little miscreant got in so you can nail them next time.

Enough of that. We are going to tell you how you can set your system up so you have this back way in. After all, where would you have been had you been unable to stop the flood from your network?

The Whys

The whys should now be obvious. Having a second communications path is always a good idea. Maybe your problem won't be a denial-of-service attack launched from your network by a bored teenager. Maybe it will simply be a bad network card that starts broadcasting junk. That would disable your network too. Dozens of things can go wrong. A common one for me since I shut down my home network with a highly restrictive firewall is forgetting to start the secure shell daemon before I leave in the morning so I can log in to my system (I must get around to adding that to runlevel 2).

In any case, having a second way in can be enormously helpful when things go wrong. If you are always at your system, you have the console. I don't know about you, but I occasionally leave the room, and once in a blue moon I even leave my house. That's when I get all twitchy unless I have a dialup backup.

The Hows

Logging in to a Linux box starts with a program called a *getty*. This stands for GET tTY. *TTY* stands for teletype, which was the brand name of the first serial communications devices. This name just sticks around like the terms *Xerox* and *Kleenex*. Nobody uses teletypes any more, but their names and terms stick around. I find it a charming bit of nostalgia in an industry that has no memory.

You use a getty any time you log in to one of your text-mode consoles. You do know about the text-mode consoles, don't you? (If you have a distribution that always boots to a graphical user interface (GUI) and you haven't been a Linuxer for some time, maybe you don't.)

Linux supports multiple virtual consoles. Every distribution I have seen uses this feature and runs at least five of them. You use the CTRL-ALT-Fn keys to switch between them. Press CTRL-ALT-F1 and you will find yourself at a text-mode login prompt. Press CTRL-ALT-F2 and you'll find yourself at another one. Most distributions I have seen put the GUI at CTRL-ALT-F7. You can press that to go back to the GUI.

The job of a getty is simple. Detect a connection on a port, match communication parameters, display the */etc/issue* file, prompt for a username, and then wait. When a username is entered, the getty program actually runs a separate program called *login*, which prompts for the password and runs whatever shell is specified for the user in */etc/passwd*.

For the desktop virtual consoles, this job is so simple (there are no status lines or modems or serial interfaces) that there is a special version of getty called *mingetty* that most distributions use for these consoles.

The mingetty program can't be used for dialup terminal login support. It doesn't know anything about serial port status lines or modem control commands and result codes. It doesn't know about baud rates, parity, start bits, stop bits, or terminal types. Maybe you don't either. That's okay—you don't really need to know.

It turns out that there is more than one kind of smart getty out there. We'll take a look at the most common ones and help you figure out how to configure them. But first, we have to talk about how to run a getty. It's not like any other process in Linux.

The */etc/inittab* File

Remember when we told you that this wasn't a book about Linux system administration? That, like so much in this book, was a half truth. What, in fact, ethics specialists call a "lie." In order to explain certain topics, we have to acquaint you with some of the less savory aspects of Linux system administration. One of these is the so-called *System V initialization model*. The heart of this is a little file called */etc/inittab*, for INITialization TABle. (By the way, did you know that an acronym made up of syllables instead of initials is called a *portmanteau* word? Don't tell me this book didn't teach you anything!)

If you hadn't heard about *inittab* before this, then you probably haven't heard of runlevels either. The System V initialization model assumes the system can be in one of a number of *states*, or *runlevels*, ranging from state 0 (shut off) to state S (single user), through levels 1–5, which will be states with different mixes of baseline services, running, all the way to state 6, which is reboot (not really a state, is it?). What services are running in each state will vary quite a bit from distribution to distribution. Also, how the system moves from state to state will vary quite a bit.

What we will show you here is the "out-of-the-box" */etc/inittab* from a SuSE Linux 6.4 system. This was chosen through an exhaustive process of systems analysis to determine which distribution had the best pedagogical potential. Also it was chosen because that was the system I was using when I typed this part of this chapter. It could have been from a RedHat system or a Debian system. There would be differences in the specifics, but the general form and function is the same.

So let's dissect an *inittab*, shall we?

```
#
# /etc/inittab
#
# Copyright (c) 1996 SuSE GmbH Nuernberg, Germany.  All rights reserved.
#
# Author: Florian La Roche <florian@suse.de>, 1996
#
# This is the main configuration file of /sbin/init, which
# is executed by the kernel on startup. It describes what
# scripts are used for the different runlevels.
#
# All scripts for runlevel changes are in /sbin/init.d/ and the main
# file for changes is /etc/rc.config.
#

# default runlevel
id:3:initdefault:

# check system on start-up
# first script to be executed if not booting in emergency (-b) mode
si:I:bootwait:/sbin/init.d/boot

# /sbin/init.d/rc takes care of runlevel handling
#
# runlevel 0 is halt
# runlevel S is single-user
# runlevel 1 is multiuser without network
# runlevel 2 is multiuser with network
# runlevel 3 is multiuser with network and xdm
# runlevel 6 is reboot
l0:0:wait:/sbin/init.d/rc 0
l1:1:wait:/sbin/init.d/rc 1
l2:2:wait:/sbin/init.d/rc 2
l3:3:wait:/sbin/init.d/rc 3
#l4:4:wait:/sbin/init.d/rc 4
#l5:5:wait:/sbin/init.d/rc 5
l6:6:wait:/sbin/init.d/rc 6

# what to do in single-user mode
ls:S:wait:/sbin/init.d/rc S
~~:S:respawn:/sbin/sulogin
```

```
# what to do when CTRL-ALT-DEL is pressed
ca::ctrlaltdel:/sbin/shutdown -r -t 4 now

# special keyboard request (Alt-UpArrow)
# look into the kbd-0.90 docs for this
kb::kbrequest:/bin/echo "Keyboard Request -- edit /etc/inittab to let
    this work."

# what to do when power fails/returns
pf::powerwait:/sbin/init.d/powerfail    start
pn::powerfailnow:/sbin/init.d/powerfail now
#pn::powerfail:/sbin/init.d/powerfail now
po::powerokwait:/sbin/init.d/powerfail  stop

# for ARGO UPS
sh:12345:powerfail:/sbin/shutdown -h now THE POWER IS FAILING

# getty programs for the normal runlevels
# <id>:<runlevels>:<action>:<process>
# The 'id' field  MUST be the same as the last
# characters of the device (after "tty").
1:123:respawn:/sbin/mingetty --noclear tty1
2:123:respawn:/sbin/mingetty tty2
3:123:respawn:/sbin/mingetty tty3
4:123:respawn:/sbin/mingetty tty4
5:123:respawn:/sbin/mingetty tty5
6:123:respawn:/sbin/mingetty tty6

#
#
#  Note: Do not use tty7 in runlevel 3; this virtual line
#  is occupied by the programm xdm.
#
#  This is for the package xdmsc; after installing and
#  configuration, you should remove the comment character
#  from the following line:
#7:2:respawn:+/sbin/init.d/rx tty7

# modem getty.
# mo:23:respawn:/usr/sbin/mgetty -s 57600 modem

# fax getty (hylafax)
# mo:23:respawn:/usr/lib/fax/faxgetty /dev/modem

# vbox (voice box) getty
# I6:23:respawn:/usr/sbin/vboxgetty -d /dev/ttyI6
# I7:23:respawn:/usr/sbin/vboxgetty -d /dev/ttyI7

# end of /etc/inittab
```

As usual in *nix configuration and script files, lines beginning with a pound sign (#) are comments and are ignored. Active lines in the file are of the form:

```
id:runlevels:action:process
```

where the following holds.

id	An identifier name of up to four characters. This is just a name. It doesn't have a great deal of significance (although there are some conventions for login accounting, so don't change names of entries that already exist).
runlevels	Lists one or more runlevels at which this entry's process is to be run.
action	One of the following

Action	Description
respawn	If the process dies, run it again.
wait	The process will be run when the specified runlevel(s) is (are) started, and *init* will wait for the process to terminate before continuing.
once	The process will be started once when the specified runlevel(s) is (are) started. *init* will not wait for the process to terminate before continuing.
boot	The process will be executed once during boot. The *runlevels* field is ignored.
bootwait	The process will be executed once during boot. The *runlevels* field is ignored. The *init* process will wait for this process to terminate before continuing.
off	Disabled entry. Same as commenting the line out.
initdefault	Specifies the default runlevel. The *process* field is ignored.
sysinit	The process will be executed once during boot. It will be run before any *boot* or *bootwait* entries.

There are other options for power failure and on-demand processing, but these do not concern us here. Consult *inittab(5)* for full details.

process	The process to execute.

The first noncomment line is:

```
id:3:initdefault
```

This line specifies the default runlevel. This is the runlevel the machine will be in when booted. Note that here this is runlevel 3.

Setting Up a getty

As we said earlier, the program that recognizes and services a connecting (non-network) user is called *getty*. There are actually a great many getty programs out there. The truth is, you probably will *not* want to use one that works just like the classic getty program. We will describe two getty variants that are particularly well suited to modem use. These are *agetty* and *mgetty*.

agetty

The *agetty* command has a number of features that suit it to modem use, including:

- It autosenses parity and character size; it can handle uppercase only (in the traditional *nix way: \EVERYTHING UPPERCASE, WITH \C\A\P\I\T\A\L\S PRECEDED BY BACKSLASHES).
- It can adjust baud rate based on Hayes CONNECT messages from a modem.
- It has configurable flow control (needed for today's high-speed modems).

The *agetty* command is fairly useful, but in my humble opinion *mgetty* is better. For completeness, however, here are the switches that *agetty* understands (as usual, we document only those you are likely to use—dig deeper if you want to know more):

Switch	Description
-h	Enable hardware flow control (RTS/CTS protocol).
-i	Do not display the contents of */etc/issue* file.
-f *issue-file-name*	Use *issue-file-name* instead of the default */etc/issue* file.
-I *initialization-string*	Set a modem initialization string to be sent before sending anything else. Often set to *ATZ* (the Hayes modem reset command). Nonprintable characters may be put in the string by inserting a backslash (\) followed by the octal ASCII value of the character as a three-digit number. For example, to send an ESC (ASCII decimal 27), you would put \033.
-l *login-program*	Specify an alternate login program. Defaults to */bin/login* if not specified.
-m	Attempt to extract the connection speed from Hayes standard "CONNECT xxx" result messages. The *agetty* program assumes the modem emits status messages at the baud rate specified as the first rate on the command line.
-n	Do not prompt for a login name. This can be used in conjunction with -l to run an alternate system, such as a BBS. Note that when *agetty* does not prompt for a login, it can't automatically set parity, word size, and other terminal options.
-t *timeout*	If a user name is not entered within *timeout* seconds, terminate the program.

(*continued*)

Switch	Description
-L	Local line. This makes agetty ignore the status of the carrier detect signal on the serial port. This might make sense if you have a terminal attached directly to a serial port, as opposed to using a modem.
-w	Wait for a carriage return or linefeed character before sending the */etc/issue* file and user login prompt. This is a very good idea, especially when using the -I option.

mgetty

The *mgetty* program is my personal preference when enabling non-network remote access. Why? Because it supports a couple of extra and useful features. Here are the advantages I see to *mgetty:*

- It supports modem initialization between calls.
- It manually answers incoming calls, so you never set your modem on "Autoanswer." This means your modem will not answer the phone if the system is not ready.
- It obeys UUCP (Unix-to-Unix Communications Program) locking protocols, so you can use the same modem for dial-in and dial-out applications simultaneously.
- It understands fax/modems, so if an incoming call is from a fax machine, it will save the incoming fax as a file and will then again be ready for either a fax or a data call.
- It has extensive logging capabilities.

If you go back to the earlier section on */etc/inittab*, you will notice a commented-out line that would set up *mgetty*. Apparently, SuSE shares my preference for *mgetty*. The only problem is their default parameters are little behind the times. For one thing, a speed of 57,600 baud might well be a bit low for today's fastest modems.

Let's go over the most important command line options for *mgetty*, and then let's choose a few to modify our sample */etc/inittab*.

Switch	Description
-k *space*	Reseve *space* kilobytes on the drive when receiving a fax. It is a very good idea to set this to a fairly large value. Otherwise you may become a victim of a denial-of-service attack through a fax machine!
-x *logging level*	Set the "verbosity" of mgetty logging. The *logging level* may be from 0 to 9, with 0 being no logging and 9 being, well, a *lot*.
-s *speed*	Sets the data rate between mgetty and the modem or terminal to an initial value of *speed* bits per second.

Switch	Description
-r	Skips modem initialization for direct-connected terminals.
-p *login-prompt*	Allows you to create your own login prompt. There are a number of special macros you can use to put information in the prompt. For example, "\D" will output the date, "\T" the time, and "@" the system name. There are many others. Consult the man and info pages for details.
-n *number of rings*	Allows you to specify which ring *mgetty* should answer on. The default is 1 (meaning the first ring).
-D	Tells *mgetty* to accept data calls only. You should set this option if your modem is not a fax/modem. Even if it is a fax/modem, this will cause fax calls to be rejected.
-F	Tells *mgetty* to accept only fax calls. No data calls will be accepted.
-C *class*	Tells *mgetty* what "class" of modem is being used. Values allowed for *class* are: • auto • cls2 • c2.0 • data (This is the same as using the -D option) The default class is *auto*, which *mgetty* will attempt to query the modem for its capabilities. The *cls2* and *c2.0* select between the "class 2 fax" and "class 2.0 fax" protocols (don't ask me whose bright idea it was to have "2" and "2.0" be different instead of, say, "2" and "2.1"). I would recommend sticking with *auto* unless you have problems.
-I *fax id*	Use the string *fax id* as the fax station ID. In the United States it is unlawful to send a fax without certain identifying information. This information must include at least the business or person's name and the fax's telephone number. Although *mgetty* doesn't normally send faxes (except for fax polling—read the info and man pages!), it is still a good idea to put this minimal information in the program, just to be "Reno-proof."
-a	This enables *autobauding*. In other words, *mgetty* will attempt to parse the "CONNECT xxxxx" messages from the modem and adjust its baud rate to match. Most modems today do not require this. They communicate with the host at a fixed rate and buffer internally to handle different connection speeds. Use this option only if your modem insists on actually changing its host rate to match the connection rate. (No 14.4k or faster modems should do this).
-m *modem chat*	Set the modem initialization dialog. The string consists of alternating "expect/send" messages. Use two double quotes for an empty expect string. Example: -m '"" ATZ OK ATH0'

Remember, this is not complete *mgetty* documentation. Still, based on this, let's take a look at how we would set up our */etc/inittab* line:

```
# modem getty.
mo:23:respawn:/usr/sbin/mgetty -k 204800 -s 115200 -m '"" ATZ OK' -I
    "(763) 555-3456 M. Schwarz" modem
```

Our options make sure that:

- At least 200MB of disk space is left free (-k).
- Baud rates up to the maximum ability of modern serial ports will be accepted (-s).
- The modem will be reset between calls (-m).
- Any faxes will be met with correct identification (-I).

Be aware that *mgetty* has several options we have not covered. It can reject calls based on caller ID (for modems that support it). It is designed to work with the *sendfax* program. It can be made to reject calls without disabling the program, and so forth. Be sure to read up on these features.

Conclusion

There you have it. You now have the power of the primitive. Every year brings great advances in communications technology, and no one, not even a technofogey (a term coined by my wife, Tina) like me, would want to give up those advances. But sometimes these advanced and high-speed communications methods break down. It is well to know something about lower-level communications technologies in these cases, because slow or limited connectivity is better than no connectivity at all.

These technologies provide a useful "second path" to back you up in the event of a failure. The getty-based dial-in may even allow you to fix your network problem without making a trip to the site. It may even let you catch a bored teenager. Leaving you with only the question "Why would I want to?"

Chapter 5

SAMBA: TALKING TO WINDOWS NETWORKS

Difficult-o-Meter: 4 (fairly high Linux knowledge required)

Covers:

Samba	*http://www.samba.org*
TkSMB	*http://www.rt.mipt.ru/frtk/ivan/TkSmb/*
xSMBrowser	*http://www.public.iastate.edu/~chadspen/*
SMB2WWW	*http://www.samba.org/samba/smb2www/*

Question: I've snuck a Linux machine onto my mostly Windows corporate network, to use as a personal workstation. There are a lot of files and documents out on the NT file servers that I'd like to be able to access. I also need to be able to print documents to the network printers. Or . . . maybe I've started my own business. My employees are more comfortable with Windows workstations, but I don't want to spring for an expensive file and print server. What can I do?

Answer: Samba provides a complete solution for sharing files and printers with Windows networks. Not only does it allow a Linux machine to act as a workstation in a Windows network, it can also make a Linux machine act as a file and print server for a Windows network. In fact, why don't you just replace both the servers and workstations with Linux machines?

One of the most important requirements for Linux to be adopted in the mainstream business environment is the ability to interoperate with Microsoft Windows networks.

Neither Windows nor Linux is going to go away anytime soon. Transparent network access that's independent of a user's choice of operating system is a worthy goal. Since Windows isn't known for its wide variety of networking protocols, it's up to Linux to fill the niche.

The software package that came to be known as Samba was originally developed in Australia by Andrew Tridgell. The project is open source and released under the GPL. A worldwide group of contributors have carefully reverse-engineered Microsoft's protocols, both documented and not so documented. The job is even more difficult because of Microsoft's strategy of making their software a moving target: changing protocols, using incompatible file formats, and so on.

Simply put, Samba provides full-featured SMB networking functionality to Linux—almost all of the functions available on a Windows machine. A Linux computer can browse shares and access files or printers on an existing Windows network. It's also easy to set up a Linux machine as a file or print server in place of a Windows NT or 2000 box. In Samba versions 2.0 and above, Linux can even serve in place of a Windows NT domain controller. Samba emulates the SMB protocol so closely that clients won't even know it's not a Windows machine. In fact, many corporate IT departments have been able to replace their Window NT servers with Linux machines with no interruption in service.

What Is SMB?

Years ago, Microsoft and IBM came up with the SMB (Server Message Block) protocol to compete with Novell's IPX-based file and print sharing. Though it's hard to believe now, there was a time when pretty much all corporate networks were running IPX and Novell Netware servers. The relatively few home networks were running IPX, while military and research networks used TCP/IP. SMB was the first protocol to run over multiple network protocols: TCP/IP, NetBEUI, and IPX/SPX. In other words, an SMB server could replace a Novell server without need of changing the rest of the network infrastructure. The promise was that of an open system—one where any server that could speak SMB could serve any SMB-speaking clients, over any of several network protocols. Bear in mind, though, that this promise would go pretty much unfulfilled for quite some time. The only servers that spoke SMB were OS/2 and MS Windows. When OS/2 failed to gather much market share, Joe User was left with an "open" solution that was available from only one vendor.

Note, as well, that this "open" solution (which, to the best of my knowledge, was never marketed as such) had nothing for Unix users. SMB was strictly PC stuff, and PC stuff was shunned by Unix users as being too dinky, too underpowered, and incapable of running a "real OS." As MS Windows quickly became a de facto standard, so did the SMB protocol. Users began using MS Windows' built-in (SMB) file and print sharing to offer new levels of data sharing. When Windows 95 came along, it got even easier. Using the standard GUI approach, anyone with a mouse and a finger to click it could set up file shares, shared printers, password-protected shares, and even drive mappings. Gone was the need for the arcane batch files required by earlier versions of Windows and by contemporary versions of Novell Netware. So today, we are left with a single great divide: the Microsoft, PC, SMB world, on the one hand, and the Unix, big iron, NFS world on the other. So what are the differences? There are quite a few, and we'll start by looking at naming.

Every machine on a Windows network is identified by a NetBIOS name, which is similar to a Linux hostname. NetBIOS names are at most 15 characters and are case-insensitive. Unlike hostnames, they also contain a resource-type byte, which describes the role or roles of the machine on the network. Multiple names and multiple types can be associated with a single physical machine. As an example, here is a listing of the NetBIOS names associated with the primary Linux box on my home network:

```
HOMER           <00> -          B <ACTIVE>
HOMER           <03> -          B <ACTIVE>
HOMER           <20> -          B <ACTIVE>
__MSBROWSE__    <01> - <GROUP>  B <ACTIVE>
WORKGROUP       <00> - <GROUP>  B <ACTIVE>
WORKGROUP       <1d> -          B <ACTIVE>
WORKGROUP       <1e> - <GROUP>  B <ACTIVE>
```

The NetBIOS names are on the left, and the hex value of the resource-type byte is shown in angle brackets. Type <00> means a standard workstation, type <03> means a WinPopup service, and type <20> means a file and print server. So my computer HOMER advertises itself as a workstation and a file server and as capable of receiving WinPopup messages.

The other name, __MSBROWSE__, is Microsoft's way of identifying a domain master browser. A master browser is responsible for periodically checking what machines and shares are available on a network and caching that information. Then when another computer wants to "explore" the network, it needs to ask only the master browser what is available instead of doing a network-intensive broadcast request.

What about the WORKGROUP entries? These describe the workgroups, or domains, to which my machine belongs. I only have one workgroup on my network, WORKGROUP, and HOMER advertises itself as a workstation (type 00) in that domain. The other two lines refer to the machine's role as a master browser, which we won't discuss in detail in this chapter.

Every machine that understands SMB advertises itself as providing certain services. These services do not have to be limited to file sharing; in a typical Windows network they include print sharing, remote administration capabilities, popup messaging, and other features. Every service has a name unique to the machine where it is offered. On a network, a service is identified with the following syntax:

```
\\machine-name\service-name
```

This notation is called the *universal naming convention* (though it's hardly universal!). Since backslashes are shell metacharacters under Linux, most of the Samba utilities will conveniently accept UNCs using forward slashes and automatically convert them to backslashes as necessary.

On a Windows file server, any directory can be defined as the root of a file-sharing service. There is no dependence on the physical layout of the file system, and the directory being shared can itself be connected to a file share on a third machine. All subdirectories of the file-sharing root are accessible through a share. Access to a share is controlled both by the permissions on the share and by the permission on the underlying file system, if applicable.

A Windows print share allows network access to a locally connected printer. The service does not provide drivers for a printer, only the ability to send a preformatted print job from a remote machine. As a result, if you intend to use a Windows printer from a Linux machine, you must have Linux drivers available to generate the appropriate control language for the printer. The Ghostscript package is included with most Linux distributions, and it provides a wide variety of filters to convert PostScript to proprietary printer-control languages. A list of directly supported printers and third-party-supported printers are available at the Ghostscript Web site.

On my machine KEARNEY, for example, the following services are available. We'll see how to list these services in the next section.

```
\\KEARNEY\CDROM    maps to E:\
\\KEARNEY\ZIPLIB   maps to D:Ziplib\
\\KEARNEY\CANON    print service for a Canon BJ-200
\\KEARNEY\IPC$      special OS service
```

Much more information is available on SMB and CIFS (Common Internet File System). NetBIOS names and scoping are described in RFCs 1001 and 1002. The book *Using Samba* (by Robert Eckstein, David Collier-Brown, and Peter Kelly; published by O'Reilly & Assoc.) is also an excellent reference for the idiosyncrasies of Microsoft's SMB implementation. It is available online as well.

Setting Up Samba as a Client

Samba can be compiled from the source distribution or installed as a Debian or RPM package. In either case, there are several different components that will be installed. The server components are:

- smbd: a daemon that shares out files and printers from the Linux system
- nmbd: a daemon that provides NetBIOS name resolution
- sambaconfig: a reconfiguration tool
- smbpasswd: an SMB password maintenance tool

The client components are:

- smbclient: an FTP-like program for accessing shares
- smbspool: a tool to send print jobs to shared printers
- smbmount, smbumount: tools to, respectively, mount and unmount SMB shares.

All of the Samba components use a single configuration file, usually located at */etc/samba/smb.conf*. The majority of configuration options in this file affect the behavior of the Samba server, but a few options need to be set correctly in order to use the client applications.

Like many other Linux configuration files, the Samba configuration file is a simple text document. Blank lines and white space are not significant (except in parameter values), and comments begin with a semicolon and extend to the end of the line. The whole file is case insensitive, so *WORKGROUP* is the same as *workgroup* is the same as *WoRkGrOuP*. Booleans can be yes/no, 0/1, or true/false. There are three special sections: [global], [homes], and [printers]. The man page covers this and more in pretty good detail.

The default configuration file is heavily commented, describing the purpose of each line. The only significant thing you'll have to do for using client applications is to change the default workgroup:

```
; "security = user" is always a good idea. This will require a
; Unix account in this server for every user accessing the server.
security = domain
; Change this for the workgroup your Samba server will part of
workgroup = WORKGROUP
server string = %h server (Samba %v)
```

Modify the line starting with workgroup = to specify the name of your Windows workgroup or Windows NT domain. Actually, this step is not strictly necessary, since the Samba client tools will also accept the -W command line option to specify a nondefault workgroup. But it's easier to use a tool if you don't have to remember (and type!) a long list of arcane options and flags.

Discovering the Local Network

As mentioned previously, a client explores the local network by locating the workgroup master browser and querying it for information. This is equivalent to the Windows concept of *Network Neighborhood*. The next section describes how to use nmblookup to find the name of the master browser, and the following section shows how to list the shares on that machine.

Now you may be saying, "We don't want the shares, just the computers!" And you would be right. But the same program that lists shares on a particular machine will also display the machines in the local workgroup. Technically, if you already know the name of one machine in the network, you don't even need to know the master browser—you can just request the shares from the one you know and find the machines on the network as a convenient side effect of the way the Samba tools work. So read on.

Looking Up Machines with nmblookup

One of the utilities in the basic Samba installation is nmblookup, which is a NetBIOS equivalent to nslookup. The primary purpose of the utility is to resolve NetBIOS names into IP addresses. Typical usages are as follows:

```
$ nmblookup KEARNEY
querying KEARNEY on 192.168.0.255
192.168.0.19 KEARNEY<00>

$ nmblookup -M -
querying __MSBROWSE__ on 192.168.0.255
192.168.0.11 __MSBROWSE__<01>

$ nmblookup -A 192.168.0.19
Looking up status of 192.168.0.19
received 5 names
KEARNEY         <00> -         M <ACTIVE>
CURTIS          <00> - <GROUP> M <ACTIVE>
KEARNEY         <03> -         M <ACTIVE>
KEARNEY         <20> -         M <ACTIVE>
CURTIS          <1e> - <GROUP> M <ACTIVE>
num_good_sends=0 num_good_receives=0
```

The first example looks up the named machine by doing a subnet broadcast (as can be seen from the .255 address). The response shows the IP address, NetBIOS name, and resource-type byte for KEARNEY. If the Windows network has a WINS server, you can specify a direct request with the `-U <ip-address>` option. The second example is a shortcut for looking up the domain master browser, while the third example performs a status inquiry on an IP address rather than on a NetBIOS name.

nmblookup has many more modes of operation. As usual, consult the man page for more information.

Listing Shares

Now that you've identified a machine, how can you find out what shares it has? This task, and most others associated with Windows networking, can be done with the smbclient program, which is part of the standard Samba distribution. The syntax for listing shares is:

```
$ smbclient -L HOMER
added interface ip=192.168.0.1 bcast=192.168.0.255
nmask=255.255.255.0
Password:
Anonymous login successful
Domain=[CURTIS] OS=[Unix] Server=[Samba 2.0.7]

Sharename  Type    Comment
---------  ----    -------
site-local Disk
c          Disk    Old Windows 95 Installation
IPC$       IPC     IPC Service (homer server (Samba 2.0.7))
lp         Printer HP Deskjet 672C

Server     Comment
------     -------
HOMER      homer server (Samba 2.0.7)
KEARNEY    Tom's Computer
SANJAY     Annie's Computer

Workgroup  Master
---------  ------
CURTIS     HOMER
```

This is actually a lot more information than you might have expected—but we'll go through it one piece at a time. I just hit Enter at the password prompt for an anonymous login. There are a few messages at first, and then the first table, which shows the shares available on HOMER, their type, and any comment that's set up in the configuration file. The second table lists the machines in the current workgroup along with their descriptions. This answers our question in the previous section, about how to find the machines on the local network. The third table describes the available workgroups and which machines are the master browsers for each. In my case, there's only one workgroup.

Now if I looked at the shares on KEARNEY, I'd get a different result:

```
$ smbclient -L KEARNEY
added interface ip=192.168.0.1 bcast=192.168.0.255
nmask=255.255.255.0
Password:
Anonymous login successful

Sharename Type    Comment
--------- ----    -------
CDROM     Disk
PRINTER$  Disk
CANON     Printer
ZIPLIB    Disk
IPC$      IPC     Remote Inter Process Communication
```

If I want to specify a different workgroup or a username (in the case of Windows NT domains), I could use the -W and -U options to smbclient, respectively.

Accessing Shares with smbclient

Although we've already used it in a noninteractive mode, smbclient is really an interactive program that looks and acts like an FTP client. Simply invoke the utility with the name of the share. Remember that the share name can be specified with forward slashes if desired, and you may specify the username and workgroup also. A sample session would proceed as follows:

```
$ smbclient //homer/site-local
added interface ip=192.168.0.1 bcast=192.168.0.255
nmask=255.255.255.0
Password:
Domain=[CURTIS] OS=[Unix] Server=[Samba 2.0.7]
smb: \> dir
  .      D        0  Tue Oct 24 18:58:00 2000
  ..     D        0  Tue Oct 24 19:09:45 2000
```

```
       archive      D        0  Tue Oct 24 18:58:21 2000
       perl-lib     D        0  Sat Aug 14 15:43:24 1999
       www          D        0  Mon Jul 31 18:00:18 2000
       sql          D        0  Tue Oct 24 18:58:18 2000
44717 blocks of size 131072. 14061 blocks available
    smb: \> cd sql
    smb: \sql\> dir
       .            D        0  Tue Oct 24 18:58:18 2000
       ..           D        0  Tue Oct 24 18:58:00 2000
       tables.sql   3042   Sun Aug 20 22:47:05 2000
       data.sql     95706  Sun Aug 20 22:14:00 2000
44717 blocks of size 131072. 14061 blocks available

    smb: \sql\> lcd /tmp
    the local directory is now /tmp
    smb: \sql\> get tables.sql
    getting file tables.sql of size 3042 as tables.sql (86.8301 kb/s)
       (average 86.8304 kb/s)
    smb: \sql\> exit
```

The program prompts for a password (unless the -N option is used), and that information is used to authenticate to the share. All of same commands are available as in a typical FTP client: dir, ls, cd, lcd, get, put, prompt, mget, and mput, to name a few. The only difference is the exit command, which replaces bye.

Another difference from FTP is that all file transfers are performed in binary mode; that is, no translations between CR and CRLF are performed. Consequently, there is no equivalent to the FTP type command. If you are retrieving text files from a Windows share, you may want to use dos2unix or Perl -pe 's/\r\n$/\n/' to perform the end-of-line translations.

Accessing Shares with smbsh and smbfs

The smbclient program is not the only way to access Windows shares. Linux provides two other alternatives: the smbsh shell and the amazingly useful smbfs file system.

The first option is smbsh, which is actually just a bash shell invoked inside a Samba "wrapper." The wrapper is a shared library that intercepts file-related system calls in order to create a virtual directory at */smb*. Any dynamically linked program run under this environment will be able to access a Windows network as if it were part of the local file system.

The virtual directory is organized as */smb/<server>/<share>/<path...>/<file>*. For example,

```
$ ls /smb
```

will list all available machines in a workgroup, and the command

```
$ cp /smb/HOMER/site-local/sql/tables.sql ./
```

will copy a file on *//HOMER/site-local* to the current directory. Keep in mind that smbsh will not work with statically linked programs, and in fact the Samba documentation refers to the SMB "wrapper" as "a hack."

Fortunately, there is a better option available: Windows shares can actually be mounted on a Linux file system just as if they were local partitions! This is equivalent to the Windows and Netware operations of mapping a network volume. However, instead of adding a volume as a separate drive letter, the share can be mounted anywhere on the Linux file system. The smbfs kernel module and the smbmount utility are responsible for this bit of magic. Support for Samba file systems is included in the kernel source distribution, but you may need to enable that support in the kernel configuration and recompile. The configuration option is under the Filesystems/ Network filesystems menu. Kernel recompilation is covered in Chapter 1.

```
# insmod smbfs
# smbmount //KEARNEY/C$ /mnt/remote-cdrom
# df
Filesystem   1k-blocks     Used  Available  Use%  Mounted on
/dev/hdc1       101075    40254      55602   42%  /
/dev/hdc5       147740    32032     108079   23%  /var
/dev/hdc6       147740     2039     138072    1%  /tmp
/dev/hdc7      1981000  1251183     627405   67%  /usr
/dev/hdc4      5723816  3859608    1567809   71%  /home
//kearney/c$    101075    40254      55602   42%  /mnt/kearney-cdrive
```

The insmod ensures that the smbfs kernel module is installed. Of course, this step is not necessary if SMB file system support is precompiled into the kernel. The standard mount command cannot build the appropriate data structures necessary for the smbfs modules, so Samba provides the smbmount command. The syntax is similar, but the first argument should be a share name instead of a device name. Share names ending with a dollar sign are not shown by Windows Explorer. This is a Microsoft-specific way to implement "hidden" shares. Samba will always show these shares, however.

In the case of authenticated shares (and none of your shares allow anonymous logins, right?), the username and domain required to connect to the share can be provided with the -o option:

```
# smbmount //KEARNEY/C$ /mnt -o username=pcurtis,workgroup=WORKGROUP,
   uid=root,gid=staff,fmask=0664,dmask=0775
   password:
```

You will need to enter a password to complete the connection. The other options set the user, group, and permissions under which the mounted files will appear. In this example, the SMB file system is made available read-only to any user on the machine, except for root and any user in the group staff.

Accessing Shared Printers with smbprint

Using a Windows printer from Linux is very simple. Aside from a little configuration, the only thing you need is the smbprint utility. Samba also provides the smbspool utility, which performs almost exactly the same task as smbprint. However, the command line argument positions are arranged so that it can be used as a spooler under the Common Unix Printing System. We will discuss only smbprint in this section.

To set up a Windows printer, you first need to create an SMB-specific configuration file. The recommended location is a directory *$SPOOL_DIR/lpd/<printer-name>*, where *$SPOOL_DIR* is the standard spool directory on your system. For example, on a Debian system the path is */var/spool*. Create this directory, and then create a file containing the print server name, share name, and password (if necessary). Save this file in the new directory, with the name *.config*. On my Linux machine, for example, I have set up a Canon BJ-200 as a remote printer:

```
$ cat /var/spool/lpd/canon/.config
server=KEARNEY
service=CANON
password=""
```

Now you can send a print job to the remote printer by running the smbprint command:

```
$ smbprint /var/spool/lpd/canon/acct < print.job
```

The first argument is the name of the accounting file where lpd should log the print job. This file does not have to exist yet, but it should be in the right spool subdirectory. smbprint assumes its configuration file is in the same directory as this accounting file. The second argument is a file containing the print job, formatted in the appropriate printer-control language. If you're unlucky enough to have a printer that doesn't understand PostScript, you may have to use Ghostscript (gs) to convert a PostScript file to a particular printer language. In the case of my Canon bubble jet printer, I have to use the bj200 driver, resulting in the following command line:

```
$ cat myfile.ps | gs -q -dSAFER -sDEVICE=bj200 -dQuality=1 -dNOPAUSE \
-sOutputFile=- - | smbprint /var/spool/lpd/canon/acct
```

On my machine, I placed this command line in a shell script so that I just have to redirect a PostScript document into the command in order to print it remotely.

The final step is to integrate calls to this script into whichever print architecture you prefer. If you use lpd/lprng, for example, you'll want to modify your */etc/printcap* entry to add this script as an output filter:

```
# /etc/printcap: printer capability database. See printcap(5).
# You can use the filter entries df, tf, cf, gf, etc. for
# your own filters. See /etc/filter.ps, /etc/filter.pcl, and
# the printcap(5) manual page for further details.

    canon|Canon BJ-200 on Kearney:\
    :sd=/var/spool/lpd/canon:\
    :af=/var/spool/lpd/canon/acct:\
    :mx#0:\
    :sh:\
    :of=/etc/printing/canon.filter:
```

Graphical Clients

In addition to the basic command line tools, there are also a number of graphical interfaces to the Samba client tools. They all provide similar functionality: the ability to browse a network, browse the computers in a domain, browse the shares on a computer, and browse the files within a share. All of the graphical clients mentioned here use the smbclient program underneath, parse the output, and present it in a easy-to-use manner.

TkSMB (Figure 5-1) is written by Ivan Volosuk, and is available at *http://www.rt.mipt.ru/frtk/ivan/TkSmb/*. As the name indicates, it is a Tk-based application.

XSMBrowser (Figure 5-2) is another Tk-based Samba network browser with a number of contributors. It is available at Chad Spencer's Web page at Iowa State University, *http://www.public.iastate.edu/~chadspen/*.

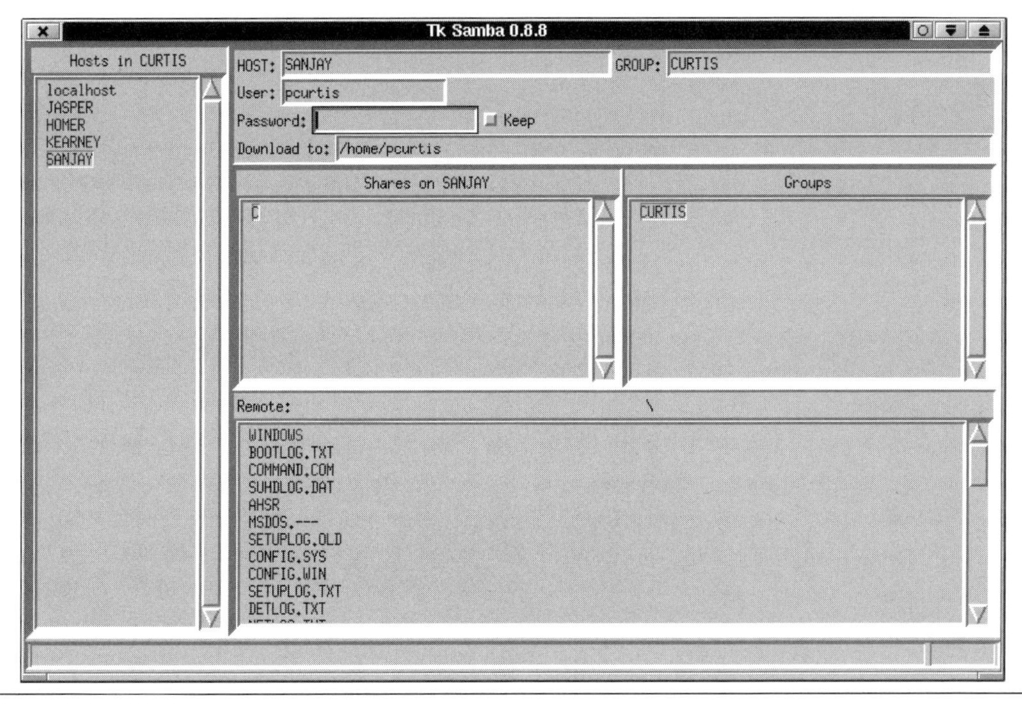

Figure 5-1 TkSMB.

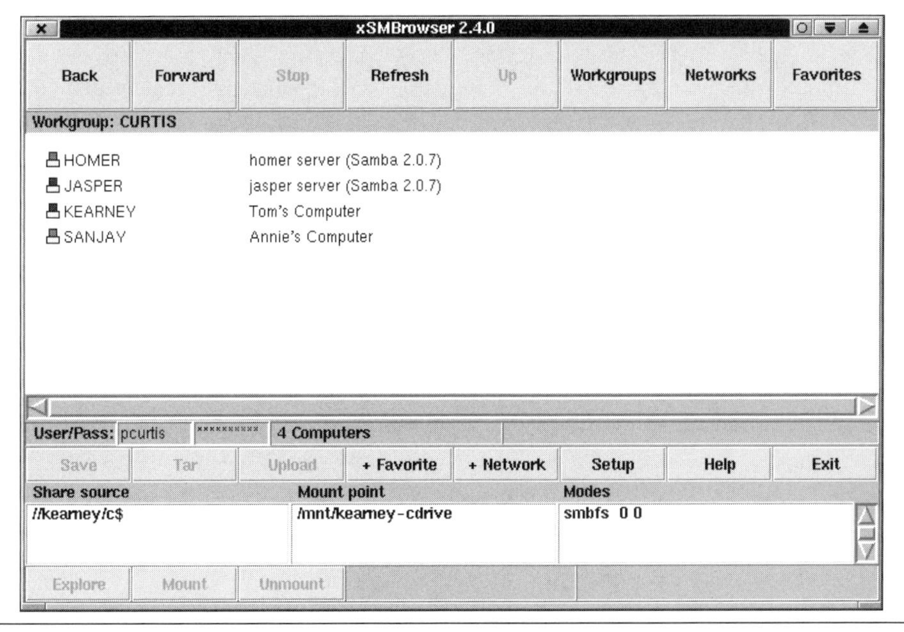

Figure 5-2 xSMBrowser.

Finally, SMB2WWW (Figure 5-3) is a Web-based interface for browsing a Windows network. It is distributed as a set of CGI scripts that access smbclient on the back end. It is available from *http://samba.anu.edu.au/samba/smb2www/*.

In addition, KDE 2.0 and higher has native support for Windows shares in Konqueror, their advanced file/Web browser. You can browse the network, shares, and mount SMB file systems, if the kernel supports it and the user account has appropriate privileges.

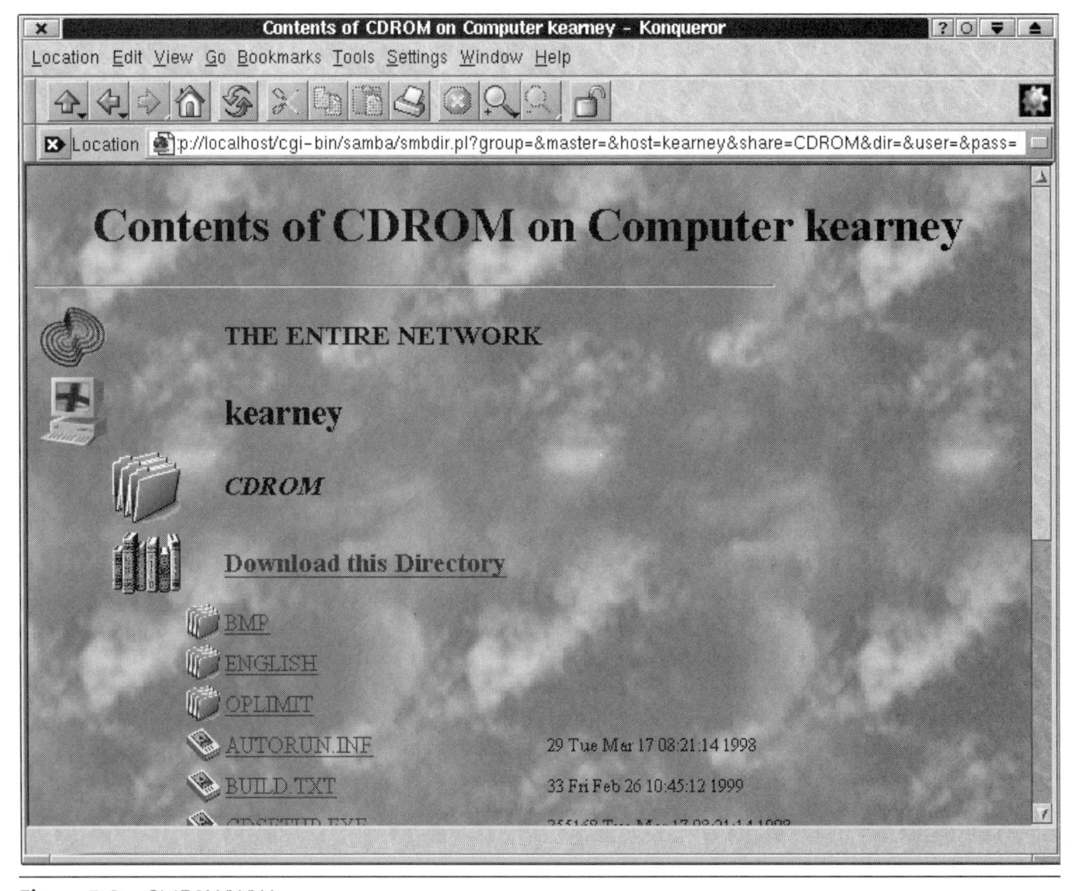

Figure 5-3 SMB2WWW.

Replacing Those Workstations

Given all these options, how would you go about replacing your workstation with a Linux box but still be able to get to all your files? Well, a simple answer would be to install KDE 2.0 or higher and use its integrated features. Of course, this answer only shows my bias toward the KDE environment. You can choose whatever desktop environment you like, and use the following Linux analogs of Windows networking operations.

All drives that should be mapped on start-up are placed in */etc/fstab*. If you want the user to feel *really* comfortable, you can mount the SMB shares as if they were drive letters:

```
# /etc/fstab: static file system information.
#
# <file system> <mount point> <type> <options>         <dump> <pass>
/dev/hda1       /        ext2    defaults,errors=remount-ro    0      1
    //HOME/PCURTIS /F:       smbfs  username=pcurtis,uid=pcurtis,
      gid=admin     0      1
    //HOME/SHARED  /G:       smbfs  username=pcurtis,uid=pcurtis,
      gid=admin     0      1
```

Make sure to create the /F: and /G: directories before you reboot.

Drives can be manually mapped and unmapped by mounting and unmounting an SMB file system. These two scripts will do the trick nicely, but they need to be run as root. If you want to give unprivileged users the ability to run them, you'll have to set up user mount capabilities and change `mapped_root` to a directory that's writable by the user.

```
#!/bin/sh
# maps a drive letter
    # usage: map F: //HOME/PCURTIS

    mapped_root="/mnt/"
    drive_dir="$mapped_root$1";
    share=$2

    # Check if this mount point is already used.
    if [ "$(mount | grep -c $drive_dir)" -ne 0 ]; then
  echo "Drive $1 is already mapped."
      exit
    fi

    # Make sure the mount point exists!
mkdir -p $drive_dir
```

```
# Mount the file system, using the current username from the
  environment.
mount $share $drive_dir -t smbfs -o username=$USER,uid=$USER,
  gid=admin || \
  echo "Unable to map drive!"
```

```
#!/bin/sh
# unmaps a drive letter
# usage: unmap F:

mapped_root="/mnt/"
drive_dir="$mapped_root$1";
share=$2

# Check if the drive is mapped
if [ "$(mount | grep -c $drive_dir)" -eq 0 ]; then
echo "Drive $1 is not currently mapped."
  exit
fi

# Try a simple unmount. This will fail if some process has open
  files on the share.
umount $drive_dir

if [ $? -ne 0 ]; then
        # Prompt the user. This is a "dialog box" of sorts.
        echo -n "Someone may be using this drive. Continue (Y/N)? "
        read ok

        # If the user says Y, try to force the unmount.
        if [ "$ok" = "y" -o "$ok" = "Y" ]; then
                umount -f $drive_dir
        fi
fi

# Finally, verify the mount is really gone...
if [ "$(mount | grep -c $drive_dir)" -ne 0 ]; then
echo "Unable to unmap drive $1, giving up."
  exit
fi

# before removing the directory
rmdir $drive_dir
```

Printers are set up by adding entries to the */etc/printcap file* (unless you're using a different print architecture, of course.) The output filter for each printer should be a script like the one shown earlier, but customized to output the right kind of printer-control language. The script doesn't have to use GhostScript; in fact, it can call a vendor-supplied driver instead. This is just what I do with my Lexmark printer.

Then to print a file, you just use this command:

```
$ lp -d SALESPRINTER sales_report.ps
```

Simple, eh? But it belies a complex chain of events going on in the background.

I'll quickly summarize this process:

- `lp` spools the input file, which is picked up by `lpd`.
- `lpd` checks the printcap entry for `SALESPRINTER` and pipes the file to your custom script.
- Your script calls GhostScript to do the dirty work of conversion.
- Then your script pipes the PCL output to `smbprint`.
- `smbprint` uses the Samba libraries to send the print job over the network.
- Your pages come flying out the laser printer in the sales department.

Problems with any one of these steps can keep things from working. If you do encounter problems, the best way to avoid frustration is to be methodical and verify each step in turn.

Let's Get Practical

Now I'll describe a task that would have been more difficult than it needs to be, if not for Samba. The example may seem trivial (or perhaps it just *is*), but it's a real-world application.

My employer has a heterogeneous network environment: Unix and IBM for the big machines, and Windows NT for the desktops and file serving. One day, while browsing one of my favorite news sites (over the lunch hour, of course), I found an interesting link and bookmarked it. When I got home, I wanted to revisit the site, but I had problems remembering the path of links that I took. So my problem was: How do I get to the bookmarks on my desktop machine at work?

If I were using a Windows machine at home, I would use the RAS connection plus SecureID provided for work-at-home employees and map a drive to my desktop to pick up the files I needed. There was a problem with that, though; I don't have a Windows system at home, just Linux. As a consequence, I had never signed up for RAS or obtained a SecureID token. My usual way in from home is through SSH to our Unix servers. But never fear, Samba is here! Here is a transcript of my session (the IP addresses are blanked out):

```
$ ssh -l pxcurtis devbox.mycompany.com
Last login: Wed Aug 2 11:31:03 2000
No mail.
bash-2.01$ smbclient //W-IS-PXC/C$ -U PXCURTIS -W MYCOMPANY
added interface ip=172.17.*.* bcast=172.17.255.255 nmask=255.255.0.0
Password:
Domain=[MYCOMPANY] OS=[Windows NT 4.0] Server=[NT LAN Manager 4.0]
smb: > cd "Program Files/Netscape/Communicator/Users/pxcurtis"
smb: > get bookmarks.htm
getting file bookmarks.htm of size 4021 as bookmarks.htm (47.4793 kb/s)
smb: > exit

[In another terminal window on my home machine]
$ scp pxcurtis@devbox.mycompany.com:bookmarks.htm bookmarks.htm
```

The first step was to SSH in to establish access to the company network. Although it wasn't too important for this application, an added benefit of using SSH was the encryption of all information traversing the public parts of the Internet. Once I got to the shell prompt on our Unix server, I ran the smbclient program to connect to a share on my desktop machine, specifically, the hidden "administrative" share set up by desktop support as C$. I made sure to specify the user and domain as well, using the command line options. Then I entered my Windows account password and used the SMB client program to change to the correct directory and retrieve my Netscape bookmarks file to the Unix server. Finally, I used scp to copy the file to my home machine, all in under 60 seconds.

Of course, this wouldn't have helped if I had shut my desktop machine off at the end of the day, like everyone else.

The Other Side of the Coin: Samba as a Server

Remember how little configuring we needed to do to get the Samba client tools working? Well, those days are over, my friend. We'll have to change a lot of options now, but we'll explain each one. Without further ado, here's the updated smb.conf.

```
;
; /etc/smb.conf
;
```

```
[global]
    workgroup = CURTIS
    guest account = nobody
    keep alive = 30
    os level = 2
    security = user
    encrypt passwords = yes
    socket options = TCP_NODELAY
    map to guest = Bad User
    interfaces = 192.168.2.102/255.255.255.0
    wins support = no

[cdrom]
    comment = Linux CD-ROM
    path = /cdrom
    read only = yes
    public = yes
    locking = no

[music]
    comment = My Music Files
    browseable = yes
    public = no
    writeable = no
    create mode = 755
    path = /MyMusic
```

- *workgroup:* All my Windows machines belong to the CURTIS workgroup, so it only makes sense that the Samba installations would be members as well.
- *guest account:* Is set to nobody. This is fairly irrelevant, since you should never grant write access to anything without a username and password.
- *keep alive:* Sets the number of seconds between "keepalive" packets, which are used to determine if clients are alive and responding. And 30 seems to be a good generic number for this—often enough to notice pretty quickly if a client hangs, but not often enough to swamp the network with "keepalive" packets.
- *os level:* Sets the importance of the samba server for the purposes of master browser elections. Windows NT workstations and servers hold regular battles to see who is in charge of things (who becomes the master browser, that is), and the higher this value is, the more likely the server is to win. I've set this rather low, since I've got another Samba server on the network, and that one has the os level set to 65—which means it will win *every* election.
- *security:* The valid options here are user, share, server, and domain. I set it up for user-based security, because that's how I think and because I specify the same username for both my windows machines and for my Unix accounts. If your usernames aren't the same between the two, you should set up share-based security. Share-based security is also good for password-free shares,

such as for printers. The security setting is the single most important aspect of your configuration file, and therefore of your Samba setup. At the very least, read the section of the man page and see what will work the best for you. At the very most, go out and read a detailed book on installing Samba.

- *encrypt passwords:* If you use windows 98 or NT 4.0 SP3, set this to `yes`. Otherwise, set to `no`. If you've got a mix of Windows flavors on your network, God help you. Seriously, though, there are known issues with mixing Windows 9x, NT, and 2000 on a single network. Again, the Samba documentation is king.
- *socket options:* TCP_NODELAY is a major performance gain. Set it.
- *map to guest:* This isn't used if your security level is set to share. Basically, this determines who becomes the guest user. *Bad User* means that if someone enters a username that does not exist in the *smbpasswd* file, that individual will be treated as the guest user. Other options include *Bad Password*, *Never*, and *Bad Andy*. *Bad Password* means that users who enter their passwords incorrectly will be treated as the guest account. *Never* is self-explanatory, and *Bad Andy* is a special case for dealing with evil sock monkeys.
- *interfaces:* This line describes IP address and netmask to use when doing broadcast queries. If these options aren't set, Samba will determine the values automatically.
- *wins support:* You shouldn't set this to true unless you have a multisubnetted network and want a different machine to be your WINS server.

Per-Share Options

- *[whatever]:* Every share must have an internal label. How else would Samba tell the difference between them?
- *comment:* Put anything you feel is appropriate in here. It will be visible if you're looking at your Network Neighborhood in Detail mode.
- *path:* Is the full path to the share on the Linux system.
- *read-only:* Sets whether or not users can write to the share.
- *locking:* This *might* be useful for read-only file systems (like CD-ROMs). According to the man page, I should never need to set this. SuSE sets it out of the box, and they're usually pretty clever, so I'm following their lead on this.
- *browseable:* Determines whether or not this share will show up in the Network Neighborhood browse window. If set to *no* or *false*, then the share will not appear.
- *public:* This is a synonym for "guest ok."
- *writable:* Determines whether or not users can write to the share. Rather the opposite of read-only, eh?
- *create mode:* The default permission for files created on this share. The format is the same as the numeric permissions argument to chmod.

Obviously, there are a lot more options. You could spend weeks learning them all, but they aren't all necessary to get you up and running right now, so we're not going to cover them. The point is: You can really, really customize Samba. It's a full-featured replacement for Windows NT server—and the price is certainly right.

smbpasswd

smbpasswd allows you to add and remove user accounts from Samba's local database as well as to change passwords. These functions are useful only if you have the *security = user* option set. This means that Samba should "roll its own" authentication rather than using an external provider like a domain controller. When someone on a Windows machine tries to connect to a share on the Samba machine, they'll need to provide one of these usernames and a valid password.

When you first start out, then, you'll need to add some users to the local database. Use the following command to do this:

```
$ smbpasswd -a username
```

Note that the users *must be valid users on your Linux machine, too*. Samba certainly isn't going to give the Windows users remote root access just because they happened to know a password. Instead, the remote users get the privileges of the Linux user account with the corresponding name. The permissions on the Linux system will have an effect on what the users can do through the share.

Other flags to smbpasswd include -x to delete a user, -d to disable a user, and -n to set a user up without a password. Please, please, please don't use -n. It's just not wise.

Now that users and shares are set up, any Windows clients on my network should be able to connect to the music share by mapping a drive to \\SAMBASERVER\MUSIC. If they're logged into the Windows network with the same username and password as one that I set up with smbpasswd, they'll be able to map it immediately. Otherwise, a new authentication box will pop up for them to enter a new username and password. I won't worry about Linux workstations, since we already know how to connect to shares with those.

Becoming a Server in an Existing Domain

Isn't it tedious to go setting up users on your Linux box that duplicate existing Window logons? And just wait until you have to deal with password changes. If you already have a Windows domain with a Primary Domain Controller, it's probably easier to tell the Samba server to use domain authentication instead.

Simply set the *security = domain* option in the configuration file, and then use `smbpasswd -j` to tell the domain master that you'd like to be added to the domain. You'll also have to set *password server = <myPDC>*. Note that your PDC can be either another Samba machine or an NT box. No matter how good an idea it seems to be, do *not* point your Samba server at itself! Can you say *infinite loop*? I knew you could. Anyway, look up the password server and security options in the documentation and knock yourself silly.

Windows 2000 Issues

What were you thinking? You paid for *another* MS upgrade? Ugh. Okay, there are known issues. Samba 2.2.0 and higher can act as a Primary Domain Controller for W2K, with some limitations in functionality. File sharing is okay, as of Samba 2.0.7. Smarter people than I are currently working on this. They'll likely have it fixed by the time this book is published, but be sure to check out the Samba Web page for documentation of this. You can get some documentation on using Samba 2.2.0 as your PDC at *http://us1.samba.org/samba/docs/samba-pdc-faq.html*.

SWAT

SWAT is the Samba Web Administration Tool. It allows you to set up and configure your *smb.conf* file via your browser. Before I go any farther, I have to say: I hate GUI configuration tools. They annoy me. They never offer anything over the command line tools, and they rarely work. That said, I have this to say about SWAT: I love it. It's a pretty slick system, and it even has password authentication.

SWAT is started via `inetd`, and has only two flags: -a and -s. -s specifies the name of the proper config file (SWAT assumes it's at */usr/local/samba/lib/smb.conf*), and -a turns off authentication. You would never ever want to use -a. Ever. Really. I'm quite serious about this.

In order actually to run it, you'll need to add a line to */etc/services* and one to */etc/inetd.conf*. Add this line to */etc/services:*

```
swat            901/tcp
```

The number "901" can be any sub-1024 port, provided that it is not already in use. The SWAT man page warns of an obscure security hole that may be encountered when using port numbers larger than 1024. For safety's sake, keep it under 2e9.

Add this line to */etc/inetd.conf*:

```
swat  stream  tcp  nowait.400  root  /usr/local/samba/bin/swat swat
  -s /usr/samba/smb.conf
```

Notice the -s option. It specifies the location of the Samba configuration file on my Debian system. After both files are changed, tell inetd to refresh its configuration:

```
# kill -HUP `pidof inetd`
```

or

```
# /etc/rc.d/init.d/inetd reload
```

Now, fire up your browser, and type *http://localhost:901/* in the address window. Away it goes!

Caveats

You should use SWAT only from `localhost`. Even though it's password authenticated, the password is sent over the network in clear text and is hence just as vulnerable to sniffing as Telnet. If you consider the risks of disclosing this password, you'll decide very shortly to avoid taking the easy way out by connecting to SWAT remotely.

And for the white-space-obsessed, be warned: SWAT removes *comment*, *copy*, and *include* options from your Samba configuration file. It rearranges entries. If you have a really customized *smb.conf* file, either avoid SWAT or back up the config file first.

Figure 5-4 shows SWAT's start-up screen, viewing the network over at Mr. Anderson's place. Figure 5-5 is the selection screen for choosing which share to manipulate. Figure 5-6 presents some of the options you can set within the share manipulation screen.

I like SWAT. It has a nice link to the Help file right by each of the options. It's a nice, easy way for you to get started creating your own shares and to manage most everything about your Samba server.

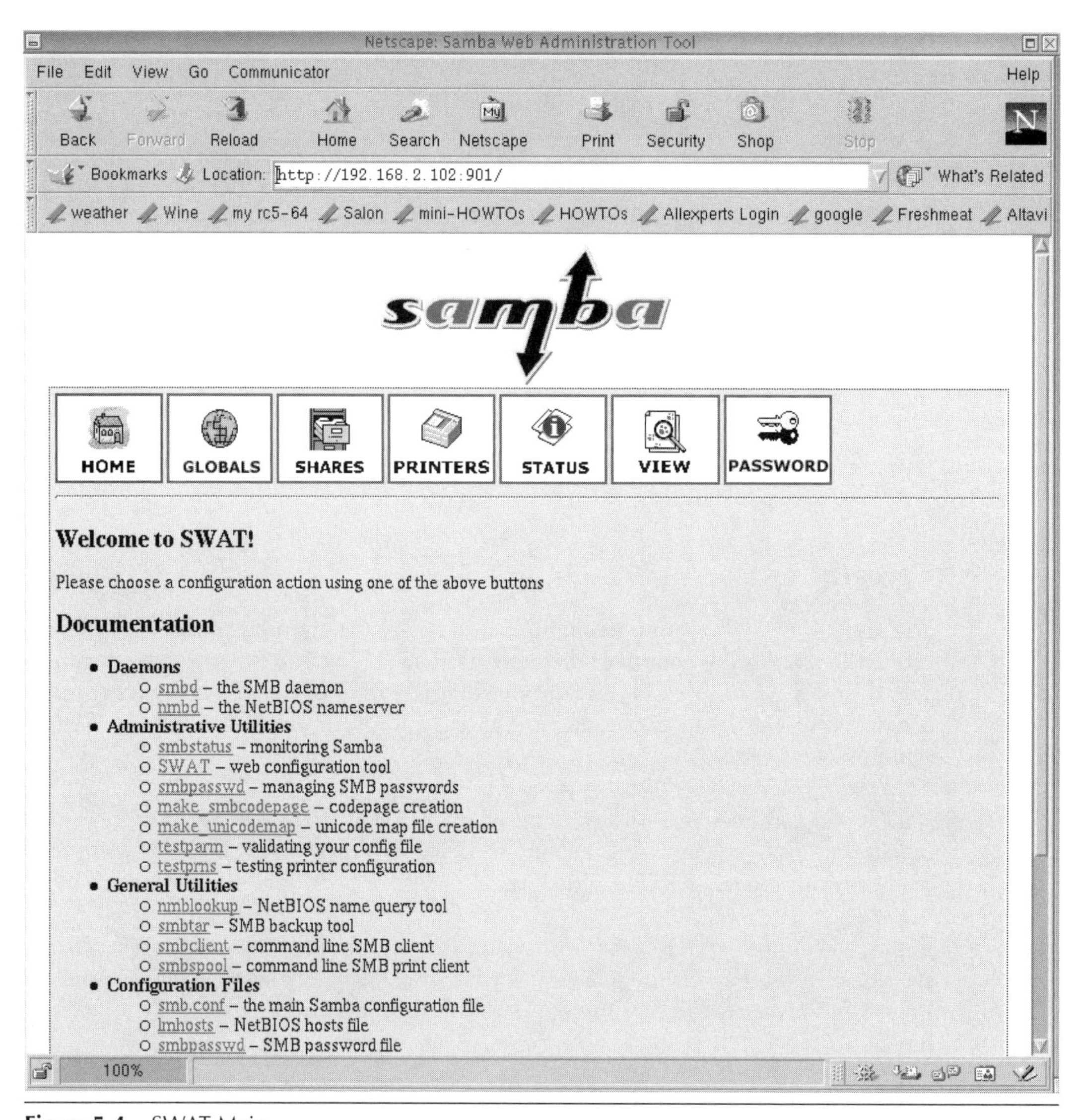

Figure 5-4 SWAT Main.

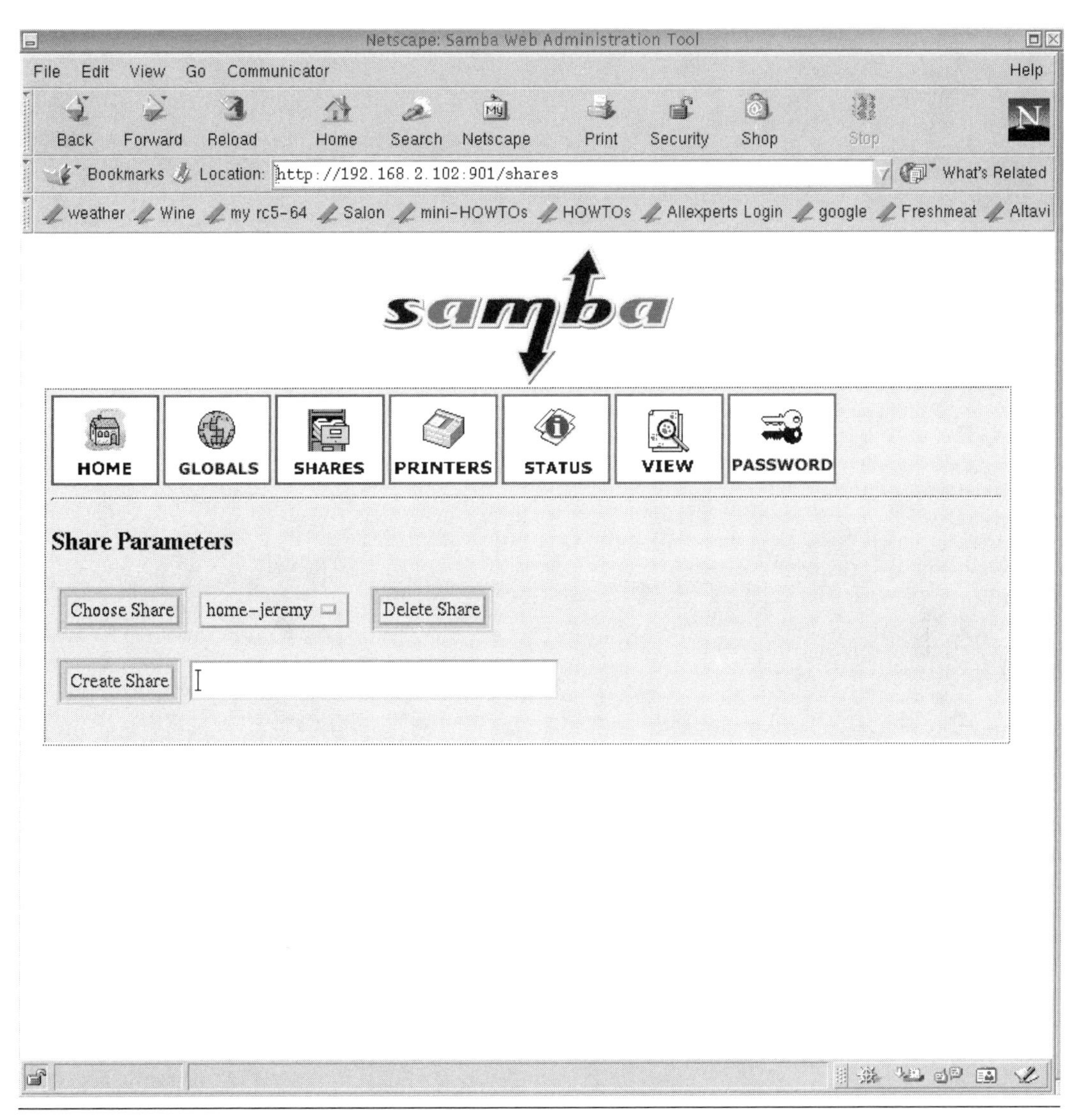

Figure 5-5 SWAT Choose Share.

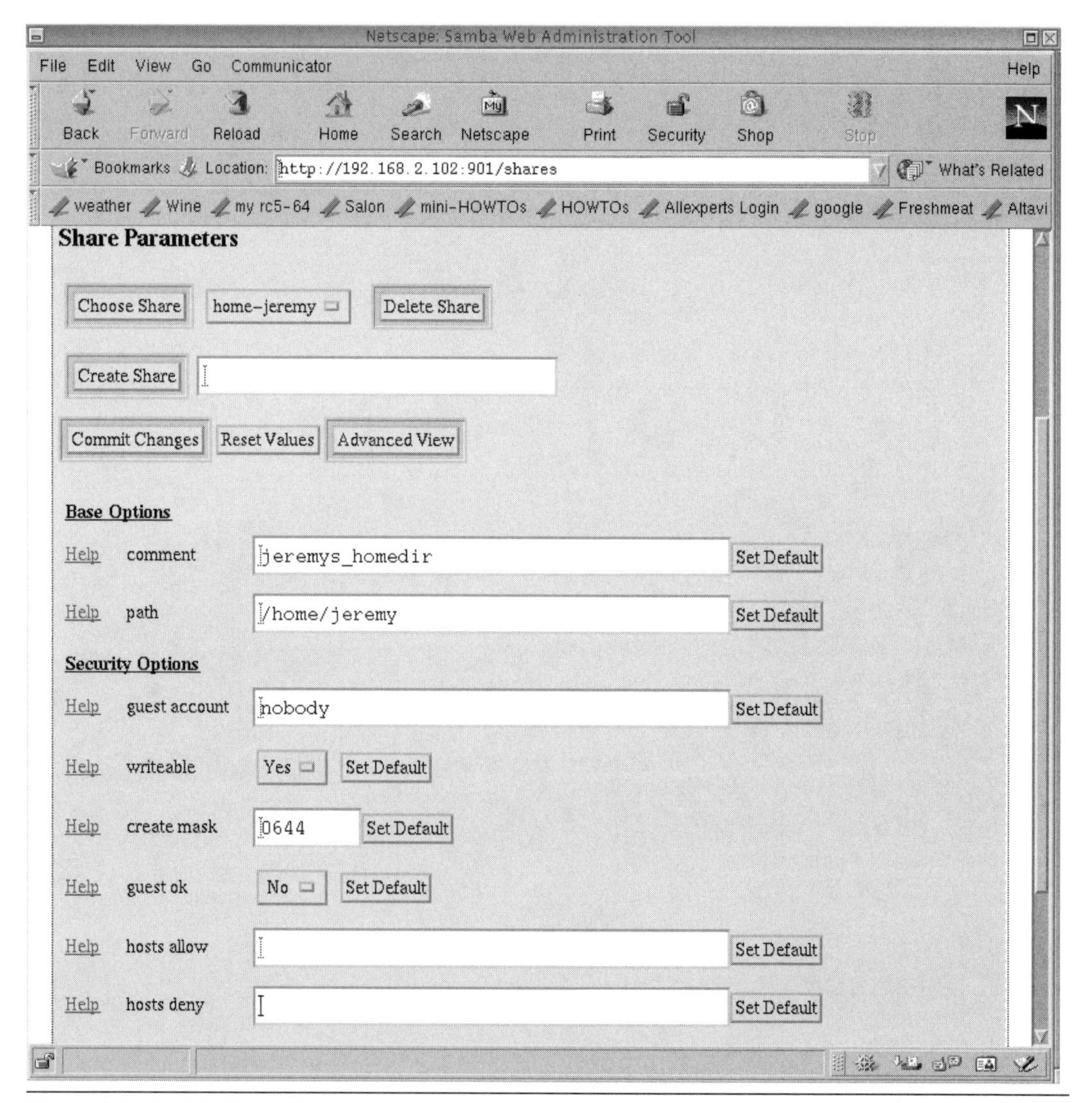

Figure 5-6 SWAT Share Manipulation.

Summary

This chapter briefly discussed the ins and outs of Windows networking and then showed several ways to access file shares and remote printers from a Linux system. It also showed that, once configured, Samba is an exceptional file and print server for your Unix *and* your MS Windows clients. It's robust, it scales remarkably well (after all, if you really need horsepower, you can throw a 16-processor IBM RS/6000 under it), and it's free. What more can you ask of server software?

References

More about NetBIOS and SMB/CIFS

- NetBIOS specifications:
  http://www.faqs.org/rfc/rfc1001.txt
  http://www.faqs.org/rfc/rfc1002.txt
- Online version of using Samba:
  http://samba.he.net/using_samba/

Samba

- Homepage: *http://www.samba.org/*
- Download:
  http://www.samba.org/samba/ftp/samba-latest.tar.gz
  ftp://ftp.samba.org/pub/samba/samba-latest.tar.gz

TkSmb

- Homepage: *http://www.rt.mipt.ru/frtk/ivan/TkSmb/*
- Download: *http://www.rt.mipt.ru/frtk/ivan/TkSmb/Arc/TkSmb-0.9.0.tar.gz*

xSMBrowser

- Homepage: *http://www.public.iastate.edu/~chadspen/*
- Download: *http://www.public.iastate.edu/~chadspen/xsmbrowser-2.4.0.tar.gz*

SMB2WWW

- Homepage: *http://www.samba.org/samba/smb2www/*

Ghostscript

- Homepage: *http://www.cs.wisc.edu/~ghost/*
- Download: *http://www.cs.wisc.edu/~ghost/doc/gnu/index.htm*

Chapter 6
UNDERNETS

Difficult-o-Meter: 2 (light Linux skill required)

Covers:

Apache 1.3.14	*http://www.apache.org/*
CVS 1.10.7	*http://www.cvshome.org*

Question: I've got a team of people who work scattered around the company. We need to share information and documents. Right now we are using a confusing mix of interoffice mailed paper documents, file-server-based file sharing, and various barely compatible groupware and e-mail products. How can Linux help me get to a single simple way to share information with my team? We have a corporate intranet, but there is a formal process to get anything on it and the intranet team controls the content. What can we do?

Answer: You can spend a lot of money on a proprietary groupware system like Lotus Notes. You can live with the long lead time from your intranet team. Or you go under the radar and implement your own Web server that you control, and you put all your team's stuff up there.

That last solution is the topic of this chapter. My co-authors and I like to think we coined the term *undernet* when we did this at HealthPartners in 1996, but a quick Web search showed us that other people have done this and called their systems *undernets*. Publish or perish, I guess.

The concept of undernets is an obvious one, and with the terms *Internet*, *intranet*, and *extranet* already taken, even the name is obvious. What else would you call a Web service set up by a small team for its own purposes and not linked to the rest of an organization's network strategy? *Undernet* is the obvious and cool choice.

In this chapter we will discuss some of the reasons to build an undernet, and we will show you how easy it is to set one up. We will even show you how to use some additional tools to make the maintenance and deployment of content as simple as possible.

The Needs

The needs are to improve coordination between team members, to share documentation, to centralize the control and update of that documentation, to reduce the cost and effort of cross training, to bring new employees and contractors up to speed quickly, and to do all of this at the lowest possible cost and with minimal impact on the rest of the business.

The Answer

The odds are that if you have a network of PCs in your business, you have a TCP/IP network. If you have a TCP/IP network and a spare PC, you have everything you need to build an undernet that will answer all of the needs.

The Structure

Virtually every Linux distribution comes with Apache, the free WWW server. We cover details of customizing Apache eleswhere in this book. See Chapter 9 for details. Different distributions place the served content in different places. SuSE, for example, puts the Apache content directories at */var/www*. SuSE 6.4 puts them at */usr/local/httpd*. For the purposes of this discussion, we will assume that the Web content is deployed in */var/www*. This does not reflect any preference on our part. It is simply less to type!

The most common tree structure under a Web server looks something like this:

```
/<basedir>   Debian uses "/var/www"
       \
        |-- cgi-bin  Debian keeps these in /usr/lib/cgi-bin
        |-- htdocs (perhaps "html")  Debian doesn't have this.
        |-- icons
```

Depending on your distribution and options you may have installed, there may be several more directories at this level, such as *logs*, *servlets* and so on.

Most distributions place some sort of standard content in this structure. Debian, for instance, puts up a slightly modified standard Apache postinstall index file. SuSE puts in a homepage with links to the online documentation and to pages that show the present system configuration. Other distributions will vary.

For the purposes of this chapter, I'm going to assume a Debian file layout. As in Chapter 4, this choice was made through exhasutive analysis of which distribution offered the greatest pedagogical potential and also because I was using a Debian machine when I wrote this chapter.

None of the pre-existing content just mentioned will be significant for your undernet. The best thing to do is to cd to the */var/www* directory and (as root) run *rm -rf ./**, which, when done, will have deleted everything in and below the *www* directory.

From this point on, you deploy documents in the */var/www/* directory. You should immediately create a file in this directory called *index.html*, which is the file the Web server will try to present whenever anyone tries to visit your machine with an empty file URL (meaning *http://your.host.com/*, which is equivalent to *http://your.host.com/index.html*).

Individual Empowerment

One of the best uses of an undernet is to enable individual team members to contribute. HTML is easy to write, and many word processors and editors will also produce HTML content. All you need now is some way to let all of your users deploy content on your undernet.

You have a lot of choices on how to do this. One way is to give all your users an account on the Linux box. After that, you must ensure that all of your users have rights to the Web directories. The simplest way to do this is to give everyone access to everything. This is fine if the machine is inaccessible to the outside world and you fully trust your network and your employees. If you work with IT professionals, this is a dubious proposition. Still, you can throw it open with the following command (run as root, of course):

```
# chmod -R 666 /var/www
```

A better way would be to create a group, where membership in that group confers the right to modify the Web content. I often create separate groups for access to the HTML content and access to *cgi-bin*, but we'll keep it simple here.

The sequence to follow to set up a secure group is:

1. Create the group.
2. Change group ownership of the Web directories.
3. Add group read and write permission to the files.
4. Add setgid on the Web directories (optional).

1. Create the Group

Groups are defined in the */etc/group* file. The format of entries in this file is:

```
GroupName:GroupPassword:GID:MemberList
```

Field	Description
GroupName	This is the name of the group. Keep this short, preferably eight characters or fewer. This is the name that will show up in long format directory listings and the symbolic name you can use anywhere a group must be specified.
GroupPassword	*Just say no!* Do not set a group password. It really creates more problems. In theory, an encrypted password here requires the user to enter that password in order to make this group the "primary group." Having a group password allows people who know the password but are not in the MemberList to become group members. I think this just adds complexity and confusion. If you create a group to keep unauthorized users away from certain files, it's a bad idea to give them a potential back door. Users also tend to take shortcuts. If a group member wants to give a nongroup member access to a file belonging to the group, they might be tempted to share the group password. Don't do it. Use MemberList exclusively to control group access.
GID	This is a unique group ID number you create. It must be unique, or you will see confusing things in your file system. (You will set the group ownership of a file to your group name, but you might see some other name when you look. This is because the two different names have the same GID. If it were just an issue of names, it wouldn't be a big deal. It is, however, also a question of security. People in the other named group with the same ID will have access to this file. You probably don't want that. Make sure this number is unqiue.)
MemberList	This is a list of user names that belong to this group. Add a user to this list to give them access to the group's files. Remove a user name from this list to take it away.

So an entry you might make could be:

```
undernet:x:5001:mschwarz,pcurtis,smurphy,janderso
```

2. Change Group Ownership of the Web Directories

You might want to create more than one group. For example, one group would have the ability to modify HTML content, the other might have the ability to write and deploy CGI (common gateway interface) programs. This distinction might be necessary if, for example, you have many people who write documents, only a few of whom are programmers.

For our purposes, our little team is able to do both. So now that we have the groups, we must set the group owner of the Web directories and files to our new group:

```
# chgrp -R undernet /var/www
```

Now the *undernet* group owns all the files and directories under the Web server.

3. Add Group Read and Write Permission to the Files

In addition to changing the ownership, you must make sure the group can read and write the files that are already there. Generally, I allow the *undernet* group to read and write everything but the undernet homepage itself. To do this, I issue the following commands:

```
# chmod -R g+rw /var/www ; chmod g-w /var/www/htdocs/index.html
```

The first chmod gives read and write on every file to everyone in the group. The second chmod takes away write permission on the undernet homepage, *index.html*.

4. Add setgid on the Web Directories (Optional)

Just because someone is a member of a group does not mean that that group is the user's primary group. Every user has a "primary group," that is, the group that will own files the user creates. It defaults to the group specified in the user's */etc/passwd* entry. The user may also change it to any group the user belongs to with the *newgrp* or *sg* commands.

As we have things now, if a member of the *undernet* group creates a new file somewhere in the Web server hierarchy, that file will be group owned by whatever group is that user's primary group. That's not what we want. We want the file to be owned by the *undernet* group automatically so that other undernet users get the correct access to it.

Fortunately, there is a very nice, and little-known, feature of the Unix permissions system that takes care of this for us. Files in Linux can have a *setgid* attribute. On an executable program, this attribute means that while that program is running, the user belongs to the group owner of the executable program, even if he or she would not normally be in that group. This attribute (and a similar attribute called *setuid*) can be used to give the users of a program permissions they would not normally have. This attribute shows up as an "s" in the execute permission spot in a long directory listing, as shown here:

```
drwxrwsr-x   7 root     wwwadmin     4096 May 31 18:22 htdocs
```

This bit has a special meaning when it is on a directory instead of an executable file. On a directory, this bit means that files created in this directory should be group owned by the group owner of this directory, no matter what the user's primary group is, so long as the user is a member of the directory's group owner. Read that again if it is confusing. Another way to say it is that if the *setgid* attribute is set on a directory and a user who is a member of that group creates a file in that directory, that file will be group owned by the group owner of the directory, no matter what the user's primary group is. Phew!

The upshot is that files the get created are group owned by the *undernet* group, just as we wish.

Since we want only directories to have this attribute, we will use the *find* command (see Chapter 15, Tools You Should Know) to apply this permission:

```
# find /var/www -type d -exec chmod g+s {} \;
```

Now all the directories in the Web hierarchy are *setgid undernet.*

The Maintenance

Let's imagine a sample team undernet (and here I would like to thank Starkey Laboratories, a marvelous hearing-aid manufacturer headquartered in Eden Prairie, Minnesota, for permission to use portions of the undernet I built during a project I did for them in the winter of 2000–2001). It looks like Figure 6-1. With this undernet, we took individual empowerment to the next level. We were already using CVS, the Concurrent Versioning System, to manage source code for several projects. One of the concerns expressed when we set up the undernet was that content needed to be backed up, and the network administrators were reluctant to put a desktop PC into their backup scheme. "No problem," I said. "I'll keep the whole Web site in the CVS repository on one of the main Unix servers."

We need to step aside from the undernet story for a moment to introduce you to CVS.

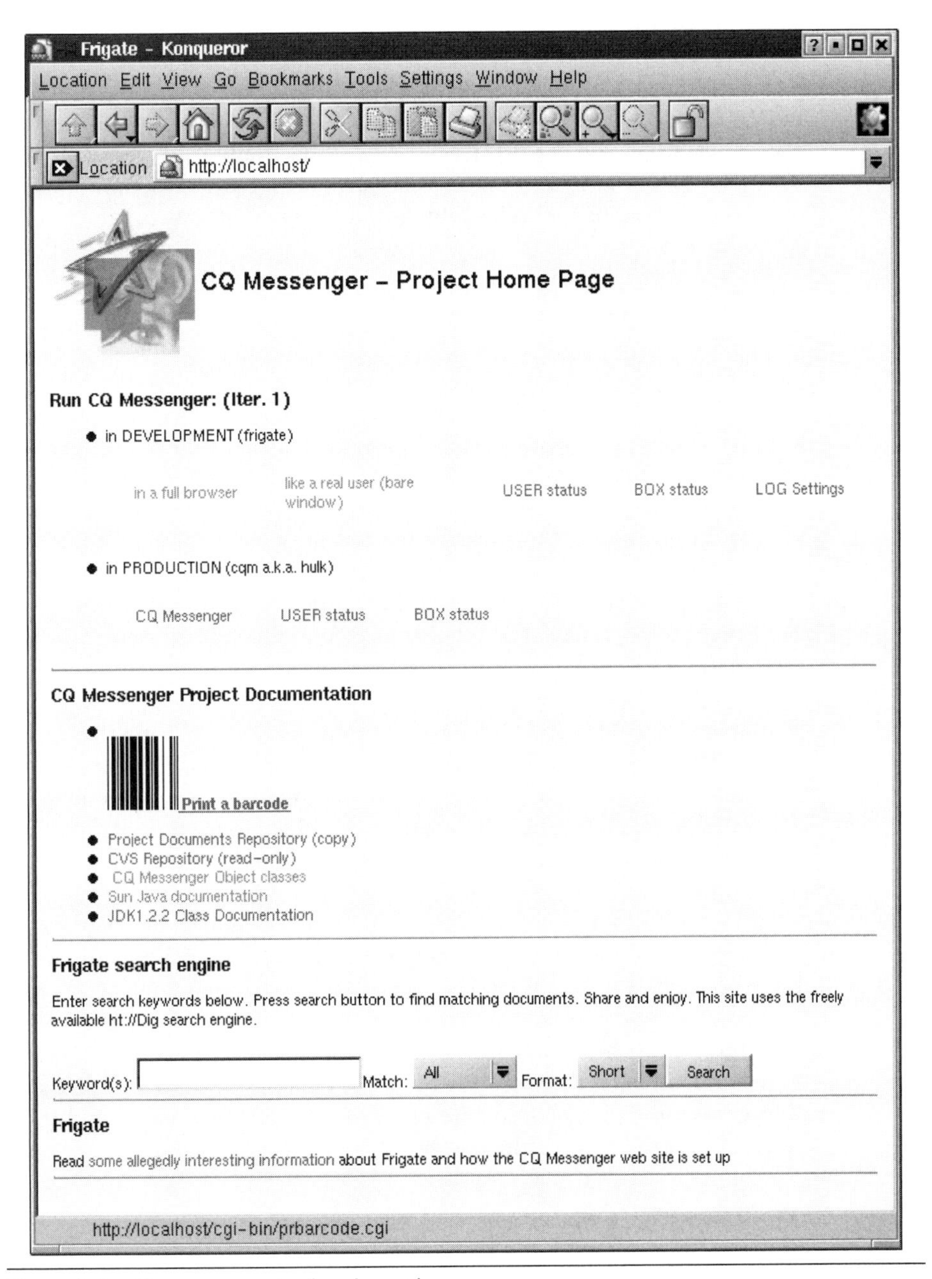

Figure 6-1 Konquerer grab of undernet homepage.

CVS Basics

Concurrent Versioning System is a very powerful and complete version-control system. It has many features and options, and fully effective use of the system has many nuances. CVS is worthy of a book in itself and is, in fact, the subject of more than one such book, the most widely used being the free *Guide to Using CVS*, by Cederqvist et. al, listed in the Bibliography section at the end of this chapter. Nonetheless, we don't wish to leave you high and dry. Here we will introduce just enough of CVS to get you going.

Core Concepts

CVS is another example of the well-known *client/server* model. There is a CVS server, which handles the central archive of files, called the *repository*, and one to many clients that manage the working copies of individual users, which we like to call *sandboxes*, because they are places where each user may play with his or her own copy of the CVS-managed files without let or hindrance from other users.

A user *checks out* a sandbox. The user then *commits* changes to the repository and *updates* her sandbox with other users' changes made to the repository since the last checkout or update.

Sometimes it will happen that another user has changed a file that our user has also changed in her sandbox. When that happens, there is a *collision*, and whoever commits last must *merge* the changes together. Most of the time, CVS is able to handle this all by itself. But if two or more users have made changes to the same parts of a file, a *conflict* occurs, and the person committing must manually resolve this conflict.

I know this is a lot to throw at you all at once, but we'll show you the commands and where each of these concepts come into play. We'll show you an example of each of these concepts and briefly explain them. Above all, don't panic! CVS really works. It is used by most Open Source projects, including wine and plex86, among many others, and it allows hundreds of developers, most of whom have never met one another, to work together on the same pile of source code at the same time. This very book was written using CVS to coordinate changes between this book's multiple authors. So relax, and let us show a little of what CVS can do.

The Repository

The repository is the base of all CVS-managed files. A CVS server can manage one to many repositories. The CVS client needs to be told where a repository is for almost all commands. You can specify the repository on the command line with each command, but it is more common to put the repository into an environment variable called *CVSROOT*. The repository may be local, in which case there really isn't a CVS server program; the client just uses the local file system. In this case the CVSROOT is just a pathname, for example:

```
export CVSROOT=/usr/local/secureprojects
```

The repository need not be local. It may be accessed using a number of methods. The general form for a remote access is

```
:<method>:<user/host spec>:<pathspec>
```

where *method* is one of the following

- *pserver:* This is CVS's own client/server protocol.
- *ext:* This uses an external program that can run the CVS command on the remote machine. The default program is *rsh*, the remote shell program. However, CVS will use any program named in the environment variable CVS_RSH to run the command. It is common to use this variable to specify secure shell (ssh/OpenSSH) instead of the insecure RSH protocol.
- *kserver:* This is the Kerberos version 4 security protocol. We won't cover this here.
- *gserver:* This is Generic Security Services API and/or Kerberos version 5. We won't cover this one here either.

The *user/host spec* is generally like an rsh/ssh login specification:

```
user@some.hostname.org
```

This is the form used both by *pserver* and *ext*.

pathspec is the path to the repository on the named host.

CVS Commands

I wish we had room to go into CVS's commands in detail. Alas, we can only offer you a glimpse and direct you to more complete resources. The general form of a CVS client invocation is:

```
cvs cvs-options cvs-command cvs-command-options [filespecs]
```

The most heavily used CVS commands are listed in the following table. This is by no means a complete list of CVS commands, nor is it even remotely complete documentation of these commands. It is meant to be enough to get you started.

CVS Command	Description and Examples
import	The *import* command is used to bring an entire subdirectory tree into the repository at once. This command is generally used when first putting an existing project into a repository. It may also be used when starting a project from scratch, but it is more common to use the *add* command to add files and directories as they are created. *Example:* `$ cvs import book addison_wesley initial` The first argument follwing the *import* command is the directory name the import will be given in the repository. **Warning!** This is unlike all other CVS commands! The import will begin at the present working directory and recurse down, with the files in the present directory being placed in the repository at the directory named by the first argument. Most CVS commands by default will work on the specified directory and all subdirectories unless told otherwise. The second argument is a *vendor tag*. This has uses well beyond our scope here, but, alas, you must specify one even if you never will use it. After the vendor tag, at least one initial *revision tag* must be specified. Revision tags are a way to give a full set of files at various revision numbers a single name, so you don't have to remember the different revision numbers of various files that make up a given release of your files. Again, you may not need this initial tag, since all of your files are probably starting at revision 1.1 anyway, but the command requires it. Most people can just make up a couple of tag names here and never care again. Consult some of the CVS resources if you would like to know more.
checkout	This command creates a sandbox. Unlike many other source-control systems, this does not lock files. You can check out the whole project and the resulting copy is yours to do with as you please. If, however, you wish to make changes that will be shared with others and become part of the project revision history, you must use the *commit* command to put your changes in the repository. If other users of the repository make changes to the files, you must use the *update* command to bring their changes into your sandbox. *Example:* `$ cvs checkout book`
commit	If you make changes to the files in your sandbox, and you wish those changes to become part of the history in the repository, you must *commit* the changes to the repository. This will make the versions of the files in your sandbox a permanent part of the history stored in repository. The commit may fail if another user has made changes to any of the same files since you last checked out or updated your sandbox. To reconcile the conflict, you must use the *update* command. When you commit, your chosen editor will open, and you may write a comment describing the changes that will become a part of the CVS log for each revised file. *Example:* `$ cvs commit`

CVS Command	Description and Examples
update	The *update* command brings your sandbox up to date with changes made to the repository by others. If you have changed some files locally, the changes from the repository are automatically merged with your changes. This usually happens automatically. Sometimes, however, other users' modifications may be to the same parts of files as yours. When that happens, the *update* command will tell you that a merge conflict has occurred and that you will have to resolve it. See the next subsection, Resolving Conflicts. *Example:* `$ cvs update`
add	The *add* command allows you to add new files to the repository. The *add* command merely marks the file or files for inclusion. You must still issue a *commit* to put the files in the repository. *Example:* `$ cvs add newfile.java newdir newdir/newpage.html` As you can see, you add directories in the same way.
remove	The *remove* command "deletes" files and/or directories from the repository. This command merely marks the files for deletion. You must still issue a *commit* to actually remove them from the repository. You must actually delete the file from your sandbox before you issue the *remove* command. Removing does *not* erase the file! Remember, CVS is a versioning system that can bring a collection of files back to any previous state, which means that "removing" a file merely means ending its "future," if you will. Files that are removed are relocated to a special directory in the repository called *Attic*. In this way, the file disappears from current and future updates and checkouts, but the file is still available when looking into the history of the repository. *Example:* `$ rm droppedfile.java $ cvs remove droppedfile.java`

Resolving Conflicts

Usually, CVS is able to merge other people's changes to files into your changed files seamlessly and quietly. Let's walk through two changes to a file, one where the other user's changes do not conflict with ours, and one where they do, so that you can see how this works.

Here is the original state of our sample file:

```
This is a sample text file that will
allow us to demonstrate how
CVS can allow many users to work
on the same files at the same
time. Not only that, but it will
show how users may merge changes
and how sometimes conflicts will
occur, and how those conflicts can
be resolved.

Enjoy.
```

Our first scenario will show the merging of two users' changes without conflicts. Let's say one user makes the following change and commits it:

```
This is a sample text file that will
allow us to demonstrate how
CVS can allow many users to work
on the same files at the same
time. Not only that, but it will
show how users can merge changes
and how sometimes conflicts will
occur, and how those conflicts can
be resolved.

Enjoy.
```

Here's what his command session looks like:

```
first@mars:~/user1/project$ cvs commit
cvs commit: Examining .
Checking in sample.txt;
/usr/local/projects/project/sample.txt,v  <--  sample.txt
new revision: 1.2; previous revision: 1.1
done
first@mars:~/user1/project$
```

Now let's assume the second user, oblivious to the changes made by the first user, modifies his sandbox copy of the file thusly:

```
This is an example text file that will
allow us to demonstrate how
CVS can allow many users to work
on the same files at the same
time.  Not only that, but it will
```

```
show how users may merge changes
and how sometimes conflicts will
occur, and how those conflicts can
be resolved.

Enjoy.
```

Now, user 2, having made this change, attempts to commit the change. This fails, as shown here:

```
second@mars:~/user2/project$ cvs commit
cvs commit: Examining .
cvs commit: Up-to-date check failed for 'sample.txt'
cvs [commit aborted]: correct above errors first!
second@mars:~/user2/project$
```

This failure tells us that the file *sample.txt* has been modified since we checked out or last updated our sandbox. The cvs update command brings our sandbox up to date with the repository. Now, you might think that this means the repository will overwrite our changes, but this is not so. If we have locally modified files, the update command will *merge in* the other user's changes. It looks like this:

```
second@mars:~/user2/project$ cvs update
cvs update: Updating .
RCS file: /usr/local/projects/project/sample.txt,v
retrieving revision 1.1.1.1
retrieving revision 1.2
Merging differences between 1.1.1.1 and 1.2 into sample.txt
M sample.txt
second@mars:~/user2/project$
```

Now let's look at the file:

```
second@mars:~/user2/project$ cat sample.txt
This is an example text file that will
allow us to demonstrate how
CVS can allow many users to work
on the same files at the same
time.  Not only that, but it will
show how users can merge changes
and how sometimes conflicts will
occur, and how those conflicts can
be resolved.

Enjoy.

second@mars:~/user2/project$
```

As you can see, the changes of *both* users are now in the file. These are still merely local. Remember, our last commit failed, so we must commit again.

```
second@mars:~/user2/project$ cvs commit
cvs commit: Examining .
Checking in sample.txt;
/usr/local/projects/project/sample.txt,v  <--  sample.txt
new revision: 1.3; previous revision: 1.2
done
second@mars:~/user2/project$
```

This makes a nice lead-in to our discussion of merge conflicts. Remember, our second user has modified the first line of the file, but the first user has neither modified it nor updated to bring in the second user's changes. Let's suppose now that our first user modifies the first line like this:

```
This is a sample flat ASCII file that will
allow us to demonstrate how
CVS can allow many users to work
on the same files at the same
time.  Not only that, but it will
show how users can merge changes
and how sometimes conflicts will
occur, and how those conflicts can
be resolved.

Enjoy.
```

Now our first user tries to commit, but he gets the same failure our second user saw before, telling him the repository copy of this file has changed:

```
first@mars:~/user1/project$ cvs commit
cvs commit: Examining .
cvs commit: Up-to-date check failed for 'sample.txt'
cvs [commit aborted]: correct above errors first!
first@mars:~/user1/project$
```

Just as before, our first user needs to use the update command to bring his sandbox up to date with the repository:

```
first@mars:~/user1/project$ cvs update
cvs update: Updating .
RCS file: /usr/local/projects/project/sample.txt,v
retrieving revision 1.2
retrieving revision 1.3
Merging differences between 1.2 and 1.3 into sample.txt
rcsmerge: warning: conflicts during merge
```

```
cvs update: conflicts found in sample.txt
C sample.txt
first@mars:~/user1/project$
```

What's this? It looks a little different from the last time we merged in another user's changes. Why? Because the two changes were made to the same part of the file, that's why. CVS couldn't figure out how to merge them without undoing somebody's work. What does it do? Well, it punts. Take a look at the file in the first user's sandbox now:

```
first@mars:~/user1/project$ cat sample.txt
<<<<<<< sample.txt
This is a sample flat ASCII file that will
=======
This is an example text file that will
>>>>>>> 1.3
allow us to demonstrate how
CVS can allow many users to work
on the same files at the same
time.  Not only that, but it will
show how users can merge changes
and how sometimes conflicts will
occur, and how those conflicts can
be resolved.

Enjoy.

first@mars:~/user1/project$
```

Yikes! What's all that junk in the file? CVS has "marked up" the file. It couldn't figure out whose changes should win, so it dumped both versions into the sandbox of the person trying to commit. Yessir, it just says, "Sorry, buddy. It's your problem." The user must edit the file, deciding for himself how to reconcile the versions. The user must also delete the "markup" CVS put in the file.

So the first user might edit the file to look like this:

```
This is an example flat ASCII file that will
allow us to demonstrate how
CVS can allow many users to work
on the same files at the same
time.  Not only that, but it will
show how users can merge changes
and how sometimes conflicts will
occur, and how those conflicts can
be resolved.

Enjoy.
```

Now the first user may commit:

```
first@mars:~/user1/project$ cvs commit
cvs commit: Examining .
Checking in sample.txt;
/usr/local/projects/project/sample.txt,v  <--  sample.txt
new revision: 1.4; previous revision: 1.3
done
first@mars:~/user1/project$
```

And that's how you resolve CVS conflicts!

This is only the very briefest of introductions to CVS. We haven't covered tagging, branching, branch merges, diffs, status, or any of a host of other topics. CVS is a powerful and multifeatured tool. Our goal here has been merely to introduce you to it.

And Now, Back to Our Story

When we last left the undernet, I had proposed keeping the critical parts of the system on one of the primary Unix servers so that no critical content could be lost in the event of a failure of the Linux PC–based undernet.

This plan was acceptable to the client, and it turned out to have enormous and unanticipated benefits for the project.

Before we get to that, let me describe how we set things up. First, we set up a very simple (almost HTML 2.0) homepage. We set this up on a Debian system, so the *index.html* file resides at */var/www*. It is shown here.

```
<HTML>
<HEAD>
<TITLE>Frigate</TITLE>
</HEAD>
<BODY BGCOLOR="#F0F8FF">
<TABLE>
<TR>
<TD>
<IMG SRC="see/images/senses_n_star.jpg" ALT="project logo"
HEIGHT=100
WIDTH=100
ALIGN=BOTTOM>
</TD>
<TD>
<H1>CQ Messenger - Project Homepage</H1>
</TD>
</TR>
```

```
</TABLE>
<P>
<H2>Run CQ Messenger: (Iter. 1)</H2>
<UL>
    <li>in DEVELOPMENT (frigate)
    <TABLE cellpadding=10 cellspacing=10><TR>
        <td><a href="/servlet/starkey.track.ui.CQMessenger">
        in a full browser</a></td>
        <td><a href="http://frigate.starkey.com/see/CQMessenger.html">
        like a real user (bare window)</a></td>
        <td><a href="/servlet/starkey.track.ui.CQMessenger?admin=users">
        USER status</a></td>
        <td><a href="/servlet/starkey.track.ui.CQMessenger?admin=boxes">
        BOX status</a></td>
        <td><a href="/servlet/starkey.track.ui.CQMessenger?admin=show">
        LOG Settings</a></td>
    </TR></TABLE><BR>
    <li>in PRODUCTION (cqm a.k.a. hulk)
    <TABLE cellpadding=10 cellspacing=10><TR>
        <td><a href="http://cqm.starkey.com/see/CQMessenger.html">
        CQ Messenger</a></td>
        <td><a href="http://cqm.starkey.com/servlet/starkey.track.ui.
          CQMessenger?admin=users">
        USER status</a></td>
        <td><a href="http://cqm.starkey.com/servlet/starkey.track.ui.
          CQMessenger?admin=boxes">
        BOX status</a></td>
    </TR></TABLE>
</UL>
<HR>
<H2>CQ Messenger Project Documentation</H2>
<UL>
        <li><a href="/cgi-bin/prbarcode.cgi">
        <H3><img src="code39.gif" HEIGHT="50" WIDTH="50">
        Print a barcode</H3></a>
        <li><a href="/CQ/docs/">Project Documents Repository (copy)</a>
        <li><a href="http://frigate.starkey.com/cgi-bin/cvsweb">CVS
          Repository (read-only)</a>
        <li><a href="http://cq-dev.starkey.com/see/XFiles/index.html">
                                CQ Messenger Object classes</a>
        <p>
        <li><a href="/javadoc/">Sun Java documentation</a>
        <li><a href="/javadoc/api">JDK1.2.2 Class Documentation</a>
        <p>
</UL>
<HR>
<H2>Frigate search engine</H2>
<p>
Enter search keywords below.  Press search button to find matching
    documents.
Share and enjoy. This site uses the freely available ht://Dig search
```

```
engine.</p>
<p>
</p>
<form method="post" action="cgi-bin/htsearch">

Keyword(s): <input type=text maxlength=80 name=words size=25>Match:
<select name="method">
<option value="and" selected>All
<option value="or">Any
<option value="boolean">Boolean
</select>
 Format:
<select name="format">
<option value="builtin-long">Long
<option value="builtin-short" selected>Short
</select>
 <input type=hidden name="config" value="htdig">
<input type=submit value="Search" name="SUBMIT">
</form>
<HR>
<H2>Frigate</H2>
Read <a href="frigateFacts.html">some allegedly interesting
    information</a> about
Frigate and how the CQ Messenger Web site is set up
<hr>
</BODY>
</HTML>
```

The critical information is in the link to */CQ/docs*. This directory, under */var/www*, was created by executing the CVS command:

```
# cd /var/www
# cvs checkout CQ/docs
```

That created a CVS sandbox (as I like to call CVS working directories). All of our project documentation is maintained in CVS. Each user has his or her own checked-out copy of the files. Some use WinCVS on windows machines, some use accounts on Linux boxes, some HP/UX, some IRIX. Because we standardized on HTML for our documents, it doesn't matter how they are written or on what system. Some users use MS Word (not me!). Some use Netscape's Composer (not me!). But the point is, it does not matter.

Each user commits and updates his or her own copies as needed. The magic lies in how the documents are deployed to the Web server. The root account on the Web server box has the following crontab:

```
frigate:~# crontab -l
*/11 5-19 * * * cd /var/www/CQ/docs; cvs update -d > /dev/null 2>
    /dev/null
```

This means that every 11 minutes, from 5 am to 7 pm, the copy of the documents under the Web server is automatically refreshed from the CVS repository. That means that whenever a user creates or modifies one of her documents, within 11 minutes of committing that change it will be up on the Web site! The user need not even have an account on the Web server box!

In the last section we described how to give a group access to the Web server documents. By making use of CVS, we can give any number of people the ability to put content on the Web server, but none of them need have any direct access. Also, because CVS is a versioning system, we have the ability to "roll" the Web content back in time to any previous set of content.

The Outcome

The project documentation was not the only thing we automated. This project is a Java language project. Java includes a documentation generator that builds beautiful linked Web-based documentation directly from the Java source code. I think you can guess where I'm going here. We periodically update our Java-class documentation directly from the CVS archive, so when the code gets changed, the online documentation is brought up to date in minutes.

Creating a project undernet had a number of tangible benefits for us:

- The developers, managers, analysts, and users had almost real-time access to information about the project and its status.
- The shared documentation repository allowed all of us to be sure that we had up-to-date information and that there was no miscommunication because people were working from old designs.
- Having the documents up on a Web server meant we could give anyone the ability to read the project documents without having to give the ability to write or change them.
- Having the class documentation constantly updated from the code archive meant that developers were always working from documentation that matched the real state of the code. This drastically reduced the impact of changes on the development process.
- Keeping the CVS archive on one of our master servers allowed all of this documentation and code, scattered around various development machines and workstations, to be backed up together. No single machine failure could have more than a tiny impact on the project.

An undernet is an inexpensive way to improve team performance.

Summary/URLs/Bibliography

We don't have time or space to provide you with even a minimal tutorial on CVS. Fortunately, there are a number of excellent online resources. Some of these we list here.

- CVS documentation
    - Cederqvist Manual, HTML format: http://www.loria.fr/~molli/cvs/doc/cvs_toc.html
    - Cederqvist Manual, PDF format: http://www.loria.fr/~molli/cvs/doc/cvs.pdf

Chapter 7

E-MAIL AS A SYSTEM CONSOLE

Difficult-o-Meter: 4 (fairly high Linux knowledge required)

Covers:

Fetchmail	*http://www.tuxedo.org/~esr/fetchmail/*
Procmail	*http://www.procmail.org/*
GnuPG	*http://www.gnupg.org/*

Question: How can I get access to my home Linux system when I'm either at work behind a firewall that only allows me to send e-mail from my workstation or when away on a business trip and the hotel firewall only allows me to surf the Web?

Answer: Create an e-mail-based console application that lets you execute commands and return results via e-mail. If you're stuck with only Web access, get a Web e-mail account and use that to send commands over e-mail to your system at home. The e-mail console is a nice way to communicate with your system when normal communications (Telnet, SSH, FTP, what have you) are unavailable.

Introduction

Have you ever been sitting around at work wishing you could execute a command on your home Linux system to get some information from it? I have, and I bet you could find lots of reasons why you would want to as well.

E-mail is simple yet powerful. But can it be used as a console to your home Linux system? You bet! I use it all the time. Why not just log in and execute commands in the traditional manner? Sure, I could do that, but that would be no fun and I would not be able say, "Try *that* with Windows NT!" (Another name we could have called our book.) Also, there are times when direct access to a system is not available. But if e-mail is available, then this will work for you. First, I'll tell you about how I arrived at developing the e-mail console; then I'll share how I did it.

My Disconnected System

If you're like me, at one time you probably connected to the Internet using a standard phone line and a local Internet service provider (ISP). I like my ISP, but they limit the number of hours I can be online each month and charge me big bucks when I go over that limit. I won't switch ISPs since they are, without a doubt, the best in my area. Because of this restriction to my online adventures, I pick and choose the times when my Linux system will be online fetching e-mail, downloading files, what have you. The problem I had with this situation was that I wanted access to my home system when I was at work. What I needed was a way to keep my home system offline until I needed it and then have it go online and stay that way until I told it to disconnect.

Some time ago I decided to make it so my system would periodically connect to the Internet and download e-mail from my ISP using a nifty program called *Fetchmail*. I wrote a few Perl scripts to automate and synchronize the connection requests from various applications, like SETI@Home and Fetchmail, which both need to connect to the Internet at various times. Plus, I needed to go online to surf around but not get disconnected when the Fetchmail utility was complete. Getting e-mail with Fetchmail allows me to spend as little connection time as possible getting and responding to e-mail. Why waste the connection time typing replies? The main goal of these scripts was to coordinate the connection and disconnection requests and to keep my system online when needed.

It then occurred to me that if I could send an e-mail to my system (which picked up e-mail once an hour) and have that e-mail parsed somehow so that a command could be executed, I could make it so that I could tell my system to stay online or disconnect. Bingo! Now all I had to do was find that e-mail-parsing, command-executing dream utility. The solution was right under my keyboard.

Getting Connected

On a piece of paper beneath my keyboard I had written down some of the utilities I thought might be useful for dealing with my e-mail, and Procmail was one of them.

Procmail, as it turns out, is a very useful utility for performing searches on incoming e-mail and then performing some kind of action. I used Procmail to parse my incoming e-mail every 15 minutes (I lowered it from an hour to 15 minutes so I wouldn't have to wait so long to access my system) and execute the command that told my system to stay online after it was done fetching e-mail. This worked like a charm. I could send e-mail to my home system with a special subject like "CONNECT REMOTE" and my system would simply stay online after fetching and processing all the e-mail from my ISP. In my Procmail configuration file, a recipe file, I searched for this string and then executed the Perl script I had written to make it so my system stayed online. I could also tell it to disconnect. It then occurred to me that with a little more work, I could write a Procmail recipe and Perl script that would execute any arbitrary command I gave it. This was the coolest thing I had ever heard of, and my NT friends would be so jealous!

Locking It Down

Because anyone can send me an e-mail, I had to work out a protocol that would allow me and trusted friends, but no one else, to execute commands. I also needed to ensure that the results were returned securely, safe from snooping eyes. The solution to all of this lies with encryption and digital signatures found in another great utility, GnuPG (see Chapter 10, Secure Your E-Mail with GPG).

The Project

Now that you know the story of how the e-mail console came to be, it's time to put together all the pieces and make a working system. You will be using the following utilities for this project:

- Fetchmail—to get the mail
- Procmail—to parse and execute the e-mail console script
- GnuPG—to decrypt the e-mail and verify the authenticity of the sender

The Disclaimer

Doing this project could seriously damage your system. If you implement this project, anyone, and I mean anyone, on the planet with Internet access and an e-mail account has the potential to execute any command, even as root, on your system. Please don't attempt this project if you are not 100% sure you can secure your system from unauthorized use. In plain English: Don't do this project unless you know what you are doing, and don't blame me if you screw it up and get your system hacked. I warn you.

You know what? Just don't do it. Just read the chapter and learn. But don't do it. You know what? Don't even read this chapter. Just skip right past it and go on to the next chapter. Okay, now I'm thinking you just shouldn't read the book at all. In fact, just return the book from wherever you bought it, just to be on the safe side. I mean, you can't be too sure this code won't jump from the book and into your computer and cause irreparable damage. If you can't return it, burn it. Do whatever it takes, but *don't do this project.*

Okay, do it if you want to, but don't say I didn't warn you about the risks. This is seriously risky stuff I'm talking about. Think about this when you try to log in one day and your hard disk has been wiped clean by some hacker who discovered he can send a simple e-mail containing a few simple commands to your system. You have been warned. Do this project at your own risk. Now, if you're still reading this chapter . . . carry on!

Understanding E-Mail

E-mail comes in. E-mail goes out. Simple, right? Ah, not so my friend. Your e-mail requirements and my e-mail requirements will probably be different. With this in mind, I'm going to take the easy way out and describe my e-mail setup and let you work out how to adapt the e-mail console to work to your needs.

I use Exim as my mail delivery agent (MDA). This delivers incoming mail to my personal mail folder/file. On a side note, a mail transport agent (MTA) delivers mail between connected mail hosts. On yet another side note, a mail user agent (MUA) is the e-mail client program you use to read and send e-mail. Fun stuff! A lot of Linux distributions use Sendmail as their MDA. Whatever works for you should be fine. The key thing to remember is that when using an MDA, local e-mail is delivered to your e-mail file, which is usually */var/mail/your_account*. Some Linux distributions might differ on this configuration. I'm going to assume you don't receive e-mail directly from the Internet but instead use an ISP to store e-mail for you. If you are set up with a DNS, a static IP, and have direct Internet e-mail capabilities, stop reading this chapter, because you probably know more about e-mail systems than I do.

When e-mail is waiting at your ISP, you have basically two ways to get it. The first is to use a client e-mail program like KMail or Netscape Mail and retrieve your e-mail via POP or IMAP. The second is to use a program called Fetchmail that will also use POP or IMAP but will deliver your e-mail to your MDA, which will deliver the e-mail to your local account's mailbox (*/var/mail/your_account*). There are other ways to get your e-mail, but they are not relevant to this discussion.

Once the e-mail is in */var/local/your_account*, you can use almost any e-mail client to retrieve it. This usually means transferring the e-mail into another folder in your home folder, *.mail* or *Mail*, or some other location.

Fetchmail

Fetchmail is one of those handy tools that makes using an operating system like Linux so much fun. It's easy to configure, has lots of functionality, and does what you want, when you want, and without much complaining. You can run it from cron or run it by executing it from the command line. If life could only be so easy.

For the e-mail console, you will use Fetchmail to retrieve e-mail from your ISP. This means that you will have to switch your current e-mail client from using POP/IMAP to picking up e-mail locally. Why do you have to do this? Well, when the MDA on your system wants to send e-mail to your account, it will first check to see if a file named *.forward* is in your home folder. If it is, then all your mail will be forwarded to the e-mail address in the *.forward* file. But wait! We don't want that to happen. What we want is for the e-mail to be sent to Procmail for processing. You'll learn how to do this in the next section. For now, just remember that the *.forward* file is the key.

Fetchmail Configuration

Configuring Fetchmail is a breeze. All you need to do is create a *.fetchmailrc* file in your home folder. You can read the man page for Fetchmail and write this file yourself, or you can use fetchmailconf and generate the *.fetchmailrc* file. I wrote my original configuration file by hand, but the fetchmailconf application is a much faster way to get things going.

Figure 7-1 shows a screenshot where I'm adding a new remote e-mail server. Figure 7-2 presents a screenshot where I'm setting up the server protocol and adding a new e-mail account. Finally, Figure 7-3 shows a screenshot where I'm configuring the e-mail account password and setting up the processing options.

Once fetchmail is configured and working, you will be able to run it from the command line or via cron. The screenshot in Figure 7-4 shows that Fetchmail got a single e-mail from my ISP and then flushed (removed) it from my ISP. When you want to automate the Fetchmail process, use cron to schedule a Fetchmail call, and make sure you use the silent (-s) command line parameter or else you'll be getting lots of messages from cron each time Fetchmail is run.

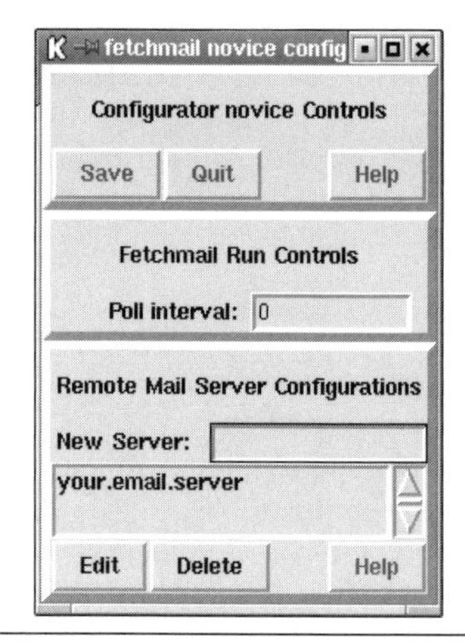

Figure 7-1 Fetchmail configuration—new e-mail server.

crontab

In order to make the e-mail console work, you must run Fetchmail at regular intervals. Cron is usually a good way to go about doing this. Here's a sample crontab entry:

```
0,15,30,45 * * * * /usr/bin/fetchmail
```

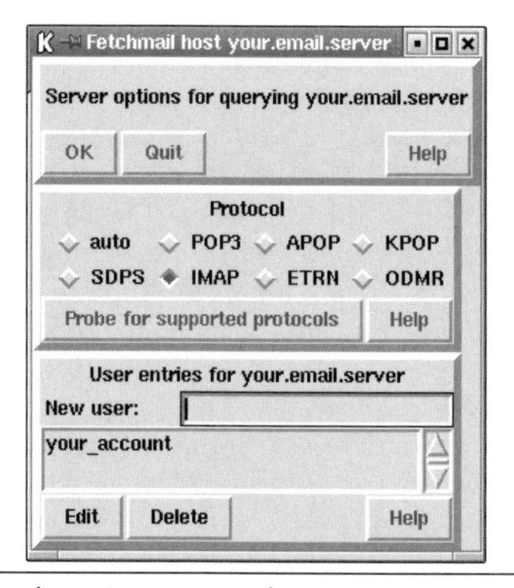

Figure 7-2 Fetchmail configuration—protocol setup.

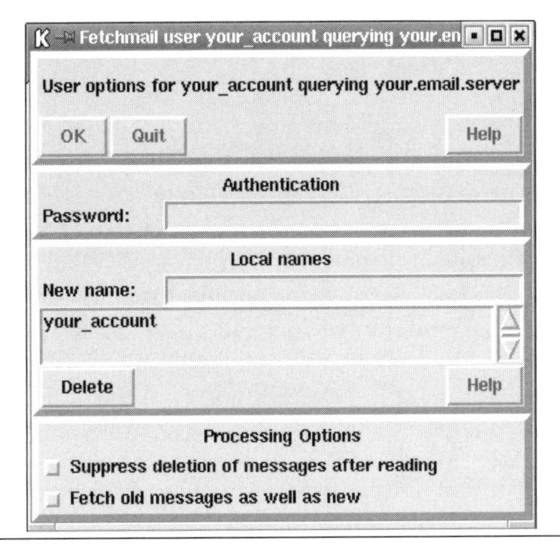

Figure 7-3 Fetchmail configuration—account setup.

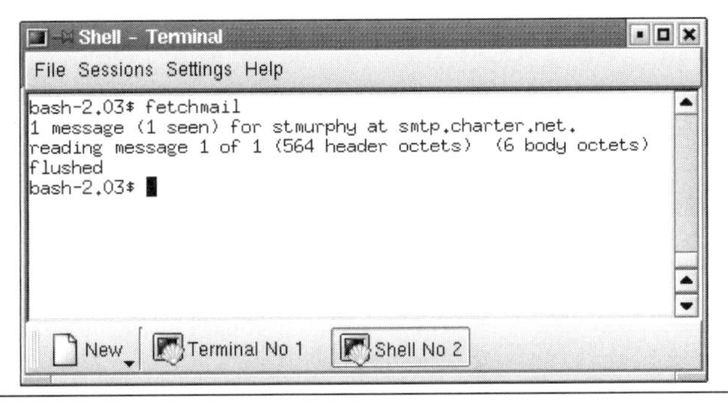

Figure 7-4 Fetchmail being executed.

Procmail

Here's where it really starts to get interesting. Procmail is the tool that makes the e-mail console possible. Procmail is a program that scans a text file (your e-mail file, which is one giant file when it comes from your MDA) looking for patterns you specify, and then it performs some kind of action that you specify on a particular e-mail within the file. You see, Procmail understands how to read this giant e-mail file and can perform either an action on the text itself or just an action in general. For instance, you might have Procmail scan incoming e-mail and for each subject line have it execute a text-to-speech program so it reads each subject to you when new e-mail arrives (see Chapter 21, Speech Synthesis, for another way to do this). Kind of cool, right?

Our use of Procmail will involve scanning the subject lines of each e-mail looking for a given pattern that indicates that the body of the e-mail holds a command sequence to be executed and that the output is to be captured and sent back to the sender of the e-mail. You could also have Procmail react to just the sender's e-mail address, but this is not as flexible and there are better ways to lock things down, as you will see in a while. So the big question you should have now is, "How do I tell Procmail how to scan my e-mail and how to do something?" Easy! You create a recipe for Procmail.

Recipes

A *recipe* is how you tell Procmail what to search for and then what to do when it finds something. A recipe is the heart of Procmail. You create a recipe for each type of thing you want to search for or an action you want to perform. There are many good resources on the Internet on creating recipes, and your best bet is to start at the Procmail Web site. So where do you put your recipes once they're created? You put them in your home folder in a file named *.procmailrc*, of course. Here is a beginning *.procmailrc* that has two recipes in it:

```
01 #---------------
02 # my .procmailrc file
03 #----------------
04 SHELL=/bin/bash  # path to your sh (try "which sh" to find it)
05 MAILDIR=${HOME}/Mail # e-mail goes here after your client gets it
06 LOGFILE=${MAILDIR}/procmail.log
07 LOG="--- Logging ${LOGFILE} for ${LOGNAME}, "
08
09 #-------------------------------------
10 # Your recipes (the order is extremely important!)
11 #-------------------------------------
12 :0
13 * ^Subject: test test test
14 /dev/null
15
16 #-----------------------------
17 # Accept all the rest to your default mailbox
18 #-----------------------------
19 :0:
20 ${DEFAULT}
```

I stuck the line numbers in so I can reference each important line for this example. You should *not* put line numbers in your file, since they would really mess things up.

Lines 04 through 07 are fairly obvious, so just follow the comments. Lines 12 through 14 make up the first recipe. This recipe will search for the string "Subject: test test test" at the beginning of a line. Remember, all your e-mails get sent to Procmail as one giant file, but Procmail knows how to logically break up the file into individual e-mails and check for whatever pattern you give it. In this case, line 13 is the pattern you want to search for. The ^ at the beginning means that the string of text you are looking for must be anchored at the beginning of the line. Line 14 directs Procmail to send the matching e-mail to the digital garbage can, black hole, or bit bucket, if you prefer. Each e-mail is passed from the first recipe to the next until a match is made. If you haven't already figured it out, the search criterion is a regular expression.

If you know regular expressions, then you already know how to enter a search string for any text you want to search for. If you don't know how to write regular expressions, then I highly recommend reading up on them. They are powerful and are used in many of the best tools available for Linux. Line 14 instructs Procmail to take the e-mail where the regular expression matches and send it to the null device. In other words, it copies the text to the null device and removes it from the e-mail file. Can you say, "spam filter"? I can think of a few rules to filter out unwanted e-mails. Of course, there are numerous examples on the Internet of spam filters for Procmail. Just search *Google.com* for them.

Another good use for Procmail is to direct e-mails from various e-mail lists into their own e-mail folder in your e-mail folder. This is beyond the scope of this chapter, but you can experiment and read some lists of frequently asked questions (FAQ) to get the answers on how to achieve this functionality. The next recipe is probably the most important recipe of them all.

The second recipe, on lines 19 and 20, is the catchall recipe for any e-mail not processed previously. When I wrote my first *.procmailrc* file, I neglected to include this recipe and my e-mail simply went away. Don't make this mistake. This last recipe tells Procmail to put all e-mail not caught by previous recipes into your normal mailbox location (*/var/mail/your_account*). Wait—I thought it was in my mail folder in my home folder? Nope. You see, when Fetchmail picks up the e-mail from your ISP, it delivers it to your MDA, and your MDA looks for a *.forward* file before writing the e-mail to the */var/mail/your_account* file. The *.forward* file tells your MDA to send the incoming e-mail to the address within. The neat thing is that you can also pipe the e-mail to a program, like Procmail. Procmail acts like a filter and has the ability to remove e-mail from the giant e-mail file. Once Procmail is done with it, the e-mail not filtered out goes to */var/mail/your_account*, where your normal e-mail client can pick it up. Make sense? I'll talk more about the contents of the *.forward* file in a later section. So what's all that other stuff, like *:0*, *, *:0:>*, and *${DEFAULT}*, all about? Here's a table that should sort it all out for you:

:0	Begin a recipe
:0:	Begin a recipe and use a lock file. Use a lock file to prevent multiple Procmails from trying to write to your mail file at the same time. (From the Procmail FAQ: "Rule of thumb: Use file locking when delivering to a file. Don't use file locking when delivering to */dev/null*."
*	Begin a condition.
${DEFAULT}	This is your default e-mail location (*/var/mail/your_account*)
|	(pipe) Execute a command

So filtering e-mail is great and all, but what about executing commands? No problem! Procmail has support for that too and can even execute scripts. The recipe I use for the e-mail console is as follows:

```
:0
* ^Subject: <console/>
|/usr/bin/perl /home/stmurphy/bin/email_console.pl
```

For our e-mail console recipe, what we want to do is look for a pattern in the subject line that indicates that the e-mail contains a command to be executed and its output e-mailed back to the sender. The best way to parse this e-mail and execute those commands is to write a Perl script and have Procmail execute the Perl script, passing the entire e-mail to the script. It's important to do it this way for reasons that will become obvious in the later section Securing Everything. You should notice that I am putting the *email_console.pl* script in a folder named *bin* in my home folder. This is just a convenient place to put stuff I want executed by my account only. Now we'll concentrate on the Perl script.

The Script

Before we get to the script, let's define some requirements. Let's say that in order for Procmail to pick up and pass an e-mail with a command to execute to our Perl script, the subject line must contain the following phrase:

```
<console/>
```

Simple enough. I'm using an XML-style tag here. I could use any word, but that leaves me open to accidents. I should be okay so long as no one sends me an e-mail with a subject line like:

```
<console/> is the XML tag I was talking about . . . let's talk
```

Of course, once you become a Procmail guru, you'll find even better ways to obfuscate the subject line. Moving on, let's also decide that the e-mail body will contain zero or more commands to execute. The Perl script should not barf on an empty e-mail and should also be capable of handling more than one command. Each command output should be separated by some kind of horizontal rule:

```
~~~~~~~~~~~~~~~~~~~~~~~~~~~~~~
```

Got it? Okay. One more requirement is that every command must be surrounded by exec tags. For example:

```
<exec>......</exec>
```

Nice huh? Well, I think so! This will make parsing the file easier. To make life really easy on us, let's also require that commands be on a single line. Parsing multiple lines for a single command block would complicate parsing too much for this basic example. Lastly, we e-mail the results back to the sender, either using the From: or Reply-To: fields. We'll use xmail to accomplish this small part, so make sure it's installed on your system.

Figure 7-5 presents an example e-mail file that I sent from my Web e-mail account, *digitalman@musician.org* (hosted by *www.mail.com*). Ouch! Lots of stuff in there, but we're almost done. In this e-mail, I am asking the e-mail console to execute three different command blocks. The first is the *free* command. The second is a set of three commands, *cd*, *pwd*, and *ls*. The final command is the *netstat* command. It's the job of the Perl script to make sense of this mess. Luckily, this is one of the last things we have to do. That is, we have to build the Perl script that parses the e-mail. Here's the code:

```
#!/usr/bin/perl

use IPC::Open3;
use Symbol;

#-----------------------
# setup vars for open3
#-----------------------
$WTR = gensym();
$RDR = gensym();
$ERR = gensym();

#---------------------------
# some handy variable defs
#---------------------------
```

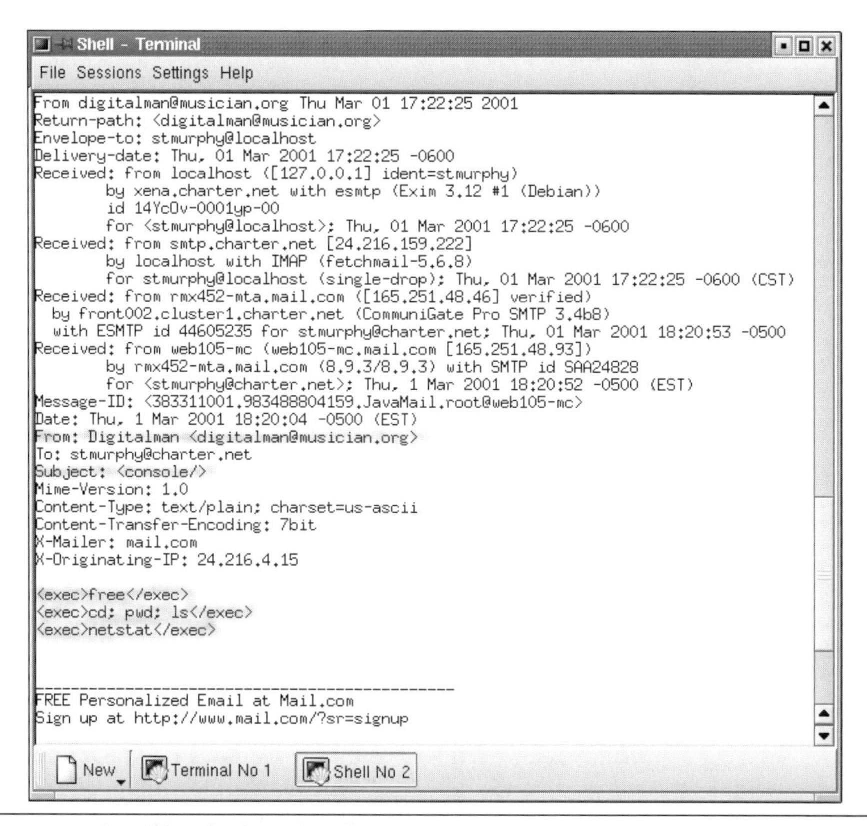

Figure 7-5 E-mail header from digitalman.

```
$logfile = "/home/stmurphy/.email_console.log";
$line_sep = 0;
$separator = "\n" . "~' x 72 . "\n";
$theOutput = "\n\n";
$reply_subject = "E-mail Console Results";
$signature_line =  "\n--\nOutput generated by the E-mail Console\n";
$no_commands_mesg = "No commands found to execute.";
$from = "";
$reply_to = "";

#---------------
# open log file
#---------------
open LOG, "<<$logfile";

#-------------------------
# our parse/execution loop
```

```
#-------------------------
while(<>) {

    #-----------------------
    # get the sender address
    #-----------------------
    if ( $_ =~ m/From: (.*)/) {
        $from = $1;
    }

    #--------------------------------
    # get the sender address override
    #--------------------------------
    if ( $_ =~ m/Reply-To: (.*)/) {
        $reply_to = $1;
    }

    #--------------------------
    # look for <exec>...</exec>
    # and process the command
    #--------------------------
    if ( $_ =~ m/^<exec>(.*)<\/exec>/ ) {
        undef $cmd_output;
        if ($line_sep) {
            $theOutput .= $separator;
        } else {
            $line_sep = 1;
        }
        $who = ($reply_to ne "") ? "F:$from R:$reply_to" : $from;
        print LOG scalar localtime() . " $who executed [$1]\n";
        $theOutput .= "Executing [$1]\n\n";

        #-----------------------
        # execute the command(s)
        #-----------------------
        open3($WTR, $RDR, $ERR, $1);
        close($WTR);
        while (<$RDR>) {
            $cmd_output .= $_;
        }
        while (<$ERR>) {
            $cmd_output .= $_;
        }
        $theOutput .= $cmd_output;
    }
}

#----------------------------
# report if there was
# no command executed at all
#----------------------------
```

```
if (!$line_sep) {
    $theOutput .= $no_commands_mesg;
}

#--------------------------
# tack on a handy dandy
# signature line
#--------------------------
$theOutput .= $signature_line;

#----------------------------
# override the from address
# with the reply-to address
#----------------------------
if ($reply_to ne "") {
    $from = $reply_to;
}

#---------------------
# close the log file
#---------------------
close LOG;

#----------------------
# send the reply e-mail
# with the execution
# results
#----------------------
exec "echo \"$theOutput\" | mailx -s \"$reply_subject\" \"$from\"";

exit;
```

I won't go line by line into the code, since it's so short. However, I will point out that there are many other possible ways to write this code. I kept this code rather simple because it gets the point across. Even so, a nice improvement would be to put in a sigalarm-catching procedure in case you tell the e-mail console to run an interactive application like *top*. If you did execute *top*, the *email_console.pl* process for that session would simply get stuck waiting for input from you—which you could never give. Looking on, the code accepts multiple <exec>....</exec> lines and executes whatever the command is in the context of the user running the Fetchmail command. This could be root if you so desired, but I would highly recommend getting some common sense before allowing the world to execute commands on your system as root via e-mail. Not a good idea! This script also allows you to chain commands using && || and ; if the shell that Perl is running under supports it. At this point, I can safely say the end of this project is nearing and things should be coming together real soon.

Gluing It All Together

The final task is to create your *.forward* file in your home folder. This is how Procmail actually gets executed by your MDA.

```
|IFS=' '  && exec /usr/bin/procmail
```

Make sure the first character is the vertical bar, or pipe, and that there are no spaces after it and before the next command. This can cause ugly problems. (From the Procmail FAQ: "IFS=' ' sets the shell's "internal field separator" to a single space. This is mostly just in order to prevent some old Sendmail hacks that were based on setting the IFS to something else.")

So there you have it. You should be able to send yourself an e-mail with <console/> as the subject and the command, free, encapsulated with the XML-style tags, <exec>......</exec>, and your e-mail console should come to life. Of course, at this point, even I could execute commands on your system if I knew your e-mail address.

Right now, the e-mail console is totally open and unsecured. (Was that redundant?) Anyway, in order to keep unwanted people from sending e-mail console commands to your system, you need to have a way to authenticate who is sending the command and determine if they are allowed to do this. Additionally, the information being e-mailed back to you is in plain text. If you don't want your command results being returned to you in plain text, you will have to encrypt the results. For these two tasks, encryption and authentication/authorization, we'll use another very handy Linux tool, GnuPG.

Securing Everything

We are now entering the part of this chapter where it starts to get really funky. Encryption and digital signatures are not new, but when it comes to your use of this technology, you might be new to it and not quite sure of how to go about using it. Don't panic! Chapter 10, Secure Your E-Mail with GPG, discusses everything you need to know about GnuPG.

Using GnuPG to Handle Authorizations

One small problem with this version of the e-mail console is that anyone is able to send an e-mail to your system and execute commands from your user account. To prevent this, we'll modify the Perl script to include support for digital signature detection and verification. When an e-mail arrives for the e-mail console, it will check for a digital signature and then check it against your special e-mail console keyring to see if it's a valid signature. This means that only people you trust can send e-mail console commands to your system. You could keep on locking it down using other techniques. For this example, we'll keep it simple and just assume your friends are trustworthy and won't try to erase all your files from your home folder. In addition to authorization, our results should be kept private until the recipient gets the results. To do this, we'll use encryption.

Using GnuPG to Encrypt the Results

So long as the digital signature verifies, we can now get down to executing the commands contained in the e-mail and placing the results in an encrypted e-mail back to the sender. We'll use GnuPG to encrypt the execution results.

We'll do this by using the e-mail address in the From or Reply-to field as the public key identifier when encrypting the results. Sounds easy enough.

Putting It All Together

Both the digital signature verification and the encryption of the results will require significant changes to the *email_console.pl* script. Here is the new version of the script:

```
#!/usr/bin/perl

use IPC::Open3;
use Symbol;

#------------------------
# set up vars for open3
#------------------------
$WTR = gensym();
$RDR = gensym();

#--------------------------
# some handy variable defs
#--------------------------
$logfile = "/home/stmurphy/.email_console.log";
$line_sep = 0;
$separator = "\n" . "~" x 72 . "\n";
$theOutput = "\n\n";
$reply_subject = "Email Console Results";
$signature_line =  "\n--\nOutput generated by the Email Console\n";
$no_commands_mesg = "No commands found to execute.";
```

```
$from = "";
$reply_to = "";

#---------------
# open log file
#---------------
open LOG, ">>$logfile";

#----------------------------
# read in the entire file
#----------------------------
@email = <>;

#---------------------------
# search for a sender to
# put as out recipient for
# the reply back
#---------------------------
foreach $_ (@email) {

    #-----------------------
    # get the sender address
    #-----------------------
    if ($_ =~ m/^From: (.*)/) {
        $from = $1;
    }

    #--------------------------------
    # get the sender address override
    #--------------------------------
    if ($_ =~ m/^Reply-To: (.*)/) {
        $reply_to = $1;
    }
}
$who = ($reply_to ne "") ? "F:$from R:$reply_to" : $from;

#------------------------------------
# check message for a valid signature
#------------------------------------
open GPG, "|/usr/bin/gpg -batch -verify -keyring ec-keyring -no-default-
    keyring
foreach $_ (@email) {
    print GPG $_;
}
close GPG;
$val = $? / 256;

#------------------------
# valid signature found
#------------------------
if ($val == 0) {
```

```
        #--------------------------
        # our parse/execution loop
        #--------------------------
        foreach $_ (@email) {

            #--------------------------
            # look for <exec>...</exec>
            # and process the command
            #--------------------------
            if ( $_ =~ m/^<exec>(.*)<\/exec>/ ) {
                undef $cmd_output;
                if ($line_sep) {
                    $theOutput .= $separator;
                } else {
                    $line_sep = 1;
                }
                print LOG scalar localtime() . " $who executed [$1]\n";
                $theOutput .= "Executing [$1]\n\n";

                #-----------------------
                # execute the command(s)
                #-----------------------
                open3($WTR, $RDR, "", $1);
                close($WTR);
                while (<$RDR>) {
                    $cmd_output .= $_;
                }
                $theOutput .= $cmd_output;
            }
        }
    }

    #-------------------------
    # invalid signature found
    #-------------------------
    elsif ($val == 1) {
        $theOutput .= "Invalid digital signature!";
        print LOG scalar localtime() . " $who - Invalid digital signature\n";
    }

    #-------------------------
    # some other problem
    # or not a signed message
    #-------------------------
    elsif ($val >= 2) {
        $theOutput .= "Not a valid Email Console email.\nA digital signature
           is required!";
        print LOG scalar localtime() . " $who - No digital signature
           found\n";
    }
```

```
#----------------------------
# report if there were
# no command executed at all
#----------------------------
if (!$val && !$line_sep) {
    $theOutput .= $no_commands_mesg;
    print LOG scalar localtime() . " $who - No commands in email\n";
}

#--------------------------
# tack on a handy dandy
# signature line
#--------------------------
$theOutput .= $signature_line;

#----------------------------
# override the from address
# with the reply-to address
#----------------------------
if ($reply_to ne "") {
    $from = $reply_to;
}

#---------------------
# close the log file
#---------------------
close LOG;

#---------------------
# encrypt the results
#---------------------
open3($WTR, $RDR, "",  "gpg --armor --output - --recipient \"$from\
    " -quiet --batch

print $WTR $theOutput;
close $WTR;

undef $theOutput;
while(<$RDR>) {
    $theOutput .= $_;
}
close $RDR;

#----------------------
# send the reply email
# with the execution
# results
#----------------------
exec "echo \"$theOutput\" | mailx -s \"$reply_subject\" \"$from\"";

exit;
```

To simplify my testing of the two versions of the e-mail console, I decided to name the second version *email_console_gpg.pl*. You should have noticed a few significant changes, such as the logging of requests. I placed the e-mail console log file in a hidden file, *.email_console.log*, in my home folder. The biggest change is the addition of the GPG code for digital signature verification and execution results encryption.

Finally, I modified the *.procmail* file to include an additional recipe that sends e-mail with the subject line <gpg-console/> to the new *email_console_gpg.pl* script. Under normal circumstances, you would not include both recipes and scripts, just the secured versions. If you leave both in there, your system will be left open to attacks. It's only included here so you can see the differences. Here's the new *.procmailrc* file with the new recipe included:

```
#-----------------------
# my .procmailrc file
#------------------------
SHELL=/bin/bash
MAILDIR=${HOME}/Mail
LOGFILE=${MAILDIR}/procmail.log
LOG--- Logging ${LOGFILE} for ${LOGNAME}, "

#-----------------------------------
# Recipes
#-----------------------------------
:0
* ^Subject: <console/>
|/usr/bin/perl ~/bin/email_console.pl

:0
* ^Subject: <gpg-console/>
|/usr/bin/perl ~/bin/email_console_gpg.pl

#-------------------------------------------
# catchall recipe
#-------------------------------------------
:0:
${DEFAULT}
```

This wraps up securing the e-mail console. However, this isn't everything you could do to secure the e-mail console utility. There are plenty of improvements waiting to be explored. And just in case you were wondering if this thing even works, here are some screenshots of the e-mail console in action. The screenshot in Figure 7-6 is of an e-mail being generated for the secured e-mail console. Figure 7-7 shows the e-mail as it is received by my system (I diverted it from Procmail for the screenshot). Finally, Figure 7-8 shows the result of the executions. Notice that KMail automatically decrypts the result. I like this feature!

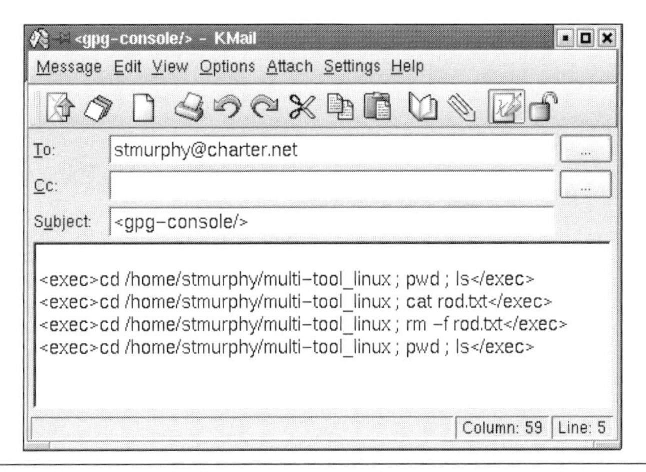

Figure 7-6 Generating an e-mail.

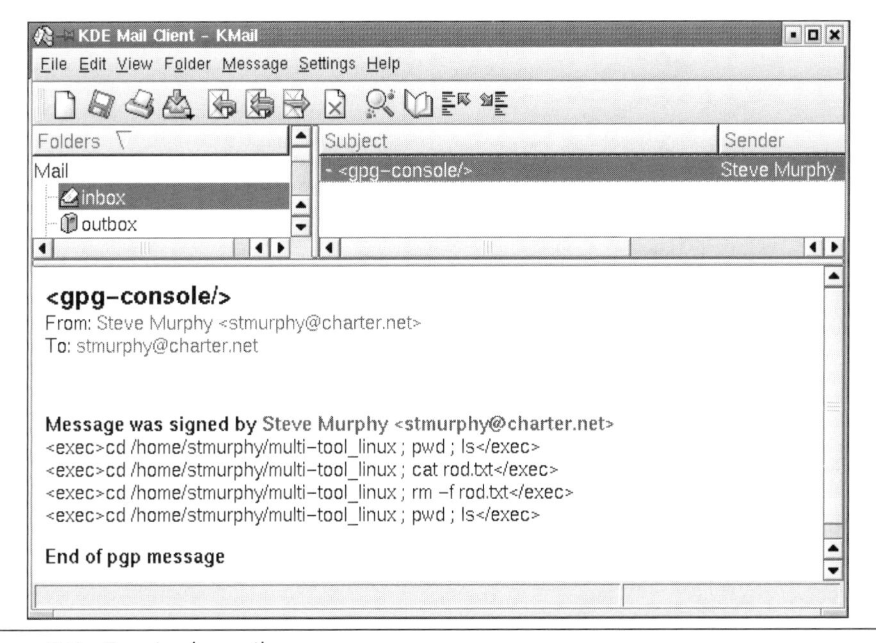

Figure 7-7 Received e-mail.

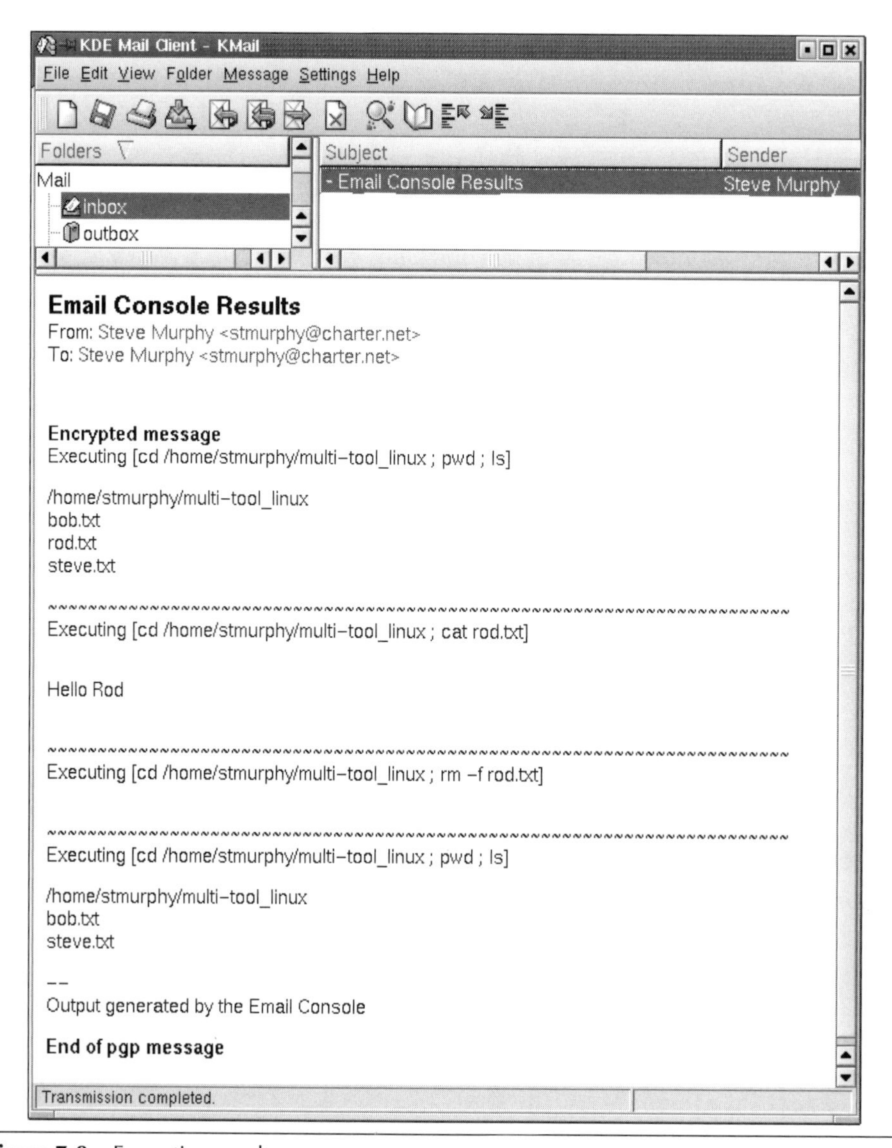

Figure 7-8 Execution results.

Summary

Here we are at the end of the chapter and with any luck I've shown you something that was not completely obvious to you. It's funny how ideas can cascade into new ideas and eventually end up coded and implemented on systems. This was the case with the e-mail console. I'm continuing to improve on the e-mail console, and I hope that you might do the same or possibly come up with other innovative ideas based on this project.

Some improvements to the e-mail console you could explore include:

- Improve how authorizations work.
- Use sudo to execute commands as other users on your system.
- Implement running commands as root with heavy-duty authentication.

There are endless possibilities that can be explored with the e-mail console. I hope I have given you enough information to stimulate some creative thinking on your part so that you can expand and extend the e-mail console, another good tool for Linux.

Chapter 8

Build a Secure Web-Mail Service Supporting IMAP and SSL

Difficult-o-Meter: 3 (moderate Linux skill required)

Covers:

Aeromail	*http://the.cushman.net/reverb/aeromail/*
IMAP	*http://www.washington.edu/imap/*
SSL	*http://www.modssl.org/*
	http://www.openssl.org/
PHP	*http://www.php.net*
Apache	*http://www.apache.org*
Required	gcc
	g++
	Perl 5.6
	sendmail
	inetd

This chapter will describe how you can set up your Linux computer to be a Web-based e-mail system for yourself or a group of friends. It will work best, of course, if you are on a dedicated Internet connection, like a cable modem or a DSL line at home. This will provide you with a secure method to check your e-mail from remote locations without having to add insecure connection methods that could be used by an attacker. While your friends and coworkers complain when their free Web-based e-mail system is inaccesible, yours will be humming along.

The combination of software we will be using is Apache with mod_ssl and PHP4, and the Web-mail package we describe later is Aeromail. We chose this combination because it is under active development (as of this writing), very easy to install, and quite feature rich. We also describe some additional Web-mail packages at the end of the chapter and provide several resources for more information.

We assume that you haven't installed a Web server or the SSL libraries on your system, which we will cover here. While it may seem like a lot of different components, it's really quite simple. Furthermore, your secure Web server can be used for other things you may wish to experiment with.

The general steps we will be using are quite direct. First we will install the basic connectivity for the mail server, the IMAP server, and secure it to accept only local connections. Secondly, we'll build a powerful Web server, one that supports secure socket layer (SSL) connections and the PHP scripting language. After that, the actual software used to display your mail on a Web page is quite simple to install.

To begin with, these are the files we have downloaded and their versions:

```
-rw-r--r--   1 jose  jose    22841 Nov 19 15:18 aeromail-1.40.tar.gz
-rw-r--r--   1 jose  jose  2847497 Oct 25 19:14 apache_1.3.14.tar.Z
-rw-r--r--   1 jose  jose  1866035 Oct 25 13:27 imap.tar.Z
-rw-r--r--   1 jose  jose   748253 Oct 25 19:15 mod_ssl-2.7.1-1.3.14.
    tar.gz
-rw-r--r--   1 jose  jose  2086131 Sep 24 11:46 openssl-0.9.6.tar.gz
-rw-r--r--   1 jose  jose  2225976 Nov  5 13:31 php-4.0.3pl1.tar.gz
```

The versions were chosen because they provide the most features and stability plus contain the latest security patches as of this writing. You're definitely encouraged to use at least these versions. The IMAP server we're using is the latest version available.

Now that you've obtained the pieces needed, we'll get to work. Building things shouldn't take too long, approximately one hour on a 300-MHz system. The longest waits are, of course, during the compilations. For reference, we will be keeping all of the archives in one directory, *webmail/*, as we build them. We'll be installing to the default Apache directory, */usr/local/apache/htdocs/*.

System Preparation

We need to install a package for the computer to handle listening services, one that's not normally installed by a workstation Linux installation. This is the inetd server, which listens for several daemons. On RedHat 6.2 installations, this is in the RPM inetd-0.16-4.i386.rpm. In earlier RedHat systems, such as 6.0 or 6.1, this was in the netkit-base-0.10 RPM.

On RedHat 6.2, these steps will install and turn on the inetd daemon:

```
rpm -ivh inetd-0.16-4.i386.rpm
/usr/sbin/inetd
/sbin/chkconfig inetd on
```

Building the IMAP Server

IMAP, or the Internet Message Access Protocol, provides a way for you to access your mail or Usenet newsgroups from a variety of computers. It works by storing the messages on a central server and allowing you to view copies of them. Then, when you delete a message locally, you can synchronize your mailboxes at your local workstation and the server. Also, you can have folders for your mail and full access to them, unlike with POP3.

First, having downloaded and verified the archive, you should unpack it:

```
$ tar -zxvf imap.tar.Z
```

Now, we're going to enter the newly formed directory and proceed to build the IMAP server. Because we're using Linux, the process is quite simple:

```
$ cd imap-2000
$ make slx
(make output omitted)
```

Installing the new IMAP server is also quite easy; we just drop it in place and it's almost ready to go:

```
# cd imapd
# cp imapd /usr/sbin/imapd
```

Now we have to tell the computer how to listen for imapd connections and how to handle them. First, we edit the inetd configuration file *inetd.conf*:

```
# vi /etc/inetd.conf
```

We will change the line that normally reads

```
#imap   stream  tcp     nowait  root    /usr/sbin/tcpd  imapd
```

to instead read

```
imap    stream  tcp     nowait  root    /usr/sbin/tcpd  imapd
```

By removing the opening pound sign (#), it becomes a directive to inetd and not a comment.

Now we have to tell inetd to reread its configuration. We do this by sending the inetd process the HUP signal. First we get the process ID of the inetd process:

```
# ps -ax | grep inetd

      7699 ?        S      0:00 inetd
```

Here, 7699 is the process ID of the inetd process. Your process ID will most certainly be different.

Now we tell inetd to reread the configuration file:

```
# kill -HUP 7699
```

Last, we will secure our inetd installation against unwanted connections. Unfortunately, a lot of hackers like to break in using the imapd service. However, we will limit connections to this server to only the local machine itself, which means that only our local Web server can connect to it. We do this using the TCP wrappers program already installed on our system. We edit two files, first the file that defines who cannot connect and then the file that lists the exceptions to that rule.

```
# vi /etc/hosts.deny
```

Then we add a line for the IMAP daemon:

```
imapd: ALL
```

Now we will edit the file that lists who is allowed to connect:

```
# vi /etc/hosts.allow
```

We then add at the end of the file the line

```
imapd: 127.0.0.1
```

That's it. The first piece of installation is done!

Configuring the SSL Libraries

Now we're going to build and install the libraries for our secure Web server. These libraries provide the functions needed for SSL, or secure socket layers. We want a secure Web server to protect your password and all of your traffic to your Web server while you check your e-mail. This will prevent someone from listening to your conversation and gathering your password.

Building the libraries and installing them is really quite simple. Starting from the directory that contains all of our archives, *webmail/*, the steps are very easy. First, we unpack the archive:

```
$ tar -zxvf openssl-0.9.6.tar.gz
```

Now we're going to configure and build the libraries. The configuration management is pretty smart, and it can figure out a lot about our system without asking us any questions. The build process is also automated.

```
$ cd openssl-0.9.6
$ ./config
(output omitted)
$ make
(output omitted)
```

Now all we have to do is become root and install the software in the default directories. Programs that use OpenSSL usually expect it in this default location (*/usr/local/ssl*), so we won't change it:

```
# make install
```

And that's all there is to that. We now have the needed libraries for our secure server to be built. Other programs can also use these libraries, as can some applications in the OpenSSL installation. See the Resources section at the end of this chapter for where to find more information about OpenSSL and the applications that use it.

Building a Secure Web Server That Supports PHP4

Now comes the most time-consuming part of the install, though it's still pretty easy to do. We're going to build a powerful Web server, one that supports the scripting language PHP4 and secure connections via SSL. To do this, we first have to merge these components into the server software and then build it.

First we unpack our sources that we will be using for this installation:

```
$ tar -zxvf apache_1.3.14.tar.gz
$ tar -zxvf mod_ssl-2.7.1-1.3.14.tar.gz
$ tar -zxvf php-4.0.3pl1.tar.gz
```

Note that mod_ssl has two version numbers, in this case 2.7.1 and 1.3.14. This is because it is a large set of patches and source additions to the Apache source code tree. Because of this, it *must* match the Apache source code version you are using, otherwise it just won't work.

The first thing we will do is to apply the source code patches from mod_ssl to Apache. The only directive we have to tell mod_ssl is where the Apache source code tree is, which is up and to the right:

```
$ cd mod_ssl-2.7.1-1.3.14
$ ./configure --with-apache=../apache_1.3.14
$ cd ..
```

Be sure to watch for errors in this step. Any errors will almost surely mess up the rest of the steps here. If you do find errors, make sure that your mod_ssl version matches your Apache version. It should apply cleanly. If you have to, remove both directories, unpack them again, and start this step over.

Now we have to preconfigure the Apache source code tree. We do this so that the PHP source code knows all about our Apache system and can prepare itself correctly:

```
$ cd apache_1.3.14
$ ./configure --prefix=/usr/local/apache --without-confadjust
$ cd ..
```

Now we can prepare PHP for its installation in Apache. This may seem a bit strange, but we're going to install it in the Apache source tree. At this stage most of the PHP module is built, which can take a bit since there's a lot of software to build. We build it also to support the IMAP client functions, which we need for Web-based e-mail using IMAP.

```
$ cd php-4.0.3pl1
$ ./configure --with-apache=../apache_1.3.14 --with-imap=../imap-2000
```

Now go ahead and install its components on your system and for Apache:

```
# make install
$ cd ..
```

Now we're ready to build our Apache server. It has SSL support and PHP4 support prepared; we just have to tell it to be sure to include them in the configuration step.

We also have to tell it where our SSL libraries reside, which we installed earlier when we installed OpenSSL.

```
$ cd apache_1.3.14
$ SSL_BASE=/usr/local/ssl ./configure \
--enable-module=ssl \
--without-confadjust \
--activate-module=src/modules/php4/libphp4.a
```

One thing to note here: *libphp4.a* does not yet exist, but this step will ensure that it is built and added into the server. Don't try and outsmart it; it's supposed to be like this!

Now we can build and install the Web server and the SSL certificates:

```
$ make
$ make certificate
```

This step will interactively generate a certificate for your server. These are used in cryptographic negotiations with your Web clients. See the Resources section at the end of the chapter for where to find more information on SSL. In the meantime, here are my suggested answers to the questions (you'll have to adjust some parameters).

```
Signature Algorithm ((R)SA or (D)SA) [R]: R
(omitted)
1. Country Name (2 letter code) [XY]: US
2. State or Province Name (full name) [Snake Desert]: Ohio
3. Locality Name (e.g., city) [Snake Town]: Cleveland
4. Organization Name (e.g., company) [Snake Oil, Ltd]: Home
5. Organizational Unit Name (eg, section) [Web server Team]: Parents
6. Common Name (e.g., FQDN) [www.snakeoil.dom]: friend.dsl.isp.com
7. Email Address (e.g., name@FQDN) [www@snakeoil.dom]: friend@isp.com
8. Certificate Validity (days) [365]: 365
________________________________________________________________________
STEP 3: Generating X.509 certificate signed by Snake Oil CA [server.crt]
Certificate Version (1 or 3) [3]: 3
(omitted)
Encrypt the private key now? [Y/n]: n
(omitted)
```

While the certificate process correctly notes that this certificate should not be used on a production system, for home use it should be just fine. Basically, there is no trust mechanism in place, so the certificate could be a forged one, allowing an attacker to listen to sensitive information. However, since it is just you, and signing a certificate can be expensive, we'll work with these certificates. If you want to host, say, a commerce site on your Web server, you should definitely get it signed by a recognized authority.

We also chose not to encrypt the private key with a passphrase. This is because this passphrase would be required if the server had to restart. If you are away from your server and it reboots and restarts, it would wait for you to enter this passphrase before it could start up. By omitting a passphrase, we allow the server to restart without you. This is not advised if you are on a multiuser machine with untrusted users, by the way.

Finally, we can install the whole server, configurations, and certificates:

```
# make install
```

To get it to understand PHP files, which the server has to process before serving, we need to edit the configuration file. While we're at it, we'll add forcing Web-mail clients to use SSL:

```
# cd /usr/local/apache/conf
# vi httpd.conf
```

We first want to change the server to understand PHP files and to interpret them. This is absolutely required for Web-mail to work. Uncomment (remove the leading # sign) the following lines:

```
    AddType application/x-httpd-php .php3
    AddType application/x-httpd-php-source .phps
    AddType application/x-httpd-php .php
    AddType application/x-httpd-php-source .phps
```

The first lines will be for *application/x-httpd-php3* and source, so just remove the 3. PHP3 is slowly being phased out, and PHP4 is backwards compatible. However, it doesn't get parsed properly if it is treated as a PHP3 file, so treat it as plain PHP.

Now we're gong to change the server to require SSL to be used if you want to read your e-mail. This way you can't make a mistake and send your password across an untrusted network in plain text, letting someone listen to it. We do this by adding the following lines, called a *Directory Directive*. Place these after the </Ifmodule> directive where PHP handling was described.

```
<Directory /usr/local/apache/htdocs/aeromail>
SSLRequireSSL
</Directory>
```

Yes, these directives read just like HTML, with a start and an end. Now go ahead and write out the configuration file. We're almost ready to start the server and test it out.

Installing Aeromail

Finally, we can install the Web-mail package, Aeromail. We chose Aeromail because it's simple and very easy to install and can be ready to run in just a few minutes after the Web server is installed.

Installation is a breeze; you just unpack it and edit a configuration file. All we have to do is unpack it under the Web documents tree.

```
# cp aeromail-1.40.tar.gz /usr/local/apache/htdocs/
# cd /usr/local/apache/htdocs/
# tar -zxvf aeromail-1.40.tar.gz
# cd aeromail
```

Now we're going to edit the Aeromail configuration file, *config.inc:*

```
# vi config.inc
```

You can change the window name at the top of the window, which is normally set to Aeromail (the program name). Maybe call it CoolMail. If you want to, you should edit this line:

```
    $PROG_NAME              = "AeroMail";
```

Because we're running our own mail server, an IMAP server, we'll use the localhost directive. If you wanted to point it to another server, say, at your ISP, you should edit that value. It's important that they be using either the Cyrus or University of Washington (UWash) server types. Other servers are not supported by Aeromail. Earlier we installed the UWash server, so again we can leave this unchanged.

The biggest one to change is the page you get redirected to when you log out or cancel a login. You should set it to your own Web server. Change this line to somewhere other than the Aeromail installation on your server:

```
    $SERVER_REDIR           = "http://the.cushman.net/";
```

Other variables, like the number of messages per screen, color theme, and even language (Aeromail supports German, English, Spanish, French, and Hungarian), are configurable. The comments in the configuration file should help you through this.

Write out the configuration file and you're ready to go.

Testing the Server

Now we're ready to take the server for a test drive. First we start up the server for both normal and SSL Web traffic:

```
# /usr/local/apache/bin/apachectl startssl
```

You should see a message like this:

```
      apachectl startssl: httpd started
```

If you don't, something happened that prevented the server from properly starting. The best place to look to help diagnose what is wrong is the error log file, in *../logs/error_log*.

Now look to see if you have two new ports listening, ports 80/TCP and 443/TCP. We will use the netstat command to look for them:

```
# netstat -na | grep LISTEN

tcp        0      0 0.0.0.0:80              0.0.0.0:*               LISTEN
tcp        0      0 0.0.0.0:443             0.0.0.0:*               LISTEN
```

Sure enough, we have two listening sockets, on ports 80 and 443 TCP ports. These correspond to the normal and SSL traffic for the server, respectively.

And now we will connect to our server and test out the secure Web-mail connection. Fire up a browser like Netscape or Internet Explorer (if you are on a Windows machine) and point it to your Web server. In our example the machine's name is *friend.dsl.isp.com*, so the secure Aeromail site would have the URL *https://friend.dsl.isp.com/aeromail/*.

The first thing you should go through is the acceptance of the certificate. For Netscape, it's a several-stage process, illustrated next.

First, we are presented with a popup window noting that the site uses encryption but Netscape doesn't recognize the signing authority (remember, we didn't have a big name sign above it). Use *Next* to move on in the process (Figure 8-1).

Second, it tells us a little bit about the certificate. If you click the *More Info* button (Figure 8-2) we can view more information, and *Next* will continue in the process.

Now we can choose to accept this certificate or not, and for how long. I usually choose to accept the certificate until it expires (Figure 8-3) and then click *Next*.

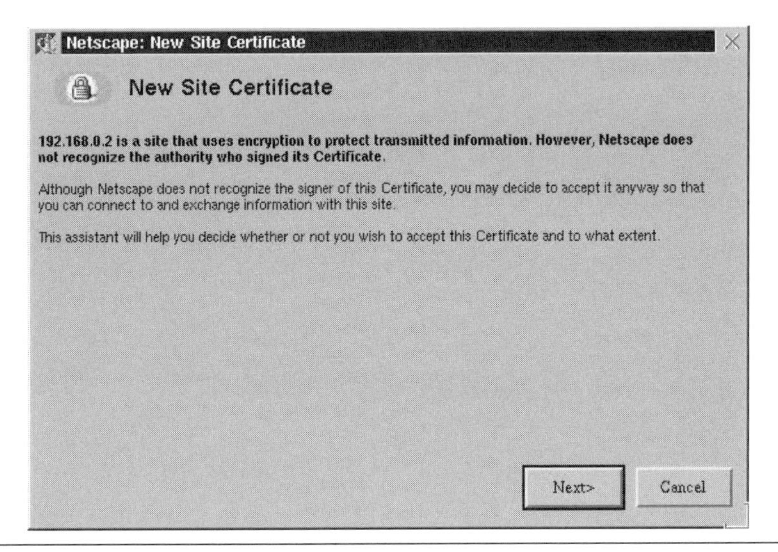

Figure 8-1 Netscape—cert2.

Then it offers you the chance of alerting you whenever you submit information (Figure 8-4). This can be useful, but with Web-mail it can also be extremely annoying. I usually ignore the warnings and don't let them pop up, and I click *Next* to continue the process.

Now we can finish the process by clicking *Finish* (Figure 8-5).

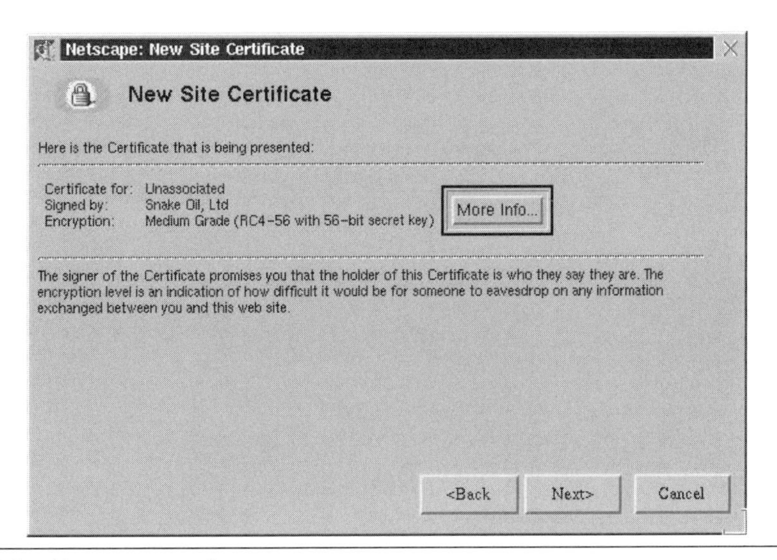

Figure 8-2 Netscape—cert3.

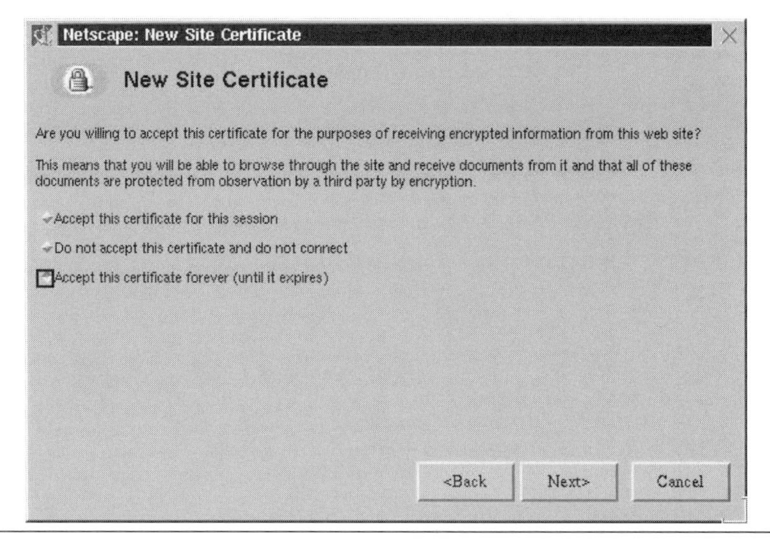

Figure 8-3 Netscape—cert4.

I often get the popup shown in Figure 8-6, since the site name that is on the certificate and the one that I am actually connecting to don't match (I'm not running a real Internet server here). I just click *Continue* and accept the certificate.

We know we have a secure connection because of three things: We have a URL that starts with *https://* rather than *http://* (Figure 8-7). And we have two indicators in the

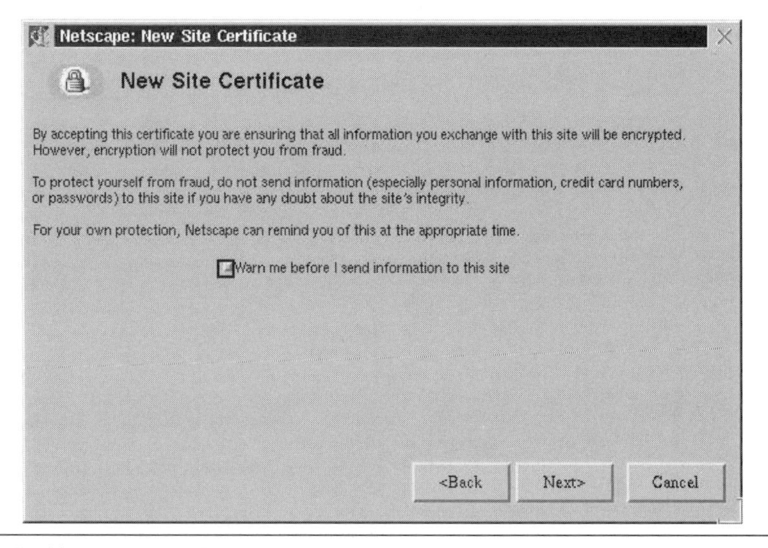

Figure 8-4 Netscape—cert5.

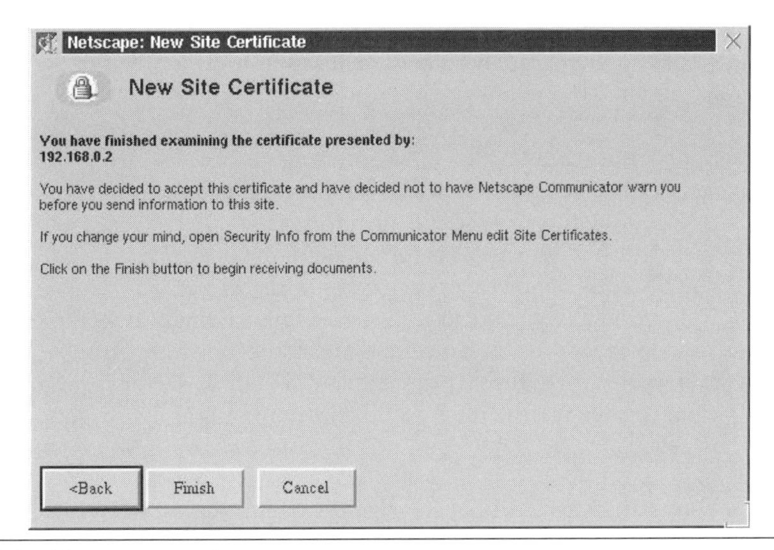

Figure 8-5 Netscape—cert6.

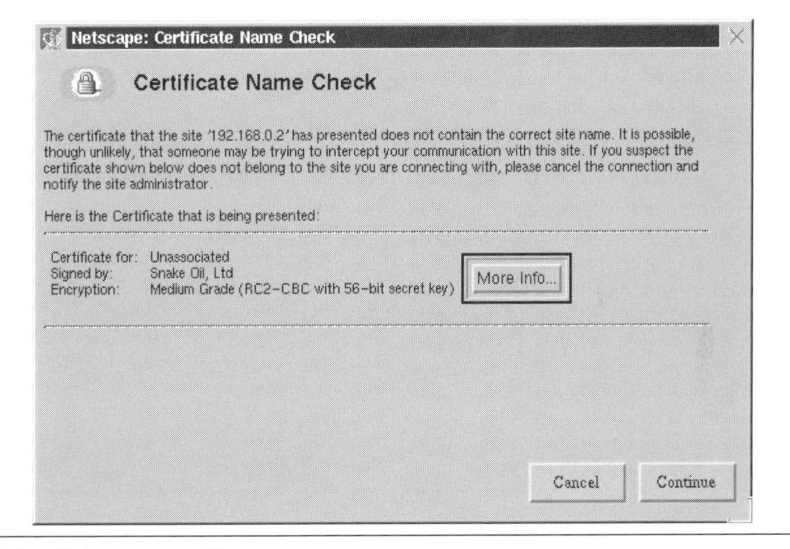

Figure 8-6 Netscape—cert7.

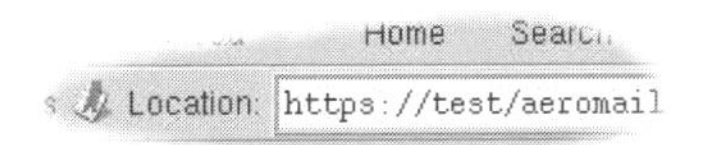

Figure 8-7 Secure—2.

browser that the connection is secure: The button bar at the top has a highlighted security lock (Figure 8-8), and the lock in the bottom left of the browser is closed and highlighted (Figure 8-9).

Should the preceding not have occurred, you need to diagnose the problem and try to remedy it. You can look in several places. First, make sure you are listening on both ports 80/TCP and 443/TCP for normal and SSL Web connections. Second, make sure that the SSL engine is turned on in the directives for the Web server. Otherwise you'll never complete a connection with the server—your browser will just hang. Last, make sure you are indeed connecting. Use netstat on the server to show that you are connecting to the server, and check the logs from Apache, both the *access_log* file and the *error_log* file, for any entries. The SSL server is pretty verbose about what went wrong, and the mod_ssl documentation is also very good at helping diagnose a problem.

You can test your PHP4 installation with a simple PHP file. Simply create the file *test.php* in your *htdocs/* directory for your Web server with the following very simple content:

```
<?php phpinfo() ?>
```

This will show you all of the information about your PHP installation if it comes up. Make sure that you have IMAP support, for one, or your Web-mail solution just won't work. If you get prompted to download the file, make sure you added the earlier directives for PHP files to the server configuration file, *httpd.conf*. When in doubt, check the documentation for each of the components, Apache, mod_ssl, and PHP, for chances are you have encountered a common problem.

Figure 8-8 Secure—1.

Figure 8-9 Secure—3.

Using Aeromail

Now that we've connected to the server, we are presented with an authentication popup window (Figure 8-10). This is just your usual username and password. They will be sent across the network encrypted using the SSL connection.

And now you have a fully working secure Web server. You can protect a lot of Web transactions using this server, like our e-mail connection.

Once we successfully authenticate, the software reads our mailbox and prepares a Web page for us. This is what is done by the PHP software: It connects to the IMAP server, logs in as us, and reads the message folder for our inbox. The server then processes the PHP and presents us with a Web page, showing us our inbox. This is illustrated in Figure 8-11, which shows an inbox containing two messages (you may

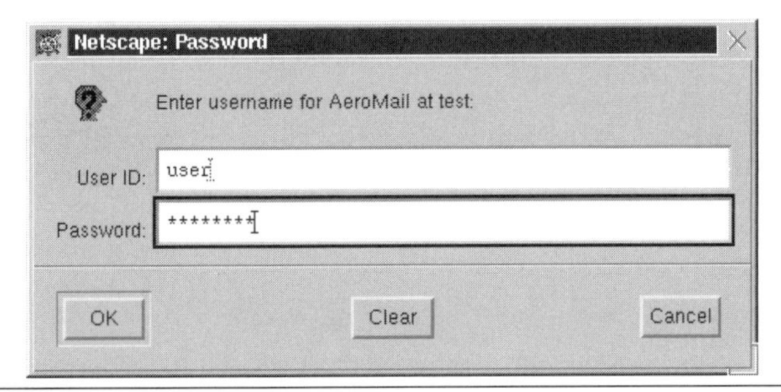

Figure 8-10 Aero—auth1.

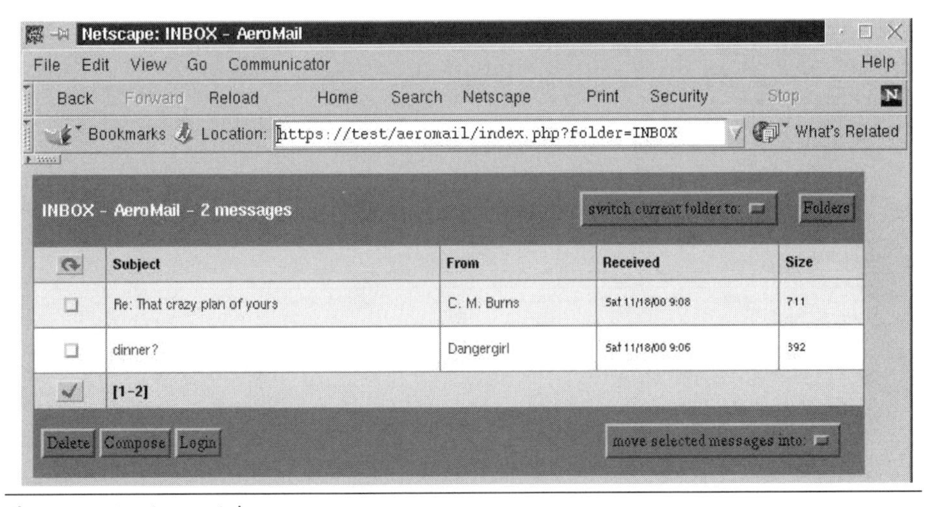

Figure 8-11 Aero—inbox.

get more mail than I do). Messages are sorted in the order of their date received, with the newest messages appearing on top. Shown are the subject of the e-mail, who it was received from, when it was received, and its size. The checkbox to the left of the message is used for selection, either to delete the message or to move it to another folder. The little check mark below that column is used to select all messages on that page. The small circular arrow at the top of that column is used to check for newly received mail. At the bottom of the message listing is the range of the messages shown on the page.

If you have more than the number of messages that can be shown on the page, you can select what range to skip to (Figure 8-12). You can determine how many messages per screen of a folder to show by editing the variable $MSG_COUNT in the configuration file *config.inc*.

One of the strengths of IMAP is that we can arrange our mail into folders remotely, on the server, and retain access to those messages. At the top right of the inbox are two folder-management selections, allowing us to change from the current folder, in this case the Inbox folder, to another folder, or to list the folders we have. This can be useful for sorting mail from mailing lists, certain topics like work or home matters, and the like. Figure 8-13 shows the folders listing, with two folders I have created. This

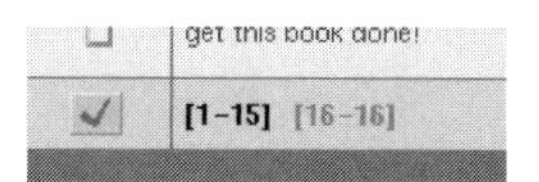

Figure 8-12 Aero—more.

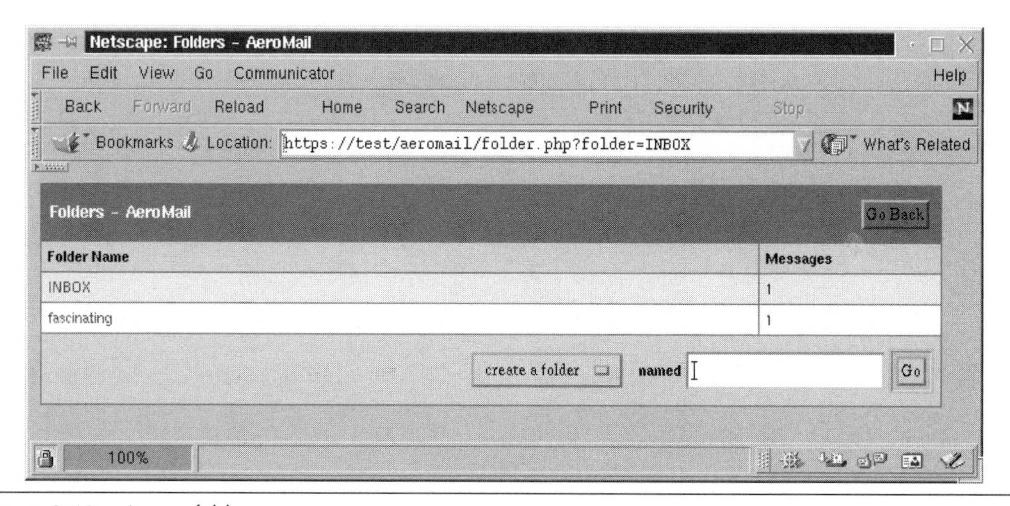

Figure 8-13 Aero—folders.

displays all of the known folders and the number of messages in each of them. We can open a folder by selecting its name, or we can create a new folder in the bottom right.

Back in our inbox, if we select a message's subject, we can view the message. If we select the sender, it brings up a reply dialog regarding that message (Figure 8-14). The message view is expanded, showing us not only the name but the e-mail address of who sent us the message, which address it was sent to, the date and the subject, and of course the message body itself. We can act on this message from here, as you would expect, replying to the author, or, if multiple recipients were specified, we could reply to everyone, or we could simply delete the message. To go back to the folder that originally held this message, we use your browser's *Back* button.

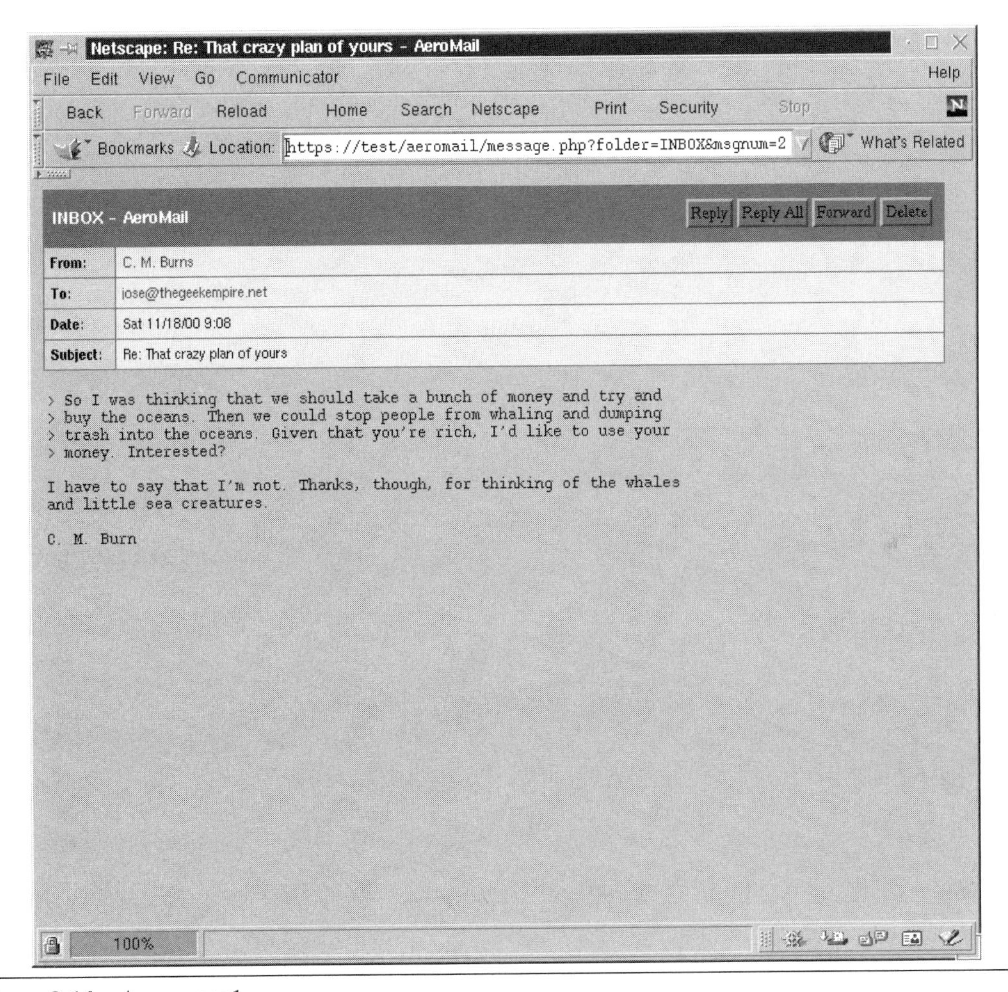

Figure 8-14 Aero—msg1.

Attachments as well are handled pretty well by Aeromail. In the folder view, such as your inbox, the message subject is followed by an "at" sign, @ (Figure 8-15).

When you view the mail, the attachment can be shown inline if it is a graphic that your Web browser knows about, such as a JPEG image, a GIF, or a PNG graphic. Note that the graphics are shown at the end of the mail, so we can't illustrate the e-mail this way (Figure 8-16).

Files or archives are not displayed, but a link is provided to them (Figure 8-17). If it is an archive, you can download it and save it locally. If it is a flat text file, you can display it as plain text in another window.

The composition window is pretty straightforward (Figure 8-18). You can edit the message recipients, of course, and even attach local files using your browser. No fancy features, like spellchecking, can be done, though. Simply click on the *Send* button in the top right-hand corner when you are ready to send your e-mail.

Simply put, Aeromail may not be feature rich, but it is fully functional and very easy to use. You can customize the color schemes in the *themes/* directory of the installation, and be sure to update your configuration in *config.inc* to chose the new one. From speaking with the author of the software, I learned that they plan to have address book support in version 2.0 but probably won't add any more features. The

☐	Use Apache! @	John Doe	Sat 11/18/00 9:34	5.2 k

Figure 8-15 Aero—attach.

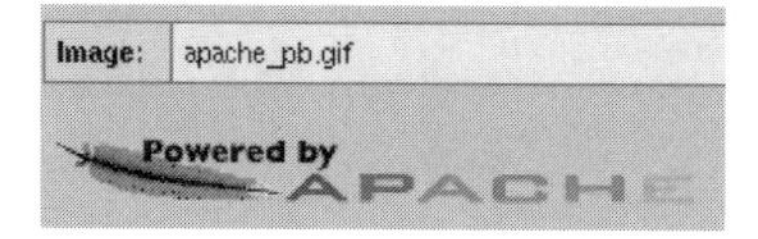

Figure 8-16 Aero—attach3.

Date:	Sat 11/18/00 9:3
Files:	minicom.log

Figure 8-17 Aero—attach2.

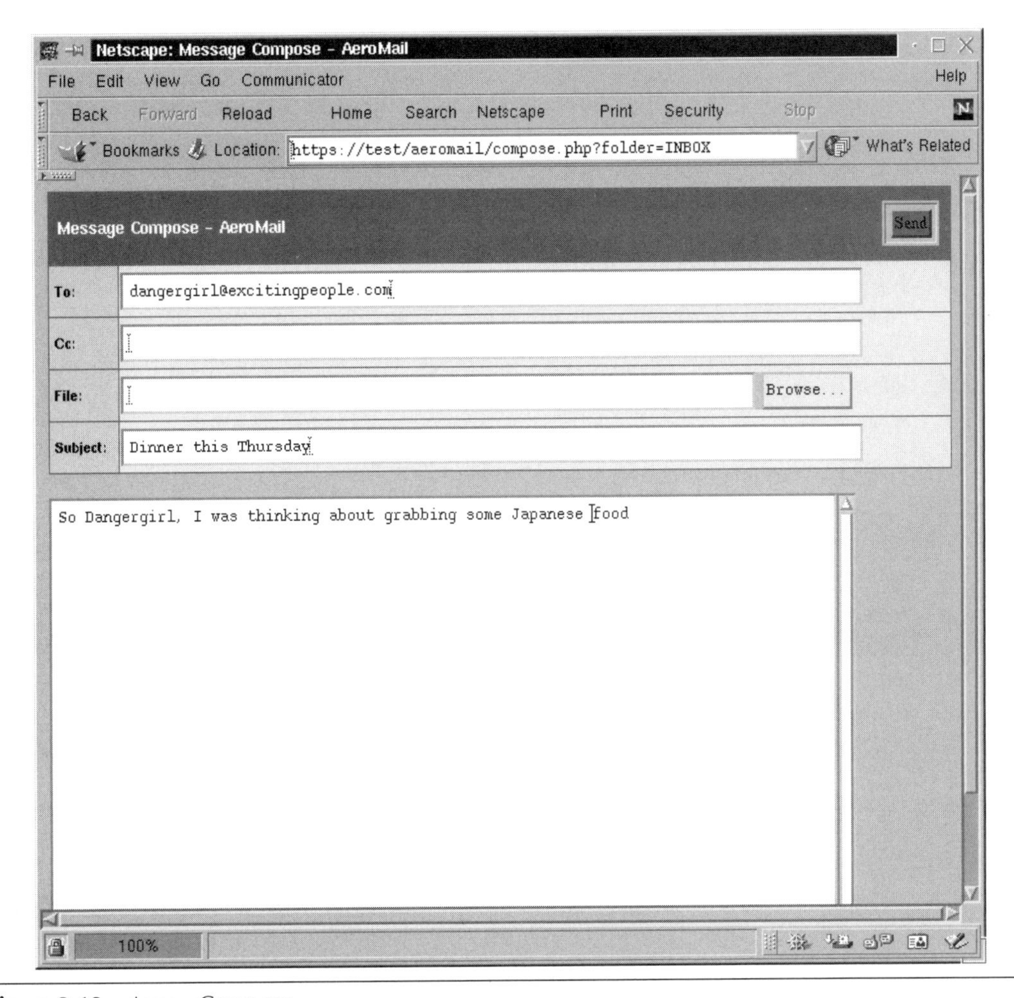

Figure 8-18 Aero—Compose.

goals have been met, a functional Web-mail client in a small package. This differs from many other packages with many more features, at the expense of simplicity or weight.

In this chapter you've set up a small, secure Web-mail client. This should give you access to your e-mail from almost anywhere in the world. Furthermore, it may wind up being more reliable than various free online Web-mail solutions. Your friends may start asking for accounts, too.

Other Web-Mail Packages

Several other Web-mail packages exist, often with more features but also with added complexity in installation. Here are some that have become well known. (A larger annotated list can be found at *http://www.cru.fr/http-mail/* if you would like to check out other solutions.)

SquirrelMail

http://www.squirrelmail.org: It uses PHP4, IMAP, and HTML 4.0 without Javascript to be a rather feature-rich e-mail client. It's pretty lightweight, too, and can integrate into a large organization's e-mail directory using LDAP.

IMP

http://www.horde.org/imp/: IMP is a powerful Web-mail system that is quite feature rich and very usable. It features great online help, a large language set that it can work with, and great scalability. Installation, however, can be a bit difficult for the uninitiated. Its biggest selling point is integration with a variety of mail server types. Because of its complexity, you may be tempted to install from precompiles and configured RPM packages.

PIMP

http://prometheus.zerodivide.net/apps/pimp/: This is a project from a former IMP developer. It strives to be feature rich without expecting fancy work on the client end. No cookies are used, no Javascript or frames, and it can utilize a large database for preferences. MySQL is required, and LDAP is not supported at this time.

TWIG

http://twig.screwdriver.net/: TWIG isn't just simply a Web-mail client, it can also work as a groupware setup. It features calendaring, messaging, and Usenet support and great usability. It's also very easy to install.

Resources

PHP

PHP is a powerful scripting language, as you can well imagine. It works on Unix and Win32 Web servers and provides massive connectivity features. It's also very well documented.

Online manuals: *http://www.php.net/docs.php*

Several books are also out there on PHP, including Web applications:

- *Development with PHP 4.0*, by Tobias Ratschiller and Till Gerken
- *Professional PHP Programming*, by Jesus Castagnetto, Harish Rawat, Sascha Schumann, Chris Scollo, and Deepak Veliath

Apache

Apache is also, as you can see, a powerful Web server that supports a multitude of options. It can also work on Win32 in addition to Unix-based systems.

Online manuals: *http://httpd.apache.org/*

Several books are also available on Apache:

- *Apache: The Definitive Guide*, by Ben Laurie and Peter Laurie
- *Administering Apache*, by Mark A. Arnold, Jeff Ameida, Clint LeMon Miller III, James D. Sheetz, and Gwen R. Rhine

SSL

Understanding SSL may be useful, either for debugging your SSL server or for working up a larger project. The mod_ssl documentation is a good place to start, as is Netscape's site on SSL:

- Online manuals: *http://www.modssl.org/docs/*
- Netscape's SSL 3.0 specification: *http://home.netscape.com/eng/ssl3/*

Sendmail

Most Web-mail packages use the Sendmail SMTP daemon for delivery. In fact, to get mail delivered to your machine you will have to set up *sendmail*. Most Linux distributions ship with it already configured. Still, you may want to change some configuration items.

Homepage and documentation: *http://www.sendmail.org*

Several books are available on Sendmail, varying in complexity.

- *Sendmail for Linux*, by Richard Blun, et al.
- *Sendmail*, 2nd ed., by Bryan Costales and Eric Allman

Chapter 9

EXTENDING APACHE

Difficult-o-Meter: 5 (as hard as this book gets!)

Covers:

Apache Web server *http://www.apache.org*

Question: I want my Web server to do something unusual, like authenticate against a proprietary data store, log to a relational database, or provide real-time statistics about the machine it's on. I've looked for packages to do these things, but I can't find anything that will work to my satisfaction. What can I do?

Answer: Consider building an Apache module. I admit this violates one of Larry Wall's three great virtues of a programmer, namely, Laziness. But sometimes nothing else will get the job done, and writing a CGI is not an option. You'll have to hold your breath and dive into the world of Apache server extensions.

Apache is the most popular Web server in the world! There, I said it. It also happens to be the most flexible, thanks to the fact that it's completely open source. Apache was built with modularity in mind, and Apache run on Linux can realize its full potential for extensibility. In this chapter, I'm going to discuss how Apache modules are used to extend the server, and show how to write your own modules.

A word of warning: If you didn't read the Difficult-o-Meter, go back and do that. This chapter will probably put you off a little if you're not experienced with Apache or used to C programming. To discuss modules I'll need to delve into the Apache source code, configuration files, and API, and I'll be writing a module in C. If you feel comfortable with the language, you should have no problems understanding the details of what follows. If not, there's still plenty to follow.

Module Basics

I'll have to admit up front that this section is already well covered in the Apache documentation. But rather than telling you to go read the manual, I'll try to provide a smooth introduction with no more information than is necessary to start building modules. If you want to find out more than I've laid out, I encourage you to consult the authoritative source. A URL is provided in the References at the end of this chapter.

Apache can be configured (and on Linux systems, it often is) to provide nearly all of its functionality through modules, which are really just shared libraries. The libraries, or *.so* files, are usually stored in a single resource directory. On my Debian system, the path is */usr/lib/apache/1.3*. The base distribution contains a number of standard modules to do URI mapping, access control, script invocation, logging, and so on. When Apache needs to use some part of a module's functionality, it dynamically loads it into memory and resolves the symbols that it needs. Linux has very good support for dynamic loading that is sometimes lacking on other operating systems, and Apache was built to take advantage of these advanced features, if they're present.

It's important to note that these modules are different from the kernel modules that are also available under Linux, and they provide extensions to the functionality of the kernel. Apache modules have an *.so* extension and run in nonprivileged user space. Kernel modules have an *.o* extension and run in kernel space with direct access to physical memory, input/output (I/O) ports, and hardware. However, the mechanism by which they are loaded is quite similar.

All the modules visible to Apache are listed in the configuration file *httpd.conf*. Modules that are not necessary for a given installation can be commented out, to reduce the memory footprint of the server and speed it up. Here is a sample of the configuration file for my server:

```
# LoadModule vhost_alias_module /usr/lib/apache/1.3/mod_vhost_alias.so
# LoadModule env_module /usr/lib/apache/1.3/mod_env.so
LoadModule config_log_module /usr/lib/apache/1.3/mod_log_config.so
# LoadModule mime_magic_module /usr/lib/apache/1.3/mod_mime_magic.so
LoadModule mime_module /usr/lib/apache/1.3/mod_mime.so
LoadModule negotiation_module /usr/lib/apache/1.3/mod_negotiation.so
LoadModule status_module /usr/lib/apache/1.3/mod_status.so
# LoadModule info_module /usr/lib/apache/1.3/mod_info.so
# LoadModule includes_module /usr/lib/apache/1.3/mod_include.so
LoadModule autoindex_module /usr/lib/apache/1.3/mod_autoindex.so
```

There are about 30 modules total, and many of them are commented out. When you create your own modules, you'll have to provide a LoadModule directive for it.

So What Do Modules Do?

When a client requests a file, the Apache server breaks down the request into several steps:

- URI mapping
- Authentication
- Authorization
- MIME-type mapping
- Replying to the client
- Logging

Actually, there are a couple of more steps, but they're not often used. Then for each step of the request, Apache walks through the list of currently loaded modules and asks each one if it would like to affect the outcome of that step. A module can indicate interest, defer to the next module, or raise a server error of some sort. If a module expresses interest, then the server will call a handler function within that module, passing it information about the request.

In the replying-to-client step, a module can actually have multiple named handlers. These names are used in the Apache configuration file when the module is being set up to handle all requests to a certain subdirectory or all requests for a particular file type. When Apache gets to the point where it needs to provide the headers and body of the HTTP response, it will call the appropriate handler function instead of using the default behavior of sending the contents of a file. By using this mechanism, a module can send dynamically generated data that does not exist on the file system. For example, the mod_dir module uses a named handler to display an HTML-formatted directory listing, and the mod_cgi module uses a named handler to invoke an external script and send the output to the client.

Most modules will never indicate interest in more than one or two steps. For example, the mod_log_config module has only a handler for the logging step. The mod_mime module, on the other hand, has only a handler for the MIME-type mapping step.

As with all rules, there are some exceptions, and you can find more detailed information in the Apache documentation. This brief introduction should describe enough about the inner workings of Apache to get started building your own simple modules.

The Apache API

Among all the other things it was meant to be, Apache is also a cross-platform server. As a result, a module developer can't rely on the availablity of POSIX libraries. Apache provides a large API to perform functions like string handling, resource management, and process management, and we'll need to know about these in order to build modules. All these functions are distinguished by the prefix *ap_* (which is a good practice in the C world.) But before I introduce some of the common functions, I'll need to describe two more concepts: the request structure and resource pools.

The Request Structure

Most of the handler functions you'll write for custom-built modules are passed a single argument, a pointer to a request structure, of type *struct request_rec* *. This structure contains everything Apache knows about the current request. Many of the Apache API functions operate on this structure and take a pointer to it as their first argument. Some of the important fields are listed next, in a liberally edited version of the *request_rec* structure. The full description is found in the header file *httpd.h*.

```
struct request_rec {
    /* General information */

    pool *pool;              /* The request's resource pool */
    conn_rec *connection;    /* Information about the connection and
                                client */
    server_rec *server;      /* Information about this server */
    const char *hostname;    /* Hostname from URI or Host: header */
    void *per_dir_config;    /* Options set in config files, etc. */
    void *request_config;    /* Notes on *this* request */

    /* Request information. Usually not changed. */

    char *unparsed_uri;    /* The unparsed URI */
    char *uri;             /* The path part of the requested URI */
    char *filename;        /* The filename to which this URI translates */
    char *path_info;       /* Additional path information */
    char *args;            /* Query string, if present */
    int header_only;       /* 0 = GET, 1 = HEAD request */
    char *protocol;        /* Protocol, as given to us, or HTTP/0.9 */
    char *method;          /* GET, HEAD, POST, etc. */
    int method_number;     /* M_GET, M_POST, etc. */

    /* Response information. Usually modified by a handler function. */

    char *content_type;         /* This should be set by the handler
                                   function */
```

```
    char *content_encoding;
    int bytes_sent;              /* Used for logging */
    int no_cache;                /* Can be set to suppress client caching
                                    */
};
```

Resource Pools

An Apache resource pool is a structure that, at its simplest, manages memory and files so that you don't have to. Resource pools can ease some of the difficulties with string handling in C. For example, if you need to concatenate two strings, traditionally you would allocate a buffer of the appropriate size with *malloc* and use *strncat.* However, you need to keep track of the pointer and free the memory when it's no longer needed. If the string is relevant only within a certain function, you can simplify things by using a character array on the stack. But if the string needs to be passed around from function to function, it's hard to know where to perform the deallocation.

Using a resource pool, on the other hand, is trivial:

```
char *new_string = ap_pstrcat(r->pool, "http://www.myserver.com", path,
    "/favicon.ico");
```

new_string is created by concatenating all the arguments provided to ap_pstrcat. It's "owned" by the resource pool, and you don't have to be concerned with deallocating it at some point in the future. It will be freed when the pool is destroyed by Apache during its normal course of operation. The Apache API provides many other resource pool functions; here is a simple way to obtain the list:

```
grep -l API_EXPORT /usr/include/apache-1.3/*.h | grep "struct pool"
```

Apache creates several types of resource pools with different scope. There is one global resource pool that exists for the lifetime of the server process. There are resource pools for the individual server threads (or processes.) But the resource pool you'll make use of as a module developer belongs to an individual request. It's created when the request is received, and destroyed when the request is finished. As we saw earlier, the request structure contains a pointer to this pool.

Commonly Used Functions

There are a number of functions from the Apache API that you'll use over and over, so I'll introduce a few of the most common ones here. It's by no means an exhaustive list; you can obtain a full enumeration of the Apache API by searching for the word

"API_EXPORT" in the header files. However, it's difficult to determine the exact behavior of a function from looking at just its signature, so it's often useful to use the Apache source distribution as a usage guide. Simply search for the function you're interested in and see how it's used in the standard modules.

Without further ado, here's my "top ten or so" list of most important functions.

```
void ap_send_http_header(request_rec *r)

void ap_send_fd(FILE *file, request_rec *r)
```

The first function forces the HTTP headers to be sent. You should always call this function before you start writing to the body of the HTTP response. The second one sends the content of a file opened with fopen directly to the HTTP response. These two functions are really all that's necessary to serve simple files.

```
void ap_rputc(char c, request_rec *r)

void ap_rputs(char *s, request_rec *r)

void ap_rprintf(request_rec *r, char *fmt, ...)

int ap_rwrite(const void *buf, int nbyte, request_rec *r)

void ap_rvputs(request_rec *r, char *s, ...)

int ap_rflush(request_rec *r)
```

These functions all send output to the body of an HTTP response. The behavior of the first four are analogous to putc, puts, printf, and write, respectively. The fifth function is a convenient time saver. It takes a variable number of arguments, all strings, and concatenates them together to the response. This allows you to write things like this:

```
char *link, *text;
ap_rvputs(req, "<a href=\"", link, "\">", text, "</a>");
```

which outputs the HTML for a hyperlink, given two variable strings. Finally, the last function allows you to flush the output buffer.

```
void ap_log_rerror(int line, int level, const request_rec *s,
const char *fmt, ...)
```

This function writes an entry to the error log. The constants for the `level` argument are defined in *http_log.h*, and the arguments following *request_rec *s* are in the same style as *printf*.

```
void *ap_palloc(struct pool *, int nbytes)

void *ap_pcalloc(struct pool *, int nbytes)

char *ap_pstrdup(struct pool *, const char *s)

char *ap_pstrcat(struct pool *, ...)

char *ap_psprintf(struct pool *, const char *fmt, ...)
```

These functions are all memory and string-handling functions. All needed space is allocated from the specified resource pool, and you don't have to worry about freeing this space later on; it will be released when the pool is destroyed. Under normal circumstances, you'll use the pool provided by the request structure, so any memory you use will be freed as soon as the request is finished.

The first two functions are worry-free versions of *malloc* and *calloc*, if you need to use variable-sized buffers in your code. Of course, you're still free to use local buffers allocated on the stack. *ap_pstrcat* and *ap_psprintf* mirror *ap_rvputs* and *ap_rprintf*, respectively, but they return new strings allocated in the pool instead of writing to the HTTP response body.

Remote Monitoring

With all this under our belts, let's try to build a simple module. I don't know about anyone else, but at times I've thought it would be nice to be able to monitor remotely certain things about my machine. Say I'm behind one of those aggressive firewalls that Mike keeps talking about, so I can't log in to my machine to check the load average. Nor can I run xload and send the display to the machine I'm on. Since HTTP is the only port I have available, why not monitor the load average from a Web browser? And thus is born the mod_proc module.

I'm going to be building a module that allows me to remotely browse the */proc* directory on my machine, with the exception of the process-specific directories. That way I can look at much more than just load average. I should be able to navigate the directories and view files within those directories. I'll avoid any fancy formatting, just to keep things simple. After all, it's just numbers that I'm after.

Of course, the easiest way to do this would be to set up a virtual server with the */proc* directory as its document root. But with the obstinancy of a true hacker, I've got my mind set on an Apache module, and nothing's going to stop me!

Writing the Code

The first thing to do is include the appropriate headers:

```
#include <sys/types.h>
#include <stdio.h>
#include <dirent.h>
#include "httpd.h"
#include "http_config.h"
```

I already know I need the first three headers, since I'm going to be opening files and reading directory entries. The remaining two are header files from the Apache distribution, which I need to access the Apache API.

Next, I need to define the module itself, its handler functions, and its commands:

```
handler_rec procHandlers[] = {
        { "proc-handler", procHandler }
};

command_rec procCommands[] = {
        { NULL }
};

module proc_module = {
    STANDARD_MODULE_STUFF,
    NULL,               /* Initializer */
    NULL,               /* Dir config creator */
    NULL,               /* Dir merger */
    NULL,               /* Server config */
    NULL,               /* Merge server config */
    procCommands,       /* Commands */
    procHandlers,       /* Handlers */
    NULL,               /* URI mapping */
    NULL,               /* Authentication */
    NULL,               /* Authorization */
    NULL,               /* Other access control */
    NULL,               /* MIME type mapping */
    NULL,               /* Fixups */
    NULL,               /* Logging */
    NULL                /* Header parser */
};
```

This module isn't interested in intercepting every single request, so most of the handlers for the different request steps are set to NULL. Instead, I'll activate this module when the requested URI has a specific format, which can be done in the *httpd.conf* file. So I only need to provide a single handler, through the procHandlers structure. Likewise, I'll define a placeholder for the commands through the procCommands structure. These three definitions set up everything that Apache needs to know to use my module.

So now I just need to fill in the procHandler function. Handler functions are passed a pointer to a request (a struct *request_rec* *) and should return an integer value indicating whether it has handled the request, chooses to ignore it, or needs to raise a server error.

```
static int procHandler(struct request_rec *r) {
    int code;
    struct stat fs;
    char *path;

    r->allowed = (1 << M_GET);
    if (r->method_number != M_GET) return DECLINED;

    path = ap_pstrcat(r->pool, "/proc", r->path_info, NULL);
    if (stat(path, &fs) < 0) return HTTP_NOT_FOUND;
    if (S_ISDIR(fs.st_mode)) {
        code = showDir(r, path);
    }
    else {
        code = showFile(r, path);
    }
    if (code != OK) return code;
    return OK;
}
```

This is a fairly simple handler that delegates the major work of reading the files and directories to another pair of functions, showDir, and showFile. The first two lines of code beyond the local variable declarations ensure that the handler will respond only to HTTP GET requests. Since this monitoring module is read-only by nature, I don't want a Web browser to be POSTing information to a matching URI. Hence, any type of request other then GET causes the handler to return the constant DECLINED.

The next line of code retrieves the path_info from the request, which is the part of the URI after the prefix I choose to invoke this handler. Then it constructs the actual path on the file system that corresponds to that URI. For example, if I choose */monitor* as the URI prefix, then a request to */monitor/uptime* will have a path_info of */uptime* and hence will map to the file */proc/uptime.*

The next line does a stat call to determine if the path is a file or a directory. If the path is not found and the stat call fails, then I return the constant HTTP_NOT_FOUND from the handler. This will invoke a 404 Not Found error, and Apache will retrieve the appropriate error document and send it to the client. If the path exists, then the appropriate delegate function will be called.

Forging ahead, I'll create the simpler of the two delegates, showFile:

```
static int showFile(request_rec *r, const char *name) {
    FILE *file;

    file = fopen(name, "r");
    if (file == NULL) {
        if (errno == EACCES) return HTTP_FORBIDDEN;
        return HTTP_NOT_FOUND;
    }

    r->content_type = "text/plain";
    ap_send_http_header(r);

    ap_send_fd(file, r);
    fclose(file);
    return OK;
}
```

The first step is to open the file and verify that it's readable. If there's an access error, I return the constant HTTP_FORBIDDEN back to the handler function, which is passed in turn back to the server. Even though this function shouldn't be called with a nonexistent path argument, I still code for that case and return HTTP_NOT_FOUND.

If the file is successfully opened, the next two lines set the content type to plain text and send the HTTP headers. Finally, I use the ap_send_fd function to append the contents of an open file to the HTTP response, close the file handle, and return OK back to the handler function. You can see how the Apache APIs make a relatively complex task simple to code, even in such a notoriously long-winded language as C.

The only thing left now is the show Dir function, which turns out to be the most complicated. I want it to output a hyperlinked list of the directory's content, so I'll need to send a content type of text/html.

```
static int showDir(request_rec *r, const char *name) {
    DIR *dir;
    struct dirent *de;
    struct stat fs;
    int is_root;

    dir = opendir(name);
    if (dir == NULL) {
        if (errno == EACCES) return HTTP_FORBIDDEN;
        return HTTP_NOT_FOUND;
    }

    r->content_type = "text/html";
    ap_send_http_header(r);
```

```
        is_root = (strcmp(name, "/") == 0) ? 1 : 0;
    ap_rputs("<dl>\n", r);
    while (1) {
        de = readdir(dir);
        if (de == NULL || de->d_name == NULL) break;
                if (is_root && isdigit(de->d_name)) continue;
        ap_rprintf(r, "<dt><a href=\"%s/%s\">%s</a>\n", name, de-d_name,
                   de->d_name);
    }
    ap_rputs("</dl>\n", r);
    closedir(dir);

    return OK;
}
```

The first five lines open the directory and perform an access check similar to the one in the showFile function. Then I set the content type and send the headers. After this, the fun starts. The next line outputs some HTML using ap_rputs, and then the code goes into a loop, reading in directory entries. Each directory entry is given its own <dt> tag and hyperlink, which is written out with the ap_rprintf function. However, if I'm in the root directory and the entry name begins with a digit, this entry must be one of the process subdirectories, so I'll skip it instead. The last three lines write out the closing HTML, close the directory, and return OK to the handler.

Compiling it

This is all the code you need to write for a simple module! Next, I need to compile it. Since I don't want to mess around with the Apache source distribution, I'll use the `apxs` tool, which is just a Perl script that sets up the correct compiler and linker options to build a module. It does require that you have the Apache header files installed under */usr/include*, either copied from the source distribution or obtained as a package. To obtain these files under Debian, I simply need to run

```
apt-get install apache-dev
```

`apxs` is distributed in the Apache source distribution (so you might have to download it anyway!). It resides in the *src/support* subdirectory. Unless you're compiling and installing from source, you'll need to modify a few lines in the script to get it working. Find the following lines in apxs and change them appropriately, using paths for your system when applicable.

```
my $CFG_LD_SHLIB      = q(gcc);                    # substituted via
                                                     Makefile.tmpl
```

```
my $CFG_LDFLAGS_SHLIB = q(-shared);                  # substituted via
                                                       Makefile.tmpl
my $CFG_PREFIX        = q(/usr/local);                # substituted via
                                                       APACI install
my $CFG_SBINDIR       = q(/usr/sbin);                 # substituted via
                                                       APACI install
my $CFG_INCLUDEDIR    = q(/usr/include/apache-1.3); # substituted via
                                                       APACI install
my $CFG_LIBEXECDIR    = q(/usr/local/lib);            # substituted via
                                                       APACI install
my $CFG_SYSCONFDIR    = q(/etc/apache);               # substituted via
                                                       APACI install
```

As you can see from the comments, these values aren't filled correctly until you actually do a make install of the source. If you have a pre-existing installation, you probably don't want to do that, so you're forced to perform these manual edits. On my system, I need to change the following two lines to the values shown. Such is the price of flexibility!

```
my $CFG_PREFIX        = q(/usr);
my $CFG_LIBEXECDIR    = q(/usr/lib/apache/1.3);
```

Now that apxs is in shape, let's try compiling the module.

```
$ apxs -c mod_proc.c
gcc -DLINUX=22 -DUSE_HSREGEX -fpic -DSHARED_MODULE -I/usr/include  -c
    mod_proc.c
gcc -shared -o mod_proc.so mod_proc.o
```

If you get compile or link errors, carefully read what they're saying. If the errors aren't in your code, they probably result from an incorrectly set path in apxs. You'll need to review the entries and ensure that everything is correct.

But it worked for me, so now I can copy the shared library into the appropriate directory. On my Debian system, it's */usr/lib/apache/1.3/*; just find where the all the other standard Apache modules are located, and that's the place to put it. If you want, you can even install it in a nonstandard place and provide the full path in the Apache configuration file. Speaking of which, I need to change that file to get this module working:

```
LoadModule proc_module /usr/lib/apache/1.3/mod_proc.so

<Location /monitor>
    SetHandler proc-handler
        order deny, allow
        deny all
        allow from *.nastyproxy.com
</Location>
```

The first line tells the server to dynamically load the module at start-up. The first argument is actually the symbol name that Apache looks for, so it *must* match the name of the `module` structure in the module source. In this case, I called it proc_module. The second argument, obviously, is the full path to the shared library. It can also be a relative path, in which case the path is taken relative to the server root.

I use the Location directive to tell Apache to invoke this module when I reference any URI starting with the string */monitor*. The SetHandler directive defines the name of the handler to use, and, as you remember, I named it proc-handler. The remaining lines provide rudimentary IP-based access control, which really wouldn't be sufficient to keep a determined attacker (or even a lazy attacker) from viewing the guts of my system. In order to make this module reasonably secure, I'd have to set up authentication and SSL by adding a few more lines to the configuration file. Although the module could probably use more verbose error logging, I can still track who might be attempting to use the interface by looking at the access logs.

The Big Moment

Now let's test the end result! I'll try to access *http://www.mymachine.net/monitor* (Figure 9-1).

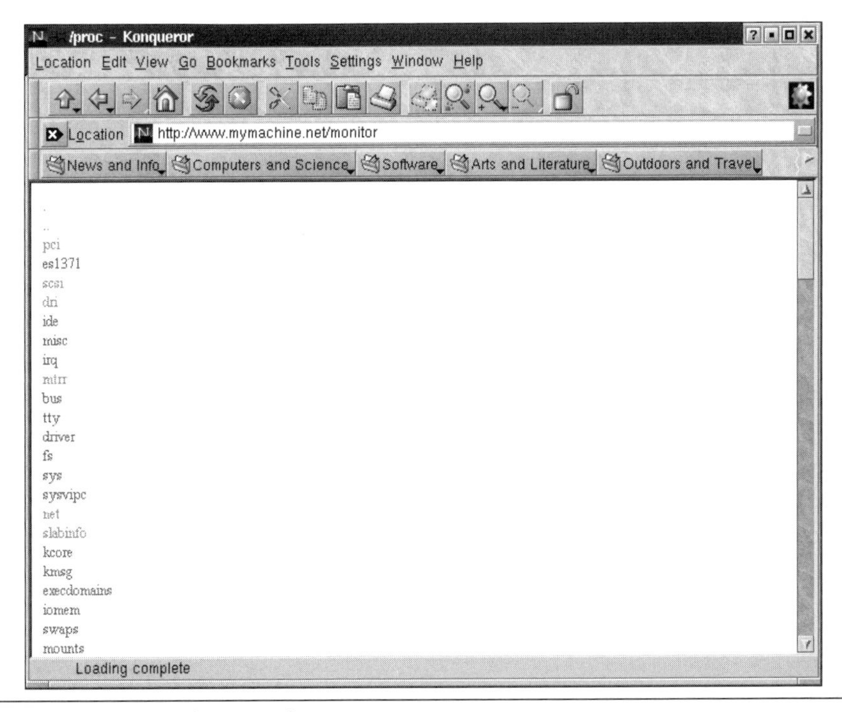

Figure 9-1 Browsing the */proc* directory.

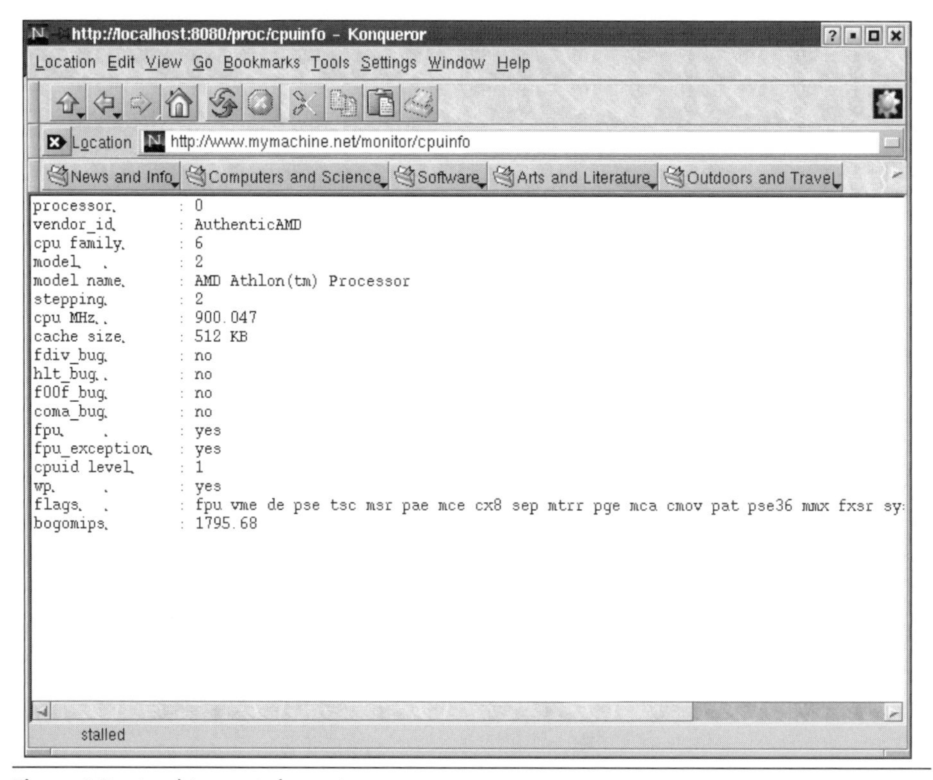

Figure 9-2 Looking up information.

There are a few things wrong here: I really don't need a parent directory link from this URI, and the directory entries are coming up in their natural order, which is far from alphabetical. But it's good enough for my purposes. Let's try clicking on *cpuinfo*. I have to scroll down to find it, but it should be there, since it's a standard file in the */proc* directory (Figure 9-2).

Perfect—this is just what I'm after. Obviously, there are still a few issues, some of them serious. For example, if I navigate to */monitor/self/cwd*, which is a symlink out of */proc*, I can freely browse the entire file system on my machine. This isn't a vulnerability I would want to expose to the world. So the moral of the story is, *Don't build this module!* At least, don't deploy it on a machine where the Web server is accessible to the outside world. Or write the module with better security. You have been warned!

Summary

In this chapter, I briefly discussed Apache modules and the process by which Apache serves content. I then built a simple module to remotely browse a Linux machine's */proc* file system. Although the usefulness of such an application might be up for debate, this chapter should have given you a foundation from which you can start building more complex and useful modules.

References

Apache

- Homepage: *http://www.apache.org/*
- Documentation: *http://www.apache.org/manual/index.html*
- Apache API: *http://www.apache.org/manual/misc/API.html*
- Apache Module Repository: *http://modules.apache.org/*

Chapter 10

Secure Your E-Mail with GPG

Difficult-o-Meter: 2 (light Linux skill required)

Covers:

gpg (GNUpg) v1.0.1 *http://www.gnupg.org/*

Question: I hear all the time about viruses spread by e-mail. How can I be sure that a message I get from someone is really from them and not some sort of autogenerated infected mail? Also, I think Tom Brokaw is reading my e-mail. What can I do about that?

Answer: This sounds like a job for . . . encryption and digital signatures! (You were expecting what, Superman?) There are very powerful free packages to solve your little problem.

Introduction

Modern life can make you paranoid. Hardly a day goes by that you don't hear that all of a company's e-mail has been seized and used in a lawsuit or that some employee has been fired for inappropriate e-mail. You hear about credit card numbers and passwords hijacked from e-mail. You also hear about vicious, nasty, evil viruses propagated by e-mail that appears to come from people you know.

Some of these problems exist because people (Microsoft) are putting too much capability into e-mail clients (Outlook). There really is no reason you need your e-mail to launch applications embedded in a message! Sure, it's nifty and cool, but it is also how these evil programs spread around.

Even so, there is one way to protect yourself fully from evil, nasty e-mail viruses, and evil, nasty password thieves, and evil, nasty lawyers, and evil, nasty employers, and even, possibly, evil, nasty foreign governments, if you're that paranoid. All of this safety can be found from one free, open program: GNU Privacy Guard, or GPG.

GPG's name is a bit of a tweak on an earlier, and formerly free, security package that was called *PGP,* for "Pretty Good Privacy." The authors of PGP chose to take their product closed and commercial (something that cannot be done with code licensed under the GPL; see Defining *Free* in Chapter 1). Not long thereafter, the GNU Privacy Guard project started. GPG is compatible with PGP and is completely free and published under the GPL.

GPG delivers you from the horrors of e-mail with two basic mechanisms: strong encryption and digital signatures. *Encryption* involves scrambling the content of your message so that none but the intended recipients are able to read it. *Digital signatures* verify the identity of the sender and validate that the message is intact (and has not been changed or defaced in transit by third parties). This is not cryptography like the puzzle in the daily paper. It is not a simple substitution cipher. It is, in fact, encryption so thorough that it should be impossible to tell the difference between an encrypted message and a stream of random noise. GPG provides this level of encryption.

Cryptographic Basics

All modern crypto systems depend on keys. A *key* is a value required to recover the message. Without burying you in the mathematics of cryptography (if you wish to delve further, the book *Applied Cryptography*, by Bruce Schneier, is an excellent resource), the idea is to employ a mathematical function that is very easy to use in combination with the key but is impossible to use without it. Such a function is called a *one-way function*. Use that term and people will think you know a lot about cryptography. Try it! It works!

A cryptographic system that requires that both parties in the communication know and use the same key is called a *symmetric-key cryptographic system*. There are quite a few of these systems. The widely used (but no longer terribly secure) U.S. Data Encryption Standard (DES) is a 56-bit key symmetric-key cipher.

GPG uses a newer and, in some ways, more useful cryptographic system. With GPG, you generate two keys. One key you keep secret. This is called a *private key*. The other key you give away. You don't care who has this key. Go ahead and give it to your enemies. This key is known as your *public key*.

To decrypt a message requires both your public and private keys. To encrypt it requires only your public key. So anyone can send you a message encrypted with your public key, but you and only you can decrypt such a message (assuming you have kept your private key properly private). Such a system is called a *public-key cryptographic system*.

If this were all you could do with a public-key crypto system, it would be little better than a symmetric one. It turns out that a public-key cypto system has one more very appealing use. You can "sign" a message with your private key. Once this is done, anyone with your public key can validate that the message is yours and that it is *exactly* the message you sent, with not a comma changed.

This is done by applying a *message hashing algorithm* to the message. A hashing algorithm is any function that takes an arbitrarily large and complex set of data and produces a fixed-size result. A function that sums all the bytes in a message and takes the low-order 8 bits of that sum would qualify as a hashing algorithm, albeit a relatively usesless one. Hashing functions have many applications in computer science, from sorting to databases, but we are concerned with their applicability to digital signatures.

For digital signatures we must have a function such that it is impossible for any two differing messages of the same length to have the same hash value. It turns out there are a number of such so-called *message digest* functions.

So to sign a message, we calculate the message digest value on the message. We then encrypt the hash value with our private key. This encrypted hash of the message serves as a signature. When our recipient gets this message, she calculates the hash of the message as received, decrypts the signature with her copy of our public key, and then compares the two values. If they match, it is absolutely certain both that the message was signed with our private key (or else our public key will not have been able to decrypt it) and that the message was not changed in any way (or the match would have failed).

The success of digital signatures depends entirely on the "split" private key/public key pair. A symmetric cryptographic system could not be used to validate identity in this way. The system depends on one and only one party in the communication having the private key.

One very important attribute of public key/private key pairs is that it is difficult if not impossible to derive one key given the other in the pair. In other words, you need two values that are easy to generate but difficult to derive. A number of algorithms for such have been put forward, but many, such as the "knapsack" algorithm, have proven to be flawed. The system used in all common public-key cryptographic systems is based on the product of primes.

Basically, it is very easy to multiply two very large prime numbers together, but it is very difficult to factor the resulting large number. Remember, GPG keys are from 512 to 2048 bits. These are truly huge numbers.

The public and private keys are not merely the two prime factors of a very large number. There are additional transformations applied to them to arrive at the key values, but the principle is the same. It's easy to make them, hard to break them. Merely possessing one half of the keypair confers no advantage in deriving the other. That is the main point.

These descriptions are somewhat simplified—there are some additional complexities in the actual implementation. We'll address those as we come to them.

Generating Keys

Before you can use GPG, you must generate a key. The first time you ever run GPG, it will probably say this:

```
[bubba@mars bubba]$ gpg -gen-key
gpg (GnuPG) 1.0.1; Copyright (C) 1999 Free Software Foundation, Inc.
This program comes with ABSOLUTELY NO WARRANTY.
This is free software, and you are welcome to redistribute it
under certain conditions. See the file COPYING for details.

gpg: /home/bubba/.gnupg: directory created
gpg: /home/bubba/.gnupg/options: new options file created
gpg: you have to start GnuPG again, so it can read the new options file
```

Unless your system administrator has a *.gnupg* directory set up for new accounts automatically, GPG must create a *.gnupg* directory and set it up with default configurations and empty private and public keyrings. A *keyring* is simply a file that stores keys. The default is to have two: *pubring.gpg* and *secring.gpg*. Your private keys are kept in *secring.gpg*, and your public key and the public keys of any of your correspondents are in *pubring.gpg*.

The other file in the *.gnupg* directory is *options*. This file may be modified to change the default settings for GPG. In its default state, it is configured to interoperate with the commercial PGP 5 software. I recommend leaving these defaults alone until the whole world wakes up and starts using GPG instead!

Once the *.gnupg* directory is set up, you generate a key as follows:

```
[bubba@mars bubba]$ gpg -gen-key
gpg (GnuPG) 1.0.1; Copyright (C) 1999 Free Software Foundation, Inc.
This program comes with ABSOLUTELY NO WARRANTY.
This is free software, and you are welcome to redistribute it
under certain conditions. See the file COPYING for details.

Please select what kind of key you want:
   (1) DSA and ElGamal (default)
   (2) DSA (sign only)
   (4) ElGamal (sign and encrypt)
Your selection? 1
```

I can't think of any reason not to generate both key types. You will then be prompted for key length:

```
DSA keypair will have 1024 bits.
About to generate a new ELG-E keypair.
              minimum keysize is  768 bits
              default keysize is 1024 bits
    highest suggested keysize is 2048 bits
What keysize do you want? (1024) 2048
Do you really need such a large keysize? yes
Requested keysize is 2048 bits
```

I'm not certain why they object to large keysizes. The truth is, all of these keysizes are more than adequate to protect you against any reasonably resourced attacker. The default 1024 keysize is such that a brute-force attack, assuming geometrically increasing computational power, should take you well past the expected life of the universe. That's pretty good. Besides which, most secrets need only be kept for a short time. Many business secrets, such as new product names and quarterly financial disclosures, need be kept only for days or weeks. After that, they need not be secret. Other secrets may need to last one or two human generations. A very few secrets must be kept indefinitely. It is certainly true that the minimum GPG keysize is more than adequate for most purposes. Even so, I elected to use a large key to show how GPG behaves. Note that 2048 is not an upper limit; you may use an even larger keysize than this. I would suggest the default keysize for most purposes.

The key-creation dialog continues thusly:

```
Please specify how long the key should be valid.
         0 = key does not expire
      <n>  = key expires in <n> days
      <n>w = key expires in <n> weeks
      <n>m = key expires in <n> months
      <n>y = key expires in <n> years
```

```
Key is valid for? (0) 10w
Key expires at Tue 12 Sep 2000 04:29:02 PM CDT
Is this correct (y/n)? y
```

Here you have the option of *expiring* your key. Once a key expires, it may no longer be used to encrypt, sign, decrypt, or verify messages. Having a key expire is probably a good idea. We set this key to expire in the realtively short period of ten weeks.

The process continues:

```
You need a User ID to identify your key; the software constructs the user
    ID
from Real Name, Comment, and E-mail Address in this form:
    "Heinrich Heine (Der Dichter) <heinrichh@duesseldorf.de>"

Real name: Leroy Macmillian
E-mail address: leroy@flatbush.nonesuch.org
Comment:
You selected this User-ID:
    "Leroy Macmillian <leroy@flatbush.nonesuch.org>"

Change (N)ame, (C)omment, (E)-mail or (O)kay/(Q)uit? o
```

So we gave the fictitious Leroy a user ID consisting of his name and his e-mail address. You may also add a comment. We chose not to here.

Finally, we have to protect the private key. To do this, we use a passphrase. A passphrase is much like a password, but the length is much greater. Just as in passwords, I recommend mixing upper- and lowercase letters and some nonalphabetic characters as well. Here's what the dialog looks like:

```
You need a passphrase to protect your secret key.

Enter passphrase:
```

Having entered the passphrase once, you are prompted again:

```
Repeat passphrase:
```

The program now starts generating your keys. In order for a key to be secure, it must be unpredictable. There are many pseudo-random algorithms, many of them rely on the nonrepeating decimal places of irrational numbers. These numbers appear random, but if you know the algorithm they are entirely predictable. Such "random" sequences are useless for generating keys.

The GPG program on Linux makes use of a rather nifty feature of our favorite operating system. Linux maintains an *entropy pool*. Linux times the clock ticks between various interrupts, such as keystrokes, disk drives, serial ports, and network interfaces. It uses these to maintain an ever-growing pool of random bits. Though in a strict mathematical sense these bits are not necessarily random, they are complex, asynchronous, and very difficult to predict. This is as close to random as you are likely to find this side of the Heisenberg principle.

As these keys are generated, this pool of random bits is depleted. It is possible that the pool could become exhausted during the key-generation process. If that happens, the key-generation process stops until user activity on the system raises the pool size to a level sufficient to continue. The user at the console may help the process along by typing or moving the mouse. Don't worry about "mixing up" the time between your keystrokes. At the speed at which the system counts things, you will never have the same value for two keystrokes no matter how hard you try.

In our example, our "random pool" was not quite large enough to do the job without stopping:

```
We need to generate a lot of random bytes. It is a good idea to perform
some other action (type on the keyboard, move the mouse, utilize the
disks) during the prime generation; this gives the random number
generator a better chance to gain enough entropy.
++++++++++++++++++++++++++++++.++++++++++++++++++++.+++++.++++++++++++++
++++++++++++++++++++++++++.++++++++++.+++++++++++++++.++++++++++........
....>++++++++++
We need to generate a lot of random bytes. It is a good idea to perform
some other action (type on the keyboard, move the mouse, utilize the
disks) during the prime generation; this gives the random number
generator a better chance to gain enough entropy.
+++++.+++++...++++++++++++++++++++++++++++++++++.++++++++++....+++++++++
++++++++++++++.+++++++++++++++++++++++++++++++++++++++....++++++++++++++
++++..++++++++++>++++++++++++++++++++>+++++.>+++++......................
.......................................................+++++^^^^^
public and secret key created and signed.
[bubba@mars bubba]$
```

If you look now, your keyrings are no longer empty.

To extract your public key so you can share it, use the following command:

```
[bubba@mars bubba]$ gpg --export --armor leroy
-----BEGIN PGP PUBLIC KEY BLOCK-----
Version: GnuPG v1.0.1 (GNU/Linux)
Comment: For info see http://www.gnupg.org
```

```
mQGiBDliXhYRBACPy47P0e71DUe+SvSSepRxi23KpM3xhLu3BsjQmKK5oNwShcPx
LivsXB3WZZpdQ0TCPbf4DiihYOCo6FtPvPqFKqlLr/xiJq4SJ0syJFIivGKgiEx2
EHApzxwxOwBuhR+Qb80/aquBpN5sQwCGolAlPN6Vawd9gut8kCXBQkBpEwCg91CO
mUEMjXa50BfYDEkABkg9J/UD/0XaXz0yny5t9pKZvzXLuuI+7ZkXSbxt3jiaJfnM
sBNro2ZmXGSWx25Fr1mz5h49TKlmgvm1/icJ9qym8b1v336xt+7lN9ZZfjOgx9A8
C+t77wPIy3ADc5hkFh70RiduylQjs3EKafqMB5ZFtXYqLqvmyZO3vp6CPtgJXirF
f6IhA/9nPBOyxD7tHNGWA7cm3VhQieVbQKbQzYmFVaMVKz62KYB6mJvOIs0EZsR9
E75CuikJ52eJwzbuZKP+sfSjzUW3PDnnKrI4ER2hnfl/p+rqtJZ4VE/jgC9PWGgZ
Ljju9W0tsXbFoxFxPDlFIKPqlyIFUxmUotYsMuqeCrLC71MdN7QuTGVyb3kgTWFj
bWlsbGlhbiA8bGVyb3lAZmxhdGJ1c2gubm9uZXN1Y2gub3JnPohcBBMRAgAcBQI5
Yl4WBQkAXEkABAsKBAMDFQMCAxYCAQIXgAAKCRCLHoAxDo+rZGf5AJ9ktBHkXffB
bQLo/ax/LwWjQBMUYQCbBxhUNJJzg07RjlVhAHfKVCDtuGC5Ag0EOWJemhAIANSs
TUaG69ly2lDbVenNLYLo4ydog8RU7GC5kLcLLwtlbDCZVd35puk9G2RzZgwmnCOc
120bGFDtgW2dC/qixspojwgxPf002tf61BAJdQyVVJzm1n7D4mdXuP+j28OGlVh+
NOZv9ImFiObUmQ2xdKnCSDBow9edbGH9IvMTNcDhkeCP87uWe3Sr6AexKx8jufOU
FedQH0ZoQHzDtGcalmpK8DMXGT1oU8+KJBYMgJ2vz6L6hYsmFHUCCmwIIteafGkl
No8VEy3/vntap45iaOYMGosgEg1dcCAs9drykFiyZ18JJh0n528w5gQfORciHM8d
W8KqE2aTy3cueQLp+H8AAwcH/1KOIOmejQADrpgDs0tC8LrwgG7hpwKXhNop6EG1
HRO6jxCkX/DVQNazfsTGkNPCDxgiNEZ+ejlR5w7i1zB67IIqAhVuFxOZ17H4FJIf
Hj7p6B5zndhX272x2ZVHNvuKiHDbqkPe4MzAC6Ju8dJCjRSbvUbSol/DANtudP5H
ndiBaxcFzSHM6ftQpGI2/ba7/d92C/7vXj0Rnpz2o0AQJ/vT327zVdIWpbtOdL+C
dpxlrC3Vp9RdFi7Do/R+DgrDJT7Hvuw+17JDe0sctFeZsm+uxmCQigo4TkCzz5gK
0WzZuKYMwoJRwNCQLLWpcOC0+UuDF2/OvlNpds17msiBV52ITAQYEQIADAUCOWJe
mgUJAFxJAAAKCRCLHoAxDo+rZIlrAJ4gzhD8Z70r4dTcY3xQFc1fMttULACgmunL
J/68lWMGBkNVrn4HEGOJMic=
=qiUY
-----END PGP PUBLIC KEY BLOCK-----
[bubba@mars bubba]$
```


So there it is. The "--armor" option causes the key to be extracted in a "text" form, suitable for e-mail. Without the "--armor" option, the key is in a binary form that will neither display nor e-mail successfully.

Using GPG to Sign and Encrypt Files

We will now cover using the GPG command line to carry out the basic operations of encrypting and signing files. We will then discuss how various e-mail clients integrate these operations into sending and receiving e-mail messages and how they may be integrated into e-mail packages that *do not* automatically support them.

To see the full set of command line options, execute

```
gpg --help
```

The program has many more options than we will present here. We are going to present the bare basic commands to sign, encrypt, decrypt, and verify signatures on plain-text messages. In other words, the basics to integrate GPG into e-mail. We will then show how some existing e-mail clients already support GPG and how some can be made to do so.

Signing Files

One of the most powerful uses of GPG doesn't actually hide your message at all. Digital signatures assure the recipient of a message of two things:

- The identity of the sender
- The integrity of the message

Let's construct an example that can have obvious consequences. Suppose our Leroy has been suspected of some sort of white-collar crime. He sends an e-mail to a good friend of his that says:

```
I did NOT commit the crime!
```

Now suppose the actual criminal has access to the mail servers. He has put a program on the mail server to deflect any mail from our Leroy to his own mailbox, where he can modify the message at will and send it on to someone else, still appearing to come from Leroy. Suppose he changes it to read:

```
I did commit the crime!
```

The ease with which such changes can be made is part of why e-mail is not that good a medium for legal purposes. Leroy can protect himself, however. Let's show how with files.

Suppose we have the original message in a file called *legal.statement* in Leroy's home directory (*/home/bubba*). He can digitally sign the file in a form suitable for e-mail with the following command:

```
[bubba@mars bubba]$ gpg --clearsign legal.statement
You need a passphrase to unlock the secret key for
user: "Leroy Macmillian <leroy@flatbush.nonesuch.org>"
1024-bit DSA key, ID 0E8FAB64, created 2000-07-04

Enter passphrase:
```

After he enters his passphrase, he will be back at his Linux prompt. But there is a new file out there called *legal.statement.asc*, and it looks like this:

```
[bubba@mars bubba]$ cat legal.statement.asc
-----BEGIN PGP SIGNED MESSAGE-----
Hash: SHA1

I did NOT commit the crime!
-----BEGIN PGP SIGNATURE-----
Version: GnuPG v1.0.1 (GNU/Linux)
Comment: For info see http://www.gnupg.org

iD8DBQE5Y0q1ix6AMQ6Pq2QRApSDAKDz/RLuUE3a71xmgTzqZmtvbPdEHACdHFR1
NWedbupPVk1TCFOUIVaJzsU=
=NPHm
-----END PGP SIGNATURE-----
```

As you can see, the original content of the message is still in there and still readable, but it is surrounded by a bunch of junk. That junk can be thought of as a GPG "envelope." Notice it actually says "PGP" in the message. Since GPG is designed to be a drop-in replacement for PGP, it has to follow the behavior of PGP exactly, right down to the structure of the "envelope." If it were changed to read "GPG," it might break other programs.

So how does this gibberish protect Leroy? Well, first let's see what happens when Leroy sends this file to me (remember, we'll get to e-mail later. Right now it is files).

As it happens, Leroy and I correspond a lot. I already have his public key and I've already marked that I trust it. So when I pass his original, unmodified message through GPG, I get:

```
mars:26:~$ gpg legal.statement.asc
gpg: Signature made Wed 05 Jul 2000 09:48:05 AM CDT using DSA key ID
    0E8FAB64
gpg: Good signature from "Leroy Macmillian <leroy@flatbush.nonesuch.org>"
mars:27:~$ ls legal*
legal.statement  legal.statement.asc
```

He sent me *legal.statement.asc* and then I ran GPG on it. This produced the file *legal.statement*, which is the original message without the envelope. It also gave me a message. The "Good signature" message tells me that the message I received was signed with the private key that goes with Leroy's public key, and it tells me that the message I got was the one he signed with that key. So long as Leroy has kept his passphrase totally secret, we both know that he sent me a message telling me he did not commit the crime.

Now suppose our evil white-collar criminal, twirling his moustache and cackling, intercepted Leroy's message and changed it to look like this:

```
mars:30:~$ cat legal.statement.asc
-----BEGIN PGP SIGNED MESSAGE-----
Hash: SHA1

I did commit the crime!
-----BEGIN PGP SIGNATURE-----
Version: GnuPG v1.0.1 (GNU/Linux)
Comment: For info see http://www.gnupg.org

iD8DBQE5Y0qlix6AMQ6Pq2QRApSDAKDz/RLuUE3a7lxmgTzqZmtvbPdEHACdHFR1
NWedbupPVklTCFOUIVaJzsU=
=NPHm
-----END PGP SIGNATURE-----
```

Boy, that surprises me! I know Leroy and I don't think he'd do something like that. And if he did, I don't think he'd send me e-mail about it. He's smarter than that. I'd better check the signature.

```
mars:31:~$ gpg legal.statement.asc
gpg: Signature made Wed 05 Jul 2000 09:48:05 AM CDT using DSA key ID
    0E8FAB64
gpg: BAD signature from "Leroy Macmillian <leroy@flatbush.nonesuch.org>"
mars:32:~$ ls -la legal*
-rw-rw-r--   1 mschwarz mschwarz       25 Jul  5 10:10 legal.statement
-rw-rw-r--   1 mschwarz mschwarz      303 Jul  5 10:09 legal.statement.asc
```

Whoa! "BAD signature" tells me this message was originally signed with the private key of my good friend Leroy but that the message text has been tampered with, because the signature doesn't match the file. Someone is out to frame my good friend!

Nothing prevents moustache twirler from creating a fake key with the same name and e-mail address as those of my friend, but it would not match the public key I have on my keyring from Leroy. If our villain tried to substitute a fake signature, this is what GPG would have told me:

```
mars:39:~$ cat legal.statement.asc
-----BEGIN PGP SIGNED MESSAGE-----
Hash: SHA1

I did commit the crime!
-----BEGIN PGP SIGNATURE-----
Version: GnuPG v1.0.1 (GNU/Linux)
Comment: For info see http://www.gnupg.org

iD8DBQE5Y1L1oHgCFwxAlJgRAlaVAJ4hHP8aV03F46hx1LxQkIeDU1pOwgCglXc+
ksM5rPYWtetrPHG7/EhcTD0=
=vODa
-----END PGP SIGNATURE-----
```

```
mars:40:~$ gpg legal.statement.asc
gpg: Signature made Wed 05 Jul 2000 10:23:33 AM CDT using DSA key ID
    0C409498
gpg: Can't check signature: public key not found
```

As you can see, I find I can't validate this message at all because I don't have the public key that goes with the private key that was used to sign this message. Suppose, however, I had received a message that appeared to come from Leroy many months ago, telling me that he had generated a second key for emergencies and here was the public key? Suppose I had accepted that key into my keyring? Suppose, instead of that message coming from Leroy, it had come from the moustache twirler? I would have had a "Good signature" on that fake message!

The integrity of keys is the absolute foundation of any crypto system. You don't care who gets your public key, but you do care very much who is giving you public keys and whether they are really from the people they claim to be.

My preferred method of exchanging public keys is face-to-face on floppy diskettes. Failing that, GPG has key-signing and trust levels. You can sign other people's keys with your private key. This allows people who trust your key to trust this other key, because they know your key and they trust that you would not sign a key you didn't trust. So long as you sign only keys that you actually know came from whom they claim to come from, this system works. Note that you can sign a key and still not trust the key owner. This is a good thing. You sign it because you know for a fact that it is "Leroy's" key, but you don't trust it because you know Leroy is dumb as a stump and would sign a key sent to him in a spam e-mail message by a stranger he'd never met.

We won't cover the details of key signing and trust here. This book introduces you to the tools, shows you the basics, and sends you on your way to learn for yourself, but issues of key management, key signing, and trust are critical to the integrity of your system.

When someone sends you a public key over an untrusted medium, you have to regard it with suspicion. Verify that key! Certainly do not sign or mark at a higher trust level any key you haven't validated.

Encrypting and Signing Files

We have shown how you can validate files and foil forgers with GPG using signatures. Now what about protecting your file or message from prying eyes?

First off, I have to make a confession. I've told you that GPG uses a so-called "public-key cipher" to encrypt messages and that the older "symmetric-key" system is not used. That was a lie. I wanted to emphasize the fact that the public–private key pair is critical to both functions. Public–private keys are so large, however, that they are impracticable for messages of any significant size. Performing the encryption algorithm with more than 1024-bit keys on messages many kilobytes long or longer can take many minutes on even the fastest of machines.

These keys must be huge because it is known that (at some level) the keys are products of primes, and thus, only prime numbers need be tried when trying to break them. That means a great many numbers need not be tried when trying to "brute-force" attack these keys. (NB: I'm oversimplifying again. Remember that the keys are actually derived using relative primes and an algorithm. The principle still holds. A public key/private key pair can be attacked in more sophisticated ways than trying every possible value.)

Since the keys are so large and thus so slow, they are used to encrypt a much smaller symmetric *session key* that is used for only the one message. The encrypted session key is sent encrypted with the public key of the recipient. The recipient and only the recipient is able to decrypt the session key and thus is able to decrypt the message encrypted with that session key. Confused? Don't worry. It works. The session key is generally 128 bits long. Since it is not a public key and is generated in a truly random manner, all possible 128-bit values are equally likely, so, unlike public keys, every possible value must be attempted in a brute-force attack. A 128-bit key ought to be safe until the sun grows cold.

Now that you know about the symmetric session key, we will not mention it again, because in encryption, just as in signatures, it is the public key/private key pair you deal with at the command line.

Let's continue in the same vein as earlier. Let's assume Leroy really did commit white-collar crime. Let's say he has been stealing pens from the office supply cabinet and returning them to Office Depot to exchange for merchandise. Let's further suppose he recently returned 1,247,114 Sharpie permanent markers and used them to purchase a desk and Palm V organizer.

The pen police are hot on his trail. Leroy, figuring a risk shared is a risk doubled, decides to tell me all about it. At least he has the sense to send me his missive encrypted. Here's how things look at Leroy's account:

```
[bubba@mars bubba]$ cat confession
I returned millions of pens I stole from TeraGigaMegaCorp and
returned them at Office Depot to exchange for a desk and
a Palm V organizer!  What am I going to do?  The pen police are on
to me!

Leroy

[bubba@mars bubba]$
```

He signs and encrypts it:

```
[bubba@mars bubba]$ gpg --encrypt --sign --r mschwarz --armor confession

You need a passphrase to unlock the secret key for
user: "Leroy Macmillian <leroy@flatbush.nonesuch.org>"
1024-bit DSA key, ID 0C409498, created 2000-07-05

Enter passphrase:
```

He enters his passphrase. His passphrase is *not* needed for encryption! It is needed for the signature. If he had not requested the signature, he would not be prompted for his passphrase. Now, he has imported my public key, but he never used it before and did not give it a level of trust. My key was also not signed by someone whose key he does trust. So he has to go through a few gyrations before he's done:

```
Could not find a valid trust path to the key.  Let's see whether we
can assign some missing owner trust values.

No path leading to one of our keys found.

2048g/EF74743B 2000-02-07 "Michael Alan Schwarz <mschwarz@sherbtel.net>"
          Fingerprint: 7226 3E60 BECE D054 4CF9  0486 B309 CF38 EF74 743B

It is NOT certain that the key belongs to its owner.
If you *really* know what you are doing, you may answer
the next question with yes

Use this key anyway?
```

I gave him the key on a floppy, so he knows he can trust it.

```
Use this key anyway? yes
[bubba@mars bubba]$ ls -la confession*
-rw-rw-r--    1 bubba    bubba         194 Jul  5 11:49 confession
-rw-rw-r--    1 bubba    bubba        1248 Jul  5 12:01 confession.asc
[bubba@mars bubba]$
```

Had he set my trust level, even if to "untrusted," he would not have had to answer that question. Note he now has two files. The first is his unencrypted confession (which, if he is smart, he will overwrite and delete). The second looks like this:

```
[bubba@mars bubba]$ cat confession.asc
-----BEGIN PGP MESSAGE-----
Version: GnuPG v1.0.1 (GNU/Linux)
Comment: For info see http://www.gnupg.org
```

```
hQIOA7MJzzjvdHQ7EAf7BGj1YuxeMpz0LOzBUHMd6GL4PlIbIECzblbJefx2MOj1
oA80kQNNNOGLVRgnvB0qMSt6zaaUt5UMyhFUbH/6wS0JSMyzpfZabcKrF9/6KCcP
LhbOIScejBVWwRF6QML2g8jJBvj/GrRnLiroS/b+fZ83DtAH/CDxGkk3ilJC2tHl
5K38JePQiSwC7sXtb0WcCsiEik5M9dusAc7cpZAOPO0VRpMm006wAEh5RCyKFhZU
TlJUO5Bc+MDyVXmecOfiKBXMV59o/RFoqTvjqH8uRVJB3YzV8HBXMhyMMVead7UC
GV5jOnLsL0zZGKqgzdC1edcJaasJ9RXDYqk3echk0wf9E2vwjo4N1HGBDINYO3WK
OXYuxY9Q6NFPJw3cO46RWrWh795JpVPaOquJi7GXzy4vJUJAyhlcxnzNbwwyZq+V
5NZQNXfAotTwgHRZybrJm3sgrWQLGQMtUVSo7fTP/im6gPXj0HEC0ofJqKFt/5uq
xmrQ6VlMahuPEQxzwAPJKg/V5P/tawQhrb/MD5rJ4s1JmiE/kJ/96etG8HDr/bf6
+4PT7gOayLe3KFYuySAPr2hzqesqp5ZPu1A2wLeU6DmKldvMVWXpiWOygFUTTxNr
Z9hgSGez9vCdKOmjsaalE3a5BtsWDhpJSQjv8ZFLSaKlYdHRoyzJ5UjXhuF9e8y9
KsnAXXGVLqaodZLelztpM/65NznBf34/lXWHTea0j9ezBjXf5Mrel/zbrqGmF2Ub
zpXNxCmBTwnEoR4cZRpMg8s2ICrtzS7sL7WobFhOeUMsWfGICY6qJxlRsQOmcY8N
zIy2TNCBIEMwgnRR95YF2UZq8SgFE2am4Y0Pfxu25Kt6MQ+xFXxjD3KbZxu6Kzro
9VDhrkX/0L7HFDxaKj8ak7CSELI3OgXRFjyiouxx8+FkzJMovO5s+ckC1rwi6Xq7
65/UXJN07vpvU/J4Ti1wJiL2Q81zUZVK2r35oa+wVnJVLOzJo/Y8EIZy5FQWcylt
bp7uKHSq1owPSks7ZKLqz7c4jJk5NtE4Q2SvhXVmWfNPuH4x3xQRVMDMYL1jyp6u
Hw==
=Fzrl
-----END PGP MESSAGE-----
[bubba@mars bubba]$
```

No one but me can read that file. Even Leroy cannot read it. Only people listed as recipients (the "-r" in his encrypting GPG command line) may read the message. It is encrypted with each recipient's public key. Only the corresponding private key can decrypt the message. Yes, you are right if you have deduced that there are multiple copies of the message if it is sent to multiple recipients.

GPG compresses the message before it is encrypted, so often the encrypted message is smaller than the original, even when sent to more than one person. Our message is so short that compression buys us next to nothing.

Now, when I get the message, this is what I see:

```
mars:106:~$ gpg confession.asc

You need a passphrase to unlock the secret key for
user: "Michael Alan Schwarz <mschwarz@sherbtel.net>"
2048-bit ELG-E key, ID EF74743B, created 2000-02-07 (main key ID
    2A43DBA2)

Enter passphrase:
```

I have to enter my passphrase, not for the signature, but for the decryption. Do you begin to see? You must type a passphrase any time you need your *private* key. Your private key is stored encrypted so that even if your private-key file is somehow stolen, it is still difficult, if not impossible, to recover your private key.

Note that the security of your private key is only as strong as the strength of your passphrase. This is potentially the weakest link in the GPG chain. I know people who are so paranoid that their secret key is kept on a single floppy, symbolically linked to their *.gnupg* directory. They insert the floppy whenever they need it, and then unmount and file it when done. If they destroy the floppy, the key is gone for good and all the stuff encrypted with their public key is then encrypted forever (or until their key is brute-forced, whichever comes first). Barring a miraculous discovery of a simple means of factoring large numbers, forever will come first.

Getting back to our story, I enter my passphrase, and then . . .

```
gpg: Signature made Wed 05 Jul 2000 12:01:17 PM CDT using DSA key ID
    0C409498
gpg: Good signature from "Leroy Macmillian <leroy@flatbush.nonesuch.org>"
```

If I look, I now find a file called *confession* in addition to *confession.asc*, the one that I got from Leroy.

```
mars:109:~$ ls -la confession*
-rw-rw-r--   1 mschwarz mschwarz      194 Jul  5 12:14 confession
-rw-rw-r--   1 mschwarz mschwarz     1248 Jul  5 12:07 confession.asc
mars:110:~$
```

Here's what I find inside:

```
mars:113:~$ cat confession
I returned millions of pens I stole from TeraGigaMegaCorp and
returned them at Office Depot to exchange for a desk and
a Palm V organizer!  What am I going to do?  The pen police are on
to me!

Leroy

mars:114:~$
```

Poor Leroy. He took every precaution but he didn't realize that I want no part of a conspiracy charge. I forward the e-mail, signed and unencrypted, to T. Laurence Pencilpusher, head of the pen police. I've since deleted Leroy's key. So ends Leroy's sad story.

Encryption without Signature: A Codicil

Personally, I always sign or encrypt and sign messages. There may well, however, be situations where you would wish to encrypt a message and leave it unsigned. One situation would be Leroy's ill-fated message to me. He could have sent this to me and then claimed never to have done so if he had encrypted it and *not* signed it. Remember, all it takes to encrypt a message is the *recipient's* public key. Anyone might have that key. The signature proved that Leroy sent that message. If he hadn't signed it, he could have denied that he ever sent it, and it would be difficult for anyone to prove otherwise.

If, however, you find yourself thinking, "Hey! That's a good idea," I would reexamine the whole idea of sending your message in the first place. It's much easier to deny a message you don't send.

Integrating GPG with Popular E-Mail Clients

Elm

Elm supports PGP "out of the box." Enabling GPG takes only a little bit of work. One very short path to support is to use a shell program that "wraps" GPG with commands that look and work like the old PGP 2.6.2 commands. This is a solution for full compatibility with a lot of old PGP supporting applications.

This compatibility package is called *pgpgpg*. Here's some info:

Package: pgpgpg

Homepage: *http://www.nessie.de/mroth/pgpgpg*

Download: *ftp://ftp.gnupg.org/pub/gcrypt/pgpgpg-0.13.1.tar.gz*

Once you have this installed, you can use the older PGP commands (which is what elm will do!) to enable PGP support.

Mutt

As of this writing, the most current version of mutt is 1.2.5i. Mutt has optional support for PGP at compilation. As with elm, you can get mutt working by using pgpgpg.

Even without direct support, you can use the "F" (filter) command to send your message attachment through GPG for signature and/or encryption. You can use the pipe (|) command on the receiving side to send your message through GPG for decryption and signature verification.

Pine

Here again someone has done all the work for us. There is a program called *gpg4pine*. Here's some info:

> Package: gpg4pine
>
> Homepage: None (alas!)
>
> Download: *http://azzie.robotics.net/*

Complete directions are included with the software. (Try this too!)

Kmail

The newest versions of Kmail support GP6 directly, but older versions can support it through a PGP compatibility wrapper. Once you have installed gpgpgp, you open *File/Settings*, and select the PGP tab, as shown in Figure 10-1.

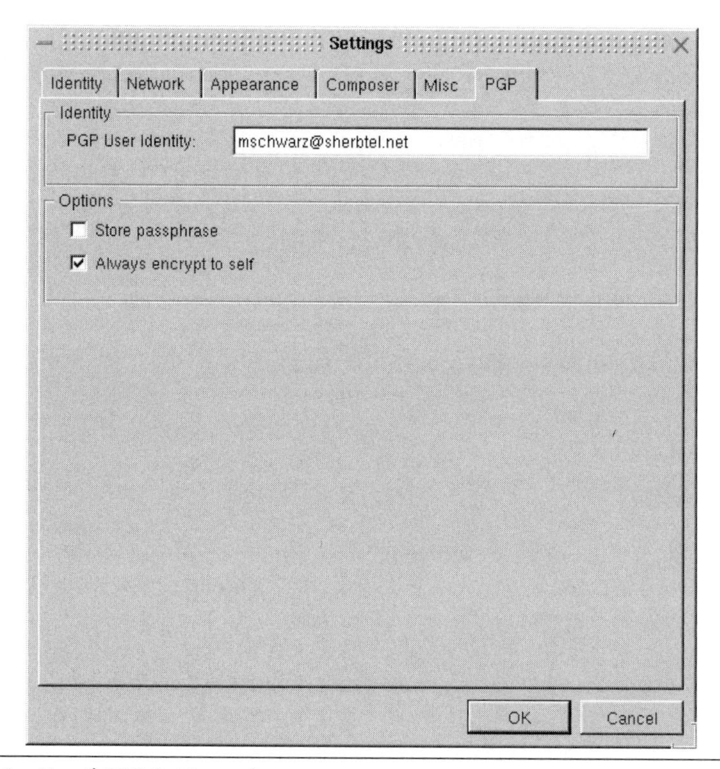

Figure 10-1 Kmail PGP Settings tab.

Mailx and Mail

These mail clients are so basic and primitive that not even I use them. As it happens, it is simple, if inconvenient, to use GPG with these programs. You must sign or encrypt your mail as a text file outside the program and then redirect the file in to send it. To read such mail, you must save the message to a file (using the *save* or *copy* commands), and then run GPG on the file directly.

Netscape

Netscape does not support GPG decently. You must "presign" and/or "pre-encrypt" your messages; you must save your messages to files to check signatures and decrypt. Sad, isn't it?

Summary

GPG is a general-purpose digital signature and encryption program. It may be used alone to sign and encrypt files. One of its most common applications, however, is integration with e-mail packages, where its capabilities may be used to verify identity and protect privacy.

Chapter 11

SNIFFING FOR IDIOTS (PUN INTENDED)

Difficult-o-Meter: 3 (moderate Linux skill required)

Covers:

sniffit	*http://reptile.rug.ac.be/~coder/sniffit/sniffit.html*
supersniffer	*http://users.dhp.com/~ajax/projects/*
tcpdump	*http://www.tcpdump.org/*
dsniff	*http://www.monkey.org/~dugsong/dsniff/*
ethereal	*http://www.ethereal.com/*

Question: Something funky is going on somewhere in my home/work network, and it doesn't make a lick of sense. What can I do?

Answer: When all else has failed, it's time to roll up your sleeves, break out your Linux box, and get sniffing!

You Want Me to *What*?

Sniffing is one of the simplest of all data-harvesting techniques. And not only is it easy to do, but people forget about it. I was at DEFCON 7, and I saw people logging in to their *root* accounts over *Telnet*! This is not something a person should do, even on a *trusted* network, much less on a malicious network like those found at a security convention!

Now, bear in mind that I don't pretend to be an expert. Well, sometimes I do, but I'm not. I cannot decode Ethernet frames in my head, I cannot merely put a CAT-5 Ethernet cable in my mouth and immediately divine what sort of traffic is on the wire. (If those two disclaimers make zero sense, worry a bit. You should know *something* about how networks work before you get this far.) But I have done some Unix administration, and I've done some network administration, and I've done more than my fair share of sniffing.

In order to understand sniffing, we should talk very, very briefly about how sniffing works. If you're old enough, you may remember the party-line telephone. This was a system in which everyone's telephone shared a single physical connection—all phones were connected on the same shared wire. If Tom, Dick, Harry, and Sally all had phones in their homes, only one of them could be using it at a time—unless, of course, Tom was calling Dick or Harry was calling Sally. It had no method to prevent eavesdropping. When Tom placed a call to, say, Chicago, he could almost guarantee that someone else was listening in on it. When a call came in from the outside, all phones would ring—and potential recipients would listen for the distinctive pattern that was *their* ring. It might be two long rings followed by a short, or six shorts and two longs.

Nonswitched Ethernet networks function in the same way. Everyone is on the same shared bandwidth; when one computer has a message for another, everyone's phone rings. Now, there are lots of technical details for how this works, but they aren't fully germane to this discussion. So we'll leave it at this: Every Ethernet card normally ignores any packets not intended for it. So, even though Tom's, Dick's, Harry's, and Sally's computers all have the potential to see the network traffic for everybody, they'll just ignore it unless it concerns them.

In order to sniff, we run a bit of software that mildly alters the behavior of our network cards. Sniffing software puts one's network card into "promiscuous" mode—in other words, it starts seeing all the network traffic out there. This is rather like becoming the person who always picks up the receiver of the party-line phone.

Why would anyone put this capability into a networking protocol? Because all our modern networking protocols were designed by engineers, not by security freaks. The engineers decided that it would be really, really useful if they could use any machine to diagnose troubles. I've got a nickel that says they never really considered the security implications. IBM, according to a rumor I once heard, did consider the implications, and produced an Ethernet card incapable of going into promiscuous mode. I've never seen one, so it may be just a rumor. And when it comes down to it, it *is* useful to be able to use any machine to troubleshoot problems.

Sniffing is the act of (and I'm sure you're already way ahead of me) examining every packet on the wire. This is a passive data-harvesting technique—it doesn't put any additional traffic on the wire, and it's rather hard to detect. It's incredibly easy to set up, and it gathers a ridiculous amount of useful information. I did an informal survey of a half-dozen Unix system administrators. They all said the same thing: They had found sniffers installed on every breached machine they had ever encountered. To believe that sniffing is uncommon is naive at best and career limiting at worst. In other words, if one of the machines on your network is compromised, you can rest assured that a sniffer has been installed on it.

Now that we know what sniffing is, and a little bit of how it works, we'll get into answering your question: How do I see what's going wrong on my network? We'll also tackle the other two uses of sniffers: offense and defense.

Troubleshooting

Problem resolution is the first use of sniffing, and it's still one of their biggest uses. Sometimes, network problems arise—anyone who has ever played with a network for more than five minutes is well aware of this. A sniffer lets you look at the individual packets and see what's going wrong. Maybe a switch is mangling a specific field in each packet, or maybe an NIC is throwing out nonsense packets at a frantic rate—a sniffer will let you see those things and let you see them quickly.

Offense

The next use of sniffing is for attack. This is how those aforementioned script kiddies use sniffing. Every successful military operation begins with good intelligence. Sniffing can get that good intelligence. It allows you to see what sort of services are being run on the target network, and it may allow you to harvest usernames and passwords. It can also be used to fingerprint operating systems—to determine exactly what operating system is on a given host—merely by examining which services (and which versions of those services) are active. Jose Nazario's paper on doing just that is at *http://www.crimelabs.com/docs/passive.pdf.*

Defense

The third use of sniffing is defense: monitoring your own network to make sure nothing out of the ordinary is going on. This can be used to ensure that: your users aren't running services they shouldn't be, there aren't any little script kiddies cruising around your intranet, and your (cough) Windows (cough) software isn't sending personal information to some server somewhere in Redmond, Washington.

The L0pht (*http://www.l0pht.com/*) is a widely respected group of white-hat crackers. They break things to reveal vulnerabilities and then contact the vendor and tell them what they need to fix. *Then* they announce the problems to the world. The L0pht uses sniffers on a daily basis—to conduct security audits and just to see what sort of things their software is communicating to the outside world. At one point, they discovered that a password-checking utility was sending a list of all the passwords from an NT server to another server, this one at another company, in order to verify those passwords. Since they were weakly encrypted to begin with, those passwords could have been intercepted by anyone (with a sniffer) between the two companies!

Tools

Here are a few tools.

Sniffit

Sniffit is an older sniffer, but it's useful nonetheless. Its homepage is at *http://reptile.rug.ac.be/~coder/sniffit/sniffit.html*. It can be downloaded from *http://reptiel.rug.ac.be/~coder/sniffit/files/sniffit.0.3.7.beta.tar.gz*.

Figure 11-1 shows sniffit looking at the result of someone else's Telnet login. Figure 11-2 shows that person's "ls" command. Note that sniffit is apparently finished—no updates have been made to the page in a year or so.

Compiling it was easy on my machine—just a standard autoconf dealie.

Dsniff

Dug Song was kind enough to work up a great sniffer in the form of dsniff—an entire package of sniffing-related tools. The homepage is at *http://www.monkey.org/~dugsong/dsniff/*, and the package can be downloaded from *http://www.monkey.org/~dugsong/dsniff/dsniff-2.3.tar.gz*.

In order to install this, I had to install Berkeley DB, OpenSSL, libpcap, libnids, and libnet. Your system may or may not need all of these installed, or it may not need any

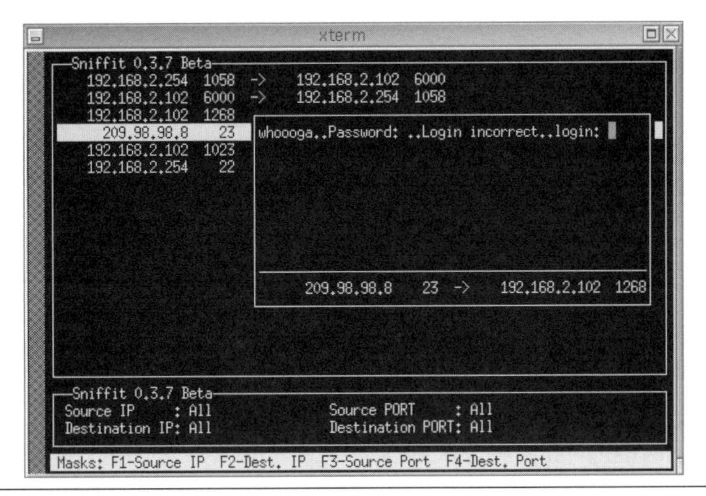

Figure 11-1 Sniffit intercepting a username and password.

of them. Some distributions ship with these packages, but, off the top of my head, I'm not sure which ones. Download dsniff and run the *./configure* program to determine which of the following packages you'll need to install. The required packages have the following homepages and URLS:

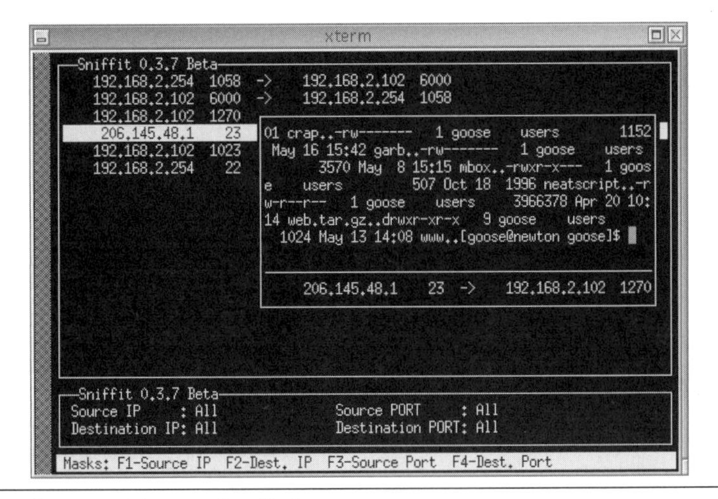

Figure 11-2 Someone's been using "ls."

Package Name	Homepage URL
Berkeley DB	http://www.sleepycat.com/
OpenSSL	http://www.openssl.org/
libpcap	http://www.tcpdump.org/
libnids	http://www.packetfactory.net/projects/libnids/
libnet	http://www.packetfactory.net/projects/libnet/

Required Packages

Berkeley DB

I grabbed version 3.2.9 of Berkeley DB and threw it into my */usr/src* directory. This was a regular autoconf build, *except* for the fact that the configure script is found in the *dist* directory, and you have to be in the *build_unix* directory when you call it. So, to simplify, here's how I did it:

```
tar zxvf db-3.2.9.tar.gz
cd db-3.2.9
cd build_unix
../dist/configure
make
su -c"make install"
make clean # gotta save some disk space, eh?
```

Compilation took about two minutes on my K6/2-450.

OpenSSL

For OpenSSL, I got version 0.9.6, the latest and greatest. It was a standard autoconf build procedure. Compilation took about 7 minutes, and installation took 1.5 more.

libpcap

For libpcap, version 0.6.1 was used. Again, a GNU autoconf-type build, and compilation took under 60 seconds.

libnids

I picked up libnids version 1.16. And while it should have been a regular autoconf build (which it was), I had to specify a command flag to get it to recognize libnids, so here's the complete build process:

```
tar zxvf libnids-1.16.tar.gz
cd libnids-1.16
```

```
./configure -with-libpcap=/usr/src/libpcap-0.6.1
make
su -c"make install"
make clean
cd ../libpcap-0.6.1
make clean
```

Apparently, libnids just can't find libpcap, because I couldn't get it to compile without explicitly declaring the libpcap build directory. Once I specified that, however, compilation took about a minute.

libnet

This one is version 1.0.1b. The autoconf-style build and installation took under a minute.

Dsniff Compilation

Dug was kind enough to use GNU Autoconf, and it was built and installed in under 60 seconds.

Figure 11-3 shows dsniff with some typical output. I had briefly considered putting in the live data I grabbed from root fest, but I decided against it for legal and practical reasons—I can't find the screenshots I grabbed back then. Regardless, it was a *prime* example of people *not thinking*. I mean, really—logging into your mail account from a hacker convention? And to top it off, after the presentation we fired up the sniffers

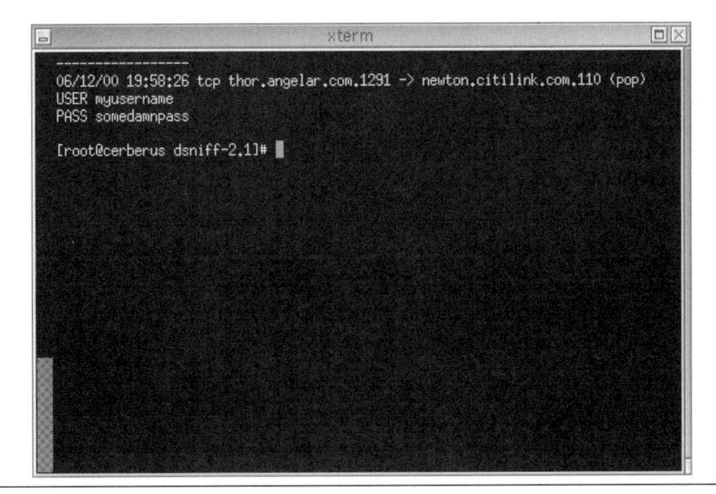

Figure 11-3 Dsniff grabbing a POP login.

again, figuring we'd get nothing. We got plenty. We got a couple of kids logging in to their mail servers, sending their passwords in clear text. And when we pointed it out, they yanked the network cables out of their machines. "How did you get past Black-ICE?!" they screamed. Sniffing isn't affected by things like BlackICE. It works on the wire. Pulling the wire out of your computer isn't somehow going to protect your mail account from me—I've already got that username and password!

Anyway, dsniff is the Cadillac of sniffers. If you haven't looked at it, go get it now. Compile it. Run it on your own machine. Be afraid.

Msgsnarf is the instant-message (IM) grabber, allowing you to eavesdrop on any IM conversations. It works with most instant messengers, I'm sorry to say. Figure 11-4 presents a shot of msgsnarf in action, catching a posed conversation between my good friend Roger Hall and me.

Mailsnarf is a handy little gadget for violating the electronic privacy act—it grabs all the SMTP traffic (that's e-mail for you newbies) and saves them into an mbox-format file, so you can browse them with elm or mutt. This actually has a good, legitimate purpose in a corporate environment—you can grab everyone's mail and check for security leaks merely by grepping* through the mbox. This is part of the dsniff package, so once you get dsniff you've got mailsnarf too.

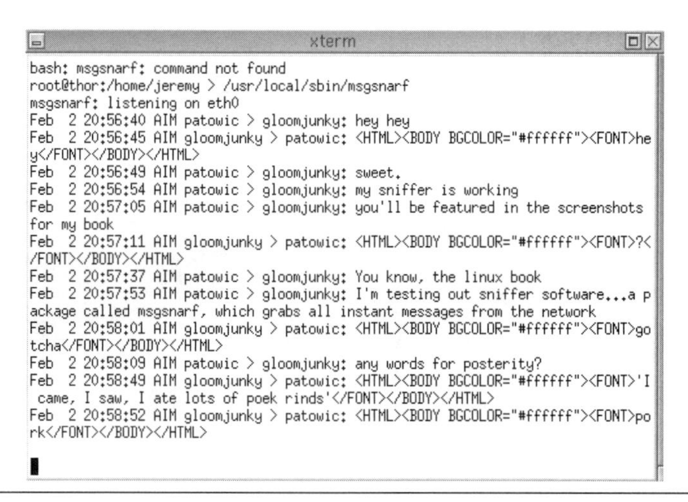

Figure 11-4 Dsniff listening to an AIM conversation.

*Meaning, use the program grep to search the mailbox file. Execute *man grep* for more info, and see Chapter 15.

URLsnarf is also part of the dsniff package; it provides a summary listing of all of the URLS that are being visited on your LAN. This is *much* better than using censorware for finding out where people are going on the net. We all know that censorware doesn't work—it fails to block pornography, and it blocks lots of nonpornography (for more details, visit *http://www.peacefire.org/*). Using URLsnarf, you can find out which users are visiting sites that are non-work-friendly and have a nice talk with them off the record. This can help some poor slob keep his job.

A simple load of *http://www.salon.com/* gave me all the URLs shown in Figure 11-5.

Supersniffer

Supersniffer is another pretty refined tool. This one is a lot more stealthy, and I'll cover why in a second. Its homepage is at *http://users.dhp.com/~ajax/projects/*, and it can be downloaded from *http://users.dhp.com/~ajax/code/ss/ss-1.3.tgz.*

I'm not going to cover compilation here, or recommend using it. It's an advanced cracker tool, and frankly I think it's overcomplex. It has clever features for avoiding detection—which puts it in a category with a disposable, silenced pistol. It has few legitimate uses. Look at the Web page, and play with it if you like. Be wary of it.

Figure 11-5 Dsniff:URLSnarf grabbing URLs.

A couple of the features I believe compromise its legitimacy are:

- Ability to appear as if it were being run under a different user name—making it easier to hide in plain view.
- Ability to detect users logging into the machine and to deactivate itself immediately.
- Ability to send all sniffed strings to a port on the machine, making the output easily accessible.
- Ability to compile without any "strings" in the binary, making it harder for an administrator to determine the purpose of the binary.
- By default, it only listens on Telnet, POP3, FTP, and login ports.

It also encrypts its output by default, but this is actually something I like—if I leave a sniffer running on one of my machines, I'd prefer that the output logs not be visible to the entire world.

Figure 11-6 shows supersniffer's output. Like I said, this is an advanced cracker tool.

TCPDump

TCPDump is the next-to-last tool I'll mention. Unless you've been completely bored with everything up to this point, don't mess with it. That said, it's a standard tool that is available on almost every flavor of Unix. It also requires a lot more knowledge of TCP/IP to use properly. And it requires libpcap. It allows the most detailed

```
xterm
-- TCP/IP LOG -- TM: Mon Jun 12 19:44:53 2000
thor.angelar.com:1286 > amethyst.tc.umn.edu:telnet [RESET] [U]
  ^C^X^_ !"'^E#^_P^X$^Xxterm#thor.angelar.com:0.0'DISPLAY^Athor.angelar.com:0.0^
A^Auser
  password

--
-- TCP/IP LOG -- TM: Mon Jun 12 19:45:09 2000
thor.angelar.com:1287 > newton.citilink.com:telnet [RESET] [ASFP]
  ^C^X^_ !"'^E#^_P^X 38400,38400#thor.angelar.com:0.0'DISPLAY^Athor.angelar.com:
0.0^Xxterm^A^Auser
  password
  elm
  x^D
--
~
~
~
~
~
~
~
~
"ss.log" 13 lines, 451 characters
```

Figure 11-6 Supersniffer sample output.

examination of the packets on the network, and it requires the most skill to make it function properly. It's included in all distributions of which I am aware, so I won't cover compilation here. You can get that from *http://www.tcpdump.org/*.

Ethereal

Ethereal is the most versatile and complete sniffer program I've seen yet. To top it off, it's free. It sits on top of TCPDump and basically makes a nice, user-friendly interface for it. The homepage is at *http://www.ethereal.org/*, and the download is at *http://www.ethereal.org/distribution/ethereal-0.8.15.tar.gz*.

Compiling Ethereal

Ethereal requires GTK-1.2 or greater (which you have if you have anything approaching a recent distribution), libpcap (which you can install using the info from the dsniff tool, previously in this chapter), and Perl (also included with any distribution). It's an autoconf-style package, and compilation only took about 7 minutes. Ethereal is actually very similar to the Windows tool NetXRay, but much easier to use and a tad more feature rich. Bear in mind, I have an old version of NetXRay, so my impressions may be wrong. Ethereal is good. (See Figures 11-7 through 11-11.) Get it. Use it. Love it.

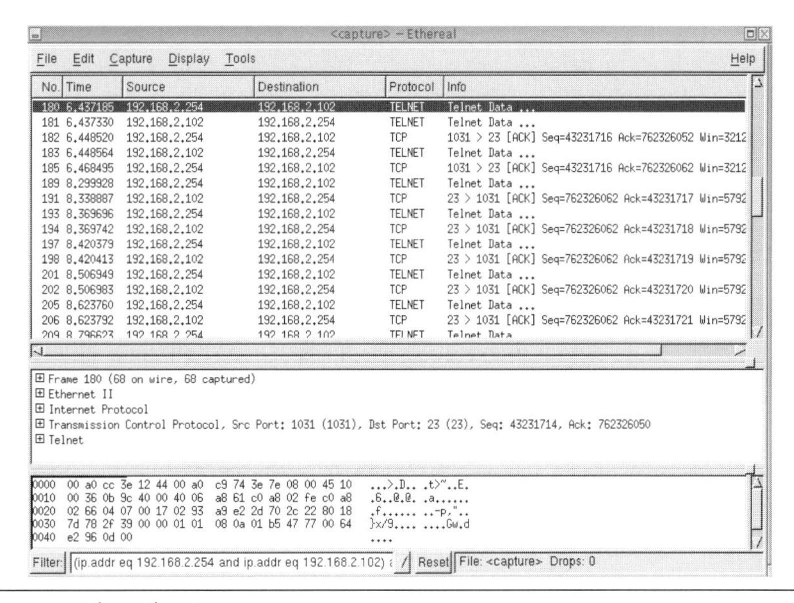

Figure 11-7 Ethereal main screen.

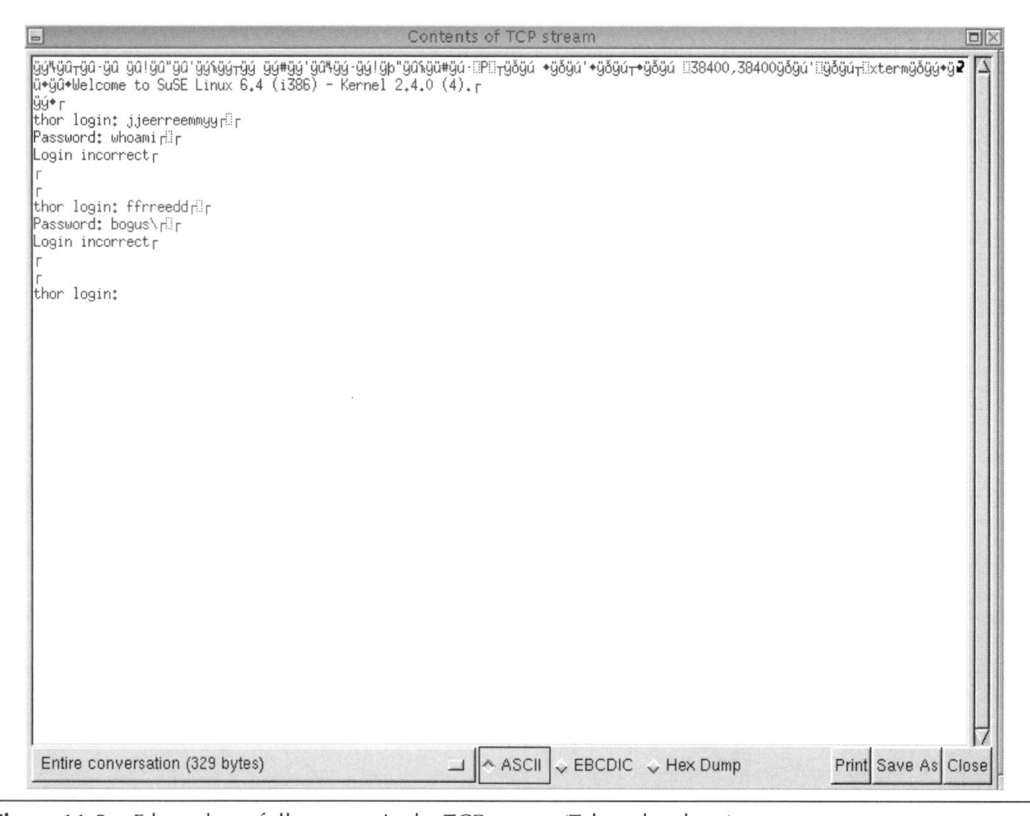

Figure 11-8 Ethereal can follow a particular TCP stream (Telnet data here).

Floppy Linux (MuLinux), the Sniffing Station

MuLinux is a rockin' multifloppy distribution available from *http://sunsite.auc.dk/mulinux*. It's full featured and includes both X-windows and sniffit. Using a copy of MuLinux, anyone with physical access to your network can create a sniffing station in a few minutes, and then leave with all the data. You'll have no evidence that you were even sniffed. See Chapter 15, Tools You Should Know, for more uses of MuLinux.

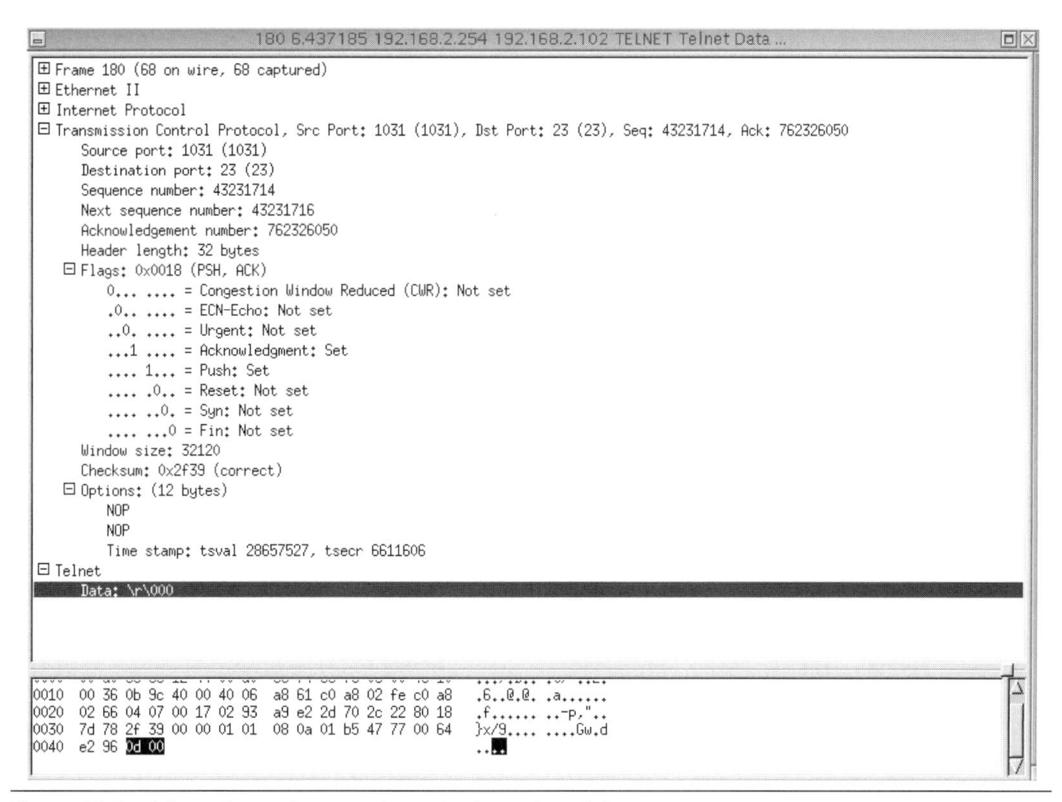

Figure 11-9 Ethereal can also examine a single packet of data.

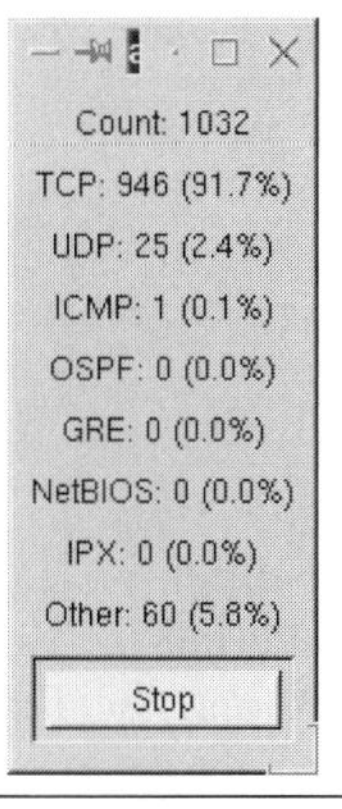

Figure 11-10 Ethereal presents overall capture statistics.

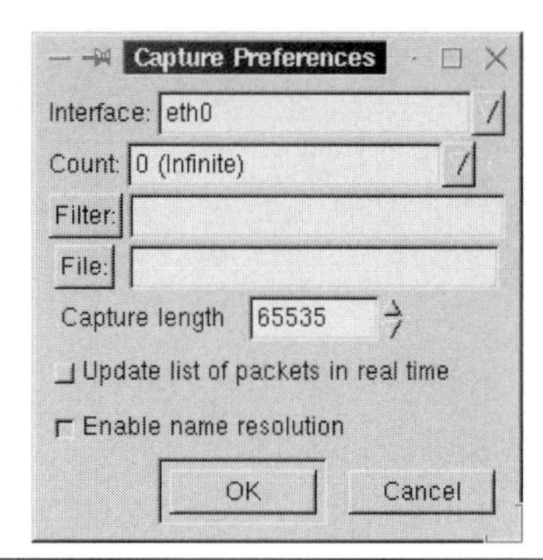

Figure 11-11 Telling Ethereal where to grab data and how much to grab.

Countermeasures

There *are* countermeasures to sniffing.

Antisniff

The first countermeasure is a package called *antisniff*, developed by Dr. Mudge of the L0pht. It's available from *http://www.securitysoftwaretech.com/antisniff/dist/anti_sniff_researchv1-1-2.tar.gz*. It's very effective at finding sniffing machines, and it uses several tests to detect them. First, it exploits a Linux kernel flaw to see if the network card is in promiscuous mode. Then it runs several other operating-system-specific tests. Then it gets really clever. It pings every computer on the network to see how fast each responds. Then it constructs a conversation between two nonexistent Mac addresses, and then it sends out *lots* of packets. Then it pings every computer again. All of the computers that are in nonpromiscuous mode are ignoring all this bogus traffic—which means they respond just as quickly as they did the first time. The sniffing station, however, is busy processing all this bogus data, so its response will be slower than it was the first time. Antisniff is very effective, but it's not foolproof. There are sniffers that will evade it. Regardless of this, it's a useful tool.

It is, however, a bit arcane. It's relatively self-explanatory to compile and run, and it has a handful of options. But after compiling it on my kernel-2.4.0 machine, I couldn't get it to detect a sniffer on another machine on my network. It apparently has limited utility on kernel-2.4 machines, or I'm simply an idiot. It's hard to say. Either of these things may be fixed in the future, but since the L0pht has sold this code to securitysoftwaretech.com (and I'm relatively uneducable), they may not.

Depth in Defense

The next countermeasure is eliminating clear-text protocols. Replace Telnet and RCP (Unix Remote Copy) with OpenSSH (see Chapter 14). OpenSSH never actually sends passwords in the clear, and it encrypts every packet. It's not unbreakable, but it will keep pretty much any nongovernmental agency from sniffing your Telnet sessions. SCP (secure copy) is SSH's remote copy program. None of my machines use FTP anymore—they use SCP instead. It's a little more difficult to use, but again it keeps me from passing things in the clear, which is good. OpenSSH is available from *http://www.openssh.org/*.

You *could* also try one-time passwords, but don't. Users will hate them.

An in-depth defense is the only real defense. Just as the Soviet Army broke the back of the Nazi German assault by using a 3-mile-deep defense at Stalingrad, you can stave off crackers by securing each machine to the utmost. Turn off services you aren't using. See Jose Nazario's presentation at *http://cwrulug.cwru.edu/talks/security/index.html*. See the Linux security HOWTO at *http://www.linuxdoc.org/HOWTO/Security-HOWTO.html*.

Summary

Get familiar with sniffing—it's too useful not to know. Get some of these tools; they're very, very handy. Check on freshmeat for new sniffers regularly—sometimes even creepier/more useful sniffers are released. Ettercap, for example, would be pretty cool if it worked. And send a thank you to Dug Song for not breaking the SSH protocol. I suspect he's more than capable, but, thankfully, he's a good guy.

Chapter 12

All Along the Watchtower

Difficult-o-Meter: 3 (moderate Linux skill required)

Covers:

Tripwire *http://www.tripwire.org/*

Question: I was sitting at home, minding my own business, when one day a bunch of police, state troopers, FBI agents, ATF agents, postal inspectors, and the Publisher's Clearinghouse prize patrol came into my house and took all my computers. Apparently, my computers had been used without my knowledge to launch a denial-of-service attack, completely blocking all access to the official Britney Spears homepage. While I am embarassed that I didn't think of doing that myself, I would have had the sense not to do that from my own computers. How can I see to it that no one uses my network in this way?

Answer: The first and simplest answer is don't have your network connected to the Internet. To some extent we tell you how to do that in Chapter 3 on firewalling. The next best answer is to know as soon as possible when miscreants come padding around your network interfaces. This chapter and the next one cover the topic of intrusion detection.

In this chapter we look at an intrusion-detection tool called Tripwire, which can detect changes to important system configuration files, files an attacker would be likely to manipulate both to hide the intrusion and to open up additional access.

Introduction

Intrusion detection is the art of knowing when a bad guy is standing in the room with you, holding a loaded gun to your head. Believe me, this can be harder than it sounds when the room is a network and its operating systems. In this chapter, we teach you how to detect the subtle and insidious acts of the typical script kiddie once he gains access to an account on your computer. In the next chapter, we will present a tool that can help you stop the barbarian at the gate so that you don't have to corner him and explain what indoor plumbing is for.

A Model of Network Attacks

This breakdown of phases in a network-based system compromise is my own taxonomy. I find it a handy way of categorizing the methods attackers use to gain access to a system and to hide their traces.

Types of Attack

There are two major categories of attacks on network machines. The first is the *denial-of-service* (DoS) attack. This is analogous to the civil disobedience protester shouting so you cannot communicate. This type of attack is most annoying when you are the vicitim, but it doesn't actually *damage* your system or the data on it.

The second major category is the *system compromise*. This is where a remote attacker actually gains access to at least read data from your system that you did not intend that party to read. At most the attacker may gain complete control of your system. Obviously, this second category is the more serious.

Phases of Network-Based Attacks

An attack leading to a system compromise is conducted in phases.

Reconnaissance

The first phase is *reconnaissance*. This comes in two flavors, *passive* and *active*. Passive reconnaissance is watching network traffic to discover hosts, addresses, resources, users, etc. Chapter 11, on sniffing, tells you about tools that may be used to do passive reconnaissance. It is very hard to detect passive network sniffing. Luckily the ability to do passive sniffing requires close proximity to the target network (or a network adjacent to the target network: Do you or should you trust your ISP?).

Active reconnaissance is where the attacker actively sends data to your network in an attempt to learn its extent, hosts, users, vulnerabilities, and so on. Tools like nmap have powerful features both for exploring networks and for obscuring the source of the attacks. You don't need such tools, however. Ping, Telnet, and finger can be used. E-mail can be used. Active reconnaissance can also be "social engineering," or outright espionage.

Think I'm paranoid? Let me tell you a little story. I have, in my consulting career, done security analysis of corporate networks. My partner got us a job trying to break into a small company's network. They never met me. We spent a little time (the time it takes to run a traceroute to their Web site) identifying their ISP. I used my color printer to make a little ID badge with that ISP's logo on it. I laminated it at the public library. The next day I paid a visit to that company with a laptop over my shoulder. I showed my badge and said I needed to change some configurations on their router. I was taken to the closet where it was stored. I plugged my laptop into their backbone. The laptop was running a little C program that captures the first 1k of data on any socket connected to port 23 (the Telnet port). I fiddled a bit with their router, not changing anything. After about 10 minutes, I asked their network guy to have everyone log in to their main machine to test. Most people did. I thanked them and left.

A couple of days later my partner went back and threw down a list of user accounts and passwords. They were flabbergasted (actually, they may not have been, but I have always wanted to use the word *flabbergasted* in a book) and had no idea how my partner had done it.

Now, I will be the first to admit that this was some time ago, when people on average were much less sophisticated about network security than they are today. Also, this was a small company with light technical expertise. But the lesson still holds. Not all your risks are technological!

Compromise

After reconnaissance comes the compromise phase. At this point the attacker knows some specific information about your network and the systems on it. He (or she) has selected one or more known vulnerabilities. He will now exploit one or more of these weaknesses to compromise one or more accounts on the system.

Obfuscation

The next phase is obfuscation. Here the attacker will try to eliminate all evidence of the intrusion.

Entrenchment

The next phase is entrenchment. Here the attacker will both enlarge the set of compromised accounts and systems and create additional holes to come through if the initial routes are found and blocked.

At this point you are pretty much done for. Your only chance to get the attacker out and keep them out is to disconnect from the Net, wipe all the machines, and install from scratch, being sure this time to apply all of those annoying security updates from your vendors.

Obviously, the earlier you can detect and head off an attack, the better. Once the entrenchment phase has been reached, it is very difficult to get the intruders out, because they generally have all the power your system administrators have, and have probably compromised multiple systems in multiple ways. The only certain way to get rid of them is to disconnect from the outside world and start from scratch, loading everything off read-only media. Even this is problematic if you have data and code you must restore from backups. Unless you know exactly when your system was compromised and have a backup that hasn't been mounted since before that date of compromise, you have no trustworthy copy of that code or data. This chapter and the next are about preventing this dilemma. This chapter covers detecting compromise. The next covers a better place to stop them: during reconnaissance.

Prints and Fibers

Just as a murderer will leave behind prints and fibers, most network host security compromisers will leave some evidence behind. Automated "exploits" combine the compromise, obfuscation, and entrenchment phases.

The emergence of these scripted attacks makes it much more difficult to detect an intrusion. Before these tools were developed, there was a considerable lag between the compromise of the system and the manipulation of system and log files to hide the attackers' presence. Nowadays mere seconds or even milliseconds may separate these events.

Obviously it becomes very important to know when these critical system files change, who changed them, and why. Often this is the only way to tell a compromise has occurred. What you need is the computer equivalent of a forensics expert, someone who can recover the prints and fibers of the scripted network-based system compromise. That expert is *Tripwire*. In this chapter we will introduce this tool and show you a little of how it works and how it can help you improve the security of your Linux system.

Tripwire

The version of Tripwire we discuss here is the version available under Debian. Tripwire is one of those products that began life as free software but was taken closed by its authors and is now a commercial product. You can find the commercial version at *http://www.tripwire.com/*, and their product is at version 2.2.1. As with SSH, the open source version has been "adopted" and is also being actively developed. The open source version can be found at *http://www.tripwire.org/* and is at version 2.3-47. The version in Debian 2.2 is 1.2-16. That's the version we cover here.

What Is It?

So just what is Tripwire? As its name suggests, it is a tool that alerts you when an intruder has been in your system. You provide a configuration file that names the files and directories to be watched, and then you specify *how* you want them watched (How much change is a change? Is a permission change a change, or only modification of the contents? Etc.). From then on, whenever a change is made to a monitored file, you will know it.

How Does It Work?

Tripwire works by using so-called message digest algorithms. This technology is similar to what underlies digital signatures. In fact, a digital signature is just a message digest that has been encrypted with a private key.

A message digest function is an algorithm constructed such that it is impossible for two different messages of a given length to have the same result. There are several such functions, and Tripwire uses quite a few of them. For those of you who care, Tripwire records all of the following functions on files included in the check:

- MD5
- Snefru
- CRC32

- CRC16
- MD4
- MD2

For those of you with a deep and abiding curiosity, you can find out about all of these functions in Bruce Schneier's excellent book, *Applied Cryptography*.

Tripwire stores all of these function results in a database file. This database should be moved on to a read-only file system. You then run Tripwire periodically to check files on the system against the database. Tripwire then generates a report of added, deleted, and changed files. This report should be checked. Expected changes should be used to update the database. Any unexpected change may indicate the prints and fibers of an intruder and should be investigated.

A (Very) Brief History of Tripwire

Tripwire began its existence at Purdue Unviversity, where it was a product of the Purdue Computer Science Department's COAST project. The COAST project is a research project dedicated to reliable computing. A great deal of research in computer security, software engineering, clustering, fail-over, and other topics of systems reliability have come from COAST. Tripwire is the brainchild of Gene Kim and Eugene Spafford.

The Painful Details

The /etc/tripwire/tw.config *file*

Tripwire configuration is controlled by the */etc/tripwire/tw.config* file. This file names all of the directories and files that are to be catalogued in the Tripwire database. You may make this as large or as small as you wish. Obviously, the more files you include, the better your protection against undetected intrusion. On the other hand, Tripwire will take longer to run, and the database will be larger.

Here's a sample configuration file for us to consider:

```
#
# tripwire.config for Linux/Debian machines
#
# I have tried to provide for a reasonable, minimal configuration file.
# You will have to tune this to your own taste and needs. -- pw.
#
# I even removed some more stuff to make it fit on a floppy. -- MM
```

```
# Define variables for searching devices, tmp directories, and logfiles
@@define DEVSEARCH E+ins
@@define TMPSEARCH E+ugp
@@define LOGSEARCH L-i

# Check all files:
# (We also mention some directories explicitly, because
#  these are often put on a separate file system)
/               R
/usr            R
/usr/local      R

# Don't do these
# (/mnt is for temporarily mounted file systems;
#  do a minimal check on /home anyway;
#  no spool files except the crontab for root):
!/mnt
=/home
!/root

#
# I don't like /var since too many files change automatically. -- MM
#
#/var           R
!/var

# Log files:
#/var/log       @@LOGSEARCH
#/var/account   @@LOGSEARCH

#  /dev, /tmp and /var/tmp
#
/dev            @@DEVSEARCH
=/tmp           @@TMPSEARCH
=/usr/tmp       @@TMPSEARCH

# No checksums for less important files (documentation, word lists):
# you might want to add /usr/X11R6/man if you have X installed
!/usr/doc
!/usr/dict
!/usr/info
!/usr/man
!/usr/src

# But do check the kernel sources
/usr/src/linux
```

For the moment, ignore the macro lines (the ones that start "@@"). The basic format is one entry per line. An entry may specify a file or a directory. When it names a directory, it really names the contents of that directory and all directories and files below it.

The basic action is to include the files specified by the entry in the Tripwire database. This behavior may be modified by a character prefix. Here are the valid character prefixes and their meaning:

Prefix	Description
!	Exclude. Excludes the file. If the entry names a directory, this excludes the contents of the directory and all directories below it.
=	Exclusive prune. Excludes all directories below the named directory, but includes the contents of the directory named. Has no effect if the entry names a file.

Following the entry is an optional "select-flag" field. I like to call this field the "watch what" field. It specifies which aspects of the file are to be included in the signature database. This specifier begins with a "+" if the attributes are to be included, or with a "−" if the attributes are to be excluded. Here's the list of attributes:

Flag	Description
p	Permission. Includes the permission and mode bits in the signature. Definitely yes!
i	Inode. Include the inode number. (For those of you at home who don't know, *inodes* are the basic directory units of the file system. This can tell you if the file is moved, even if the rest of its attributes and contents are intact.)
n	Number of links. As you probably know, more than one directory entry can point to a single physical file. This can be an important one to watch. Detecting when someone manages to get a link to an important file can matter.
u	User ID. Detects changes in file ownership. Definitely yes!
g	Group ID. Detects changes in group ownership. Definitely yes!
s	Size. Size of file. Yes!
a	Access time. This will tell you when someone looks at a file. For a very few files, yes, you care. For most, not.
m	Modification time. This will tell you when somebody modifies a file. Note that this depends on the timestamps' not being interfered with. It's okay to use this, but don't rely on the modification timestamp without also including at least one of the strong file signatures (see later).
c	inode creation/modification timestamp. This is usually the date/time the file was created. However, changes in the ownerships or permission bits of a file change this date.

(continued)

Flag	Description
0	Null signature.
1	MD5 message digest signature.
2	Snefru, the Xerox secure hash function.
3	CRC32 signature. This is a POSIX 1003.2 compliant cyclic redundancy check.
4	CRC-16. This is a 16-bit CRC algorithm, *not* the CCITT 16-bit algorithm.
5	MD4 message digest signature.
6	MD2 message digest signature.
7	SHA, secure hash algorithm, from NIST.
8	Haval. A strong 128-bit signature algorithm.

Now, you may think that's rather an intimidating list. And you would be quite right too. Fortunately, there are some shortcuts to common combinations. All of the shortcuts are single-character uppercase flags that map to combinations of the base flags. Here are those special flags:

Shortcut	Flag Equivalent	Description
R	+pinugsm12-ac3456789	This is the default combination. It is for watching files that may be freely read but whose contents, ownerships, and permissions are not to change.
L	+pinug-sacm123456789	Log files. This is intended for files whose contents change frequently but whose ownerships, permissions, and locations are meant to be fixed.
N	+pinusgsamc123456789	Ignore nothing. This watches *everything*.
E	-pinusgsamc123456789	Ignore everything. This watches *nothing*. You might think this was equivalent to using the "!" prefix on an entry, but that's not so. These shortcuts may be combined with the other flags, so, for example, you might choose to watch only file access by using "E+a" after an entry.

Tripwire also supports a preprocessor and macro system. We won't cover that here, except to point out its use in our sample file. The sample shows only the macro definition capability, which lets you name a bit of text and then use the name instead of the theoretically less readable text. Our sample uses this for a few basic flag combinations.

Database Setup

There are several "modes" in which the Tripwire executable may be run. The first is this one. Before Tripwire can do anything, you must create the database.

One tip: It doesn't do much good to create a Tripwire database on a system that is already compromised. Be certain. Create your Tripwire database on a freshly installed system that has not yet been on the Internet. Failing this, make every effort to be sure that your system has not been compromised. Look for *setuid* root programs that do not need to be *setuid* root. Look for accounts in */etc/passwd* that you did not create. Look for files in */bin*, */sbin*. */usr/bin*, */usr/sbin*, */etc*, and so on whose size and content don't match those on your distribution media. We don't have time or space to give you a full rundown on how to check your system integrity. For some help on this, look to such books as *Practical Unix & Internet Security*, by Garfinkle and Spafford, and *Network Intrusion Detection, An Analyst's Handbook*, by Stephen Northcutt.

To create your database based on the rules specified in your */etc/tripwire/tw.config*, as root, run the following command:

```
# tripwire -init
```

The machine will chug, producing output that may look like this:

```
### Phase 1:   Reading configuration file
### Phase 2:   Generating file list
### Phase 3:   Creating file information database
###
### Warning:   Database file placed in ./databases/tw.db_mars.
###
###            Make sure to move this file and the configuration
###            to secure media!
###
###            (Tripwire expects to find it in '/usr/lib/tripwire/
###            databases'.)
```

It will create a directory called *databases* in the directory below that in which you run it. It is important to know that this file will *do you absolutely no good there*. You must move this file to the directory where Tripwire expects to find it.

As configured in Debian, this is */usr/lib/tripwire/databases*, and, although the file is created root owned with permissions mode 400 (only readable by owner), this is not considered secure enough. You should *immediately* transfer the file to a read-only file system (write-protected floppy or CD-R media). You should then mount the file system at the */usr/lib/tripwire/databases* directory.

Another tip: Run the init command while the machine is in single-user mode or at least while all of the machine's network interfaces are down. Why? Well, while the chance is small, it would be handy to an attacker to get a chance to modify the database file before it is transferred to the read-only media.

Database Maintenance

From time to time you will deliberately make changes to files that Tripwire is watching. If you have Tripwire set up to produce periodic reports (which you should), you probably won't want to continually receive reports for files you legitimately modified. That leads us to another mode in which Tripwire will run. That mode is called *update*. You can ask Tripwire to update its entry in the database for a specific file or directory. It's done like this:

```
# tripwire -update /etc
```

Don't trust a copy of the database you've left on your read/write media! Be sure to copy the read-only database to a root-writeable-only directory prior to running the update.

When you run the update, it will look like this:

```
### Phase 1:   Reading configuration file
### Phase 2:   Generating file list
Updating: update file: /etc
### Phase 3:   Updating file information database
###
### Old database file will be moved to 'tw.db_mars.old'
###            in ./databases.
###
### Updated database will be stored in './databases/tw.db_mars'
###            (Tripwire expects it to be moved to '/usr/lib/tripwire/
###            databases'.)
###
```

As before, this should be done in single-user mode or with all network interfaces down to prevent tampering with the database file while it is on a writeable file system. Also, as before, transfer this database to where Tripwire expects it to be, and this should be mounted on a read-only file system.

Running Tripwire

Now, you want to periodically execute Tripwire in yet a third mode. This mode, which is Tripwire's default mode, is *integrity check* mode. To run this manually, be logged in as root and run:

```
# tripwire
```

A good way to do this is with a daily cron job. Debian, in fact, runs the following script daily:

```
#!/bin/sh

DATABASE="/usr/lib/tripwire/databases/tw.db_'hostname'"
DATABASEGZIP="/usr/lib/tripwire/databases/tw.db_'hostname'.gz"
LOG=/var/log/tripwire

#
# set to user to actually send mail
MAILTO=mschwarz

#
#
# which binary do we use?
#
[ -f $DATABASE ] && TRIPWIRE=/usr/lib/tripwire/tripwire
[ -f $DATABASEGZIP ] && TRIPWIRE=/usr/lib/tripwire/ztripwire

#
# do not run if there is no database file
#
[ -z "$TRIPWIRE" ] && exit 0

#
# rotate the log file if it exists
#
if [ -f $LOG ]; then
        savelog -p -g adm -m 640 -u root -c 7 $LOG > /dev/null
fi

#
# run the check
#
$TRIPWIRE -q > $LOG

#
# if the temporary file is empty, do not send mail
#
[ ! -s $LOG -o -z "$MAILTO" ] && exit 0

(cat <<EOF;
This is an automated report of possible file integrity changes,
    generated by
the Tripwire integrity checker.

Changed files/directories include:
EOF
cat $LOG
) | /usr/bin/mail -s "File integrity report" $MAILTO
```

The report thus generated looks like this:

```
From root@schwarz Mon Mar 26 12:23:23 2001
Envelope-to: mschwarz@schwarz
Received: from root by mars.n0zes.ampr.org with local (Exim 3.12 #1
          (Debian))
         id 14hbeF-0000Pv-00
         for <mschwarz@schwarz>; Mon, 26 Mar 2001 12:23:23 -0600
To: mschwarz@schwarz
Subject: File integrity report
Message-Id: <E14hbeF-0000Pv-00@mars.n0zes.ampr.org>
From: root <root@schwarz>
Date: Mon, 26 Mar 2001 12:23:23 -0600
Status: RO

This is an automated report of possible file integrity changes, generated
    by the Tripwire integrity checker.

Changed files/directories include:
added:   -rwxr-xr-x root          98 Oct 19 13:51:31 1998 /usr/bin/cup
added:   -rwxr-xr-x root         260 Oct  5 20:45:46 1998 /usr/bin/jlex
added:   -rwxr-xr-x root       10128 Jan  4 07:55:10 2000 /usr/bin/pwgen
added:   drwxr-xr-x root        4096 Mar 26 11:58:02 2001 /usr/share/CUP
added:   drwxr-xr-x root        4096 Mar 26 11:58:02 2001
    /usr/share/CUP/java_cup
added:   -rw-r--r-- root       14331 Oct 19 13:51:31 1998
    /usr/share/CUP/java_cup/Main.class
added:   drwxr-xr-x root        4096 Mar 26 11:58:02 2001
    /usr/share/CUP/java_cup/runtime
added:   -rw-r--r-- root        1055 Oct 19 13:51:31 1998
    /usr/share/CUP/java_cup/runtime/Symbol.class
added:   -rw-r--r-- root        8564 Oct 19 13:51:31 1998
    /usr/share/CUP/java_cup/runtime/lr_parser.class
added:   -rw-r--r-- root        1587 Oct 19 13:51:31 1998
    /usr/share/CUP/java_cup/runtime/virtual_parse_stack.class
added:   -rw-r--r-- root       13125 Oct 19 13:51:31 1998
    /usr/share/CUP/java_cup/CUP$parser$actions.class
added:   -rw-r--r-- root        1215 Oct 19 13:51:31 1998
    /usr/share/CUP/java_cup/action_part.class
added:   -rw-r--r-- root         637 Oct 19 13:51:31 1998
    /usr/share/CUP/java_cup/action_production.class
added:   -rw-r--r-- root         363 Oct 19 13:51:31 1998
    /usr/share/CUP/java_cup/assoc.class
added:   -rw-r--r-- root       12367 Oct 19 13:51:31 1998
    /usr/share/CUP/java_cup/emit.class
added:   -rw-r--r-- root         651 Oct 19 13:51:31 1998
    /usr/share/CUP/java_cup/internal_error.class
added:   -rw-r--r-- root        3901 Oct 19 13:51:31 1998
    /usr/share/CUP/java_cup/lalr_item.class
```

```
added:   -rw-r--r-- root        3930 Oct 19 13:51:31 1998
   /usr/share/CUP/java_cup/lalr_item_set.class
added:   -rw-r--r-- root        9967 Oct 19 13:51:31 1998
   /usr/share/CUP/java_cup/lalr_state.class
added:   -rw-r--r-- root        1618 Oct 19 13:51:31 1998
   /usr/share/CUP/java_cup/lalr_transition.class
added:   -rw-r--r-- root        5201 Oct 19 13:51:31 1998
   /usr/share/CUP/java_cup/lexer.class
added:   -rw-r--r-- root        3326 Oct 19 13:51:31 1998
   /usr/share/CUP/java_cup/lr_item_core.class
added:   -rw-r--r-- root        3715 Oct 19 13:51:31 1998
   /usr/share/CUP/java_cup/non_terminal.class
added:   -rw-r--r-- root         702 Oct 19 13:51:31 1998
   /usr/share/CUP/java_cup/nonassoc_action.class
added:   -rw-r--r-- root         764 Oct 19 13:51:31 1998
   /usr/share/CUP/java_cup/parse_action.class
added:   -rw-r--r-- root        1077 Oct 19 13:51:31 1998
   /usr/share/CUP/java_cup/parse_action_row.class
added:   -rw-r--r-- root        2355 Oct 19 13:51:31 1998
   /usr/share/CUP/java_cup/parse_action_table.class
added:   -rw-r--r-- root         521 Oct 19 13:51:31 1998
   /usr/share/CUP/java_cup/parse_reduce_row.class
added:   -rw-r--r-- root        1390 Oct 19 13:51:31 1998
   /usr/share/CUP/java_cup/parse_reduce_table.class
added:   -rw-r--r-- root       16045 Oct 19 13:51:31 1998
   /usr/share/CUP/java_cup/parser.class
added:   -rw-r--r-- root        8191 Oct 19 13:51:31 1998
   /usr/share/CUP/java_cup/production.class
added:   -rw-r--r-- root        1072 Oct 19 13:51:31 1998
   /usr/share/CUP/java_cup/production_part.class
added:   -rw-r--r-- root        1241 Oct 19 13:51:31 1998
   /usr/share/CUP/java_cup/reduce_action.class
added:   -rw-r--r-- root        1223 Oct 19 13:51:31 1998
   /usr/share/CUP/java_cup/shift_action.class
added:   -rw-r--r-- root        1106 Oct 19 13:51:31 1998
   /usr/share/CUP/java_cup/sym.class
added:   -rw-r--r-- root         962 Oct 19 13:51:31 1998
   /usr/share/CUP/java_cup/symbol.class
added:   -rw-r--r-- root        1555 Oct 19 13:51:31 1998
   /usr/share/CUP/java_cup/symbol_part.class
added:   -rw-r--r-- root        2747 Oct 19 13:51:31 1998
   /usr/share/CUP/java_cup/symbol_set.class
added:   -rw-r--r-- root        2335 Oct 19 13:51:31 1998
   /usr/share/CUP/java_cup/terminal.class
added:   -rw-r--r-- root        2598 Oct 19 13:51:31 1998
   /usr/share/CUP/java_cup/terminal_set.class
added:   -rw-r--r-- root         560 Oct 19 13:51:31 1998
   /usr/share/CUP/java_cup/version.class
added:   -rw-r--r-- root         184 Oct 19 13:51:31 1998
   /usr/lib/menu/cup
added:   -rw-r--r-- root         192 Oct  5 20:45:46 1998
   /usr/lib/menu/jlex
```

```
added:   drwxr-xr-x root         4096 Mar 26 11:58:03 2001 /usr/lib/JLex
added:   drwxr-xr-x root         4096 Mar 26 11:58:03 2001
    /usr/lib/JLex/JLex
added:   -rw-r--r-- root          653 Oct  5 20:45:46 1998
    /usr/lib/JLex/JLex/CAcceptAnchor.class
added:   -rw-r--r-- root         1003 Oct  5 20:45:46 1998
    /usr/lib/JLex/JLex/CAccept.class
added:   -rw-r--r-- root         2477 Oct  5 20:45:46 1998
    /usr/lib/JLex/JLex/JavaLexBitSet.class
added:   -rw-r--r-- root         1072 Oct  5 20:45:46 1998
    /usr/lib/JLex/JLex/CAlloc.class
added:   -rw-r--r-- root          819 Oct  5 20:45:46 1998
    /usr/lib/JLex/JLex/CBunch.class
added:   -rw-r--r-- root          809 Oct  5 20:45:46 1998
    /usr/lib/JLex/JLex/CDTrans.class
added:   -rw-r--r-- root          896 Oct  5 20:45:46 1998
    /usr/lib/JLex/JLex/CDfa.class
added:   -rw-r--r-- root        19984 Oct  5 20:45:46 1998
    /usr/lib/JLex/JLex/CEmit.class
added:   -rw-r--r-- root         2997 Oct  5 20:45:46 1998
    /usr/lib/JLex/JLex/CError.class
added:   -rw-r--r-- root         2129 Oct  5 20:45:46 1998
    /usr/lib/JLex/JLex/CInput.class
added:   -rw-r--r-- root        27688 Oct  5 20:45:46 1998
    /usr/lib/JLex/JLex/CLexGen.class
added:   -rw-r--r-- root         5413 Oct  5 20:45:46 1998
    /usr/lib/JLex/JLex/CMakeNfa.class
added:   -rw-r--r-- root         5984 Oct  5 20:45:46 1998
    /usr/lib/JLex/JLex/CMinimize.class
added:   -rw-r--r-- root         1370 Oct  5 20:45:46 1998
    /usr/lib/JLex/JLex/CNfa.class
added:   -rw-r--r-- root         5462 Oct  5 20:45:46 1998
    /usr/lib/JLex/JLex/CNfa2Dfa.class
added:   -rw-r--r-- root          642 Oct  5 20:45:46 1998
    /usr/lib/JLex/JLex/CNfaPair.class
added:   -rw-r--r-- root         1082 Oct  5 20:45:46 1998
    /usr/lib/JLex/JLex/CSet.class
added:   -rw-r--r-- root         3260 Oct  5 20:45:46 1998
    /usr/lib/JLex/JLex/CSpec.class
added:   -rw-r--r-- root         3173 Oct  5 20:45:46 1998
    /usr/lib/JLex/JLex/CUtility.class
added:   -rw-r--r-- root         1031 Oct  5 20:45:46 1998
    /usr/lib/JLex/JLex/Main.class
deleted: drwx------ root         4096 Mar 23 09:23:18 2001
    /usr/lib/tripwire/databases
deleted: -rw------- root     13318151 Mar 23 09:30:17 2001
    /usr/lib/tripwire/databases/tw.db_mars
deleted: -rw------- root     12973625 Mar 23 09:23:28 2001
    /usr/lib/tripwire/databases/tw.db_mars.old
changed: -rw-r--r-- root         3688 Mar 26 09:52:05 2001
    /lib/modules/2.4.2/modules.dep
changed: drwxr-xr-x root        32768 Mar 26 11:58:03 2001 /usr/bin
```

```
changed: drwxr-xr-x root         4096 Mar 26 11:58:02 2001 /usr/share
changed: drwxr-xr-x root        32768 Mar 26 11:58:03 2001 /usr/lib
changed: drwxr-xr-x root         8192 Mar 26 11:58:03 2001 /usr/lib/menu
changed: drwxr-xr-x root         4096 Mar 26 11:27:24 2001 /etc
changed: -rw-r--r-- root          359 Mar 26 09:52:02 2001 /etc/motd
changed: -rw-r--r-- root          201 Mar 26 11:27:24 2001 /etc/mtab
changed: -rw-r--r-- root           45 Mar 25 23:46:36 2001 /etc/adjtime
changed: -rw-r--r-- root         1150 Mar 26 11:54:17 2001 /etc/passwd
changed: -rw-r--r-- root          394 Mar 25 20:38:45 2001 /etc/fstab
changed: -rw------- root           60 Mar 26 09:52:02 2001
    /etc/ioctl.save
changed: drwxr-xr-x root         4096 Mar 26 11:58:11 2001 /etc/X11/twm
changed: -rw-r--r-- root        18315 Mar 26 11:58:11 2001
    /etc/X11/twm/menudefs.hook
changed: drwxr-xr-x root         4096 Mar 26 11:58:11 2001
    /etc/X11/WindowMaker
changed: -rw-r--r-- root        14127 Mar 26 11:58:10 2001
    /etc/X11/WindowMaker/menu.hook
changed: -rw-r--r-- root          553 Mar 26 11:58:11 2001
    /etc/X11/WindowMaker/appearance.menu
changed: -rw-r--r-- root           46 Mar 26 09:53:17 2001
    /etc/resolv.conf
changed: -rw-r--r-- root         3822 Mar 26 09:52:05 2001
    /etc/modules.conf
changed: -rw-r--r-- root         3822 Mar 26 09:52:05 2001
    /etc/modules.conf.old
changed: -rw-r--r-- root         4843 Mar 26 11:52:58 2001
    /etc/enscript.cfg
changed: prw-r----- root         4096 Mar 26 10:28:58 2001 /dev/xconsole
changed: -rw-rw-rw- root            0 Mar 26 10:13:07 2001 /dev/log
```

Tripwire Forensics

The report Tripwire gave us was rather lengthy. That's because I deliberately did a number of things to the system. Some were routine activities (installing a new software package, unmounting the read-only file system that contains the Tripwire database, and so on), and some were deliberate *acts of pure evil!* Now, I happen to know which were which. But if you did not, how would you go about finding out which were innocent activities and which were the *acts of pure evil?* There's no empirical way, but we can offer you a few suggestions.

First of all, when you see files added in normal system directories, you should know about it, because only root should be able to do this and only you (or your fellow system administrators) should have root authority. If this is your home desktop system and only you install software on it, be very suspicious of any such changes you don't recognize. If you are part of a group that has root authority and you don't know about these added packages, be suspicious, ask everyone else who has that privilege, and then take appropriate action. If you know (as I did) that you installed pwgen, cups, and JLex, then all is well with those added files.

One thing I would do systematically with added files, however, is to check to see if any of them are setuid root. Any new setuid root file is suspicious. If you don't know what this means, check out the man pages for the chmod command.

Next, the deleted files aren't really. As I said earlier, I had unmounted a copy of the Tripwire databases. Note that it was a copy. Had I unmounted the copy Tripwire used to compare, then the compare would not have worked!

That leaves the changed files. Some of the changed files are directories and correspond to some of the file adds and deletes. Some of the changes, such as */etc/enscript.cfg*, were changes I made deliberately to the configuration of certain programs. Changes that should stand out are those made to critical system files. In this case, the ones I would be most concerned about are */etc/passwd*, which defines users allowed to log in to the system, and */etc/modules.conf*, which specifies loadable kernel modules. If you haven't changed your kernel configuration and this file has changed, I would definitely look into it.

Sure enough, these are the right things to check out. The */etc/modules.conf* change turned out to be innocent, but the */etc/passwd* change was more suspicious. Now, this wasn't a real crack attempt—I made the change to make the point—but have a look at what Tripwire caught:

```
...
...
root:x:0:0:root:/root:/bin/bash
telnetd:x:101:101::/usr/lib/telnetd:/bin/false
mysql:x:102:102:MySQL Server:/var/lib/mysql:/bin/false
ftp:x:103:103::/home/ftp:/bin/false
badboy:x:0:0::/:/bin/bash
...
...
```

I would be mighty suspicious of a second account that is user ID number zero. "badboy" is a mighty unusual account! This might be one of several ways an attacker might try to entrench him- or herself.

Summary

Tripwire is a useful part of a complete system defense. It is, however, only a part, and it is, in fact, rather the last bastion of a defense in depth. It detects system changes made by an intruder already in your system. With the tools available to the modern script kiddie, by the time Tripwire detects, your system is probably pretty messed up. Fortunately, if you have been keeping your Tripwire database on CD-R media, you can use it to undo everything the intruder has done.

No Linux system that spends any time connected to the Internet should be without Tripwire. But likewise, no such system should rely on Tripwire as its sole protection. A defense in depth should include a firewall, which is covered in Chapter 3, plus a network monitor such as the one discussed in Chapter 13.

Chapter 13

All Along the Watchtower, Part Deux

Difficult-o-Meter: 5 (as hard as this book gets)

Covers:

snort *http://www.snort.org/*

This Q & A is a work of fiction. Any similarity to the Q & A from the previous chapter is entirely coincidental.

Question: I was sitting at home, minding my own business, when one day a bunch of police, state troopers, FBI agents, ATF agents, postal inspectors, and the Publisher's Clearinghouse prize patrol came into my house and took all my computers. Apparently, my computers had been used without my knowledge to launch a denial-of-service attack, completely blocking all access to the official Britney Spears homepage. While I am embarassed that I didn't think of doing that myself, I would have had the sense not to do that from my own computers. How can I see to it that no one uses my network in this way?

Answer: The first and simplest answer is don't have your network connected to the Internet. To some extent we tell you how to do that in Chapter 3 on firewalling. The next best answer is to know as soon as possible when miscreants come padding around your network interfaces. This chapter (and Chapter 12) cover the topic of intrusion detection.

In this chapter we look at a network-surveillance tool called *Snort,* which lets you monitor your network connection to look for signs of suspicious activity and to take programmable action when that activity occurs. This is normally the province of the most expensive of expensive tools. Snort gives you most of the same capabilities in a Free Software package. This is the best way to keep intruders out of your accounts.

Introduction

In the last chapter we taught you how to detect the subtle and insidious acts of the typical script kiddie once she gains access to an account on your computer. In this chapter we will present a tool that can help you stop the barbarian at the gate.

Here we present a brief introduction to Snort, a self-described "lightweight intrusion-detection system." Snort is a kind of a supersniffer. It is a sniffer that can use rules to select out packets seen on a network interface and take selective action based on those rules. In this chapter we will present the basics of writing Snort rules, a discussion of the "standard" rulesets and why you may wish to use them, and a few observations on how Snort might fit into the security scheme of various installations.

This chapter presumes that you have a fairly extensive knowledge of the TCP/IP suite of internetworking protocols. If you do not, I would refer you to a basic text on the subject, such as Douglas E. Comer's excellent *Internetworking with TCP/IP, Volume 1: Principles, Protocols, and Architecture*.

You, as the reader, shouldn't have to care about my problems as the author, but this tool (and this chapter) is one of those that has us walking that tightrope between being too light to be useful and too heavy to be understood. Bear in mind that the overall goal throughout this book is to show you some of the exciting things you can do with Free Software. We are not writing documentation or tutorials. That said, we do aim to make the information we present in each chapter practical and useful. If I fail here, it is certainly not for want of trying.

Packet Monitoring, Logging, and Triggering

Like sniffers (described in Chapter 11), Snort watches all the packets on a given network interface. Unlike sniffers, however, Snort doesn't just dump them out to a screen or a file. No, instead it takes some sort of programmed action when packets match certain criteria. These critera and actions are specified in Snort *rules*, which we will describe in some detail later.

So Snort monitors all packets. When a packet matches a rule, the action for that rule is taken. That action may be to log the packet for later examination. It may be to alert to a serious condition. It may even be to trigger the activation of additional rules. We'll talk about how this may help a little later on.

The goal of all of this is to watch what is going on on your network, to recognize when certain kinds of activity are coming from certain places, and to make sure that activity gets noticed in time for you to do something about it.

Remember the attack sequence described in the last chapter? One of the first things a remote attacker will do is reconnaissance. He or she will probably begin by scanning hosts on your network. With Snort, you can recognize and detect the scan itself and perhaps be able to do something about it long before the intruder gets in and starts messing with your files.

In the last chapter we told you how to detect the "prints and fibers" of an intruder who has been messing about with your systems. If Tripwire is analogous to a forensics team collecting evidence after the crime, Snort is analogous to a nosy neighbor calling the cops when he sees someone skulking around your home. I don't know about you, but I would rather the miscreant were apprehended before he got into my home and began to redecorate it.

Writing Snort Rules

A Snort rule must be a single line of text. It further consists of two major parts: the rule header and the rule options. The rule header specifies the action, the protocol, the source and destination IP addresses, netmasks, and ports. The rule options follow the header on the same line and are enclosed in parentheses. A rule option is not required. Let's first go over the rule header, then we'll cover options in greater depth.

The Rule Header

The general form of a rule header is:

```
action protocol sourceAddress sourcePort direction destAddress destPort
```

None of these entries is literal text. Here's a description of each, with examples.

Action

Action	Description

alert	Generate an alert when this rule is matched. Snort is capable of generating multiple alert types. Default behavior is to write the alert to */var/log/snort*, into a subdirectory whose name is the source IP address of the IP packet that matched the rule. A file describing the alert is created in that directory. That file's name is the protocol, followed by the source port, followed by the destination port. For example, *44.94.17.30/TCP:62077-80* is one such alert file capture generated when I ran an nmap stealth scan against one of my Linux PCs that was running Snort. I chose "full" logging, so this file's contents look like this:
	`[**] SCAN nmap TCP [**]`
	`04/25-22:49:26.071117 44.94.17.30:62077 -> 44.94.17.26:80`
	`TCP TTL:43 TOS:0x0 ID:19504 IpLen:20 DgmLen:40`
	`***A**** Seq: 0x47100003  Ack: 0x0  Win: 0x1000  TcpLen: 20`
	`=+=+=+=+=+=+=+=+=+=+=+=+=+=+=+=+=+=+=+=+=+=+=+=+=+=+=+=+=+=+=+=+=+=+=+=+=+=+`
	So what is this telling us? This tells us that on April 25 at 10:49 PM (and 26.071117 seconds) an nmap TCP scan from 44.94.17.30, port 62077, was made against my machine (44.94.17.26) port 80 (the Web server port). It then gives me some additional detail about the structure of the IP datagram and TCP envelope. An nmap scan is a very common first sign of reconnaissance.

log	The packet is written to the packet log. By default, this is a human-readable decode of the packet. You can have the log written in the "standard" tcpdump format by specifying the -b switch when you run Snort.
pass	Ignore the packet.
activate	Generate an alert, then turn on another *dynamic* rule. This is useful for adding detailed alerting or triggering detailed logging when a known attack profile start is seen. This way, Snort can turn on rules that would normally generate many false positives when a trigger condition is met. It also allows Snort to be running a relatively small ruleset, increasing its capacity in normal operation.
dynamic	Idle until switched on by an *activate* rule. It then acts like a *log* rule.

By using an advanced feature (which we will not cover here), you can create your own action types and associate output plug-ins with them. Snort is another of those tools that can fill a book of its own. We won't cover output plug-ins here.

Protocol

One of *tcp*, *udp*, or *icmp*. At the moment, these are all of the protocols that Snort will examine. The Snort rules documentation from *www.snort.org* does, however, say that there may be support for additional protocols coming. It mentions *arp*, *igrp*, *gre*, *ospf*, *rip*, and *ipx*. The routing protocols would be of particular interest to any site with multiple subnets. The average home user does not have to worry about these, since in almost all cases routing is done exclusively with default routes. But if you actually use routers, it would be nice to explictly trigger on those protocols.

Don't think, however, that this means Snort can't alert on things like route spoofing. It can. You just have to use rule options to do it. We'll show you the rudiments later in the Rules Options section.

sourceAddress, sourcePort, destAddress, destPort

These are all of similar format, so we cover them together. All four of these may be lists, with list items separated by commas. White space is *not* allowed. So, for example, your *sourceAddress* might be:

```
192.168.0.0/16,10.0.0.0/24
```

The address lists specify one or more addresses that will have to match in order for the rule to be triggered. Note in this example that the netmask bits specification is allowed to name a block of contiguous addresses.

Snort will never use the Domain Naming System (DNS), so you cannot use host names in rules. Why? Several reasons actually. DNS resolution takes time and generates network traffic. Since Snort is looking at every single packet, this can get very expensive. DNS queries generally block for a considerable period of time if the DNS server is not available. DNS is also quite easily spoofed. What good would an intrusion-detection system be if it could be blocked for minutes at a time merely by doing a DoS (denial-of-service) attack on your DNS server? It will annoy you at times when you are writing rules, but remember, names are unavailable for good reasons.

You can also use the wildcard keyword *any* in any of these lists. It means what you would think: The rule will match "any" source address, port, whichever one of the fields you put *any* into.

The port lists may be comma-separated explicit lists, the *any* wildcard, or ranges specified in this format:

```
min:max
```

So if you wanted to alert on any attempt to connect to a port below 1024 on any machine from any machine, the rule would be:

```
alert tcp any any -> any 1:1024
```

(We haven't explained the arrow yet. It is important. We cover it in the next subsection.)

You can reverse the sense of any address or range with the "!" operator. So you could modify the preceding rule to exclude your local network as a source (assuming your local network is 192.168.0.0/16) like this:

```
alert tcp !192.168.0.0/16 any -> any 1:1024
```

Direction

The direction operator may be one of "->", "<-", or "<>". Earlier we suggested that the source address and port lists came first, followed by the destination address and port lists. This is true if the *direction* operator is "->". If the *direction* operator is "<-", then this is reversed. The "<>" direction operator means "bidirectional." In this case the source and destination of the packet are each considered against both address/port lists in the rule. This is useful for logging both sides of a bidirectional protocol like Telnet.

Rule Options

Rule options modify the Snort rule. The basic format of an option is:

```
keyword: arguments;
```

One or more options appear after a rule header, all enclosed in parentheses.

Rule options are very powerful, but their use is a bit muddy. Some of them just set values. Some of them further narrow whether the current packed is logged or an alert generated. Some of them alter the data in the packet. We'll mention all of the options here, but we will not fully document them. Some descriptions will be complete, and some will be full of bona fide hand waving. Be patient. We're honest, and we won't leave you wondering which is which.

Option	Description
msg	Add a descriptive message to the alert or log. The message is enclosed in double quotes. You must escape colons, quotes, and semicolons with a backslash. Example: `alert tcp any any -> 10.0.0.0/24 22 (msg: "Attempt to access SSH port";)`

(continued)

Option	Description

ttl, tos, id	These three options allow you set conditions on triggering the rule based on attributes of the IP datagram. The *ttl* option will trigger the rule if the datagram matches the specified time-to-live exactly. This can be used to try to detect traceroutes.
	The *tos* lets you match on a specific type-of-service value. The TOS field is often ignored by many IP protocol stacks and thus can be a handy subchannel for *carrying pure evil!* (NB: *pure evil* is my "technical" term for data sent to a system with malicious intent.)
	The *id* option lets you match on a fragment ID value. Some hacking tools (and let's not open the "hacker" versus "cracker" debate) set this field to particular values, such as 31337 (supposed to suggest "elite," apparently to someone who cannot spell).
	Examples:
	`alert tcp any any -> 192.168.0.0/16 any (ttl: "1"; msg: "Traceroute detect";)`
	`alert tcp any any -> 192.168.0.0/16 any (id: 31337; msg: "Stupid ELEET cracker";)`
	`log tcp any any -> 192.168.0.0/16 any (tos: 8;)`

ipopts	This allows you to condition triggering of the rule by the options portion of the IP datagram. Valid arguments are: ■ eol: end of list ■ lsrr: loose source routing ■ nop: no operation ■ satid: stream identifier ■ sec: IP security option ■ ssrr: strict source routing ■ ts: timestamp ■ rr: record route Only one option may be specified per rule. For details on IP options, consult a book like Comer's, or see RFC* 791, section 3.2.
logto	This lets you specify that any packets matching this rule be logged to a special, separate output log file. This can be useful when you want to log all activity of a certain type to a single place for special analysis.

(*continued*)

*Request For Comments. These are the documents that exhaustively detail proposed Internet standards. Every Internet standard began life as an RFC. RFCs are relentlessly technical. You have to really want to know everything to enjoy reading them.

Option	Description
	Example: `alert tcp any any -> any any (ttl: "1"; logto: "/var/log/traceroute.snort";)`
fragbits	This option allows you to test the fragmentation bits in the IP datagram. There are three frgamentation bits. The Reserved bit, the Don't Frgament bit, and the More Fragments bit. You may test if these are set by using the letters R, D, and F, respectively. Whichever bit or bits you test, you may append any of the following characters to condition the meaning of the bits specified: ▪ +, match if all specified bits are set, ignoring other bits. Without this character, having unspecified bits set is considered *not* to match. ▪ *, match if any of the specified bits are set. ▪ !, match if the specified bits are not set.
dsize	This option lets you trigger on the data size of the datagram.
flags	This option allows you to test the TCP flags for a match. Snort supports testing for eight flags. ▪ F: FIN ▪ S: SYN ▪ R: RST ▪ P: PSH ▪ A: ACK ▪ U: URG ▪ 1: Reserved bit 1 ▪ 2: Reserved bit 2
content	This is the heart of Snort's most powerful features. The *content* option lets you search for specific bytes or text in a datagram and trigger rules based on that content. This gives you nearly infinite flexibility in detecting attacks (and, alas, in generating false positives). The *content* option may contain text to match, or it may contain binary data to match. Binary data is generally included by putting the pipe character (|, the vertical bar) followed by the binary data in ASCII-encoded hexidecimal, and ending with another pipe character. The test is case sensitive. There are a number of additional options that have meaning only in conjunction with the *content* option. ▪ *offset:* This sets the start position for the content search. Content searches are expensive (they take a lot of time compared to the other tests Snort does), so if you can limit the content search it is wise to do so. Of course, you must try to avoid limiting the search so much that you miss an attack.

(*continued*)

Option	Description
	■ *depth:* This sets the maximum position in the datagram that will be searched by a *content* option. ■ *nocase:* This makes a content search case insensitive.
content-list	This option is like the *content* option and may take the same modifier options. The argument to content-list is a file name. That file contains one or more content specifiers, just like the ones for the *content* option. Each physical line of the file is taken as one content specifier. A line beginning with a pound sign is ignored. Example: `log tcp any any <> $EXTERNAL_NET 80 (content-list: "/etc/snort/ badweb.content";)`
seq	This tests whether the TCP datagram has a sequence number set. According to the Snort documentation, this is pretty much useless and "was included for the sake of completeness."
ack	Most of the time this would be as useless as the preceding option. However, one of the most popular network reconnaissance tools, nmap, does a little trick to see if a host is active. It sets the TCP header's *ack* field (which is the stream position being acknowledged) to zero and then sends a packet with the TCP ACK flag set. Any working TCP stack will respond to such a packet. So this otherwise-useless option, which checks for a nonzero *ack* field, becomes quite useful for quickly and efficiently detecting basic nmap network scans.
itype	This option triggers on the ICMP packet type field.
icode	This option triggers on the ICMP code field.
icmp_id	This one is pretty simple on its face, but it is part of a tool for checking for some of the sneakiest network attacks. Every ICMP echo request and reply has an ID field. Normally, this is a monotonically increasing integer designed to distinguish one ping packet from another when the replies come back, since these may definitely arrive out of sequence. Very crafty network attackers have, however, realized that they can put data in ICMP datagrams and use an invariant value in this field to make it like a TCP or User Datagram Protocol (UDP) port number. If ICMP Echo requests and replies are allowed through your firewall (and the RFCs say they should be, but it really isn't absolutely necessary), then this becomes a "stealth channel" for any old data an attacker wants to pass in and out. A number of naughty people have used this. Usually, a user on the attacked network is tricked into running a program (a Trojan horse) that will open a server that listens for ICMP packets with a particular ID. This opens the channel for any data to move in and out of your network, probably undetected. For some examples, grep -i for "stacheldraht" in the Snort rules library files.

(*continued*)

Option	Description
rpc	This option lets you match for hits on a Remote Procedure Call (RPC) to a given application, procedure, and version. Each of these three is expressed as a number. You must match on the application number exactly, but you may use an asterisk (*) as a wildcard for the procedure and version numbers. A tutorial on RPC is well beyond our scope here. Be aware, however, that RPC lies at the heart of a very important protocol in *nix networks: NFS. So, if you are not familiar with at least the rudiments of the Remote Procedure Call protocol, it is worth your study.
session	The *session* option lets you log the contents of an entire TCP session using a single rule. This is a very expensive operation and, when Snort is watching a busy high-speed interface, may lead Snort to miss packets. It is better to use this option when running Snort against a binary log file. That said, if you are on a low-speed connection or on a DSL or cable modem and have a very fast machine, this can be very useful. This takes one of two arguments: *printable* or *all*. When you use *printable*, only printable ASCII characters are logged from the stream. When you specify *all*, nonprintable characters are logged as ASCII-encoded hexidecimal. Example: `log tcp any any <> 216.17.15.13/24 23 (session: printable;)`
resp	Now we get to something really cool. We've talked about Snort as a more or less passive process, monitoring for intrusion attempts across a network. Snort is also, in its most recent versions, able to act as an instrument of policy enforcement. The *resp* option allows Snort to take action when a rule is matched. The actions that may be taken are: ■ rst_snd: Send TCP RST packets to the sending socket. This is like the receiving socket closing the connection. ■ rst_rcv: Send TCP RST packets to the receiving socket. This is like the sender closing the connection. ■ rst_all: Combine both of the preceding actions. ■ icmp_net: Send an Internet Control Message Protocol (ICMP) Network Unreachable packet to the sender. ■ icmp_host: Send an ICMP Host Unreachable packet to the sender ■ icmp_port: Send an ICMP Port Unreachable packet to the sender. ■ icmp_all: Send all of the preceding ICMP packets to the sender. Multiple actions may be specified in the option. Separate them with commas. Example: `alert any any -> any 23 (msg: "Telnet access forbidden"; resp: rst_all,icmp_all;)`

(continued)

Option	Description
	This feature will work best if Snort is running on the firewall box, because then it has the best chance of sending its RST/ICMP packets before the original packets are seen by the local host. It will still close a connection even if it is running on just an internal machine, but the internal target could conceivably respond first and exchange some data before Snort closes it.
react	This is another fun one (although I have certain reservations about the implementation, which I will enumerate shortly). This works similarly to the *resp* option, except it is intended specifically for blocking Web accesses. The arguments to this option are: ■ block: Close the connection and send a message to the browser. ■ warn: Send a message to the browser. ■ msg: Include the text from the *msg* option in the visible message to the browser. ■ proxy: Send the message to the proxy port specified. This option allows you not only to close the connection, but to put up a readable notice on the Web browser attempting access that explains that this is an inaccessible site or service. If you use this option in conjunction with the *content* option, you can try to block all access to sites whose content contains certain keywords, for example. I have a few problems with the implementation of this feature. First, the HTML of the text returned is hard coded in the *sp_react.c* file in Snort. It contains a hard-coded mailto: anchor tag that will send mail to someone in Poland, which I'm guessing you do not want to do. It only sends its HTML content if the traffic is bound for port 80. It is, of course, possible to make HTTP connections to other ports. The HTML code as shipped in *sp_react.c* includes JavaScript. Not every Web browser supports JavaScript, and JavaScript has some painful variations between browser products. If you want to use this feature, I strongly advise you to get the Snort source code and customize the HTML embedded in *sp_react.c*. The port 80 limitation is another thing to bear in mind. Your users could find their way around it.

There are a couple more things you can put in a Snort rules file. For one, you will use some of the same network address specifications over and over again. Instead of typing 10.0.0.0/24 all over the place, you may create a variable:

```
var INTERNAL_NET 10.0.0.0/24
```

The other thing you can do is to "bring in" rules from other files with the *include* directive:

```
include: "/var/lib/snort.rules"
```

Attack Profiles

Attacks fall into patterns. One of the common ways to break into a system is through inherently insecure protocols, such as Network File System (NFS) and Trivial File Transfer Protocol (TFTP). So you might decide to write yourself some rules that detect any attempt to use these protocols from anywhere outside of your trusted network.

As we said in the last chapter, many attacks begin with reconnaissance using tools like nmap and queso to identify hosts and systems on your network and to look for potentially vulnerable services running on that network. Thus, another thing you might want is a collection of rules that can recognize a port scanner like nmap.

This is beginning to sound a bit daunting, isn't it? If you have to think up rules for every possible way your network might be probed or attacked from the outside, why, you could spend the rest of your life writing Snort rules, couldn't you? Yes, you could. But this is Free Software, remember. Someone has probably done most of this work already. I'll tell you more about that.

The Rules of the Game—The Snort Rules Library

Luckily for you and your keyboard, rules to detect a great many of the possible *acts of pure evil!* out there have already been written, and Snort comes with quite a library of them. Here's a quick list:

- backdoor.rules
- ddos.rules
- dns.rules
- dos.rules
- exploit.rules
- finger.rules
- ftp.rules
- icmp.rules
- info.rules
- local.rules
- misc.rules
- netbios.rules
- policy.rules
- rpc.rules
- rservices.rules

- scan.rules
- smtp.rules
- sql.rules
- telnet.rules
- virus.rules
- web-cgi.rules
- web-coldfusion.rules
- web-frontpage.rules
- web-iis.rules
- web-misc.rules
- x11.rules

Once again, we could write an entire book on Snort. We're just trying to get you started. I won't give you details on each of these predefined collection of rules, although I will go over how to set up to use them. We'll concentrate on how you would set up Snort from scratch to use one or more of these predefined rulesets as a base for an intrusion-detection system for your network. But first, I want to give you a warning you will almost certainly ignore.

The Unbearable Lightness of False Positives

The temptation when you get access to a powerful new toy, er, tool like Snort is to overuse it. At first you will turn on every single rule. You will set them to the detailed alert mode. You will have the alerts send you pages on your cell phone. Don't!

The rule library is very conservative. Many of the rules will be triggered by ordinary activity on a large and complex network. You will be paged perpetually. These events are called *false positives*. The real problem with them is not that you will be pestered and hounded but that you might raise so many things to an alert level that you will miss the real cracking attempts because you are buried up to your eyes in employees accessing E-bay.

Another mistake is to use the rule libraries without giving any thought to the details of your environment. If you use only Apache Web servers, you probably don't need the rules in *web-iis.rules*. Are you using Snort on a single box to watch for attempts to break into just that box, or are you using it in your DMZ to watch all attempts to get through your firewall?

I haven't got room to tell you how to design an intrusion-detection system. I'm just showing you the basics of Snort. Remember that while the tool may be one-size-fits-all, you do actually have to pull in the drawstrings if you are going to keep the rain out.

Keep some of these elements in mind when you are figuring out how to fit Snort into your setup:

How many networks, hosts, routers do I want to watch?

What potentially vulnerable services do I want to monitor?

Do I or can I trust my internal hosts?

How many "ports of entry" do I have, and can Snort see them all?

How much computer power do I need? Snort can easily watch a 28.8-kbps PPP link running on a 486, but to watch an asynchronous transfer mode (ATM) router you might need a bit more than that.

That's not an exhaustive list by any means. It's just the start of the sort of questions you must ask yourself when planning to deploy Snort or indeed any other IDS (intrusion-detection system) tool.

Defending Your Home

I'm going to assume a medium-small (extra medium?) case. Let's assume that you have a home network consisting of multiple PC-type boxes. Some are running Linux, some are running some other operating system. I'll assume you have a dialup ISP using PPP that assigns you a dynamic IP address. I'll further assume that your Linux box does the dialup on demand and that it acts as a simple masquerading firewall, allowing the rest of your PCs to share that one dialup link to the network over an IP Ethernet.*

We're not done making assumptions yet. Let us further assume that the internal network is implemented with a nonrouting IP network address—in this case, 10.0.0.0—and we'll use a netmask of 255.255.255.0, or 24 bits. We'll assume the dialup is implemented on interface ppp0 and the internal network is on eth0. We will assume that simple masquerading is being used, rather than explicit firewall rules, and that there is no DMZ (if these terms are unfamiliar, consider taking a look at the IP-firewalling HOWTO document).

---

*By a remarkable coincidence, this is exactly what my home network looks like. I know, what kind of a geek am I to still be on a dialup link? I blame my wife (sorry, honey!). You see, she's into horses, so we built out in the sticks. I am sitting at the end of the longest analog phone line in my entire county. That's no exaggeration. So no DSL for me. Cable? Hah! If you get enough of your friends to buy this book, maybe I'll lay in an FDDI line.

Let us further assume that we will use the predefined Snort rules libraries to set our detector. You will notice that the library makes use of a few variables. The most important of these are $EXTERNAL_NET and $HOME_NET. These variables allow you to specify the network addresses and netmasks of your internal and external networks. Given the assumptions we have made, the best choice would be to set $HOME_NET to 10.0.0.0/24 and $EXTERNAL_NET to !10.0.0.0/24.

The simplest way to make use of the library is to define your own "master" rules file. I frequently see this named *snort.conf* and located in */etc/snort*. Here's what I would put in our *snort.conf* file:

```
# Local snort configuration file, sample for Multitool Linux
# $Id: chapter13.html,v 1.1.1.1 2001/11/02 03:12:25 mschwarz Exp $

var HOME_NET [10.0.0.0/24]
var EXTERNAL_NET [!10.0.0.0/24]

include: "/etc/snort/ddos.rules"
include: "/etc/snort/scan.rules"
include: "/etc/snort/exploit.rules"
```

There are other variables used in the Snort rules library. Many of these specify the addresses of servers running specific services. Snort will tell you if you include a rules file that has variables you have not yet defined.

Note that this is for illustration only. I do *not* recommend this particular configuration. Which rule libraries you choose to use should be based on comparing the rule-sets against the kind of services you run and the kind of network you have. You should also make some decisions based on whether you want to know about any attempts on your network or only reports of attempts that get through.

One common thing to do (if you have machines to spare) is to set up Snort to detect only the most serious issues "outside" the firewall and to have one set to detect absolutely everything inside the firewall. That way, you see only the most dangerous attacks when they are made on the outside, whether or not they succeed, and you see any suspicious activity that makes its way to the inside.

Running Snort

Snort can be executed in many ways. It can be started to run in the foreground or as a daemon. It may be started to watch a network interface, or it may be started to read a binary dump from a tool like TCPDump. We will not cover all of the command line options for Snort. You have a Snort man page (or should) for that. We will basically show you how to use our example *snort.conf* file to watch your dialup interface and do it as a daemon. Here's the command line to do that:

```
# snort -A full -c /etc/snort/snort.conf -D -h 10.0.0.0/24 -i ppp0
```

Here, briefly is what these arguments do: The -A argument specifies how alerts will be formatted. The "full" option produces the output shown in the "alert" box of the action table. The -c argument specifies the rules file, in this case, the *snort.conf* file we made that includes a number of the Snort rules library files. The -D flag tells Snort to run as a daemon. The -h flag names the local network. Alerts from nonlocal addresses will be placed in */var/log/snort* in a subdirectory whose name is the dotted decimal IP address of the remote computer that triggered the alert. The -i flag tells Snort to sniff packets from the ppp0 interface.

For details on the many command line options to Snort and their use, consult the Snort man page.

Why You Should Know How to Do It Yourself

The Snort rules are updated frequently and it is tempting to rely on them entirely. To a large extent, this is a good idea. But it is a mistake to rely on these externally defined rules to the exclusion of understanding the construction and purpose of the Snort rules language.

Why? First, there is the basic issue of trust. How do you know that the person or persons constructing those rules are reliable, capable, and trustworthy? I'm not for a moment suggesting they are not, but you are trusting your network to them. If your network is like mine, you have your personal data, your personal and business financial data, work in progress for clients, and the odd manuscript or two on it. Now ask yourself again if you trust rulesets from someone you have never met who has intentions unknown to you.

To borrow an adage from Cold War arms control negotiations, "Trust but verify." You should review the rulesets you use so that, at a minimum, you understand what the rules are doing so that you know something about what an alert actually means when you get one. Also, you should be comfortable "tuning" the rules to your own needs. You might want to send certain alerts to syslogd with a fixed prefix you can use to trigger a Perl script that sends you a page message, for example.

Second, the sad but simple truth is that using an intrusion-detection system you don't understand is little better than having no such system. In some ways it is worse, because you now have a false sense of security. You assume that the absence of alerts means no attempts are being made and your system is secure. This is the reason we presented Tripwire first. To borrow from the Cold War again (and this is an apt metaphor, because it is fair to say that crackers and defenders are engaged in an arms race of attack versus defense tools), you need "defense in depth."

Snort is an extremely effective part of your network defense, but it can be much more effective when used as part of a system of defense. I recommend a minimum five-part defense:

1. Snort on the outside, set to alert only on extremes.
2. A properly configured firewall; at minimum a transparent outbound masquerade with no back channels. Ideally explicit rules set for outbound traffic as well as inbound.
3. Snort set to alert on practically everything on the inside network.
4. Tripwire on all hosts to monitor for changes on host file systems.
5. Proper ownership/permissions/setuid settings on all files, checked periodically on all hosts.

That seems like a simple list, but the devil is in the details. I recommend reading *Practical Unix and Internet Security*, by Garfinkle and Spafford, particularly Part 5, to learn some of the intricacies involved.

What We Didn't Cover

Snort has *preprocessors* that can defragment IP datagrams before the rules engine sees them, decode HTTP protocol strings so the URI Escapes are undone before you check packets with the *content* option, do portscan detection, perform TCP stream reassembly, and even do statistical packet-anomaly detection. These are very useful and powerful features and you should learn them.

We didn't cover defining your own rule actions (for the C literate, this is a kind of "typedef" for Snort rules).

We didn't cover output modules. (Note to Debian users: As of this writing, the version of Snort available in Debian 2.2 doesn't have output module support.) Output modules allow you to specify a series of "postprocessors" (Snort calls them *output plug-ins*) that will be handed packets that match a rule. Snort comes with a number of these predefined, and you may write your own if you wish (remember, it is *your* source code). This is another powerful capability, and some of the provided plug-ins, like Xml and Alert_unixsock can greatly expand the capabilities of Snort. This is another area you should explore on your own.

Summary

Snort is a very powerful tool for improving the security of whole networks. It is only as good as you are, however. This tool is not best used by someone who doesn't understand the IP, ICMP, TCP, UDP, and RPC protocols at a fundamental level. It is also most effective as part of a defense in depth.

If you are not particularly knowledgeable about TCP/IP and Linux administration, don't let the difficulty of this topic and this chapter drive you away from Linux and into the comforting but feeble arms of "easier" systems. Any operating system that implements any service using TCP/IP (and if you use the Internet, then your system is using TCP/IP) is potentially vulnerable to these types of attack. There is nothing about Linux that makes it more vulnerable, and there are some things about it, such as its user-level system security, that make it less vulnerable, certainly, than the "non-server" PC operating systems.

There are commercial products that have some capabilities Snort lacks, but this is a book about free software. I would also say that argument I made about trusting rules supplied by others applies in spades to security products for which you do not have the source code. The one good argument for trusting closed-source security products is that companies have a strong economic incentive to keep your trust. Experience has shown, however, that this pressure has not been sufficient to get companies to close security holes in a timely manner. Snort is an important part of a complete security plan, but it is not, in itself, a security solution.

References

Snort

- Snort FAQ: *http://www.snort.org/FAQ.html*
- Rules Documentation: *http://www.snort.org/writing_snort_rules.htm*
- White Paper (old): *http://www.snort.org/lisapaper.html*

Chapter 14

SECURE CONNECTIVITY

Difficult-o-Meter: 2 (light Linux skill required)

Covers:

OpenSSH 2.1.1 *http://www.openssh.com*

This chapter is in two major sections. The first covers secure login and file transfer. The second covers getting through a firewall (breaking security) and then applying tools to make secure firewall penetration possible.

Question: I've been logging in to various machines using Telnet for several years now. Apparently people can see everything you type when you use Telnet. I found this out when the bank called asking when they could expect my next payment on the QE-2 and when the very polite Secret Service man asked me to explain my e-mail to the First Lady. Now that I've cleared up these little misunderstandings, how can I avoid these problems in the future? Also, my boss is mad at me because I sent a certain patient's medical records by FTP to his new doctor and shortly thereafter he got a phone call from Tom Brokaw asking just exactly how the senator got syphilis. How can I avoid *that* little problem in the future?

Answer: You've learned yet another lesson. It isn't just e-mail and Web activity that needs protection from prying eyes. You should secure everything you use. There is a wonderful tool called *secure shell*, or SSH, that can secure your logins and your file transfers (and—as you will see if your read the next section as well—so much more). We'll here introduce you to a completely free implementation of SSH called OpenSSH. Let's be careful out there.

We've all used Telnet to log in to another machine. We've all used FTP to transfer files to and from our accounts on Linux boxes. We've all been running around a global network, offering everyone out there the keys to our computers. "What's that?" you say. "I've done no such thing! I have strong passwords and I change them every month. No one can get into my system." Sure. And I've got a bridge to sell you.

If you use Telnet and FTP, you have been broadcasting your user names and passwords all over the Internet. Don't believe me? See Chapter 11, and then come back here with a renewed sense of fear and dread. This chapter will take away that fear and dread. I'm going to show you both how to log in to remote machines and how to transfer files between machines in such a way that not only will it be impossible to see your passwords, but it will also be impossible to see what you are typing or what you are transferring.

Secure Shell (SSH)

We've already looked at public-key cryptography and we've shown you how you can use GPG to secure your e-mail. Now we are going to show you another program that uses similar cryptographic techniques to encrypt data streams between client and server programs on different machines. This section will show the basics: Using SSH to have "encrypted Telnet" sessions and using SCP (secure copy) to have "encrypted FTP." In the next section we will go over advanced applications of SSH, such as using it to go through firewalls but in a secure manner.

If you are already familiar with the *R tools*, RSH (remote shell) and RCP (remote copy), then you can think of SSH and SCP as encrypted work-alikes. If you are not familiar with the R tools, do not bother. Using RSH is like leaving your Porsche running with the door open while you go for a five-hour walk. Many system administrators simply remove these tools from their systems—they are that big a security hole. Instead, we will concentrate on comparing SSH to Telnet, and SCP to FTP.

In a Telnet session, a TCP socket is opened from the client machine to the server machine. There is some application-level protocol activity to set some terminal behavior preferences, but once the connection is established, it is literally keystrokes in one direction and screen output in the other. All the data passes over the network "in the clear." It is trivial, as demonstrated in Chapter 11, to reconstruct everything communicated in a Telnet session, including login passwords.

SSH works differently. SSH uses a public-key crypto system similar to that used by PGP. It's a bit more complicated, since keys are used to authenticate hosts to one another, and they may optionally be used also to validate users at hosts.

When the SSH server, known as SSHD, is first installed, a key pair is generated. Actually, two key pairs are generated, one for encryption and the other for DSA, the Digital Signature Algorithm. You generally don't need to worry about these. The key-generation process looks like this:

```
Generating RSA keys:  ...ooooooO.......ooooooO
Key generation complete.
Your identification has been saved in /etc/ssh/ssh_host_key.
Your public key has been saved in /etc/ssh/ssh_host_key.pub.
The key fingerprint is:
f8:fc:e8:43:be:15:59:c4:b5:44:48:ae:1b:d1:9e:a1 root@mars
Generating DSA parameter and key.
Your identification has been saved in /etc/ssh/ssh_host_dsa_key.
Your public key has been saved in /etc/ssh/ssh_host_dsa_key.pub.
The key fingerprint is:
f9:cc:4d:9c:da:50:ea:ad:a7:12:3a:4b:2d:11:50:13 root@mars
```

Once the host key exists, the server may be started.

```
[root@mars /root]# sshd
[root@mars /root]#
```

Of course, you should check to see if it is already running!

Now let's see what happens when you attempt to connect for the first time:

```
mars:22:~$ ssh alienmystery
The authenticity of host 'alienmystery.planetmercury.net' can't be
    established.
RSA key fingerprint is 58:f1:d0:f7:db:86:81:76:60:e2:7c:dd:d9:ff:f1:4e.
Are you sure you want to continue connecting (yes/no)?
```

Danger, Will Robinson! Danger! Harken back, if you will, to Chapter 10. Once again, you are dealing with cryptographic keys and trust. Only you can decide whether to trust the host key. Once you have done so, it is trusted for all time. Key discovery by connection is very risky. It is easily foiled by a "Man in the Middle" attack (MITM). You could be connecting to a spoofed host, where they are feeding you a key of their own creation. They will then make a connection of their own to the real host.

Just as with GPG, I prefer to ship host keys in person. In this case, however, let's throw caution to the wind and proceed:

```
Are you sure you want to continue connecting (yes/no)? yes
Warning: Permanently added 'alienmystery.planetmercury.net,216.17.15.13'
    (RSA) to the list of known hosts.
mschwarz@alienmystery.planetmercury.net's password:
```

Now when we enter the password, it is encypted and sent to the far end. It is utterly impossible for a third party to eavesdrop on it.

```
mschwarz@alienmystery.planetmercury.net's password:
Last login: Wed Jun 28 02:49:03 2000 from 209.105.15.162
Have a lot of fun...
alienmystery:~$
```

Not just the password is encrypted, however. All traffic from this point on is encrypted. No one but the two endpoints can see anything you do. No sniffer can observe your activity. Your login is secure.

Let's take a brief digression here and increase your level of paranoia. Even when your communications are fully encrypted with the kind of encryption that can defeat the resources of major governments, it is still possible to learn things about you and your communication. There is a discipline called *traffic analysis*. Some very fundamental facts are not hidden by SSH (or GPG for that matter). An observer can tell who is communicating. There is no way to obscure the addresses in communication and still get the messages delivered. Next, we can watch how much data moves in each direction, how many pauses occur and when, and from this we can deduce some things about what kind of communication is taking place. Over time we can build up a profile showing with whom you communicate securely and when. From this we can try to reach conclusions about who you are and what your intentions are. We might even have observed any and all of your open communications and be able to reconstruct your message with some accuracy if there are patterns to the pauses and rhythms of your typing.

Don't think for a moment that this is a mere academic exercise. As we learned to our horror on September 11, 2001, communications are essential to certain kinds of coordinated activity. Even if the parties involved had been communicating securely, the sudden increase in communications activity that must have taken place just prior to the attacks on the Pentagon and World Trade Center could have tipped us off.

This brings us to another question. Should cryptography be restricted or under government control? Sadly, the idea is appealing in light of recent horrible events. Unfortunately (or perhaps fortunately) it is already too late. The genie is out of the bottle. There is no way to take encryption away from the criminals. They already have it. We can only take it away from those who would use it for legitimate reasons.

File Transfer

File transfer is done with *scp*, which works just like the Linux *cp* command, with a bit of a filename extension:

```
Syntax:

scp [[<username>@]<hostname>:]<path> [[<username>@]<hostname>:]<path>

Where:  username        Name of user on host
        hostname        Name of host on which path resides
        path            Directory or filename to copy, wildcards allowed
```

Items in brackets are optional. An example should makes the case clear.

```
mschwarz@alienmystery.planetmercury.net's password:
nmap-2.12-1.i386.rpm 100% |*******************************|   175 KB  00:00
openssh-2.1.1p2-1.i3 100% |*******************************| 84117     00:00
openssh-clients-2.1. 100% |*******************************|   112 KB  00:00
openssh-server-2.1.1 100% |*******************************| 98106     00:00
```

As you can see, we copied all the RPM files from our present working directory on mars to mschwarz's present directory on the host "alienmystery." (Generally, the "." directory will be the specified user's home directory.) You can do recursive copies. You can copy to or from the remote host. All the traffic is encrypted, so no one can know what you are transferring—very nice and very secure.

X11 Forwarding

One more feature and our introduction to SSH is complete. Once you have used the client, an *.ssh* directory will appear in your home directory. You can create a configuration file in there called *config* to set options for SSH, either for all of your connections or on a host-by-host basis. I have set one up for alienmystery:

```
mars:45:~$ cat .ssh/config
Host alienmystery
ForwardX11 yes
```

Note the *ForwardX11* option. Watch what this does:

```
mars:49:~$ ssh alienmystery
mschwarz@alienmystery.planetmercury.net's password:
Last login: Wed Jun 28 03:22:22 2000 from 209.105.15.162
Have a lot of fun...
alienmystery:~$ echo $DISPLAY
alienmystery:10.0
alienmystery:~$ xload -fg blue -bg gray &
[1] 2760
alienmystery:~$
```

Notice, I started on mars, used SSH to log in to alienmystery, and then looked at my DISPLAY environment variable. Remember how displays are usually ":0" or ":0.0"? Well, ":10" isn't an X-server really. It's ssh. The sshd program on alienmystery is "listening" to display 10. If we open any X-windows, it will grab the traffic, encrypt it, *over the same link as the login session*, and pass it to the X-server on the client side! Perhaps Figure 14-1 will make it clear.

Not only is that alienmystery xload not local, but all the X-protocol data is mixed in on the same socket as our SSH login session and fully encrypted. Someone watching our network sees one open socket between us and alienmystery, no matter how many X-windows we have open. They can't tell encrypted X-traffic from our encrypted shell session.

The SSH programs provide fully secure, encrypted network login and file transfer. We shall see even more of what SSH can do for us in the next section.

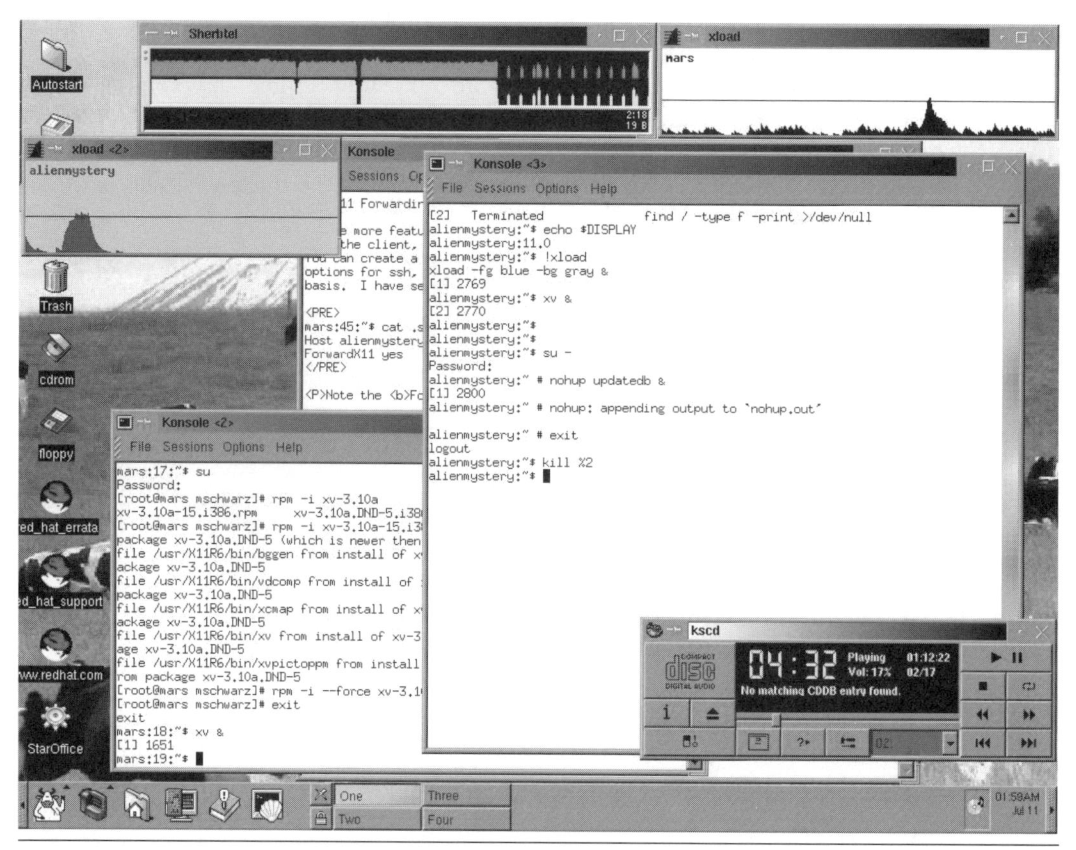

Figure 14-1 Desktop showing forwarded xload.

Telecommute through Aggressive Firewalls with SSH and Tunneling

Difficult-o-Meter: 4 (fairly high Linux knowledge required)

Covers:

OpenSSH 2.1.1	*http://www.openssh.com*
httptunnel	*http://www.nocrew.org/software/httptunnel.html*
mailtunnel	*http://www.detached.net/mailtunnel.html*
icmptunnel	*http://www.detached.net/icmptunnel/*

Problem: My office machine is behind a proxy firewall that disallows any outbound connections except FTP, Telnet, smtp, http, and httpd. It also does not allow any connections outbound that originate on the "privileged" (i.e., port numbers less than or equal to 1024) ports, no matter what service is requested on the outside. I live so far from my work site that dialing in to their terminal servers would be a long distance call, and yet I must be able to reach certain hosts and ports inside the office from my home in order to carry out my support duties. I also need to be able to do so in a manner that does not compromise the security so carefully set up by this firewall.

A Note about This Part of the Chapter

This part could be said to belong in the Networking and Communications section of the book (Chapters 2–9), since it is all about communicating effectively through firewalls. However, because OpenSSH involves authentication and encryption, and because tunneling is sometimes called *firewall piercing*, it seemed to belong in Privacy and Security as well. We chose to put it here.

I've said it before, I'm a consultant. I work for many clients. Some of these clients are in industries where security is very important indeed. Some of these clients are dealing with Other People's Money. This trust, while not, perhaps, sacred, is certainly subject to heavy-duty laws, regulations, and consequences if abused.

Let's imagine I'm working for a bank, the Fifth State Bank of Refuse. Let's imagine that they have a firewall like the one just described in the problem. Believe it or not, the scenario described there is one I really had to deal with, although it was not a bank, let alone the Fifth State Bank of Refuse. Many firewalls shut you down cold from the outside, but I had never before encountered one that shut you down so cold from the *inside*.

We'll go through two distinct paths to show how connectivity of all kinds may be given through such a firewall. The first one will illustrate the principles and demonstrate the widest range of SSH capabilities, but, as we will discover, it has fatal flaws from a security point of view. The second method is less educational but fully secure.

Beyond Login and File Transfer: SSH as Virtual Private Network

SSH is capable of much more than mere logins and file transfers. Some of this capability was suggested in the first part of the chapter when we covered X11 forwarding. It turns out we can do more. Much more.

The *.ssh/config* File

Most of this part of the chapter will concern itself with the the *.ssh/config* file located off your home directory. It is possible that this file does not yet exist. If it doesn't, create it, and then set its permissions to be at least as restrictive as 0644. A mode of 0600 is probably better. This is definitely a file you want writeable only by you.

Let's look at a sample *config* file:

```
Host alienmystery
ForwardX11 yes
LocalForward 2023 oopsbuzz:23
```

As you can see, many options may be set. We'll cover many (but by no means all) of these options in this part of the chapter. Consult the man page for OpenSSH for full details.

We will also cover a number of items in the SSH daemon option file, typically */etc/ssh/sshd_options*. We'll cover the client options first.

SSH CLIENT OPTIONS

Attribute	Description
Host	This specifies the host to which the following options will be applied. Note that this host name must be what is actually passed on the command line. If, for example, you specify an IP address on the command line and the host's DNS name appears with this option, the options will *not* be applied, because the name passed doesn't lexically match this option. Wildcards of "*" and "?" may be used (where these characters have the same meanings as in file matching); thus "Host *" may be used to set options for all hosts, and "Host *.bakery.org" may be used to set options for all hosts in the bakery.org domain. All options following a "Host" specification apply only to hosts matching the argument to this option, until another Host option is encountered, of course.
Compression	Argument must be "yes" or "no." Specifies whether data should be compressed before it is encrypted and sent. Whether this is beneficial will depend on the speed of your link and of your processors at each end. Generally, if you have fast processors at both ends of a slow link, compression is probably a good idea.
CompressionLevel	Specifies compression quality on a scale from 1 to 9, where 1 is fast but poor compression and 9 is slow but good compression. The default is 6. This seems to work well in most cases.
ForwardX11	Argument must be "yes" or "no." For X11 forwarding to work, the server side must also be set to allow this. This option is demonstrated in the X17 Forwarding section of this chapter.
GatewayPorts	Argument must be "yes" or "no"; defaults to "no." This specifies whether remote hosts will be allowed to connect to locally forwarded ports. See the later section titled "Getting Out" and the entry for *Local-Forward.*
KeepAlive	Argument must be "yes" or "no"; defaults to "yes." This specifies whether the client and the server will send periodic "keep-alive" message to one another. If a keep-alive gets no response, the connection is dropped. Usually this is desirable, since it allows either or both ends to clear their sessions if there is a loss of connectivity. This may be undesirable on a low-reliability network, since the login session and all forwarded connections and X11 windows will close.
LocalForward	See the later section, Getting Out. This command allows a port on the local (client) machine to be "forwarded" over the encrypted link to a given host and port from the remote (server) machine. This is a secure "outbound tunnel." Let's consider an example. Suppose you work for a consulting firm and you need to visit the company Web site from time to time, but company private information is kept there. You are only supposed to access it from internal machines. Well, if you have an SSH server running on your company's internal network, it is no

(continued)

SSH CLIENT OPTIONS (*cont.*)

Attribute	Description
LocalForward, (*cont.*)	problem. Put an entry like *LocalForward 2080 intranet.bodyshop.com:80* in your *.ssh/config* file. When you SSH to your SSH server (perhaps *secure.bodyshop.com*?), you will find it opens a socket *on the client machine* on port 2080. If you point your browser at *localhost:2080*, you will actually connect to port 80 on *intranet.bodyshop.com*. Not only that, but the connection will appear to come from *secure.bodyshop.com*, not from your client machine. Moreover, anyone looking at the network the client is on will just see more gibberish traffic over the single SSH connection you have open! That's right. The login shell, the X11 forwards, and the forwarded ports are all passed encrypted over the one open connection. Now you can see what the *GatewayPorts* option is for: When off, it prevents someone on any host other than the client from connecting to port 2080 on the client and getting sent through to *intranet.bodyshop.com*. There may be times when you do want to let others share the hole you open, but generally not. That's why that option defaults to "off."
Port	Specifies the port to connect to on the SSH server. Default is 22. See the later section, Maniacally Restrictive Firewalls, for more information on the use of this option.
RemoteForward	See the later section Getting In. This option is the complement of *LocalForward*. This option takes a port number to use on the server side and specifies a host and port to connect from the client. An example may make this clearer. Suppose that, in order to support the software *Bodyshop.com* has developed for a client, they need access to Telnet on a certain internal server. Let's even assume that the server has no name and is on a purely internal (10.x.x.x) network. Your client box can SSH to the outside (to *secure.bodyshop.com*) and can also reach the 10.x.x.x network. You put the option *RemoteForward 5023 10.5.1.40:23* in your *.ssh/options* file. When you SSH to *secure.bodyshop.com*, you will find a LISTEN socket open on that host on port 5023. If you were on *secure.bodyshop.com* you could then execute *telnet localhost 5023* and you would get the Telnet login prompt from 10.5.1.40 on the client network! Again, just as with the *LocalForward* scenario, the connection to 10.5.1.40 would appear to be coming from the SSH client machine and not from *secure.bodyshop.com*. Moreover, anyone sniffing anywhere from the client's firewall all the way back to *bodyshop.com* would see no Telnet traffic at all, but, rather, additional gibberish over the one open SSH connection. Together *LocalForward* and *RemoteForward* practically eliminate the need for any other type of Virtual Private Network.

(*continued*)

Attribute	Description
RSAAuthentication	Argument must be "yes" or "no." So far, all of our examples have used traditional password authentication. SSH can use many alternative methods of authentication. See the later section, Alternate Authentication Methods for details on this and some passing mention of still other methods SSH supports.
UsePrivilegedPort	See the later section Maniacally Restrictive Firewalls for details on this option.
User	Normally, SSH will try to connect to the specified host with the same username as the user running the SSH client on this host. But what if you have different usernames on different systems? You can specify the username on the SSH command line, but it is nice not to have to remember to do so. Use this option to specify your username on a given host.

There are many more options. Take a look at the SSH man pages for more details. This is quite enough to be getting on with for now.

There is also a configuration file for the SSH server. This is usually in */etc/ssh/sshd_config*. We'll take a look at some of the more interesting server options in the next table.

SSH CLIENT OPTIONS

Attribute	Description
AllowUsers	This allows you to restrict secure login to a list of users. By default, login is allowed for all users defined on the box. This keyword may be followed by a white space–separated list of names. The "*" and "?" wildcards are allowed.
DenyUsers	This command also allows you to restrict who may log in. Where *AllowUsers* allows only matching users in, *DenyUsers* allows everyone *except* matching users.
GatewayPorts	Specifies whether remote users (users connecting from other hosts) may use ports forwarded from this host by sshd for SSH clients. Unless you absolutely need this, I strongly recommend against setting this to "yes." If your server is on the "outside" (by which I mean on an unsecured public network) and you use an SSH client to forward a private port from the "inside" (by which I mean a secured private network) to the server box, you expose the port to the entire Internet! The one case where this makes sense to me is where the port you are forwarding to the outside

(continued)

SSH CLIENT OPTIONS (*cont.*)

Attribute	Description
GatewayPorts, (*cont.*)	from the inside is an sshd server port. Then it does not (in theory) decrease security to allow access to the port from the whole Internet, since you will still be using an encrypted and cryptographically authenticated connection end to end. Argument must be "yes" or "no"; defaults to "no."
ListenAddress	Specifies which local address SSHD should listen on. On a multi-homed host (a host with more than one network interface and/or more than one address per interface), the default is to accept connections from all local addresses. You may wish to restrict access to a certain interface. For example, you might configure one SSHD server with a certain set of options to listen only to the public network interface while configuring another SSHD server instance with a totally different set of options (perhaps less restrictive) to listen only to the internal network interface. This option must be preceded by the *Port* option.
PasswordAuthentication	Specifies whether an SSH client may connect to a user's account using only that user's password. So far we have shown you only this form of authentication. For most purposes, this is sufficient. If you presently use Telnet, you are so exposed to attack that simply replacing Telnet with SSH will dramatically increase your security. There are other methods of authentication that are much more secure. You might choose to use those. Argument must be "yes" or "no"; defaults to "yes."
PermitEmptyPasswords	When password authentication is allowed, this specifies whether or not login to accounts without passwords is permitted. Argument must be "yes" or "no"; defaults to "no." Never set this to "yes."
PermitRootLogin	This determines whether or not one may SSH into the root account. Argument may be "yes," "without-password," or "no." The "without-password" option disables password login for root while still allowing it for other users (depending on the setting of *PasswordAuthentication*, of course). With that setting, some other form of authentication must be used for root login. Defaults to "no." Leave this set to "no." There are other ways to gain root privilege after establishing a secure encrypted connection to an unprivileged account.
Port	Specifies the port to listen on. More than one port directive may appear.
RSAAuthentication	Specifies whether pure RSA authentication is allowed. Must be "yes" or "no"; defaults to "yes." See the later section on "Alternate Authentication Methods" for details.

(*continued*)

Attribute	Description
StrictModes	Specifies whether sshd should check permissions and modes on user SSH files before allowing login. This is a good idea, since some users leave critical files writeable, such as the key file, which totally destroys the security of the system.
X11Forwarding	Specifies whether or not X11 forwarding is permitted. Must be "yes" or "no"; defaults to "no."

As with the client options list, this is not a complete list of all the options, nor does it fully document all of the aspects of the options described. Be sure to take a look at the man pages to get the full picture.

Getting Out

Here we assume that you are inside a network that is either restrictive or highly monitored or both. Let's assume there are a couple of services you wish to reach outside. The first is your mail server (which you access via IMAP and SMTP), and the second is a Web site you wish to visit without being monitored by your network's transparent proxy. Legitimate reasons to do so abound:

- You work for a contracting company and must access company private information while at a client site.
- You need to communicate with your physician.
- Your immediate supervisor (and local network administrator) is engaged in illegal activity and you wish to report it anonymously to law enforcement authorities.

This last reason may seem unlikely, and indeed it is; but it is certainly not impossible. The first and second reasons are so commonplace that they are scarcely worth pointing out.

Let me take a moment to advise you not to abuse the capabilities we describe here. If an activity is illegal, immoral, or against company policy, the mere fact that you *may* be able to hide it from your administrators or employers doesn't change the act. If you are thinking, "Aha! This will let me surf dirty picture sites at work!" or "Aha! This will let me run my Internet stock 'Pump and Dump' scheme at work!" then let me warn you that there is more than one way to find you out. Your own computer keeps copies of Web sites you visit. Your history list may be queried when you connect to internal sites.

Step 1: Find Yourself an OpenSSH Server Outside

Before you can get out, you need someone on the outside. You need an account on a box outside the firewall. That box has to be running SSHD (the secure shell daemon), the server for SSH.

Let's assume you have a box on a DSL connection and you are running Linux on that box. Furthermore, let's assume that you have SSHD up and running on that box. The box is called *frosting.bakery.org*.

From inside you need a Linux box and the OpenSSH client. We will assume that you have connected to "bakery" for logins and file transfers as shown in the previous chapters. This means that you have generated all the keys and that the hosts know one another's public keys already.

Step 2: Check the Server Configuration

Make sure your client location is allowed in (check the *AllowHosts* and *DenyHosts* settings). Be sure to set *GatewayPorts* as appropriate for your security requirements (if forwarding a secured service, go ahead and use *GatewayPorts;* otherwise say "no.")

Step 3: Check the Client Configuration

Let's assume the client does not have an entry in your *.ssh/config* file yet. Let's add one:

```
Host frosting.bakery.org
Port 22          # This isn't really needed, 22 is the default
```

There's your base. Now let's get you access to your mail and that Web site you wish to reach unbeknownst to your client.

Step 4: Secure Access to the Server Box

Remember that you want private secure access to your e-mail services from within your client's network. You need to be able to read your mail using IMAP and to send your mail using SMTP. In all of these cases, I am going to assume that you have clients that can be made to use ports other than the defaults. If this is not so, either you may have to jump through some hoops, or you may be out of luck.

First you must select some ports on the client machine to use as "proxies" for the services you wish to receive. I like to pick a "base" port and then use the standard port numbers for services relative to the base. For example, IMAP is port 143 and SMTP is port 25. I would select a "base," like port 15000, and then I would put IMAP at 15143 and SMTP at 15025. If I ever forward any other services I would likewise move them up 15000 ports.

To make this mapping, add the following lines to *.ssh/config:*

```
Host frosting.bakery.org
Port 22         # This isn't really needed, 22 is the default
LocalForward 15143 localhost:143
LocalForward 15025 localhost:25
```

Remember, *LocalForward* is a directive to the client to forward the given port on the client machine to the given address and port *from the point of view of the server machine.* Thus, *localhost* means the server machine itself, not the client. Once you connect to the server, these port forwards are active. Now just tell your mail software to use IMAP to pick up messages from *localhost* (meaning the client) port 15143 and to send mail to *localhost* port 15025. Although insofar as the mail client is concerned it is connecting to abnormal ports on the local machine, SSH "tunnels" the protcols through to the correct ports on *frosting.bakery.org*.

Step 5: Secure Tunnel to an Insecure Service

Okay, so we have tunneled through to services on the same box as the SSHD process. That's handy. But what about reading private and sensitive company information from within a client site?

Assuming that your outside machine (*frosting.bakery.org*) has access to the Web site in question (let's call it *corporatesecrets.bodyshop.com*), we just add another line to our *.ssh/config* file:

```
Host frosting.bakery.org
Port 22         # This isn't really needed, 22 is the default
LocalForward 15143 localhost:143
LocalForward 15025 localhost:25
LocalForward 15080 corporatesecrets.bodyshop.com:80
```

As you can see, the forward doesn't have to be on the same box as the SSH server (SSHD). It may be on any box that the server box can reach.

One Section That Will Pay for the Book

I'm going to reveal a secret here that will singlehandedly make this book worth your purchase price. Once you start port forwarding, you will discover an annoying side effect. If you are connected to a remote server in a shell session that has forwarded ports in either direction and you then attempt to SCP (copy files) to or from the same remote host, you will get a message like:

```
mschwarz@mars:~  scp pubkey.asc mschwarz@frosting.bakery.org:.
mschwarz@frosting.bakery.org's password:
bind: Address already in use
Disconnecting: cannot listen port: 15143
lost connection
mschwarz@mars:~
```

You are getting this message because SCP uses SSH to do the copying, so the same *.ssh/config* entry is being used to configure the SCP session. Great, right? Well, not once port forwarding is involved. Only one process can open a socket for listen. When you try to SCP to the same host you are SSH'd in to, the connection fails because there is already an SSH session listening to (in this case) port 15143.

You might think you are completely stuck. But this is Linux. There's a simple dodge. It turns out that *.ssh/config Host* entries are matched on *exactly what is passed on the command line*, not on any real or resolved address. By this I mean that if *frosting.bakery.org* has a numeric IP address of 112.211.122.221 (which it doesn't—I just made that IP address up, although I'm sure someone has it), you can use both:

```
Host frosting.bakery.org
```

and

```
Host 112.211.122.221
```

in your *.ssh/config* file and give them totally different options. For example, you can use the named entry to do port forwarding but have no port forwarding on the numeric one, and then you will be able to use that to do SCP even while SSH'd in.

Note that you can make this even easier. If you have root access to the client box, you can use the */etc/hosts* file to create several aliases to the same box. Each alias name can have its own configuration in the *.ssh/config* file.

Telling you this up front will save you a lot of hassle. See? We told you this book was worth buying!

Getting In

Step 1: Find a Server Outside

In order to open a path in through a firewall, you still need an SSH server on the outside.

Step 2: Check the Server Configuration

The server must be configured to allow port forwarding. If you intend to open an insecure (that is, "nonencrypted") service, then I strongly recommend that you limit access to the SSH server box itself by setting the server *GatewayPorts* option to "off." If you don't, you are effectively exposing the service to the entire Internet. This totally defeats the purpose of the firewall. Your network manager would almost certainly not approve.

Step 3: Check the Client Configuration

We are going to assume you are talking to the same server as in the "Getting Out" example. At this point, your client-side configuration file looks like this:

```
Host frosting.bakery.org
Port 22          # This isn't really needed, 22 is the default
LocalForward 15143 localhost:143
LocalForward 15025 localhost:25
LocalForward 15080 corporatesecrets.bodyshop.com:80
```

Step 4: Make the Connection from the Inside

To open the inbound door, we have to do another port forward. This one is a bit different. Let's assume that what you want to do is to be able to log in to a Unix box called *netteam.somesuch.com*. They are so confident in their firewall and they trust their employees so much that they use just Telnet. They aren't using SSH themselves.

The Telnet protocol uses port 23. Here's what you might add to allow yourself to Telnet in securely from home:

```
Host frosting.bakery.org
Port 22          # This isn't really needed, 22 is the default
LocalForward 15143 localhost:143
LocalForward 15025 localhost:25
LocalForward 15080 corporatesecrets.bodyshop.com:80
RemoteForward 7023 netteam.somesuch.com:23
```

What this does is to make SSH *on the server side* set up a listener on port 7023. When you connect to port 7023 on *frosting.bakery.org*, you are actually carried through the encrypted connection to the client side, where the box running the client will connect to port 23 on *netteam.somesuch.com*. Note that this means you must SSH to *frosting .bakery.org* before you leave work in order for the connection to bc up.

Step 5: Make the Connection from the Outside

Here's what you would do when you are logged in to *frosting.bakery.org* from home and you want to connect to work:

```
$ telnet localhost 7023
Trying 127.0.0.1...
Connected to localhost
Escape character is '^]'.
Welcome to SuSE Linux 6.4 (i386) - Kernel 2.2.14 (1).
netteam login:
```

That's all there is to it! So long as you have limited connections by setting *Gateway-Ports* to "no," you are just as secure as always (assuming you can be trsuted to keep your home machine secure, which may be a big assumption) because everything you type or display actually travels on the pre-existing SSH connection you made from *inside* the firewall. It is all encrypted.

The Only Tunnel You Will Ever Need

In the preceding example we showed you how to "export" an internal port to the outside world. We also told you to limit connections on the exported service to the SSH server box so you would not expose any traffic to prying eyes. Well, there is a way to export a service that you can safely access from anywhere, a service that will allow you to connect to anything on the inside, whether or not you exported it from the inside!

If it hasn't already occurred to you, I am talking about forwarding an OpenSSH server you have on the *inside* of the firewall to the outside! This may seem goofy, but it works. With this, you export an SSH server to a port on *frosting*. You can then SSH from any box on the Internet to the forwarded SSH port on *frosting*. You are authenticating not to the SSH server on *frosting*, but rather to the SSH server inside the firewall. You can, on your client machine, specify any LocalForward or RemoteForward connections you wish and you can reach anything at all inside or outside. Not only that, but the links are totally secure, because everything is encrypted end to end, with a little bit of double encryption as things pass through the forwarded and encrypted SSH connection.

Personally, this is the *only* "Getting In" that I do. It is the only way to have absolutely everything encrypted and the only way to make the machine inside the firewall authenticate everything and everybody. When you RemoteForward other ports, you are in essence trusting that the machine outside is properly authenticating. When you remote forward SSH, you are merely giving outsiders a chance to authenticate to the SSH server properly configured and ensconsed inside the firewall. This is a very powerful and secure way to enable remote access over untrusted networks.

Maniacally Restrictive Firewalls

I did encounter one wrinkle when trying to SSH out from behind the firewall at, er, the Fifth State Bank of Refuse. They did allow machines inside to connect to machines on the outside, but not from ports on the inside below 1024. I'm not exactly sure why, but openSSH likes to use ports below 1024 (if anyone can tell me why, I'd like to hear it). I beat my head against a brick wall for a long time trying to figure out why. Then I actually RTFM'd. There it was: *UsePrivilegedPort*. Once I set that to "no," through I went—well, almost. Turns out they would only allow me to connect to ports 21, 23, 25, 80, and 149 on the outside. So I used the *Port* option on my *server* side to run SSHD on port 21. (I felt this was a good choice since I would no longer need FTP service if I had SSH).

Alternate Authentication Methods

I'm not going to go into too much depth here, because for most of us strong encryption with password authentication is plenty mucho security. You can, however, use a number of different ways to authenticate, including S/Key and Kerberos. If you do not know what these are, you almost certainly aren't using them.

The alternate authentication method I like best is the RSA/DSA authentication method. In this method, each user generates a key pair (using *ssh-keygen*), and this key is used to authenticate the user.

Hosts always authenticate to one another using public-key and private-key pairs. A user may also authenticate to an account using a public-key and private-key pair. This can be much more secure, for several reasons:

- A passphrase is used to "unlock" the private key when the connection is made. A passphrase is much longer and much harder to guess than a password.
- A key may be tied to a host. Thus you can limit the hosts from which a key may be used.

- A script or program may be triggered on successful authentication. This can let you restrict a key to performing a single activity, like a backup.
- Port forward or X11 forwarding may be disabled on a key-by-key basis.

All of these things are done by creating a file called *~/.ssh/authorized_keys*. This file exists in a user's *.ssh* directory, and it contains all of the public keys that will be allowed in. In order for someone to get in, they must have the private key that matches the public key, and that means that they must have both the key file and the passphrase that protects the key. This is considerably stronger than mere eight-character password authentication.

You generate a key by running *ssh-keygen*, which creates a secret key and a public key. The public key can be found in your *.ssh* directory in a file called *identity.pub*. You must add the contents of the file to the *.ssh/authorized_keys* file of any user account to which you will have access.

This brings up something I had neglected to mention. Suppose you do not have the same username on two different boxes? You can specify which user account you are trying to log in to, in two ways. One is with the *-l* command line switch:

```
$ ssh -l altname frosting.bakery.org
```

The other (and, I find, preferable) way is this:

```
$ ssh altname@frosting.bakery.org
```

I think the second method is more intuitive. You may have figured out by now that you can share your account with hordes of people this way. You could put the public keys of 50 people into your *.ssh/authorized_keys* file. I don't recommend this practice. Remember that anything they do in your account will look like you did it. They will be able to send e-mail as you, read any file you can read, or give themselves a *setuid* copy of a shell owned by you (which would let them become you at will, even if you delete their key from your *.ssh/authorized_keys* file).

Getting back to our story, once you have your public key in the authorized keys file, your login looks a little bit different:

```
mschwarz@mars:~  ssh alienmystery
Enter passphrase for RSA key 'mschwarz@mars':
You have old mail in /var/spool/mail/mschwarz.
Last login: Fri Oct 13 01:16:34 2000 from localhost
Have a lot of fun...
alienmystery:~$
```

Some notes: If you have *StrictModes* set to "yes" (and I recommend that you do), you will find that the files in *.ssh/* will have to be set to 600 (read and write for owner *only*) permissions or nothing will work. When SSH creates files, it generally gets this right for you, but when you create your own *authorized_keys* file, you must remember to do this.

If you do not have *StrictModes* set to "yes," then anyone with write permission on your *authorized_keys* file will be able to put a public key in there and gain full access to your account! This is what we computer security professionals call "a bad thing."

Once you have your authorized keys all worked out, I recommend you disable *PasswordAuthentication*. That will require that users attempting to connect *must* have the secret key that goes with a known public key, or they can't get in at all. This prevents anyone from attempting to use SSH to crack passwords through multiple attempts.

Nonrouting Networks

Our journey does not end here. Oh, no. There are networks still more fanatically isolated. There are, out there, networks that do not allow any directly routed IP datagrams in or out. Yes, indeed.

I have encountered networks where the only outbound communications permitted are through HTTP proxy servers and e-mail servers (where only the mail machine is allowed to send traffic—all mail users first forward their mail to the master server).

Personally, I consider such draconian networks to be severely misguided, as I suspect the rest of this chapter will make clear. Why? Because if you have a hole, any hole, in your network balloon, then it is always possible to pass the air that is network traffic through it. In other words, phhhffffthhhhhh! Your security balloon has deflated.

Let's posit a network far more restrictive than that described earlier in this chapter. This network does not allow any packet originating from the internal network to leave the building. The exceptions to this are proxied HTTP requests and e-mail routed through the corporate mail server.

What Is an HTTP Proxy?

An HTTP proxy is a special box that "mediates" outbound HTTP requests. It may be fairly transparent, or it may aggressively deny or modify HTTP requests and replies. Generally, a Web client is configured to go to a proxy instead of attempting direct network connections to servers. (More than likely if you are using a proxy you will find that no outbound traffic is allowed to traditional HTTP ports on addresses outside the local network.) This is done for the following reasons (of variable soundness).

Obscures Internal Network Details

Since all Web accesses will appear to originate from the proxy machine, no one on the outside can discover anything about the network behind the proxy by merely observing HTTP activity (mostly—some information may still be gleaned from data within the HTTP request itself, unless the proxy filters or modifies it, and, yes, some do so).

Deflects Some Browser-Based Attacks

Some evil HTTP or HTML can trick some browsers into sending information or writing files and so forth. Some of these techniques are fooled merely by proxying. Still others may be blocked by filtering or header modification at the proxy.

Site Blocking

Most HTTP proxies allow the blocking of access to particular sites. If there are inappropriate sites being accessed from inside, the proxy administrator may block them.

Employee Watching

The proxy knows what sites were accessed, when, and by whom. This is a great way to pat your employees down without their knowledge. This is also perceived as a way to limit corporate liability should an employee attempt to access illegal or obscene sites that may result in an employee civil action. (Consult your attorney! I have been told that putting in a filter may *increase* liability. It establishes a pattern of company responsibility for Web access. If someone then brings up an unblocked obscene site and a suit results, it becomes reasonable to ask why the proxy administrator failed to block the site in question. These same people tell me that it is better to establish a "no tolerance" policy, to inform employees that their Internet use *may* be monitored, and then to leave the employees free to access any site. Then it is undoubtedly the one employee's fault when they access the inappropriate site. Remember, I am not a lawyer!)

Tunneling

Tunneling is carrying one protocol in another protocol. Modems are actually an example of this. Think about it. The phone network is a system designed to carry sound from one point to another point. A modem is a device that "tunnels" data in sound. In our case, we will be talking about carrying a standard application protocol (Telnet) "tunneled" through a completely different application protocol (HTTP).

The httptunnel Package

Introduction

The *httptunnel* package is, like SSH is in part, a port forwarding system. It lets you set up a "server" that looks to the Internet like an HTTP server. It lets you set up a client that to the Internet looks like a Web browser.

Server-Side Setup (HTS)

First, you must set up a server. This server looks like a Web server to anything that connects to it. It is, however, a server that expects data for some totally different protocol carried in HTTP requests.

Server setup is quite simple. Here's one I use to pierce an http-proxy-only firewall:

```
# hts -F localhost:22
```

The HTS program listens on port 8888 by default. This is why I did not have to specify a listen port. The "-F" option lets me specify what I really want to contact when an httptunnel client connects to this server. In this case, I am connecting it to SSH. An httptunnel server can create a tunnel to exactly one port. That's why SSH is a very good choice. Even though you have only one port tunneled through the firewall, by using SSH you can pass any number of ports in or out that one port, as we've already described exhaustively. That's it for the server side.

The HTS program has many more options. Run *hts —help* to see the complete list. Remember, we are introducing here. We want to leave you with some things to discover!

Client-Side Setup (HTC)

The client side can be quite a bit more complex. Here's what I use right now:

```
$ htc -A schwarzm:d0ntsf0 -B 4k -c 2k -F 20022 -P 211.100.233.100:8080
    alienmystery.planetmercury.net:8888
```

Now that looks complicated! Don't worry. It's not as bad as it seems. It would help if there were a configuration file you could specify. Instead you have to tell HTC everything on the command line every time.

So what's going on here? The "-A" argument specifies a user name and password for the proxy. If, when you open your browser, you are prompted for a username and password no matter what Web site you first try to visit, you probably need this. If you are not prompted, you probably don't need it. I did.

The "-B" option lets you specify a buffer size for the proxy. Some proxies require a minimum request size. I had to play around to find a value that would always work. Try your connection without this at first. If it doesn't work, set this to very large value (say 32k) and try again. If it works, great! If not, try the "-c" argument.

The "-c" argument specifies the "chunk size" of your HTTP requests. This is slightly different from the "-B" argument. This fixes the actual size of each request packet no matter how much data they carry. If you are doing a lot of typing through the tunnel, you probably want this fairly small. If you are doing a lot of file transfers, you probably want this fairly large! (Small is 1k to 5k. Large is probably anything 16k or greater.) The truth is, I have not dug in to figure out what precisely the -B and -c arguments do in the code. I tried values until I got something that works. You may have to do the same (or dig even deeper than I did! Remember, it is *your* source code!)

The "-F" argument specifies what port on the client side will be listened to for traffic to tunnel. I chose 20022. That means my *.ssh/config* contains an entry that looks like this:

```
Host localhost
Port 20022
```

The "-P" argument specifies the address and port of the HTTP proxy. I made this IP address up. It is not the real address of the proxy I pierced. You would substitute the address of your proxy.

Finally, you name the server side (the HTS HTTP tunnel server). When you hit Enter, the tunnel begins running in the background. You can now do this:

```
mschwarz@mars:~  ssh localhost
Enter passphrase for RSA key 'mschwarz@mars':
You have new mail in /var/spool/mail/mschwarz.
Last login: Fri Oct 13 01:47:39 2000 from localhost
Have a lot of fun...
alienmystery:~$
```

Now, you will probably find this to be a bit erratic and slow. Remember that each time you type a character, you perform the equivalent of a Web query and result! That's a lot of overhead. This is certainly not the optimal way to communicate, but it exists and it does work.

Tunnels within Tunnels: SSH over httptunnel

Remember, just as with any other situation where you use SSH, you can now add *LocalForward* and *RemoteForward* entries to your *.ssh/config* file to use the one HTTP tunnel to open any number of tunnels to any number of services. And because you chose to use SSH to do it, all of the traffic is cryptographically secure. Remember, httptunnel doesn't do any authentication or encryption itself. I highly recommend that if you must use it, you use it only to tunnel SSH.

Truly Terrifying Tunneling

It doesn't even end here. Suppose you have no HTTP proxy. Do you have e-mail? That's right. If you simply must connect to the outside world, you can do it by tunneling through e-mail! This is fairly insane, but it can be done. Read about the work of the maniacs behind *mailtunnel* at: *http://www.detached.net/mailtunnel.*

We won't cover *mailtunnel* here. Consider a new job or a new network before you seriously consider tunneling through e-mail.

There's still more. Even if no UDP or TCP traffic is allowed out, it is very possible that ICMP (the protocol used for "ping," Internet Control Message Protocol) does go through. If you can ping the outside world, you can tunnel anything you want. That's right. You can tunnel data in ICMP messages.

Once again, this is so maniacal that we will not cover it in detail. You can read about it from the fine folks at: *http://www.detached.net/icmptunnel/.*

Summary

If you are a network administrator, I hope you will take one lesson away from this chapter: Don't bother with heavy-handed restrictions on external connectivity for internal users. By this I do not mean that you shouldn't use proxies and NAT/masquerade to hide details of your internal network from external attackers. Those measures make perfect sense. No, I'm merely arguing that the only way to prevent internal users from reaching any resource on the outside that they wish to use is to disconnect from the outside world completely.

If you allow any data to leave the network, then there is a way to use that path to carry data for other purposes. The very existence of tunneling renders moot restrictions on internal access to outside. Rather than impose restrictions that have dubious security benefits, concentrate on external security, proxies, and NAT. The more you restrict internal users, the more you will drive insecure activity underground where you cannot see it.

Frankly, you are much more likely to prevent internal abuse if you give internal users more trust. A user is much less likely to use an encrypted tunnel, thus totally denying you any ability to monitor, if you simply allow activity in the open.

If you are *not* a network administrator, please remember that the purpose of this chapter is not to encourage abuse of private networks. The purpose of this chapter is to show how you might achieve a legitimate goal, such as telecommuting or remote support in a secure and authenticated manner, even where the network infrastructure is not quite ready for such capability.

I would strongly advise you not to start setting up virtual networks and tunnels on the QT. In many organizations, such activity can certainly get you fired. If your company or organization has provision for safe external communications, by all means use that. Besides which, you can use SSH over those media as well.

Chapter 15
TOOLS YOU SHOULD KNOW

Difficult-o-Meter: 3 (moderate Linux skill required)

Covers:

A lot of tools (just read on)

Introduction

Gathered here is a collection of what we consider to be some of the more useful Linux tools. What qualifies them to be included in this chapter? For starters, the majority are command line tools. Being command line junkies and programmers, we feel some of the best tools are those that can be typed, piped, and batched. Additionally, these tools are used almost daily by all of the authors for a host of daily functions. Some qualify because they have been staples of the Unix operating system since the 1970s. Accompanying each tool listed in this chapter is a short explanation of its function and how it is used most often.

The tools are loosely organized into categories. Obviously some tools cross multiple categories, so the grouping is mostly arbitrary. Besides, it's just easier to read something in outline form. No ranking was considered when making this list.

Why is this chapter in the middle of the book? We've already introduced a lot of tools and many uses for those tools. This seemed to be a good place to pause and reflect on some specific tools that we felt needed special attention. Consider this a break from the normal style each chapter uses to introduce the various tools available.

Regular Expressions

The first tool you should start learning is *regular expressions*, or REs. A regular expression is a string of characters that matches patterns and/or does substitutions. Regular expressions are used in a great many Linux and Unix tools, from grep to sed to Perl (where they reach perhaps their greatest functional height). Mastery of regular expressions is the mark of the Unix fluent, and once you start using them intuitively, you will wonder how you ever lived without them.

Pipes and Redirection

Pipes and redirects are basic Linux and Unix skills. Most command line programs in Linux take input from standard input, usually the keyboard, and write to standard output, usually the display terminal. Redirection allows you to change where standard input comes from or where standard output goes to, for example:

```
echo -e "larry\ncarry\nbarry\nmary" > myfriends.txt
```

In this example, I created a list of my friends using the echo command and then put them into a file by redirecting the standard out of the echo command to the file *myfriends.txt*. But what if I wanted a sorted list? Read on.

A pipe performs a similar thing to redirection, but in many ways it is more useful. A pipe allows you to connect the standard output of one program to the standard input of another. Expanding on my friends examples, let's make that friends list, sort it, and finally put it into a file:

```
echo -e "larry\ncarry\nbarry\nmary" | sort > myfriends.txt
```

The list is now being piped from the echo command into the sort command, where the list is sorted. The default behavior of the sort command is to print out the results to standard out. I redirected the output of sort to the file *myfriends.txt*. The file now contains the sorted list of my friends. Not only do I have a pathetically small number of friends, but apparently I also have a bizzare attraction to people with similar names.

Files and More

If you use Linux, you will have no choice in working with text files. Text files make up 99.9% of the configuration files. If you have an Apache Web server running, you'll need to manipulate the text configuration file. Adding a hard disk to your system will require you to edit the *fstab* configuration file if you want the new disk to be checked and mounted at boot time. Text files make up most of what Linux is, and so it stands to reason that there is a vast number of tools that assist in the manipulation of text files.

Compiled here are the utilities we feel will aid you in your daily administrative tasks, programming and debugging, configuration management, file manipulation, and much more.

Vi

"Real" Unix hackers use vi exclusively. With so many Windows programmers around using GUI-based programmer editors and Integrated Development Environments (IDE), you'd swear vi was a relic. What keeps vi around? Simple answer, really: It works very well and can be found on almost every Unix and Unix-variant system. For programmers, vi offers amazing functionality. Admittedly, it is not the sexiest of editors, but that too is a noteworthy feature. vi is small and fast and works nicely over a 1200-baud modem link with a VT-100 terminal. Unlike Emacs, it won't suck up 20–200MB of disk space. Finally, clones of vi are also available on every OS in existence, thus making vi the most widely available program on Earth and nearby planets.

Sed

The stream editor program allows you to transform the data flowing through a pipeline.

Dd

This program is more than just a copier program, it can also perform conversions and other important functions. Input can be blocked, chopped, skipped, or converted. The data can be converted from ASCII to EBCDIC and back if you need that kind of thing. Trust me, if you're in an information system (IS) shop that includes mainframes, you'll need this ability.

Diff

This tool allows you to compare two files and finds the differences between them.

Od

Octal dump. If you don't want octal, then try one of the other formats it supports, like hex. This tool is great for finding unwanted data in a text file. For instance, when your EDI trading partners insist that they sent you clean files, you can find their junk data by using od to print out a dump of the files. Then just sit back and wait for the apologies.

Ispell

Didn't think there was a spellchecker for Linux? Guess again.

Tar

tar stands for "tape archive." Don't let the *tape* part fool you, though. tar is a handy tool for creating a collection or archive of files. It's like the zip utility found on the old MS-DOS OS but without the compression. Of course, compression utilities, like gzip, can be used in combination with tar. Look for filenames with *.tar.gz* or *.tgz*.

G[un]zip

gzip uses Lempel-Ziv coding (LZ77) to compress files. Look for the extension *.gz* (in most cases) to indicate a gzipped file. Use gunzip to uncompress the file.

B[un]zip2

Yet another file compression tool. Bzip generally makes files smaller than gzip.

CVS

Concurrent Versioning System is used to keep track of changes between files. Typically, this tool is used for source code, but it can be used for other files as well. For instance, the authors of this book used cvs to manage a central repository for the chapters in this book, which were written in HTML. Then a cron-executed script was used to extract the latest version of each chapter from the archive and place them into a Web server document root. The authors then had a central place to view each other's chapters as they were being written. It also allowed our publisher and reviewers to view the progress of the book.

Cut

cut is an invaluable tool for pulling out a single field or character of data from an entire line. Many Unix utilities, like *ps*, like to show you only a whole line of data. Often, you only want one piece—like a PID (process ID). Using cut, you can simply grab out the PID and discard the rest of the line. This means that tasks such as figuring out the PID of a daemon process and issuing a SIGHUP (restart) signal can be done in one mongo line, such as:

```
kill 'ps waux | grep inetd | cut -c10-14'
```

More

more is a great way either for viewing the output of another command in a screen-by-screen mode or for viewing text files. Unlike *less*, it automatically exits when you get to the end of the file and hit the space bar. Unlike *more* on almost all other forms of Unix (except for AIX, which has a proper version), it allows you to scroll backwards through the input.

Perl

The *pathologically eclectic rubbish lister* is the single most useful scripting language you can ever learn. Perl runs on many operating systems (including VAX/VMS, MVS/ESA, and MacOS), and it is the undisputed king of text-processing tools. Using Perl, you can simulate *cut* or *sed* or *awk* or *diff* or build anything else you might need—such as a little program that looks at three or four text files and tells you which entries do not appear in all of them. You can write CGI scripts for your Web server; you can use it to automatically parse error logs and issue pages. Heck, you can even write a Telnet daemon (or any other daemon for that matter) in Perl.

File

file will tell you what kind of data is in a file. Using the data from */etc/magic*, it will let you know if that file named *real_slim_shady.mp3* is actually an mp3 file or not. This is very useful when downloading files from those pesky Mac users—who seem to think that file extensions aren't really necessary.

Strings

Use the strings command to get a list of the printable strings in a file. Try this command against a binary file such as */usr/bin/perl*. Interesting things can be found using this command.

Shells and Such

Bash

The *Bourne-again shell* is generally the defacto shell for Linux distributions. It's stable, full featured, and very backwards compatible. Moving from the Korn shell to bash is as easy as falling in love (unless you're moving from the superior ksh93 to bash, in which case it's rather less comfortable). Moving backwards again isn't all that much harder. Automatic tab-completion of filenames is one of the nicer features. Learn to use bash. It's your friend.

Sudo

Ever try to execute a command but couldn't because you weren't root? Enter sudo. This nifty tool lets you execute commands as root or any other user. Of course, don't expect to get full rights to a system, because sudo has to be configured to allow you to execute those commands. System security is always an issue, and sudo can help.

SSH

You're at work and need to log into your Linux system at home, you Telnet to it, log in, and do whatever it is you needed to do. Later, after you get home, you find your system was hacked and all your files are gone. Some jerk was snooping the network and caught your Telnet login and was able to get your clear text password. Prevent this situation from ever happening by using SSH, the secure shell.

Pidof

pidof is a simple program that takes the name of a process and returns its PID number. If there is more than one process with the same name, it returns all of the PIDs of all of the so-named processes in a nice, simple list. This is a great time saver for killing processes, since you don't have to use something like

```
ps waux | grep inetd | cut -blah blah blah
```

Which

"Which," I often ask myself, "file is being executed when I type 'ls'?" Simply typing 'which ls' will give you the full pathname to the program that will be executed. This can be used to troubleshoot problems with your PATH or just to find a specific binary.

Finding Stuff

Grep

Need to search for text within a file or a bunch of files? grep is what you've been looking for. If you work on a Linux system regularly, then grep should be one of the first tools you master. By "master," I mean learn its options, the use of regular expressions, directory traversing, and combining it with other tools.

Find

Speaking of combining with other tools, find is a tool that searches for files in a directory hierarchy. Combine this with the exec option, and you've got a very powerful tool to perform operations on the files find locates. If you are going to master any other tool beyond grep, master this one.

Lsof

lsof is the nosy system administrator's best friend. Its basic mode of operation is to display all open file descriptors for a process or group of processes, including regular files, sockets, and device files. Say you're trying to unmount a volume and keep getting a "Device is busy" message. Use lsof to find out which processes have a current working directory on the file system you're trying to unmount, and then zap them. Or say netstat shows that you have an unusual TCP connection that you're not familiar with. Use lsof to find out which process is holding the socket open. Say you want to find all processes that are currently using a particular shared library. Once again, lsof comes to the rescue. You'll need root privilege to use the command, but it's an invaluable time saver.

Nslookup

When you're using a browser and you type *www.linuxdoc.org*, the browser needs to look up the IP number associated with the name *www.linuxdoc.org*. You can also do the same by using the nslookup command. This command talks to your domain name server to translate IP names into IP addresses and also the reverse of this.

Nmap

This scans large networks for hosts and services. If you're looking for systems on a network and want to know what each host has to offer, nmap is a tool you should learn. You are able to use a variety of seach techniques and can detect such things as operating system type and downed hosts.

Wget

Have you ever wanted a simple command line tool to retrieve Web pages? wget can retrieve one Web page or recursively download a whole Web site over HTTP. You can set it to use many options like HTTP authentication, report a specific user agent, even add arbitrary headers and cookies. wget is even capable of doing single or bulk transfers from FTP sites, even ones requiring a username and password. The rich feature set puts it head and shoulders above other file-retrieval tools.

Getting Help

Help! I need some info. Help! Not just any info. Won't you please, please help me?

Man

Before Web pages there were man pages. Don't even get me started. I like the Web, but when you're at a command line trying to remember some bizzare combination of parameters to an application, who wants to wait a minute to start a browser and then go looking for documentation on that tool? Just type

```
man the-tool-that-bugs-you
```

and get the info right at the command line. What could be easier?

Info

info is another format for documentation. Some stuff can only be found in info pages.

You've Got Spam

E-mail. Can you live without it? I could. I did. But do you really want to give it up? Didn't think so. E-mail is becoming as standard a communication method as the phone system. Here are a few tools to help you deal with your e-mail.

Fetchmail

Your Linux system probably has a fully capable e-mail system configured and ready to do business. Most of the time, however, it doesn't do anything because you probably use an e-mail client that is configured to talk directly with your ISP to pick up and deliver your e-mail. In cases where you want your local Linux system to deal with the e-mail, use Fetchmail to transfer the e-mail from your ISP to your local system. The e-mail console chapter (Chapter 7) uses this tool.

Mailx

Mailx is a quick-and-dirty e-mail program. Need to get an e-mail out quickly and know where you're sending it? Fire up mailx and go. Use it to get your local e-mail as well.

Elm

Need more power in your e-mail client? Check out elm. This e-mail client is text based, so it's fast and efficient to use.

Mutt

Mutt is the king of e-mailers. It runs on almost every flavor of Unix, it's lightweight, it offers good integration with PGP and GPG, and it has almost all the same keystrokes as elm. Plus, it generally understands MIME attachments (those gobbledygook-filled messages that MS Outlook users insist on sending out) very, very well.

Tin

People will try to tell you that there are other Linux newsreaders. Don't listen to them. Only tin is worthwhile. It automatically assembles portions of binaries (though not to the degree that Forte's Agent does), it handles kill files, it even keeps track of everything you've ever posted (which could be good or bad, depending on what you post). It can integrate with your spellchecker, and it can also send e-mail to a post's author. It's quite stable and rather featureful.

Noteworthy GUI tools

Okay, so GUIs are here to stay. And if I must use one, at least I should have some tools that make my time with GUIs a little easier. There are so many GUI applications available and a lot of them are noteworthy, but here are a few we feel highlight the points.

KDE and GNOME

Setting aside any personal biases, both of these desktops have achieved respect from every corner of the Linux (and Unix in general) community (with the possible exception of Jeremy). Even some commercial Unix vendors are moving from the commercial CDE to KDE or GNOME. The authors of both desktop systems and accompanying applications should be commended for their hard work. And regardless of political debate, it's great to be able to pick and choose the user interface for our Linux systems.

Blackbox

Blackbox is the leanest, meanest window manager out there. Programmed in a mere 50,000 lines of code, and nowhere near a 1.0 release, it has stability and speed to which Gnome 2.0 and KDE 3.0 will still be aspiring. It's very easily configured, it uses all three mouse buttons, and themes can be whipped up in three or four minutes. (Ever tried to whip up an Enlightenment theme? Good luck!) For sub-1-Ghz systems, blackbox is the ideal window manager. Available from *http://blackbox.alug.org/*.

The GIMP

The GIMP has been one of Free Software's champions for a while now. Not only does this GPL'ed application deliver amazing quality, it comes with oodles of support, third-party add-ons, and heaps of documentation. You would be hard pressed to find a graphics manipulation program of a higher caliber than the GIMP.

Dia

Diagramming has come to Linux in the form of Dia. Use Dia to whip out that flowchart for your boss who can't read code. And don't worry, your boss will never figure out that you keep handing over the same flowchart each time. This is just a little trick of the trade I like to share from time to time.

XMMS

XMMS is the cross-platform multimedia system, as mentioned in Chapter 20, Music Production, and Chapter 24, Video Production. It's the king of Linux multimedia players for a reason. Use it, love it.

xv

When you just want to peek at a graphics file and not edit it, xv is *the* tool for it. Again, it runs on pretty much all flavors of Unix, it does very, very nice screen captures (Mike and Jeremy did nearly all of their screenshots using xv), it supports PNG, JPG, GIF, and most everything else.

MuLinux

When all you've got is one floppy disk and you need a fully functional form of Linux, what're you gonna do? Simple—you're going to find a machine with a working Net connection, head off to *http://sunsite.auc.dk/mulinux/*, and grab this full-featured floppy distribution. Using from one to five floppies (at my last count), this variant was developed by an insanely clever Italian by the name of Michele Andreoli (send him a postcard or two—he deserves them). Mr. Andreoli went so far as to rewrite almost all command line utilities as shell scripts in order to save space. Based on the x series of kernels, there are add-on floppies for Perl, SSH, tcl/tk, X-windows and even *more* things.

A Web browser and server are included, and this is a perfectly viable system for a single user. It runs entirely out of RAM (quite well, provided you've got at least 16MB of it), so it's a great platform for tinkering around with Linux when you don't want to repartition your hard drive. It's also a great way to learn how to shell script—simply examine how Mr. Andreoli rewrote grep, for example.

It's also a fabulous sniffing station and hardware verifier. I've used it to determine if video cards and NICs really are bad, or if it was just the primary OS that was misconfigured. I've also used it to turn an abandoned PC into a network sniffing station, making this alternately a convenient tool for a network administrator and a cracker's dream.

MuLinux is really, really cool. Check it out. I carry a couple of MuLinux floppies in my pack—you never know when you just might need a tiny version of Linux!

Web Sites You Shouldn't Live Without

A Web site is a tool? You bet it is! Presented here are Web sites all the authors frequent regularly.

www.linux.com

This is a good starting place if you're new to Linux. It's got news, downloads, stuff for developers, games information, hardware information, jobs, and a whole lot more.

www.linuxdoc.org

The Linux Document Project is a fantastic resource for all things Linux. This site is a huge repository of guides, HOWTOs, FAQs, and man pages. It also includes the Linux Gazette, an online magazine. This is definitely a stopping point on the Web for most anyone interested in Linux.

www.freshmeat.net

A massive index of open source software, *freshmeat.net* has been an absolute favorite source of information, links, and more on any software for Linux and other operating systems too.

www.sourceforge.net

Got an open source project? Want a free place to host the Web site and CVS archive? Do I need to continue? I think not.

www.slashdot.org

"News for Nerds. Stuff that matters." Need I say more? Not really, but I'm going to. Have you ever tried to get to a page on a Web site only to get a "timed out" error from your browser? Chances are the network is acting funny, the Web site is poorly designed or not working, or the page you are trying to access is being "slash-dotted." *Slashdot.org* is so popular that when particularly interesting news blurbs appear, its readers have this knack of saturating the Web sites the news blurbs refer to. If you need a daily dose of techie news, *Slashdot.org* is definitely for you.

www.lwn.net

News on Linux—lots of news on Linux. Where do they get all this stuff? My work is starting to suffer because there's so much to read on Linux. Life is good!

www.google.com

One of the best tools for the Internet is a search engine. I mention Google because of their technology, a massive cluster of Linux systems. Their use of tools, such as Linux, is a prime example of how effective open source software can be to achieve a goal.

www.lokigames.com and *www.linuxgames.com*

I'm sorry if I make a typo here. My fingers are cramped from an all-night Quake session on my 1Ghz Linux system! Games on Linux? Sure! Take a break from the grind and put your mind into gamer mode. Games on Linux is a reality my friend. If you didn't know about these sites or that there were games for Linux, then I suggest removing the very large rock off your person and getting to these sites. Support these companies! We want more games!

www.jabber.org

I just had to include this site. Jabber is an open source messaging system with an implementation of an instant messenger, like the infamous ICQ (Phonetic acronym

"I seek you") and AIM (AOL Instant Messanger) clients. The key here is that Jabber is open source, and thus you don't get the same infighting you get with giant corporations hell-bent on making yet another dollar from you and me.

Summary

That's it? Hardly. Explore. Find stuff. Learn. Use your knowledge for good. And if you can't do that, well, umm, go play in traffic or something—I don't know. We hope you're stimulated by our efforts to inform you on some of the more interesting tools available to you. Tools are what make a good operating system. Good design makes it great! The Unix model of computing is a great design and can serve you very well so long as you're willing to put in the time and effort to learn the tools that are at your fingertips. Enjoy!

Chapter 16

Use Your Palm-Connected Organizer

Difficult-o-Meter: 3 (moderate Linux skill required)

Covers:

pilot-link	*http://sourceforge.net/projects/pilot-link*
pilot-manager	*http://www.moshpit.org/pilotmgr/*
kpilot	*url http://www.kde.org/*
jpilot	*http://jpilot.org/*
malsync	*http://www.tomw.org/malsync/*

Question: Doesn't switching to Linux mean that I will have to give up my Palm computing device (or PalmPilot as most humans still call them)?

Answer: Absolutely not! You have an embarassment of options for linking your Palm, Sony Clie, or Handspring Visor to Linux. Which one of the host of choices you select will depend on your needs, your desktop choice, and your personal tastes. Heck, I actually use more than one of the packages every single day. It is a lot of fun!

Introduction

PalmOS devices, including the PalmPilot, the Palms III, IIIx, V, Vx, VIIx, m100, and now m500, etc., the Handspring line of personal digital assistants (PDAs), the Sony Clie, and so on are the most widely used type of PDA in the market, recent inroads by the so-called PocketPC notwithstanding.

These devices are particularly popular with the techno-geek crowd, to which your bending author himself belongs. Linux was, of course, built from the ground up by techno-geeks. It follows quite naturally that good support for PalmOS devices would indeed be available on the platform.

The support ranges from very traditional command-line-based tools through general-purpose GUI tools, through tools closely tied to particular X desktop managers, and on to tools for actually writing PalmOS applications. (Yes, that's right. Not only does Linux make available industrial-strength development tools for PCs, it also offers all the tools needed to build Palm applications!)

In this chapter we will introduce some (but by no means all) of the tools that allow you to make use of your Palm-type PDA with a Linux-based PC. We will in passing mention some of the development tools. But since this is not a programming book, we will do little more than tell you where to find more information. We will also spend a little time talking about some of the third-party applications for Palm-type PDAs and some of the issues they present when using such a device with Linux.

Also, this chapter will seem to be a completely gratuitous attempt to inflate our page count, because it has more screenshots in it than any other chapter. I won't apologize for this. Those of you who have PalmOS devices already know what we are talking about here. What you want is some guidance to help you choose the tool that's right for you. Seeing how these packages do their work is the only way to make that choice, hence all the pretty pictures (so perhaps this is a bit of an apology after all).

One more note: We will use the terms *palm*, *Palm*, *pilot*, and *PDA* interchangeably throughout this chapter. In every case we mean one of the PalmOS-based personal digital assistants, without regard to a particular model or manufacturer.

The Handspring Visor: A Brief Digression

I recently bought a Handspring Visor Deluxe when I accidentally ran over my long-used and much-loved Palm V. The Visor won me over because, despite its larger size and use of AAA batteries, its Springboard expansion slot would offer me both the

Palm VII's wireless abilities plus the ability to plug in a GPS system. These features appealed to my inner geek and I went to the Visor like a moth to a flame, despite oodles of affection and admiration for my departed Palm.

You don't care about any of this. What you do care about is that the Handspring Visor Deluxe comes with a USB sync cradle. Why do you care? Because if you have such a cradle you may find yourself really annoyed. Depending on the version of the Linux kernel you have, you may not be able to use your USB cradle at all. If you have a recent 2.2.x kernel or a 2.4.x kernel, you will be able to use your USB cradle, but you may find some software working in an annoying way.

Basically, most of the Linux sync software is written to work with a traditional old serial port. You can set up a USB port that works like a serial port. "Aha!" you think. "I'm saved!" Well, yes and no. You see, the Visor's cradle is only "on" the USB bus when the button has been pressed and a sync is actually in progress. This means you must press the hotsync button *before* running your program. This is a minor inconvenience when using tools like pilot-tools and malsync, which are "run once" sync programs, but it is a pain when using a daemon-based sync tool like kpilot.

If you don't mind these inconveniences, I will say that USB is many times faster than the serial interface. I use the USB cradle with my laptop and I just fire up daemon-based services (if I use any) after pressing the sync button. I shut them down again afterwards. I did buy a serial cradle, but I leave that attached to my desktop machine.

Until such time as sync software for Linux is written with USB services in mind, I would recommend spending the $30 or so it takes to get a serial cradle for your Handspring. USB support was quite recently added to Linux, so I expect to see support come along quite quickly now that it is here.

Pilot-link

Start simple. The pilot-link tools are a set of command-line-based utilities for syncing PalmOS-based PDAs. These tools all default to a port of */dev/pilot* and a baud rate of 9600. You can override these with the environment variables PILOTPORT and PILOTRATE.

Pilot-xfer

The main tool is called pilot-xfer. If you run that without arguments, it dumps out its help screen:

```
mschwarz@mars:~$ pilot-xfer
Usage: pilot-xfer [-p port] command(s)

Where a command is one or more of: -b(ackup)  backupdir
                                   -u(pdate)  backupdir
                                   -s(ync)    backupdir
                                   -r(estore) backupdir
                                   -i(nstall) filename(s)
                                   -m(erge)   filename(s)
                                   -f(etch)   dbname(s)
                                   -d(elete)  dbname(s)
                                   -e(xclude) filename
                                   -P(urge)
                                   -l(ist)
                                   -L(istall)
                                   -v(ersion)
                                   -h(elp)

The serial port to connect to may be specified by the PILOTPORT
environment variable instead of the command line. If not specified
anywhere, it will default to /dev/pilot.

The baud rate to connect with may be specified by the PILOTRATE
environment variable. If not specified, it will default to 9600.
Please use caution setting it to higher values, as several types
of workstations have problems with higher rates.

 -b backs up all databases to the directory.
 -u is the same as -b, except it only backs up changed or new db's
 -s is the same as -u, except it removes files if the database is
    deleted on the Pilot.
```

The *backup* switch saves all programs and data from your PDA to the named directory. The *update* command moves only new programs and changed data to the directory, but it doesn't erase data from the directory that has been removed from the pilot. The *sync* command works like update, except it does erase things from the directory that have been erased on the pilot. The *restore* command will load everything in the directory into the pilot. This is great for restoring the pilot if you let the batteries die.

The *install* switch loads a *.prc* file (a pilot program) into the pilot. This is how you add new Palm applications.

The *merge* switch is one you aren't likely to use very often. It allows you to add the data stored in a file in your backup directory to your Palm. This might be used if you have a Linux application that adds data to such a file. *Note:* If you add a file that is already loaded, you might end up with multiple copies of data records on your palm (for example, two copies of all your memos). Fortunately, the pilot-link package contains a program, *pilot-dedupe*, that eliminates duplicate records from your palm.

The *fetch* switch allows you to pull a single database out of the palm. This is another option you are unlikely to use unless you are developing or debugging a palm application.

The *delete* switch allows you to erase a database from the palm. Once again, I wouldn't use this one as a matter of routine.

The *exclude* switch allows you to name one or more directories to omit from a backup, update, sync, or restore operation. You must specify this option on the command line before the operation you intend it to modify.

The *list* switch will give you a list of the databases in your palm:

```
mschwarz@mars:~$ pilot-xfer -l
Waiting for connection on /dev/ttyS0 (press the HotSync button now)...
Connected
Reading list of databases in RAM...
'AvGoPref'
'AvGoVersion'
'QuickenCategories'
'AvGoChanMQ'
'Auto Log DB'
'CityTimeDB'
'Datebk3HDB'
'HSAdvCalcDB'
'AddressDB'
'DatebookDB'
'ExpenseDB'
'LauncherDB'
'MailDB'
'MemoDB'
'NetworkDB'
'WWJournal'
'SolitaireFreeData'
'ToDoDB'
'DiddleDB'
'AvGoDocsMQ'
'DiddleIDB'
'Untitled'
'AvGoMUrlMQ'
'QuickenMemorized'
'Auto Log Notes'
'AvGoNtShMQ'
'HSPrefs'
'AvGoTimeMQ'
```

```
'QuickenTransactions'
'HandyShop2'
'Auto Log'
'AvantGo'
'Diddle'
'Hearts'
'MobileLink'
'PktQuicken'
'YAtzee'
'GraffitiDemo'
'WW Journal'
'SolFree'
'MBlnDeviceInfo'
'libmal'
'Graffiti ShortCuts'
'Unsaved Preferences'
'AvGoRecent'
'Net Prefs'
'System MIDI Sounds'
'Saved Preferences'
'MBlnProfile'
List done.
```

The *Listall* (note the capital) switch will list all databases, including system databases. You normally shouldn't be messing about with system databases.

The *purge* switch will remove all deleted records from the palm device without doing a sync. This does no harm. I would think you should prefer to do a sync, however.

Backup

Here it is in action. First, we do a complete backup:

```
mschwarz@mars:~$ pilot-xfer -b visor
Waiting for connection on /dev/ttyS0 (press the HotSync button now)...
Connected
Backing up 'visor/AvGoPref.pdb'... OK
Backing up 'visor/AvGoVersion.pdb'... OK
Backing up 'visor/QuickenCategories.pdb'... OK
Backing up 'visor/AvGoChanMQ.pdb'... OK
Backing up 'visor/Auto Log DB.pdb'... OK
Backing up 'visor/CityTimeDB.pdb'... OK
Backing up 'visor/Datebk3HDB.pdb'... OK
Backing up 'visor/HSAdvCalcDB.pdb'... OK
Backing up 'visor/AddressDB.pdb'... OK
Backing up 'visor/DatebookDB.pdb'... OK
Backing up 'visor/ExpenseDB.pdb'... OK
Backing up 'visor/LauncherDB.pdb'... OK
Backing up 'visor/MailDB.pdb'... OK
```

```
Backing up 'visor/MemoDB.pdb'... OK
Backing up 'visor/NetworkDB.pdb'... OK
Backing up 'visor/WWJournal.pdb'... OK
Backing up 'visor/SolitaireFreeData.pdb'... OK
Backing up 'visor/ToDoDB.pdb'... OK
Backing up 'visor/DiddleDB.pdb'... OK
Backing up 'visor/AvGoDocsMQ.pdb'... OK
Backing up 'visor/DiddleIDB.pdb'... OK
Backing up 'visor/Untitled.pdb'... OK
Backing up 'visor/AvGoMUrlMQ.pdb'... OK
Backing up 'visor/QuickenMemorized.pdb'... OK
Backing up 'visor/Auto Log Notes.pdb'... OK
Backing up 'visor/AvGoNtShMQ.pdb'... OK
Backing up 'visor/HSPrefs.pdb'... OK
Backing up 'visor/AvGoTimeMQ.pdb'... OK
Backing up 'visor/QuickenTransactions.pdb'... OK
Backing up 'visor/HandyShop2.prc'... OK
Backing up 'visor/Auto Log.prc'... OK
Backing up 'visor/AvantGo.prc'... OK
Backing up 'visor/Diddle.prc'... OK
Backing up 'visor/Hearts.prc'... OK
Backing up 'visor/MobileLink.prc'... OK
Backing up 'visor/PktQuicken.prc'... OK
Backing up 'visor/YAtzee.prc'... OK
Backing up 'visor/GraffitiDemo.prc'... OK
Backing up 'visor/WW Journal.prc'... OK
Backing up 'visor/SolFree.prc'... OK
Backing up 'visor/MBlnDeviceInfo.pdb'... OK
Backing up 'visor/libmal.prc'... OK
Backing up 'visor/Graffiti ShortCuts.prc'... OK
Backing up 'visor/Unsaved Preferences.prc'... OK
Backing up 'visor/AvGoRecent.pdb'... OK
Backing up 'visor/Net Prefs.prc'... OK
Backing up 'visor/System MIDI Sounds.pdb'... OK
Backing up 'visor/Saved Preferences.prc'... OK
Backing up 'visor/MBlnProfile.pdb'... OK
Backup done.
```

Sync

Now there is a copy of every program and database from my Handspring Visor Deluxe stored in the directory *~/visor*. From now on, I will probably use the sync option to bring in only my changes.

That operation looks like this:

```
mschwarz@mars:~$ pilot-xfer -s visor
Waiting for connection on /dev/ttyS0 (press the HotSync button now)...
Connected
```

```
No change, skipping 'AvGoPref'.
No change, skipping 'AvGoVersion'.
No change, skipping 'QuickenCategories'.
No change, skipping 'AvGoChanMQ'.
No change, skipping 'Auto Log DB'.
No change, skipping 'CityTimeDB'.
No change, skipping 'Datebk3HDB'.
No change, skipping 'HSAdvCalcDB'.
No change, skipping 'AddressDB'.
No change, skipping 'DatebookDB'.
No change, skipping 'ExpenseDB'.
No change, skipping 'LauncherDB'.
No change, skipping 'MailDB'.
Backing up 'visor/MemoDB.pdb'... OK
No change, skipping 'NetworkDB'.
Backing up 'visor/WWJournal.pdb'... OK
No change, skipping 'SolitaireFreeData'.
No change, skipping 'ToDoDB'.
No change, skipping 'DiddleDB'.
No change, skipping 'AvGoDocsMQ'.
No change, skipping 'DiddleIDB'.
No change, skipping 'Untitled'.
No change, skipping 'AvGoMUrlMQ'.
No change, skipping 'QuickenMemorized'.
No change, skipping 'Auto Log Notes'.
No change, skipping 'AvGoNtShMQ'.
No change, skipping 'HSPrefs'.
No change, skipping 'AvGoTimeMQ'.
No change, skipping 'QuickenTransactions'.
No change, skipping 'HandyShop2'.
No change, skipping 'Auto Log'.
No change, skipping 'AvantGo'.
No change, skipping 'Diddle'.
No change, skipping 'Hearts'.
No change, skipping 'MobileLink'.
No change, skipping 'PktQuicken'.
No change, skipping 'YAtzee'.
No change, skipping 'GraffitiDemo'.
No change, skipping 'WW Journal'.
No change, skipping 'SolFree'.
No change, skipping 'MBlnDeviceInfo'.
No change, skipping 'libmal'.
No change, skipping 'Graffiti ShortCuts'.
Backing up 'visor/Unsaved Preferences.prc'... OK
No change, skipping 'AvGoRecent'.
No change, skipping 'Net Prefs'.
No change, skipping 'System MIDI Sounds'.
Backing up 'visor/Saved Preferences.prc'... OK
No change, skipping 'MBlnProfile'.
Backup done.
```

When you have something large and with as much data in it as AvantGo, which is a Web-clipper application, the complete backup can take a long time indeed. The sync, however, usually takes only a few seconds. If you are an AvantGo user, be patient, you can indeed use this service with Linux, but it isn't part of this package. If you can't wait, skip to the later section on malsync.

Restore

If you ever lose the contents of your palm because your batteries die, you are forced to do a hard reset, or if you accidentally leave your palm on top of your car at a gas station like a moron and then some other moron comes along and rolls an SUV over it (My poor Palm V! My poor Palm V!), then be glad you have made this little backup and have been keeping it in sync! You can now restore all your former data with a single command. That looks like this:

```
mschwarz@mars:~$ pilot-xfer -r visor
Waiting for connection on /dev/ttyS0 (press the HotSync button now)...
Connected
Restoring visor/libmal.prc... OK
Restoring visor/AvantGo.prc... OK
Restoring visor/Auto Log.prc... OK
Restoring visor/Untitled.pdb... OK
Restoring visor/SolitaireFreeData.pdb... OK
Restoring visor/SolFree.prc... OK
Restoring visor/MobileLink.prc... OK
Restoring visor/MBlnProfile.pdb... OK
Restoring visor/HSPrefs.pdb... OK
Restoring visor/HandyShop2.prc... OK
Restoring visor/AvGoDocsMQ.pdb... OK
Restoring visor/DiddleIDB.pdb... OK
Restoring visor/DiddleDB.pdb... OK
Restoring visor/HSAdvCalcDB.pdb... OK
Restoring visor/Auto Log DB.pdb... OK
Restoring visor/AvGoChanMQ.pdb... OK
Restoring visor/QuickenMemorized.pdb... OK
Restoring visor/QuickenCategories.pdb... OK
Restoring visor/PktQuicken.prc... OK
Restoring visor/Hearts.prc... OK
Restoring visor/Diddle.prc... OK
Restoring visor/WW Journal.prc... OK
Restoring visor/YAtzee.prc... OK
Restoring visor/GraffitiDemo.prc... OK
Restoring visor/Net Prefs.prc... failed.
Restoring visor/WWJournal.pdb... OK
Restoring visor/Saved Preferences.prc... OK
Restoring visor/Graffiti ShortCuts.prc... failed.
Restoring visor/AddressDB.pdb... OK
```

```
Restoring visor/System MIDI Sounds.pdb... OK
Restoring visor/LauncherDB.pdb... OK
Restoring visor/ToDoDB.pdb... OK
Restoring visor/MemoDB.pdb... OK
Restoring visor/Unsaved Preferences.prc... OK
Restoring visor/NetworkDB.pdb... OK
Restoring visor/QuickenTransactions.pdb... OK
Restoring visor/DatebookDB.pdb... OK
Restoring visor/CityTimeDB.pdb... OK
Restoring visor/AvGoPref.pdb... OK
Restoring visor/AvGoVersion.pdb... OK
Restoring visor/MBlnDeviceInfo.pdb... OK
Restoring visor/AvGoTimeMQ.pdb... OK
Restoring visor/AvGoMUrlMQ.pdb... OK
Restoring visor/AvGoNtShMQ.pdb... OK
Restoring visor/AvGoRecent.pdb... OK
Restoring visor/ExpenseDB.pdb... OK
Restoring visor/MailDB.pdb... OK
Restoring visor/Datebk3HDB.pdb... OK
Restoring visor/Auto Log Notes.pdb... OK
Restore done
```

Most of the time, that is all you will do with pilot-link. It serves primarily as a backup for your palm. It is capable of a great deal more, however. It has "conduit" programs to allow you to link your calendar and mail applications and so forth. I will go over some of these additional programs briefly. Note that this is not a complete list, nor is it complete documentation. Once again, we aim to get you started in the right direction. Half the fun of using Linux is learning to figure it out for yourself (with a little help from other users and, of course, the source code).

Program	**Description**
addresses	This program will read your addressbook database and write it to standard output in a fairly useful format.
pilot-addresses	This will export and import your addressbook.
read-todos	This will output the to-do lists in your palm to a text format.
install-todos	The function complementary to the *read-todos* program. This will take a text file of to-do items and store them in your palm.
pilot-schlep	This will turn your palm into a one-file file system. You can save any disk file (that will fit in your palm's free memory) on your palm and then use this program to extract it again. Very James Bond.
pilot-mail	This will read mail from a POP3 account into your palm's mail application and will send any mail coming from your palm using the *sendmail* program.

There are many more programs in this package, including ones that allow you to hot-sync over a network, ones that will synchronize your datebook with ical or netplan, and ones that will capture your pilot's ROM (for use in some of the palm pilot emulators used to develop palm applications). What we have shown you here should be enough to get you going.

pilot-manager

This is the first GUI palm sync program we will look at.

The first time you run *pilot-manager* (as a GUI—it may be run as a command line utility—run *pilot-manager -?* for details), the screen looks like Figure 16-1. Once you read and close this screen, the main application screen comes up, also in a "first time" mode, to help point you at setup and use. That screen looks like Figure 16-2.

Here, follow the program's advice. Select the Properties screen from the menu. The Properties screen looks like Figure 16-3. This Properties screenshot shows the application configured for my system. Note that the program comes with a number of conduits that you may use to interface certain PDA applications with certain Linux applications. It is left as an exercise for you to explore these conduits.

After the first run, the application screen is more basic (Figure 16-4).

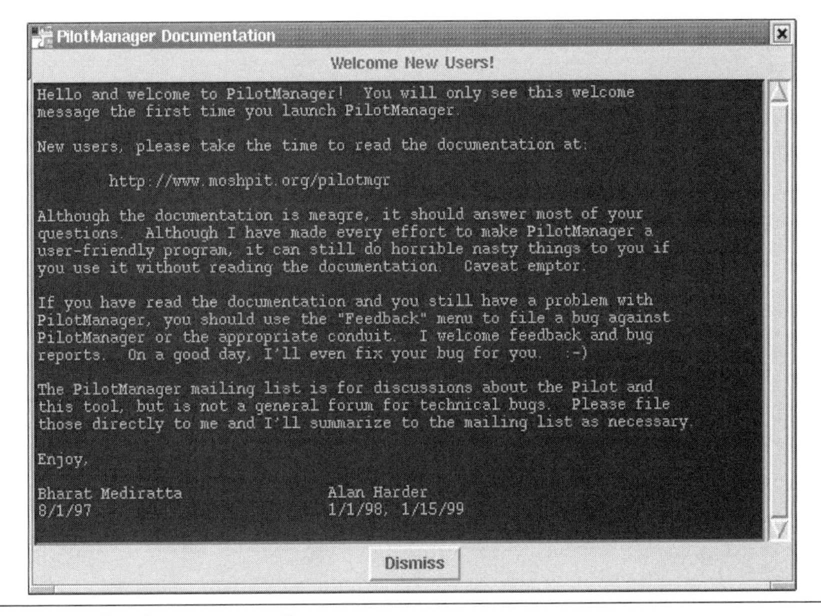

Figure 16-1 First time you run pilot-manager.

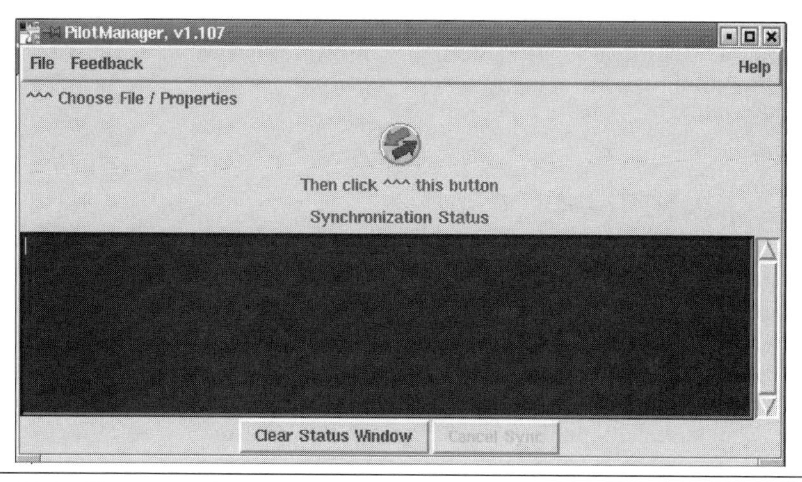

Figure 16-2 First-run application screen.

To actually perform the sync, click on the hotsync icon. A sync status window will open that has a progress bar. It looks like Figure 16-5. After the sync is completed, you will find the log of the sync on the main application screen (Figure 16-6).

The pilot-manager program is a perfectly sound option for Palm backup and synchroization.

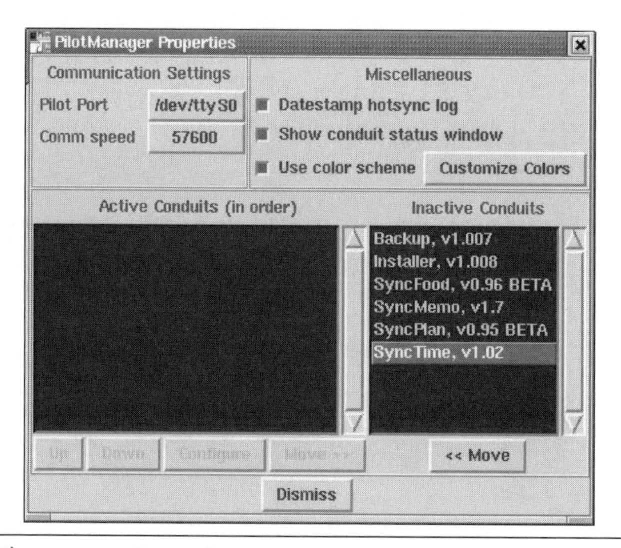

Figure 16-3 Pilot-manager Properties screen.

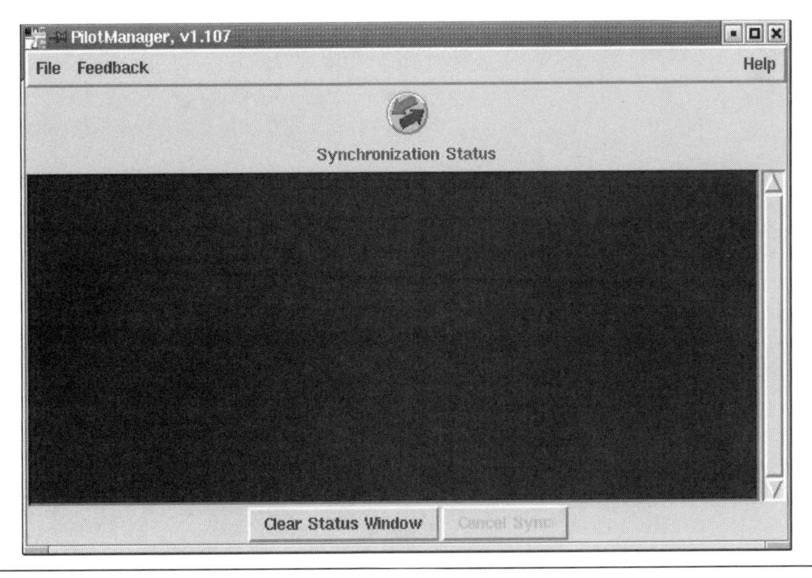

Figure 16-4 Normal application screen.

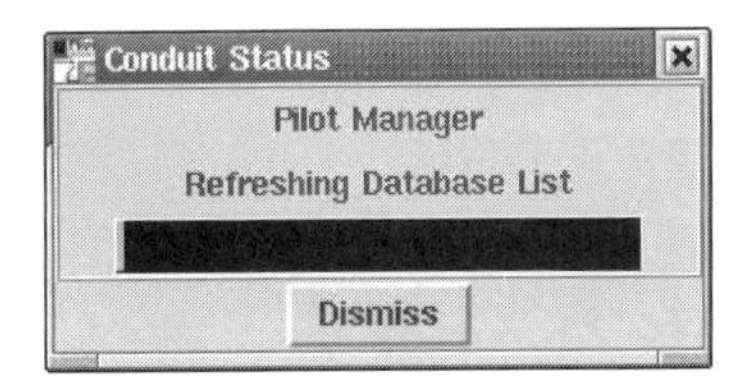

Figure 16-5 Sync progress window.

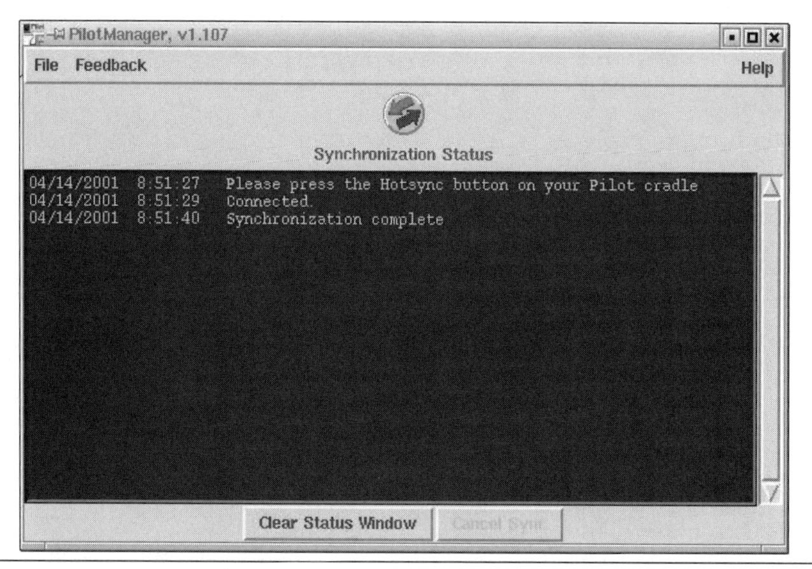

Figure 16-6 Main screen after sync.

Kpilot

The kpilot program is the KDE Desktop system's answer to the PDA sync problem. It consists of two parts, a daemon (called, not unexpectedly, *kpilotDaemon*), which may be run to constantly watch for synchronizations, and a GUI client program called *kpilot.* You control the settings of both programs through kpilot.

The kpilot program is a bit more complete than pilot-manager in that it provides built in viewer/editor screens for certain standard palm databases. When you start kpilot, you get the screen shown in Figure 16-7.

If you haven't already set up kpilot, you must do so by selecting File -> Settings. That will pop up the dialog box in Figure 16-8. Note that this dialog box has four tabs. This one, the likely default, allows you to set baud rates, port, and daemon preferences. (As an aside, kpilot is probably the poorest at dealing with USB cradles, but it is very good in other respects, as you will soon see.)

The second tab, which looks like Figure 16-9, allows you to set the import and export format for your address book using a series of macros that correspond to the data fields in the standard palm addressbook application.

Figure 16-7 Kpilot—Start.

Figure 16-8 Kpilot-Settings—General.

The remaining tabs, DB Specials and Sync, allow you to specify databases to be backed up only or to be skipped altogether, and to specify alternative sync behavior (such as always having the desktop override the pilot, or to do a full backup instead of only a sync). It is left to you to explore these options in depth if you have need of them.

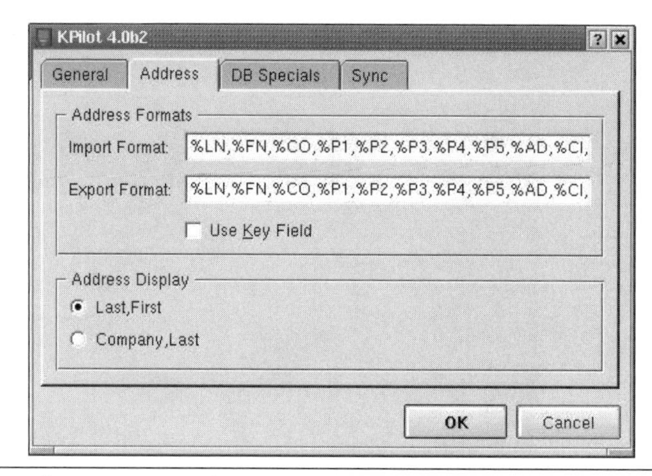

Figure 16-9 Kpilot-Settings—Address.

kpilot includes native conduits for three applications: Memos, Addressbook, and File Installer. You may access these under the Conduits menu entry, or by the dropdown list on the top right of the main application screen.

Let's take a quick look at each. The Memos conduit provides a desktop view of the memos in your palm. It allows you to view, export, import, and delete memos. In other words, it is very like the Windows-based Palm Desktop software for the same purpose. When you have a memo on the screen, you can click on the memo and edit it. Figure 16-10 presents a screenshot.

The Address Book conduit looks like Figure 16-11. The Export and Import buttons are where that Address Settings tab we showed you earlier come into play. As you can see from the other buttons, you can edit, delete, and create new entires.

The File Installer looks like Figure 16-12. Pressing the Add File button opens the standard KDE file selection dialog box. Pressing the Clear List button will, of course, clear the list. Tricky, that. Files specified here will be loaded into the palm on the next sync.

All of that is always built into the kpilot application. But, just as with the pilot-manager application, it is possible to write additional conduits for kpilot. Several have been included with kpilot as distribuited by KDE.org. You access them from the Conduits menu (Figure 16-13). Select External and you will get the screen shown in Figure 16-14.

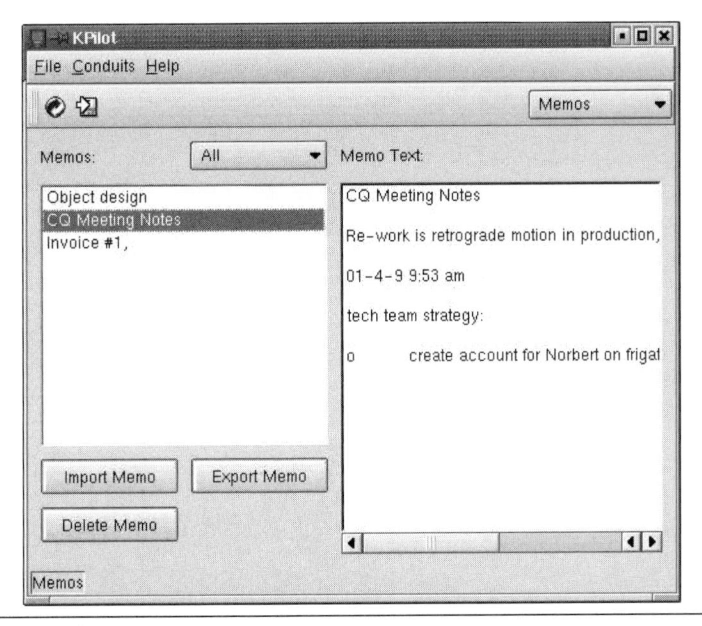

Figure 16-10 Kpilot—Memo.

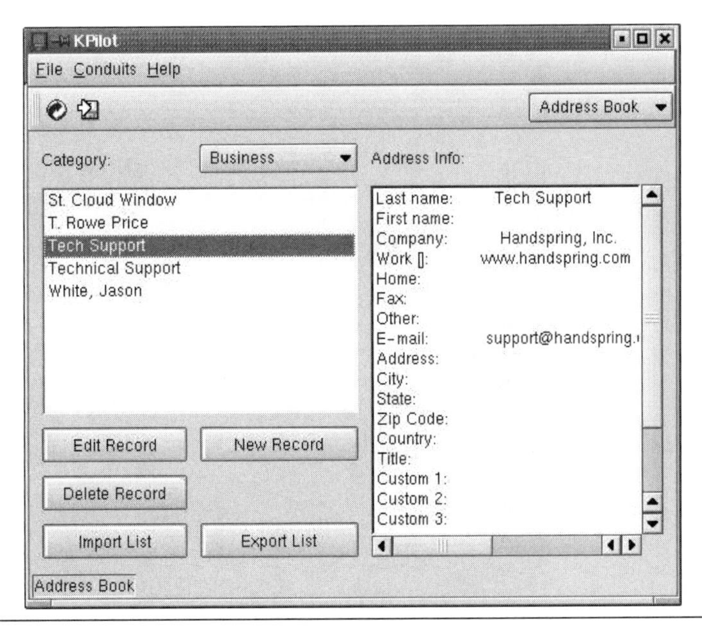

Figure 16-11 Kpilot—Address.

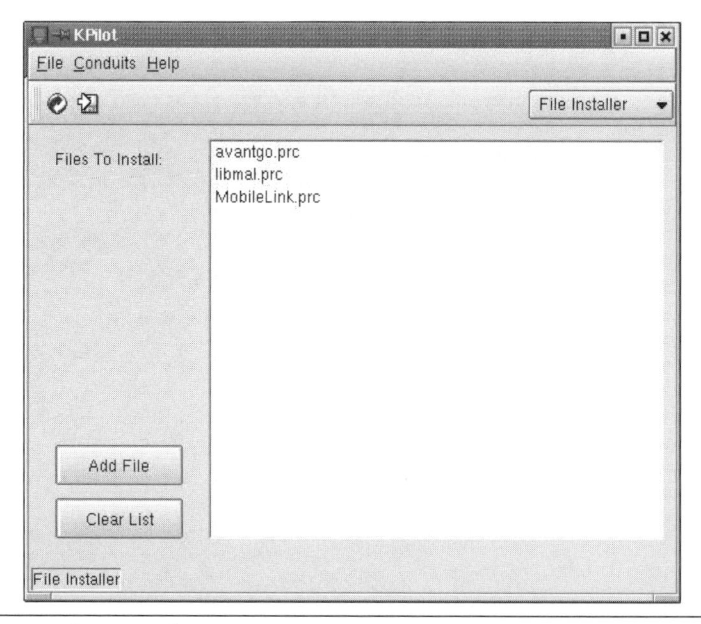

Figure 16-12 Kpilot—Install.

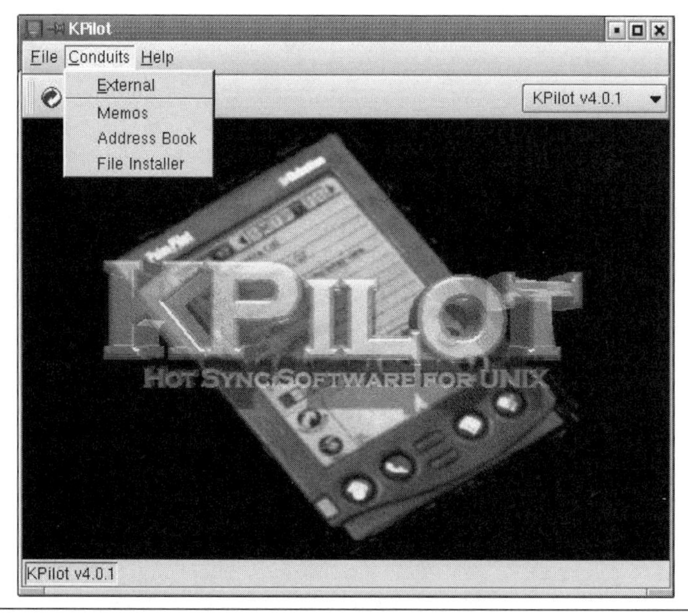

Figure 16-13 Kpilot-Conduit—Menu.

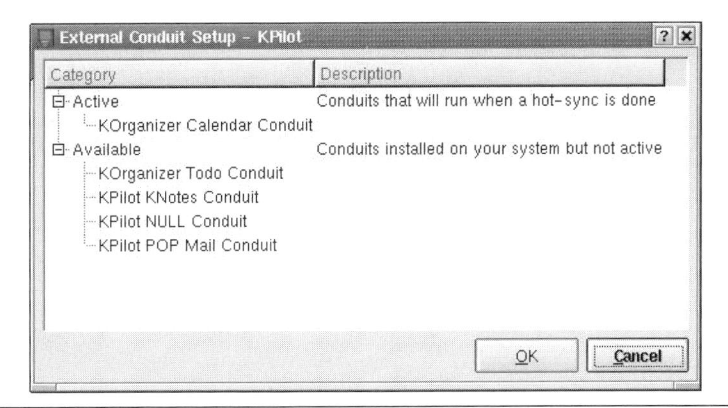

Figure 16-14 Kpilot—External.

As you can see, I have the KOrganizer Calendar Conduit working. That means my appointments in my Palm Datebook are kept in sync with those in my KDE Korganizer application. To make one of these conduits active, drag and drop it from the Inactive entry to the Active entry. Likewise, to deactivate one, drag and drop from Active to Inactive.

To configure one, simply click on it. For example, clicking on the KOrganizer Calendar Conduit brings up the screen shown in Figure 16-15. As you can see, this conduit is set up to store appointments in my Korganizer Calender file (*mike.vcs*), and it is set to prompt me before making changes to it.

During an actual sync operation, a small window showing current activity opens. Figure 16-16 presents an example.

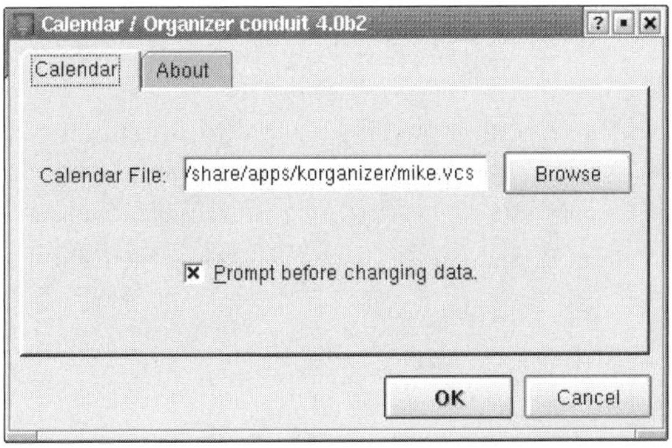

Figure 16-15 Kpilot-korg—cal.

Figure 16-16 Kpilot—sync.

So, if you happen to be a KDE user, you might find that kpilot is one of the best choices for synching your PalmOS PDA. Because of its daemon-based sync listener, however, it is a poor choice for USB-based Handspring users.

Jpilot

Jpilot is another full-featured Palm Desktop sync application. It is probably the better choice for Handspring users than kpilot because it is not daemon based. It was written using the GTK toolkit, and thus is also very Gnome-friendly, for those who have a desktop preference (it seems to work fine under every window manager I tried, as did kpilot).

Interestingly, jpilot uses the pilot-link command line applications underneath, as we shall see shortly.

When you first open jpilot, it's a featureless wasteland (Figure 16-17).

The File menu has the following options:

- *Search:* This works like the Find feature on the Palm device itself (Figure 16-18). Just click on an entry, and the main screen will bring that database entry up. Note the application understands only the Memo, Addressbook, To-Do, and Datebook applications. It won't find data records from other applications in your Palm. (By the way, sorry for scrambling some content—some of my personal records just don't belong in your book!)
- *Install:* This is the application installer for jpilot. When selected, it opens the dialog window shown in Figure 16-19. Here I have selected a *.prc* (PalmOS application) file to install the next time I sync.
- *Preferences:* The "Preferences," or setup, screen for jpilot looks like Figure 16-20. You see it here set up for my USB Handspring (which I have symbolically linked to */dev/pilot*).
- *Quit:* This quits jpilot (duh!).

Okay, back at the main screen. You see the four "buttons" that look like the buttons on the Palm III that correspond with the Datebook, Addressbook, To-Do, and Memo

Figure 16-17 Jpilot—start.

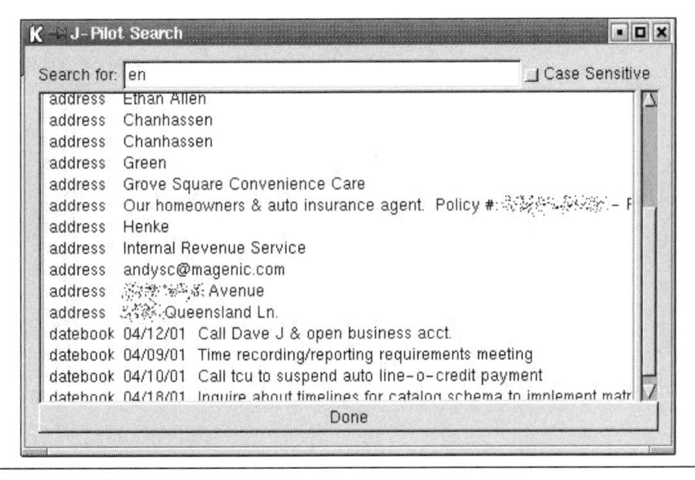

Figure 16-18 Jpilot—search.

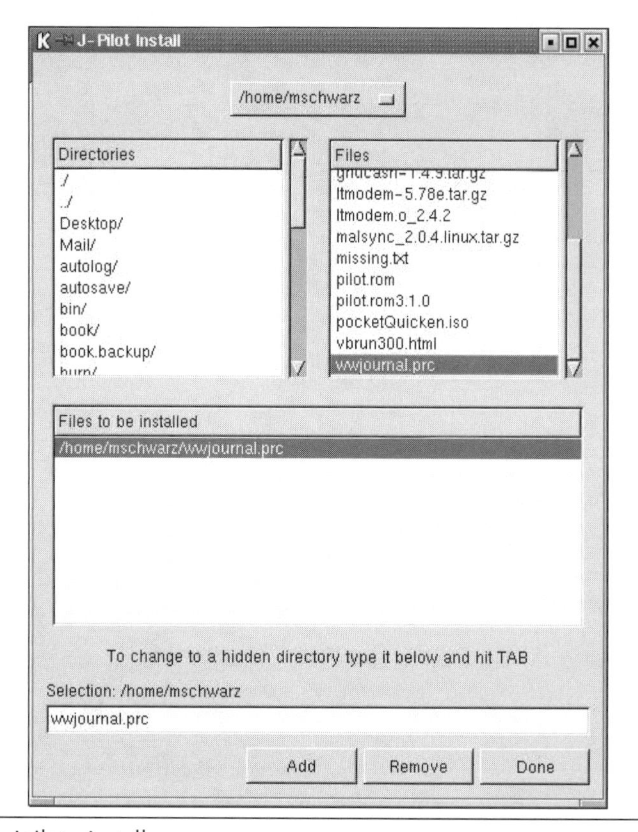

Figure 16-19 Jpilot—Install.

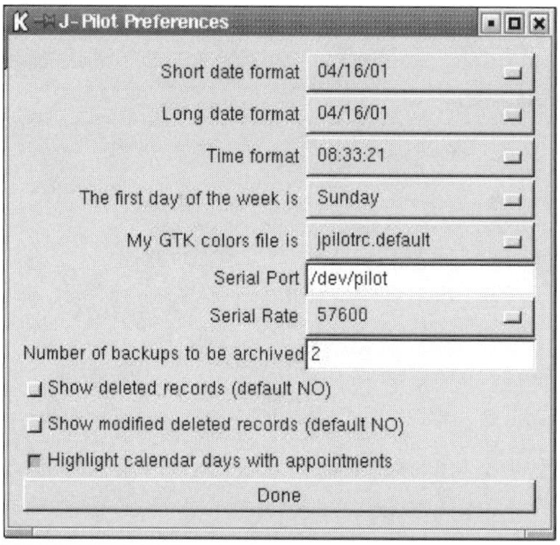

J-Pilot Preferences
Short date format 04/16/01
Long date format 04/16/01
Time format 08:33:21
The first day of the week is Sunday
My GTK colors file is jpilotrc.default
Serial Port /dev/pilot
Serial Rate 57600
Number of backups to be archived 2
Show deleted records (default NO)
Show modified deleted records (default NO)
Highlight calendar days with appointments
Done

Figure 16-20 Jpilot—Prefs.

applications? Well, press any of them and you will get the jpilot user interface (UI) for those. Figure 16-21 shows what you get when you select the Datebook button (you can also select an application UI with the F1–F4 function keys or via the View menu).

Feel free to explore the other jpilot interfaces. They are clean and easy to understand. They correspond well with the "Official" Palm Desktop that runs on another operating system, whose name shall remain Windows.

Now let's get to some fun. How do I know that jpilot uses pilot-link? Well, let's hit the Backup button. Figure 16-22 shows the screenshot. Does this look familiar? Sure enough, it is the output of the *pilot-xfer-backup* command! Backup does a full backup. Sync does a sync *of only the four jpilot-supported applications.* This is an important point and one that bears repeating. The Sync button on jpilot syncs only the Addressbook, Datebook, Memo, and To-Do applications *and nothing else.*

This leads us to the major deficiency of jpilot. It has no provision for adding conduits for additional applications. It can back up the data in your other applications, but it cannot process it in any way. However, this may be less of a restriction than it seems.

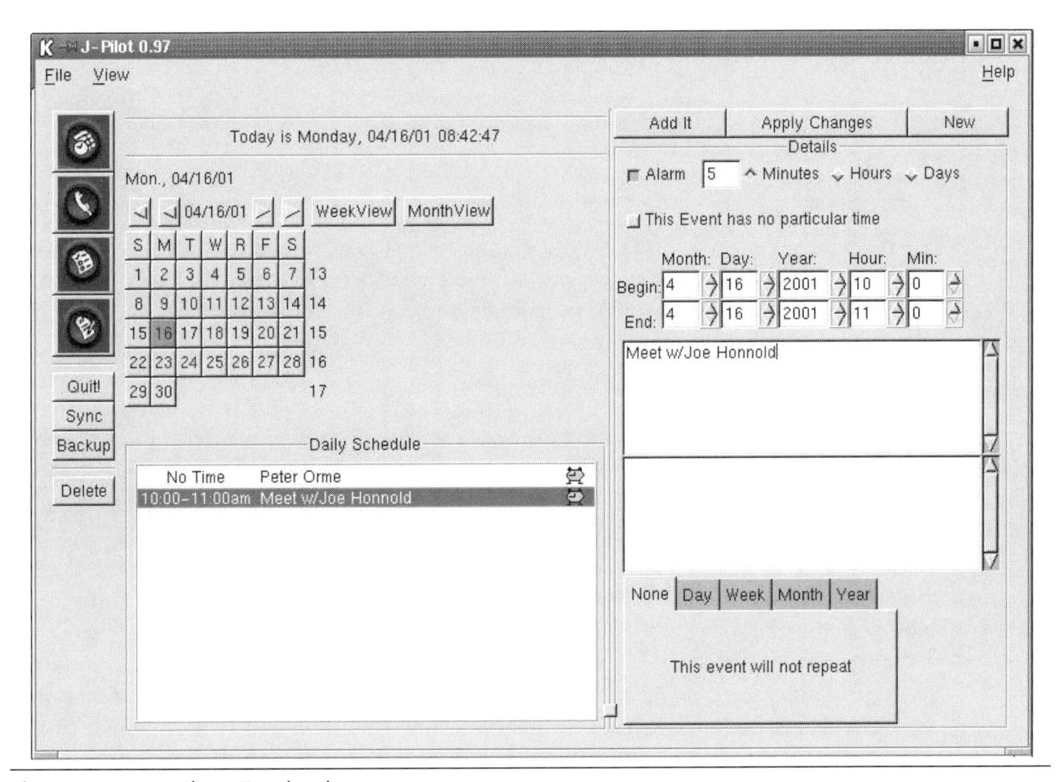

Figure 16-21 Jpilot—Datebook.

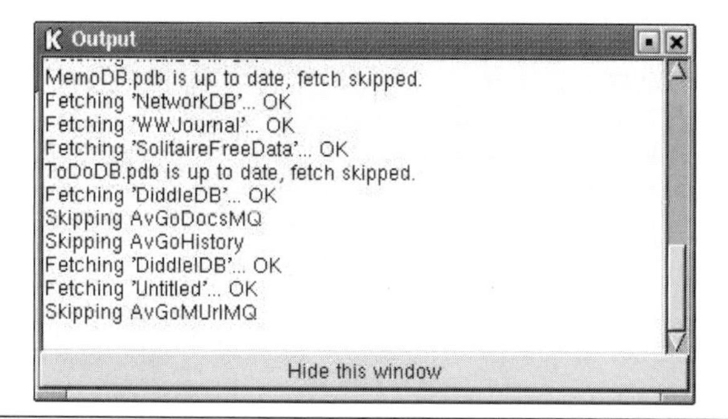

Figure 16-22 Jpilot—backup.

Unless you are a programmer yourself, you are unlikely to be able to write a conduit for pilot-manager or kpilot, the two products listed in this chapter that *do* support add-on conduits. Plus, due to the fact that Windows remains the majority OS, most PalmOS software authors who do have conduit applications (such as LandWare's Pocket Quicken, one that I use personally) write the conduits for that platform only. Still, it is one mark against jpilot that it has no provision for add-on conduits. In every other way, I found it to be the best sync GUI I've seen so far.

Malsync

I would be remiss if I didn't mention this one, at least in passing. One of the most popular "after-market" software packages for the PalmOS-based PDAs is AvantGo, which is basically an offline Web browser or Web page–"clipping" service. You can use your Linux-based PC to connect to MAL servers like AvantGo. Here we will show you how.

In this discussion, I will assume that you are already have AvantGo or some other MAL-based Web-clipping application set up on your Palm device and you currently sync it using that *other* OS. If you don't know anything about this, start at *http://avantgo.com*, learn about the product, and then come back here.

So you have a Web-clipping server and your own account on it. You have your channels set up and now you want to use Linux to sync it so you can finally jettison that other operating system. Well, you've come to the right place! First, you need to get a little program called *malsync* from *http://www.tomw.org/malsync/*. You can get source and compile it, get RPMs, or get a binary tarball. I recommend either the first or the last choice (in this rare instance, I would recommend the last choice, because the first choice may ask you some setup questions you aren't ready to deal with unless you are a programmer).

As I said, I assume you already have an AvantGo account and you have the Palm software installed and configured. If you don't, the malsync tarball includes them. You will have to install the software and then use the menu on the AvantGo application on your palm to select Options -> Server Preferences, where you will enter your AvantGo (or other MAL) server address and account information.

To synchronize, you have to run the malsync program and hit the Hotsync button on your palm cradle. malsync respects the PILOTPORT and PILOTRATE environment variables. It also supports both HTTP and SOCKS proxies (if you are behind a firewall). Basic operation looks like this:

```
mschwarz@mars:~$ malsync
Waiting for connection on /dev/pilot (press the HotSync button now)...
Connection successful...
Searching for updated Web pages...
.
..............................Removing out-of-date Web pages...
.
......
Saving updated channels...
.
..........
Saving updated Web pages...
.
..........................
Finishing...
```

Not very pretty, is it. That's okay—if we wanted pretty we'd be using a Mac. It does get you your Web pages on your palm, and that was the point.

Things That Don't Work

I use PocketQuicken, but not on Linux. Even though I can run Quicken under Wine, I have not yet been able to get the Palm Desktop and PocketQuicken conduit working under Wine. It may be possible, but I haven't figured it out yet. Any palm application that requires a special conduit (as opposed to the standard default backup conduit) will probably give you problems on Linux, unless, of course, the software comes with a conduit program of its own for Linux or someone has invented their own (use a Web search to look for "*programname* linux conduit," that's how I found malsync) or you write one for one of the "custom conduit"–capable sync programs.

Chapter 17

Necessary Evils: Running MS Windows Programs

Difficult-o-Meter: 4 (fairly high Linux knowledge required)

Covers:

wine *http://www.winehq.com*

Question: How can I run MS Windows programs from Linux?

Answer: Use Wine.

Repeat after me: Wine is not an emulator (WINE). It's not, really. Emulators . . . well, emulate different hardware. Wine runs Windows programs in the Linux environment, but the hardware is all the same—Intel x86. As such, it's really a program loader and a massively reverse-engineered shared library system. If none of that makes sense to you, just remember this: Wine lets you run your MS Windows programs under Linux.

Wine is probably the most ambitious Linux-based project since Linux itself, and it's done by a set of developers who have recognized that alternative software sometimes just doesn't cut it. Sometimes, one simply *must* run MS Windows software to accomplish a given task. This is particularly true of games.

Wine is aiming at a moving target—it's attempting to emulate all of MS Windows, in all versions, simultaneously. Amazingly enough, it's actually managing to do this. Not everything is perfect, that's for sure. There are font-size problems in certain windows. Some applications will cause your instance of X-windows to crash. Some games will hard-hang your entire machine (it sounds like a perfect copy of certain MS Windows behaviors, doesn't it?). DirectX support is still spotty, and graphics under X are slower than under MS Windows. But for the most part, it's functional.

Bear in mind that Wine is still technically a developer-only release. This means that documentation is often either sparse or outdated, sometimes both. Sometimes new releases of Wine will not run applications that worked fine under previous versions (though this is happening less and less). It's not terribly space-optimized yet. You'll want to have 300MB of space free on your hard drive to compile and install Wine. As of the more recent versions, you no longer need to have an MS Windows installation at all! Wine can load and run programs directly from the ext2 file system. Support for installer programs has come a long way, so the installer can be run through Wine, and all the registry entries will be properly installed.

Applications run with different degrees of success, depending on whether or not your system has a real copy of MS Windows installed somewhere. The authors all run varying setups and have experienced some minor differences in how applications run. We've noticed that this occurs both ways, in fact—sometimes, having MS Windows negatively affects how an application runs, and sometimes it nets a positive effect. As always, your mileage may vary.

Getting Wine

Point your browser at *http://www.winehq.com/*. Dig through the site to grab the latest source code, and download to your */usr/src* directory.

```
tar zxvf Wine-blah-blah.tar.gz
cd wine-blah
./tools/wineinstall
```

The *wineinstall* program will configure, compile, and install Wine for you. You'll want to be root for this, by the way. It'll even detect if you're on a dual-boot system and fill in the proper paths for the registry. Once the compile is running, you've got some time to kill. Wine takes a while to compile, but it is worth it.

If you're not root when this is running, however, it'll build everything as simply a normal user. You can then install the software by running *wineinstall* as root.

Your *wine.conf*

Stored in either *~/.winerc* or */usr/local/etc/wine.conf*, this file is the Wine version of *system.ini*. It even follows the same format.

Here's my *wine.conf*, followed by an explanation.

```
WINE REGISTRY Version 2
;; All keys relative to \\Machine\\Software\\Wine\\Wine\\Config
;;
;; MS-DOS drives configuration
;;
;; Each section has the following format:
;; [Drive X]
;; Path=xxx       (Unix path for drive root)
;; Type=xxx       (supported types are 'floppy', 'hd', 'cdrom' and
                  'network')
;; Label=xxx      (drive label, at most 11 characters)
;; Serial=xxx     (serial number, 8 characters hexadecimal number)
;; Filesystem=xxx (supported types are 'msdos'/'dos'/'fat',
   'win95'/'vfat', 'unix')
;;   This is the FS Wine is supposed to emulate on a certain
;;   directory structure.
;;   Recommended:
;;   - "win95" for ext2fs, VFAT and FAT32
;;   - "msdos" for FAT16 (ugly, upgrading to VFAT driver strongly
       recommended)
;;   DON'T use "unix" unless you intend to port programs using Winelib!
;; Device=/dev/xx (only if you want to allow raw device access)
;;
[Drive A]
"Path" = "/mnt/fd0"
"Type" = "floppy"
"Label" = "Floppy"
#Serial=87654321
"Device" = "/dev/fd0"

[Drive C]
"Path" = "/loki"
"Type" = "hd"
"Label" = "loki"
"Filesystem" = "win95"

[Drive D]
"Path" = "/fenrir"
"Type" = "hd"
"Label" = "fenrir"
"Filesystem" = "win95"
```

```
[Drive E]
"Path" = "/cdrom"
"Type" = "cdrom"
"Label" = "CD-Rom"
"Filesystem" = "win95"
; make sure that device is correct and has proper permissions!
"Device" = "/dev/cdrom"

[Drive F]
"Path" = "/dvd"
"Type" = "cdrom"
"Label" = "Toshiba"
"Filesystem" = "win95"
"Device" = "/dev/hdd"

[Drive G]
"Path" = "/tmp"
"Type" = "hd"
"Label" = "Tmp Drive"
"Filesystem" = "win95"

[Drive H]
"Path" = "${HOME}"
"Type" = "network"
"Label" = "Home"
"Filesystem" = "win95"

[wine]
"Windows" = "c:\\windows"
"System" = "c:\\windows\\system"
"Temp" = "g:\\"
"Path" = "c:\\windows;c:\\windows\\system;e:\\;e:\\test;f:\\"
;Profile=c:\windows\Profiles\Administrator
"GraphicsDriver" = "x11drv"
; <wineconf>

[DllDefaults]
"EXTRA_LD_LIBRARY_PATH" = "${HOME}/wine/cvs/lib"
;DefaultLoadOrder = native, builtin, so
"DefaultLoadOrder" = "builtin, so, native"

[DllOverrides]
"kernel32, gdi32, user32" = "builtin"
"krnl386, gdi, user" = "builtin"
"toolhelp" = "builtin"
"comdlg32, commdlg" = "builtin, native"
"version, ver" = "builtin, native"
"shell32, shell" = "builtin, native"
"lz32, lzexpand" = "builtin, native"
"commctrl, comctl32" = "builtin, native"
```

```
"wsock32, winsock" = "builtin"
"advapi32, crtdll, ntdll" = "builtin, native"
"mpr, winspool.drv" = "builtin, native"
"ddraw, dinput, dsound" = "builtin, native"
"winmm, mmsystem" = "builtin"
"msvideo, msvfw32" = "builtin, native"
"mcicda.drv, mciseq.drv" = "builtin, native"
"mciwave.drv" = "builtin, native"
"mciavi.drv, mcianim.drv" = "builtin, native"
"msacm.drv, midimap.drv" = "builtin, native"
"w32skrnl" = "builtin"
"wnaspi32, wow32" = "builtin"
"system, display, wprocs" = "builtin"
"wineps" = "builtin"
"icmp" = "builtin"

[x11drv]
; Number of colors to allocate from the system palette
"AllocSystemColors" = "100"
; Use a private color map
"PrivateColorMap" = "N"
; Favor correctness over speed in some graphics operations
"PerfectGraphics" = "N"
; Color depth to use on multidepth screens
;;ScreenDepth = 16
; Name of X11 display to use
;;Display = :0.0
; Allow the window manager to manage created windows
"Managed" = "Y"
; Use XFree86 DGA extension if present
"UseDGA" = "Y"
; Use XShm extension if present
"UseXShm" = "Y"
; Enable DirectX mouse grab
"DXGrab" = "N"
; Create the desktop window with a double-buffered visual
; (useful to play OpenGL games)
"DesktopDoubleBuffered" = "N"
; Code page used for captions in managed mode
; 0 means default ANSI code page (CP_ACP == 0)
"TextCP" = "0"
; Use this if you have more than one port for video on your setup
; (Wine uses for now the first 'input image' it finds).
;; XVideoPort = 43

[fonts]
;Read documentation/fonts before adding aliases
"Resolution" = "96"
"Default" = "-adobe-times-"

[serialports]
"Com1" = "/dev/ttyS0"
```

```
"Com2" = "/dev/ttyS1"
"Com3" = "/dev/modem,38400"
"Com4" = "/dev/modem"

[parallelports]
"Lpt1" = "/dev/lp0"

[spooler]
"LPT1:" = "|lpr"
;LPT2:=|gs -sDEVICE=bj200 -sOutputFile=/tmp/fred -q -
"LPT3:" = "/dev/lp3"

[ports]
;read=0x779,0x379,0x280-0x2a0
;write=0x779,0x379,0x280-0x2a0

[spy]
"Exclude" = "WM_SIZE;WM_TIMER;"

[registry]
; Paths must be given in /dir/dir/file.reg format.
; Wine will not understand dos filenames here...

;These are all booleans.  Y/y/T/t/1 are true, N/n/F/f/0 are false.
;Defaults are read all, write to Home
; Global registries (stored in /etc)
"LoadGlobalRegistryFiles" = "Y"
; Home registries (stored in ~user/.wine/)
"LoadHomeRegistryFiles" = "Y"
; Load Windows registries from the Windows directory
"LoadWindowsRegistryFiles" = "Y"
; TRY to write all changes to home registries
"WritetoHomeRegistryFiles" = "Y"
; Use new file format
"UseNewFormat" = "Y"
; Registry periodic save timeout in seconds
; PeriodicSave=600
; Save only modified keys
"SaveOnlyUpdatedKeys" = "Y"

[Tweak.Layout]
;; WineLook=xxx  (supported styles are 'Win31'(default), 'Win95',
    'Win98')
;WineLook=Win95
"WineLook" = "Win98"

[programs]
"Default" = ""
"Startup" = ""

[Console]
;Drivers=tty
```

```
;XtermProg=nxterm
;InitialRows=25
;InitialColumns=80
;TerminalType=nxterm

[Clipboard]
"ClearAllSelections" = "0"
"PersistentSelection" = "1"

# < /wineconf >
```

I'm not going to talk about how the drives themselves are configured, since the configuration file is (as you can see) pretty much self-explanatory. The last nine-tenths of the file are automatically generated. I set up the C, D, E, F, and G drives myself. If you don't have two win98 drives, and two CD-ROM drives, your setup will probably be a bit simpler. The *wineinstall* tool will really set up almost all of Wine for you—including your *config* file. It's getting to be quite newbie-proof.

At this point, you might be thinking you'll have MS Windows running in a window under Linux. Wine doesn't really work like that yet—you'd need something like vmware or plex86 to do that. Wine is still rather application based, meaning that you fire off instances of Wine with the argument of the program you'd like started. To demonstrate, let's look at some concrete examples: AIM, Solitaire, MS Word, and Stars!

AOL's AIM Client

Now, there are lots of AIM clients for Linux these days, but the MS Windows AIM client works under Wine quite well. It's also a small, network-centric application (and what fun is a computer without an Internet connection these days?). Starting it is quite simple. Change into the directory where it's located—which in my case is */loki/progra~1/aim95/*, and start Wine with an argument of the program name. (As you may or may not know, *Program Files* can be abbreviated as *progra~1*) I also give my X-window manager control of the application's window, using the -managed flag. So the command looks like this:

```
cd /loki/progra~1/aim95/
wine -managed ./aim.exe &
```

Note how I pop Wine into the background. That's because it takes a while to load—somewhere between 15 seconds and 2 minutes (or more) depending on how fast your hardware is. The newer versions of Wine also seem to load faster than the old ones. Figures 17-1 through 17-3 show what the AIM client looks like under X-windows.

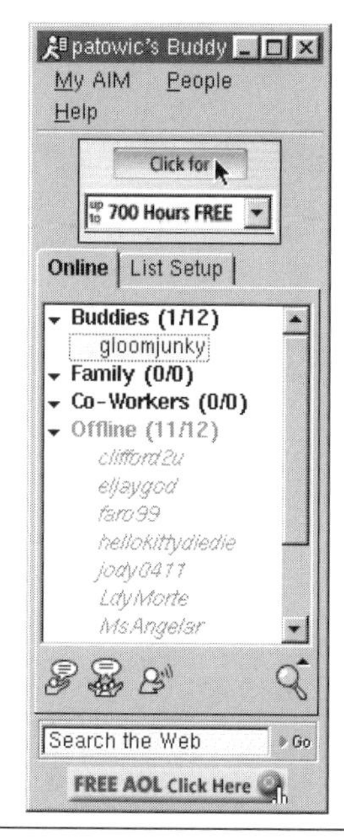

Figure 17-1 Emulated AIM Buddy list.

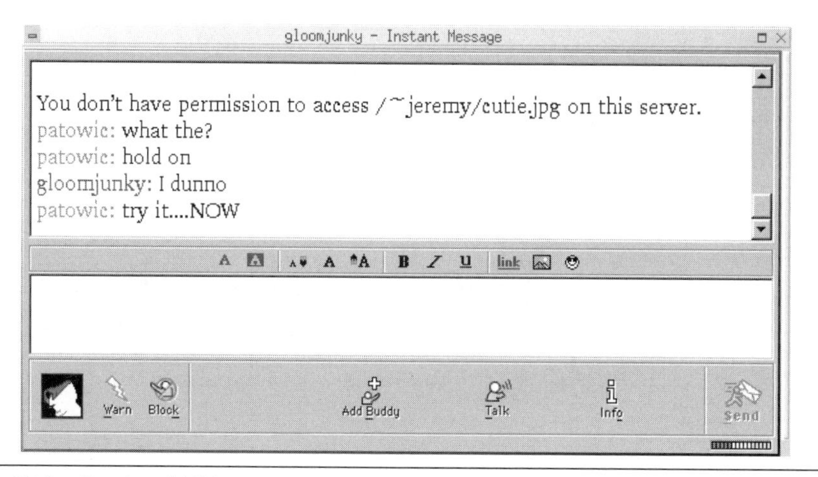

Figure 17-2 Emulated AIM message.

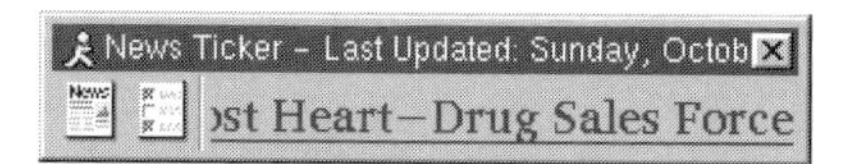

Figure 17-3 Emulated AIM news ticker.

Solitaire via Wine

You want slow? Try firing up a game of solitaire over a T-1 via Wine. Yikes! It does load, though, and I'm betting that with a fat enough pipe, it'd be playable. On the local machine, it's quite usable, and if you're a real solitaire addict this is just what you're looking for. It starts with the simple command of

```
wine -managed /yourhd/windows/sol.exe
```

and it's more than happy to have multiple instances up at once (Figure 17-4).

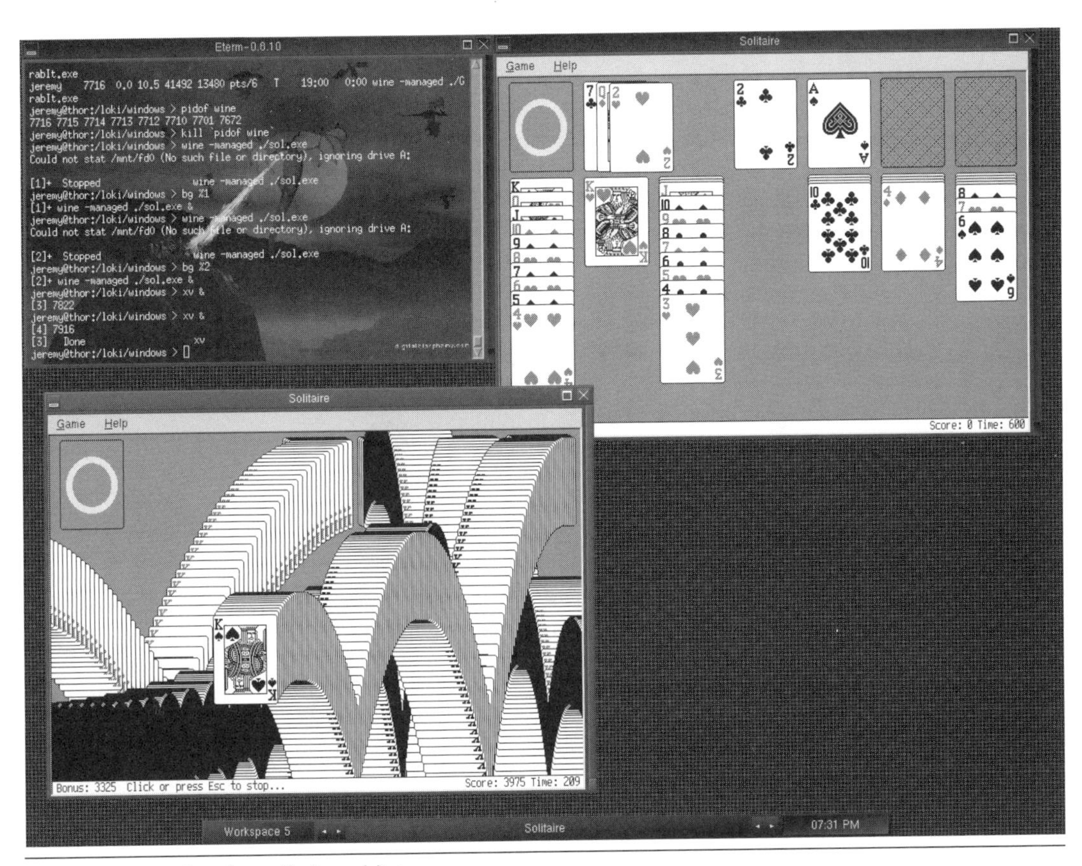

Figure 17-4 Wine for solitaire addicts.

MS Word 97 via Wine

Again, this is just as simple as changing directories to your mounted Windows drive, changing into program files, then Microsoft Office, then Office, and running

```
wine -managed winword.exe
```

As we can see in Figure 17-5, it loads and runs just fine.

But check out the word it doesn't recognize in the spellcheck (Figure 17-6): *Linux*. In 1998 it still didn't recognize Linux. But it *did* recognize Bill Gates. Hmm.

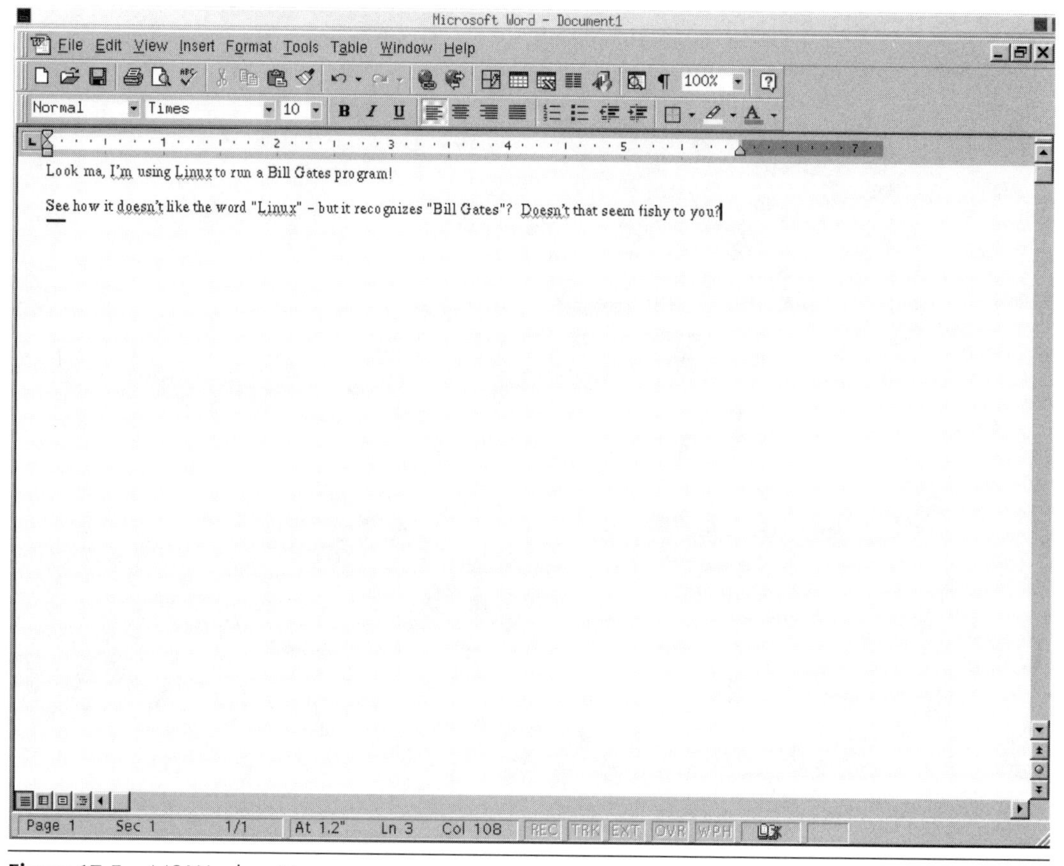

Figure 17-5 MS Word on Linux.

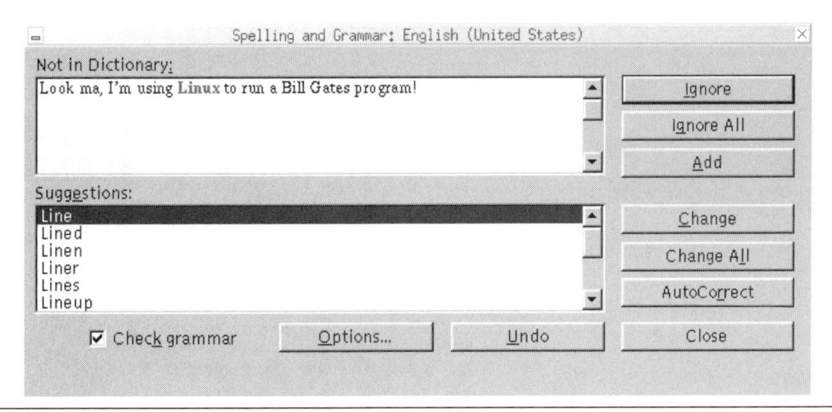

Figure 17-6 MS Word spellchecking.

Stars!

Stars! is a turn-based galactic conquest game that actually runs okay under Wine. It was one of the reasons I started looking at the demo, got hooked, and bought it. I'm willing to bet the next version, Stars! SuperNova, won't run worth a dang on it, but I probably won't even buy that version. Why, you ask? Well, allow me to answer that question in the form of shameless self-promotion: I've been plugging away on Stellar Legacy, a multiplatform game of similar purpose at *http://stellarlegacy.sourceforge.net*. Stars! *does* run on Wine, but every time it starts up, it says, "Hey, your machine configuration changed! Re-enter your serial number." This is a pain, and it's really, really weak copy protection. Figure 17-7 shows the basic screen, happily running under the January 12, 2001, version of Wine (20010112).

The trick is not to watch any of the combat scenes. They'll hang up Wine right quick, though they worked about four months ago. This is unfortunately the way Wine works sometimes. It's just as well, really. If Stars! worked flawlessly under Wine, I'd never have finished this chapter, much less the book. Thankfully, Rogue Spear doesn't run at all under Wine! Interestingly enough, when Stars! bought the farm (that is, the copy running under Wine crashed hard), it took AIM down as well—but stealthily. AIM *appeared* to be working fine, but it wasn't sending or receiving anything.

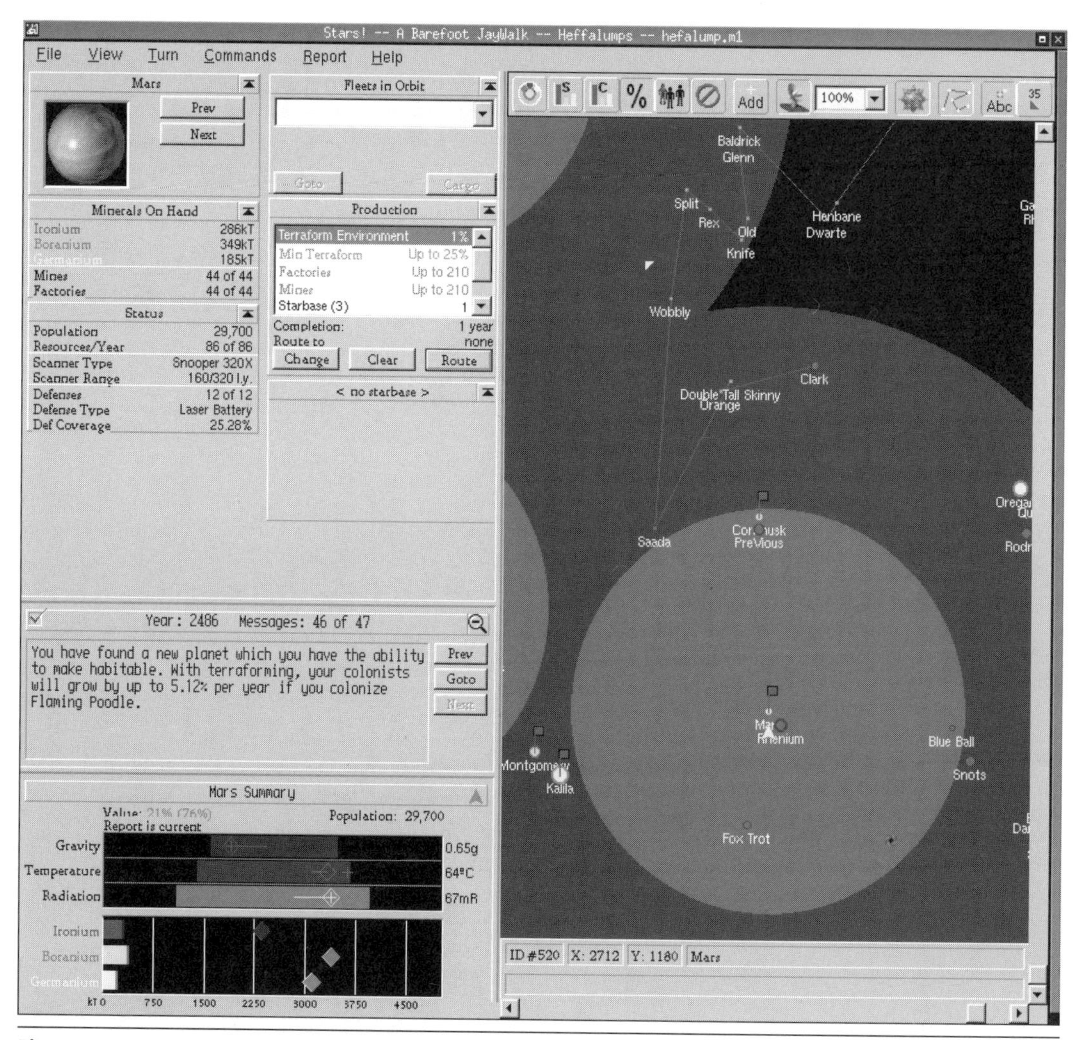

Figure 17-7 Stars! main screen.

Total Annihilation, Wine, and Other DirectX Games

Total Annihilation supposedly runs under Wine. I've had only a little luck when forcing my X-server to 640 × 480 and 8-bit color. Even then, it had a few hard hangs, dropping my entire Linux box. Wine isn't really up to running games yet. There are teams working on this, however. You can find some games that do run on it, and limited notes on how to do it, at *http://www.linuxgames.com/wine/*. The guys at *http://www.transgaming.com/* take gaming under Linux seriously. They're porting DirectX to Wine very quickly, and they're on a subscription basis. If enough people give them money, they'll GPL their work. While I don't really like being extorted like this, it is a viable model for generating revenue. Really, a few dollars is a cheap price to pay when one considers what a stable platform Linux can be for gaming.

Basically, you *can* run games like these on wine, but you're into serious geek land by the time you get there. I've been playing with Wine on and off for some time now, and I can't reliably get Total Annihilation (or other DirectX) games to run. And when they do run, they're noticeably slower and buggier than in Win9x. This isn't what I look for when I'm gaming. Wine 1.0 will be different. And the subsequent versions will be much, much, much better.

Network Applications

Some network applications work great under Wine. Forte Agent works fairly well. mIRC runs fine but cannot handle DCC transfers. AOL's AIM works just fine. If the application is going to work, it'll pretty much work automatically—the Wine folks have successfully implemented enough of the Windows code base to emulate a good portion of MS Windows network connectivity.

Serial- and Parallel-Port Support

Serial- and parallel-port support also vary from release to release. There are reports of applications working wonderfully on one release, only to break with the next. The more people that try, the more data will be gathered, and the more effort will be exerted by Wine's developers.

Summary

Wine is great for running regular Windows programs, and office productivity applications. Quicken, according to Mr. Schwarz, runs flawlessly under Wine—and it has since the fall of 2000.* If you do use it, be prepared for occasionally lacking documentation and for odd behavior. And please advise the maintainers of any bugs you find. That's the only way this can improve, and improve it has. The difference in the last 60 days alone, in terms of MS Word support, is huge. What I gave a B+ when I first started this chapter now gets a solid A.

*Mr. Schwarz here: Mr. Anderson overstates the case somewhat. Quicken runs well enough to be usable under Wine. There are still a number of font and dialog box problems. I recently tried to export my Quicken data to QIF under Wine20010510 and it just plain crashed when I clicked the OK button to start the export. I do, however, fire up Quicken under Wine to key in my daily transactions. I then back these up to a floppy right away. I then "restore" from that floppy into my "official" copy of Quicken, which, yes, is still running under a "real" version of Windows. I'm just starting to fiddle with GNUCash, a Free Software GUI accounting package that runs under Linux. Alas, I don't know enough yet to include a chapter on it in this book, but if you want to look into this, check out *http://www.gnucash.org/* to learn more.

Chapter 18

REMOTE CD BURNING

Difficult-o-Meter: 2 (light Linux skill required)

Covers:

cdrecord	*http://www.fokus.gmd.de/research/cc/glone/employees/joerg.schilling/private/cdrecord.html*
mkisofs	*http://www.fokus.gmd.de/research/cc/glone/employees/joerg.schilling/private/mkisofs.html*
xcdroast	*http://www.xcdroast.org*
CD-Writing HOWTO	*http://www.ibiblio.org/pub/Linux/docs/HOWTO/CD-Writing-HOWTO*

Question: How do I burn CD-Rs on my Linux machine? Where do I start?

Answer: In the summer of '00 I was right where you were at. I couldn't find an exact document that would teach me how to do what I wanted to do—which was throw an IDE* CD-RW in a P133 I had sitting around and then burn CDs unattended. Thus this chapter was born.

I'd had the remote-burn approach in mind when I bought my Mitsumi CDRW drive. I'd made sure it was listed in the CD-Writing-HOWTO as one that was supported (the HOWTO is at *http://www.ibiblio.org/pub/Linux/docs/HOWTO/CD-Writing-HOWTO*).

*Integrated Device Electronics, as opposed to SCSI.

You might want to check and make sure yours is supported. It likely is. When I got my Mitsumi CR-4802TE, it was not listed as 100 percent supported, but there were hints from people that it was, so I gambled.

It's really up to you whether you want your CD recording device (hereafter referred to as a *burner*) in your workstation or in some other machine. I'm paranoid and work under the assumption that even hitting the Shift key while burning a CD-R will result in a failed burn (and this is obviously not true), so I put it in a machine that doesn't do much else. When I want to burn a CD, I SSH into the burning station ("Surt"), transfer the files, create the iso image, and cut the CD. The only CPU-intensive process that runs on that machine is the burning software itself—even though CD-Rs are less than $1 each these days, I still hate to waste them. When you're picking the machine you're going to put the burner in, don't forget disk space. If you're going to cut full 650MB CD-Rs, you're going to need 2 × 650MB, or 1.3GB of free space. Why that much? Because we don't cut CDs on the fly—that's a good way to waste blanks. So we need 650MB for the files that will be on the CD and another 650MB for the *.iso* image we'll create from those files: 650 + 650 = 1300.

Now that you've found almost 1.5 gigabytes of free space, and made sure it's in the proper machine, you get to install your burner. If you've got a small computer systems interface (SCSI) burner . . . well, you're obviously either a genuine power user, a hardware snob, or both, so skip ahead to where I'm talking about installing the requisite software.

Getting Linux to Grok Your IDE Burner

Well, we already know your burner is supported, right? So all we have to do now is convince Linux that your IDE burner isn't a regular CD-ROM drive. Unfortunately, when you booted, Linux decided that it *was* a regular CD-ROM drive. In order to convince it otherwise, we're going to have to tweak your *conf.modules* settings, recompile your kernel (or set up a module for insertion), and . . . reboot!

It's been said that the only reason to reboot in Linux is to add new hardware. While there are rare instances when this isn't true, it most certainly is true here. Basically, we're going to convince Linux that your IDE burner is actually an SCSI burner. That's because all the burning software in the world is pretty much written to the SCSI (at least in the Linux world. I have no idea how Windows handles the dirty work, but I'm sure it's messy). The reason for this is simple: IDE/ATAPI doesn't have a full command set, so you can't properly drive a CD burner with it.

Let's not go modifying your *conf.modules* yet, at least not until we have a new, working kernel compiled. I'm going to assume that you want to compile the driver into your kernel. I'm a firm believer in having the core drivers compiled *into* your kernel—this means they can't be inadvertently deleted, and you have access to those devices just as soon as the system loads the kernel.

Jump into your kernel source directory. On my system, at the time of this writing, the kernel source is at */usr/src/linux*, and it's version 2.2.16. Even though I detest X-windows for being slow and bloated (don't even talk to me about the Enlightenment Window Manager), I almost always use *make xconfig* for my kernel configurations. Figure 18-1 shows the generic Kernel config screen. Figure 18-2 shows the SCSI device setup, where I've selected SCSI-emulation, SCSI CD-ROM support, and generic SCSI support. Figure 18-3, on the other hand, shows the Block devices setup, where I've disabled IDE/ATAPI CD-ROM support. I don't need it, because I'll never be addressing my CD-ROM as an IDE device anymore. If, and only if, you have an additional IDE CD-ROM device in your machine should you leave this enabled. If you don't, pull it out. It'll make your kernel smaller and faster.

Now go into *Filesystems*. Undoubtedly, you're going to want to be able to understand a PC-formatted CD-R someday, so we're going to enable Joliet file system support. Joliet is a way to get long filenames onto a CD-ROM (longer than 8.3 characters, anyway), and to have deep directories and what not. Naturally, Microsoft has added their own extensions to this (surprise, surprise!), and we're going to compile those extensions directly into the kernel. Again, we do this for ease of configuration and speed.

Now exit and save your kernel configuration. We're about to rebuild the kernel. The sequence of commands we want to follow is this:

```
make dep
make clean
make
make modules
su -c"make install && make modules_install"
```

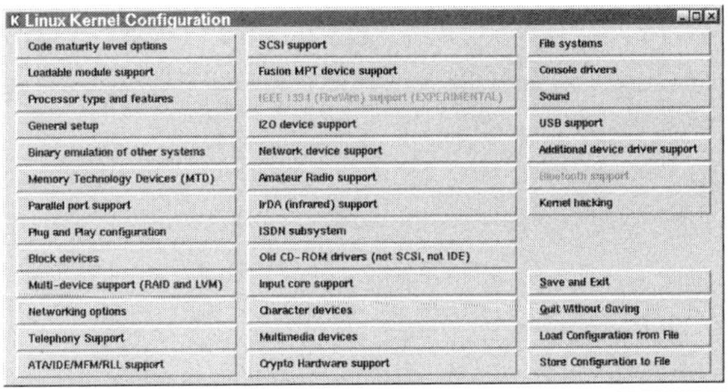

Figure 18-1 Kernel Configuration main menu.

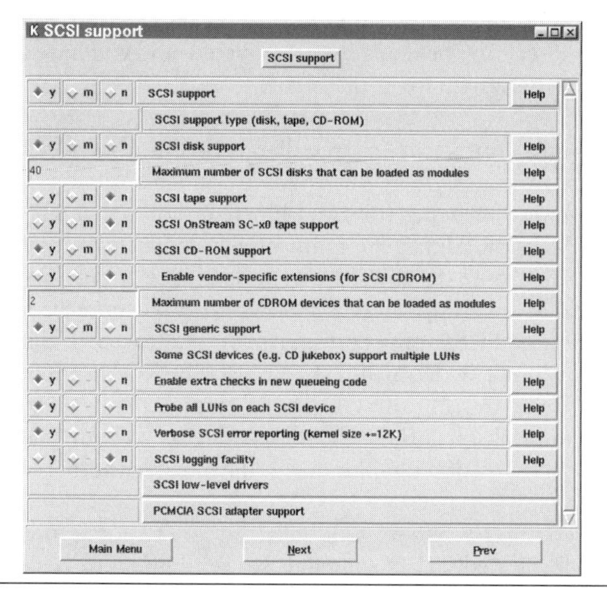

Figure 18-2 Kernel Configuration SCSI menu.

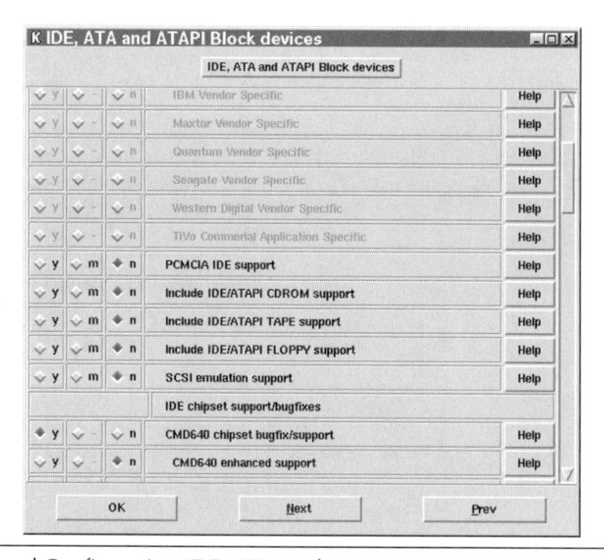

Figure 18-3 Kernel Configuration IDE, ATA, and ATAPI menu.

I give some of my friends major conniptions when I do things this way:

```
jeremy@thor:/usr/src/linux > make dep &&make clean &&make &&make modules
    &&su -c "make install && make modules_install" && /sbin/lilo && reboot
```

The double ampersands require that each previous command complete successfully before the next will be run. If any command in the list errors out, no subsequent commands will be run. Personally, I think it's pretty cool. When I run the whole thing as root, I don't even need the "su -c" bit—my machine just recompiles the kernel and modules, installs them, reruns LILO, and reboots. I hit Enter, go get myself a soda, talk to my wife for an hour or so (or maybe wrestle with the bloodthirsty beast I call a dog), and come back to the new system. Note that we can't do that nice über-command here, because we haven't yet made all the necessary modifications to */etc/conf.modules*. We'll do those now.

If you're taking the kernel module approach, you'll have to have the following lines in your */etc/conf.modules:*

```
alias scd0 sr_mod
alias scsi_hostadapter ide-scsi
options ide-cd  ignore=/dev/hdX  #where X is the letter of your device
```

If you're compiling everything into the kernel, ignore the preceding stuff. It's all extraneous.

Now we modify */etc/fstab* to reflect the new nature of your CD-ROM drive.

Open up */etc/fstab* in your favorite editor, and find the line with */cdrom* in the second field. Mine looks like this:

```
/dev/hdc         /cdrom                         auto
    ro,noauto,user,exec 0    0
```

Change it to look like this:

```
/dev/scd0         /cdrom                        auto
    ro,noauto,user,exec 0    0
```

Did you notice that the only change is that *hdc* became *scd0*? That's all you had to do.

Now it's time to reboot. Note that you'll need to make the above changes to your */etc/conf.modules* only if you decided to ignore my advice and go with the modules approach. If you left IDE CD-ROM drivers in the kernel, you'll need to have all three options in your */etc/conf.modules*, or it won't work.

Now that you've rebooted, it's time to test your setup. Throw a CD-ROM into your drive, and type

```
mount /cdrom
```

If it returns without error and you can now browse the CD, you've done everything right. It's time to start installing burning software. If it *doesn't* work, then you've done something wrong. Go back to the beginning and double-check all your entries. If you're trying something funky, like a machine with one IDE CD-ROM drive, a SCSI burner and an IDE DVD-ROM drive . . . well, try disabling some of the hardware and doing it again.

mkisofs, cdda2wav, cdrecord

Check out the links at the opening of this chapter for where to download mkisofs. This is the first tool we'll install, because without it we won't get anywhere. mkisofs will create an iso9660 file system (isofs, get it?)—the standard format of CD-ROMs everywhere. Most PC CD-ROMs have Joliet extensions too, but ISO9660 came first. Basically, mkisofs takes a directory structure and turns it into one big iso image. Then cdrecord will throw that iso image onto a recordable CD.

Building mkisofs is easier than you'd think, and it also ends up building most everything else you need to write CDs. Basically, head to the FTP directory referred to earlier and grab the latest stable version of cdrtools—that'll contain cdrecord, mkisofs, and all the other goodies. (Be sure to grab the latest *stable* version. I had difficulty getting the experimental versions to work on my system.)

Building the whole works is a little different than one's average package. This is probably due to the fact that the author (Mr. Schilling) has made a genuinely multiplatform release here. It compiles and runs on most everything. I've saved you a little work, since I went through the READMEs and promptly decided that they were wrong. They ordered me to unset some variables in SuSE Linux and to run a special command. Well, SuSE didn't *have* that variable defined, so I guessed that the documentation was out of date (it certainly appears to be). All I had to do to get the system to build was to change into the directory, type *make*, and then follow that up with a *make install*—but don't run the *make install* until after you've read the next paragraph!

The make doesn't take that long, but it defaults to installing the binaries in */opt/schily/bin*—which isn't really a typical Linux way of doing it. */usr/local* seems like a better place for this stuff, but no matter how I tried, I could only get it to run from */usr/bin*! I played with three versions of the software (1.8, 1.9, and 1.10a4), all compiled from source, and one installed via RPM. For no good reason, the cdrecord binary refused to run from any location other than */usr/bin*. I even tried putting a soft link in */usr/bin* to the real location, and it didn't work. I don't understand why this is, but it's consistent. I'm chalking it up to some kind of hardcoding in the cdrecord code.

cd DEFAULTS

```
edit Defaults.linux
change all instances of /opt/schily to /usr
NOW run the 'make install' :)
```

The next little thing I do is to introduce a security hole in my system. setuid programs are to be avoided whenever possible, but sometimes they save a lot of nuisance. I usually put the setuid bit on cdrecord—because one has to be root in order to access the CD burner. I'm the only user on my burning station, so the security risk is quite small. I wouldn't *dream* of doing this on a shared machine—in that case I'd use a nifty little utility called *sudo* (see Chapter 15).

Okay, so now we've got cdrecord and mkisofs installed on the system. Whatever do we do with them? We make CDs, of course!

Making the iso Image (or How I Learned to Master My Data)

I fear buffer underruns. A buffer underrun occurs when the system can't feed data to the burner fast enough, and the end result is a coaster—a CD-R that can't be read. With fast machines, it *is* possible to stream the data directly to the CD-R, but I don't like to do that.

Get all the files you want on a CD-R into the directory structure you want on the CD. That is, if you've got a bunch of photos you scanned and a handful of wav files you made and some old e-mail you want to categorize, you can try a structure like this:

```
cdstuff
  +-> email
  +-> photos
  +-> sounds
```

Get everything in its proper place. Once you cut the CD, you can't redo it without using another blank. CD-R drives are technially WORM drives: "write once, read many." So this is definitely a case where you want to measure twice—because you can only cut once.

Watch your size, as well. I usually keep it to a total of 645MB or so—I'd rather waste 5MB than a blank CD. The *du -sh* command will give the size of any directory and its contents in megabytes.

Now that you've got all the files there, you're ready to cut yourself a data CD. The mkisofs will take all your data and massage it into a CD-ready format. The format is pretty simple, though the man page is a bit daunting. I always burn my CDs with Joliet extensions enabled. This ensures I can read them if I don't have access to a Linux box. I've pretty much memorized the following string, and feel free to copy it. First, the generic format:

```
mkisofs -hide-joliet-trans-tbl -J -p <preparer> -V <volume-name> -r -A
    <some comment> -o <output-file> <directory-name>
```

In practice, it tends to looks like this:

```
mkisofs -hide-joliet-trans-tbl -J -p me -V old_email3 -r -A "just some
    crap I want to keep" -o email3.raw /home/jeremy/email3_dir
```

See all those neat error messages you get for deep files (ones in multiple directories)? Those are just the way mkisofs says, "Hello! I'm doing something!" Don't worry too much about them. If you really want to know why they're there, check out the mkisofs man page. At the end, you get a nifty summary, which looks something like this:

```
Total translation table size: 0
Total rockridge attributes bytes: 115029
Total directory bytes: 256000
Path table size(bytes): 946
Max brk space used a1424
4783 extents written (9 Mb)
```

Make sure that the size listed is about the same size as the sum of the files you wanted on the CD. Then use isovfy to verify it:

```
isovfy email3.raw
```

It'll say something like

```
Root at extent 1c, 12288 bytes
[0 0]
No errors found
```

and you can continue on to the next phase: mounting it.

This is relatively simple—just mount the ISO file to a mount point, and look at it for a few minutes and make sure everything is there. This command should get you up and running:

```
su -c"mount -o loop -t iso9660 /data/email3.raw /mnt/cdrom"
```

Feel free to substitute any mount point for */mnt/cdrom*, and be sure to specify the proper name of your iso file. I always call mine *.raw* instead of *.iso*. I don't know why, it's just something I do. If you want to call yours *.goofy*, knock yourself out—this is Linux, after all. A file extension doesn't have to mean anything.

Great, now we've got a working iso image. Go ahead and unmount it. If you weren't able to browse the image properly, make sure you have plenty of disk space on your system. Running out of disk space can mess up an iso image (and lots of other things, too). It's time to think about cutting it to a CD-R or CD-RW.

Finding Your CD-R/CD-RW Drive

Just look at the front of your PC. It's just about that easy. Run the cdrecord with the scanbus flag. Look at the output. Mine looks like this:

```
[extraneous data snipped]
scsibus0:
        0,0,0     0) 'MITSUMI ' 'CR-4802TE       ' '1.3C' Removable CD-ROM
        0,1,0     1) *
        0,2,0     2) *
        0,3,0     3) *
        0,4,0     4) *
        0,5,0     5) *
        0,6,0     6) *
        0,7,0     7) *
```

It looks like my cdrecord is device 0,0,0. From now on we'll refer to that as dev=0,0,0 (because that's how cdrecord likes to think of it).

Blanking a CD-RW

Aha, you say, now you mention CD-RWs! There must be some type of trick, some strange and arcane incantations to be performed for us to access the holy grail of CD media . . . *rewritable media*! Well, sorry to disappoint you, but there's no real trick at all. Since CD-RWs come preformatted with the Universal Disk Format (UDF) file system (the same as used on DVDs), the average Linux box can't read it. UDF file systems aren't automatically supported under pre-2.4 kernels (see *http://linux-udf.sourceforget.net/* if you'd like to add this support into your kernel, but be warned—it's not a trivial task), so we'll have to figure out how to clean that nasty old UDF file system off of the CD-RW. (Even if you have kernel 2.4 up and running, read/write UDF access is still marked as experimental, so you may not want to fool around with it.) Thankfully, purging the UDF file system off a CD-RW is pretty easy to do—it just takes one little command you need to run on it before you start burning:

```
cdrecord -v -speed=2 blank=fast dev=0,0,0
```

Be sure to replace the "2" after *speed* with the actual maximum RW speed of your CD-RW drive (it'll almost certainly be the slowest number in the AxBxC speed specification of the drive). And even if it gives you an error message, it probably succeeded. When I blank my CDs, I get this sequence of messages:

```
jeremy@surt:/data > cdrecord -v -speed=2 blank=fast dev=0,0,0
Cdrecord 1.10a04 (i586-pc-linux-gnu) Copyright (C) 1995-2000 Jörg Schilling
TOC Type: 1 = CD-ROM
scsidev: '0,0,0'
scsibus: 0 target: 0 lun: 0
Linux sg driver version: 2.1.38
Using libscg version 'schily-0.4'
atapi: 1
Device type    : Removable CD-ROM
Version        : 0
Response Format: 1
Vendor_info    : 'MITSUMI '
Identifikation : 'CR-4802TE       '
Revision       : '1.3C'
Device seems to be: Philips CDD-522.
Using generic SCSI-3/mmc CD-R driver (mmc_cdr).
Driver flags   : SWABAUDIO
Drive buf size : 1638400 = 1600 KB
Current Secsize: 2048
ATIP info from disk:
  Indicated writing power: 5
  Reference speed: 2
  Is not unrestricted
  Is erasable
  ATIP start of lead in:  -11080 (97:34/20)
  ATIP start of lead out: 335100 (74:30/00)
  speed low: 2 speed high: 2
  power mult factor: 3 5
  recommended erase/write power: 3
Disk type:    Phase change
Manuf. index: 11
```

```
Manufacturer: Mitsubishi Chemical Corporation
Trying to clear drive status.
cdrecord: Drive needs to reload the media to return to proper status.
Blocks total: 1166730 Blocks current: 1166730 Blocks remaining: 1166880
Starting to write CD/DVD at speed 2 in write mode for single session.
Last chance to quit, starting real write in 1 seconds.
Blanking PMA, TOC, pregap
Blanking time:    1.713s
 cdrecord: Input/output error. prevent/allow medium removal: scsi
    sendcmd: retryable error
CDB:  1E 00 00 00 00 00
status: 0x2 (CHECK CONDITION)
Sense Bytes: 70 00 05 00 00 00 00 06 00 00 00 00 2C 00 00 00
Sense Key: 0x5 Illegal Request, Segment 0
Sense Code: 0x2C Qual 0x00 (command sequence error) Fru 0x0
Sense flags: Blk 0 (not valid)
cmd finished after 0.000s timeout 40s
```

Lots of stuff, no? Like the error message at the end, which tells me that a track that was smaller than the minimum size was expanded to the minimum size. In other words, it *succeeded*. I suspect that this is because I have an early CD-RW drive, but it may be entirely normal. I also specified the verbose flag, which may be part of the problem, but even with the -v *not* specified, I get this string of output:

```
jeremy@surt:/data > cdrecord -speed=2 blank=fast dev=0,0,0
Cdrecord 1.10a04 (i586-pc-linux-gnu) Copyright (C) 1995-2000 Jörg Schilling
scsidev: '0,0,0'
scsibus: 0 target: 0 lun: 0
Linux sg driver version: 2.1.38
Using libscg version 'schily-0.4'
Device type    : Removable CD-ROM
Version        : 0
Response Format: 1
Vendor_info    : 'MITSUMI '
Identifikation : 'CR-4802TE       '
Revision       : '1.3C'
Device seems to be: Philips CDD-522.
Using generic SCSI-3/mmc CD-R driver (mmc_cdr).
Driver flags   : SWABAUDIO
cdrecord: Drive needs to reload the media to return to proper status.
Starting to write CD/DVD at speed 2 in write mode for single session.
Last chance to quit, starting real write in 1 seconds.
cdrecord: Input/output error. prevent/allow medium removal: scsi sendcmd:
    retryable error
CDB:  1E 00 00 00 00 00
status: 0x2 (CHECK CONDITION)
Sense Bytes: 70 00 05 00 00 00 00 06 00 00 00 00 2C 00 00 00
Sense Key: 0x5 Illegal Request, Segment 0
Sense Code: 0x2C Qual 0x00 (command sequence error) Fru 0x0
Sense flags: Blk 0 (not valid)
cmd finished after 0.000s timeout 40s
```

See how similar the output is? The only difference is that I didn't get a "blanking time" piece of information. Heck, that's why I usually run things verbose—might as well see what's going on, eh?

Danger Will Robinson! Do *not* attempt to blank a CD-RW twice in a row! When I did this inadvertently, it knocked my CD-RW drive offline—I couldn't access it from the operating system until I rebooted. This may be a peculiarity of the Mitsumi CR-4802TE, but why take the chance?

Burning Data to a CD-R/CD-RW

This is the fun part—the part of the chapter that tells you the last piece of information you need to know in order to put down this book and start burning CDs like there's no tomorrow. (Note, though, that in a later section I'll tell you how to *duplicate* a data CD, so there is at least some small incentive to continue reading.)

As you saw before, we ran the cdrecord command to blank a CD-RW. Now we'll run the cdrecord in normal recording mode. The command looks like this:

```
cdrecord -eject -v -speed=4 dev=0,0,0 /data/myimage.raw
```

Why the *-v*? Because if you don't specify it, you won't get a status update as the CD is cut. On my machine, cutting a full (650MB) CD-R takes about 18 minutes. I get nervous when I don't get any screen output from a program in that amount of time. Bear in mind that CD-RWs will cut only at CD-RW speed. So even after I've blanked a CD-RW, it takes me 37 minutes to burn a 650MB image to one (my Mitsumi handles CD-RWs at only 2×). Needless to say, I prefer to use CD-Rs, but CD-RWs do have their place.

The *-eject* tells the system to open the drive and eject the media. I did this so that when I walk by my machine and see the drive hanging open, I know the burn completed successfully. I simply pull out the burned disc, label it, and pop a new blank in.

Be sure to substitute your drive's speed in the *-speed* area. It should save you some time. I've seen 12× and even 20× CD-R speeds in some ultraexpensive drives. Since 1× = 74 minutes for 650MB of data, a 12× CD-R can cut a 650MB CD in just over 6 minutes.

And be sure to put the name of your actual image file in the last field, or you won't get what you want at all.

I have had difficulty with some ultracheap CD-R blanks in my drive. Sometimes burns will fail due to inferior media. If this is happening to you, try moving to a name-brand media for a bit. I've found Maxell and Imation to be quite reliable.

Verifying the Freshly Burned CD-R/CD-RW

Well, one way to verify it is to mount it and look around the CD to make sure everything is kosher. That is, in fact, the only way I've found to ensure everything is the same without using X-CD-Roast (see the later section on "Using X-CD-Roast to Verify the Freshly Burned CD-R/CD-RW").

Duplicating Data CDs from the Command Line

Use the dd command line utility to create an ISO image file from the /dev/cdrom device as follows:

```
dd if=/dev/cdrom of=mycd.raw
```

Make sure you have /dev/cdrom as your CD-ROM or linked to your CD-ROM device. dd will read the device file completely, making an ISO image file that is ready to burn to CD using the cdrecord utility. What could be easier?

Using a GUI

I still use X-CD-Roast (see Figure 18-4), since it's the only way I know how of duplicating a data CD. It's really, really self-explanatory. If any of the foregoing stuff frightened you, you might as well start off with X-CD-Roast, since it's incredibly painless. The screenshots in Figures 18-5 and 18-6 show the X-CD-Roast way of doing the things I've already talked about.

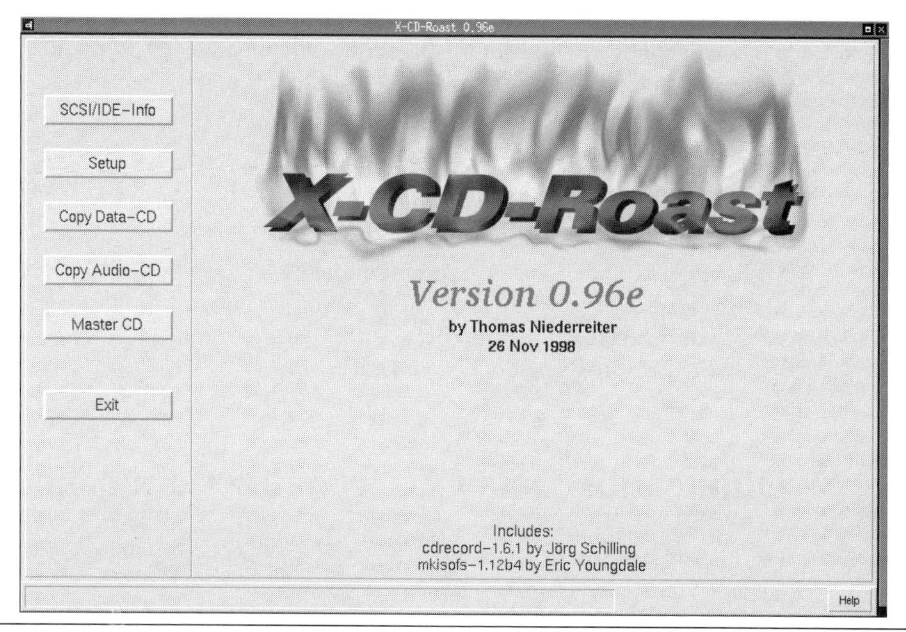

Figure 18-4 X-CD-Roast main screen.

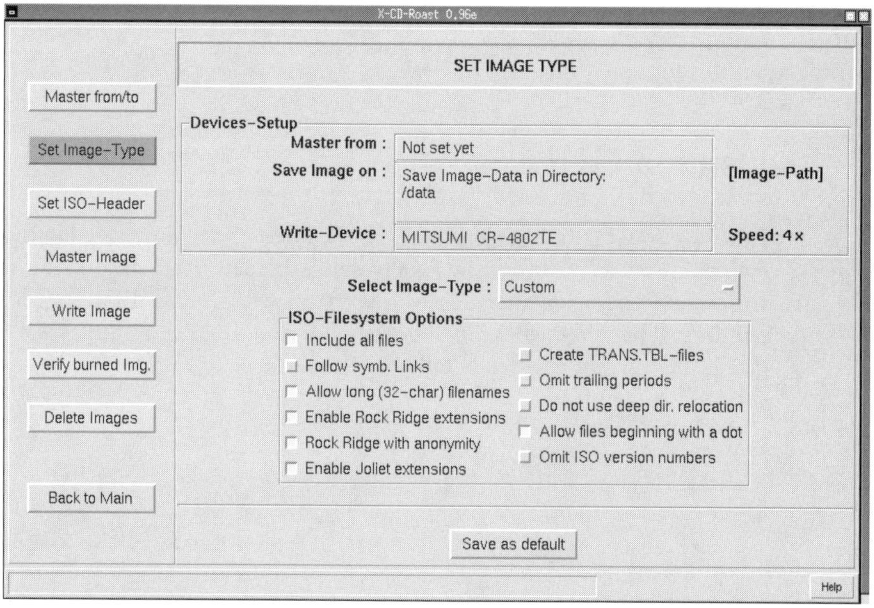

Figure 18-5 Set Image options, such as using Microsoft's Joliet extensions.

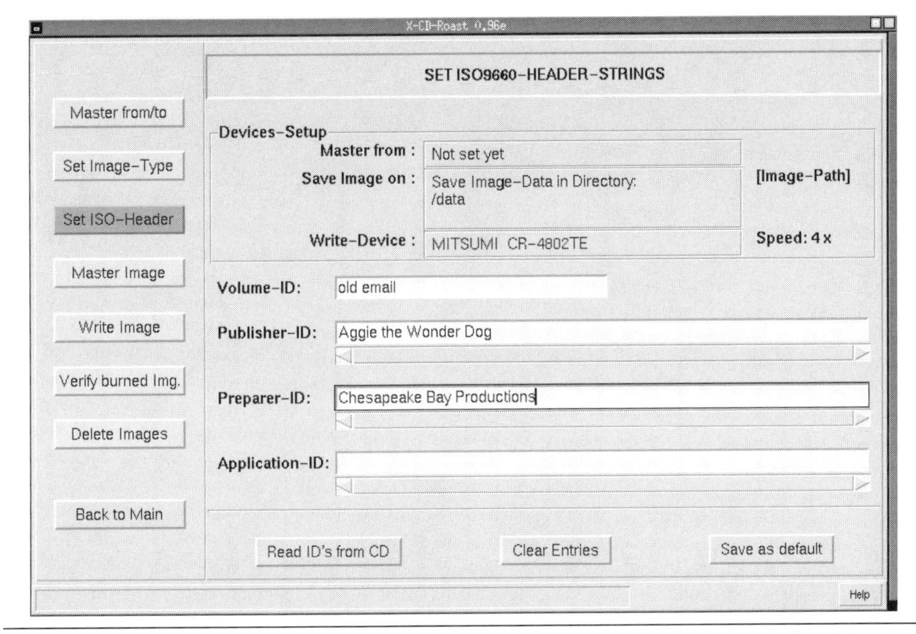

Figure 18-6 Setting the image header in X-CD-Roast—looks like my dog populated these fields.

Duplicating Data CDs with X-CD-Roast

This is really very easy. I'm sure it can be done from the command line, but X-CD-Roast is just so darn easy that I haven't gotten around to learning to do it the hard way (you've read my disclaimer about this already). Basically, just throw the CD to be copied into the CD-R/CD-RW drive, and bring up xcdroast (as root, mind you). Then select the *Copy Data CD* option, and you'll get Figure 18-7.

Click on down to the Read Image section, and fill in an appropriate filename. In Figure 18-8, I just used the default name of *image1.raw*.

Continue on to verifying the image you've just pulled off, and then write it to a CD. Anytime you buy software, the first thing you should do is to make a couple of backup copies—then lock the original away in a safe place. This is especially true of really expensive stuff, like Adobe Photoshop. After I carelessly scratched up my copy of Rogue Spear, I was quite relieved that I'd made a couple of backup copies. Remember, making backup copies does *not* violate license agreements unless you give copies away to your friends.

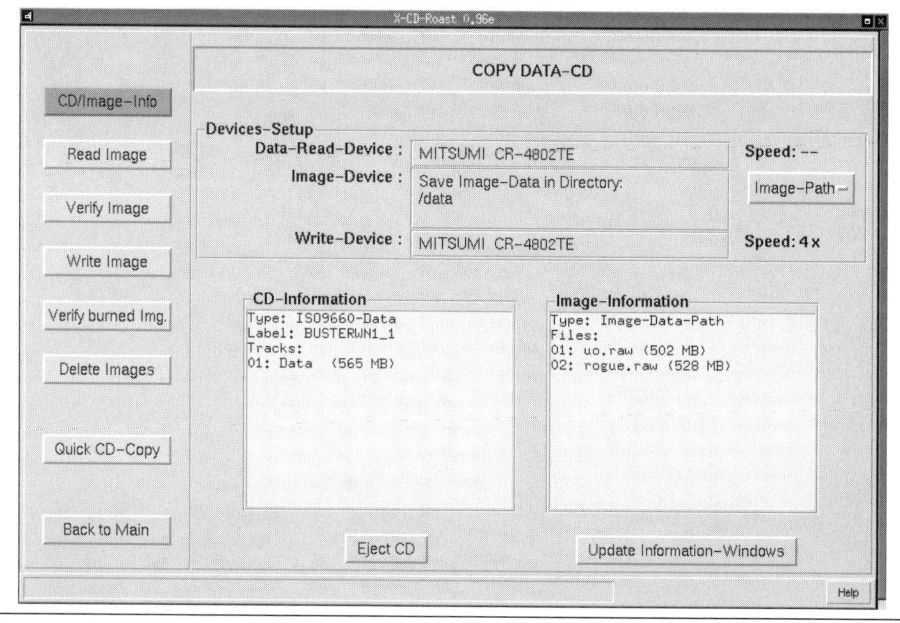

Figure 18-7 Copy CD dialog.

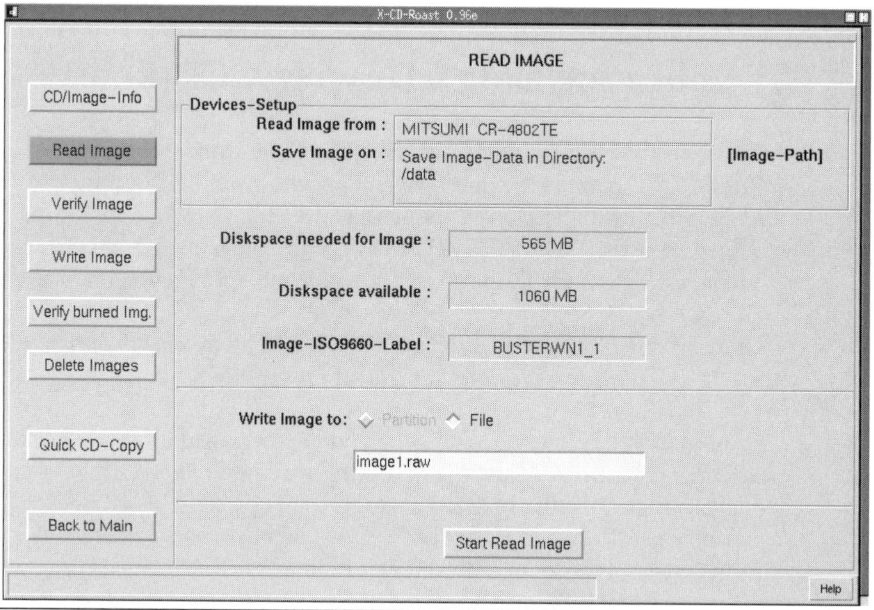

Figure 18-8 Read Image dialog.

Using X-CD-Roast to Verify the Freshly Burned CD-R/CD-RW

If you're duplicating data CDs, simply use the *verify burned img.* button, as seen in Figure 18-7. It's quite self-explanatory. If you've instead mastered your own CD (either with X-CD-Roast or from the command line), you can just use that option as well—or you can run the *verify burned img.* option from the *Master CD* button, as seen in Figure 18-4. Select the proper image file, and verify away.

Burning Audio CDs

I'll spare you the rant on why I like MP3 better than AudioCD format, and simply direct you to Chapter 19 and the section Saving Your Old Vinyl. It has a very nice discussion on cutting audio CDs.

Making Bootable CDs

Much like duplicating data CDs, this is something I can't figure out how to do. It's big, it's complex, it can't be done with xcdroast. I've made several dozen attempts to create a bootable CD, but so far I haven't produced anything but a stack of coasters. On the upside, I do have a nice set of matching CD-R coasters. On the downside, I have nothing for this section. Making a bootable CD is . . . well, beyond the scope of this chapter for the simple reason that I couldn't figure it out. Bootable CDs are a rather advanced topic. Perhaps *Son of Multitool Linux* will mention it.

80-min/700MB CDs

In order to do these, just make a bigger iso image and insert the larger media. cdrecord seems to detect the extra size with no problems, and the CD-Rs are readable under both Linux and Windows (and on my portable MP3 CD player).

Summary

Using xcdroast, cdrecord, and mkisofs, you should now be able to burn all the CDs you'll ever want. If you figure out how to burn bootables and can explain it to a caveman like me, drop me a note.

Chapter 19
Audio Processing

Difficult-o-Meter: 3 (moderate Linux knowledge required)

Covers:

cdparanoia	*http://www.xiph.org/paranoia*
SOX	*http://home.sprynet.com/~cbagwell/sox.html*
bladeenc	*http://bladeenc.mp3.no*
LAME	*http://www.mp3dev.org/mp3/*
Ogg Vorbis	*http://www.vorbis.com/*
FreeAmp	*http://www.freeamp.org*
cdrdao	*http://cdrdao.sourceforge.net*
dd	*http://www.gnu.org*
cdrecord	*http://www.fokus.gmd.de/research/cc/glone/employees/joerg.schilling/private/cdrecord.html*

Question: I've heard that Linux works really well as a platform for music and audio, so I want to set up a jukebox. I want to record a demo tape of my songs to give to the local radio station. I want to archive all my old tapes and vinyl records (and 8-tracks, though I'm embarrassed to admit owning any!). But I'm not sure how to go about doing this.

> *Answer:* Hold on there—that's a lot of things you want to do! Linux has a plethora of utilities you can use to record, transfer, clean up, and archive digital audio clips. We won't cover all the possibilities, but we'll describe digital audio concepts and show a few of the most useful utilities. Finally, we'll present a practical example of preserving your old vinyl records.

The past couple of years have seen an explosion in the popularity of digital audio. Music lovers are digitizing and archiving their collections. Some people are already using their computers for playback instead of their CD players. Amateur musicians can now record their own music in unprecedented fidelity, without needing to purchase expensive pieces of specialized equipment. It's definitely an exciting time, and Linux is right there in the thick of things. It's an excellent platform for doing all of the things I've mentioned. In this chapter, though, I'll talk more about digital audio concepts and about how to record, clean up, and even distribute your own recordings.

Types of Digital Audio

There are two major methods for storing digital audio: amplitude based and frequency based. The amplitude-based method takes samples of the sound waveform at very small time intervals, converts the analog voltages into integers, and stores the resulting values sequentially. Usually the sample rate will be between 8,000 and 44,000 per second. The quality of recording will go up with an increase in sample rate, and down with a decrease; CD-quality sound has a standard rate of 44,100 samples per second. Sample rates higher than this don't add any additional sound quality.

The quality of the sound is also affected by the resolution of the analog-to-digital (A–D) conversion. If each sample is stored in any less than 8 bits, the sound quality degrades rapidly. CD-quality sound is recorded with 16 bits of accuracy, and many sound cards advertise the ability to record incoming signals to 20 or more bits of accuracy. The number of bits used for each sample is called the *bit depth*.

The amplitude-based method is more commonly known as *PCM*, short for "pulse code modulation." This terminology comes from the early days of digital audio, when the results of the A–D conversion were re-encoded into trains of pulses for transmission over a serial line. These days, of course, those results simply go straight to a hard drive or some other process.

PCM storage is simple and intuitive. If a stream of PCM samples stops (for example, due to a network problem), the sound simply stops. If a PCM file is played at a sample rate different from the one at which it was recorded, it sounds speeded up or slowed down, like a record player at the wrong setting. In fact, records and cassette tapes both store a replica of the analog waveform on physical media, and thus could be called *analog PCM*.

The frequency-based method of storing audio is much more recent and has no physical analog. In the 18th century, Fourier proved that any repeating waveform, no matter how complex, can be represented as a sum of pure tones of different volumes. Sustained notes from a flute, a bassoon, or an electric guitar approximate periodic waveforms and can all be represented this way. The flute has more of its volume in the high-pitched pure tones, which is what gives it its "brightness." Similarly, the bassoon has more of its volume in the low-pitched pure tones, which gives it its "throatiness."

The basic idea of frequency encoding is first to chop the audio waveform into frames that last only a fraction of a second. This frame rate is much slower than PCM sample rates but too fast for the human ear to perceive as independent. Then a mathematical transform is performed on the frame that obtains the pure tones and their corresponding volumes. The operation is repeated for the next frame, and those values are stored. Often the values for one frame won't be that different from the values for the next frame, and this makes it easier to compress the resulting lists of numbers.

This basic concept can be enhanced in many ways. For example, some of the values that don't contribute much to the sound of the audio clip can be discarded. In this respect, frequency encoding of audio is similar to the JPEG encoding of image data (see Chapter 22, Image Processing). How much information is retained is determined by a parameter called the *bit rate*. Low-bit-rate files have poor quality; the quality gets better and better as the bit rate increases.

In constrast to PCM encoding, if a frequency encoding stream stops or skips, the sound does not simply stop. Instead, it "freezes" at a particular tone until more data is received. If the stream is delayed, as in a slow network connection, the sound appears to "drag," or slow down, without altering the pitches used in the clip. This interesting effect isn't possible with a PCM file (in that case, the audio would slow down, but the pitch would be changed also).

Finally, many audio clips support more than one channel of sound. One channel means *monaural*, and two channels mean *stereo*. High-end audio applications can handle audio clips with many more channels (for example, 5.1 stereo surround sound). Most of the clips that you'll work with, though, will involve two channels.

So which method is right for your recordings? The answer depends on what you want to do with the files. If you want to trim or add dead time, add digital effects, or reduce noise, it's best to use an uncompressed PCM format. If you have limited storage space, or when you actually want to distribute your files, frequency-based encoding is often a good bet due to its considerably smaller size. For each of these two methods, there are several commonly used file formats.

RAW Format

RAW format is basically raw PCM data in a file, with nothing else. Its major drawback is that the file contains no information about the size of the samples, the sample rate, or even the endianness* of the data. On the other hand, if you pick a standard such as CD quality (44.1 KHz, 16 bits, 2-channels, little-endian), you can use Unix utilities like cat and dd to cut and paste audio clips. What could be simpler? I'll show you an example in the upcoming section Cut and Paste.

WAV Format

Another major type of PCM file is the WAV, which is familiar to Windows users. WAVs contain multiple chunks of data, each tagged with a type code and a size. The two required chunks are a header, tagged WAVEFMT, and PCM audio data, tagged DATA (surprising choice of name, isn't it?). The header contains the information lacking in a RAW file: sample rate, number of channels, and bit depth, as well as other optional fields. WAV files are found on many different platforms, and practically all Linux sound-processing utilities support them to one degree or another.

MP3 (MPEG Layer 3) Format

In recent years, the MP3 format has become extremely popular on the Internet. An MP3 file consists of header information, followed by a number of encoded frames. The frames have a very short duration (<1/20 of a second), so individual frames blend together in a continuous perception. The data in each frame is frequency encoded, and certain heuristics are used to preserve only the elements of a waveform that are important in human perception. These tricks allow a very high compression ratio over a comparable WAV file, easily as high as 10:1. Even the highest-quality MP3 encoding can still produce a 4:1 compression.

The quality of an MP3, and in fact most frequency encodings, is determined by a parameter called *bit rate*. The de facto standard bit rate is 128,000 bits per second, or

---

**Endianness* refers to whether given data is stored "little-end-first" (*little-endian*) or "big-end-first" (*big-endian*).

128 kbps. Compare this to the number of bits of a PCM file that must be sent to a soundcard each second:

$$44{,}100 \text{ samples/sec} \times 16 \text{ bits/sample} \times 2 \text{ channels} = 1{,}411 \text{ kbps}$$

This is a factor of 10 more than the bit rate of an MP3. Small wonder, then, that frequency-encoded formats are the best for distributing audio files.

Since MP3s are frequency encoded, the data in the file bears little resemblance to the actual waveform. It must be decoded before any but the most simple operations can be performed on it. Consequently, playing or modifying MP3 files takes a good deal of processing power. Luckily, most modern machines have little difficulty keeping up. However, RAW or WAV files are still far better for editing and filtering audio clips.

Depending on your software philosophy, there may also be another problem with MP3s. The MP3 encoding algorithm is patented by the Fraunhofer Group, which requires anyone who builds an MP3 encoder (but not a player) to pay a license fee. Despite this situation, when MP3s became the "next big thing," many encoders appeared, some under dubious circumstances. The resultant wide access to free encoders helped propel MP3s to the popularity they enjoy today.

In addition, in their latest release of Windows, XP, Microsoft has de-emphasized the ability to create MP3s in favor of Windows Media Format. The default recorder settings for MP3s make them sound considerably worse than the default setting for WMA. It would be a sad situation indeed if this trickery causes the majority of music lovers to switch to a proprietary format simply because it "sounds better," not because of any real quality differences. In the long run, the popularity of MP3s may already have peaked.

Ogg Vorbis Format

Luckily, the open source movement comes thundering back! The Ogg Project is an ambitious and worthy attempt to build a set of fully open source, nonproprietary, non-patent-encumbered audio and video storage algorithms (referred to as *codecs*). Although development is happening on many fronts, the audio codec, called *Vorbis*, is mostly completed. It is technically similar to MP3 but sufficiently different that it does not violate any patents held by Fraunhofer or other industry groups. All of the Ogg Vorbis source is freely available under the BSD license. Support for this format has already found its way into XMMS, and players are available for Windows. So perhaps there is some hope after all.

Preparing Your System for Audio Work

Obviously, the first step is to install a soundcard. You don't have one? Well, go get one! And make sure it works with Linux. I won't cover installing the kernel drivers and installing the new kernel; these procedures are discussed elsewhere in the book (see Chapter 1). However, when installing a soundcard for the first time, you might run across a nonobvious problem. You can verify that the kernel drivers are installed and loaded correctly by checking the output of dmesg for a soundcard-related entry:

```
es1371: version v0.30 time 19:26:05 Oct  5 2001
es1371: found chip, vendor id 0x1274 device id 0x1371 revision 0x08
es1371: found es1371 rev 8 at io 0x9400 irq 5
es1371: features: joystick 0x0
ac97_codec: AC97 Audio codec, id: 0x4352:0x5913 (Cirrus Logic CS4297A
    rev A)
```

But even if the drivers are installed correctly, you still need to have device files set up so your applications can *communicate* with the drivers. On some distributions those files are not installed by default or are installed with incorrect permissions. To fix this, you can run the following commands:

```
# cd /dev
     # ./MAKEDEV audio
     # ls -l /dev/audio
     crw-rw----     1 root     audio     14,   4 Oct 17 21:37 /dev/audio
     # adduser myself audio
```

The MAKEDEV command creates the character devices in /dev that are necessary for communication with the soundcard drivers. Then we verify that the permissions are correct; we want the device file to be owned by root and to be readable and writable by members of the audio group. Finally, we add nonprivileged users to the audio group.

If this setup isn't done, either manually or by a distribution's installer, it can be quite maddening trying to track down why the soundcard doesn't work. You may be tempted to recompile the kernel a half dozen times, or even try exchanging the card for a new one. It seems whenever you have a problem with Linux, the solution turns out to be simple. It often turns out to be obscure, as well.

Input Gain, Output Volume, and Clipping

The next step is to set the properties of one of these audio devices, namely, the mixer. Input gain and output volume control are important considerations when dealing with digital audio files. If the output volume is set too high, audio files that contain perfectly good samples can overdrive the soundcard, causing a type of distortion called *clipping*. Clipping is often described as a "crunchy" or "crackling" sound that usually occurs during the loudest parts of an audio file. To avoid clipping, you can turn down the output volume just far enough to remove any audible crackling.

Likewise, if the output volume is set too low, you may have to turn up the volume significantly on whatever system is receiving your soundcard's output (your audio receiver, a stereo, PC speakers, etc.). This can introduce additional noise during playback, which is not very desirable from a fidelity point of view. *Improper volume adjustment is one of the major causes of problems and complaints with digital audio.*

There are a variety of ways to adjust the output, or PCM, volume on Linux systems; players like XMMS or FreeAmp have a volume control that adjusts the PCM volume. Under KDE, the kmix program is accessible from the Control Center. The PCM volume is the second slider from the left, with the waveform icon above it (Figure 19-1). On my system, I need to turn the PCM volume down to 58% to avoid clipping during audio playback.

Analogous problems can occur while recording. Recorded audio files can be clipped, or too quiet, depending on the input gain. Luckily, quiet files can be boosted in volume (see the later section, Sound Effects and Filtering), although this may introduce some noise. On the other hand, clipped files cannot easily be repaired. The solution is to ensure that the input gain is near the top of the optimum range *before* you begin recording.

The optimal input gain depends on the properties of your soundcard, so you'll need to determine the appropriate value by trial and error. Use a recording source that is optimally loud; the line out of a CD player is usually a good bet (refer to the later

Figure 19-1 KDE volume control utility.

section, Writing Your Own Audio CDs). Note that the CD player's volume control does not affect the volume of the line-out signal, only the volume of the speakers. You'll need to play a CD and try recording short clips using various values for the input gain. Make sure that the clips you record are the loud parts of the CD, or you'll overestimate the required gain. Finally, pick the highest gain that does not exhibit clipping when you play it back from the computer. On my system, I have to turn the input gain all the way down to 25% to avoid clipping.

Creating Audio Files from CDs

Most audio CDs have a relatively simple format. The beginning of the disc contains a table of contents, which describes the starting point and length of each track on the CD. The unit of measurement is the sector, which equals 1/75 of a second. Therefore, a song exactly 4 minutes long would have a length of $4 \times 60 \times 75 = 18{,}000$ sectors. Each sector consists of 588 16-bit samples on both left and right channels. This adds up to 44,100 samples per second, with four bytes per sample. See now why this sample rate is considered to produce CD-quality sound?

A track does not need to start directly after the end of the previous track. There are usually gaps of up to a few seconds between tracks. These gaps can be blank, or they can contain nonaudio data. In fact, some recent audio CDs include multimedia presentations in the leftover space at the end of the disc. Ultimately, audio CDs look much like a number of raw PCM files stored on a physical medium (there are some technical differences, but I won't go into them).

cdparanoia is one of the best tools to record, or *rip*, CD tracks. It works for either IDE or SCSI CD-ROMs, and includes automatic jitter and error correction. It is capable of rereading areas of the disc that may be scratched or dusty, to try to obtain the best-quality recording possible.

cdparanoia has a number of options, all available from the man page. To list a CD's table of contents, use the *-Q* option.

```
$ cdparanoia -Q
cdparanoia III release 9.6 (August 17, 1999)
(C) 1999 Monty &lt;monty@xiph.org&gt; and Xiphophorus
Report bugs to paranoia@xiph.org        http://www.xiph.org/paranoia/

Table of contents (audio tracks only):  track length begin copy pre ch
===========================================================
1. 14348 [03:11.23] 32 [00:00.32] no no 2
2. 13752 [03:03.27] 14380 [03:11.55] no no 2
```

```
3. 13783 [03:03.58] 28132 [06:15.07] no no 2
4. 12845 [02:51.20] 41915 [09:18.65] no no 2
5. 14032 [03:07.07] 54760 [12:10.10] no no 2
6. 11155 [02:28.55] 68792 [15:17.17] no no 2
7. 10128 [02:15.03] 79947 [17:45.72] no no 2
8. 11570 [02:34.20] 90075 [20:01.00] no no 2
9. 18842 [04:11.17] 101645 [22:35.20] no no 2
10. 10600 [02:21.25] 120487 [26:46.37] no no 2
11. 23330 [05:11.05] 131087 [29:07.62] no no 2
12. 18413 [04:05.38] 154417 [34:18.67] no no 2
13. 14072 [03:07.47] 172830 [38:24.30] no no 2
14. 24080 [05:21.05] 186902 [41:32.02] no no 2
15. 17873 [03:58.23] 210982 [46:53.07] no no 2
16. 13225 [02:56.25] 228855 [50:51.30] no no 2
```

This tells the utility to search for a CD-ROM drive and, if one is found, to query its contents. To rip audio tracks, use the following syntax:

```
$ cdparanoia 2 track-2.wav
$ cdparanoia 1-16 onebigfile.wav
$ cdparanoia -B
```

By default, the output format is a WAV file. You can also rip portions of tracks, basically from any sector to any other sector, regardless of their relationship. Use the *—help* option for details on the start and end syntax. Another useful option is *-B*, which will rip all the tracks on a CD and place each into its own WAV file, named *track01cdda.wav*, *track02cdda.wav*, and so on.

Since cdparanoia saves all songs as uncompressed WAV files, you can imagine how your disk space will be rapidly depleted. A single CD's worth of songs averages about 650MB when stored as WAVs, so you want to have a large scratch space and to convert the files into MP3 or Ogg format before ripping the next CD. I use the leftover 2GB partition on my Windows drive as a storage area for massive audio and video files. Under all circumstances, you don't want to use your root partition or the */var* and */tmp* directories unless you know you have enough space.

If all you want to do is rip songs from a CD and convert them into MP3s, there are a number of utilities to do everything in one step. In fact, it seems you can't turn around these days without seeing another ripper/encoder application. My personal favorite is the GTK-based grip. But cdparanoia and similar applications are much better if you actually want to go outside that narrow scope, for example, if you want to sample a few seconds from a song for your newest techno tune.

Recording Your Own Audio

So you're an amateur musician with a few songs you want to record, and you're not sure you want to spend $50 an hour on studio time. But you do have a guitar, a microphone, and a little mixing board. You're ready to record onto your computer . . . but how? Well, assuming you have the output of the mixer attached to your soundcard, here's how:

```
$ rec mysong.wav
Send break (control-c) to end recording
```

It's that simple. *rec* is part of the SOX package, which I discuss in the upcoming section, Converting Between File Formats. The command line explains itself—it records audio data into the file *mysong.wav*, in WAV format. `rec` knows what format to use by looking at the file extension. If you provide a *-t*-type option, it will use that type instead. When you're done playing, press Control-C to finish writing the file.

To play back the file, simply type:

```
$ play mysong.wav
```

play is also part of the SOX package, the complement to *rec*. But when *mysong.wav* plays back, it sounds terrible! What went wrong? Let's try a different playback tool, one that displays some information about the file:

```
$ wavp mysong.wav
WavTools 1.3 Written by Colin Ligertwood.
This software is provided as is. No warranty is offered, implied, or
    included.
Playing [FILE: mysong.wav] [LENGTH: 987494]
[RATE: 8000] [BPS: 8000] [DEPTH: 8] [CHANNELS: 1]
[TIME: 00:00:00]
```

The ubiqituous *file* command will also work:

```
$ file mysong.wav
mysong.wav: RIFF (little-endian) data, WAVE audio, Microsoft PCM, 8 bit,
    mono 8000 Hz
```

Aha! The rate is 8000 (samples per second), the depth is 8 (bits), and the number of channels is 1 (mono). This is definitely not CD-quality sound! We will need to provide options to *rec* to specify the appropriate values:

```
$ rec -r44100 -c2 -sw mysong.wav
Send break (control-c) to end recording
```

The file sounds much better now. As usual, consult the SOX man page for more information about the available options.

rec can do only the simplest kind of one-track audio recording. If you want to do professional quality multitrack recording, well, Linux can help you with that, too! The next chapter, Music Production, has a section about multitrack hard disk recorders that are available for our favorite operating system. These applications are quite a bit more sophisticated and allow you to lay down a number of tracks and then play them back while simultaneously recording an additional track.

Cut and Paste

Now that you have a decent recording, how can you make it sound more professional? There are several ways to do this; a good first step is to remove dead space at the beginning and end of the audio clip. You can do this visually with the audacity waveform editor (Figure 19-2):

```
$ audacity mysong.wav
```

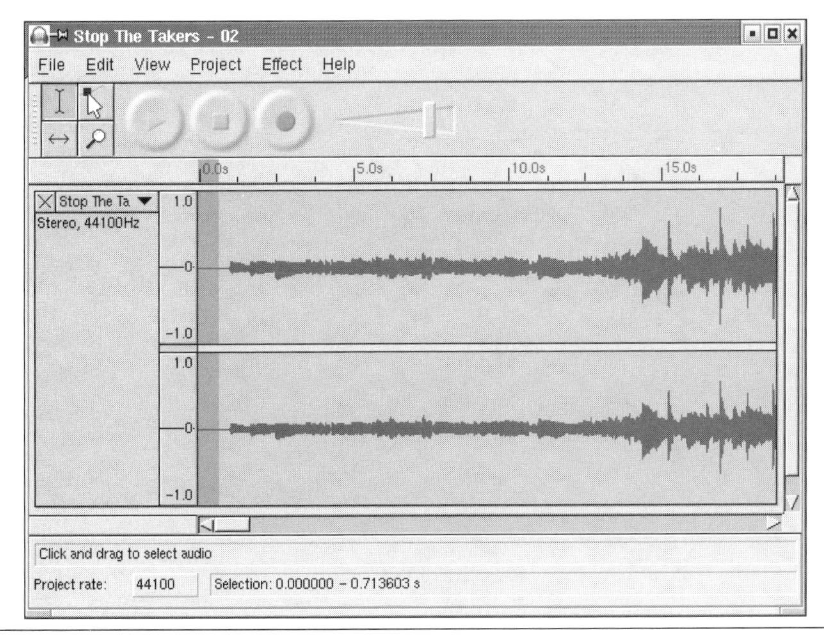

Figure 19-2 Cutting a section from an audio file with the audacity utility.

I selected the first half second of the song, shown in darker gray. Next, I would go to Edit/Delete to remove this little bit of silence. I could also modify the volume and apply audio effects to all or part of the file. Finally, I would export the audio clip as a New and Improved WAV file.

In this version of audacity, exporting is not as simple as it sounds. You must split the stereo track into left and right channels before exporting, or both tracks will be mixed down into a monaural WAV file. You can do this by right-clicking on the track name (next to the little X) and selecting Split Audio Track. Then right-click on each of the mono tracks and set the channel (left or right), as in Figure 19-3:

If you record your files as raw PCM samples, you can even use basic Unix utilities to do the same kind of thing. For example, to shave a half second off the beginning of a

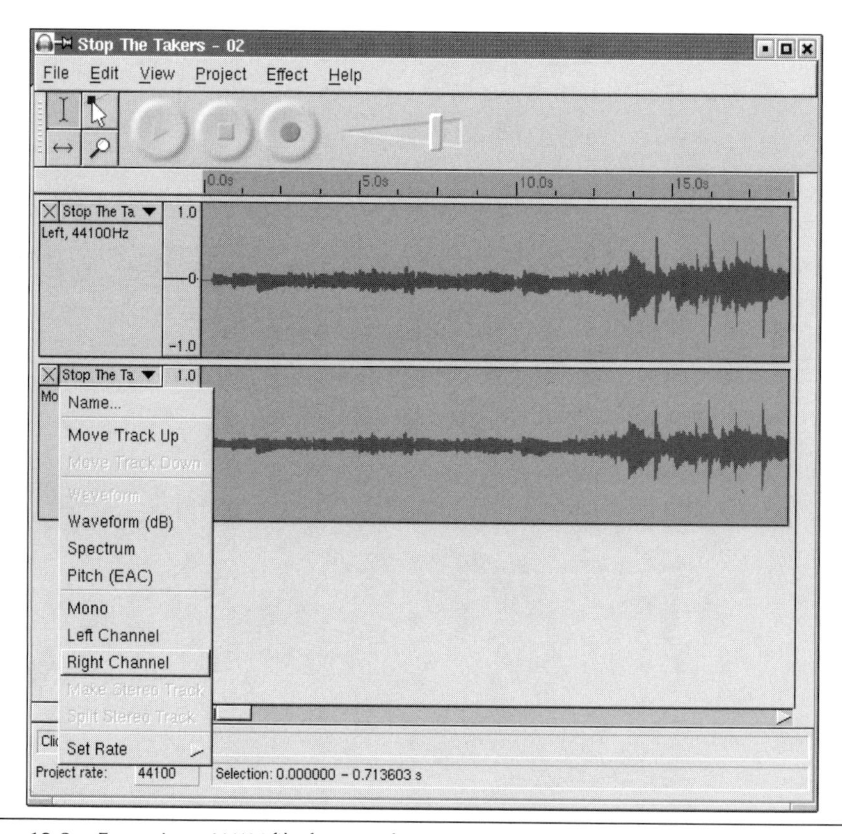

Figure 19-3 Exporting a WAV file from audacity.

song, you can use the *tail* command. The first line is there to calculate how many bytes to remove:

```
$ perl -e 'print 44100 * 4 * 0.5'
88200
$ tail -c +88200 mysong.wav > newsong.wav
```

Assuming the raw file is at standard CD quality, there are 44,100 4-byte samples every second. So a half second is 22,050 samples at 4 bytes per sample, or 88,200 bytes. We'll use dd in the same way in the Trimming sections later in this chapter.

Sound Effects and Filtering

The next step is to apply effects or filtering to modify the sound quality of your recording, if necessary. One situation where filtering might be useful is when capturing live audio from a microphone. Depending on the quality of the microphone and the acoustics of the recording space, you may need to perform frequency filtering or apply minor effects to give the recording a fuller sound.

Volume Adjustment

Despite the precuations you may have taken setting the correct recording volume, sometimes an audio clip is just too quiet. If you've obtained the clip from somewhere else, you may have no choice in the matter. It's easy to use SOX to boost the volume level of the file. In fact, this can be done simultaneously with any other operation SOX supports. The first step is to find out *how much* the volume must be boosted:

```
$ sox mysong.wav -e stat
Maximum amplitude: 0.803
Minimum amplitude: 0.000
Mean    amplitude: 0.006
Maximum delta:     0.690
Minimum delta:     0.000
Mean    delta:     0.003
Volume adjustment: 1.245
```

The command runs some statistics on the samples in the file and prints the results. For us, the important one is the Volume adjustment suggestion. This indicates that we need to boost the volume about 24%. And we can immediately do this:

```
$ sox mysong.wav -v 1.245 newsong.wav
```

newsong.wav is created, with an optimal volume. This technique can also be used to soften the volume of an audio clip. Keep in mind, though, that if the recording volume was too high when the clip was recorded, lowering the volume of the file will not make the crackling go away. It will just be softer, like the rest of the file.

If graphical applications are your thing, you can use audacity to do exactly the same thing. The menu option is under Effect/Amplify. You also have the option of boosting the volume of certain sections, instead of applying the change to the entire file.

Frequency Filtering: High-Pass, Low-Pass, Band-Pass "Graphic Equalizer"

Frequency filtering is most familiar in the sense of a graphic equalizer. In the earlier section Types of Digital Audio, I discussed how frequency encoding converts an audio clip into a set of volumes. Frequency filtering is a mathematical operation that changes these volumes relative to one another. Figures 19-4 and 19-5 show a sample frequency encoding. The spikes you see are the pure tones with the highest volumes. Notice how, in Figure 19-5, the lower-pitched frequencies are suppressed.

Although frequency filtering can be done very precisely, the human ear generally recognizes three broad categories: treble, midrange, and bass. Too much bass or too little

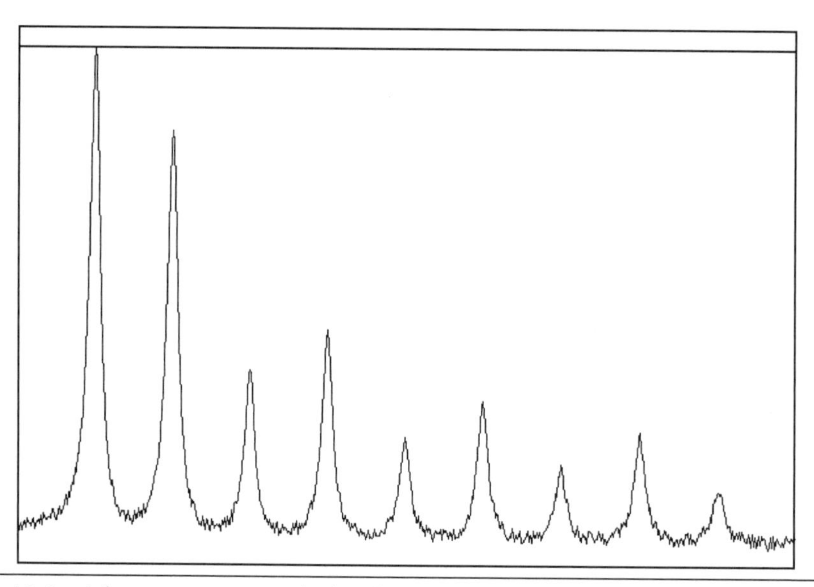

Figure 19-4 A frequency spectrum before filtering.

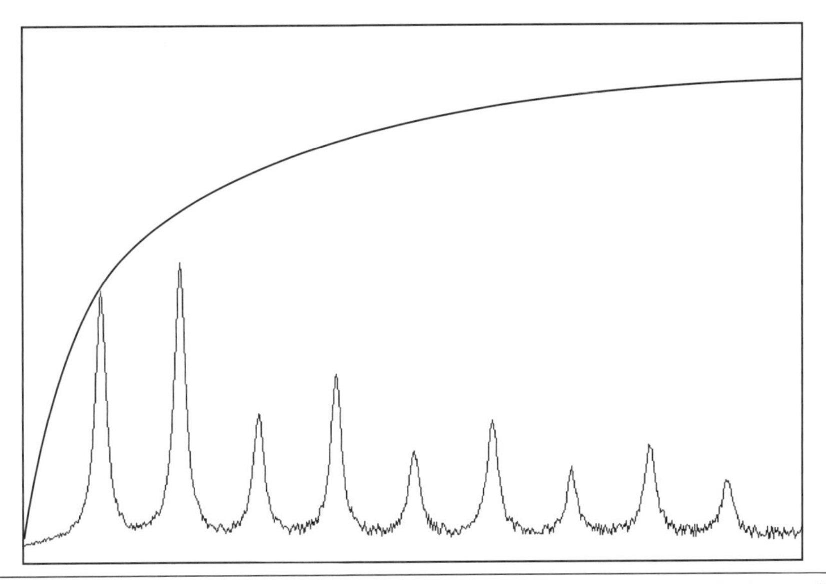

Figure 19-5 The same frequency spectrum as in Figure 19-4 after applying a high-pass filter.

treble leads to a "muffled" sound, whereas too much treble or too little bass leads to a "tinny" sound. The human voice generally falls in the lower end of the midrange frequencies, so vocals can be enhanced by boosting the midrange. Karaoke machines work by selectively filtering in the 2- to 4-KHz range while allowing other frequencies through.

Again, SOX excels at performing equalization. SOX provides low-pass, band-pass, and high-pass filters, which decrease the amount of treble, midrange, and bass, respectively. The filter called *tape-deemph* is also useful when recording directly from a television or DVD audio signal. All of these filters can be invoked during file format conversion. Consider the following commands:

```
$ sox infile.au tape-deemph outfile.wav
$ sox outfile.wav highp 4000 outfile-hp.wav
```

The first command performs a format conversion while applying the tape-deemph filter, and the second applies an additional high-pass filter centered at 4KHz and saves the recording into a new WAV file. SOX is restricted to one filter per invocation, but it supports pipes for input and output, so the previous pair of commands could be reduced to the following command line:

```
$ sox infile.au tape-deemph - | sox - highp 4000 outfile-hp.wav
```

A word of caution: Many audio players for Linux, such as XMMS, have built-in graphic equalizers. If you are using one of these players to preview the "before" and "after" of frequency filtering, make sure that all the equalizer knobs are set to a central position. Otherwise, the "after" file that sounds best on your own system may not sound that good on someone else's system, defeating altogether the purpose of doing this kind of processing.

Sound Effects: Chorus, Delay, Echo, Reverb, Stereo Offset

Sound effects are even more complex than frequency filtering; they include such well-known effects (especially in electronic music) as reverberation, echo, delay, flanging, and chorus. The SOX utility can add all of these effects to any uncompressed sound file, using the same syntax as earlier:

```
$ sox mysong.wav -e reverb 1.0 500 250 mysong
```

Did I mention that audacity can apply effects to all or part of a file, as well? There's more than one way to do it in the Linux world.

Converting between File Formats

Sometimes you will run across file formats that haven't been discussed in this chapter. As long as the codecs aren't too new, it's a good bet that SOX will be able to convert these files to a WAV or raw file. SOX automatically does a conversion if you provide different extensions for the input and output files:

```
$ sox infile.au outfile.wav
```

When dealing with raw files, you need to provide options specifying the number of channels, sample rate, and bit depth just before the file name. The following command line converts *mysong.wav* into a raw file at CD quality:

```
$ sox mysong.wav -r44100 -c2 -sw mysong.raw
```

SOX supports a huge variety of PCM file formats. Not to seem repetitive, but you can read the man page or documentation at the SOX homepage for more information.

Newer codecs, such as Windows Media and AAC, are frequency encoded, more similar to MP3 and Vorbis than they are to WAV files. Many of these new codecs are also proprietary and can be read only by certain applications on certain platforms. For this reason, you may have trouble finding a Linux tool to convert these files. It would be most unfortunate if industry pressures cause larger numbers of people to start using these closed formats.

However, MP3 and Vorbis format are still available to everyone. SOX cannot handle frequency-encoded files, so you will need different tools. The Ogg Vorbis distribution includes two command line tools that can be used to convert WAV files into Vorbis files, oggenc and ogg123. To encode a WAV file:

```
$ oggenc mysong.wav -b 128 myfile.ogg
```

To decode an OGG file:

```
$ ogg123 -d wav mysong.ogg
```

Now you can play the *.ogg* files with Ogg's own player or with XMMS.

The popularity of MP3s has spawned a massive number of encoding tools. Many of them are integrated into rippers and provide playlist management, particularly on the Windows side of the fence. Many of these utilities are also asymmetric; they will convert PCM files into MP3s, but not back into WAV or raw files. You'll need to do the latter if you're processing a pre-existing audio clip. One example would be if you clip out a sample from a popular song to use in music made with a loop-based sequencer (see Chapter 20, Music Production).

bladeenc is a simple command line encoder that can work on multiple files. It is useful for encoding in a background window while you are performing other tasks. As is typical of MP3 encoders, it will encode only WAV or AIFF files. It will support bit rates of 64 through 320 kbps, with a default of 128. As of version 0.93, it does not support variable-bit-rate encoding (which isn't always necessary).

bladeenc is used as follows:

```
$ bladeenc -b128 file1.wav file.mp3 file2.wav file2.mp3
```

LAME is a more complex encoder that features a pluggable architecture and compiles for many systems other than Linux. It has similar features and syntax to bladeenc, but it also supports variable bit-rate encoding and includes psychoacoustic plug-ins that can squeeze out maximum compression for a given sound quality.

What about decoding MP3s? This can be useful if you want to clip a segment from an MP3 file or apply volume adjustments or effects to it. The file must be uncompressed to perform these operations, but you don't want to play it (yet). Surprisingly, it's harder to find decoders than encoders (at least, decoders that don't just play the audio!). One option that works well is the *towav* utility that comes with the FreeAmp distribution. If you have the FreeAmp source distribution, you can build it with the following command:

```
$ cd freeamp
$ make -f Makefile.towav
```

The utility takes two arguments, the name of the MP3 file and the name of the WAV file, respectively:

```
$ towav infile.mp3 outfile.wav
```

XMMS has an output plug-in that will send audio output to a file rather than to the soundcard. You can also use this for decoding any file type that XMMS supports. After the file is decoded, you can process it as desired and re-encode using one of the previously mentioned tools. When decoding a file, remember that the output file will be about 10MB per minute of audio, so make sure you have sufficient disk space.

Writing Your Own Audio CDs

Finally, your files are in good shape. They're clipped to the appropriate length and sound balanced between treble, midrange, and bass. Now you want to burn them to an audio CD to preserve for all posterity (or maybe just to make some money selling it). There are several Linux utilities you can use, but all of them require the audio files to be in a PCM format, usually WAV. Because the files are uncompressed, a full CD's worth of WAV files will take up about 650MB. So you'll need to make sure you have plenty of disk space.

cdrecord is one of the most common command line CD-burning tools, but I'll wait to discuss it in the Audio CD Creation section of this chapter. Another good option is *cdrdao*, which is capable of writing audio, data, or mixed audio/data disks. To use cdrdao, you first create a table of contents file:

```
CD_ROM
CD_TEXT {
    LANGUAGE_MAP {
        0 : EN
    }
    LANGUAGE 0 {
        TITLE "My CD"
        PERFORMER "Me"
```

```
        DISC_ID "XY12345"
        }
    }
}
TRACK AUDIO
CD_TEXT {
    LANGUAGE 0 {
            TITLE "My First Song"
                PERFORMER "Me"
        }
}
FILE "mysong-01.wav" 0
        :
        :
        more tracks...
        :
        :
TRACK MODE1
CD_TEXT {
    LANGUAGE 0 {
            TITLE "Video clip from First Avenue, 4/17/2000"
                PERFORMER "Me"
        }
}
DATAFILE "first-avenue-show.mpg" 0
```

The man page for cdrdao describes the format of this file in detail; this example is fairly complex. The CD created by the file just listed would contain a number of audio tracks (however many the ellipses refer to) followed by a final data track containing an MPEG movie. Each track would have title and performer text associated with it. In contrast, a simple audio-only CD would use a first line of CD_DA, and have only alternating TRACK AUDIO and FILE "xxxx" 0 lines.

After the table of contents file is created, run the command and give it the filename:

```
$ cdrdao --device=0,0 --driver=generic-mmc toc.txt
Cdrdao version 1.1.4 - (C) Andreas Mueller <mueller@daneb.ping.de>
  SCSI interface library - (C) Joerg Schilling
  L-EC encoding library - (C) Heiko Eissfeldt
  Paranoia DAE library - (C) Monty

Check http://cdrdao.sourceforge.net/drives.html#dt for actual driver
    tables.
0,0: YAMAHA CRW8824E    Rev: 1.00
Using driver: Generic SCSI-3/MMC - Version 1.0 (data) (options 0x0000)
```

Assuming the table of contents file is correct and all the files are available, the program will warm up the laser on your CD-RW drive and display a 10-second countdown. At the end of those 10 seconds, it will begin writing the disk. A word of caution: If you are using an IDE CD-RW with SCSI emulation, you do *not* want to try canceling the write process. IDE-SCSI emulation under Linux does not handle errors very gracefully, and I've been able to completely lock up my machine by trying to cancel a write in progress.

Notice the cryptic way in which I specify the CD writer:

```
--device=0,0
```

This is related to the way the Linux handles SCSI; it is described in more detail in the Audio CD Creation section of this chapter.

There are also a number of graphical CD-writing programs you can use, such as xcdroast and gtoaster. But since, like my co-authors, I qualify as a command line bigot, I won't discuss them here. If you've had any experience obtaining documentation for open source programs, you should have no trouble finding out how they work.

Saving Your Old Vinyl

So, finally, how do I put all this good information to use? I'll illustrate some of the finer points from this chapter in an example. In this example, we'll be saving our old vinyl records from the dust pile.

The great thing about Linux is the abundance of high-quality, free applications. I feel that some of the best applications for Linux are the ones that have been around for years. Like those applications, some of the best albums in my collection are the old vinyl records. My old comedy albums, for example, bring back childhood memories and are still hilarious to listen to. I've always wanted them on CD, but I didn't want to buy them all over again. So I did the next best thing: I converted them into CDs myself. The best part of doing this is listening to all those old comedy bits again. Of course, it's also hard to keep track of where you are in the recording process when you're on the floor all teared up and laughing.

This section will walk you through all of the steps of transferring your old record collection to CDs. Not only will this save you money, it will allow you to preserve records that may not even be available on CD because the copyright owner decides it's not "profitable" to rerelease the old recordings and that the masters should instead decay in a musty vault somewhere.

Preparation

As with most things, preparation is the key to success. Before you begin your recording process, make a plan of what you want to do. It may seem simple, but once you're into it, you don't want to start changing things around. Figure out how you want to organize your collection. Some of the questions you should ask yourself are:

Do I want one record per CD?

Do I want a CD full of MP3 files or playable audio for a compact disc player?

Do I want fancy CD labels and case inserts?

Do I want to keep a copy of each track on my hard drive?

Do I have time to do this today?

Here was my plan for saving each of my Bill Cosby albums:

1. I want one CD per record.
2. I want fancy labels and jewel case inserts.
3. I want to end up with a playable audio CD *and* MP3 files for my computer.
4. I will make a project directory called *comedy_albums* to hold all the albums.
5. In the *comedy_albums* directory I will make a project directory for each album.
6. Each file will be named according to the track number (trackxx, where xx is 01, 02, 03, and so on).
7. Each file will be stored in CDR format at 44.1 khz (suitable for audio CD production).
8. I will convert from CDR format to MP3 at 128kb.
9. After burning all tracks in an album directory, I will erase all the CDR files, leaving the MP3 files.
10. Finally, I will create a playlist for each album and store it in each album directory.

Cleaning

A common problem with CDs and records is that they need to be cleaned periodically. I highly advise you to obtain a good cleaning solution and cloth suited for records. Because you're not remastering the audio from the original tape recordings, your recordings from the album will reproduce, in digital clarity, every pop, click, and hiss a record has to offer. A dirty record is not a good way to begin a recording session.

System (Space, Tools, etc.)

If you've ever downloaded an MP3 file, you know they can be fairly large. The longer the song and the higher the quality of the MP3 file, the larger it will be. For example, a three-minute song with a bit rate of 256 will produce somewhere in the neighborhood of 5 to 6 megabytes, depending on the software used to encode it. This same song at 44.1 khz in WAV format might be 50 megabytes. A typical CD-R will hold about 70 minutes of audio (a two-second gap between each track should be taken into account). It is important that you have enough space available on your hard disk to hold an entire album of audio. As my former boss used to say, "Disk is cheap." Do yourself a favor and buy another hard disk if you need more space. Trying to work with a limited amount of disk space will certainly make the project a lot more frustrating than it has to be.

Audio System

Record players require an amplifier. In order to record onto your PC, you must first boost the signal from the record player, using an amplifier. Most of us don't have professional recording equipment at our disposal. If you have an ordinary home amplifier with phono RCA jacks and TAPE IN and TAPE OUT RCA jacks on the back, you have all the audio gear you'll need.

There are several audio system configurations you can choose from, depending on your needs. My needs are probably different from most because I also create music and videos with my Linux system. I have a mixing console, multiple amplifiers, monitor speakers, and several audio devices in my configuration. Your configuration may simply include your record player, amplifier, and computer with attached speakers. Chapter 20, Music Production, contains a diagram of the more complex audio configuration.

Figure 19-6 is a picture of how you might configure your audio system for recording from a record player to your computer. In this picture you will notice a special cable connecting an RCA jack to mini-headphones. These cables are inexpensive and can be found at most consumer electronics stores. In order to record from the record player, you must connect the record player to the amplifier, which provides the preamplification for the record player. Then, treating the computer as a tape recorder, you attach your computer soundcard's LINE-IN to the amplifier's TAPE-RECORD, or TAPE-OUT, RCA jacks. In this configuration, no other connections are needed, since sound will be played on your computer speakers. Make sure you turn off the amplifier's speaker, if possible.

If you cannot do this, then use the configuration shown in Figure 19-7, a slightly more complex configuration that includes speakers attached to your amplifier. This

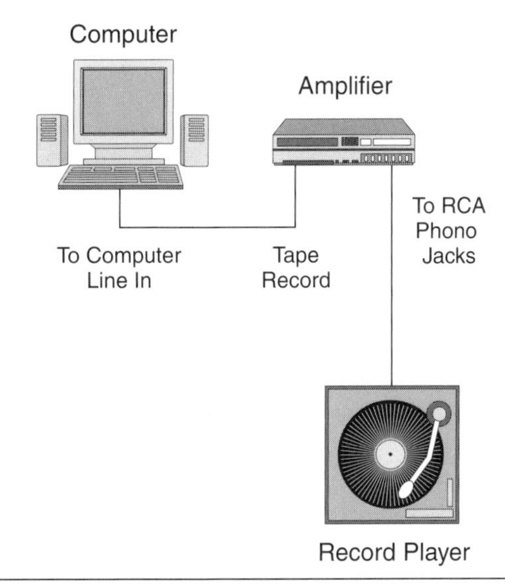

Figure 19-6 Audio system configuration 1.

allows you to play your recordings and any other music on your system through your home audio system. In this picture, the soundcard's LINE-OUT jack is connected to the amplifier's TAPE-PLAY or TAPE-IN RCA jacks. This provides an excellent way to hear those MP3 files on your hard disk through your home stereo, which is probably a lot better than your computer speakers.

Recording

Now that you have your audio hardware configured, you are ready to begin the recording process. Following your plan is a good starting point. For me, I decided to record each track of the record to its own file and then burn all the files onto a single CD. Recording is probably the easiest part of the process, since it only involves recording each track of the record to a file. The software you choose to do this will determine exactly how easy this task will be.

Software

The software used for the recording can range from GUI-based WAV recorders to text-based sound utilities that serve many functions. We discussed some of these earlier, and I chose to use SOX to record and play back my sound files. Visual editing of WAV files with audacity or similar tools might be required for some projects, but recording tracks from a record requires nothing more than simply recording the

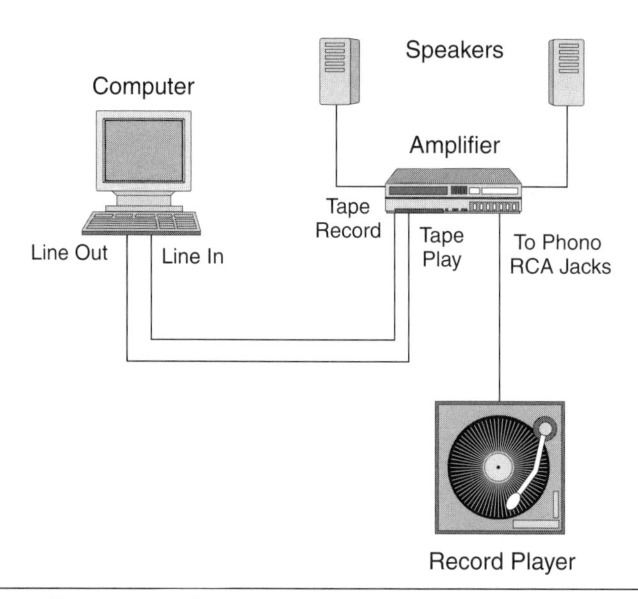

Figure 19-7 Audio system configuration 2.

tracks to a file. Because of this, I also chose to record my tracks into CDR format. CDR is the format for an audio file that can be written directly to a CD-ROM disk without conversion. It is basically a CD-quality RAW file (again, CD quality is 44.1 kHz, 16 bits, 2 channels, little-endian).

My distribution of SOX includes a script that simplifies the recording and playing of audio files. Even so, I still found it valuable to make my own script to simplify the recording process down to a single, simple command line:

```
$ cdr track_name
```

cdr is a script in my personal *bin* directory. Here is the source to cdr:

```
rec -s w -c 2 -r 44100 $1.cdr
```

This is the same command line I showed when we first discussed SOX. *rec --help* will give you all of the available recording options. I chose to record to a filename that is the cdr parameter with an added file extension.

The trickiest part of the recording process is to make sure to ready the command line for each track on the record with a new filename and to press Enter in time before the track starts. To record a track off my record, I change to my project directory for the album and ready my command line as follows:

```
$ cdr track01
```

Then I set the needle on the record, wait for what I feel is an appropriate time, and then press Return to begin the recording process. If I'm lucky, the recording starts before the record begins playing. Eventually, all the tracks for both sides of the record will be recorded. Now it's time to process the audio files in order to get them ready to be burned onto a CD-R.

If your audio equipment and computer are set up to work together properly, you should be able to listen to your record player through your soundcard and computer speakers. If not, check your connections with the diagrams given earlier. When playing back your track, use the play utility that comes with SOX.

If you end up with a huge file of silence after you finish recording a track, make sure the recording source is set correctly in your mixer. Next, make sure the input gain is set to the proper value. I mentioned how to do this earlier in the chapter. The volume slider for LINE IN will not affect the recording volume; rather, it determines how much of the LINE IN signal gets passed through to the output of the mixer.

Cleaning Up

The least fun, but most necessary part of this project is that of cleaning up all those audio files you just recorded. They are probably not perfect, but they can be made better. SOX is a great tool. Once you understand how it works, you will be working like a pro, but without the expenses.

Removing Clicks, Pops, and Hiss

Records are not perfect. They pop, click, and have a nasty hiss to them. But that's what makes this project so fun. The challenge is not to remove the pops and clicks, but to reduce them so they're not so annoying. I actually prefer to hear a few clicks now and then to remind me of just how old some of my records really are. Listening to a remastered comedy album, for instance, just isn't the same without hearing the needle of the record player grind over old scratches from many years of constant play.

SOX provides everything you need to reduce hiss, pops, and clicks in your audio files. As is my style, I use a shell script to simplify the processing of the audio files, since they can all be processed with the same SOX command line options. My script, clean, takes a filename as the only argument. It writes the SOX output to a temporary file, deletes the original, and then renames the new file back to the original name. Here is the source to clean:

```
#------------
# clean
------------
mv $1.cdr $1.orig.cdr
sox $1.orig.cdr $1.cdr lowp 4000 deemph
rm $1.orig.cdr
```

Now simply execute the *clean* command for each file in the project directory, as follows:

```
$ clean track01
$ clean track02
        :
        :
```

Or even:

```
$ for num $(seq -w 1 12); do clean "track$num"; done
```

Your files are almost ready to be burned to a CD-R. There is, however, the problem with time before and after the recorded audio. If you're like me, you probably overcompensated for the start and end of the record track. This can lead to long delays before the audio actually begins playing. With a two-second delay between CD audio tracks, this silence at the beginning and end of a track can add up to annoyingly long pauses between tracks. What is needed is a way to trim the excess silence from the beginning and end of the audio files.

Trimming

You could use audacity to trim excess space from the beginning and end of file, but luckily there's a more obscure way. *dd* is a utility for copying a file while applying a particular format or conversion to the file. For example, dd can be used to convert between ASCII and EBCDIC, which is very useful if you routinely trade files with an EBCDIC-based mainframe. It also has the ability to skip blocks from the beginning of a file. This is the feature that will enable you to trim off the excess time from the beginning of the file.

Timing is everything. In this case, it's crucial. The first part of trimming the beginning of the file is knowing that a CDR audio file is formatted in 2352-byte blocks and that each block lasts 1/75 of a second (remember these numbers, from before?).

Knowing this, it's easy to remove any number of blocks from the beginning of a file by telling dd to skip a given number of 2352-byte blocks. This is done with the following command line:

```
$ dd bs=2352 if=track01.cdr of=track01.trim.cdr skip=300
```

The following table explains the command line options in detail.

bs=2352	This sets the block size to 2352 bytes.
if=track01.cdr	This specifies the input file.
of=track01.trim.cdr	This specifies the output file.
skip=300	This specifies the number of 2352-byte blocks to skip from the beginning of the input file.

As is my usual style, I have written a small shell script to assist in the trimming process, called *trimb*:

```
#---------
# trimb
#---------
dd bs=2352 if=$1.cdr of=$1.trim.cdr skip=$2
if [ "$3" = "save" ]
then
  rm $1.cdr
  mv $1.trim.cdr $1.cdr
else
  play $1.trim.cdr
fi
```

The idea behind this script is to allow for trial and error. Basically, it's a guessing game when it comes to determining the number of blocks to trim from the front of the file. For this reason, the script plays the file after trimming so you can hear if the number of blocks entered was the right number of blocks to skip. If not, hit Control-C and try a larger number:

```
$ trimb track01 100
   (control-C)

$ trimb track01 200
    (control-C)

$ trimb track01 255
    (control-C)
```

Once you've found a number that works, simply reissue the command and add the word *save* as an additional parameter and your trimming will be made permanent:

```
$ trimb track01 255 save
```

We now move on to trimming the end of the file. The best way, of course, is not to have to trim the file at all. This means listening to each track as it is being recorded and hitting Control-C to end recording at the end of the record track. Otherwise, this part of the process is going to seem somewhat odd. Simply put, the audio will be reversed, trimming will be applied to the silent audio at the front of the reversed file, and then the audio will be rereversed to its final state. For this, we'll use a slightly modified version of the *trimb* script, which I call *trime:*

```
#----------
# trime
#----------
sox $1.cdr $1.reversed.cdr reverse
dd bs=2352 if=$1.reversed.cdr of=$1.trim.cdr skip=$2
rm $1.reversed.cdr
if [ "$3" = "save" ]
then
  rm $1.cdr
  sox $1.trim.cdr $1.cdr reverse
else
  play $1.trim.cdr
fi
```

The process is the same as trimming the beginning of a file, except the audio you hear will be reversed. Just listen for the silence and keep increasing the number of blocks to skip until you're satisfied with the amount of silence at the beginning (which is really the end of the audio):

```
$ trime track01 50
    (control-C)

$ trime track01 80
    (control-C)

$ trime track01 100
    (control-C)
```

When you've found the right number, add the *save* parameter, and your file will be trimmed and reversed back to normal:

```
$ trime track01 100 save
```

Once you've trimmed all of your audio files, you're ready for the final step in the project, preserving those tracks for future listening.

Preserving Your Work

There are a couple of methods which you might choose to save your newly created CDR tracks. The most obvious is to simply keep the CD-R or WAV files on your hard disk and play them back when desired. But this requires a lot of disk space and is not practical if you have a large library like I do. Your choices are basically limited to your available resources and system hardware configuration. If you have a CD-R or CD-RW, you can save your audio files to an audio CD-R and be able to listen to your new audio CDs in your car or on your home stereo (assuming you have a CD player in your car or home). If not, your other choice would be to convert the audio files into a format that conserves disk space while maintaining audio quality. A good format for this is the MP3 audio file format; Ogg would serve equally well.

Audio CD Creation

Linux offers a variety of tools for audio CD creation. Many of the GUI tools are simply front ends to command line programs. Some include libraries that implement the same features as the command line program, which are made from the same library. I, being a command line junkie, chose to use the cdrecord program for its relative simplicity and its nice set of features (most of which I never use).

In case you haven't guessed, simplicity is my goal. In fact, it's a lifestyle. If I can take something complex and simplify it, I will. With this, I offer up my *burnaudio* script:

```
cdrecord -v speed=2 dev=0,0 -audio $1*.cdr
```

While it may look simple, it hides lots of complexity. Actually, I just don't like typing the same thing over and over again.

The options for cdrecord are numerous. Luckily, the ones we need for audio CD creation are few and are detailed in the following table.

-v	Be verbose. Tell us what's going on during the recording process.
speed=2	Set the recording speed to 2×. Set this to the speed of your CD-R burner. Check the man page for cdrecord for acceptable values.
dev=0,0	This is a rather complex option. Basically, it tells cdrecord where to find your CD burner in your SCSI subsystem. It means SCSI Controller 0, Bus 0, and, implicitly, Device 0 and LUN 0. Yours may be different, something like 0,0,6,0. Use cdrecord —scanbus to find the values that are right for you.
-audio	This tells cdrecord that you are burning an audio CD-R as opposed to a CD-R with data on it.
$1*.cdr	This is a wildcard filename passed to my script. If you named all of your tracks as suggested, track01.cdr, track02.cdr, and so on, you should simply be able to pass the word *track* as a parameter to *burnaudio*.

So to burn a CD-R with all of the tracks just recorded, simply execute the burnaudio command as shown:

```
$ burnaudio track
```

If all goes well, you will have a perfect CD-R of your favorite old record album. If all does not go well, you will need to consult the documentation for your specific distribution of Linux in order to resolve any problems you might have, such as enabling the ability to use an IDE based CD-R drive or how to configure user access to your CD-R drive so you don't have to be root every time you wish to burn a CD-R.

MP3 File Creation

Lastly, even though you might have a CD-R with the audio tracks you just created on it, you might want to have instant access to your audio files from your computer. As mentioned before, storing the CDR or WAV files on your hard disk as a long-term solution can be very costly in terms of disk space, and eventually money, for when you run out of space and need to purchase a second or third hard disk. Compressing the audio files is the best alternative to storing them uncompressed. To do this, it is recommended that the files be converted to the MP3 format, which can save a significant amount of disk space while maintaining a reasonable level of quality in your recordings.

As usual with Linux, there are several programs to choose from to convert your files into MP3 format. I prefer bladeenc for its speed and quality. The following command line will encode an audio file:

```
$ bladeenc track01.wav -128
```

The command line options are amazingly simple and are explained in this table.

track01.wav	The input file to be converted.
-128	The bit rate determines the quality the resulting MP3 file will have. Generally, the higher the bit rate, the higher the quality and the larger the resulting MP3 file will be. Considering the source for your audio, a bit rate of 128 should be sufficient for your needs and will keep the file at a reasonable size. You could probably get away with 96 kbps if you're a real disk space hoarder.

You might have noticed that the source file for bladeenc was a WAV file and not a CDR file. For this reason, I have one last shell script to assist in the process of converting a CDR file to an MP3 file:

```
#----------
# cdr2mp3
#----------
    sox $1.cdr $1.wav
bladeenc $1.wav -$2
rm -f $1.wav
rm -i $1.cdr
```

The script converts the CDR file to a WAV file and then encodes the WAV file into an MP3 file at the provided bit rate. Finally it removes the unwanted WAV file and prompts for the removal of the CDR file. Execute the cdr2mp3 for each file, as follows:

```
$ for num $(seq -w 1 12); do cdr2mp3 "track$num" 128; done
```

Summary

In this chapter, I described some of the different audio file formats and their strengths and weaknesses. I showed how to rip files from CDs and record your own music. Then I showed some techniques for cleaning up and filtering these files. I also discussed ways to preserve and distribute your music, by converting it into MP3 or Vorbis files or burning it to CD. Finally, I gave you a real-world example of how to apply the techniques introduced in this chapter.

References

cdparanoia

- Homepage: *http://www.xiph.org/paranoia*

SOX (SOund eXchange)

- Authors: Chris Bagwell and others
- Homepage: *http://home.sprynet.com/~cbagwell/sox.html*
- Download: *http://download.sourceforge.net/sox/*
- Audio format FAQ: *http://home.sprynet.com/~cbagwell/AudioFormats.html*

bladeenc

- Author: Tord Jansson
- Homepage: *http://bladeenc.mp3.no/*
- Download: *http://bladeenc.mp3.no/skeleton/source.html*

LAME (Lame Ain't an MP3 Encoder)

- Authors: various
- Homepage: *http://www.mp3dev.org/mp3/*
- Download: *http://www.mp3dev.org/mp3/download/download.html*

Ogg Vorbis

- Authors: various
- Homepage: *http://www.vorbis.com/*
- Download: *http://www.vorbis.com/download.html*

FreeAmp

- Authors: various
- Homepage: *http://www.freeamp.org/*
- Download: *http://www.freeamp.org/*

cdrdao

- Authors: various
- Homepage: *http://cdrdao.sourceforge.net/*
- Download: *http://cdrdao.sourceforge.net/download.html*

cdrecord

- Authors: various
- Homepage: *http://www.fokus.gmd.de/research/cc/glone/employees/joerg.schilling/private/cdrecord.html*

Chapter 20
MUSIC PRODUCTION

Difficult-o-Meter: 1 (monkeys can do it)

Covers:

MIDI	*http://www.midi.org*
Tracking	*http://www.united-trackers.org*
Jazz++	*http://www.jazzware.com*
Trommler	*http://muth.org/Robert/Trommler/*
TiMidity++	*http://www.goice.co.jp/member/mo/timidity/*
SoundTracker	*http://www.soundtracker.org*
MixMagic	*http://mixmagic.sourceforge.net*
XMMS	*http://www.xmms.org*
mpg123	*http://www.mpg123.de*
Additional hardware	mini-DIN -> stereo cable

Question: How do I use Linux to make music? What tools are available to me, and how do I know which tool is right for my needs?

Answer: You will find Linux well suited for music production, with its large assortment of sound-generating, sequencing, and audio-recording applications.

Introduction

This chapter will introduce some of the tools you might use for music production. The introduction of new Linux tools is an almost daily occurrence, as is the improvement of existing tools. It is up to you to keep up with what's new and improved. This chapter will get you started down the road to creating music with an operating system thought of mostly as a corporate server or something that only programmers use. What you will learn in this chapter is that Linux has a lot to offer the creative musician. Here are some of the topics you will learn about:

- MIDI sequencers
- Mod trackers
- Software synthesizers
- Software drum machines
- Multitrack hard disk recorders
- Loop-based sequencers
- Musical notation editors

Scores of musicians use all sorts of electronic musical equipment to aid them in creating music. Technology has changed the way music is created, recorded, and performed. In this chapter, we will explore many technologies that can be used to produce sound or music under Linux. It's probably best to start at the beginning, when the technology behind the music really took off with the introduction of MIDI.

What Is MIDI?

MIDI (Musical Instrument Digital Interface) has had by far the most influence on music creation and performance. Simply put, MIDI allows a musician to connect one musical device to another for a variety of purposes. For instance, a drummer can connect a specialized drum pad via MIDI to a synthesizer module. When the pad is triggered by the drummer hitting it with a drum stick, the pad sends a MIDI signal to the module (or *brain*, as it is typically called) to play an assigned part. It can also trigger other events if the pad is connected to other MIDI-capable devices, such as lighting controllers, digital recorders, and computers. There are many technologies that a musician can take advantage of. MIDI is the glue that binds the music and the technology together.

By today's standards, MIDI is a relatively simple technology in terms of its use with computers and musical instruments. For each device there are MIDI in and MIDI out ports. In addition, a MIDI through port, used for chaining devices together, is also available on some hardware. Connecting a synthesizer to a computer is a simple

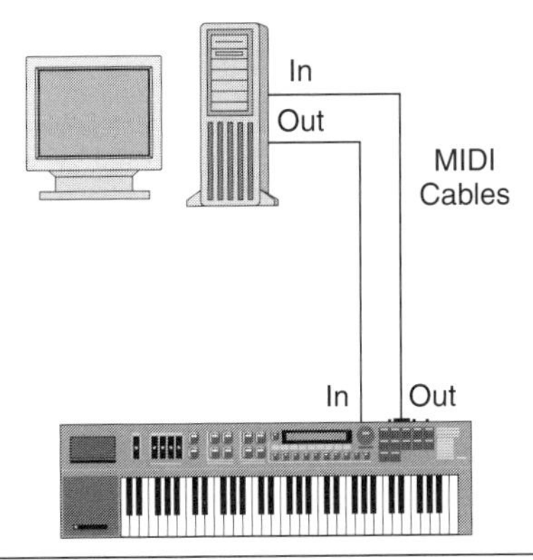

Figure 20-1 MIDI synthesizer connected to computer.

matter of connecting the out port of each device to the in port of the other device, as illustrated in Figure 20-1.

When recording, the synthesizer or MIDI controller (a special keyboard for generating only MIDI events—it doesn't produce sound itself) generates the MIDI events and the computer records them using sequencing software. (More information on MIDI can be read at *www.midi.org*. There is also an excellent introduction to MIDI at the Jazz++ Web site, *http://www.jazzware.com*.) For playback, the computer will send the recorded MIDI events to a sound-generating device, such as a synthesizer module or synthesizer keyboard, or some other device.

Computer Hardware

For a computer to send and receive MIDI events, it needs to have a MIDI device. This device can either be a dedicated MIDI board, such as a true MPU-401 MIDI board, or a soundcard with MIDI support, such as my Creative SBLive. Whichever you choose, you'll want to make sure the MIDI device is supported by the Linux kernel you are using. Dig into the documentation directory of the kernel sources. It's a great source of information about which devices are supported by the included drivers. MIDI devices have been around long enough that support is almost assured.

Once your MIDI device is recognized by the kernel, you should have access to it through a */dev/midi* device file. Your sequencing software will use this device file to communicate with your computer's MIDI ports and ultimately your synthesizers.

MIDI Sequencing

There are a number of GPL'ed MIDI sequencing software packages. A search on *www.freshmeat.net* for MIDI will produce a moderately sized list of applications, such as:

- Anthem
- Brahms
- Gseq
- Jazz++
- Rosegarden
- Melys
- MusE

The specifics of each program would be too much to write about, and most aren't even at release 1.0 yet. Instead I will be writing about a program that I've used over the years, Jazz++. Recently GPL'ed, Jazz++ has been a cornerstone of the Linux MIDI sequencing scene for years. What scene? Okay, no scene. However, I remember using Jazz+ years ago and then discovering Jazz++ and wanting to buy it. But I could never get Jazz+ to work with my Creative Sound Blaster AWE32. Of course, a lot has changed since then, like better driver support and Jazz++ going GPL! During this time, I had a brief lapse in judgment and purchased, along with my Roland XP-30, Steinberg CuBase VST, a MIDI/audio sequencing application for Windows. Once I regained my senses, I realized that I'd wasted over $300 for a product I will never use. Why? Because I'm 100% Linux!

Now, don't get me wrong. I think Microsoft Windows is okay for my mother-in-law and my wife. But for me, "Just Linux" is the motto. Interestingly, Brahms' claim to fame is that it intends to be the Steinberg CuBase VST for Linux. CuBase VST is really good. (For what I paid for it, it better be good!) This is why I like GPL'ed software. If you make a mistake and choose an application that's not right for you, you're only out the time you spent learning the product. Knowledge is never wasted, however. Whatever you learn will be applied somehow, sometime. Money, on the other hand, can be wasted. We'll have to wait and see if Brahms lives up to its claim, because as I write this, Brahms is not even at a 1.0 release and will probably be at release 4.0 when it finally comes close to CuBase VST. But this is okay. The effort is appreciated and encouraged. The best thing about software is that there are plenty of people who will use one product over another, for whatever reason, and will always fuel the need for new applications of the same genre. Speaking of genre, my musical genre preference is techno, so using synthesizers to create music is right up my alley. Enough talk about hardware and software. Let's get started creating our next big chart buster.

Making It Work

One area that might prove to be difficult is figuring out how to make your sequencing software work with your synthesizer. Every synthesizer works differently. It would be impossible for me to describe how they all work, so instead I will take the easy way out and describe how mine works. Hopefully, this will help you discover how best to work with your synthesizer and sequencing software.

My sequencing application of choice is Jazz++. You may use whatever you like, of course, but you will probably find it easier to follow along if you install and configure Jazz++ for now. I will only be describing how to make Jazz++ work with my Roland XP-30. This should give you enough information to make it work for your synthesizer.

The first thing you will have to do is configure Jazz++ for your MIDI card and then your synthesizer. Make sure your card is selected in the OS config, and then compile and install your kernel. Easy right? Check out the HOWTOs and other chapters in this book for information on how to recompile your kernel. This chapter is about Linux music, not the kernel. Next, you need to tell Jazz++ what type of synthesizer you have. You have only a few choices, and most of the time it will be general MIDI (GM). See the Jazz++ help for a good explanation of the choices. Configuring the synthesizer is the next step.

The Roland XP-30 is a multitimbral synthesizer. This means that it can receive multiple channels of MIDI and play a separate part (or sound, if you will) for each channel. This is like having multiple synthesizers but not quite as good. Why? Because instead of using the full capabilities of a synthesizer for each part, the synthesizer must share its sound-generating resources with each part being played. This can seriously limit the number of simultaneous sounds that can be generated. However, having five synthesizers for five different parts of a song is expensive, so it's best to start out with one and gradually add to your collection as you need. The XP-30 is good because it's relatively inexpensive, has a huge sound bank, and is capable of playing a lot of sounds at the same time. For starting out, I cannot think of a better synthesizer. Configuring the XP-30 is also very simple to do.

The XP-30 has three modes in which it operates: part, performance, and rhythm. *Part* mode is used to play a single part (sound). It is good for playing a song with just a piano sound, for example. *Rhythm* mode turns your synthesizer into a drum machine. Lastly, *performance* mode is for both layered sounds or multitimbral work. *Layered sounds* is a mode in which you layer many parts from the XP-30 sound bank so that they get triggered together when a note is played. The results can be quite pleasing, but it's not all that good for producing a song that has four or five separate parts, each with a different instrument. Instead, the XP-30 performance mode can be configured to play multiple parts (without layering), which makes it capable of playing each instrument on its own MIDI channel (1 through 16). Channel 10 is always preassigned as the rhythm track, by the way.

On the main screen you will see the tracks laid out (see Figure 20-2). Each track can be assigned a different program, bank, and MIDI channel. With MIDI there are 16 channels on which to communicate. This allows you to address different devices on a single MIDI port.

To make Jazz++ work with the Roland XP-30, it was a simple matter of figuring out what was required by both the synthesizer and the sequencer. I dabbled with changing the bank and program numbers in Jazz++ but this limited me to GM only. General MIDI is restricted to 127 of probably the worst-sounding parts imaginable. Every time I wanted to record or play a song, Jazz++ reset my synthesizer and jammed me back into GM mode. The solution was to disable the resetting of the synthesizer by Jazz++ (see Figure 20-3). Now my synthesizer wasn't being jammed into GM mode anymore. Through trial and error I discovered that my synthesizer should be configured to have a part (sound) for each bank, or MIDI channel. In performance mode, I can choose from two submodes, layered and part. In performance/part mode, I can assign any of the 1500 different parts to one of the 16 available performance parts, and each one of these is assigned a specific MIDI channel (1 through 16). (I mentioned this before, but now I'm getting specific.) After figuring this out, I decided to choose some interesting sounds and assign each to one of the 15 available MIDI channels. Now all that was left was to figure out how to get Jazz++ to talk to each of the 16 channels.

As mentioned before, each track in Jazz++ can be configured to play on a specific bank, program, and MIDI channel. MIDI channel? Ah ha! Leaving the bank and

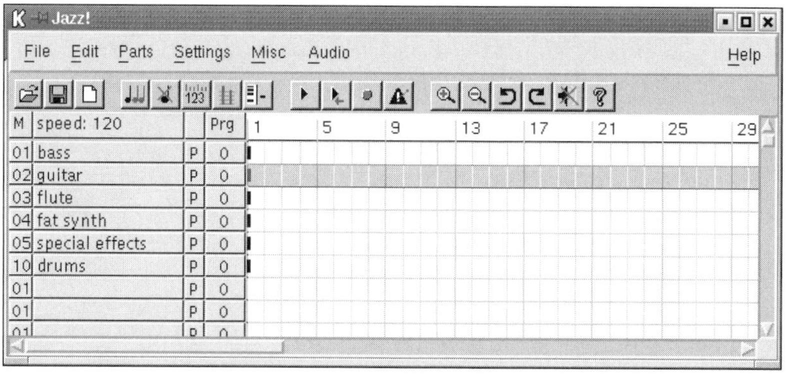

Figure 20-2 Jazz++ tracks window.

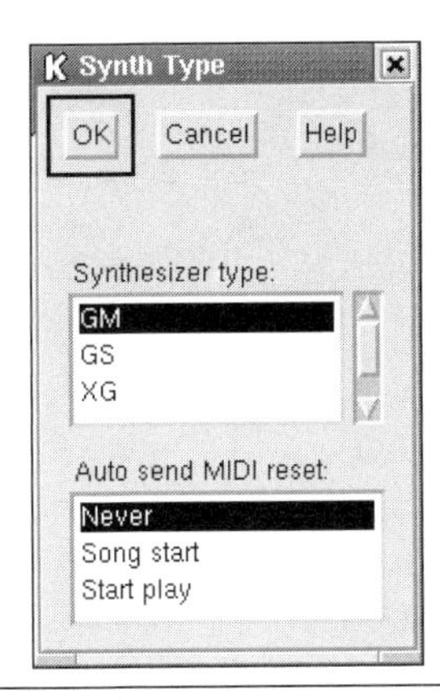

Figure 20-3 Jazz++ Disable Reset Dialog.

program fields alone, I configured track 1 for MIDI channel 1, track 2 for MIDI channel 2, and so on, which worked great. I can now have any track be assigned to any MIDI channel (track 56 assigned to MIDI channel 4, for instance). Now that we have a workable hardware and software solution and are able to record and play back, we should be able to work on a project.

Recording

Everyone will have a different method for attacking a music project. My way may or may not work for you. Over time you will develop your own style. I like beginning my project by recording a scratch track. This is a single reference track to help me understand where I want to go with a song. It's not meant to go into the final product. I usually record this reference version on track 1.

From there I build up around the scratch track, filling in an intro sequence, special effects, drums, bass, leads, and whatever else is needed for the song. It would be difficult to convey exactly how to go about building a song in whole, but with a little experimentation and persistence you will become more and more comfortable with the process involved in making a song via a MIDI sequencer. I can tell you that, at least for me, it involves a lot of repetition, cutting and pasting, and patience.

Because we all can't play the stock market like pros, some of us have to make do with one, maybe two synthesizers. If you have a particularly complicated piece that extends beyond the capabilities of your single synthesizer, you should definitely check out TiMidity. Quoting from the Web site, "TiMidity is a MIDI-to-WAVE converter and player that uses Gravis Ultrasound(*)–compatible patch files to generate digital audio data from general MIDI files." This very handy program can turn your stale MIDI file into a full-bodied masterpiece.

Once you have your masterpiece created, you'll want to be able to record it on paper. For this we'll move into the area of musical notation. MIDI is great for musical notation, since MIDI records the actual notes being played and those notes can be used to print notes on a staff.

Musical Notation

Assuming you have a Postscript printer or a printer that is configured to print graphics (like from a browser or The GIMP), you should be able to print your music. There are only a handful of programs that can be used, or claim they can be used, for musical notation. Here are just a few:

- Brahms
- Rosegarden
- GNU Lilypond

If you need music notation, make sure the program you choose accepts standard MIDI files as output by your MIDI sequencer program. The focus of this chapter is music creation, so I will not spend any more time on music notation. It's available, it's useful, and I encourage you to explore this subject if you have a need for it.

Software Synthesis

Thus far we have concentrated on music creation using MIDI and external sound-creation devices such as synthesizers, but what if you want to use your computer as a synthesizer? No problem!

What is a software synthesizer? Considering what a synthesizer does, converting electricity into sound, it stands to reason that a computer with a soundcard would also be able to convert electricity into sound. The only hitch is that you need a fairly powerful computer to do this, which is why MIDI is so nice—it doesn't require a 1-GHz system to achieve amazing results. Of course, the trade-off is the expense of the synthesizers. However, if you find yourself with an extra dozen CPU cycles lying around doing nothing, give a software synthesizer a try. Here's a few from *www.freshmeat.net* that might meet your needs:

- aRts: analog real-time synthesizer
- BacteriuM: virtual analog matrix synthesizer
- Cumulus: asynchronous grain synthesizer
- Freebirth: integrated bass synthesizer/step sequencer/sample player
- gAlan: modular synthesizer–drum machine–sequencer–effects unit for Linux
- SpiralSynth: a software synthesizer

So what do they do? Using your soundcard, they shape bit patterns into sound. They model old-style analog synthesizers that had lots of knobs, buttons, and switches and produced very rich sound. If you like to tinker with stuff, you will probably like analog modeling synthesizers, as they are known, because they allow you to fiddle with all aspects of sound, from waveforms to filters and more.

The interesting thing about these tools is that the sound you create can be stored to a file. So then what? Later in this chapter you will learn how to use these stored sounds in two other types of music creation applications for Linux.

Drum Machines

Since a lot of songs need some form of percussion, you might want to check out a drum machine and drum pattern maker. These nifty devices let you create drum patterns you can use for your compositions.

Essentially a form of software synthesizer, a drum machine typically will let you do one thing, produce a pattern of repeating sounds. This pattern can then, usually, be saved as a WAV file to be used elsewhere. Of course, you will probably find these applications just fun to play with. Some let you shape your own sounds, some you load WAV files with drum sounds, and others come preloaded with their own sounds. Regardless, they ultimately allow you to work within the confines of a set number of measures and allow you to determine the tempo and when each sample is to be played.

Like software synthesizers, these are highly specialized applications and also require a lot of CPU to be effective. Here are some drum machines to look at:

- gAlan: modular synthesizer–drum machine–sequencer–effects unit for Linux and Win32
- Green Box: next-generation drum machine
- RhythmLab: displays and sounds polyrhythms
- The Real Thud: a simple WAV mixer most useful as a drum machine

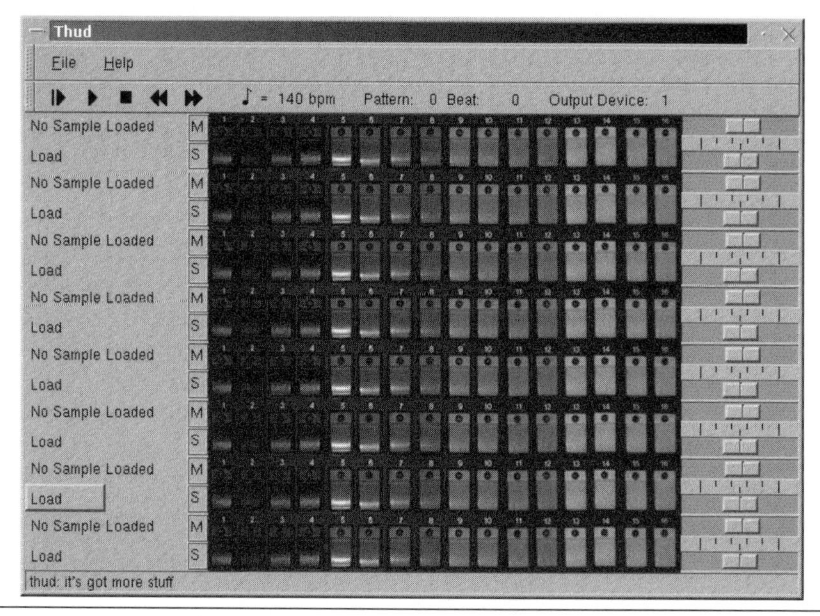

Figure 20-4 Drum machine.

Figure 20-4 presents an example of what a drum machine might look like. This is a screen shot of Thud. Most have the same look, which is basically modeled after their hardware ancestors.

The generation of sound is a key element of creating music with Linux. However, just generating cool sounds and awesome drum patterns doesn't do you any good if you can't put it all together into a song. This is where sequencers (not MIDI) come into play. Somehow, you have to put all those sounds together into patterns of music. For this, you have a couple of options, a MIDI sequencer that also supports audio, a tracker, or loop-based sequencer.

Trackers

What's a tracker? Really, the first question should be "What's a MOD?" A MOD is a type of music file that is not quite MIDI and not quite WAV, but more a combination of the two. MODs came out of the demo scene of many years ago. What's a demo? Back in the DOS days, very talented individuals formed groups all over the world. These groups usually consisted of a programmer, a musician, and an artist. Each group showed off its talents by producing computer programs that showed amazing

3D graphics, great techno music, and stunning artistic pictures and text. In fact, you might have seen some demos running at a local computer store in your area. The coding that went into making a demo was equally impressive—getting the most out of a 10-MHz IBM PC/XT and later a 386.

MODs came around about the same time demos were becoming known. A MOD file is a file that contains audio samples of instruments and sequence information on when to play each sample. A pure audio file (WAV or AU file) is a file containing a digital representation of a song in wave form. A MP3 file is a highly compressed version of this. A MIDI file stores just the notes; a separate device is needed to make the sounds you hear. So how do you make a MOD file? You use a tracker, of course. Now we get back to our original question, "What's a tracker?"

A *tracker* is a program similar to a MIDI sequencer but that requires a much finer attention to detail. In fact, unless you like composing music note by note, event by event, and down to a level of detail that is almost the equivalent of programming in assembly language, a tracker is probably not for you. Music composition using a tracker is an art form. Many projects have come and gone that tried to implement a tracker. Some died due to lack of interest, while others died due to the complexities of the MOD file formats. Because MODs were created in the days before the Internet and high-speed connections, the file formats where kept extremely small. Some files are only 400K for a song that is three minutes long. An MP3 song encoded at 128 bits might require a few megabytes, while a WAV file would be somewhere between 20 and 30 megabytes. Of course, the more samples your MOD-based song has, the larger the file will be. What's a sample?

Samples are the files you employ to create the actual sound used in the tracker. Samples can be made via a software synthesizer or a drum machine, or they can be downloaded from the Internet or even captured from a synthesizer using an audio-capture program. Samples are the sound files a tracker uses to produce the music you hear. You lay out the sequence of when and how you want a sample played by the tracker or by a MOD player that plays only the resulting MOD files trackers create. Figure 20-5 shows the main sequencer screen of SoundTracker, lifted from their Web site. Most trackers will have a sequencer that looks similar. As you can see, the screen is a bit confusing. Not to worry, though—once you understand what's going on with a tracker, you'll be creating very interesting songs. Visit The Mod Archive at *www.modarchive.com* for a huge collection of MOD songs. To create your own tracker-based songs using Linux, you first have to get a tracker and some samples. Here is a list of trackers found via *www.freshmeat.net*:

- SoundTracker
- tektracker
- Voodoo Tracker

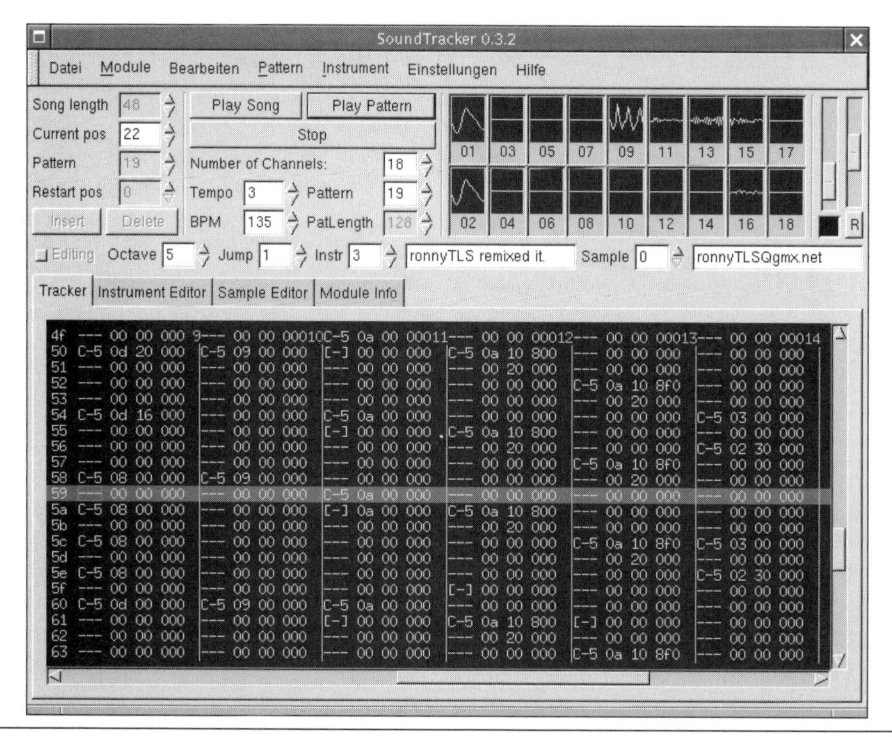

Figure 20-5 SoundTracker main screen.

More information about trackers can be found at *www.united-trackers.org*. If you are dead set on creating music with a tracker, I suggest searching the Net for all the information you can get on trackers and sample archives. It can be frustrating, or it can be the most enjoyable music creation experience you have.

Loop-Based Sequencers

If trackers aren't your bag, then there is yet one more type of tool you can use that requires even less musical skill than sequencers or tracker: loop-based sequencers.

Back in 1998 I happened upon Magix MusicMaker (*www.magix.com*), a Windows application. At the time, I had both a Windows system and a Linux system. Since the program was only $20 I decided to check it out. To my surprise, it turned out to be a program that allowed me to create music, rich music, by dragging and dropping sound files (*loops*) onto a track in a sequencer. I could then stretch the loops to increase the length of time the loop was played. I was amazed at the simplicity of the entire process. In less than an hour, and without reading the manual, I was able to create a three-minute song I named "The Chase," which can be found at *www.mp3.com/digitalman*. In less than six months I had created a total of 14 songs. My first CD, *It's Just the Galaxy*, is now available at *MP3.com*. My second CD, *Majestic Relics*, is on its way or might be there by the time you read this. Go to *MP3.com* and listen to music that is possible with a loop-based sequencing program. You might be impressed.

In addition to plugging my own music, I want to point out that loop-based sequencers, though easy to use, can be a little limiting on your creativity. It really depends, however, on your source of sounds. Similar to trackers, loop-based sequencers use sound files to produce the audio you hear. This means you will have to provide your own sound files for the sequencer. What sequencer, you ask? Well, since I had taught my wife how to log in and use a browser in Linux, I no longer had a need for a Windows system (you didn't think I actually used Windows for anything other than MusicMaker did you?). So my search for a loop-based sequencer for Linux began. I'm happy to report that I found one, MixMagic, at *mixmagic.sourceforge.net*.

MixMagic is described not as a loop-based sequencer, but as "a hard drive sound-mixing program." It's just semantics. Figure 20-6 shows the main composition window. You'll see that the loops (or samples) are layed out horizontally and that the tracks are layed out vertically. On the left is a directory list for your loops. You simply click-and-drag samples from the left over to the composition window on the right. Then you position the loop somewhere on the track and adjust its parameters to suit your needs. What could be easier? ("Turn on the radio" is not allowed as an answer.) All you really need to know about music is whether the samples you dragged to the right-side composition window sound good together. You see, each track plays left to right, as expected. All tracks are mixed together into a single stereo signal and played. This is similar to the final type of software technology I will be introducing, the digital multitrack recorder.

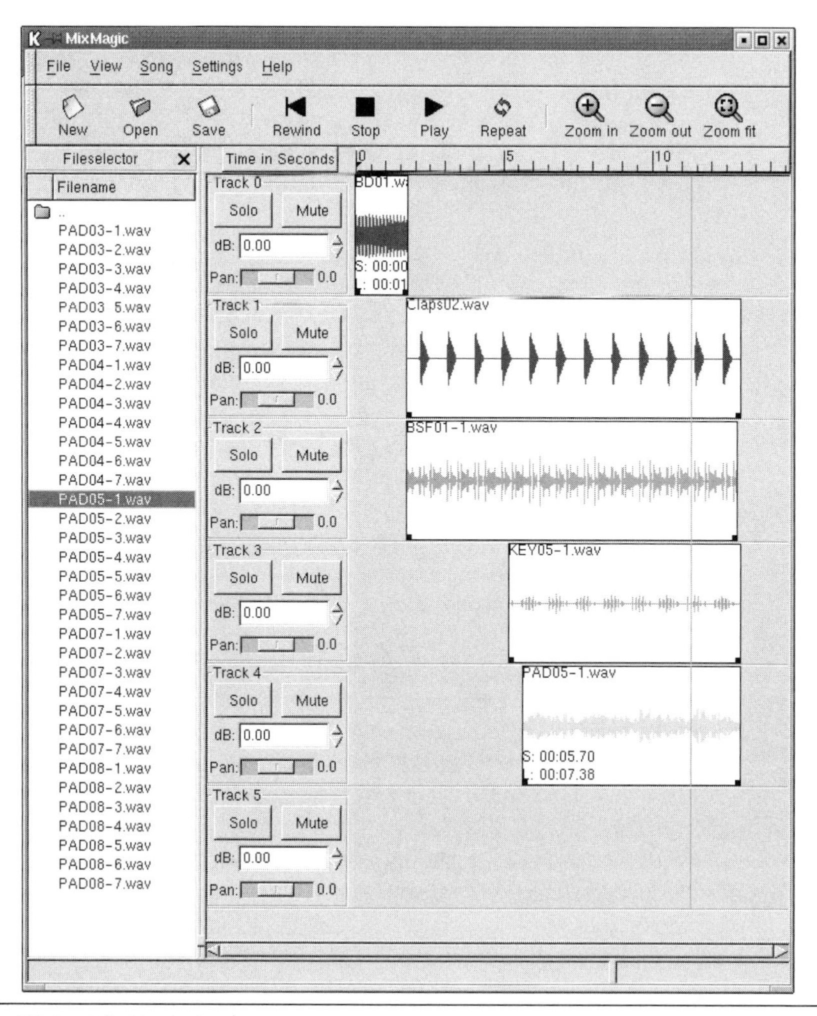

Figure 20-6 MixMagic tracks screen.

Multitrack Hard Disk Recorders

Unlike MixMagic, a digital multitrack recorder records what you play, on either a synthesizer or some other electronic instrument, or what you record with a microphone. You record to each track separately. Normally you play back previously recorded tracks while recording the next track. Hardware-based multitrack recorders can costs thousands of dollars and digital multitrack recorders even more. With Linux, however, a free alternative to expensive hardware is almost always available:

- Audacity: cross-platform multitrack audio editor
- ecasound: sound-processing, multitrack recording and mixing
- hdrbench: tool to measure real-world audio multitrack HD recording
- PROTUX: free professional audio tools for Linux

This short list represents the current offering of multitrack recording applications distributed under the GPL. So how do you use a multitrack recorder? The specific process required of each application would certainly be too much to go into here, but in a nutshell you would do the following:

1. Record audio to track 1.
2. Play back track 1 while recording track 2.
3. Play back tracks 1 and 2 while recording track 3.
4. And so on until you have all your tracks recorded.

If this seems a bit wasteful to you, I couldn't agree more. But multitracking has a purpose and a place. For someone with just one synthesizer, it's a way to record a song that a single synthesizer couldn't possibly do if it were being played by a MIDI file. The point is, use whatever tools you need to get the job done.

Playing Your Masterpiece

So you've gone and created tons of music and now you want to play it for the masses at one of your 100-hour-long rave parties. Well, read on, because now we'll discuss the creation of an MP3 jukebox to play your music.

Sixty to 80 hours of music is a pretty decent demand. An average CD holds a maximum of 74 minutes of audio. Those of you with CD-Rs and a good memory for arcane data will remember that 74 minutes of audio equals 650MB of data. So if we were to convert those time demands into minutes, we'd have 4800 minutes of music required. Well, since 74 goes into 4800 about 65 times, that means you get 65 CDs worth of music, or 42GB. Now, it is conceivable that you've got 42GB of spare space on your hard drive, particularly with the plummeting cost of storage these days. But if you're a college freshman, you've probably got an inordinate number of games on that PC (taking up a good portion of disk space) and some copies of the purity test as well. So we'll have to figure out a way to fit your 42GB of music into something less than 42GB of space.

Thankfully, we've got a trick up our sleeve: compression. A few years ago, a few clever gents came up with an audio-compression format called MP3. MP3 is actually shorthand for the full name of the compression: MPEG layer 3. MPEG compression is useful on sound and moving images (such as movies). What it does is basically shave off the highs and lows. We can get away with this because the human ear, while quite sensitive, is generally incapable of detecting all the quality that a CD can deliver. We can take a 74-minute CD and compress it down to about, oh, 75MB without losing a noticeable amount of quality. That's about a meg per minute. That means we can fit your 80 hours of music in 4800 MB, or 4.8GB. Not too shabby! With a little bit of overhead, we can simplify the formula a little more to say that 1GB of MP3s equals about 15 hours of good-quality music. This gets particularly attractive in light of what hard drives are costing these days. My employer just paid $150 for a fast 31GB drive, and that was far too much money. By the time you're holding this book, 30GB drives will probably be sub-$100 items.

Of course, once you've got a big pile of MP3s sitting on your Linux box, you're stuck without a cable that will let you plug your soundcard into your stereo. Why run a cable from your PC to your stereo? Because most complaints about PC audio are due to the low quality of PC speakers. MP3s that sound tinny or short on bass when played on my PC speakers sound fine when piped through my 12-year-old Fisher (now *there's* a high-quality name for audio!) stereo system. Make sure the cable you get is long enough to string from your PC soundcard to your stereo, and try to avoid linking extenders together. If worse comes to worst, you should be able to fabricate your own cable with a solder gun, a couple of connectors, and some cable.

Okay, so now you've got a big pile of MP3s and a PC that's wired into your stereo. What now? Good question! We'll need to find software that not only can play your MP3s, but also can randomize the list. (You wouldn't want people knowing the exact order of the music at your parties!)

XMMS: The Cross-Platform Multimedia (MP3s, too) Player

The easiest player is XMMS—the evolution of x11amp (a previous MP3 player for Linux). It's got a very Windows-like interface that makes playing a few MP3s very easy. XMMS also ships standard with several distributions and is available at *http://www.xmms.org/* (direct download at *http://www.xmms.org/download.html*). Now, SuSE does ship with XMMS, I do believe, but I neglected to install it when I set up my workstation, so I had to download and compile it.

Compiling is, as always, a very simple affair. After grabbing version 1.2.4, I just followed the directions for a normal, autoconf-style compile, which means configure, make, make install. Compilation and installation took about 15 minutes on my K6/2-450. I did not install all of the myriad options that can be had for XMMS, since

XMMS is a suboptimal jukebox anyway. I've got no way to run it remotely (unless I've got a second machine with an X-windows server on it), which is what I'm striving for in this system. Still, it'll allow me to play a few MP3s and to verify that everything is set up properly for the next phase.

Once you've fired up X (if you don't know what this means, never mind), simply type *xmms* at a command prompt. This will fire up a copy of the Cross-Platform Multimedia System (and all this time you've been wondering what XMMS stands for) and give you the image seen in Figure 20-7.

Look for the little *pl* button on the right middle side of the window. I've circled it in Figure 20-8.

Click that button (or use the keyboard shortcut of Alt-E) and the window in Figure 20-9 will show up.

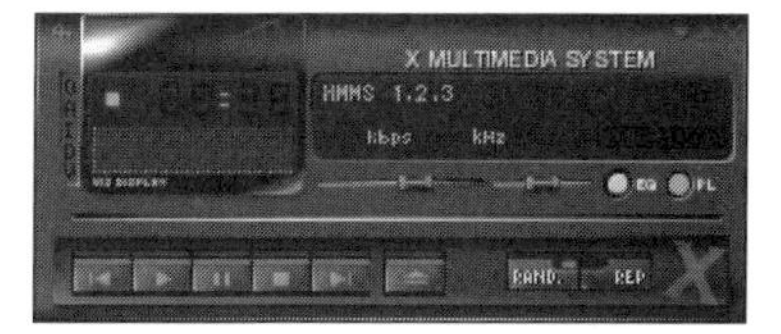

Figure 20-7 XMMS main window.

Figure 20-8 XMMS Playlist button circled.

Figure 20-9 XMMS Playlist Editor.

In the lower left corner is the little button labeled *+file*. Click on that to add an MP3. This will bring up the window in Figure 20-10. Select one of your favorite MP3s. You'll note that I've selected "Dream Universe" by Crystal Method. Note that you can select mutliple files by simply Ctrl-clicking, and you can select ranges by Shift-clicking. Once you've got some files added, you can click on the *Close* button.

You can also bring up the Load files dialog by clicking on the little *Eject* button, which is circled in Figure 20-11, or by hitting *l*.

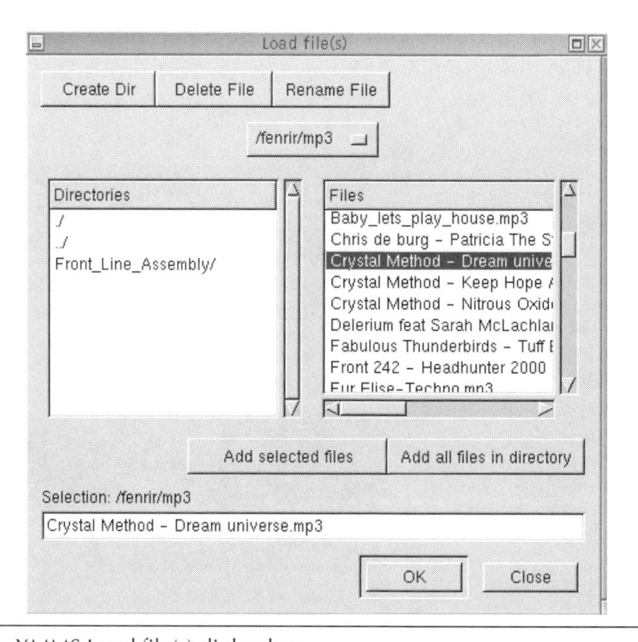

Figure 20-10 XMMS Load file(s) dialog box.

Figure 20-11 XMMS Eject button circled.

Increase Your Technogeek Appeal: Text-Only Commands!

You've got to admit that using just XMMS isn't as whiz-bang cool as it could be. Ideally, wouldn't it be nice to have a machine that didn't need a monitor attached to it? Yes, if you want to be technical, XMMS can be run over the network, so your MP3 player doesn't need a monitor. But wouldn't it be nice to save the space required for X for more MP3s? If you want to do that, you'll need a console-based MP3 player. There is a wide variety of choices: mpg123, mpg321, freeamp, madplay, and so many more.

I prefer to use freeamp, because it has a command line mode that lets you play, pause, and skip files from a text terminal. It's fantastic to use over SSH. I've got an old Pentium 90 I'm turning into an MP3 jukebox (and it's short enough on space that I can't afford to install X—I intend to run CD-Rs burned with MP3s in it for parties), so I just follow the standard process for an autoconf-style package. I intend to upgrade the PCs around the house. My wife's K6-200 will become the MP3 player and CD burner.

So now I've got freeamp installed. What can I do with it? Well, I can very, very, *very* easily build a list of songs to listen to. To test out the format of the list file, I just changed into the directory where I keep the soundtrack from 1998's version of *Godzilla* and did this:

```
$ ls > zilla.m3u
$ freeamp -ui freeampcmd zilla.m3u
```

and *bang!* it's a text player console:

```
Command Line Interface
 * q    Quit
 * +/=  Next Song
 * -    Prev Song
 * p    Pause / UnPause
 * s    Shuffle

 * f    Fast forward 10 seconds

 * b    Skip backwards 10 seconds

Playing:
```

Self-explanatory, isn't it. You can press *s* to tell freeamp to go bounce through your list, selecting songs willy-nilly.

To get a listing of all the MP3s in your MP3 hierarchy and then to play them, you can try this:

```
$ find /mp3dir -name '*.mp3' -print > songs.m3u
$ freeamp -ui freeampcmd songs.m3u
```

Away goes the player!

Real-World Problems

It'd be nice to sit back and enjoy. But that's easier said than done because no matter how you try to keep on top of your MP3 collection, you'll always end up finding a song that you can't stand. How to skip that song? Very easy . . . just hit = or +, and freeamp will go on to the next song.

So it's five minutes until the party is going to start, and you want some tunes. Well, it's time to start things up. Run freeamp with the right playlist, and turn off the monitor, or move it, or hide it. Away goes the music. When that damned Barry Manilow tune comes on (why'd you keep that one, anyway?), just stroll over to the jukebox's keyboard like the techno-wizard you are, and hit = (just once, mind you). And away goes the evil tune and the next one is started. If you mess up and hit it too many times, you can go back by pressing -. (And do us all a favor after the party—delete that song you don't like anymore.)

You know it'll happen, sooner or later—you'll fill up your 40GB drive, and you'll have to start using CD-Rs full of MP3s. Well, that takes just a hair of configuration work. You'll need to modify your */etc/fstab* so that a normal user (yourself) can mount and unmount CD-ROMs. The appropriate line is:

```
/dev/hdc       /cdrom       auto       ro,noauto,user,exec    0    0
```

Now go ahead and test that you can successfully mount and unmount CD-Rs and CD-ROMs. Once you've verified that, it's time to alias a couple of things.

Script That Bad Mamma Jamma

Now come the shell scripts. We want a brief script that will mount a CD, take an inventory of all the MP3s on it, and then start *freeamp*. When the player exits, we want to unmount and eject the CD, and then hope the partygoers won't be too perturbed by the break in the music. So here it is:

```
#!/usr/bin/bash
# cdr.bash -- the mounting & playing & unmounting script
mount /cdrom && \
    find /cdrom -iname '*.mp3' > /tmp/songs.m3u && \
    freeamp -ui freeampcmd /tmp/songs.m3u
    rm /tmp/songs.m3u && \
    umount /cdrom && \
    eject /cdrom
```

That's a mouthful, eh? Now just make sure it's executable, and test it. Since it'll work if you typed it in just as seen here, I'll explain the logic.

- It declares what shell it's using. We use bash, because it's nice and consistent and is included in almost all distributions (I haven't seen a Linux without it, in fact).
- Mount the CD-ROM, and if that succeeds,
    - do a *find* command that will find anything ending with *.mp3*, *.Mp3*, *.MP3*, or *.mP3* and then dumps all matching filenames into */tmp/songs.m3u*. If that succeeds,
        - Start a new copy of freeamp, using the new playlist as fodder. When that exits,
            - Unmount the CD. If that's successful,
                - Eject the CD.

This isn't a terribly advanced shell script—I'm sure you'd be able to improve it with a little thought. Since it's executable, and in a logical place (you always put your shell scripts in a logical place, right?), we just need to define some aliases. I put my scripts in */home/jeremy/juke_scripts*. And then I set up this alias:

```
alias m='/home/jeremy/juke_scripts/cdr.bash'
```

Voila! Now, during a party, you need only hit *m* to start the player. When the CD finishes, or you cancel freeamp by pressing *q*, the CD will eject. Then put in the fresh CD-R, and type *m* again—the CD tray will close, and the music will start as soon as a playlist has been composed.

There you are. You've got yourself a pretty cool MP3 player that's the utmost in simplicity.

Here's the final piece of advice: **Don't follow the directions in this chapter.** Unless you've got a big spare hard drive and a relatively fast processor (at least a Pentium 90) sitting idle (not to mention a keyboard, a good soundcard, and some time to kill), this is going to cost you a good $200. Run, don't walk, to your nearest electronics retailer and buy yourself a piece of hardware like the Apex DVD player or the Rio Volt. Such a device will play CD-Rs burned with MP3s, and can almost completely substitute for the system we've spent the last few pages building.

Summary

The goal of this chapter was to introduce you to a variety of technologies available under Linux that will aid you in creating music. I hope I have convinced you that it is possible to use Linux for more than a file server, DNS, or Web server. It can be a truly useful music workstation if properly configured with the right software. Given that, I have to confess that there are even more tools "out there" that I did not cover, such as:

Audio editors

Audio recorders

Effects processors

Format converters

Oscilloscopes

Patch editors and librarians

Samplers

Spectrum analyzers

More software is appearing for Linux every day, giving the Linux community a continually growing list of quality music-creation applications to choose from. Choosing which applications are appropriate for your projects will be the hardest part of the process. I've already got my list of favorites and, hopefully, you will find yours.

Chapter 21

SPEECH SYNTHESIS

Difficult-o-Meter: 4 (fairly high Linux knowledge required)

Covers:

rsynth	*ftp://svr-ftp.eng.cam.ac.uk/pub/comp.speech/sources/*
Festival	*http://www.cstr.ed.ac.uk/projects/festival/*

> *Question:* I think it would be cool to have my Linux system talk to me, maybe to tell me when mail arrives and who it's from or to remind me of appointments if I'm deep into coding. How can I do this?
>
> *Answer:* Read this chapter! This is a situation where you should be glad you're running Linux, since you'll need to piece together many different tools to do the job.

Actually, there are two major ways to speech-enable a Linux system: the hardware way and the software way. Many companies sell internal or external hardware devices for synthesizing speech, targeting their products at disabled computer users. This chapter is not about accessibility under Linux; there are already good online references discussing this issue, and the major desktop environments all have some degree of support for accessibility. Instead, this chapter is concerned with the no-cost route of software synthesis and, more importantly, with tying in speech synthesis with all the other tools available on a Linux system to create a program that is more than the sum of its parts. I'll begin by discussing some concepts underlying speech synthesis, and then jump right into some applications with (in my opinion) a pretty high "cool factor."

Analyzing Speech Synthesis

As lifelong users of spoken language, we find speech synthesis (or "generation") a simple task. Many of us probably don't remember a time when we weren't capable of conversing with the people around us. But getting a computer to speak intelligibly is a surprisingly complicated process.

The simplest approach is to record audio clips of the desired words or phrases and then to play them back as required by the application. This is the approach used by answering machines, voice mail, and VRU systems. It has the advantage of not requiring much processing power, but it doesn't scale to the case of arbitrary phrases. Every conceivable phrase that the system can utter would have to be recorded by a human voice.

A trade-off can be made between flexibility and smoothness: Instead of recording every possible phrase, a human will record every possible word that can be uttered by the system. The words are then strung together to create the appropriate phrases. However, without the natural rise and fall of pitch through the phrase, it sounds jerky or stilted and sometimes can lead to a comical-sounding situation: (female voice) "Please wait by your car for parking officer Steve . . ." (deep male voice) "Grebowski" (female again) "between the hours of 9 and 5."

As computing power has increased through the years, dynamic synthesis of voice waveforms has become a less expensive proposition. Nevertheless, there are still many different programmatic steps required to convert a string of words to an output waveform. Speech scientists have identified these steps in great detail, but for our purposes four will suffice. In order, from the human-centric level to the machine-centric level, they are: tokenization, phrasing and accenting, phonetics and intonation, and waveform generation.

Not all speech synthesis packages provide all the higher-level components. For example, a simple synthesizer may perform only the waveform-generation step, which requires the application to specifically create the appropriate string of sounds and embedded intonation hints.

Tokenization

Tokenization is the process of breaking up an input string into words, identifying punctuation marks, and often includes conversion of special characters into their alphabetic equivalents. For example, a typical tokenization would be:

```
The time is 8:04 PM, July 24th.
the time is eight oh four P M  <comma> july twenty fourth <end>
```

Sometimes some of these steps are part of the phrasing and intonation step, to be described shortly.

Tokenization rules can quickly become complicated. Even in our short example, we can see that the following rules must be defined somewhere:

- Numbers are expanded to their word equivalents (8).
- A colon surrounded by numbers is skipped.
- A zero following a colon becomes "oh."
- Unrecognized words are spelled out (P.M.).
- A number followed by an ordinal suffix is expanded to the corresponding ordinal word (24th).

Phrasing and Intonation

The next step in speech synthesis is to take the list of tokens, identify parts of speech, and divide them into plausible phrases. Punctuation marks, like commas and periods, are critical to this process. If the machine has a knowledge of the correct grammar as well, the dependent and independent clauses can be recognized in order to provide additional hints. In our example, the phrasing rules would break the sequence of tokens into two parts:

```
the time is eight oh four P M
july twenty fourth
```

Usually commas and semicolons will indicate the end of a phrase, followed by a brief pause, and periods will indicate the end of a phrase, followed by a longer pause.

Now, the words within each phrase must be assigned accent, which describes variations in the pitch and speed of the spoken word. Accented words tend to have a heavier, slower intonation, and other words are spoken more quietly and quickly. Phrase-level accenting is a highly language-specific property.

Here is an example of the importance of phrase-level accenting (in English, of course) (the accented words are underlined):

```
Alice is telling Bob about her appointment:
A: I'm supposed to be there at eight. (flat tone, falling at end)

Alice thought her appointment was at seven, but Bob has just told her
    differently:
A: I'm supposed to be there at eight? (rising sharply at end)
```

```
Alice, reminding herself of the right time:
A: I'm supposed to be there at eight. (rising a little at end)
```

All three sentences contain the same words, but they imply very different things, depending on the intonation. It's difficult to tell the appropriate intonation just from the written words. Some speech synthesizers allow special marker symbols to provide accenting hints at this step.

Phonetics

Next, each word needs to be decomposed into its specific phonemes. *Phonemes* are the specific, small units of sound that make up the characteristic sound of a language. The International Phonetic Alphabet describes a universal way of writing each of these sounds and all their subtleties. One of the more familiar uses of phonemes is probably on your bookshelf: The pronunciation guides in dictionaries spell each word phonetically.

Decomposition into phonemes is difficult for an irregular language like English, where the spelling of a word does not bear as much relation to its pronunciation as in other languages. Most speech synthesizers use both a dictionary of known words and a set of rules for unknown words to derive the correct pronunications.

There can be more than one pronunciation dictionary for a given language, corresponding to the quality commonly known as *accent* but more properly termed *dialect*. For example, the Festival speech synthesis package comes with several English phoneme databases, including a British English male speaker, two American English male speakers, and a Castilian Spanish male speaker.

Once the appropriate phonemes and their accents are looked up in the pronunciation dictionary, the information is combined with the overall intonation of the containing phrase to derive the appropriate pitch and duration for each phoneme. This process provides continuity between words and avoids a monotone effect.

After this step is completed, our time-and-date example is reduced to the following sequence of phonemes:

```
th (pitch normal)
<weak vowel>
t
ah
ee
m (longer)
<stop>
```

```
ih (pitch decreasing)
z
ay (pitch higher than normal)
t(s)
<stop>
oh (long)
f (pitch normal)
aw
r
```

Of course, the description of each phoneme is not as complete as the software would generate, but many of the more important aspects are shown.

Waveform Generation

Finally, the waveforms for each phoneme are generated, either by looking them up in a file or by a more sophisticated wave envelope synthesis. This is the point at which different voice qualities can be simulated. For example, the voice of a man or woman or a child, a gravelly voice, a smooth voice, and a whispering voice are all distinguished and generated at this step. The waveforms for each phoneme are adjusted for pitch and duration and then blended into a final waveform, which can be stored to a file or sent directly to an audio device.

Speech Synthesis Packages

At this point you may be asking, “Okay, enough about the theory. I just want a program that will work.” Never fear; there are several packages that will work under Linux. In a later section we’ll see how to combine them with the other tools on a typical Linux system to perform useful tasks. However, it still helps to know what the software is doing, in order to better make it do what you want.

Rsynth

Rsynth is one of the simplest, fastest speech synthesizers available for Linux. It is a public domain program that originally appeared on the *comp.speech* newsgroup. Unfortunately, due to its simplicity it has relatively poor sound quality. The basic usage is:

```
say -d a "Hello world."
echo "Goodbye cruel world." | say -d a
```

The *-d* option describes which pronunciation dictionary to use: *a* means American, and *b* means British. The pronunciation dictionaries must be set up in a library directory, usually */usr/local/lib* (*/usr/lib/dict* on Debian systems). Rsynth can be used without a pronunciation dictionary, but due to the irregularities of the English language, it performs atrociously. Luckily, the software comes with a utility called *mkdictdb*, which converts plain-text dictionaries into specially indexed dictionaries that rsynth can use.

There are many plain-text pronunciation dictionaries available online. One of the most commonly used American English dictionaries is available from Carnegie Mellon University. You will need to convert it to rsynth format in order to use it:

```
$ wget ftp://ftp.cs.cmu.edu/project/fgdata/dict/cmudict-0.6.gz
$ gunzip cmudict-0.6.gz
$ mkdictdb cmudict-0.6 /usr/local/lib/aDict.db
```

If you don't already have it, wget is a nifty utility to retrieve known URLs. See Chapter 15, Tools You Should Know, for a discussion of wget. The final line of code runs the utility to index the dictionary and place the output file in the directory that rsynth expects.

There is also a British English pronunication dictionary available at the following URL:

```
ftp://svr-ftp.eng.cam.ac.uk/pub/comp.speech/dictionaries/beep-1.0
    .tar.gz
```

Rsynth allows you to insert specific phonemes in the plain text. This provides an easy way to correct for the cases in which a word is not in the pronunciation dictionary and rsynth's internal rules produce the wrong pronunciation. For example, when rsynth is given the word *Linux*, it pronounces it "Line-ux", instead of "Lin-ux." The proper pronunciation is obtained by supplying the list of phonemes enclosed in brackets:

```
say -d a "[lInVks]"
```

The correspondence between characters and phonemes follows the same standard as the prebuilt pronunciation dictionaries. Rather than detailing the codes for each phoneme, it's actually easier to experiment a little to find the correct pronunciation for a word. A good approach is to look at the encoding for a word that sounds similar and try modifying it as necessary.

Festival

Festival is an open source speech synthesis package developed primarily at the University of Edinburgh Centre for Speech Technology Research. It is distributed under an X11-style license. The core speech engine, written in C++, includes a command interpreter based on Scheme, one of the many dialects of LISP. Inveterate users of the advanced features of Emacs should feel right at home in the Festival command interpreter. Festival aims to provide a complete set of tools addressing all levels of speech synthesis, and it is deliberately built to support multiple (human) languages.

Festival can be obtained as a RedHat or Debian package, and can be downloaded directly from the University of Edinburgh:

```
http://www.cstr.ed.ac.uk/projects/festival/
```

Festival provides several pronunication and phoneme dictionaries, and additional voices are available from other sources at no cost or for a small fee. The basic package includes:

- *voice_rab_diphone:* A British English male speaker. The accent is linguistically known as *RP*, which would be most familiar to nonlinguists as the "voice of the BBC."
- voice_don_diphone: Another British English male speaker, which sounds better than *rab*.
- voice_ked_diphone: An American English male speaker.
- voice_kal_diphone: Another American English male speaker, which sounds better than *ked*.
- voice_ell_diphone: A Castilian Spanish male speaker.

Despite its underlying complexity, Festival is actually very easy to use. The simplest method of invocation is via the *—tts* option (text to speech). It will read a file or standard input and speak the incoming words:

```
fortune | festival --tts -
```

Without the text-to-speech option, Festival invokes a Scheme interpreter that takes commands from standard input. For example,

```
festival <<END
(Parameter.set 'Audio_Method 'linux16audio)
(voice_kal_diphone)
(SayText "Hello, world!")
(SayText "You can hear me now!")
END
```

This example shows a few of the features of Scheme. Commands are executed by enclosing the command name and arguments in parentheses. Strings are represented by enclosing them in double quotes (not single quotes.) Festival populates the interpreter environment with a number of commands, but the two basic ones you need to know are the (*voice_**) commands, which set a particular voice to use, and the (*SayText* "...") command, which does exactly what it would appear to do, that is, parse a phrase and speak it to the audio device.

The remaining command (*Parameter.set*) is used to set the audio output method. If you are using an audio server that has a large output buffer, Festival may start sending a sentence to the audio mixer before the previous one is done, resulting in an unexpected muddle of voices. To avoid this problem, you can specifically set the audio output method in the interpreter to linux16audio, which tells Festival to use the */dev/audio* device.

You can also modify the interpreter's initial environment to specify a different default voice and audio mode. Included in the Festival distribution is a file called *init.scm;* its location in the file system may vary depending on whether you compiled Festival from source or obtained it as a DEB or RPM. This file contains most of the default settings and can be hand-edited to set the desired parameters.

Festival was originally built on Unix-based systems, and as a consequence it is easily integrated with the other Unix command line tools. We'll see an example of this later in the chapter. It also has an excellent set of documentation, which is always an asset when learning to use new software!

My Computer's First Word Was "Linux!"—Some Examples

Check Your Internet Mail at Login

Many Internet mail clients offer the option to periodically check whether there is any unread mail in your inbox. Sometimes there is a small applet or tray icon that changes color or shape to indicate new mail. But why stop there? Keeping with the spirit of the Unix philosophy, this example shows how to set up your machine to talk to you when new mail arrives and also to notify you of mail when you first log in.

The example is written in the Swiss Army chainsaw of languages, Perl. Without further ado, I'll present the code and then explain the various pieces. Of course, if you're already comfortable with Perl, you can certainly skip over the explanations.

```
1   #!/usr/bin/perl
2
3   # Daemonize myself
4   exit if (fork() != 0);
```

```
5   close STDIN;
6   close STDOUT;
7   close STDERR;
8
9   use Socket;
10
11  $POP_SERVER = "pop.myserver.com";
12  $POP_PORT = 110;
13  $POP_USER = "pcurtis";
14  $POP_PASSWORD = "notmyrealpassword!";
15
16  socket(S, PF_INET, SOCK_STREAM, getprotobyname("tcp"))
17      || die "Can't create socket: $!";
18  connect(S, sockaddr_in($POP_PORT, inet_aton($POP_SERVER)))
19      || die "Can't connect: $!";
20
21  select S; $| = 1; $line = <S>;
22  print "USER $POP_USER\n"; $line = <S>;
23  print "PASS $POP_PASSWORD\n"; $line = <S>;
24  if ($line =~ /^\+OK/ && $line =~ /has (\d+) mail messages/i) {
25          $count = (0 + $1);
26          $word = ($count || "no") . " message"
27          . (($count != 1) ? "s" : "");
28          &say("You have $word.");
29          &say("Bedder cheg it now.") if ($count == 1);
30  }
31  print S "QUIT\n";
32  close(S);
33  exit;
34
35  sub say {
36          my ($string) = @_;
37          $string =~ s/'/\\'/g;
38          open(FH, "| festival");
39          print FH "(voice_kal_diphone)\n(SayText '$string')\n";
40          close FH;
41          sleep(2);
42  }
43
```

Save this program to whatever directory with whatever name you prefer, and make sure to set the executable bit in the file permissions. Then, add a call to this command in your *.profile* file. Some mail clients also allow you to run an arbitrary command when new mail is detected. You can place a call to this command there as well. For example, to configure kmail, the KDE 2 mail client, select *Settings* > *Configuration* from the menu, select the *Miscellaneous* category, and modify the box labeled "New mail notification."

The foregoing Perl script doesn't rely on external utilities; it actually implements a very small portion of the POP3 protocol, just enough to retrieve the number of messages on the server. The script will have to be adjusted if your mail server cannot handle a POP3 protocol or if the message formats returned by the POP server are slightly different.

Lines 3–7 cause the process to fork and close all its handles, putting it in the background. This will keep a misbehaving script from locking up your mail client or blocking your login scripts from running. You do want to be able to log in, right?

Line 9 defines the library required to use socket routines. It is provided as part of the standard Perl distribution. Lines 11–14 set up the appropriate parameters for your mail account.

Lines 16–19 are where the action starts; the first two commands create a new socket and try to connect to the given port on the POP server. Once a connection is established, line 21 tells Perl to print to the socket and then reads the first "hello" line sent by the mail server and throws it away. Lines 22 and 23 send the username and password, reading the response lines each time. For simplicity, the script isn't written with error checking at each step.

Line 24 is where the first response line is examined. My POP server returns this line after the username and password are provided (and are correct!):

```
+OK User pcurtis has 2 mail messages
```

The *if* statement checks that the lines starts with *+OK* (part of the POP protocol) and then matches the text surrounding the number of interest. If your POP server returns a slightly different string, you may have to adjust that second regular expression.

If the response has the expected form, lines 25–29 build an appropriate text string to send to Festival. Since Festival provides a sophisticated semantic layer, it's okay to put just the number into the string; it will be spelled out. Then the *say* function is called to speak the given text. And line 29 causes the script to tell you that you "better check it." Notice the intentional misspelling, which actually makes the generated speech sound cleaner on my system.

In case we haven't yet changed the *init.scm* script, we provide a separate subroutine for saying a phrase using a nondefault voice. We could have used the *--tts* option to Festival, but a separate subroutine is more flexible. The *sleep* command isn't strictly necessary, but helps if the audio device is not completely synchronous; it gives the audio time to be output before the subroutine returns.

It's easy to think of a number of ways to enhance this program; some of them could be enlightening exercises:

- More robust error checking.
- Implementing more of the protocol to retrieve message sizes, headers, From: fields, and so on.
- Providing command line options for different behaviors. For example, a *—just-new* option, which would not log into the POP server, just verbally inform you of new mail. This could be the command run from a mail monitor. You could cause the mail client (or some other application) to be automatically launched.
- Just running the script from cron makes a simple but effective mail monitor. It would have to be modified to wait until you are logged in, perhaps by looking at the output of the *who* command.

The Lazy Man's File Browser

The next example would stand a good chance of winning a Most Gratuitously Useless award, if such an award existed. It uses Perl to glue together an IRMan infrared remote control, Festival, and XMMS to make the ELM jukebox. ELM stands for "extremely lazy man's" jukebox; the "lazy man" would be me. Even though XMMS already has a plug-in for the IRMan, it is only set up to use the standard "CD player" commands: *play*, *pause*, *next track*, and so on. If you want to add songs not on the playlist, you still have to select them from a dialog box. I want to be able to walk through my music collection using the remote control, with vocal feedback about my current location. Then, once I locate a song, I want to send it to XMMS to play. I chose to use Festival over rsynth because of its superior ability to handle the complex semantics of typical filenames: things like slashes, numbers, and abbreviations.

In case you're wondering, IRMan is a very cool and inexpensive piece of hardware that reads remote control codes from almost any universal remote (Figure 21-1). It plugs in to a serial port and has a simple, openly implemented communication protocol. To be specific, it dumps a six-byte code to the serial port every time it receives a key press. You can use it to remote-control-enable almost any application with only a little programming. Even better, some applications have built-in support for IRMan. Go out and buy one *right now*!

When you first run this program, you start with a current directory and a current position within that directory. You navigate by changing the current position; if the currently selected item is a subdirectory, you can descend into it. Every time you change the current position, the program tells you the name of the file. If you change the current directory, you will hear the directory name and the number of files it contains.

The six file-navigation commands are: *Forward*, *Back*, *Forward half*, *Back half*, *Up*, and *Down*. *Forward* and *Back* move to the next or previous file in the current directory,

Figure 21-1 IRMan remote control receiver.

respectively. *Forward half* moves from the current position halfway to the end of the directory, and *Back half* moves from the current position halfway toward the beginning of the directory listing. *Up* moves to the parent directory, and *Down* descends into a subdirectory. The other two commands, *Play* and *Stop*, will tell XMMS to start or stop playing the currently selected song, respectively.

As an example, say I start in the root of my music collection. I would use *Forward* and *Forward half* to navigate to the artist I wanted to hear and then use *Down* to descend and hear the number of files in that subdirectory. Then I would use *Forward* and *Forward half* again to pick an album or song name. Finally, when I picked the song I wanted to hear, I would use *Play*.

The following script is easily adapted to become a general-purpose file browser, with added features such as following symbolic links, launching various applications depending on file types, and so on. Navigation through long directory listings could also use some refinement.

```
1   #!/usr/bin/perl
2
3   use Socket;
4
5   use constant FORWARD_1 => 1;
6   use constant FORWARD_HALF => 2;
7   use constant BACK_1 => 3;
8   use constant BACK_HALF => 4;
```

```
9   use constant UP => 5;
10  use constant DOWN => 6;
11  use constant PLAY => 7;
12  use constant STOP => 8;
13  use constant QUIT => 100;
14
15  my %KEYS = (
16      "660000000000" => FORWARD_1,
17      "460000000000" => FORWARD_HALF,
18      "620000000000" => BACK_1,
19      "420000000000" => BACK_HALF,
20      "750000000000" => UP,
21      "640000000000" => DOWN,
22      "710000000000" => QUIT,
23      "700000000000" => PLAY,
24      "730000000000" => STOP
25  );
26
27  my $QUIET = 0;
28  my $FEST_PID = &forkOff("festival", "--server");
29  sleep(2);
30
31  my ($dir, @files, $index);
32  &gotoDirectory("/home/mp3");
33  while (1) {
34      if (!$QUIET && $index >= 0 && $index < @files) {
35          my $tmp = $files[$index];
36          $tmp =~ s/\.mp3$//;
37          &say($tmp);
38      }
39      $cmd = $KEYS{&readKeypress};
40      next if !$cmd;
41      if ($cmd == QUIT) {
42          kill 15, $FEST_PID;
43          wait;
44          exit;
45      }
46      elsif ($cmd == FORWARD_1) {
47          $index = ($index + 1) % @files;
48      }
49      elsif ($cmd == BACK_1) {
50          $index = ($index - 1) % @files;
51      }
52      elsif ($cmd == FORWARD_HALF) {
53          $index = int(($index + @files) / 2);
54      }
55      elsif ($cmd == BACK_HALF) {
56          $index = int($index / 2);
57      }
58      elsif ($cmd == DOWN) {
59          if (!-d "$dir/$files[$index]") {
```

```
60              &say($files[$index] . " is not a directory.");
61              $QUIET = 1;
62          }
63          else {
64              &gotoDirectory("$dir/$files[$index]");
65          }
66      }
67      elsif ($cmd == UP) {
68          $dir =~ s/\/[^\/]*$//;
69          $dir = "/" unless $dir;
70          &gotoDirectory($dir);
71      }
72      elsif ($cmd == PLAY) {
73          my $tmp = "$dir/$files[$index]";
74          if (!-f $tmp || $tmp !~ /\.(mp3|wav|ogg)$/) {
75              &say($files[$index] . " is not a playable file.");
76              $QUIET = 1;
77          }
78          else {
79              &forkOff("xmms", "-p", $tmp);
80              $QUIET = 1;
81          }
82      }
83      elsif ($cmd == STOP) {
84          &forkOff("xmms", "-s");
85          $QUIET = 1;
86      }
87  }
88
89  sub readKeypress {
90      my ($k, @k);
91          open(FH, "/dev/ttyS1");
92          read(FH, $k, 6);
93          close FH;
94      @k = unpack("C6", $k);
95      $k[5] = $k[5];
96      return join("", map {sprintf("%02x", $_)} @k);
97  }
98
99  sub gotoDirectory {
100     my ($d) = @_;
101     my @list;
102     $dir = $d;
103     opendir(DH, $dir);
104     while (defined (my $file = readdir DH)) {
105         next if ($file =~ /^\./);
106         push @list, $file;
107     }
108     closedir DH;
109     @files = sort @list;
110     $index = -1;
```

```
111     (my $tmp = $d) =~ s/^\/usr\/local\/music\/Old By Name\/?//;
112     &say("$tmp. " . scalar @files . " files.");
113 }
114
115 sub say {
116     my ($string) = @_;
117     $cmd = "(Parameter.set 'Audio_Method 'linux16audio)\n
           (voice_kal_diphone)\n(SayText \"$string\")\n";
118     socket(SOCK, PF_INET, SOCK_STREAM, getprotobyname('tcp')) ||
           die "socket: $!";
119     connect(SOCK, sockaddr_in(1314, inet_aton("localhost"))) ||
           die "connect: $!";
120     print SOCK $cmd;
121     close SOCK;
122 }
123
124 sub forkOff {
125     my ($cmd, @args) = @_;
126     my $pid = fork();
127     die "Error in fork()" if ($pid < 0);
128     unless ($pid) {
129         close(0); close(1); close(2);
130         exec ($cmd, @args);
131     }
132     return $pid;
133 }
```

Because this script has to manage many processes, it uses a separate subroutine, *forkOff()*, to start a child process. It starts out by running *Festival* in server mode, so it can simply open a socket to port 1314 and send Scheme commands. This is done in the *say()* subroutine. Then it sets the current directory and position and goes into a continuous loop where it reads the remote control key presses via *readKeypress()* and updates the directory and position appropriately. If the key press is Play or Stop, the script will launch XMMS to handle that file. Admittedly, this program is pretty roughly done, but it shows how you can take many different tools and put them together to do something totally different.

In order to use this program effectively, you will have to enter the appropriate IRMan codes in the %KEYS hash. You can use the configuration dialog for the XMMS IRMan plug-in to find the various codes. Simply bring up the dialog and press any of the action buttons. Another dialog will pop up telling you to enter a code or press a button on the remote. When you press a button, a 12-digit hexadecimal code will appear in the text box. These are the codes you need to insert into the script.

I'm also getting away with a little simplification in the *getKeypress()* subroutine: In order to communicate with the serial port, you must set the appropriate baud rate for IRMan. This is done through the *tcsetattr()* system call, which isn't part of the Perl core language. You will have to obtain the Device::SerialPort module from CPAN and use it to set the baud rate and serial port attributes required to use that particular piece of hardware.

Summary

In this chapter, I discussed some concepts underlying speech synthesis, and showed some of the major packages that can be used under Linux. Then I provided some examples that combine these packages with various Linux tools to perform some interesting tasks.

References

Linux Access HOWTO

- *http://www.linuxdoc.org/HOWTO/Access-HOWTO.html*

RSynth

- Download: *ftp://svr-ftp.eng.cam.ac.uk/pub/comp.speech/sources/*

Festival

- Homepage: *http://www.cstr.ed.ac.uk/projects/festival/*
- Download: *http://www.cstr.ed.ac.uk/projects/festival/download.html*
- Documentation: *http://www.cstr.ed.ac.uk/projects/festival/manual/festival_toc.html*

Chapter 22

IMAGE PROCESSING

Difficult-o-Meter: 2 (light Linux skill required)

Covers:

The GIMP	*http://www.gimp.org*
Imagemagick	*http://www.imagemagick.org/*
xscanimage and SANE	*http://www.mostang.com/sane/*
gphoto	*http://www.gphoto.org*

Question: I'm thinking of putting together a Web site, and I want to put a bunch of images on it: my vacation photographs, baby pictures, the newspaper photo where my face was in the corner, and so on. How can I use Linux to help me make those images look good?

Answer: Learn about digital imagery, and then get familiar with the variety of image manipulation tools that come with your Linux system.

The rise of the World Wide Web has opened a world of rich content that is accessible at the click of a mouse. On many modern Web sites, administrators often find that the most requested files are, contrary to expectation, not HTML files. Instead, they are images! Considering the ubiquity and importance of image files, Web site designers should take care to understand how digital images work, how they are stored, and how they can be manipulated.

Linux provides a number of powerful tools that make it an excellent platform for image processing. And this means more than just making images for a Web site: It can include document archiving and preservation, scene rendering and creation of textures for computer games, artistic endeavors, and optical character recognition, to name a few. In this chapter, we'll discuss some of the popular types of image formats, their strengths and weaknesses, and ways to convert between them. We'll then discuss various types of image retouching, primarily oriented toward Web presentation. And we'll learn how to use various Linux tools along the way.

Types of Image Formats

Raster vs. Vector

One of the most fundamental distinctions between image formats is whether the image information is represented in raster form or vector form (Figure 22-1). *Raster* images describe a picture by dividing the image into square or rectangular cells, called *pixels*, and specifying the color of each pixel. Smaller pixels can represent more detail, but this obviously requires a larger number of pixels to represent the entire image. The *resolution* of an image describes the size of the cells, usually specified in *dpi*, or dots per inch. An image that has 300 dpi contains 300 cells in one linear inch, which means 90,000 cells in every square inch.

Typically an image displayed on a monitor has about 96 dots per inch. In contrast, the a traditional film photograph can have upwards of 2000 dots per inch, depending on the grain of the film used. Digital cameras create raster images with an intermediate resolution of 200–400 dots per inch.

If a raster image could be exemplified by a photograph, then a vector image could be described as an "Etch-a-Sketch" drawing. Vector images are specified not by the colors of contiguous pixels, but by drawing commands such as "Move to this point," "Draw a line to this point," "Draw a circle here," and "Draw a word using this font." The major advantage of vector images over raster images is that they can be made smaller or larger and still retain perfect detail.

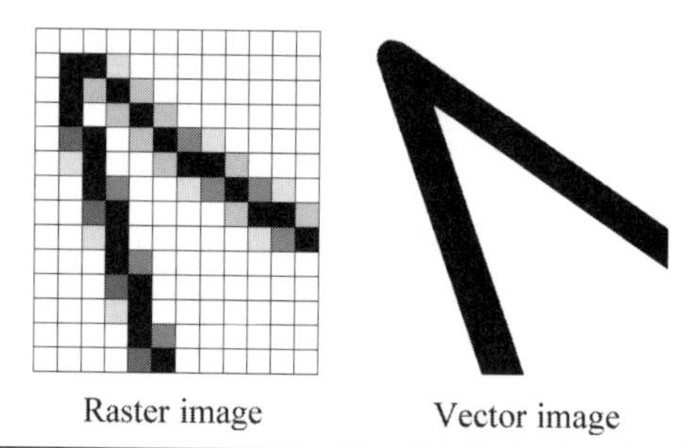

Figure 22-1 The difference between raster and vector images.

Not every raster image can be easily expressed as a vector image. For example, a typical photograph is not well described in terms of sequential drawing commands. However, every vector image can be converted into a raster image at a certain resolution. The higher the resolution, the more accurate the rendition as a raster image.

Ultimately, raster and vector are just two different ways of describing image information, and which method is the better depends on the type of image being described.

What about Compression?

In the previous section, we noted that a 300-dpi raster image contains 90,000 pixels in every square inch. For a large and detailed image, the size of an image file can balloon to many megabytes. Fortunately, there are patterns in the colors of the pixels: many pixels have the same color, and similarly colored pixels are often adjacent. Certain image formats exploit these patterns to compress the image data, often reducing the file size 10–20 times. There are actually two ways of compressing image data: lossless and lossy. *Lossless* compression does not reduce file size quite as much, but it retains the exact colors of each pixel when it is decompressed. *Lossy* compression accepts some modification of pixel colors or brightness, in return for increased compression.

As we saw in raster vs. vector, the type of image is the factor that determines the better compression method. Lossy compression works well for photographs and images that have swaths of smoothly varying color with few sharp edges. Lossless compression is preferable for clipart-type images that contain only a few distinct colors and have many edges with high contrast.

Color Palettes

Another distinction between image types is the number of colors they contain. Icons and clipart often involve no more than a few tens of different colors, whereas photographs contain smoothly varying hues that must be very closely approximated. This requirement pushes up the number of colors used in such an image; the most common types are High Color (65,536 colors) and True Color (16 million colors.) Such images specify color by means of RGB (red-green-blue) triplets. Each component of the triplet describes the relative intensity of the three primary colors or light: red, green, and blue. True Color images use 8 bits of precision, or 256 possible values, for each of the three color channels.

If the number of distinct colors is small, however, it is a waste to store the entire triplet for each pixel. Instead, the image contains an index of colors, called a *palette*.

Each triplet that occurs is assigned a single number, and that number is used to represent the pixel color. It's much like a paint-by-number kit you may have used as a child. For a large image, the savings in going from three bytes to one for each pixel can really add up.

A Smorgasbord: GIF, JPEG, PNG, TIFF, XPM, Etc.

There is a wide variety of image formats in common use, and each has its strengths and weaknesses. The rise of the World Wide Web and the widespread use of Web browsers has driven the popularity of threee image formats in particular: GIF (Graphics Interchange Format), JPEG (Joint Photographics Experts Group), and PNG (Portable Network Graphics). These three formats alone have support in all the major Web browsers. We'll also discuss a number of other formats that you may commonly encounter.

XPM (X pixmap) is a format commonly used for icons on Linux and other Unix systems that use the X-windows system. An XPM file is actually a snippet of C code conforming to a certain format. It can be included in the source code of an application, or it can be read in dynamically using Xlib. It is an uncompressed raster format and consequently can become very large for large images.

BMP (bitmap) is a format introduced in early versions of Windows. Like XPM, it is a lossless raster format and does not include any compression. It can use a palette or can be stored in True Color. Because the representation of the data in a BMP file is so similar to its required visual representation, encoding and decoding BMP images is a trivial task. However, the files can often be quite large.

GIF (Graphics Interchange Format) is one of the first standard image formats. It was originally used for exchanging graphics files on Compuserve's bulletin boards, before the days of the Internet. It is an uncompressed raster format and requires a palette of no more than 256 distinct colors. The low number of allowed colors keeps GIF from being an acceptable format for many photographic images. The image data is compressed using the very efficient LZW compression algorithm, so GIF files can achieve extremely small sizes (a few tens of bytes) when applied to small, icon-like images.

GIF images also support multiple images in a single file. GIF viewers can display these images in sequence, producing a crude animation. This has become very popular on the Web as an attention-grabbing feature, often used in advertisements.

A major drawback of the GIF format is that the LZW compression scheme is patented by Unisys. Periodically Unisys' corporate lawyers have surfaced, threatening to sue

Web site operators who use GIFs on their sites and challenging them to prove that the GIFs were created using a licensed tool. The inherent limitations of GIF files, combined with the encumbrances and uncertainty so generously provided by the LZW patent, have led to the development of an alternative file format, known as PNG. The Burn All GIFs Web site is dedicated to promoting the use of PNG images rather than GIF images and to encouraging Web site operators to use the new format. The URL is provided in the references at the end of this chapter.

PNG (Portable Network Graphics) is another raster, lossless image format that was designed as a patent-free successor to GIF. PNG corrects some of the deficiencies of the GIF format, including the limitation to a 256-color palette, and increases the number of compression options. PNG was specifically designed not to be animated, that is, PNG files do not contain multiple frames in a single file. Netscape Navigator and Internet Explorer both partially support PNGs, enough so that most GIFs can be replaced with PNGs with no impact to the end user.

TIFF (Tagged Image File Format) is more of a specification than a specific format. TIFF files support multiple chunks of data within a file, and each chunk has a "tag" associated with it that describes its functions. Some tags are universally recognized, and applications are free to insert their own types of tags. On occasion, this can confuse a second application that may interpret the custom tag as one of its own custom tags. TIFF provides a high degree of flexibility, but I have experienced some application support problems while using this format.

Even the venerable and versatile PostScript language is sometimes used as an image format. EPS (Encapsulated PostScript) can be loosely defined as a set of PostScript commands that leave the interpreter state unchanged after they are executed (hence "Encapsulated"). Any of the drawing operations supported by PostScript can be included within an EPS file, and it is the only format that supports both raster and vector image types. Since PostScript's raster support has no clear advantages over the other image formats we've mentioned, EPS is typically used more for vector images, such as line art. One advantage of EPS files is that they can be trivially integrated into PostScript output. Considering the importance of PostScript to printing on most Unix-based systems, there remains a use for this unusual format.

JPEG is named after the group that created the format specification, the Joint Photographics Expert Group. As is to be expected from the name, the format is meant for encoding of photographic information. In contrast to the formats previously mentioned, JPEG accepts the trade-off of lossy compression for decreased file size. That is, converting an image to JPEG and back again produces a slightly degraded copy of the original image. The degradations will accumulate if the image is converted back and forth multiple times. When encoding a JPEG image, you can also specify the amount of compression you prefer and, consequently, the amount of image loss.

Compression values range from 0 to 100, and typically the range 75–90 will produce the best trade-off between file size and quality.

JPEG images can achieve compression ratios of 10 or higher over the uncompressed image data. It is interesting to look briefly at the JPEG encoding algorithm to see how this magic is performed. The encoding steps are typical of the types of algorithms used in most lossy image formats, and the high-level concepts are actually quite similar to audio encoding algorithms.

The philosophy behind the JPEG encoding scheme is to preserve the parts of an image that are most important to the human eye and accept inaccuracies in the parts that are least important. In fact, this is the same philosophy behind the wildly popular MP3 format, which achieves similar compression ratios by accepting inaccuracies in the unimportant parts of an audio stream. In both case, the relative importance of various image or audio features was determined by actual psychological studies, and this information went into the design of the encoding algorithms. In the case of images, the JPEG capitalized on two major facts:

- The human eye is less sensitive to changes in hue than to changes in brightness.
- Most photographs have swaths of smoothly varying color and fuzzy edges, rather than swaths of identical colors separated by sharp edges.

Given these requirements, the encoding algorithm works as follows.

Step 1: Color Space Conversion. Most raster images are specified in RGB, that is, each pixel has a particular amount of red, green, and blue light. The JPEG algorithm "rotates" this color space into one grayscale and two colored components, where the gray component ranges from 0 to 1 and the colored components can range from -1 to $+1$. Negative values for a component can be thought of as "anti"-color; for example, red's "anti"-color would be cyan, and blue's "anti"-color would be yellow. The advantage of changing the color space in this way is that the varying values of the colored components can be encoded with less precision than the gray component, thus taking into account the first of the preceding bullet points. JPEG is built with support for several different color systems.

Step 2: DCT. For each of the three color components, the image is broken up into 8×8-pixel blocks. Each of these 64-pixel blocks then undergoes a mathematical operation known as a two-dimensional DCT (discrete cosine transform). The transform converts the square of pixels into an equal-sized square of coefficients that, when the DCT is reversed, can exactly reproduce the original pixels. But if the squares are the same size, each containing 64 numbers, it seems like nothing has been gained, right? Not so! First, when there is a smoothly varying swath of color across the pixel block, the higher-order DCT coefficients are very small compared to the lower-order ones. In fact, some of these higher-order terms can be dropped completely, and the reversed transform will still appear very close to the original image. Thus, for parts of the image without much detail, which are considerable based on the second assumption listed earlier, the algorithm can get away with using less than 64 coefficients—perhaps as few as 32–40.

Step 3: Quantization. Another property of the DCT is that the coefficients do not have to be specified with the same accuracy as the original pixels. Hence, each of the remaining DCT coefficients can be reduced in accuracy by using only the high-order bits and dropping the low-order bits. This process of *quantization* does not have to be the same throughout the entire image or even within the same block. In fact, the colored components are quantized more aggressively than the grayscale component.

Step 4: Compression. Each of the sets of coefficients from the previous steps are then organized and compressed. The most commonly used compression algorithms are Huffman encoding, arithmetic encoding, and entropy encoding. Consult an outside resource for details about the differences between these algorithms. Suffice it to say that this step reduces the data size considerably, in some cases to a few bytes overall for each 8 × 8 block of pixels.

Step 5: Encapsulation. The image header information, various flags, the compression tables, and the compressed data are all tagged and placed into a single file. Other types of tagged elements, such as comments, copyrights, and color correction tables, can be added to the file at this step. In this respect, the outer appearance of a JPEG file is similar to that of a TIFF file. However, a JPEG decoder must reverse the steps of the algorithm to obtain the image data, which is not a trivial task!

The Future: MNG and JPEG2000

The collective experience gained from the development of the World Wide Web has suggested which types of image formats are most practical and improvements that can be made on these image formats. As we look toward the future, there appear to be some promising file formats on the horizon. None of these formats has yet been implemented in a mainstream product, but all have been successfully prototyped, and the theory behind each encoding has been proven.

MNG (Multiple-image Network Graphics), designed by many of the same developers behind PNG, is intended as a replacement and extension of animated GIFs. MNG supports multiple frame types, has excellent compression, and handles complex animations, although they are not as detailed as Macromedia's Flash format.

Like PNG, MNG is an openly specified, patent-free format with free library source code available.

JPEG2000 is an exciting new image format from the Joint Photographics Experts Group, intended as a successor to the popular JPEG format. The original JPEG format achieves lossy compression with a discrete cosine transform, and the mathematical theory behind DCT (Fourier transforms) has been known for hundreds of years. JPEG2000 uses the related but much more recent discovery of wavelet transforms to simultaneously achieve higher compression ratios and better image quality than the original JPEG format. JPEG2000 is also capable of compressing different parts of an image differently, based on the amount of detail in that area; it is not limited to 8×8 blocks and a global compression-quality parameter. Currently very few applications support JPEG2000 images, although it is the author's personal hope that this will change.

Which Image Format Is Right?

The answer to this question really depends on the qualities of the image you are working with. A few simple rules of thumb will suffice for 90% of cases.

- If you want to preserve images precisely but don't really care about displaying them in a Web browser or about having extensive application support, you can use Windows BMP format, TIFF, or PNG. Keep in mind that there are sometimes interoperability problems between different TIFF implementations; some software will insert tags that aren't recognized by other applications, which can confuse them to the point of being unable to open the image.
- If the image is a photograph and you can tolerate a little bit of loss, you can't beat the JPEG format. PNG may also be acceptable if the image is small or needs high fidelity.
- If the image is an icon or is clipart with a limited number of colors, use PNG or GIF, depending on your preferences and application support. Remember that both of the major Web browsers currently support PNG and that PNG has some advantages over GIF.
- If the image is animated, you will probably have to use animated GIFs for the moment, until there is better application support for MNG.
- If you need complex animations or line art, you may want to investigate the Flash format from Macromedia. Although the Flash player is free for most platforms as a browser plug-in, Flash is a proprietary format, and you must purchase Flash creation software.

If all else fails or you're not really sure what to do, you can always try the experimental approach. Save the image in more than one format and see which has the best combination of quality and file size. When I design Web pages, I routinely save almost every image as a GIF, PNG, and JPEG with at least two different quality settings (unless I know from experience which will work best). Then, of the ones with acceptable image quality, I pick the one with the smallest file size. The result is professional-looking images with very fast load time.

Image-Processing Utilities

The GIMP

Beyond a doubt, the best image-processing program available for Linux is called the GIMP, or GNU Image Manipulation Program. It is released under the GNU General Public License, so source code is available, and it is built to allow easy integration of third-party extensions. It is often compared to Adobe's Photoshop in the breadth of its features. Like Photoshop, the GIMP also has a considerable learning curve, but the time investment is well worth it if you need to process images on a regular basis. The GIMP has been in development for many years now, and plentiful reference guides and tutorials are available on the Web. There is even a site oriented toward artists, rather than techies, who would like to investigate the creative possibilities of this package and other Linux-based image-processing tools.

ImageMagick

For command line image processing, one of the best tools is ImageMagick. It is provided as a shared library and a set of binaries, and supports even more image formats than the GIMP (if that's possible!). The commands can be combined with shell or another scripting language to perform batch processing on large numbers of images.

The *convert* command can be used to convert between image formats, scale, crop, rotate, or merge images, add borders to an image, adjust brightness and contrast, and perform many other operations. Not surprisingly, you can check the man page to get an idea of all the available options. ImageMagick also includes commands to display images to the screen (*display*), create photo montages (*montage*), and create animations (*animate;* can you see a pattern in the command names?).

The general form of the *convert* command is:

```
convert [options] input-file output-file
```

As a simple example, suppose you have a number of BMP images that were scanned from a set of photos. The sizes of the images vary, and the brightness and contrast vary moderately from photo to photo. The following command line will convert all the photos to approximately 250 × 250 pixels while preserving aspect ratio, adjusting the brightness, and adding a 10-pixel white border:

```
for file in *.bmp; do
        convert -border 10x10 -bordercolor #FFFFFF -equalize -geometry 250 \
                $file 'echo $file | sed 's/bmp/jpg/'';
done
```

What's *aspect ratio*? Simply put, it's the ratio of width to height. If we didn't preserve this value, the image would look squashed horizontally or vertically, and we don't want that.

As usual, a Linux software environment shines at automating a task that could potentially be highly repetitive. Try retouching 50 images using a traditional application; each image might take 10 or 15 mouse clicks. That would definitely not be a well-spent hour, and that estimate assumes you're highly proficient with a mouse! In this situation, a command line solution is far quicker.

Creating Images

Scanners

If you already have traditional photographs that you want to digitize, you'll need to scan them. Linux supports a wide variety of scanners, both paper-feed and flatbed, as long as the appropriate bus type is compiled into the system. Older scanners are SCSI-based and will require an SCSI adapter card, unless your motherboard has an integrated SCSI controller. Newer scanners use USB.

Once the hardware issues are worked out, all you need is the xscanimage program and the SANE plug-ins. SANE is the Linux answer to TWAIN, a common API that was developed for Windows software to communicate with a variety of scanners. Each scanner manufacturer provides an interface between the TWAIN API and its own proprietary protocols. With this simple architecture, a single image program can use almost any type of scanner without having to support it directly. Such is the case with xscanimage.

I'd show you how these programs work, but I can't do that since I don't own a scanner. But you can visit the Web sites listed at the end of this chapter to obtain information and tutorials on these applications.

Digital Cameras

Another popular way to obtain digital images that is now within the reach of the public is via a digital camera. Digital cameras use a semiconductor device called a CCD (change-coupled device), which is light-sensitive like traditional film. However, the CCD is broken up into pixels, and the amount and color of light hitting each pixel can be read out by an on-board microprocessor and converted directly into an image file. Typically this will be a JPEG file, taking advantage of the good compression provided by that format. The current generation of digital cameras have a resolution from 1 to 5 megapixels, which corresponds to an image width of 1200–2500 pixels, and a slightly lower height.

If you have a digital camera, retrieving the images from it is a breeze. Simply download the gphoto package: a GTK-based application that currently provides the widest support for different types of digital cameras. Unfortunately, some manufacturers use proprietary communications protocols, and some (oh, horrors!) even use proprietary file formats. If you're unlucky enough to have one of these cameras, you may have to use the development snapshots of gphoto, bother the manufacturer, or even be reduced to using the manufacturer's Windows-only software just to do the download. Since I was personally running Linux before I bought a digital camera, I made sure to do my research and found a camera that met my needs for resolution, open file format, and gphoto support.

There are two ways to connect digital cameras: Almost all of them have a traditional serial port connector, and most modern cameras now have USB ports. gphoto has support for both types of connectors, but there are some limitations on the USB cameras supported. Personally, I use a plain old serial port connector, which works fine for my purposes.

The gphoto Web site has a list of supported cameras and instructions on how to use the application. In fact, it's simple enough to figure out just from looking at the menu options. The first time you start the program, it will ask which port the camera is connected to. Assuming you are using a traditional serial port, just select the appropriate */dev/ttySx* device and you should be ready to go. Also, make sure that the cable is securely connected and that the camera is powered on and set to the appropriate mode to communicate with the computer. In the majority of cases it will simply work. Figure 22-2 shows the main application window after I've downloaded image thumbnails from the camera.

The images you obtain from a moderately priced digital camera of 2–3 megapixels will be in the range of 2000 × 1500 pixels. This will be quite large when viewed on a relatively low resolution display like a monitor. The major operation you'll need to perform on such an image is a resize; typically, you'll want to scale each image to about a quarter of its original size. You can quickly do this with ImageMagick:

```
$ convert bigphoto.jpg -scale 640 webphoto.jpg
```

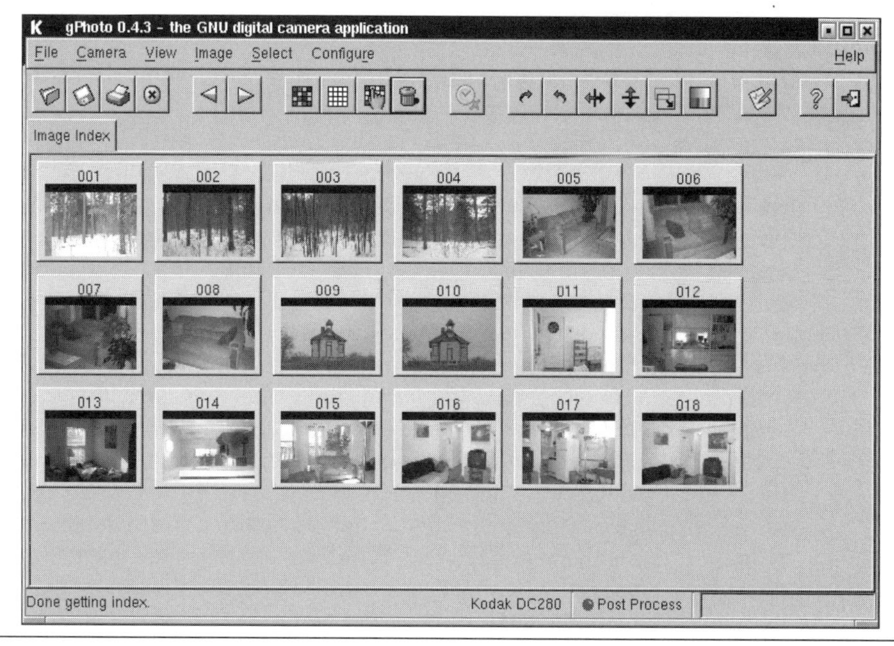

Figure 22-2 gPhoto main application window.

This scales a large photo down to a width of 640 pixels and preserves the aspect ratio. In the next section, I'll show you some other ways to enhance digital photos or any other kind of image.

Image Retouching

Now that you've created an image, there are a number of things you can do to improve image quality before posting it on a Web site, sending it to Grandma, and so on. As a group, these techniques are called *retouching*. There are many fine references that explain the how and why of digital photo retouching. This section introduces a few techniques that I've found useful, but it certainly isn't meant to replace a good tutorial.

Cropping

One of the first techniques I'll discuss is familiar even from the days before computers, when it was commonly applied to photographs. I'm referring to *cropping:* the process of trimming off irrelevant parts of an image in order to better highlight the intended subject (or subjects) of the picture. The technique remains important in the digital age. Proper use of cropping will always lead to better esthetics, no matter what the medium. This is really a graphic design issue, which is important when designing a Web site, for example.

From a technical perspective, cropping can significantly reduce the size of an image file. There's no point in making someone download or manipulate unnecessary data. As an example, consider a 4" × 6" photograph with 3/4 inches of unnecessary space around each edge. The entire photograph takes up 24 square inches, but the area of interest is only 2.5" × 4.5", for a total of just over 11 square inches. In this case, proper cropping of the image can reduce the file size by more than half. For a 300-dpi uncompressed image, this saves about a megabyte of disk space.

Although the space savings is not as important for the smaller images common on the Web, the esthetic benefits remain. Here is an example of a fictitious family homepage, where "Bob" and "Mary" are telling their online friends about their summer vacation. Figure 22-3 shows their Web site, with an image exactly like the original photograph.

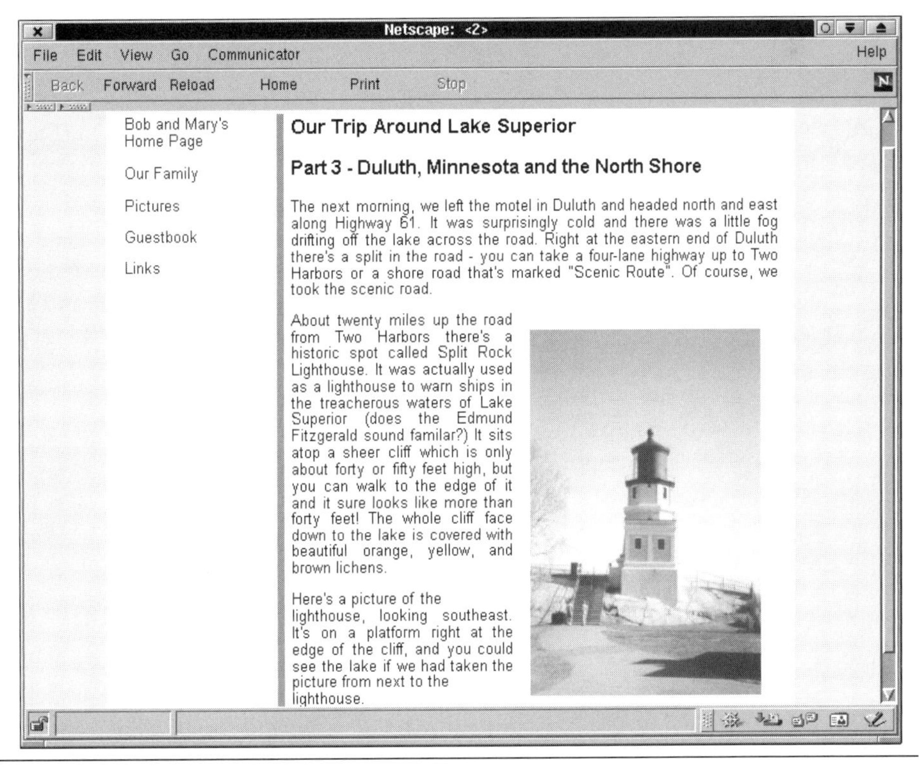

Figure 22-3 Fictitious homepage before cropping.

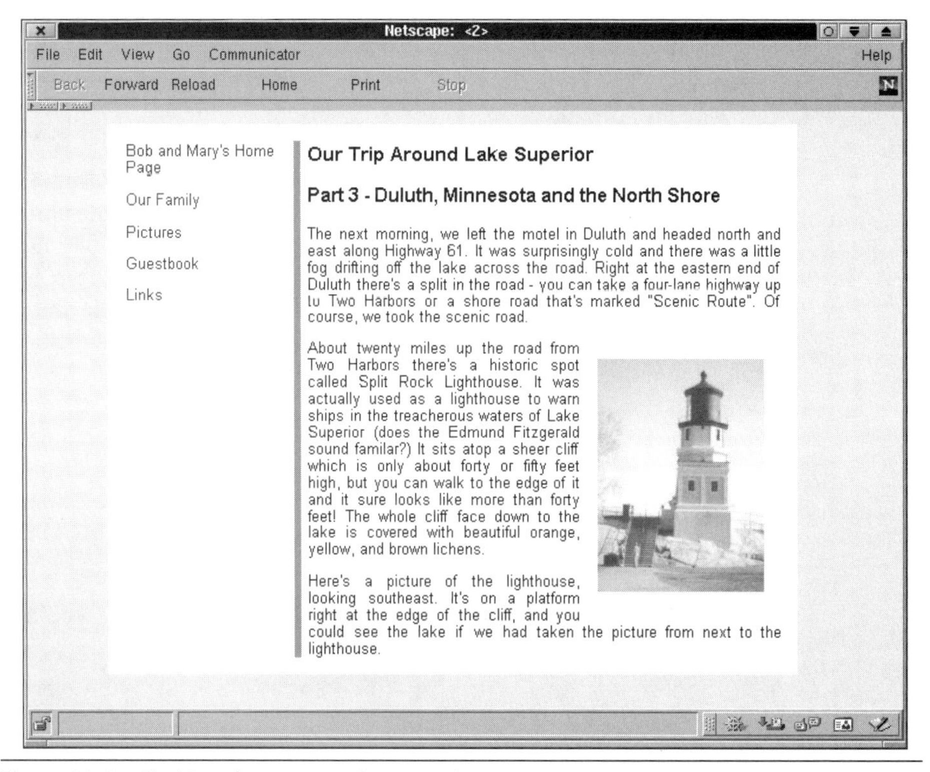

Figure 22-4 Fictitious homepage after cropping.

Notice the image needs to be fairly large in order to show the detail of the lighthouse. In Figure 22-4, the excess sky and ground have been removed, and the image has been somewhat reduced in size. When saved as a PNG, the file size goes from 42K to 30K, a 28% reduction. Of course, if Bob and Mary had wanted to present the lighthouse as only a small, lonely building on the edge of a cliff, the wider-angle uncropped image might have been appropriate. Or if they'd wanted to provide more detail, a larger, cropped image might have been appropriate. But esthetics is a matter for another book.

Brightness, Contrast, and Tone

Most people understand the concepts of *brightness* and *contrast*, if only from twiddling the knobs on a television or monitor. But these are also important ways to increase image quality. Practically all image-processing programs allow for adjustment of brightness and contrast, sometimes automatically. But often it is more useful to work with a similar concept, called *tone*. Tone adjustment is the process of remapping the brightnesses in an image, without affecting the color. For example, a washed-out image has a disproportionate number of bright pixels. Such an image can be tone-adjusted to darken appropriate pixels, thus providing an increase in contrast.

The easiest way to explain is with some examples. Let's use the picture of the lighthouse from Bob and Mary's vacation. Just on first sight, the picture looks a little washed out; everything's too bright. Using the GIMP, I can right-click and select *Image > Colors > Levels* from the menu, and I obtain the window in Figure 22-5. The jagged line with black underneath is a *histogram*, which shows me the relative number of pixels with different brightness values. The brightnesses are shown in the gray-shaded bar directly underneath. My visual impressions are confirmed by the histogram; most of the pixels are over toward the white, or bright, end of the histogram, and there are no pixels at all below a certain shade of dark gray!

To remedy this situation, I can drag the black triangle underneath the brightness bar to the right, just to the left edge of the histogram. This will map the dark gray colors in the image back down to true black and set the brightnesses of other pixels in the image proportionately. Since the Preview box is checked, I see the results as soon as I let go of the triangle. Although the changes to the image can't easily be included here, trust me, the image looks much better just after this one operation!

In the case of a dark-toned image that doesn't have any pixels near white or completely white, you could also move the upper white triangle to the left. Basically, you want to use the black and white triangles to bound the limits of the pixel brightnesses

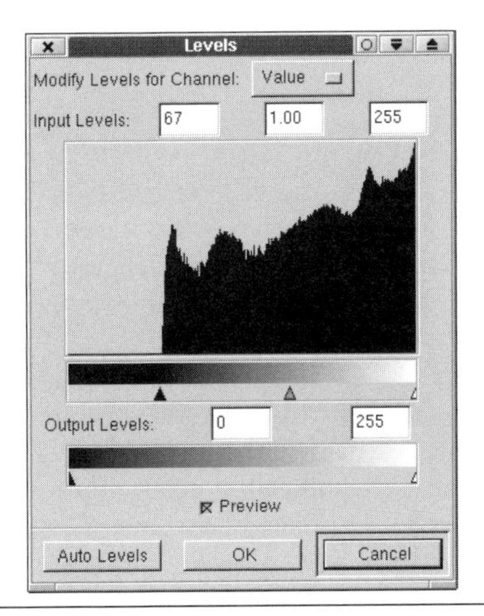

Figure 22-5 Levels dialog from the GIMP.

displayed on the histogram. Then the darkest pixels in the original image will be mapped close to black, and the lightest pixels will be mapped close to white.

How about that third triangle? That controls the tone, or balance between light and dark. Moving the triangle to the left will bring more of the dark pixels into the "light half," and moving the triangle to the right will bring more of the light pixels into the "dark half." Generally the ratio of light to dark pixels should be from 1.5:1 to 2:1. In terms of the histogram, this means there should be a little less than twice as much area under the curve to the right of the middle triangle as there is to the left. In the case of our lighthouse image, the middle triangle looks just about right where it is. The best advice, of course, is to use the GIMP's preview feature to experiment with an image and see what tone suits it best.

The visual representation of tone that the GIMP provides can perform the same functions as brightness and contrast adjustments, and more, and is more intuitive in that you can estimate beforehand the type of change required to get a desired effect. Typically, adjusting only the brightness and contrast of a digital image is still comparable to an old television set: Twiddle the knobs until it looks good.

Color Adjustment

Sometimes you may find that the color in scanned photographs is slighly "off." This can be due to an actual color imbalance in the photograph or may be an artifact of the scanner that was used. For example, a picture taken in the woods on a sunny summer day may have too much green light illuminating the objects of interest, and this effect can be exaggerated when it is scanned. There are two major types of operations that can be useful in these cases: saturation adjustment and color balance.

Saturation refers, roughly, to the "amount of color" in an image. Completely saturated colors are bright and glaring, much like magic marker colors or neon lights. Moderately or lightly saturated colors have pastel-like shades, and completely unsaturated colors are not really colors—they are shades of gray. Saturation adjustment is often available on televisions, where it is typically called "color."

If an image seems too gaudy or too drab, the solution is probably a saturation adjustment—a decrease in the first case, and an increase in the second case. In the GIMP, the adjustment is available by right-clicking on the image, selecting Image > Colors > Hue-Saturation, and adjusting the Saturation slider. The Hue and Lightness adjustments in this particular dialog box are not usually of interest for retouching photographs, but they can be very useful for other applications (one example is making color variants of a texture for 3D rendering).

We discussed saturation first because the second color operation is much easier to perform if the saturation is correctly adjusted. *Color balance* allows you to adjust the relative amounts of red, green, and blue in an image. In the GIMP, color balance can be changed by right-clicking on the image, and selecting Image > Colors > Color Balance from the menu.

Each of the three color levels can be either increased or decreased; if all the levels are increased equally, there is no net color shift, just an increase in brightness. Likewise, decreasing each of the three color levels equally produces only a decrease in brightness. To maintain the brightness of an image while adjusting its color, try to keep the sum of changes in the three primary colors to zero. For example, in an overly green photograph, a good adjustment might be Red +5, Green -10, Blue +5.

As we discussed earlier, in the section about JPEG compression, the human eye isn't the greatest at detecting absolute colors. We tend to judge a color based on the colors surrounding it; hence, obtaining a neutral color balance can be surprisingly tricky. An excellent indicator of color balance can be obtained if there are light-colored flesh tones in the image or photograph. In this case, use your hands or other, neutral-colored windows to block out extraneous parts of the photograph, and focus on the flesh tones. Are they appropriately colored? Are they too red? Adjust the color balance until these tones are close to correct, and the rest of the photograph will probably look fine.

Halftone Images

One of the most common ways of displaying photographs or other smoothly colored images in print is the process of halftoning. The image is created so that lighter-colored pixels are drawn as small dots of ink and darker-colored pixels are drawn as large dots. When viewed from afar, the dots appear to merge into a continuously colored image relative to the background color. In the usual applications, this is white paper. Halftone images work quite well to fool the human eye, but they pose a problem when scanned. Typically, the dot size is large enough that scanning the image at any more than 100 dpi will pick up the individual dots. The result is a digital image with strong moire patterns that can sometimes make it difficult even to see the intended image.

Luckily, there are ways to successfully scan a halftone image. The key is to actually scan the image at as high a resolution as possible and to then average the image before scaling it down. Usually a scan resolution of 400 dpi or higher is preferable. The averaging operation smears together all the pixels within a certain distance of each other. The best radius for the averaging is about the same factor as you intend to scale the image, perhaps even 1 more. After the image is resized, the moire patterns will be almost completely gone.

As a concrete example, consider a 2" × 3" halftone black-and-white photograph in an old newspaper. Using the GIMP, the following steps will work to successfully digitize this image.

1. Scan the image at 400 dpi. The resulting image will be about 800 × 1200 pixels. Assume we want to scale it down to about 200 × 300 pixels, a factor of 4. Since it's a black-and-white photograph, you may want to right-click and select Image > Grayscale to remove any yellow tint resulting from the old paper.
2. Right-click and select Filters > Blur > Gaussian Blur from the menu. Gaussian Blur will work to average the pixels in the necessary way. In the Radius box, enter 1 more than the scale factor, namely, 5.
3. Now go to Image > Scale and enter the appropriate pixel sizes in the dialog box. The image will be resized, and at this point it will probably show no trace of the original halftoning.
4. You can also try Filters > Enhance > Sharpen to see if it improves the image. Whether or not it helps depends on the type of image.

Summary

In this chapter, I discussed some concepts underlying digital images and showed how to acquire, create, process, and convert images to meet a variety of needs. I hope I've been able to show that Linux is a full-featured image-processing platform comparable in power to any other system out there. Okay, not comparable to an SGI Origin 2000, but what do you expect from a PC? It turns out you can expect quite a lot from a PC with open source software!

References

Burn All GIFs

- Homepage: *http://www.burnallgifs.org/*

PNG and MNG Specifications

- PNG: *http://www.libpng.org/pub/png/*
- MNG: *http://www.libpng.org/pub/mng/*

JPEG and JPEG2000 Specifications and Documents

- JPEG: *http://www.jpeg.org/public/jpeglinks.htm*
- JPEG2000: *http://www.jpeg.org/JPEG2000.htm*

The GIMP

- Homepage: *http://www.gimp.org/*
- Download: *http://www.gimp.org/download.html*
- Artists' site: *http://www.linuxartist.org/*

ImageMagick

- Homepage: *http://www.imagemagick.org/*
- Download: *http://imagemagick.sourceforge.net/http/*

xscanimage and SANE

- Homepage: *http://www.mostang.com/sane/*
- Download: *http://www.mostang.com/sane/source.html*

GPhoto

- Homepage: *http://www.gphoto.org/*
- Download: *http://www.gphoto.org/download.html*

Chapter 23

3D Graphics Production

Difficult-o-Meter: 2 (light Linux skill required)

Covers:

PovRay *http://www.povray.org*

Question: How can I use Linux to make 3D graphics like I see in pictures, movies, and games?

Answer: There are quite a number of tools available for Linux that can be used to produce all sorts of graphics. From simple raster paint utilities to complicated 3D modeling, rendering, and animation applications, Linux is one of the best platforms for 3D graphics production. This may be just my opinion, but I feel this way because of what I've read and learned about how the industry is using Linux for all sorts of graphics-related projects.

Introduction

My first exposure to 3D graphics was quite a while ago, when Linux was still relatively new. I was at a new job and wanted to learn something about 3D graphics. I decided to make a 3D version of the company logo. A friend suggested I use a program called PovRay. The company logo turned out great and I learned a lot from the project. I learned something about 3D art and also about messing with a company logo (they get kind of upset at that sort of thing). I used PovRay to dive deep into the world of 3D art. PovRay is a great first step into 3D art and will teach you a lot about the subject in a short amount of time. So what, exactly, is PovRay?

PovRay is a ray-trace engine. What is ray tracing? The concept is straightforward. Each pixel on the screen is calculated based on several factors, such as lighting, color, texture, and reflection. All of this and more is combined to determine how the pixel is displayed, or, more to the point, what color the pixel should be. Ultimately, this is what it all comes down to, a pixel on the screen is assigned a color, from black to white and everything in between. As it turns out, PovRay was the best thing to come my way for learning all about 3D graphics. Why? Because you get right down to the nitty gritty of 3D graphics.

This chapter is about 3D graphics under Linux. To explore this topic, first I'll introduce the various types of utilities for general graphics production. Then I'll talk about a challenge I gave myself to create a 2D logo and transform it into 3D space using PovRay. Finally, I'll review what other tools are available for 3D graphics production under Linux.

The Basics

Let's start at the beginning. This section is devoted to the various types of graphics possibilities that exist on computers. Keep in mind that everything in this chapter is simply about putting a colored pixel on the screen, even though the process of doing so might not be that easy at times.

Raster Vector Painting

Raster and vector image formats are explored in Chapter 22, Image Processing. What's important to know is that there are programs designed specifically to work with both formats. As a digital artist, you work visually with pixels or objects to produce what is seen on the screen. To get a triangle or circle on the screen, either you have to draw it by hand using a mouse or tablet, or you use some application feature to assist you in the creation of the figure. Either way, it is your skill and and your hand/eye coordination that gets the images drawn on the screen. This is not the only way to produce computer graphics, however. Another is to describe a scene and have a program draw it for you. This is what you do when using a ray tracing application.

Ray Tracing

Ray tracing is a process by which elements of light—color and intensity—are calculated with respect to other elements in an environment. Here are a few ray trace applications for Linux.

Blender	http://www.blender.nl
K-3D	http://www.k-3d.com
MagicLight	http://home.bip.net/mikael_aronsson
PovRay	http://www.povray.org/

In order to create an image, you create a scene file that describes the environment and objects that will appear in the image. A ray-trace engine reads the scene file and generates the output image. This is the method employed by PovRay. PovRay takes a standard ASCII file, the scene file, as its input and delivers a graphic image as its output. Other tools that integrate modeling and rendering components store their data in formats similar to a scene description file. If this sounds confusing, don't worry, it will start making sense later in the chapter. The point to get here is that the scene file is not made up of binary data that maps to bits of an images, but rather is a description of the objects and their properties as they would appear after being rendered.

Like a lot of Linux tools, PovRay has a complex set of command line arguments and options. Managing those arguments and options can be challenging, so tools have been created to ease the pain.

Front-Ends

A front-end is a program, typically GUI based, that assists in the operation of another program, typically command line, that has a lot of parameters and options. There are a lot of front-ends written for PovRay. PovRay has many command line options. A front-end application can assist in managing those options and help you to understand which options to use to produce the best results when rendering a scene. A front-end will not help you produce a better scene file.

Here's a sample of some PovRay front-ends:

Gpfe	http://digilander.iol.it/2g/tcltk-e.htm
gPov	http://www.nasland.nu/software.php?program=gpov
modray	http://kcopensource.org/modray.php
Peflp	http://mogzay.multimania.com/
povfront	http://perso.club-internet.fr/clovis1/
tkRender	http://members.nbci.com/raydarx/
XPovRay	http://www.metroweb.co.za/~r0cknr0l

If you would rather work visually, then perhaps you should use an application that lets you see your scene file graphically as you work on it. This application is called a modeler.

Modelers

Did you create the typical ashtray back in your elementary school art class? I did. Did the teacher show a picture of a real ashtray before letting you loose to create your own masterpiece? The process, which probably resulted in something that almost resembled an ashtray, was modeling. You took a primitive substance, in this case a lump of clay, and formed and shaped it, removed bits and pieces, added some back on, and then smoothed and roughed it up. This is modeling. And this is exactly what you do with a 3D modeling application.

Some modelers only produce a scene file; they don't render the scene. Others are packaged with a rendering engine. Finding a modeler suited to your needs may take a while, since each one is in a different stage of development. If you are working with PovRay for rendering, then you will want to find a modeler that outputs a PovRay scene file.

Here's an interesting list of modeling applications to get you started:

3dom	http://threedom.sourceforge.net/
3dPM	http://rupert.informatik.uni-stuttgart.de/~kraftts/
Blender	http://www.blender.nl/
Extreme Wave	http://agnews.tamu.edu/~jpalmer/ewave/
g3d	http://condor.stcloudstate.edu/~hebl9901/g3d/
Giram	http://www.giram.org/
gSculpt	http://gsculpt.sourceforge.net/
Innovation3D	http://innovation3d.sourceforge.net/
K-3D	http://www.k-3d.com
MagicLight	http://home.bip.net/mikael_aronsson/
MindsEye	http://mindseye.sourceforge.net/
mg^2	http://www.op.net/~finklesk/3d.html
Pygmalion	http://web.kyoto-inet.or.jp/people/tantaka/pygmalion/pygmalion-en.html
Sced	http://http.cs.berkeley.edu/~schenney/sced/sced.html

A 3D modeler lets you place primitive shapes on the screen (cubes, cones, pyramids, etc.) that can be manipulated using a variety tools. These tools allow you to combine, separate, shrink, and otherwise mangle the figures. As with vector painting, each object on the screen is a unique object capable of being selected for moving, shaping, or anything else you can image. The end result is that you sculpt your objects into more sophisticated objects. For example, from spheres, cubes, a lathe tool, and possibly some other objects and tools, you can construct a chess piece. The process can be quite detailed.

In addition to shaping, you can determine the color and/or texture for the surface of the objects you construct. Attributes such as reflectiveness, granularity, and hue, among a host of others, allow you to control almost every aspect of the appearance of your object. Don't like your wood-textured chess piece? Change it to a shiny black-onyx texture using a simple properties change. Modelers are the word processors of 3D graphics.

Once you've created a collection of objects, you might want to try your hand at putting them in motion.

Animation

Classic animation hasn't changed much over the years. The concept behind animation is simple: Draw each frame of an animation, changing the shapes on each frame ever so slightly, and then flip through those frames really fast. If done properly, the shapes will appear to move and change shape smoothly. The human brain can be fooled into thinking that a series of still images with an object that changes position or shape is real motion. Your mind compensates for the gaps of time in between the frames. Without this ability, we probably wouldn't have movies, television, or computer monitors. Luckily, we do, and computers have introduced a new way of making animation easy, even for the nonartist.

Here's a sample of some animation applications:

Blender	http://www.blender.nl/
K-3D	http://www.k-3d.com
MindsEye	http://mindseye.sourceforge.net/

Computer animation is essentially the same as classic animation. You produce a series of still images and then play back the series very rapidly on the computer monitor. A bouncing ball is made by drawing a ball on each frame, progressively different for each frame. The physics involved in the ball bouncing is totally up to you, the animator, to determine. In one world, balls may gain energy when they hit a wall and begin to move faster as they hit more and more walls. Of course, with computers, we have the ability to describe a behavior of an environment and properties of the balls and walls so that the computer can calculate how a ball should react when striking a wall. This frees you from the task of managing every little object in a scene.

Consider the problem you would have if you wanted to animate a bee flying over a field of tall grass on a windy day. Animating each one of the thousands of blades of grass for each frame of video would leave you so mentally exhausted, you would probably leave out the bee or give up entirely. With animation applications, the amount of work you have to put into an animation varies with the sophistication of the application. It will be some time before the Linux animation applications get to a level equivalent to the tools used to make major motion pictures, but with a little work you can achieve some very nice results. Even so, there are some cases where you need the computer to do most of the work for you, such as a 3D scene in an arcade game. In this environment the graphics generation is specialized and geared toward a single purpose: real-time 3D graphics presentation.

3D Game Engines

A new breed of 3D animation tool is the 3D game engine. Popularized by the many 3D shooters available today, these engines are designed to optimize the presentation of a scene for real-time game play. In traditional computer animation, the rendering of thousands of frames could take days or weeks for just an hour of video. This obviously wouldn't work too well for a game, so designers aimed specifically at the goal of real-time 3D graphics generation.

Here are a few notable 3D game engines:

Crystal Space	http://crystal.linuxgames.com/
DUMB	http://samba.anu.edu.au/dumb/
QuakeForge	http://quakeforge.net/
World Foundry	http://wf-gdk.sourceforge.net/

Like PovRay, Crystal Space uses a standard ASCII text file to describe scene data for the engine. Rendering is not ray-trace quality, but it is real time, and the quality is good enough.

Now that you have a general understanding of the types of applications for graphic production, let's introduce 3D graphics techniques by exploring PovRay.

Introduction to PovRay

PovRay is not GPL, but its license makes it freely available—even the source code. Installing PovRay is a simple matter, since it's available in many executable forms. Simply find one for your Linux distribution and install it.

So why PovRay? Is this a chapter about PovRay? Well, yes and no—mostly yes. In order to understand 3D graphics, you will need a foundation to build on. I learned by using PovRay. That was a while ago, when there weren't too many quality tools to choose from. Today, you could pick up a fancy 3D application (modeler, renderer, animator) and go to town. But learning the basics is what it's all about, and I can't think of a better product than PovRay to do that. This won't be a PovRay tutorial, but more of an introduction to PovRay and the concepts of 3D art. Once you understand the concepts of 3D art, you'll be better prepared for the other tools available for 3D graphics production under Linux.

Getting Our Feet Wet

Working with PovRay is easy. Even though I'll go over a few PovRay features, it would be best if you read the PovRay documentation to get a better foundation. However, you can choose to simply follow along, but I can't promise I won't skip over or around some key items you would probably benefit from. Luckily, this stuff is pretty simple to grasp, so let's continue and see where this leads.

To start off, let's draw a simple box. Using a text editor, you will construct a scene file that describes how PovRay will render the scene. For example, you might draw a box by giving it the box command with some coordinates:

```
// Persistence of Vision Ray Tracer Scene Description File
// File: box_1.pov
// Auth: Steve Murphy

#include "colors.inc"

background { color White }

camera {
  location <2, 2, -10>
  look_at  <2, 2,  0>
}

light_source { <5, 5, -15> color White}
```

```
box {
  <0, 0, 0>, <5, 5, 5>
  pigment { color Gray }
}
```

This is a scene file. It has a simple format and is loaded into the PovRay engine for rendering a scene. The scene, once rendered, is saved as a graphic image file, such as PNG. To generate the image file, type in the following command line:

```
povRay +i box_1.pov +o box_1.png +Fn16 +A0.1
```

The command line options for PovRay are numerous, but for this example we need only four:

+i box_1.pov	Specify the input scene file to read.
+o box_1.png	Specify the output image file to write to.
+Fn16	Specify the format of the output file as a PNG file with 16 bits per pixel to represent color.
+A0.1	Anti-aliasing: remove the jaggies and smooth out the edges.

The image produced is a very simple box (Figure 23-1).

Did we really draw just a simple box with all that text? Well, of course not. With a simple adjustment to the camera position only, we are able to shed some more light on the scene, so to speak:

```
camera {
  location <10, 10, -10>
  look_at  <1, 1,  2>
}
```

Figure 23-1 Image of a box.

Figure 23-2 Image of a 3D cube.

Make this small change to the scene file and then rerun the previous PovRay command line. It produces the result shown in Figure 23-2. Oops! We actually drew a cube and not a box. However, all we did was move the camera around. We did not draw a different box. So what happened? When you read the word *box*, think of a square packing box and not a simple square shape. You now have to begin thinking in three dimensions. Each coordinate in PovRay is a three-dimensional coordinate in space. The days of *X*,*Y* are out and *X*,*Y*,*Z* are in, my friend.

A good way to remember the coordinate system is to hold up your left hand like you are pointing a gun. Your thumb points straight up. This is the *Y*-axis. Your index finger points away from your chest. This is the *Z*-axis. Now uncurl your middle finger and point it perpendicular to your index finger (to your right). This is the *X*-axis. PovRay uses a left-hand coordinate system. OpenGL, on the other hand (pun intended), uses a right-hand coordinate system.

Special Effects

If everything were green, we'd either be in the Army or on the island of Guam. In your scene, you will typically have objects of different colors and textures. Each object can have different characteristics. There are many factors involved in determining how an object in your scene will appear: color, texture, lighting, camera angle, etc. Let's explore these in more detail.

Colors, Textures, and More

A red ball is red because its material is dyed with red coloring. You also see it red because of a whole lot of technical details about light spectrums and frequencies, the biology of your eyes, etc. You get the point. In a similar manner, you are able to apply color to your PovRay object by specifying its pigment. This tells PovRay that you want to color the entire object in one color. This does not mean, however, that the object will be that exact color for every pixel that makes up the object. In real life, even a red ball is not entirely the same red as viewed by your eyes. There might be shadows cast on the ball, creating darker shades of red. The sun might be to the left of the ball, making the left side of the ball lighter than the right side. So, in fact, what you are seeing is a variety of colors from a ball whose pigment is red. The same is true for the objects in your scene.

Objects in a scene, as rendered by PovRay, are subject to the same physical effects as those in real life. Light sources, shadows, colors, reflections, obstructions, and more all affect how the object is rendered as an image. This is ray tracing. We are not limited to just simple colors. In fact, PovRay lets us define all sorts of attributes for objects, like textures and finishes.

It's probably safe to say that most objects in nature have texture. Wood has a grain, glass is smooth and reflective, metal is smooth and shiny or is brushed or coarse, marble is a random mixture of colors and patterns. Texture makes up the majority of what we see in life. In your scenes, textures will play a huge part in communicating your thoughts and emotions. You are now armed with probably the most important aspect of 3D art, an understanding that textures and materials make up every object in a scene, and your choices will affect that scene in a dramatic way.

Lighting

You've probably heard it before: "Lights, camera, action!" You're not only the artist and cameraperson, but you're the lighting technician as well. Lighting plays a very important role in your scene. Everything reflects light to some degree. Even objects that are black reflect some light. The absence of reflective light leaves us with a hole in our field of vision.

In PovRay, you control every aspect of light. There are a variety of choices when it comes to lighting a scene. I've used a simple area light to illuminate my objects. However, with some fancy tricks, some dramatic effects can be achieved. (Figure 23-3 represents a grayscale version.) In this example I've positioned a solid white wall on the left and a glass wall on the right. The left wall is not white because it falls inside the shadow of the wall on the right. A blue spotlight is pointing at the center of the right wall, so the blue light will shine through the glass wall and produce a circle of blue light on the left wall. A small cube centered next to the right wall obstructs some of the light passing through the glass wall. The results can be seen on the left wall. Even the shadow from the cube can be seen on the left wall.

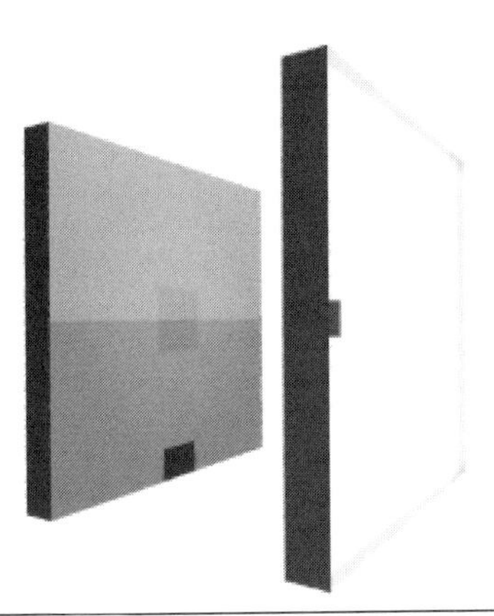

Figure 23-3 Image of two walls.

Such simple effects can produce dramatic results when combined with other special effects. And here's the really nice thing—the code for this example is really simple:

```
// Persistence-of-Vision Ray-Tracer Scene Description File
// File: walls.pov
// Auth: Steve Murphy

// ==== Standard POV-Ray Includes ====
#include "colors.inc"   // Standard Color definitions
#include "textures.inc"
#include "glass.inc"

background {color White}

// here I am!
camera {location <28,10,-20> look_at  <10, 10, 10>}

// area light to light up the scene
light_source {<30, 30, 10> color White}

// large white wall
box { <0, 0, 0>, <2, 20, 20>
        pigment { color White }
}

// large glass wall
box { <16, 0, 0>, <18, 20, 20>
        texture { T_Glass3 }
}
```

```
// small box in the center
box { <11, 9, 9>, <12, 11, 11>
        pigment { color Black }
}

// the blue spotlight
light_source {
    <22, 10, 10>
    color Blue
    spotlight
    radius 15
    falloff 25
    tightness 10
    point_at <18, 10, 10>
  }
```

If you look closely at the left wall, you'll notice the shadow of the right wall splitting the left wall horizontally. This is due to the area light that is above and to the right of the wall on the right.

Another aspect that can have a dramatic impact on a scene is the camera characteristics. Let's explore a little more on this subject, and then we'll jump into the logo project.

Camera Positioning

Cameras are simple, right? Wrong! There are many different types of cameras: perspective, orthographic, fisheye, ultrawide angle, omnimax, panoramic, and cylinder. Cameras have a position within the scene and can be directed to look at any point in the scene. They can focus on specific areas of a scene while making the rest of the scene blurred, something seen in movies and television. You don't have to use this blur effect, but sometimes it makes a scene more realistic. Although cameras play a very important role in a scene, they are often considered only after a scene is created.

I think camera perspective is the most important aspect of a scene. Even though your scene is rendered in three dimensions, your camera presents a two-dimensional view. Combined with fancy lighting techniques, you can achieve some dramatic effects.

Consider, as a project, the view a fish has from inside its aquarium. You've got water and a glass or plastic tank wall to look through and then the objects around the room. The camera becomes the fish. It's a living object in your scene.

The 2D Logo

Let's dive right into this project by showing a picture of the 2D logo I want to convert to 3D (Figure 23-4). I used basic building blocks, or *primitives*, in my logo to be more effective at showing the conversion from 2D to 3D. As you can see, it's a fairly simple design. You should have noticed that the design is a repeating pattern. That's good, because it simplifies the task a bit. You'll see how later on. In PovRay, all measurements are in units. This makes it easy to describe in the PovRay language, but can be tricky when translating from a real-world object.

My first task was to draw out the logo on graph paper so I'd know exactly how many units each figure in the logo should be. This step paid off later, since it eventually helped me out with the 3D model. With the coordinates mapped out, it was a simple matter of entering a bunch of box, sphere, and triangle commands into my scene file, *2d_logo.pov*.

```
// Persistence-of-Vision Ray-Tracer Scene Description File
// File: 2d_logo.pov
// Auth: Steve Murphy

// ==== Standard POV-Ray Includes ====
#include "colors.inc"   // Standard Color definitions

background { color White }

camera { location <0, 0, -30> look_at  <0, 0, 0> }

light_source { <0, 0, -10> color White }
light_source { <0, 12, -50> color White }
```

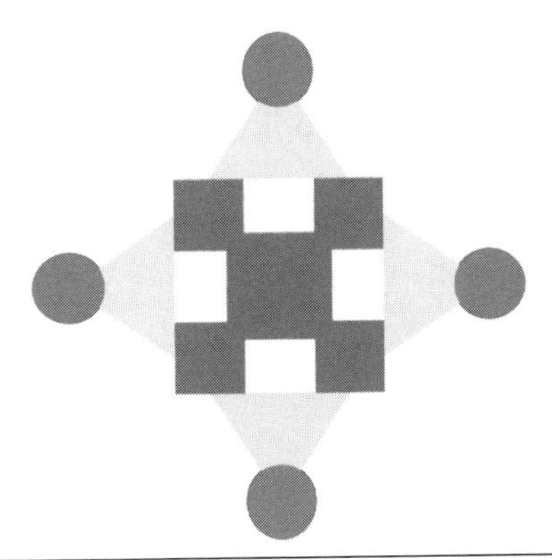

Figure 23-4 Image of 2D logo.

```
light_source { <0, -12, -50> color White }
light_source { <-12, 0, -50> color White }
light_source { <12, 0, -50> color White }

// larger box in the center
box {
        <-3, -3, 0>, <3, 3, 0>
        pigment { color Blue }
}

// make a box object
#declare myBox = box {
        <-2, -2, 0>, <2, 2, 0>
        pigment { color Blue }
}

object { myBox translate <-4, -4, 0> }
object { myBox translate <-4, 4, 0> }
object { myBox translate <4, 4, 0> }
object { myBox translate <4, -4, 0> }

// make a triangle object
#declare myTriangle = triangle {
        <-4, -3, 0>, <0, 3, 0>, <4, -3, 0>
        pigment { color Green }
}

object { myTriangle translate <0, 9, 0> }
object { myTriangle rotate <180, 0, 0> translate <0, -9, 0> }
object { myTriangle rotate <0, 0, -90> translate <9, 0, 0> }
object { myTriangle rotate <0, 0, 90> translate <-9, 0, 0> }

// make a sphere object
#declare mySphere = sphere {
        <0, 0, 0>, 2
        pigment {color Red}
}

object { mySphere translate <0, 12, 0> }
object { mySphere translate <12, 0, 0> }
object { mySphere translate <0, -12, 0> }
object { mySphere translate <-12, 0, 0> }
```

There's a lot of bulk here, but nothing too complex. Still, I'd recommend reading the PovRay documentation file to learn about the not-so-obvious commands. In reading the documentation myself, I discovered a real time-saver. I could create objects and then call the objects into play like a subroutine in a computer program. This meant I could define the three pieces in the logo as objects and simply reuse them whenever

I needed them. With some fancy rotations and translations, I was able to shorten the scene file.

Translations? What's that? When designing a PovRay object, it's best to center the object at <0,0,0>. Then use the *translate* command to place the object somewhere in your scene. *Translate* moves the object relative to coordinate <0,0,0>. Proper object rotation is also achieved when the object is designed around <0,0,0>. The first mistake you might make is to design a scene with objects at absolute positions within the scene. This will lead to complications when you need to move things around.

The next step was to determine what it would take to transform this image into three dimensions. As you probably figured out, the end result will be a slight modification to the 2D logo scene file.

The 3D Logo

After some thought about how to project this image into a three dimensional space, I came up with the image in Figure 23-5.

I've included several area lights to make the logo appear brighter on all the visible sides so that it will show up better in this book. The code for this logo is really simple:

```
// Persistence-of-Vision Ray-Tracer Scene Description File
// File: 3d_logo_1.pov
// Auth: Steve Murphy

// ==== Standard POV-Ray Includes ====
#include "colors.inc"   // Standard Color definitions
```

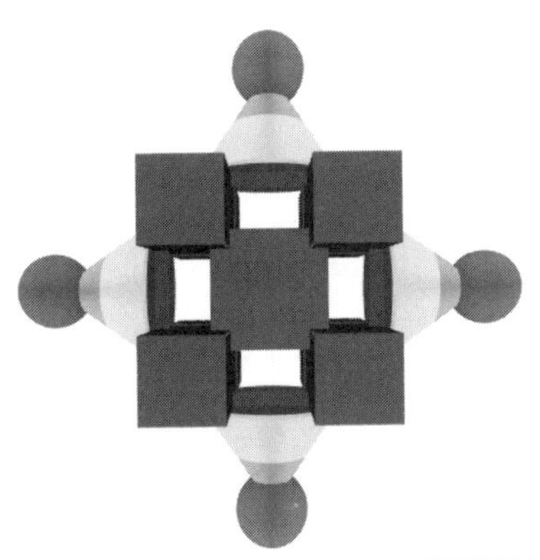

Figure 23-5 Image of 3D logo.

```
background { color White }

// camera { location <0, 20, 0> look_at  <0, 0, 0> } // top
camera { location <0, 0, -30> look_at  <0, 0, 0> } // front
// camera { location <-20, 0, 0> look_at  <0, 0, 0> } // left
// camera { location <10, 10, -30> look_at  <0, 0, 0> } // perspective

light_source { <0, 0, -130> color White }
light_source { <130, 0, 0> color White }
light_source { <-130, 0, 0> color White }
light_source { <0, 130, 0> color White }
light_source { <0, -130, 0> color White }

// larger box in the center
box {
        <-3, -3, -3>, <3, 3, 3>
        pigment { color Blue }
}

// make a box object
#declare myBox = box {
        <-2, -2, -2>, <2, 2, 2>
        pigment { color Blue }
}

object { myBox translate <-4, 4, -4> } // tlf
object { myBox translate <-4, -4, -4> } // blf
object { myBox translate <-4, 4, 4> } // tlb
object { myBox translate <-4, -4, 4> } // blb
object { myBox translate <4, 4, -4> } // trf
object { myBox translate <4, -4, -4> } // brf
object { myBox translate <4, 4, 4> } // trb
object { myBox translate <4, -4, 4> } // brb

// make a cone object
#declare myCone = cone {
        <0, -3, 0>, 4
        <0, 3, 0>, 0
        pigment { color Green }
}

object { myCone translate <0, 9, 0> } // top
object { myCone rotate <180, 0, 0> translate <0, -9, 0> } // bottom
object { myCone rotate <0, 0, 90> translate <-9, 0, 0> } // left
object { myCone rotate <0, 0, -90> translate <9, 0, 0> } // right

// make a sphere object
#declare mySphere = sphere {
        <0, 0, 0>, 2
```

```
        pigment {color Red}
}

object { mySphere translate <0, 12, 0> }
object { mySphere translate <12, 0, 0> }
object { mySphere translate <0, -12, 0> }
object { mySphere translate <-12, 0, 0> }
```

The first thing we do is set up the general stuff like the lighting and camera position. Then we define our basic shapes, or building blocks. Next we use our blocks to form each side of the logo. Each object is rotated and translated into its proper relative location from the coordinate <0, 0, 0>.

Once you're done with this example, try changing some textures or pigments, or add some new primitive objects to the scene and see what else you can come up with. Try to get fancy with it.

Getting Fancy

I decided to get a little fancy with the logo and came up with the image in Figure 23-6. I changed only the coloring and texture for each of the objects. I also added the front and back structures to complete the look. Here's the code to get you thinking about it.

```
// Persistence-of-Vision Ray-Tracer Scene Description File
// File: 3d_logo_2.pov
// Auth: Steve Murphy

// ==== Standard POV-Ray Includes ====
#include "colors.inc"   // Standard Color definitions
#include "glass.inc"    // Glass finishes and textures
#include "textures.inc"
```

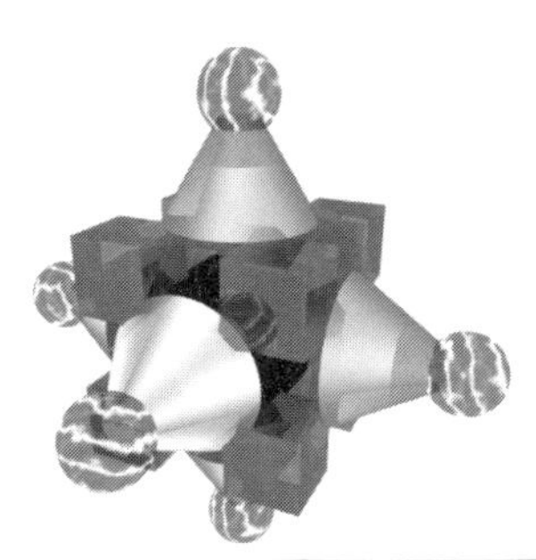

Figure 23-6 Image of fancy 3D logo.

```
background { color White }

// camera { location <0, 20, 0> look_at  <0, 0, 0> } // top
// camera { location <0, 0, -30> look_at  <0, 0, 0> } // front
// camera { location <-20, 0, 0> look_at  <0, 0, 0> } // left
camera { location <15, 15, -30> look_at  <0, 0, 0> } // perspective

light_source { <0, 0, -40> color White }
light_source { <40, 0, 0> color White }
light_source { <-40, 0, 0> color White }
light_source { <0, 40, 0> color White }
light_source { <0, -40, 0> color White }

// larger box in the center
box {
        <-3, -3, -3>, <3, 3, 3>
        texture { Starfield  }
}

// make a smaller box object
#declare myBox = box {
        <-2, -2, -2>, <2, 2, 2>
        texture { T_Ruby_Glass }
}

object { myBox translate <-4, 4, -4> } // tlf
object { myBox translate <-4, -4, -4> } // blf
object { myBox translate <-4, 4, 4> } // tlb
object { myBox translate <-4, -4, 4> } // blb
object { myBox translate <4, 4, -4> } // trf
object { myBox translate <4, -4, -4> } // brf
object { myBox translate <4, 4, 4> } // trb
object { myBox translate <4, -4, 4> } // brb

// make a cone object
#declare myCone = cone {
        <0, -3, 0>, 4
        <0, 2, 0>, 1
        texture { Chrome_Texture }
}

object { myCone translate <0, 9, 0> } // top
object { myCone rotate <180, 0, 0> translate <0, -9, 0> } // bottom
object { myCone rotate <0, 0, 90> translate <-9, 0, 0> } // left
object { myCone rotate <0, 0, -90> translate <9, 0, 0> } // right
object { myCone rotate <-90, 0, 0> translate <0, 0, -9> } // front
object { myCone rotate <90, 0, 0> translate <0, 0, 9> } // back
```

```
// make a sphere object
#declare mySphere = sphere {
        <0, 0, 0>, 2
        texture {  Lightening1 }
}

object { mySphere rotate <5, 6, 7> translate <0, 12, 0> } // top
object { mySphere rotate <10, -8, 20> translate <12, 0, 0> } // right
object { mySphere rotate <-19, 17, 22> translate <0, -12, 0> } // bottom
object { mySphere rotate <-29, 87, -87> translate <-12, 0, 0> } // left
object { mySphere rotate <12, 18, -91> translate <0, 0, -12> } // front
object { mySphere rotate <-19, -16, -14> translate <0, 0, 12> } // back
```

So that's it for the 3D logo. Your introduction to 3D art is not complete by any means. There's a whole lot more to PovRay, and it's worth exploring on your own. PovRay isn't the only avenue for you to explore either. These days there are many new tools available to you.

More Tools

The list from *freshmeat.net* is quite large, and I can't possibly explore them all here. But I will draw attention to some I've kept tabs on over the years.

- 3dom: general-purpose 3D object modeler
- 3dPM: modeler for PovRay 3
- Crystal Space: free and portable 3D engine based on portals
- Extreme Wave: A libre 3D modeler being developed for Linux
- g3d: 3D polygonal modeler built with GTK+
- Giram: modeler written in GTK+
- gSculpt: 3D modeler
- Innovation3D: 3D modeling program
- K-3D: 3D modeling, animation, and rendering system
- MagicLight: 3D modeler and renderer for Linux and Windows
- mg^2: trueSpace work-/look-alike 3D modeler using GTK and OpenGL
- Blender: Extremely fast and versatile 3D rendering package
- MindsEye: 3D modeling program for Linux

Over the years I've tracked the progress of many of the 3D applications available for Linux. PovRay is still a required tool for me and is a joy to work with, but some of these newer applications offer some exciting new features. Let's explore a few.

Crystal Space

If you want to write a Quake-like 3D shooter or simply need real-time 3D graphics, then check out this 3D game development kit. It offers great graphics, speed, and functionality. Visit their Web site at *http://crystal.linuxgames.com* for an extensive list of features and how you can use it to produce your own real-time 3D graphics application.

MindsEye

This project has been in my scope for a while. It's got real promise and helped me lose the Windows platform for good. My addiction to Caligari's trueSpace held me on my Windows platform for a couple of years longer than I desired. But hey, I have to have the applications, right? It's all about the applications. Linux is fantastic, but without a 3D modeler, rendering, and animation package, I was stuck using Windows. But then a friend told me about MindsEye. It got me off Windows, and this is a good thing. Check out *http://MindsEye.SourceForge.net* for the latest.

Blender

Blender is basically your full-featured modeling, rendering, and animation package. It used to cost money to use, but has since seen the light. I highly recommend checking out this package if you are really serious about your 3D. Visit *http://www.blender.nl* for more information.

Summary

With your basic knowledge of 3D art and some tools to help you explore the subject, you should be well on your way to creating a work of art. 3D art can be very time consuming and even frustrating at times. Don't get discouraged. It takes time to learn the techniques others have already mastered. They've put in their time, you can be sure of it. You can achieve some fantastic results with just a little practice. One suggestion is to find some images on the Internet and try to recreate them. Be careful to choose images that are very basic and that don't overchallenge you.

Start off doing something simple, like the typical colored shiny spheres on a glossy surface (Figure 23-7). This one is great eye candy and always impresses the non-3D artists, and you will have the satisfaction of knowing just how easy it was to create.

Figure 23-7 Image of 3D spheres.

```
#include "colors.inc"
#include "textures.inc"
#include "glass.inc"

background { color White }

camera {location <20, 20, -18> look_at  <15, 9, 0>}

light_source {<12, 20, 12> color White} // above
light_source {<-5, 12, 12> color White} // left
light_source {<12, 12, 25> color White} // in back
light_source {<29, 12, 12> color White} // right
light_source {<12, 12, -5> color White} // front

box { <0, 0, 0>, <24, 1, 24> texture { Glass } }

#declare theSphere = sphere { <0, 0, 0>, 4 texture { T_Glass4 } }
object { theSphere pigment { color Yellow } translate <7, 4, 7> }
object { theSphere pigment { color NeonBlue } translate <7, 4, 17> }
object { theSphere pigment { color Aquamarine }   translate <17, 4, 7> }
object { theSphere pigment { color Red } translate <17, 4, 17> }
object { theSphere pigment { color Magenta } translate <12, 12, 12> }
```

Testimonial

After reading an early draft of this chapter, Greg Albing, the fifteen-year-old son of an author's friend, crafted the following scene file:

```
#include "shapes.inc"
#include "colors.inc"
#include "metals.inc"
#include "woods.inc"
```

```
#include "stones2.inc"
#include "glass.inc"
#include "skies.inc"

#declare pipe = union{
        cylinder{
                <0,1,0>,
                <0,5,0>,
                0.5
                open
        }
        cone{
                <0,0,00>, 0.0
                <0,1,0>, 0.5
                open
        }
        texture { T_Chrome_2D }
}

#declare goldPipe = object{ pipe texture { T_Gold_3D }}
#declare woodPipe = object { box {<0,0,0> <1,8,1> texture { T_Wood13 }}}
#declare hornPipe = union {
        cone{
                <0,-1,0> 0.0
                <0,-1,-3> 0.3
                open
        }
        cone{
                <0,-1,-3> 0.3
                <0,-1,-4> 0.4
                open
        }
        texture { T_Copper_4B}
}

#declare pue = union {
        box{<00,2,0><8,5,1>}
        box{<0,0,0><1,2,3>}
        box{<7,0,0><8,2,3>}
        box{<0,1,1><8,2,3>}
        pigment{Brown}
        rotate y*180
}
background{ color White }
light_source { <10,0,-20> color White}
light_source { <-10,0,-20> color Maroon }
light_source { <0,0,1.5> color White }

//      some middle range pipes
object { pipe translate <-5,0,0> scale <1,.5,1>}
object { pipe translate <-4,0,0> scale <1,.6,1>}
```

```
object { pipe translate <-3,0,0> scale <1,.7,1>}
object { pipe translate <-2,0,0> scale <1,.8,1>}
object { pipe translate <-1,0,0> scale <1,.9,1>}
object { pipe translate <0,0,0> scale <1,1,1>}
object { pipe translate <1,0,0> scale <1,.95,1>}
object { pipe translate <2,0,0> scale <1,.85,1>}
object { pipe translate <3,0,0> scale <1,.75,1>}
object { pipe translate <4,0,0> scale <1,.65,1>}
object { pipe translate <5,0,0> scale <1,.55,1>}

//      the BIG honkin' pipes
object { goldPipe translate <0,0,2> scale <1.7,2.1,1.5> }
object { goldPipe translate <1,0,2> scale <1.7,2.3,1.5> }
object { goldPipe translate <-1,0,2> scale <1.7,2.2,1.5> }
object { goldPipe translate <2,0,2> scale <1.7,2.5,1.5> }
object { goldPipe translate <-2,0,2> scale <1.7,2.4,1.5> }
object { goldPipe translate <3,0,2> scale <1.7,2.7,1.5> }
object { goldPipe translate <-3,0,2> scale <1.7,2.6,1.5> }
object { goldPipe translate <4,0,2> scale <1.7,2.9,1.5> }
object { goldPipe translate <-4,0,2> scale <1.7,2.8,1.5> }
object { goldPipe translate <5,0,2> scale <1.7,3,1.5> }
object { goldPipe translate <-5,0,2> scale <1.7,3,1.5> }

//      the wood pipes, usually somewhat large
object { woodPipe translate <0,0,0> }
object { woodPipe translate <1.1,0,0> }
object { woodPipe translate <-1.1,0,0> }
object { woodPipe translate <2.2,0,0> }
object { woodPipe translate <-2.2,0,0> }
object { woodPipe translate <3.3,0,0> }
object { woodPipe translate <-3.3,0,0> }
object { woodPipe translate <4.4,0,0> }
object { woodPipe translate <-4.4,0,0> }
object { woodPipe translate <5.5,0,0> }
object { woodPipe translate <-5.5,0,0> }
object { woodPipe translate <-6.6,0,0> }

//      the trumpet pipes ( it's supposed to look like a trumpet's bell )
object { hornPipe translate <0,0,0> }
object { hornPipe translate <1,0,0> }
object { hornPipe translate <-1,0,0> }
object { hornPipe translate <2,0,0> }
object { hornPipe translate <-2,0,0> }
object { hornPipe translate <3,0,0> }
object { hornPipe translate <-3,0,0> }
object { hornPipe translate <4,0,0> }
object { hornPipe translate <-4,0,0> }
object { hornPipe translate <5,0,0> }
object { hornPipe translate <-5,0,0> }
object { hornPipe translate <6,0,0> }
object { hornPipe translate <-6,0,0> }
```

```
//camera{location<9,15,-18> look_at <0,6,0>} // up and right
camera{location<0,-09,-38> look_at <0,0,0>}   //center and back
// the platform that all of the pipes sit on
box {<-10,-10,0> <10,0,7> texture {T_Wood18}}

// the stone blocks on either side
box {<-20,-10,0> <-10,20,7> texture {T_Stone28}}
box {<10,-10,0> <20,20,7> texture {T_Stone28}}

// the stone behind the pipes
box {<-10,0,7> <10,20,7> texture {T_Stone29}}

// the wooden walls and floor
box {<-20,-10,-15> <-20,20,0> texture {T_Wood19}}
box {<20,-10,-15> <20,20,0> texture {T_Wood19}}
box {<-20,-10,0> <20,-10,-38> texture {T_Ruby_Glass}}

// the pews
object { pue translate<-05,-10,-25>}
object { pue translate<13,-10,-25>}

// the ceiling
box {<-20,20,7><20,20,-15> texture{T_Cloud3}}
```

Figure 23-8 shows that scene as rendered by PovRay.

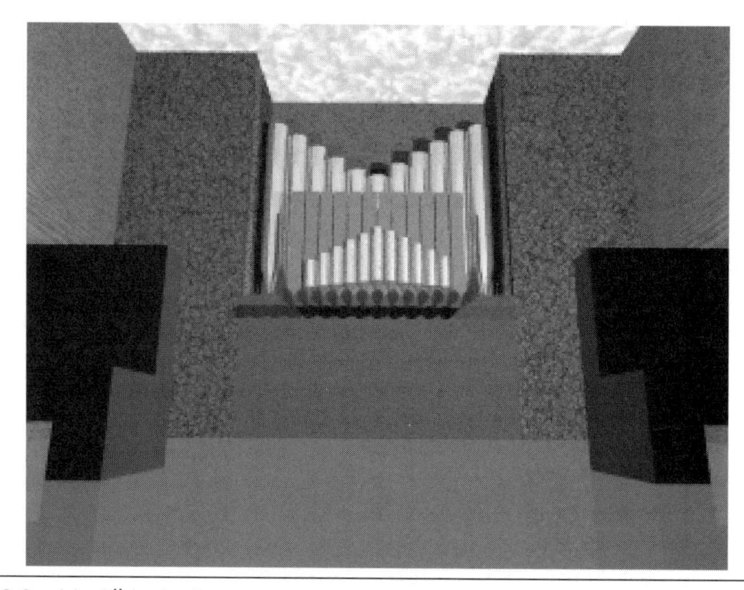

Figure 23-8 Mr. Albing's pipe organ.

Chapter 24

Video Production

Difficult-o-Meter: 4 (fairly high Linux knowledge required)

Covers:

MJPEG tools	*http://mjpeg.sourceforge.net/*
Broadcast 2000	*http://heroinewarrior.com/bcast2000.php3*
XMMS	*http://www.xmms.org*
QT	*http://www.trolltech.com*
SDL	*http://www.libsdl.org*
smpeg	*http://www.lokigames.com/development/smpeg.php3*
avifile	*http://divx.euro.ru*
Various video codecs	*ftp://divx.euro.ru/*
XMMS-avi	*ftp://ftp.xmms.org/xmms/plugins/avi-xmms/*
XMMS-smpeg	*ftp://ftp.xmms.org/xmms/plugins/smpeg-xmms/*
RealPlayer	*http://www.real.com*

Question: How can Linux help me get on TV or make my own movies or videos?

Answer: By learning about video4linux and the tools available for video production, you'll be able to produce a video. With a little help from me you might even get your mug on the tube.

Introduction

Your mission, should you choose to accept it, is to get your face on TechTV. Why? Because it's there. Video production under Linux is not only possible, it's inexpensive. If you're willing to put in a little time, dig into to specifics of recompiling the kenel, some drivers, and applications, and spend around $100 on new hardware, then you'll have the makings of a decent video production studio.

This chapter is all about how to capture video from your video camera, edit the captured video clips, and, finally, combine several video clips into a video work of art. I'll also cover sending your creation to your monitor and saving it to a VCR or VCD. Why not DVD? Because DVD still costs way too much for the average consumer. The goal of this chapter is to educate you on the process of creating a video under Linux and possibly getting that video on television. To this end, I offer you my journey of endurance and perseverance with the trials and tribulations of video production under Linux.

Video4Linux

One good thing that can be said for commercial operating systems is that they have multimillion-dollar companies behind them with the resources to invest in such things as common APIs for just about everything. Linux, you might think, does not have this resource pool. Sure, there are many individuals writing drivers for various devices. A lot of those drivers make it into the official kernel—some don't. But when a group pools its resources and organizes a concerted effort, you get some amazing results. This is what Video4Linux is all about. It's about an effort to produce a common interface for multimedia devices.

Video4Linux can be thought of as a collection of kernel drivers adhering to an API for multimedia features. From FM radio cards to video capture cards, Video4Linux makes it possible for a diverse set of hardware components to operate within your distribution of Linux.

What's really exciting about Video4Linux is that it offers those amazingly talented device driver authors a standard to write their code to. The inclusion of a multimedia subsystem in the kernel will help move Linux into a world dominated by commercial operating systems.

To begin our journey into video production, it is helpful to have a background in the various technologies that may be used. You may already be familiar with some, such as MPEG and AVI, while there are others you may not have been exposed to, such as MJPEG and DivX. Let's explore a bit and get you up to speed on a few things you'll need to get started.

The Formats

There are several video file formats used for storing video. Here is a short list of the more common ones.

MPEG-1	A standard optimized for CD-ROM. Video data is played back at a rate of 1.5 Mbit/sec.
MPEG-2	A newer standard designed for video data rates of 15.2 million samples/sec. Some common devices using this standard are direct broadcast satellite system, digital cable system, and HDTV.
AVI	Developed by Microsoft to play videos in the Windows environment.
Quicktime	Developed by Apple Computers to play videos in the Machintosh environment.
DivX	A new format intended for streaming video over the Internet.

In addition to file formats, you have to consider the compression/decompression algorithm, or codec, used to encode a video data stream. For example, many different codecs can be used for the AVI file format. The one I will be focusing on is MJPEG, since this is the codec used by the software that works with the frame grabber device I have installed in my computer.

The Video Hardware

When considering a video production project using Linux, it is absolutely required that you research the kernel-supported hardware for video capturing. Make sure you have a list of the currently supported Video4Linux video capture devices handy when you go to your local computer retail store to buy a video capture device. I researched the drivers, the hardware, and the prices and then decided to get what I felt was the best bang for my buck, the Pinnacle Systems Studio DC10 Plus video capture card.

I found the price to be right in my budget range, and the driver was available for download from a Web site. The driver is not yet included in the Video4Linux list of kernel drivers, but it is Video4Linux compliant.

As you are probably aware, support for various hardware devices under Linux comes very infrequently, mostly because a few talented individuals devote some of their time and their knowledge of hardware and programming. Some also rely on getting hardware donated to them by manufacturers not willing to put in their time to support Linux (a huge mistake, if I may say so) or by fellow users or programmers who really want a particular piece of hardware supported. Not all of us can write device drivers, but we can support those who do with free hardware, praise, or thanks.

Frame Grabbers

Frame grabber—what a strange name for something! But the name serves it well because it describes what's going on. In lay terms, a frame grabber is a device that converts an analog video signal into a digital representation of video frames. The frames are stored on your hard disk, a process known as *video capture*, by various methods using different techniques of encoding and compression.

Video Cameras

In doing your research for supported hardware, you should consider your video playback device. By this I mean your camera or VCR. Is your camera a digital camera with Fire Wire output, or does it have the more common analog output device? This makes a huge difference in your choice of supported hardware. I have a Sharp Viewcam VL-E650, which is not a digital camera. It outputs a standard analog signal. A simple cable connects my camera to a video capture card, or frame grabber, using standard RCA connectors for the video signal and the sound.

Your camera should have some way of connecting to a VCR using RCA connectors. If not, then you might have to play your videotape from a VCR using a tape adapter cartridge in order to capture the video. If your camera is like mine, it does not have stereo outputs, so use a Y splitter to give you left and right sound cables. It won't be stereo, but at least the sound won't come from only one of your stereo speakers.

Webcams

Webcams can also be used to capture video. It should be noted, however, that many Webcams do not have a very good picture quality, and their frame rates can be very slow. They are intended mainly for transferring video between computers over the Internet.

For this purpose, they work quite well, since video quality is usually not an issue among friends in a video conference. The other downside to Webcams for my projects is the fact that they have to be connected to a computer in order to capture video.

For the project I'm writing about, I needed to be able to take my video camera to the local R/C racing track to shoot video. I positioned the camera in various places to get the best shots of my R/C (Radio Control) monster truck flying through the air. You can't do that while tethered to a computer. This is why a supported video capture device is crucial to my projects.

Your System

Video production, capturing, editing, and storing requires a beefy system. You'll want to have plenty of memory, lots of hard disk space, and a decent-speed CPU. My configuration is as follows:

MSI K7T Pro-2A motherboard (with UDMA100)

AMD Athlon 1-Ghz CPU

512MB memory

Western digital 7200 RPM 30GB UDMA100 hard disk

Creative SBLive! Value soundcard

PowerColor PowerGene MX (GeFORCE 2 MX) video card

Pinnacle Systems Studio DC10 Plus analog video capture card

Due to the amount of data being transferred from your capture card to your hard disk, I highly advise you to use a hard disk of at least 7200 RPM and at least UltraDMA/33 as the interface. The faster the hard disk and interface speed, the less likely it will be that you'll get lost frames during the video/audio capture process. If your hard disk or interface is slower, you might try increasing the number of frame buffers so that the system has time to write to disk while it's capturing the video/audio frames. Playback is also where a faster drive and interface really come into play, because the drive may simply be too slow to load enough video frames into memory to play at 30 frames a second.

The Video Software

The one thing that can be said about working with video is that the files are not small. In fact, depending on the codec, video can consume from 500MB to 10GB (gigabytes!) for only 30 minutes of video. Uncompressed frames require much more space.

Consider how much space is needed when you are capturing images at 640 × 480, 30 times a second in full color. This is your data rate, and it can range from 1MB to 11MB per second, sometimes less, sometimes more, depending on your drivers, the hardware, and the codec.

Because of the amount of data being moved around in your system, you will want a beefy system. My system is beefy enough to be suitable for nonlinear video editing. *Nonlinear* means that you have random access to any part of a video without having to wait for a tape to fast forward or rewind. This almost always means a computer is involved. I'll get into editing video later in the chapter, but first we have to capture the video and store it on a hard disk. For this we'll use tools that are Video4Linux compatible and that work for my hardware configuration and, hopefully, yours.

Drivers

Before you begin your video production project you'll need to do some research on the available drivers for your specific video setup. My setup included a standard video camera, nondigital interface, so I needed a video capture card to add to my system. Because there are so many video capture cards available, it's a wise thing to research which of these cards a Linux driver is available for. Otherwise, you might get stuck with an unsupported video capture card and no way to get the video from your camera into your PC.

My research began by looking on the Web for video capture devices supported under Linux. Google produced many results, as any good Web search engine should. What I found were a lot of cards based on the same chip sets. Chip sets are basically the chips on the video capture card that make it work. The most common driver I found was for the BTTV chip set. I also found a card called the LML33 from Linux Media Labs. Eventually I settled on a card that met my budget requirements, the Pinnacle Systems Studio DC10 Plus. I found the driver at this Web site: *http://www.cicese.mx/~mirsev/Linux/DC10plus/*. A search on *www.freshmeat.net* for "DC10" will also get you to the driver's home. The driver has been integrated into the MJPEG Tools project, so get the latest driver from that Web site.

The current author of the driver, Sergei Miridonov, was kind enough to help me with kernel recompiling issues. Once I got past the fact that my RedHat 7.0 kernel was a modified kernel, I downloaded and compiled an official kernel (*http://www.kernel.org*) and got to work on my video project. The driver for the DC10+ card is not yet part of the official Video4Linux set of drivers. It is Video4Linux compliant, with extensions to provide MJPEG compression and decompression (the codec I mentioned earlier). The tools I will use to capture and play back my video create both Quicktime and AVI file formats.

Capture and Playback Tools

There are several tools for capturing and playing back video under Linux. The tool set you use will be determined by the capture/playback device you have and the device drivers. In addition, codecs play a large part in the tools you will use. Some tools support only specfic codecs. I'm using the MJPEG Tools package, since it supports my hardware with drivers and applications. Within the MJPEG Tools package is a set of tools called *lavtools*, used to do the actual capture and playback of video.

The Linux Audio Video Tools is a package of command line tools for working with video. The two main command line programs are *lavrec*, for capturing video, and *lavplay*, for playing video. There are other utilities in the package as well, but these two will be used the most.

In order to simplify my projects, I always like to create simple shell scripts to keep me from making typing mistakes at the command line. Plus, since the parameters are usually the same every time I run the *lavrec* command, it just makes sense to keep it simple. After playing around with different parameter settings, I settled on the following script, called *vidrec:*

```
lavrec -t${2} -in -fq -d1 -q50 -a16 -s -r44100 -l-1 -R1 -w /clips/${1}.mov
```

lavrec has many command line options, which are defined in the source file, *lavrec.c*. I have used the following command line options:

-t	Record for a specific number of seconds
-i	Input source (composite vs. SVHS, PAL vs. NTSC or SECAM, etc.)
-f	Output file format (AVI, Quicktime, etc.)
-d	Used to set the decimation
-q	Quality setting
-a	Bits resolution for audio (0, 8, or 16)
-s	Enable stereo audio
-r	Audio sampling rate (44,100 Hz for CD-quality sound)
-l	(That's a lowercase *L*) Recording volume (-1 to use mixer setting)
-R	Audio recording source (line, microphone, or CD-ROM)
-w	Wait for me to get ready

I pass only two parameters to my shell script, the filename and the number of seconds I want to record. In my shell script, I automatically place video files on my hard disk in the */clips* directory.

lavplay will play back your video file by sending the output to the video output port of the frame grabber board. If you have this connected to the video-in RCA jack on your TV or VCR, you should see the video playback on your TV. If not, check your VCR's recording source. The geometry and decimation parameters I have in my *vidrec* script make the video playback full screen. Playback was nice and smooth.

So far, all we've done is capture and play back video with our frame grabber device. The real fun begins when you take all your separate video clips and put them together, insert some clever transitions betwen them, add some music, a voice-over, and precede it with a fancy title and you've got yourself a full-fledged video production on your hands. To make this masterpeice, you'll need nonlinear video editing software.

Nonlinear Editing Tools

Nonlinear video editing is a very CPU- and memory-intensive process. The slowness of your processor and the amount of memory you have will limit the size of your projects. So what does *nonlinear* mean? It simpy means you don't have to fast-forward and rewind a tape to get to a point on a video. In other words, you have random access. Later in the chapter I'll tell you more about what tools are available. To get you started making your own video, the next section will be a very high-level conceptual overview of how you might put together a video using the tools I've talked about so far.

Making Your Video

Before we move on, let's get to a checkpoint. If you are going to work on a video project, you should have done the following:

- Researched current video capture drivers
- Researched video capture boards within your budget
- Acquired (if you don't already have one) a video capture board
- Downloaded and compiled a compatible kernel for the driver
- Downloaded, compiled, and installed a driver for your video capture board
- Downloaded, compiled, and installed applications for your video production process
- Tested the capturing and playback of video

The Gopher

In your production, you have several parts to fill. In addition to producing the video, you might also be the director, the musical talent, or the actor. You are definitely the gopher. On the other hand, you might be lucky and have plenty of friends willing to work for beer or food. Either way, you're in control and in charge. The success of your video project depends greatly on your organizational skills and planning.

As with any project, you need an idea to start things rolling. The idea for my project was to videotape my R/C truck, the Traxxas T-MAXX (*http://www.traxxas.com* and *http://www.t-maxx.com*), doing all sorts of jumps, crashes, and speed runs while putting the whole thing together with some nifty stills and some kickin' rock-n-roll music. To start my project I created a script of how the video was going to play out, from start to finish.

The Story, Script, Screenplay, Whatever!

Your screenplay or script will be the starting point for your video. My project had no actors and, because I'm not a professional filmmaker, I didn't feel the need to research how a real screenplay should be written. So I came up with what I call a *video sequence guide*. This is a guide to help me determine in detail the sequence of events thoughout the video. I'm a big fan of "winging it." Figure 24-1 shows a sample of my video sequence guide.

The basic idea is that you have an idea of what you want to do before you begin shooting video and taking pictures. A video sequence guide will assist you in this. You'll be able to work out what music you want, make notes for yourself for when you're shooting, and be able to work out the timing.

Though such a guide helps keep you organized, it doesn't always give you a good feeling for the visual aspects of your project. This is where the storyboard comes into play.

The Storyboard

The pros do it and so should you. Forget for the moment that your drawing skills might be as poor as mine. The storyboard is your way to make sure your video will come out the way you intend. It will help you focus on camera angles and avoid plot deviations and will serve as a guide as you shoot video footage and prepare graphic images or animations.

There is really nothing Linux specific about this concept—it's just a good idea to do. As you become familiar with more Linux tools, you might try using them to create the storyboard images. I find it easier to simply scratch out my ideas onto 3 × 5 index cards. I'm no artist, but I get my point across.

T-MAXX Fever

Title Sequence
Video: Black screen 1 second
Video: Fade in "Evil Penguin Productions" screen
Music: Play sinister laugh audio
Video: Fade to black
Video: Fade in "T-MAXX Fever" title screen
Video: Fade to black
Video: Black screen 1 second

Sequence 1
Video: Play jump01 (1 minute)
jump01 should start with the T-MAXX launching off a ramp and landing on the ground. On the landing is when the music starts.
Music: "Tom Sawyer" by Rush (3.00 minutes)
Video: Transition to *jump02* (1.00 minute)
Video: Transition to *jump03* (1.00 minute)
Video: Transition to black screen as music fades out
Video: Black screen 1 second

Sequence 2
Music: "Bad to the Bone" by George Thorogood (2.50 minutes)
Loop for entire song:
Still: tmaxx photo set 1 (3 seconds each photo)
Video: transition to next still
End loop
And so on.

Figure 24-1 Sample video sequence guide.

Lights, Camcorder, Action!

Once you have an idea of what video you will need, it's time to head to the set and start shooting. For me, the set was the local R/C track. Luckily, the guys at the track were very nice and allowed me to walk all over the track to position my camera in various places for the best shots. Keep track of what video you will need to shoot. Your script and storyboard cards should come in very handy at this point.

When shooting your video, it's always a good idea to have some extra time at the front and end of each take. And it's always a good idea to have at least two takes of each action item. This will give you something to choose from when editing your video clips together. It will also help to build your library of stock footage for future video projects.

Up to this point, I've concentrated on the organization of the video project and getting the video recorded. Now we move on to the next stage: video capture and editing. The specific aspects may be different for you and your project, but you will probably follow the same basic steps for any video project. Before you begin, however, make sure your video production studio is configured properly.

Your Studio Setup

If you already do music production with your Linux system, adding video to the mix is not that difficult. If you only have a set of speakers attached to your computer to listen to MP3 files, then you have a little bit of setup ahead of you. The configuration of your production environment will vary greatly with your needs. My studio consists of mixing equipment, amplifiers, speakers, a TV and VCR, a camera, several synthesizers, and computer speakers. Needless to say, I have cables running all over my computer room/studio (I also have a drum set in the corner). To get basic video and audio into your computer, you need at a minimum a video capture card and a soundcard. You will need to connect your camera to the video-in and audio-in ports on each card. To view your work, you will need to connect the video-out and audio-out ports to the video-in and audio-in ports on your VCR or TV. Figure 24-2 diagrams a simple configuration.

If you plan to perform your own music or have additional audio sources, you might want to add a mixer to your setup. Also, having multiple video sources might come in handy, so a video source and destination switch might be useful. Figure 24-3 presents an example of a more complicated configuration.

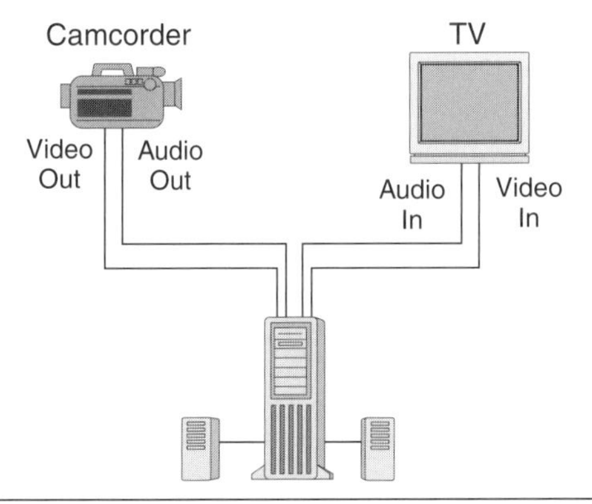

Figure 24-2 Simple studio configuration.

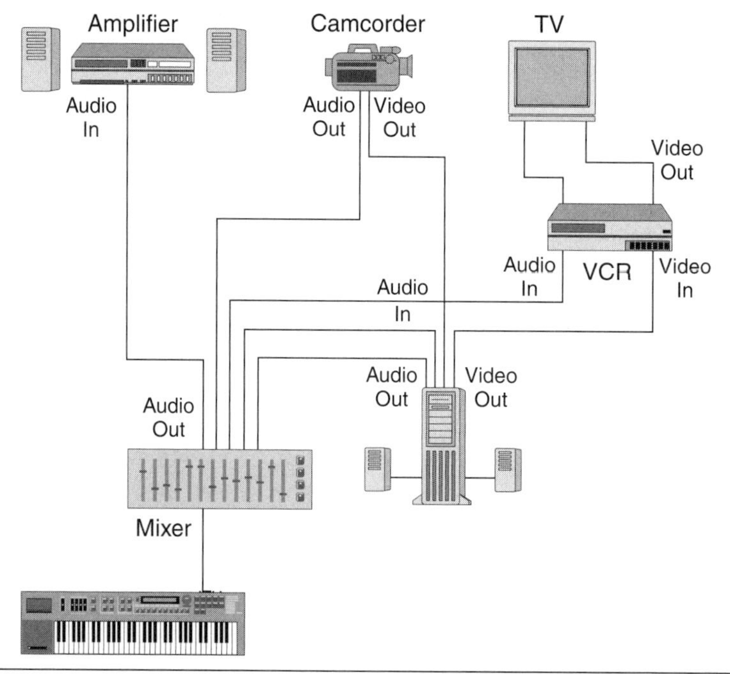

Figure 24-3 Complex studio configuration.

Capture Your Video

After spending five hours on a Sunday afternoon at a dusty R/C racing track, I managed to shoot three hours of videotape. Using my video sequence guide and storyboard cards, I was able to record all of the required footage, along with a lot of extra suff for filler and stock footage for future projects. I also got some real nice snapshots using my digital camera. All I had to do was get the video into my computer to be able to "digitally join" everything together.

Using the recording script, *vidrec*, will help me avoid making endless typos at the command line. For each segment of video shot, I captured the video using the *vidrec* command, naming each file according to the video sequence guide.

```
$ vidrec jump01 60
$ vidrec jump02 60
     :
     :
```

lavrec displays status information while capturing the video. It is a good idea to monitor this output to determine if any frames were lost during the recording process.

Depending on the hardware and software you choose to use, you may see a much different screen. Figure 24-4 shows the output from one of my capture sessions. As you can see, I've captured 60 seconds of video.

Once the video is captured, it's time to review it. I created a very simple script, *vidplay*, that executes the *lavplay* program and takes a single parameter:

```
lavplay -C /clips/${1}.mov
```

Executing *vidplay* will play the video file through the frame grabber's video-out connector. If you have this connected to your TV or VCR and have your setup configured correctly, you should be able to see the captured video playing on the TV. Status information from lavplay will be written to the text window where you ran the program. Figure 24-5 presents an example of the playback status of a video file.

Editing Clips

We're at the part of the project where your creative skills meet up with your technical skills to put together all the peices of video, music, and sound to create your masterpiece. Nonlinear video editing is a relatively simple process. We won't go into the more complex subjects of digital compositing or including graphic animations along

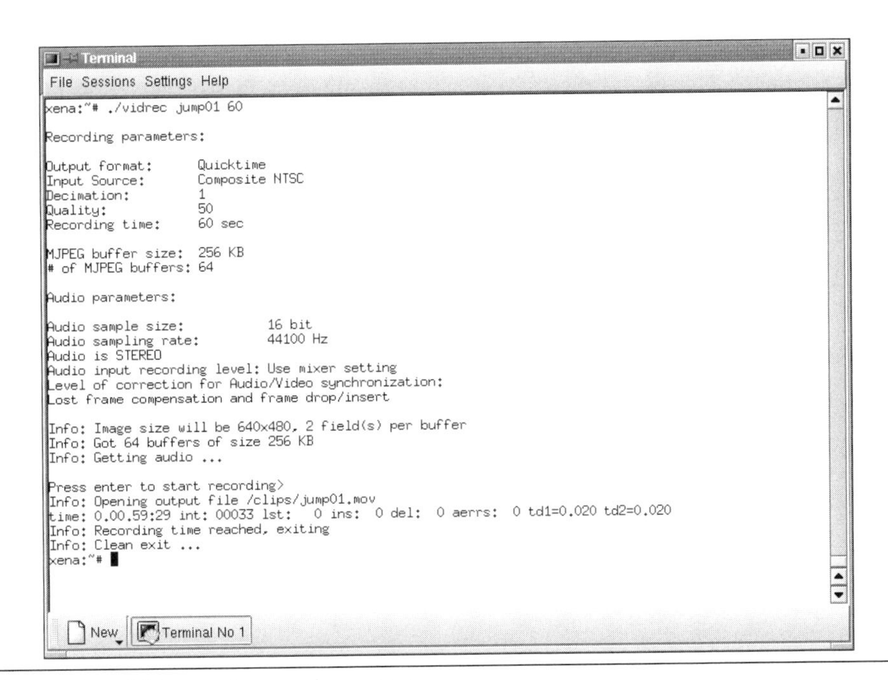

Figure 24-4 Video capture session output.

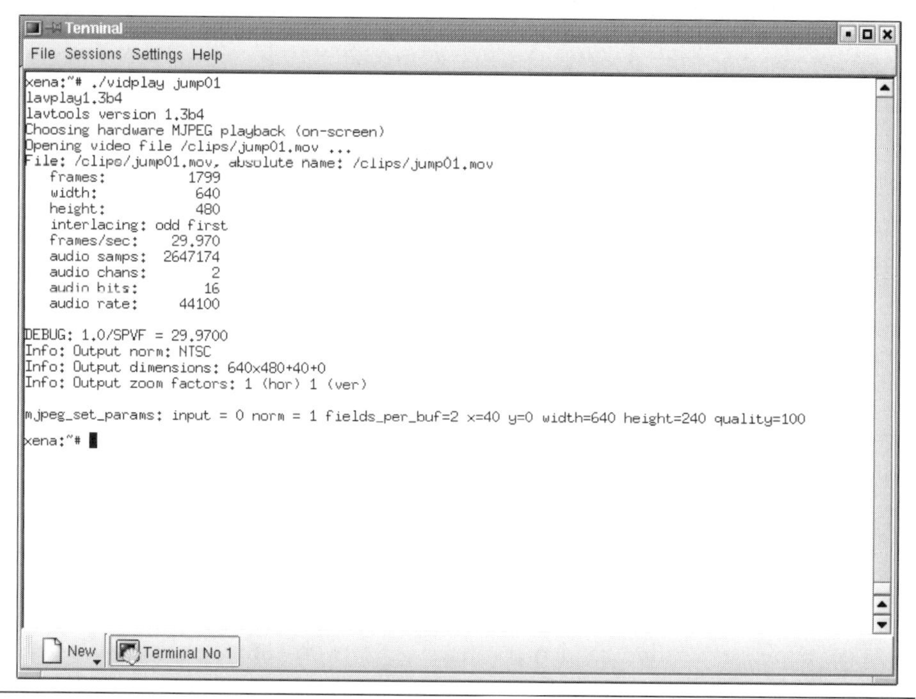

Figure 24-5 Video playback session output.

with live video, subjects that could fill an entire book. Instead, we will cover the very basics in order to get you over the learning curve and into simple video production with Linux. These include:

- Adding video tracks
- Creating transitions between video tracks
- Adding background music
- Adding voice-over narration
- Creating text titles

For my project, I used Broadcast 2000 for my nonlinear video editing. When I began writing this chapter for the book, Broadcast 2000 was available as a GPL product. This is no longer true. In fact, the product is currently not available to anyone. The owners claim "excessive liability" as their reason for pulling the product. So where does that leave us for nonlinear video editing software? A good and inexpensive commercial alternative to broadcast 2000 is MainActor from MainConcept (*http://www.mainconcept.com/products/mainactorLinux.shtml*). Considering this book is about Free Software, I have reluctantly included this plug for MainActor because it is currently the only low-cost alternative to Broadcast 2000.

Timeline

To get started, you will be presented with a timeline onto which video clips will be added. These clips are the files you captured onto your hard disk. The timeline represents the time for a video clip. You are able to move your cursor to any point in time within the clip and play the video or make adjustments to its parameters (Figure 24-6).

Transitions

In between each clip, you will be able to add transitions. Transitions create a smooth bond between two different video clips. Without transitions, video clips simply run from one to the next with a sudden switch. Sometimes, this is the desired effect and that's okay. But sometimes you want to emphasize the change from one video clip to another, and for this you use transitions. A transition can be thought of as a special video clip that goes between two clips you want join together. Figure 24-7 is a diagram illustrating the basic idea behind a transition.

The key point to remember is that transitions take time from each end of the two clips you want to join. They require time from the end of the first clip and the beginning of the next clip. Allow for this when shooting and capturing your video. Once you are more familiar with the transitions, you'll get the timing down and you'll be able to work the transitions into your video sequence guide from the beginning, complete with time requirements.

Once you've connected the video clips together, it's time to get some music into your video.

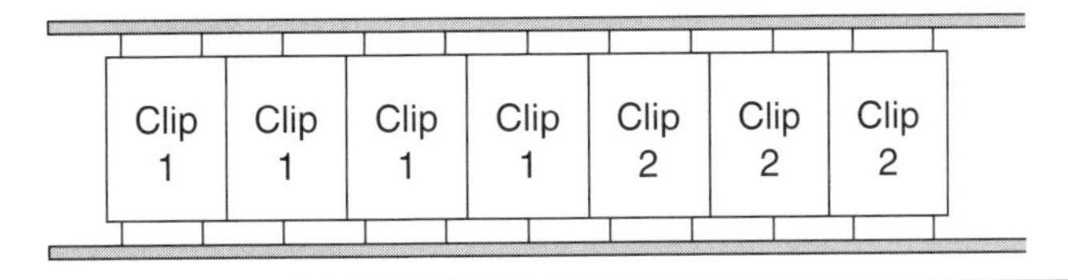

Figure 24-6 Video clip timeline concept.

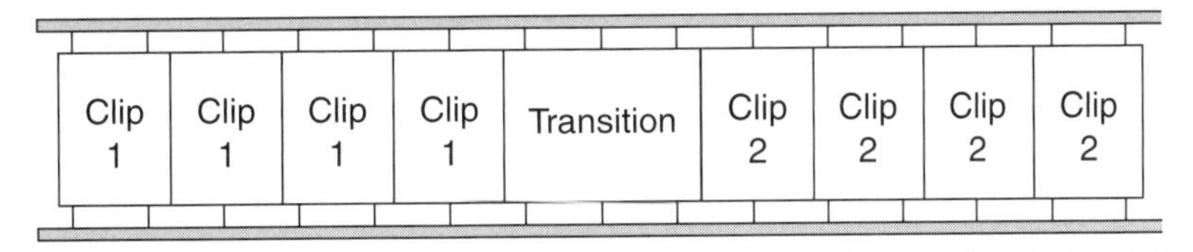

Figure 24-7 Video clip transition concept.

Voice-Overs and Music

Voice-overs can make or break a video project. Use them sparingly and only when absolutely necessary. Voices-overs can add to a video when the subject matter is not entirely understood or when a story is being told and narration is required. Otherwise, it's best just to have really good music in the background.

Music is used all the time in movies to establish a particular tone or to invoke a particular feeling. The same can be accomplished in your videos. For my *T-Maxx Fever* video I used two songs I felt brought out the feelings I wished to invoke in my audience. Adding music is as simple as adding a video clip to your project. Generally, you will add either a WAV file or an MP3 file, depending on what the editor application supports. The music will be displayed on the timeline, along with the video clips and transitions, and it should show the waveform image as a guide for aligning the music to the video or the video to the music, whichever is needed.

Once the music is synced to the video, all that's left is to title your work and to create the final video file.

Titles

Titling a video is your one chance to say, "Hey, this is mine!" Titling is your way of communicating to your audience that what they are about to see or have just seen was made by you. It gives credit where credit is due. It also gives you a chance to come up with a nifty production company name (mine is Evil Penguin Productions). Have fun with your titling, or at least let those viewing know the name of your video.

Titling usually involves adding text or a still-image file with text to the timeline before, after, or during video clips. Play with the various transitions between your text images to get some fancy titling, like the big guys in Hollywood.

Final Rendering

The final step in your project will be to render your video, complete with music, transitions, voice-overs, and titles, to a single AVI, Quicktime, or MPEG-1/2 file, depending on what the editor application supports. Regardless, you should be able to convert your video to a different format once you've rendered your project in one of these formats.

Commercial Music

If you intend to make a video that will be for anything other than private use, it is a good idea to employ music that you create yourself or have purchased the rights to. I've included examples of songs from very well known artists. I am doing this without their permission or without compensating them for the use of their songs. If I were going to sell this video, I'd have to get permission or send them lots of money. Since I have neither, I'll stick to playing the video in the comfort of my home and only for my friends.

But what about our goal? What about getting our video on TechTV? For that, I swapped out the Rush and George Thorogood songs for a couple of my own, just in case TechTV objected. This also helps promote my own music and keeps the lawyers off my back.

Video Playback

When I was working on the book, my wife's little brother sent me a video called "*teasingc.mpg*"—a cute little movie of two housecats wrestling—actually a kitten who antagonizes a full-grown cat into tackling him. Relatively funny. But I didn't know that, because I use Linux to read e-mail, and I didn't have a multimedia player installed on my system. The little MPG aggravated me. I wanted to watch it—after all, it had taken a couple of whole *seconds* to come down through my cable modem. To top it off, I had a handful of other little movies that friends had mailed to me—a couple of AVIs, an ASF file, and some more MPEGs. Determined to remedy this situation, I headed off to *freshmeat*, and started researching.

I found that there was software to play video files, but it involved a near-dizzying array of package dependencies, which took me the better part of two days to figure out. While chatting with the other authors, they admitted they'd never managed to get AVI/MPG playback working on their systems. This, I thought, was a worthy subject to include in this chapter. I'll cover what packages you need to install, but I'm going to do it in the reverse order in which I found them—because every package I found had three packages that had to be installed before it. So I'll hand you the packages in the order they need to be installed.

I got MPG playback to work first and then worked on AVI playback. I had long since given up on viewing AVIs under Linux—after all, AVI is an MS Windows–only format, pretty much. Have you ever tried to watch an AVI on the MacOS? I tried years ago, and didn't have much luck (things have probably changed by now). But while researching MPEG playback, I stumbled on the release of *avifile* on *freshmeat*. Sure enough, it was *exactly* what I needed.

Now, remember how I mentioned I would do things in reverse order? I'm going to cover AVI/ASF first, because I can.

XMMS

Requires: GTK and GLIB > 1.2.2

Before I could play any multimedia, I needed a little program called XMMS, the Cross-Platform Multi Media System. XMMS, available from *http://www.xmms.org/*, is probably the coolest MP3 player I've found, and it even has support for the 3DNow! extensions offered by my AMD processor. If you've got an AMD K6/2, K6/3, or Athlon, you'll want to enable the 3DNow! bit. I downloaded version 1.2.4, copied it to my */usr/src* directory, and did the following:

```
tar zxvf xmms-1.2.4.tar.gz
cd xmms-1.2.4
./configure –with-x –enable-3dnow  #I have an AMD K6/2.  If you use an
    AMD CPU, enable this
make
su -c"make install"
```

Simple, eh? It's a quick compile, at about six minutes, so there's no need to leave your computer for this one.

qt-2.2.2

Requires: Removing old QT first, or major wizardry

Yarg! I had to upgrade the QT library for the next-to-be-mentioned package, avifile-0.51. QT is a graphics library that allows a nice standard library for developers. Because of this, it's widely used. It's a prerequisite for KDE. Changing this was not something I really wanted to do. Conveniently enough, I don't use KDE, so I just removed all traces of KDE and QT from my system. This required repeated use of the infamous "rpm —erase <package>" command and left me with some extra empty disk space. After that, I pointed my copy of netscape to *ftp://ftp.trolltech.com/qt/source/* and grabbed qt-2.2.2. Note that qt-2.2.3 is now available, and by the time you get this book qt-2.2.4 will likely be there as well. Might as well grab the latest, eh?

After you've done that, extract the package with a simple *tar zxvf*. I extracted the package and compiled it thusly:

```
cd /usr/src/qt-2.2.2
export QTDIR=/usr/src/qt-2.2.2
./configure -platform linux-g++ -shared
make
su -c"make install"
```

Note that I didn't bother compiling it with JPEG or PNG support. If you really want those, you can look at the *./configure —help* screen to see where to get those. Compiling this took some time—1.5 hours on my machine. You might want to consider doing something else while your machine chugs along.

What should you do if you're a heavy KDE user? Upgrade QT from the RPMs. I've tried compiling KDE several times and never had any luck.

SDL

Requires: a soundcard

Next, I had to upgrade my copy of SDL! SDL is the simple direct media layer, which is required for *avifile*. Basically, it's designed to give quick access to your video and audio devices—so the sound is nice and the video plays back at a watchable speed. Like most of the packages, downloading, compiling, and installing it was simple. I grabbed libsdl-1.1.7, which was the most recent version, and went to compiling it. Thankfully, this was a plain, simple *autoconf* build, so there's no point in burdening you with the details.

Take note that SDL does require a soundcard. Since there aren't many machines without them these days, I'll assume you've already got one. SDL can also benefit from some hardware acceleration under Xfree86 4.0.1, so this may be a good enough reason for you to consider upgrading your X-windows installation. The compile took about 25 minutes on my K6/2-450. With SDL installed and ready to go, I could move on to the next piece.

avifile-0.53.2

Requires: QT > 2.1.0, XFree86 3.3.x or 4.0.x with Shared Memory Support

I originally tried using avifile-0.51 but had great difficulty getting it to grok the ac3dec I'd just installed. I gave up at the time, but as I turned my jumbled notes on video playback into a chapter, I decided to revisist *avifile*, and found that a new release was out!

Surely, I thought, avifile-0.53.2 will fix these pesky compile problems. Wrong I was. Despite spending a few hours trying to get *ac3dec* to compile into *avifile*, I had absolutely no luck. I'm not sure what it takes to get it included, but I must be doing *something* wrong.

After a bit more analysis of the files available on *freshmeat*, I started to wonder whether using libMPEG3 might be a better approach—but without a word from the documentation for *avifile*, I didn't feel like messing with it. I have run into nothing with ac3 audio so far—or at least nothing I'm aware of. The homepage for *avifile* is at *http://divx.euro.ru/*. Get it now, before Microsoft sics their lawyers on the author for daring to decode ".asf" files as well. Microsoft is claiming that the whole format is proprietary and that an open source attempt to decode it is copyright infringement. This sounds like spurious reasoning to me, but I'm a Unix administrator, not a lawyer. Your mileage may vary. I downloaded *avifile.tar.gz* to my */usr/src* directory, and did the following:

```
tar zxvf avifile.tar.gz
./configure -with-qt-dir=/usr/src/qt-2.2.2/ -enable-release
make
su -c"make install"
```

At this point, *avifile* is quite happy, but we need to install codecs, or it won't be much fun. From *http://divx.euro.ru/* you can also get the *binaries.zip*, which contains pretty much all the codecs that *avifile*'s author has found. I'd love to give credit to the author by name, but he's carefully kept it off his Web site. Still, he's done good work on this code, and it was mighty kind of him to compile all these codecs for us. To get the codecs in place, do this:

```
su root
cd /usr/lib
mkdir win32
cd win32
cp /usr/src/binaries-001222.zip .  #substitute the proper filename here
unzip binaries-001222.zip
rm binaries-001222.zip
exit
```

Avifile expects the codecs to be in */usr/lib/win32*, so all we did was put them there. The aforementioned compilation took only about 10 minutes for me. Now it's time to move on to the next piece.

AVI-XMMS-1.2.1

Requires: SDL > 1.1.5, Avifile > 0.51

Here's the piece of the puzzle that'll actually let XMMS play *.avi* and *.asf* files. It's called AVI-XMMS, and it requires that you have avifilei0.52 or greater. It can be found at *http://www.xmms.org/plugins_input.html#122*. Since we've already installed *avifile* (and the codecs) and SDL, we can start installing it as we would any other *autoconf* package.

Compilation took all of 30 seconds for me, and I don't have that terrifically fast a machine. Once installed, you're ready to go watch some AVI, ASF, or WMV movies!

Adding MPEG Support

With AVI/ASF/WMV movies now happily playing on your machine, you can think about adding MPEG support. MPEG is a more universal standard for encoding video and audio, and players are available for almost every operating system out there. Linux is no exception—there are several players out there. But since we're already using XMMS to listen to MP3s (which are actually MPEG-3 compressed audio files) and watch our AVIs, ASFs, and WMVs, doesn't it make sense to extend XMMS? On that theory, we're about to begin adding MPEG video support to our XMMS application.

smpeg

Requires: SDL > 1.1.4

smpeg is Loki Entertainment's (yep, the company that ports games to Linux) first open source project, and it's pretty cool. It's a full MPEG video library and even includes a minimal MPG viewer. smpeg-0.4.2 was the version used, and I downloaded it from *ftp://ftp.linuxgames.com/loki/open-source/smpeg/*. Then I handled it like any other autoconf-style package.

Compilation took a whopping three minutes. Off I went to get the XMMS plug-in to use smpeg. Tired of compiling yet? (The minimal MPEG viewer is GTV, by the way.)

smpeg-XMMS

Requires: SMPEG > 0.4.0, SDL > 1.1.4, GLIB > 1.2.2

The last of our XMMS plug-ins is the one that actually lets us view the MPG that started off this chapter. smpeg-XMMS is available from the XMMS input plug-ins page at *http://www.xmms.org/plugins_input.html*, and is quite small. Download, configure, compile (autoconf-like).

It took 7 whole seconds to compile. We're *done*! With AVI MPG, at least. We might as well get RealPlayer while we are at it. Sometimes, one will run across videos encoded in RealPlayer format.

RealPlayer

This is available from *http://www.real.com/*, in RPM format. Install the RPM and you're ready to go.

Quicktime Movies

You're SOL. There's no comprehensive *.mov* player available for Linux. If someone finds one, let me know, and I'll include it in the next edition of *Multitool Linux*.

Screenshots!

Figures 24-8 and 24-9 present a couple of screenshots of the XMMS display window in action.

There, we have it. You can now watch all the little movies you'd like. These packages will no doubt be updated fairly regularly, and perhaps someone will add a QuickTime player for me someday (I'd like to be able to watch *Troops* again without rebooting into Windows, you see).

Figure 24-8 Motorcyclist dragging his knee through a roundabout.

Figure 24.9 Different motorcyclist, performing a stoppie.

Publishing

The final leg of our journey involves the publishing of our video to a medium external to our computers. Playback of video on a computer consumes enourmous resources and is usually done in a tiny window. Full-screen video is possible, but be prepared to have a beefy system with a fast video card. To be able to share your work you should put your finished product on videotape or burn it onto a playable video CD.

Videotape

You should already know how to record your video to a VCR. You've already played back numerous video clips during your capture and review process. The same playback is all you need to record to videotape. Just be sure to have the audio-out and video-out RCA jacks from your audio card and frame grabber card, respectively, connected to the video-in and audio-in jacks on your VCR, or else you'll record static.

Creating a Video CD for Your VCD/DVD Player

Video CDs are curious creatures. Some DVD players don't support them, some do. Those that do, however, may not support CD-Rs, and so they don't support VCDs you might create on your computer. If you're lucky enough to have purchased a DVD player that does read CD-Rs and can play video CDs, you might try creating a video CD instead of recording your video to tape. So how do we go about creating a video CD?

A video CD uses the same media as an audio CD or CD-R, to be specific. Encoded on the CD is compressed MPEG-1 video. The resolution of video CDs is comparable to VHS tapes with a resolution of 352 × 240 (NTSC) or 352 × 288 (PAL). You will be able to get about 60–70 minutes of video on a VCD, but don't expect DVD quality. There are a couple of tools available for VCD creation under Linux:

- VCDImager: GNU VideoCD Image Maker
- VCD-Tools

First, you have to convert your video file from whatever format it's in to MPEG-1. If it's already in MPEG-1, then no conversion is needed. Also, make sure you change the frame size as described earlier, or else your video will not fit on the screen correctly. Then, using one of the listed tools, you create a VCD image from the MPEG-1 file. From there you use *cdrdao* to burn the image to the CD-R.

Here are some other tools and resources that may help you when working with VCDs:

http://www.vcdgear.com/

http://www.vcdhelper.com/vcdtools.htm

http://www.vcdhelper.com/vcd.htm

http://linux.about.com/compute/linux/library/weekly/aa011501.htm

http://www.reptechnic.com.au/vcd.html

http://www.hvrlab.org/~hvr/vcdimager/

http://www.nocrew.org/software-vcdpad.html

TechTV

TechTV. Let me say it again, TechTV. I get tingles every time I hear that name. What techie doesn't love TechTV? Okay, enough free plugs. This television network loves to get video e-mails, known as *v-mail*. V-mails can range from show promotions to computer questions. I was lucky enough to get one of my videos on the show *You Made It!* Unfortunately, the show was canceled.

Check their Web site for video submission guidelines. Generally, if you can make an AVI or Quicktime video, they should be able to view your video. Now, will they use it? That depends on you and your video production skills.

Summary

It's not a pretty process. What I didn't go into more detail about were the hours I spent downloading and recompiling the kernel, drivers, and tools, debugging code, and buying hardware to make my system work as fast as it possibly could without resorting to buying a new computer altogether. Will you have to go through what I did? That depends on your kernel versions, drivers, hardware, and software.

The most important thing that I can say is this: Do your research. Research the hardware and software before deciding on how to proceed with video production under Linux. It's only going to get better as more hardware is supported and the software becomes more sophisticated.

Chapter 25

AFTERWORD

Unprovided with original learning, unformed in the habits of thinking, unskilled in the arts of composition, I resolved to write a book. —EDWARD GIBBON

There is at present something called the software industry. In my humble opinion we have a software industry for three fundamental reasons.

1. *Compilation is tantamount to encryption:* When source code is compiled, information is lost. While it is possible to disassemble a compiled binary, it is provably impossible to reconstruct the full source code of the program. In fact, with highly optimizing compilers it is possible for several different source code versions of an algorithm to have identical resultant binaries. Thanks to compilation, *there is an artificial shortage of technique*. This artificial shortage raises the price of software and supports the continuance of software as an industry.
2. *Capital cost of software distribution:* When the software industry began, it was necessary to manufacture and distribute media (disks and books) in order to get software into the hands of users. Now we have the Internet, which, while presently a bit too slow, will one day totally replace physical software distribution. The capital cost to distribute your program to every computer user on Earth is now so close to zero as to be hardly worth mentioning.
3. *Human capital:* Again, when the software industry began it was necessary to gather large numbers of skilled people in one place to develop any software beyond a certain level of complexity. Once again, we now have the Internet. And as projects like Linux and Apache and others firmly demonstrate, large and complex software projects can be built by hundreds, even thousands of people, most of whom have never met one another. The capital cost of combining talented people is now so close to zero as to be hardly worth mentioning.

I imagine you are beginning to see my idea, which is that software will cease to have value and that *talented programmers* will have the value. The vast majority of programmers work not for the software industry, but in management information systems

(MIS), where they adapt systems of hardware and software to the specific needs of specific businesses and processes.

This is just as it should be. After all, a computer and its software has little inherent value. The only value it has is how it lets us do what we would have done without it faster, better, and with fewer errors. Software is a tool. It is only of value if you have something you want to build.

I believe that Free Software is the very beginning of a major shift in the value proposition of software. I believe that software design and development will evolve from its present state, analogous to laborers in industrial production, into a profession more akin to architecture, engineering, law, and medicine.

What if some of the other established professions worked like the software industry? Imagine you are a heart surgeon. You develop a new heart bypass technique. You would, of course, keep this technique secret. You would invent a way to pass the technique on to other heart surgeons so that they could perform it but not understand it or pass it on to others. Moreover, you would keep some things you already know would improve the technique from being included with the technique so that you could later sell an enhanced version. This is what medicine would be like if it worked like the software industry.

Fortunately, medicine is a field where *skilled practitioners* are highly desired and therefore highly compensated. They give away their techniques in medical journals, seminars, and schools (schools that charge tuition, of course—there's nothing that says you can't charge for a skilled person's time). They disclose it all and subject it to the public review of their peers. Surgeons are not units of production in a manufacturing enterprise; they are professionals.

An interesting counterexample is where the medical model *does* follow the manufacturing model. Pharmaceutical companies do keep their techniques secret (well, they publish them, but they obtain patent protection). This makes some sense, however, since there is an actual physical product that requires raw materials and physical plant. It cannot be distributed to more people without diminishing supply. This is quite different from software, which, as we see with the advent of the Internet, may be reproduced and distributed infinitely without increasing cost or diminishing supply.

If Free Software continues (as I believe it will) to replace the artificially scarce and therefore artificially expensive supply of software, how will programmers make money? Surely Free Software is at best an anticapitalist idea that threatens an entire economic sector?

I think not. Are physicians paupers? Do surgeons have to hitch rides to work? Are they diminishing in number? How about lawyers? How about architects? All of these professionals are paid not for the secrets they keep, but for the quality of their practice. As I said before, most programmers do not work for companies that manufacture and distribute commercial software. Most work in MIS, writing software and/or integrating systems to make them meet specific needs. Demand for this will only increase as the cost of baseline systems software and development tools drops to zero. There will be more work and more money to be made, because it is not the software that has value; it is the quality of the programmer's practice that has value.

There will be considerable resistance to this conversion of programming from industrial job to true profession. This resistance will come largely from practitioners of the art. There was considerable resistance to the conversion of medicine to scientific and statistical methods as well. This resistance came because of the sheer number of quacks and incompetents in the profession. Who can doubt that this is true of software when Weinberg's second law still seems so true: "If builders built buildings the way programmers write programs, then the first woodpecker to come along would destroy civilization." Proprietary software, by hiding poor design and implementation from peer review, helps to keep the state of the art primitive. It is part of why user experience of computers is so poor.

Free Software's rise to prominence would have been impossible without the Internet. I believe the disappearance of packaged closed software will be a natural consequence of the Internet. A fundamental shift has already occurred in the economics of software production and distribution. It will take some time for the shift to reach throughout the system, but the economics will drive it.

The best part is that by making software open and free, all of us who write software will be better prepared to be skilled practitioners. The next best part is that all of us who use software will have a lot more money to pay people for their skills, to put money into segments of the economy that produce goods with real value. It is an exciting time to be working in technology.

—MICHAEL SCHWARZ

About the Authors

Michael Schwarz

I dedicated this book to my father, Gene Schwarz. There's a simple explanation. He is the sole reason I have a career in computer programming, and, thus, he is the reason I had the opportunity to write this book.

My father was an electrical engineer working for Control Data in the mid-1970s when he began to build our first microcomputer in our basement. We cobbled together an S-100 bus microcomputer using kits and wire-wrap boards, and even began doing our own photo-etched printed circuits. We built the machine around the cutting-edge Zilog Z-80. A friend of his wrote the original BIOS and monitor program, but, before long, I was adding routines required for newer versions of the CP/M operating system.

By the time we stopped developing on that machine and bought in to the PC craze, we had a machine with 64k of static RAM and a 4MHz processor. We were hot stuff.

One of the first programs I wrote converted an entire SSSD 8-inch floppy from EBCDIC to ASCII. I will never forget the first time code of mine made those old CDC BR-803 floppy drives seek to track 0 (tracks, not cylinders—single sided floppies, remember?) and load the head. It was magical, and I was hooked.

As the PC industry grew, that magical feeling became more and more remote. The PC became an appliance. And while programming skillfully still held pleasure, it was getting to the point where monkeys could write software that, to unskilled eyes, seemed to work just fine. The excitement was gone.

Then, in 1993, I started to hear about Linux. I had already worked with Unix, starting with machines from a failed CDC venture into SOHO Xenix machines, built by Altos. I had continued to use Unix skills at work on "beefier" systems.

The idea of running Unix (or at least something like it) on my PCs was exciting. I stayed late at work (no Internet at home yet), downloading the Texas A&M University (TAMU) Linux distribution. It was something on the order of 18 floppy disk images for the whole thing.

I managed to configure and boot that, and I've been addicted ever since. It has brought excitement back to computing. Every day is a day on the frontiers of knowledge and progress. In the rest of the (Microsoft) world, you don't get to do that. You get to play in the box they provide. Want your own box? Too bad. Either come to work for Microsoft, or play where you are told to play.

I try to keep up, at least in passing, with the Windows world, but I sure don't plan to go back.

From 1993, with a crashing kernel and a bash prompt, to today, with Linux doing massively parallel supercomputing, multiprocessor, and clustered computing right up there with the big boys, Linux has been a very exciting ride, and a chance to learn so much about the most fundamental elements of computing. I hope this book helps you to enjoy Linux as much I do.

Of course, I have to thank everyone involved in this project. My co-authors, of course, who came through even when life demanded they be elsewhere. My wife, Tina, for putting up with the process and my absentmindedness. I have to thank everyone at Addison-Wesley for their hard work and patience. I also wish to thank everyone who reviewed our manuscript. Their suggestions made this a much stronger book. Where weakness may still exist, the fault is mine and not theirs.

Of course, I also thank Messrs. Thorvalds and Stallman for god-fathering so much software to write about.

—MICHAEL SCHWARZ
JANUARY 2002

Jeremy Anderson

I've run into a lot of new Linux users, and the first thing they invariably say is "Wow. This is neat! What do I do with it?" The problem has hit me on occasion, as well. Linux is an extremely competent OS—more stable than Windows, with a wider base of software support than any BSD Unix (OpenBSD, FreeBSD, and NetBSD are competing free operating systems), easier to set up than most any Unix, and widely available. It's not the best OS out there—there is, in fact, no such thing as a best OS. An operating system is really just a tool, like a screwdriver. Some tools are better suited to certain purposes. Linux has quickly found its niche as the jack-of-all-trades OS. I guess that's why I like it so much.

- It doesn't have the fastest TCP/IP stack (FreeBSD's is much better).
- It isn't the most secure (both OpenBSD and FreeBSD best it here).
- It isn't the easiest to configure (for all that I dislike it, Win9x is still easier for the general user to configure—if for no other reason than it arrives pre-installed on the computer).
- It doesn't have the widest base of software support (MS Windows has it beat hands down).
- It's not entirely standard (the differences between distributions are often as wide as the differences between commercial Unixes).
- It's often quick-and-dirty (MacOS and BeOS shame Linux with the ease of their user interface, while OpenBSD shames it by showing how security *should* be done).
- Most importantly, it does just about everything you could ever want it to do, and does it well enough.

When Linux doesn't do something well enough, it's generally just a matter of time until it does. It's evolving—at a pace that amazes me every day. Sure, at the time of this writing, kernel 2.4 is still wet behind the ears, but Linux now supports USB devices—fully two years behind the advent of USB support in Microsoft products. Even OpenBSD and FreeBSD beat Linux in this respect. But in its short life, Linux has already managed to outstrip not only the performance and reliability of the Windows 9x file system, but also the kernel—*and* it's developed the ability to read and write the native Win9x file system as well!

As mentioned in Chapter 17, on Wine, Linux is even developing the ability to run MS Windows software natively. I remember slapping a CP/M card into my Apple][+ in the early 1980s and being amazed at how cool it was that I could run a few CP/M apps. One doesn't even need an additional card to run a wide variety of supposedly Windows-only applications on Linux. All this is so in spite of an almost geometric growth in software complexity in the last decade or so.

Linux is quickly turning into the *Homo sapiens* of the operating system realm. Humans don't run particularly quickly, nor do we swim terribly fast or have terrific vision. We can't grow fur to adapt to cooler temperatures, and we spend an inordinate part of our lives in a juvenile state. But unlike every other creature on Earth, we can run, swim, see, make clothes to keep from getting cold, and team up to protect our young. Linux isn't the best at any one thing—but it's *the* best at doing everything.

The other authors have covered why software should be free (I agree) and why Linux is keen. I, on the other hand, am having a hard time keeping to just Linux in this. I'm not even sure, in fact, how I got roped into contributing to this book. I think I might've made some sort of flip comment over lunch to Mr. Schwarz. I seem to remember his saying he was thinking about writing a book, and I carelessly mentioned that I'd just reviewed a chapter at Addison-Wesley and had a contact there. Then, in the ensuing months, I failed to back out of the deal before I'd agreed to write entirely too much in too short a time.

Sure, I had months to write chapters before the contract was signed, but that would have been proactive, wouldn't it? Now I find myself in a race with three other men to complete my work ASAP, while fighting off the urge to play computer games, work on the design and code of a fledgling Turn-based game of galactic conquest (*http://stellarlegacy.sourceforge.net/*), tinker with one of my four motorcycles (the newest of which isn't even broken in yet, and the oldest of which hasn't run in better than five years), play with my dog, spend time with my wife, or rant on any and all subjects political, religious, technical, and ethical. This is trying. My only consolation was that I *did* make the deadline.

So as you read these chapters which I have written (and some which I have reviewed), try to keep a little kindness in your heart. Mine were written in the wee hours of the morning, under the influence of strong black coffee and Wild Turkey. My computer systems were fighting me with all the silicon treachery they could muster, and my fellow authors were plotting my demise in order that they could divvy up my share amongst themselves. Should you become aware of imminent danger to my life, please drop me a note at *patowic+linuxbook@jurai.net*.

—JEREMY ANDERSON
OCTOBER 2001

Peter Curtis

Working in the information technology (IT) industry can be a grind, sometimes relegating you to the role of a underequipped tailor, as you try to sew together incompatible products, write code under impossible deadlines, and constantly explain why a project isn't as simple as it seems. It's easy to go home at night and not want to hear or see a thing about computers or Microsoft or Sun or ASPs or Web sites or e-commerce, ad infinitum. It can wear you down. But Linux came along, and it turned out to be one of those things that keeps me interested, even excited, about computers.

I was really a latecomer to the world of Linux. But when I started to learn about it, there was so much that appealed to me about its simplicity and power. In hindsight, it was simply the Unix philosophy that attracted me, but Linux was an embodiment of that philosophy that could actually run on my own system! So I *very carefully* installed Linux and set up my system for dual boot. As time went on, I found myself spending more and more time in Linux, especially as more and more useful applications starting coming out of that nebulous cloud known as the Internet. I switched to using Linux full time about two years ago, and I haven't looked back since, although I admit that my *lilo.conf* still has an entry to boot Windows 95.

Time to step in the way-back machine: My family got their first computer in 1982, when I was about 8 years old. It was a Timex Sinclair ZX81, now considered as much a classic among the computer set as the Model A Ford is among the classic-car set. I remember being fascinated with writing little BASIC programs and trying to fit them all inside the 2k of memory that came with the system. And I remember being *really* fascinated when my father found a clever little piece of software that gave the ZX81 an incredible 320 × 200-pixel high-resolution screen! I played around with it a little bit, but mostly I just wondered, "How does it work?" The rest, as they say, is history.

I ended up teaching myself Z80 assembly language. Shortly thereafter, we got a new computer—a venerable Commodore 64—and I dropped Z80 assembly like a hot potato and picked up 6502 assembly. The 6502 was a classic chip! To this day I remember the 6502 instruction set with perfect clarity. As the CPU for the Commodore VIC-20, 64, and 128, not to mention the Apple II and III, it really powered the personal computer revolution in a way that Intel could only dream of years later. We had that computer for several years, and by the time we got our first Intel-based PC I had already written some very complex programs, including a role-playing game inspired by the Ultima series and a two-tasking system complete with virtual consoles. A 1-MHz clock and a fixed stack made that last exercise a little mind bending!

Programming in assembly language *forces* you to think about algorithms and about how computation is done. It forces you to think about decomposing a problem into its basic parts and putting them back together in the form of code, which are probably some of the same principles that Ritchie and Thompson had in mind back in 1969 when they created Unix. And that, in turn, explains my natural affinity for the Unix philosophy.

In the time I've used Linux, I've consistently been impressed by its enabling ability. As many people have observed, there's very little you *can't* do with Linux. The trick is to be creative, to know how to put things together to create something that's greater than the sum of its parts. This process is mirrored in the worldwide Open Source and Free Software communities; connected by the Internet, they become greater than the sum of their parts. And in the process, they've built a fantastic operating system and application collection that's both disturbing and elating the entire software industry. I hope this book can convey that sense of energy and creativity to you, the reader. And if you haven't used Linux much, I hope this book will convince you to give it a serious try, to see how Linux can help you do the things you want to do.

—PETER CURTIS
APRIL 2001

Steven Murphy

At one time in my life, computers were my hobby, my job, and the love of my life. All that's changed now. I find myself much more interested in hobbies that don't directly relate to computers, like music and video production and R/C vehicle racing. Of course, computers are still the love of my life (*Note to self:* Always tell wife she is my only love), so I have to work computers into my hobbies somehow.

I recently began enjoying the hobby of R/C vehicles. *R/C* stands for "radio controlled." My first vehicle was a one-tenth-scale monster truck, the Traxxas T-Maxx (*www.traxxas.com*). This hobby is fun—pure, noncomputer-related fun. Of course, I want to create a Web site to share my fun (computer related!). And I also want to create cool videos of my truck flying ten feet in the air as it soars off a ramp at 25 miles per hour. Getting my videos on TV would be even more cool.

Ever since I moved to a city whose cable system offered TechTV, I have devoted a good portion of my evenings to getting my face on that network. It's there now. My mug shot goes scrolling by with every promo of their Netcam Network. Unfortunately, I made the mistake of buying video capture hardware before researching my options under Linux. I'll never make that mistake again. I bought a device that had a USB connector and my Linux kernel didn't support USB at the time. Anyway, as I said, I got my face on TechTV.

Now my goal was to get my new hobby, R/C monster truck racing, onto TechTV in a show called *You Made It*. I decided to do this using Linux as the only system (no commercial operating systems). Of course, what awesome video of dirt-spitting R/C monster trucks would be complete without an equally awesome soundtrack to go along with it?

My long-time passion has been playing music—no, not the radio, though I do play a good radio. I'm referring to real musical talent. Of course, I have very little. I make up for that by pretending to be good and just faking it for my friends. Okay, so I played guitar in three bands in my youth. I still can't read or write music. And yes, I did just buy a drum set and basically sat down and started playing as if I had been playing for years. But this is just a result of my training through persistent pencil tapping during my 12 years of schooling before I left to pursue an easier degree in data processing at a technical college. Also, owning a synthesizer makes up for the lack of any real ability to play the piano, because sequencers let you input music note by note. Who needs someone standing over him with a knuckle-cracking ruler yelling, "Tempo! Tempo!"?

As it turns out, my hobbies and my love for computers go hand in hand. This a good thing, and it keeps my life interesting and challenging. Linux is also one of those things that came along at the right time in my life. But more on that later.

My first exposure to computers was at the age of 16 while on the island of Guam. My father bought an Atari 400 but returned it and got the 800 instead. I was hooked. Before that, I had no idea what I was going to do with my life, beyond following in my father's footsteps by joining the Navy and traveling the world. I had already lived in Japan for four years and was currently in Guam, so what else was there? Anyway, I had a love/hate relationship with my Atari computer. I loved showing off the cool things I came up with to my friends, who simply hated their non-Atari computers, which paled in comparison. Eventually, I moved up to an Atari 1040ST and taught myself C. I now live in the house where I learned C by reading the white K&R book (ouch!). But what a fun time I had. Eventually, my schooling came to an end and I found myself in a job surrounded and dominated by the "Personal Confuser."* Not an Atari in sight. I knew how things were going to be from then on.

I am not one who listens to mainstream music or watches the most popular movies or television shows. I also don't go with the pack when it comes to computer operating system. When I finally decided to sell my Atari 1040ST and buy Intel-based PC hardware, I did so knowing DOS and Windows were nowhere on my agenda. Instead I bought QNX from QNX Software Systems, Inc. QNX ruled then and it rocks now. Unfortunately, it wasn't free, and my first job did not pay that well. I bounced around from OS to OS, trying OS/2, Windows 95, Windows NT, but none of them felt right. QNX felt right, but I simply couldn't justify the expense at the time. Then along came this little-known operating system called Linux.

I remember installing Slackware from 50 diskettes. I was simply amazed this thing was free. And then I discovered Free Software, GPL, Debian, and XFree86. A whole new world had suddenly opened up to me. All this and the Internet too. I've had my good times and my bad times with Linux. As easy as some marketing people might tell you Linux is these days, don't be fooled. It's still not for my mother-in-law, and she can write Microsoft Word scripts for multipage data-entry forms. But if you're willing to put in the effort and learn a thing or two about Linux and *nix in general, I know you will find as much joy and satisfaction in using Linux as I have. There's a lot of software just waiting to be discovered. This book will hopefully enlighten you on the possibilities with Linux and the plethora of applications available for it.

—Steven Murphy
December 2001

Personal confuser: A term I first heard used by Leo Laporte while watching his show *Call for Help* on TechTV. This term pretty much sums up the entire PC industry.

Index

M

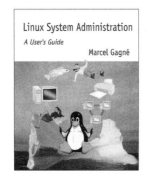

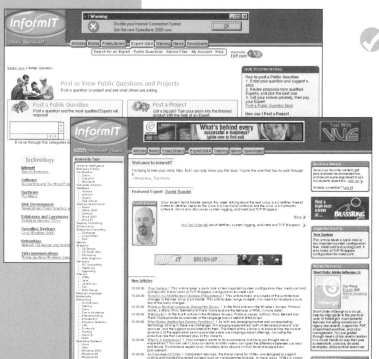